AMERICAN LODGING EXCELLENCE

THE KEY TO BEST PRACTICES IN THE U.S. LODGING INDUSTRY

By

Laurette Dubé, Ph.D.
Cathy A. Enz, Ph.D.
Leo M. Renaghan, Ph.D.
Judy A. Siguaw, Ph.D.

Cornell University
School of Hotel Administration
The Center for Hospitality Research

Funded by American Express in partnership with the American Hotel Foundation

ACKNOWLEDGMENTS

From the Authors

The authors would like to thank Erik Nisbet, project manager, for his diligence and hard work in helping to make this project possible. Without Erik's administrative expertise this project would not have been possible. The American Hotel Foundation and American Express are to be commended for their recognition of the importance of conducting this type of study and for their financial support of this project. We further appreciate the support and involvement of the American Hotel Foundation advisory board and our own industry advisory group of Cornell University alumni.

We wish to acknowledge the assistance of several different individuals and organizations who played important roles in this research endeavor. First we wish to note the involvement of Meinrad and Realtime Hotel Reports in providing databases for the Phase I portion of this project. Assistance in preparing case studies during Phase II was provided by Glenn Withiam (editor of the *Cornell Quarterly*), Rupert Spies (a Cornell faculty member in the food and beverage area), and the consultants of Cayuga Hospitality Advisors. The authors are grateful to Merat Hamedi and Sylvie Morin for the data coding and analysis in Phase III as well as Linda Carlisle for her detailed and faithful administrative support throughout the project. Thanks also go to Plog Research for its contributions during the market research portion of Phase III of this project.

Finally, we would like to thank our families for their support and understanding while we worked on this project.

From the Publishers

Publishing is the end result of a task accomplished. In this process many persons and organizations assisted the American Hotel Foundation:

- American Express for its financial support with a gift to the Hospitality 2000 campaign, a portion of which was used to create this landmark study. American Express not only provided the financial support, but also was an active partner in the development and implementation of this study and in the publication and distribution of the results.
- The Center for Hospitality Research, School of Hotel Administration, Cornell University, and the persons who gave time and effort beyond their original expectations to assure the best possible study. These include the authors, Laurette Dubé, Cathy Enz, Leo Renaghan and Judy Siguaw, who should be commended for their willingness to undertake and produce such a comprehensive study. Their drive and determination resulted in the successful and professional execution of an important work for the hospitality industry. Equally important is the project manager, Erik Nisbet, whose desire and passion to bring success to the project is hereby acknowledged.
- Early in the process, the Foundation and American Express appointed an advisory committee that reviewed the progress of the study from its beginnings to its conclusion. They willingly gave their time and expertise to assist Cornell, the Foundation and American Express in our tasks. The members were:
  Dan Bethlamy, American Express
  Maryellen Van Royen, American Express
  Ric Pastorino, American Express Tax & Consulting Services
  Douglas Viehland, American Hotel Foundation
  William Fisher, American Hotel & Motel Association
  Jack Craver, Horizons Hotels
  Gene Ference, Ference & Associates/HVS International
  Andy Devine, University of Denver
- *Lodging* Magazine, especially Larry Wilhelm, and the Educational Institute of AH&MA, George Glazer, who became the vehicles for the publication of the results by their publication and distribution expertise. This became a project that benefited from the expertise and involvement of each of the national components of the American Hotel & Motel Association.

FOREWORD

Lew Taffer
General Manager and Senior Vice President
American Express

American Express is proud to have collaborated with the American Hotel Foundation in bringing to fruition this landmark study of the lodging industry. American Express has a long history of working alongside our industry partners to help them grow and succeed.

We are especially pleased to be part of this first of its kind research that was especially designed to help hoteliers improve their business by learning from their colleagues who have been identified as the best in the industry.

Partnership is a sharing of responsibilities, and we would like to acknowledge some of our partners in this initiative:
• American Hotel Foundation as the publisher of this study and their tireless effort to see it to its successful conclusion.
• Cornell University as the research institution for seeking out these practices and documenting their use in the industry.
• *Lodging* magazine for ensuring that the study was moved from manuscript to final publication.
• Educational Institute of the AH&MA for its role in the sale and distribution of the publication.

Finally, we would like to thank and acknowledge the persons who really made this study possible. They are the individuals, the lodging properties and the corporate offices that contributed to this study by permitting their best practices to be included.

To all of you and others in the lodging industry, we salute you and pledge the ongoing support of American Express.

PUBLISHER'S OVERVIEW

Douglas Viehland
President
American Hotel Foundation

Upon review of the technical manuscript submitted by the authors, the publisher determined two items of importance were needed. First, a publication this large required a guide on how it is organized. Second, the detailed methodology and appendixes (survey instruments used in the study) added over sixty pages to a document where the major interest was in the results. This overview provides that guide and a summary of the methodology.

A Guide to Use of this Publication

The *Summary of Findings* is the one page overview of what the study discovered about the best practices in the lodging industry.

The *Introduction* is for readers seeking to know about best practices in general and their implications for the lodging industry. The authors are professors at The Center for Hospitality Research, School of Hotel Administration, Cornell University. The writing is academic style including use of the collective word "we" and citation of important references. This is the case in other sections as well. The references cited throughout the publication are listed on page 385.

The *Methodology* is a detailed statement of the processes used to conduct the study. Those interested primarily in the results of the study may prefer to read the Summary of Methodology that follows in this section and skip these eleven pages. Those readers wanting even more detail can obtain a separate bound copy of the methodology and all related and supporting appendixes by contacting the American Hotel Foundation.

Functional Best-Practice Champions is the largest section, pages 19 through 248. The overall champions follow in a separate section. Building from individual pieces to make a whole, the authors first present best-practice champions who have achieved a best practice in a functional area such as human resources, sales and marketing, accounting, etc. The case summaries are presented alphabetically (beginning with Abbey Resorts and ending with Wyndham Hotels & Resorts) rather than by function because many best practices were found to be applicable to several functional areas. The applicable function areas are noted in "flags" on each case summary.

The *Alphabetical Listing* on pages 21-23 can be used to learn what properties and corporate offices are named as functional best-practice champions and to obtain an overall review of the case summaries. To learn what properties and practices were selected as best-practice champions in a certain functional area, use the *Listing By Function* which begins on page 24. This latter listing will be especially valuable for someone in, for example, the area of human resources to quickly learn what are the best practices in human resources. Once finding an applicable practice, this person can find that specific case summary using the alphabetical name of property or corporation.

The section on *Overall Best-Practice Champions* begins on page 249. Overall champions differ from functional best-practice champions in two ways.

- First they are noted for their best practice in a competency area (profitability, customer service, quality, etc.) rather than a functional area.
- Second, best-practice champions were selected based on product segments such as deluxe, economy, extended stay — upper tier, and casinos. The product segments utilize the Bear Stearns Industry Classification Scheme. Champions were selected in both the corporate area and by individual property for each product segment.

The *Alphabetical Listing* on pages 251-252 lists the 29 properties and corporate offices named as overall best-practice champions. To review the listing of corporate champions or the listing of property champions, refer to the two listings on pages 253 and 254. All three of these listings are alphabetical by name of property or corporation. To identify the competency area (quality, profitability) or segment (economy, extended stay, casino), the reader will need to look in the second column. The listing is short and finding the best-practice champion in a particular area is easy.

The format for the case summaries is different from the functional case summaries. As noted by the authors in the methodology "a different case format is used to convey the richness of philosophies, strategies and the behaviors of these champions." In addition, the customer's perspective is added to many of the case summaries based on the results of Phase III of the study.

The *Customer's Perspectives on the Lodging Industry Best Practices* comprises Phase III of the study and begins on page 335. For those wanting a quick review of this section, several of the findings are included in the summary of findings and others are included in the case summaries of the overall best-practice champions.

The *Conclusion* section presents comments of the authors regarding the emphasis and direction of the current lodging industry practices. Again, for those wanting a quick review of conclusions please refer to the summary of findings.

The *References* section cites the various sources of information found throughout the publication, but primarily in the Introduction.

Two *Classification Indexes* are provided to again aid the reader to find a best practice that fits a particular context. The listing of all 144 best-practice champions is indexed by product segment (deluxe, upscale, economy) and by operating structure (chain, franchisee, franchisor, REIT).

The *Biographies of Principal Investigators* provides information on each of the authors who conducted the study and the expertise that they brought to this landmark work.

Summary of Methodology

This study involved three phases. In Phase I of the research the authors asked a national sample of more than 13,400 managers at both corporate and property levels, stratified by several key factors, to identify from the entire U.S. lodging industry those companies, brands, hotels or individuals they perceived as best-practice champions. The definition used throughout this study is shown in the box accompanying this text.

> **Definition: A Best-Practice Champion has developed a highly effective and profitable practice that represents the best in the industry.**

This included 2,059 corporate managers and 11,400 property managers. The corporate managers were drawn from functional areas such as chief executive officer, marketing, human resources, design/architecture, etc. At the property level, the sampling was based on product segment (economy, extended stay), operating structure and room size. Within these groups, it included managerial functions of general managers, marketing/sales, human resources, room division, food and beverage and controller. A disproportionate number (40%) of the sample was general mangers reflecting their awareness of all functions and their multi-responsibilities across several functional areas in economy properties. Efforts to collect the mailed survey results included follow-up phone calls, faxed surveys and a Web site for on-line nominations.

A total of 3,528 nominations were received in Phase I. In Phase II the authors first evaluated and reduced the number of potential candidates to 549. Fifteen-to-25-minute pre-screened interviews were conducted with each potential candidate to obtain more detailed information on the nature of the practice. If the initial discussion confirmed the nominee as a champion, he/she was then invited to participate in an in-depth telephone interview. A total of 157 were selected for the in-depth interview. Several refused to participate further, could not be re-contacted or or refused to provide permission for their practice to be published after the interview was conducted. The final number of 144 persons are included in this publication.

In Phase III, the authors interviewed a national sample of 194 travel agents, 123 meeting planners and 536 persons who were frequent-stay customers of one or more overall best-practice champions. First, customers discussed their purchase motives, their experience with one of the hotel champions, and their intention to remain loyal. Second, customers reported their experience with one of those hotels that they considered, industrywide, as champions on each of a series of hotel attributes (location, brand name, physical property, guest room design, etc.).

During each step in this process an expert panel of industry experts assembled by the American Hotel Foundation or by the authors provided advice and suggestions for executing the study, including pilot testing the survey and review of key components of the study prior to publication.

TABLE OF CONTENTS

Acknowledgments ii

Foreword iii

Publisher's Overview iv

    Guide to Use of this Publication...iv

    Summary of Methodology v

Summary of Findings..1

Introduction 3

    What Are Best Practices?..3

    Review of the Best Practices Literature 3

Methodology 7

Functional Best-Practice Champions...19

    Introduction and Overview..19

    Alphabetical Listing 21

    Listing by Function 24

    Case Summaries of Functional Best-Practice Champions 33

Overall Best-Practice Champions..249

    Introduction and Overview..249

    Alphabetical Listings...251

    Case Summaries of Overall Best-Practice Champions..255

Customers' Perspectives on the Lodging Industry's Best Practices:

    Introduction 331

    Customer Value Created by Overall Best-Practice Champions 332

    Value Drivers in the Hotel Experience 342

    Customer Value Created by Top Performance In Functional Practices.....................346

    Value Created for Intermediaries 346

    Intermediaries' Outlook on Hotel Practices Underlying Value Drivers.....................349

    Customer Value Created by Top Performers in Functional Areas 350

    Comparing Customers' and Managers' Perspectives on the Lodging Industry Best Practices....365

Conclusions 369

References 381

Classification Index 382

    Case Listings by Segment...389

    Case Listings by Operating Structure...399

Biographies of Principal Investigators 397

SUMMARY OF FINDINGS

- Of the 115 functional best practices, the largest number of champions was in the area of human resource management, followed by operations, corporate management, and sales and marketing.

- The functional champions were evenly split between corporate and property locations, while owner/operators and chains were the operating structures with the largest number of functional champions.

- Employees were extremely important to best-practice champions in every product segment from budget to deluxe. Employee involvement was frequently cited as a key to successful implementation of the functional and overall practices, and as a key to improving levels of customer satisfaction.

- The functional champions repeatedly observed that they should have started the practice sooner, moved slower in implementation, and established an approach to monitoring results along the way. Additionally, functional champions stressed the importance of senior level commitment to the practice as a major component in ensuring successful implementation.

- The 29 overall best-practice champions did many things well, and worked from a strategic business model stressing the importance of understanding customer needs and creating value, with a focus on profitability. In particular they were skilled at creating value for the owners, employees, and customers that was in line with the key strategies of their business model.

- Execution and attention to detail were keys to success for the overall best-practice champions. At the property level the involvement of the general manager in the daily life of the hotel was viewed as critical to the overall champions.

- According to the customers sampled, the six most powerful motives behind their purchase behavior were location, brand name and reputation, public spaces (e.g., exteriors, lobby, and landscape), guestroom design and amenities, value for money and functional aspects of the service. These customer value drivers were found to correspond to the practices reported by the overall champions.

- Customers stated that the public spaces, the guestroom, the interpersonal and the functional aspects of service, as well as the hotel food and beverage services were the primary creators of unique value during the hotel experience.

INTRODUCTION

Many hotels are testing new practices or activities conceived to improve effectiveness and performance. The desire to learn from these hotel companies and then experiment with bringing new ideas, approaches, and processes into another organization is at the heart of a best-practice study. The Best Practices in the U.S. Lodging Industry study, the first of its kind, fulfills this fundamental goal of helping the industry learn from itself by stimulating creativity and providing ideas for improvement that might trigger the desire to change and encourage innovation in hotel operations.

Given today's fierce global competition, the identification and use of best practices is a critical component of managerial excellence and a means of producing the best possible performance (Rogers, 1997).* Examination of the practices of other companies requires investigating new ideas, activities, or managerial processes and determining which organizations have the most effective or profitable approach.

The adoption of best practices has been shown to benefit companies through lower operating costs, increased revenue, and the more effective use of monetary and human capital (Rogers, 1997; Sullivan, 1995), as long as these adopting companies have the quality infrastructure in place to make the major transformations that may be required (Hequet, 1993). Consequently, efforts to delineate and embrace best practices are occurring in every business sector, but may still yield failure. O'Dell and Grayson (1998) revealed that many companies have excellent practices within their own organizations but are unable to transfer and share their own best practices. The inability of many companies to share practices highlights the difficulties of using and managing knowledge. One challenge for those using this book of best practices is to develop effective mechanisms to share these insights and to help the good practices within your own operation to be passed on internally.

What Are Best Practices?

While many definitions exist to define best practices, generally they refer to "any practice, know-how, or experience that has proven to be valuable or effective within one organization that may have applicability to other organizations" (O'Dell and Grayson, 1998). Best practices are exemplary or successfully demonstrated ideas or activities, viewed by some as top-notch "standards" for guiding benchmarking and making comparisons. A best-practice champion is a person or organization that supports and defends an approach, idea, or practice that has proven to be valuable.

It is essential to realize in any study of "best practices" that no single practice works in all situations, and hence the word "best" is defined in context, is situational, and means "best for you" (Hiebeler, Kelly, and Ketteman, 1998). The term "best" is constantly evolving in a world in which good practices must change to respond to new environmental conditions. To label any practice as best immediately raises the possibility of dissenting voices from other companies or properties within the same organization. In addition, the term "best" may suggest that there is only one way to do things. Therefore, the terms "excellent" or "successful" could replace the term "best" to avoid the disagreements that can result when too rigid an interpretation is placed on the collection of "best" practices.

Review of the Best Practices Literature

A review of the literature reveals a paucity of published best practices related to the service industries in general (Stank, Rogers, and Daugherty, 1994), and more specifically, to the lodging industry. A few well-known hotel chains have been recognized and discussed, most notably Ritz-Carlton, but a broader-based industry-specific review of best practices is absent from the current literature. This lack of managerial insight from research in best practices in the service industries in general, and in the lodging industry in particular, is unfortunate because in this sector of the economy, balancing best practices aimed at controlling cost with those aimed at building revenues is particularly challenging. Not surprisingly, Fornell, Rust, and Anderson (1997) recently found that the last five-year wave of downsizing and process reengineering had a far more detrimental impact on customer satisfaction for the service industries than it had in the manufacturing sectors. In fact, the national level of customer satisfaction (American Customer Satisfaction Index [ACSI], Fornell et al., 1996) for services has consistently decreased in the United States since 1994. To further

* all citations are included in References, page 385

complicate matters, the lodging industry has distinctive characteristics that require a particular approach to the study of its best practices. Thus, the lodging industry may not be able to simply borrow universal or general practices that work in other industries (Keehley et al., 1997; Young, 1996).

The pressure is on lodging firms to seek new practices to improve their effectiveness and performance for several reasons. First, competition is intensifying, bringing the industry once again close to the point where lodging supply will be greater than lodging demand. Second, consolidation in the industry has resulted in the difficult corporate task of instilling targeted behavior and practices into large, diverse hotel operations so that all properties function effectively, although distinctively, under a common corporate umbrella. Third, the realities of today's stock markets require publicly traded companies to show continuous improvement in financial performance. The "winning" lodging firms will be those that identify, adopt, and evolve the best of these practices.

Certain distinctive characteristics of the lodging industry were influential in our decisions when designing this study. The first characteristic of the lodging industry considered in formulating this best-practice research relates to the intricate relationship between corporate and property-level operations and management. To build a strong brand for a hotel chain, managers cannot rely primarily on advertising, as is done to a large extent in the selling of manufactured goods. Lodging brand equity is based upon each property's ability to deliver on the core component of the concept while responding each day to specific needs of its clientele in a profitable way. In one of the few best-practice studies within the industry, Enz and Corsun (1996) found that best practices promoted and instituted at the corporate level were often unrelated to profitability at the property level. The singular relationships among management companies, owners, brands, and other critical partners in hotel operations make the success of selecting and implementing best practices far more complex than in many businesses. In this study we elicit and analyze best practices at both corporate and property levels to account for the particular relationships that exist inside the lodging industry.

The second characteristic of the lodging industry that shaped the design of this study is the experiential nature of the product (Brown, 1997) that calls for excellence in two types of practices: *overall practices* that reflect the strategic decisions that guide the champion toward balancing the benefits to the key stakeholders (i.e., owners, employees, and guests), and specific *functional practices* that are needed to deliver on the multitude of details necessary to create a satisfactory hotel experience. Many of the best-practice cases feature core competencies that focus on factors critical to the success of this industry. These two levels of best practices are interrelated. As Parson (1995, p. 88) noted, "Total customer satisfaction increases customer retention and employee satisfaction. Employee satisfaction increases sales and profits. A momentum builds that drives sales and productivity up while it pushes costs and employee turnover down." A limited number of studies conducted on best practices in the lodging industry (e.g., Cline and Rach, 1996; Enz and Corsun, 1996; Renaghan and Green, 1993) have shown that some best practices can be identified in specific functional areas such as quality control of operations (e.g., regular inspections) or cost management (e.g., strategic alliances with major suppliers). However, the implementation of best practices is still nascent in many functional areas (Enz and Corsun, 1996).

Finally, a key aspect of the lodging industry that calls for a creative approach to the study of its best practices is the pervasive presence of the customer at the core of service operations. Recent research has shown that customers' evaluation of a hotel and their decision to patronize it do not depend so much on what services are provided as on how the firms go about delivering on many aspects of the service experience being purchased (Dubé et al, 1997; Dubé, Johnson and Renaghan, 1999). That is, the organization and operation of the staff, the information systems, the facility configuration, the hotel environment, and other resources are part of the product the customer is purchasing and important to satisfaction and repeat patronage. In a recent study on best practices in service industries in the United States (including lodging), more than 50 percent of the best practices judged by business executives as most important to firm success were related to the interface between the firm and the customer (Roth, Chase and Voss, 1997). Moreover, even the numerous management practices that remain imperceptible to the customer are ultimately justified by the extent to which they contribute to some specific aspects of customers' needs and expectations. Therefore, it is crucial to assess customers' perspectives to have a comprehensive representation of the best practices in the lodging industry.

In sum, the existing literature gives evidence that the identification and sharing of best practices produces positive outcomes. In addition, most work on best practices examines general, broad, multi-industry, and universal processes. This, the Cornell University Best Practices Study, is the first known comprehensive study to examine overall and functional best practices in the lodging industry, at corporate and property levels, and across industry product categories and key competency areas. This study is also distinctive because it builds in customers' perspectives as a fundamental component of best practice.

We define successful lodging operations as those that make a hotel a compelling place to stay for the guest, a compelling place to work for the staff, and a compelling place to invest in for the owners (Rucci, Kirn, and Quinn, 1998). Lasting success relies upon managers' abilities to develop the core competencies needed to make these three components work in balance. The lodging industry has distinctive characteristics that make balancing these three components a challenging task. Different customers in the same hotel have different, sometimes conflicting, needs and wishes. Regardless of the nature of customer needs, their successful fulfillment relies upon strategies and tactics that yield programs, practices, processes, and activities that are planned by management at both property and corporate levels. The practices and processes that have been designed are ultimately delivered by frontline employees, in the pervasive presence of the customers. Customers have developed expectations regarding what and how things should happen during the hotel stay, but they also will perceive and judge a hotel at each visit on the basis of its ability to deliver on these expectations, giving no consideration to managerial or operational constraints. Hence, the route to success in the lodging industry is likely to be paved by sustained competitive advantage, intricately linked to sustained management action, in a way that makes a hotel, as we said, a compelling place to stay, to work, and to invest in. Our strategy for the analysis of best practices in the lodging industry was to unravel the practices of the top performers keeping this balanced view of success in mind.

Thus, this study presents a compilation of strategies and techniques used by the lodging industry's "Best of the Best" in different segments, across different functional areas, and at both corporate offices and property locations; this study also examines lodging practices that are perceived as the best by the customer. The best-practice champions we feature in this study have experimented with new ideas, or creatively applied existing ideas, in the lodging industry to achieve results.

METHODOLOGY

The American Hotel Foundation and American Express jointly sponsored this research by soliciting competitive grants in February 1998. Upon selection of Cornell University as the investigators of this study, the research team assembled an expert panel of industry executives to provide advice and suggestions for executing the study. This expert panel was extremely important in helping the team define the most critical functional areas in the industry, and the most meaningful definitions of product segments and operating structures. These classifications were essential in ensuring adequate and representative reach to all segments and areas of the lodging industry.

Overview of Research Design

The goal of this research was to surface and summarize practices of use and value to the entire lodging industry. As a means to this end, we organized the study into three distinct phases. In the first phase, based on our literature review in the area of best practices, prior research, and the guidance of our expert panel, we selected three approaches to gathering data. Nominations for best-practice champions were obtained via mailed, faxed, and Internet surveys to the industry. The second phase involved in-depth interviews with carefully selected and prescreened best-practice champions derived from the nominations of Phase I. The final phase involved interviews with customers of the overall best-practice champions identified and interviewed in Phase II. In this section of the report we will summarize the research methodology employed in each phase.

Phase I — Nomination of Champions

The first phase of this study was designed to surface the names and practices of possible champions from managers across the United States. Multiple versions of an open-ended survey were distributed to a national sample of 13,400 managers at both corporate and property levels, stratified by product segments (e.g., Budget, Midscale with F&B, etc.) and functional areas (e.g., Human Resources, Food & Beverage, etc.). These lodging industry managers were instructed to write in their nominations of individuals, hotels, chains, or companies they considered best-practice champions; that is, those individuals and companies they know who have superior practices and processes and the results to prove it. The definition we provided our Phase I survey respondents to guide them in nominating a best-practice champion is highlighted in the box below.

> **Definition: A Best-Practice Champion has developed a highly effective and profitable practice that represents the best in the industry.**

Survey Design

The survey was designed and pilot-tested for feedback and input by the American Hotel Foundation (AHF) advisory committee and a group of industry managers. Revisions and additional pretesting were conducted to assure a user-friendly, reliable, clear, and meaningful Phase I questionnaire. The survey consisted of two series of questions to nominate best-practice champions. One set of items focused on overall practices in each of the eight product segments and five key competency areas. The second set of items focused on identifying nominees in the key activities of 10 specific corporate functional areas and six property-level functions. All respondents completed the first series of questions for nominations on overall practices, whereas only those respondents with responsibility for a particular function in their company or hotel nominated the champions in that functional area. The final survey contained unique versions for corporate and property-level managers, and for each of the functional area managers.

In open-ended questions, respondents were presented with the definition of best-practice champions, and asked to nominate champions. By creating special surveys for corporate and property levels and functional areas, a total of sixteen different versions of the Phase I survey were prepared and distributed by mail and fax. A Web site also was established for on-line nominations. The on-line survey provided some of the most comprehensive responses to our survey because it permitted the respondent to elaborate on his or her reasons for selecting the best practice. The approach is visually presented in Figure 1.

Figure 1: The Creation of Sixteen Versions of the Phase I Survey

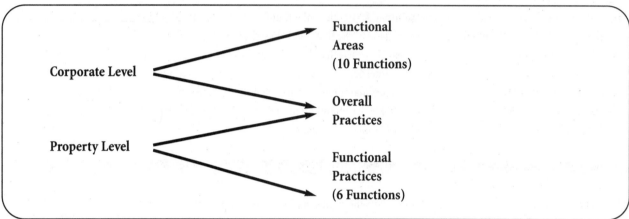

The sixteen versions of the survey reflected our desire to capture the differences and unique best practices that exist in corporate versus property settings and within various functional areas of expertise. In addition, we felt that functional experts would be more familiar with what others in their own area of expertise were doing in the industry. For example, we reasoned that the information technology experts in one company would be familiar with what others in their field of expertise were doing that was exemplary. In short, the purpose of this design was to obtain the expert opinion of functional managers in their own area, and to account for the unique operating features of the lodging industry. The use of multiple versions of the survey in the nominating process, while complex to administer, helped to ensure that the search would have the depth necessary to solicit and reach those managers who are in the best position to bring forth functional nominations of champions at both corporate and property levels.

Sampling Strategy

Surveys were mailed to 2,059 corporate managers and 11,400 property-level managers using a stratified random sample of names and addresses obtained from the Meinrad database. The database is proprietary and contains a listing of nearly 40,000 hotels in the United States. It includes information necessary to segment the industry on the basis of product category, operating structure, and hotel size, while also providing the names of all general managers affiliated with each property.

At the corporate level, we relied on the Meinrad database and the electronic version of the *1998 Directory of Hotel and Motel Companies* published by the American Hotel & Motel Association. This sample included approximately 200 lodging companies and brands organized in one of five operating structures of interest: franchisors, chain management, independent management, owner-operator, and owner. Corporate executives in the following managerial functions were invited to participate: (1) owner, chief executive officer (CEO), chief operating officer (COO), brand manager, or executive vice-president (EVP); (2) design/architecture; (3) business development; (4) information technology/system; (5) marketing; (6) sales; (7) human resources; (8) room divisions/ operations; (9) food and beverage; and (10) chief financial officer (CFO)/corporate controller. Thus, the corporate-level sample size was 2,059 managers in ten functional categories.

At the property level, the sampling was stratified by product categories, operating structure, and property size (fewer than 250 rooms; 250-650 rooms; more than 650 rooms), with representation of each stratum in the sample being proportional to that of the population. The sample of respondents was culled from the Meinrad database. At the property level, samples of respondents were randomly selected within the stratification by product categories, operating structure, property size, and function. The following percentages of the overall sample were drawn from six managerial functions: (1) general manager (39.6% of the sample); (2) marketing/sales (11.8% of the sample); (3) human resources (8.7% of the sample); (4) rooms division/operations (including front office, reservations, and housekeeping) (22.4% of the sample); (5) food and beverage/catering (5.6% of the sample); and (6) controller (11.9% of the sample). By randomly selecting managers we avoided the systematic bias due to all functional managers in a given hotel participating in the study. The sample size for general managers was 4,515 and the sample size for the five other managerial functions was 6,885. General managers were intentionally oversampled because of their important position at the core of decision-making in hotels, and the likelihood that they would perform many of the functions in the limited-service segments that the full-service segment would rely on department heads to perform.

Following the stratified sampling plan, a total of 13,459 hotel managers at the corporate and property level were mailed questionnaires. A personalized cover letter from the dean of the School of Hotel Administration accompanied the survey to all managers. The functional managers received the questionnaire and a general cover letter, mailed to the general manager with instructions to distribute to specified department heads since the contact names of department personnel were not available from the database. Follow-up calls, surveys, and faxes were sent to nonrespondents after the initial mailing within underrepresented strata. Additionally, a drawing to receive free a week of executive education on the Cornell campus during the summer Professional Development Program was offered as an incentive to facilitate quick and high levels of survey response. A total of five free weeks of executive education were given away in this phase of the study. Figure 2 provides a breakdown of the survey sampling plan for the Phase I survey.

Figure 2: Sampling Strategy for Phase I

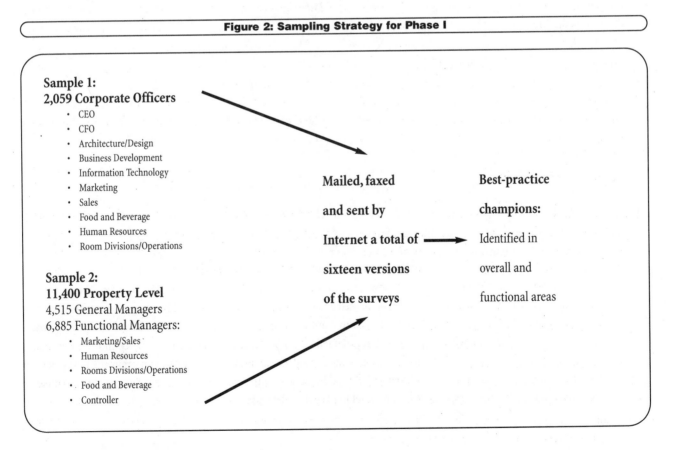

Sample 1:
2,059 Corporate Officers
- CEO
- CFO
- Architecture/Design
- Business Development
- Information Technology
- Marketing
- Sales
- Food and Beverage
- Human Resources
- Room Divisions/Operations

Sample 2:
11,400 Property Level
4,515 General Managers
6,885 Functional Managers:
- Marketing/Sales
- Human Resources
- Rooms Divisions/Operations
- Food and Beverage
- Controller

Mailed, faxed and sent by Internet a total of sixteen versions of the surveys

Best-practice champions: Identified in overall and functional areas

Respondent Profiles

A total of 610 managers responded to the Phase I nomination survey, of which 558 provided demographic information. The profile characteristics of the average manager who responded to our survey was a 40-year-old male who has been in the lodging industry for fifteen years. A summary of the respondent profile information is presented in Table 1, and it reveals that a large percentage of our respondents were general managers. The balance of corporate and property-level management responses is representative of our original sampling strategy.

Table 1: Respondent Profiles

General Information

Sex	66.4% Males	33.6% Females
Years in Industry	**Mean**	**Standard Deviation**
	15.3 years	9.12
Age	39.8 years old	9.15

Job Titles	Percent of Managers
Corporate	21.6% Total
President/COO/CEO	5.2%
Senior VP/VP	5.8%
Regional Manager/Division Head	7.2%
Manager	3.4%
Property	77.8% Total
General Manager	54.3%
Assistant GM	5.2%
Department Head/Director	18.3%
Other (e.g., Consulting)	.6% Total

To enhance the modest response to the Phase I survey we conducted the following follow-up activities. First we telephoned 100 nonresponding property-level general managers to discover why they had not completed the survey. This phone poll revealed that the general manager to whom the questionnaire had been addressed had left the property in 59% of the hotels called. Other explanations for nonresponse included: "I didn't get around to it "(10%), "I was out of town/on vacation" (2.5%), "It's in the mail back to you" (2.5%), or the phone rang at the hotel with no pickup for an extended time (7.3%). Finally, 20% of those called indicated they had not received the survey. The quality of address information in existing databases is an important consideration in any industrywide survey. In this study a total of 175 surveys were returned with bad addresses. After the phone poll we faxed shorter follow-up surveys to randomly selected hotel properties using the Realtime Hotel Reports Inc. database.

At the conclusion of Phase I a total of 3,448 nominations of best-practice champions were received. As with all studies of people's opinions, the nominations in Phase I are subject to potential error. People do not always know or have contact with the best-practice providers. To ensure that some of the best of the best were not missed via the survey, a review of the trade and industry literature also was conducted. The extensive literature review produced an additional 80 nominations. Hence, at the close of Phase I a total of 3,528 best-practice champions had been nominated for their efforts at developing highly effective and profitable practices that represent the best in the industry.

Phase II — In-depth Interview of Champions

In Phase II, the 3,528 nominations surfaced in Phase I were evaluated and reduced to 549 potential champions, using the criteria discussed below. A telephone interview prescreening procedure reduced the nominees further to a group of champions. The selected best-practice champions were notified by mail of their selection and interviews were scheduled. A total of 115 functional champions and 29 overall champions were interviewed in Phase II. Figure 3 provides a visual overview of this phase of the project.

Figure 3: An Overview of Phase II

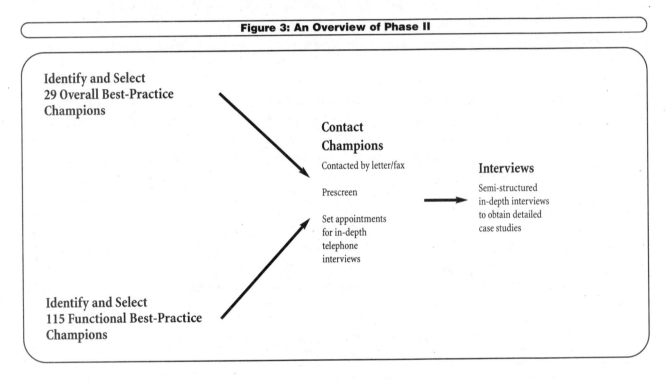

The primary objective of this phase of the study was to learn from the interviews with each best-practice champion, in as much detail as possible, what was done, why it was done, how it was done, and how it will be improved or evolve in the future. It is this richness that will provide the concrete understanding and generate the enthusiasm among others in the industry to experiment, adapt, and adopt these practices.

Criteria for Selection of Nominees

The principal investigators categorized and analyzed the entire set of 3,528 nominations. Using the frequency counts on the number of respondents who nominated each potential champion and reading each best practice independently, the four researchers scored and then assembled a subsample of potential champions. For the functional best-practice champions, the nominees whose practices most clearly adhered to our definition of a best practice, and had a high frequency of mention, were included in our prescreen process from which we selected the finalists. The overall best-practice champions were selected differently. The highest frequency of mention was calculated across all respondents for all brands, hotels, or individuals mentioned within each segment and nomination category (i.e., upscale, economy, profitability, quality, etc.) and the finalists selected from the results.

This phase of the project provided a broad, segmented, and practice-focused list of overall and functional best-practice champions. The 549 most frequently nominated and/or highest scored nominations were then prescreened in preparation for Phase II. Fifteen-to-25-minute prescreen interviews were conducted with each potential candidate to obtain more detailed information on the nature of the practice. If the initial prescreen discussion confirmed the nominee as a champion, he/she was then invited to participate in an in-depth telephone interview. The nomination as a best-practice champion and the request to participate in an in-depth interview were confirmed via a letter that was faxed to each nominee.

In-depth Interview Structure and Approach

The core interview questions, numerous probes, and a detailed interviewer manual were developed to guide the interviewers through the in-depth interview and to standardize the process of gathering information from the numerous functional best-practice champions. The overall best-practice champions were interviewed using a different set of interview questions that were broader in focus and less structured.

The interviewers initially contacted the best-practice champions and arranged an interview time. This step in the process frequently required the interviewer to make multiple telephone calls and transmit numerous faxes given the busy schedules and obligations of the champions. Once a time was established, a comprehensive interview was conducted using the carefully established questions and numerous probes. The probes were designed to assist the interviewers in eliciting sufficient information from each champion to prepare the initial case summaries.

Functional Best-Practice Champions

A total of 115 functional best-practice champions were interviewed in this phase of the project. In each case eight core questions were asked and a case synthesis was prepared following the template provided in Figure 4. Each interview was tape-recorded for future reference. The researchers reviewed each case, listened to tapes when needed, and called champions a second or third time to obtain more information and clarify information when needed.

Figure 4: Template for Summary

Description:	Provide an overview of the best practice. What? Where? When? (When completed? Length of time required?) Who? (Source of practice? People affected?) Why? (Why adopted? What were the problems/issues?)
Execution:	What was the approach for implementation? How was the practice implemented? What tactics were used to introduce the practices? (Steps and in what order? Coalition building? Trial? Full adoption? Sustaining practice?) What communication strategies were used for employees, customers? What influence strategies were used? Were new skills needed? How were they developed? Were new resources required or were resources reallocated? What was the cost of implementation?
Outcomes:	How successful was the practice in accomplishing staff, customer, and owner goals? How were results monitored? What have been the benefits of the practice?
Insights:	What are suggestions for implementing the practice? What lessons have been learned? Insights that can be offered? How might the practice be evolved for the future?
Contact:	Provide the name, address, phone, and fax of the best-practice champion or contact person.

An interview summary form was completed after each interview to capture the attitude of the champion toward the interview process and to identify any problems or issues that the interviewer may have experienced during the interview. This interview summary form, the prescreen interview notes, the in-depth interviewer notes, the case summary using the template format, and the tape recording of the interview along with any additional material that the champion provided were reviewed by the research team in preparation for the final short, content-driven case write-ups. The information obtained in the interviews was assembled to prepare a comprehensive set of case studies, and then each case study was reviewed by the interviewee to ensure accuracy. This set of case studies is provided in the next chapter of this report.

Overall Best Practice Champions

A total of 29 overall best-practice champions also were interviewed in this phase of the project. Several of the overall champions had been selected and interviewed as functional champions for specific practices, but were interviewed again because of their distinction in a variety of different domains. Because of the broader scope of practices employed by these champions, a different case format was used to convey the richness of the philosophies, strategies, and behaviors of these champions. In addition, a limited number of customers for the majority of the overall best-practice champions were interviewed, and this guest perspective was incorporated into these cases. These "overall" cases follow the chapter of functional cases.

Phase III — The Customers' Perspectives

The objective of Phase III was to assess customers' perspectives on best practices in the lodging industry by surveying the customers of the overall champions. The interview was divided into two parts. In the first part, respondents were asked to identify which hotel attributes were perceived as determinants of value in their purchase decision and in the hotel experience provided by the overall champion. The second part aimed at eliciting customers' perspectives on functional best practices. Respondents described the customer value created by what they considered as top performers in the lodging industry on a series of attributes tied to the various functional areas of a hotel in the customers' words (e.g., the personnel, the physical property, the check-in/out, etc.). These functional areas paralleled to a large extent the diversity of functional practices covered in Phase II. The content of both parts of the interview was analyzed to determine the hotel attributes that drive customer value and influence purchase behaviors and loyalty.

The survey consisted of open-ended, partially structured phone interviews. For each overall champion, we interviewed 12 customers within each segment. We considered three end-user segments, i.e., leisure, business transient, and business meeting/convention, and two intermediary segments, i.e., travel agents and meeting planners. Thus, depending on the market basis of the champion, we interviewed up to 36 end-users and 24 intermediary customers. Overall, 853 interviews were conducted (536 end-user customers, 194 travel agents, 123 meeting planners).

Description of the Samples: End-users

Four hundred sixty-nine out of the 536 end-user respondents were frequent business and frequent leisure travelers, selected on a convenience basis from Plog Research's proprietary list, the USA Travel Bank. This list is one of the largest and most comprehensive national databases available in the travel industry with more than 350,000 respondents. The remaining end-user respondents were selected on a convenience basis from customer lists provided by those overall champions whose market basis was geographically limited (individual properties). For these champions, we requested a sample list of customers who had stayed at the property within the past year. However, only a limited number of property champions were able to provide a customer list. As a result, the customers' perspectives on the property-level overall champions are not as comprehensively covered as that of the brand-level champions. Because we could not control the selection bias in the customer lists provided by the champions, we chose to use this data for the customers' perspectives in the overall cases studies only, with a mention that respondents were sampled according to this procedure. In addition, we excluded this data from the industrywide analysis of customers' perspectives presented in the customers' perspectives chapter.

Respondents were first screened on frequency of usage of hotels for one of three purchase occasions (leisure, transient business, business meetings/convention). Segment-specific frequency criteria were:

- *Leisure:* two trips within the past year primarily for leisure.
- *Transient business:* three business trips within the past year consisting of one or more hotel nights on each trip.
- *Business meetings/convention:* attendance within the past year at two business meetings (company meeting or convention that included at least two nights stay and two days of meetings on each trip).

Once respondents were screened for frequency, eligible respondents were those frequent users who had stayed at least once over the last year at one of the champion brands or properties. In Table 2, we present the demographic profile of the end-user respondents. Across customer segments, the age of the respondents was around 50 years, for an overall average of 51.0 years. The overall sample of end-users was about evenly divided between men and women. However, the relative proportion of men and women in the sample varied across segments. For instance, the relative participation of men was especially high in the business transient segment, reflecting the gender profile in the population of frequent business travelers. Women represented a larger proportion than men in the leisure segment. In terms of education, most respondents had a college education.

Table 2: End-user Respondent Profile

Demographics	Total	Leisure	Transient Business	Business Meetings Conventions
Age (Average)	51.0 years	53.4 years	48.8 years	52.8 years
Gender (# of respondents)				
Male	267	86	116	65
Female	269	168	52	49
Education (# of respondents)				
Less than high school	7	6	0	1
High school	49	32	10	7
College, no degree	129	60	41	28
Undergraduate	239	107	79	53
Graduate studies	95	40	33	22
Post-graduate	15	7	5	3
Refused	2	2	0	0
Total	536	254	168	114

Description of the Samples: Intermediaries

Intermediaries' perspectives were assessed for brand-level champions only. Travel agents were selected on a convenience basis from Plog's comprehensive travel agency database, TravelEdge. This list, which is regularly updated, consists of approximately 30,000 full-service U.S. travel agencies. Meeting planners were selected on a convenience basis from the Meeting Planners International (MPI) association membership lists. MPI represents 14,500 members and we selected 6,000 meeting planners from its membership list who possessed two years or more of experience.

Intermediary respondents were screened on two criteria: (1) minimum of five years' experience as a travel agent or meeting planner, and (2) having been a customer of one of the brand-level overall champions within the past year. A total of 194 travel agents (153 women and 41 men) and 123 meeting planners (104 women and 19 men) were interviewed. The average numbers of years of experience were, respectively, 13.4 and 9.6 for travel agents and meeting planners.

Interview Structure and Approach

The interviewers used an open-ended, half-structured approach utilizing a computer-assisted telephone interviewing (CATI) system. A CATI system is a type of software application that enables the interviewer to probe, clarify, and follow up on responses to open-ended questions. In this procedure, after having been familiarized with the topic of the interview and armed with a repertory of typical consumer responses, trained interviewers can type detailed notes as the phone interview unfolds. The content of these notes is then submitted to analysis.

The interview procedure and tools were pretested within each respondent segment for a resulting average interview duration of 25 minutes. Various versions of the questionnaires were developed for the three segments of end-users (leisure, transient and meeting planners) and two segments of intermediaries (travel agents and meeting planners). The interview was divided into two parts: The first part focused on the respondent's experience with the champion hotel for which he/she had been screened; the second part centered on his/her experience with industrywide top performers based on a series of attributes related to key functional areas in a hotel. In both parts of the interview, linkages were established among customers' perceptions of hotel attributes that drive customer value, the benefits derived from these hotel attributes, and their impact on purchase and loyalty decisions.

Customers' Perspectives on Overall Practice Champions

To assess customers' perspectives on the overall best-practice champions, respondents were asked to indicate what attributes of the hotel champion made them first decide to stay at this hotel. They then indicated whether the champion actually delivered on those attributes (yes, no, more or less). They also identified the actual practices related to the champion's ability to deliver on these hotel attributes, as well as the set of benefits they derived from these attributes. This part of the questionnaire provided the information from which we identified the source of customer value at purchase in subsequent analyses.

Customer value created by the overall champions during the hotel experience was studied by asking respondents to indicate whether they had liked anything in particular during their last stay at the champion hotel (yes, no). If respondents said yes, they were then invited to elaborate on those hotel attributes that created value during the hotel experience, the same way they had done for purchase. All respondents concluded their discussion of the overall champion by indicating whether they were likely to go back on the next similar occasion (definitely yes, definitely no, maybe).

Customers' Perspectives on Functional Practice Champions

Ideally, to assess customers' perspectives on the functional practices, we would have preferred to interview customers of our 115 functional best-practice champions, as we did for the overall best practices. This research, unfortunately, was beyond the scope and resources of this project. Instead, as part of the interview, we asked respondents to move away from their experience with the overall best-practice champion, and to think about all the hotels they ever stayed at for the same purchase occasion. They were then instructed to identify the hotel that they considered the best for two broad functional areas of a hotel, to specify those hotel attributes that created value for them, and to denote the benefits they derived from these attributes. They finally indicated whether the fact that a hotel was the top performer in a given functional area made them more likely to give priority to this hotel over competitors on the next occasion. Thus, the assessment of customers' perspectives on the best functional practices in the lodging industry is not made, as for the overall practices, in reference to the champions that were selected by the managers. Instead, customers' perspectives are presented from the point of view of what they consider as being the top performance in the lodging industry in a given functional area.

Altogether, customers provided their perspective on a set of functional areas that to a large extent paralleled the diversity of practices covered in Phase II. Specifically, end-users were asked to talk about the personnel, the physical property (separately for public spaces and guestrooms), the quality standards (separately for check-in/out and in-stay services), the brand name/reputation, the marketing to the end-customers, and the perceived value-for-money. To respect the time constraint, each respondent elaborated upon two functional areas that were randomly chosen from the preceding list. Travel agents and meeting planners were interviewed regarding communication with the intermediaries and the quality of deals and incentives as intermediary-specific functional practices. Travel agents only were interviewed on brand name and reputation, and value for money for the end-user. Pilot testing indicated that the customers' perspectives in these two areas emerged as important choice motives for travel agents. Meeting planners were interviewed on three additional areas: meetings and conventions facilities design and accommodations, services related to meetings and conventions, and guestroom and various nonmeeting-related services and accommodations for the guest. The next table indicates the number and types of respondents who described their perspective on each functional area.

Table 3: Number and Type of Customers By Functional Area							
Area	Total End-users	Leisure	Transient Business	Mtgs/Conv Business	Total Intermediaries	Travel Agents	Meeting Planners
Personnel	156	58	61	37	na	na	na
Public spaces	128	48	44	36	na	na	na
Guestroom	134	50	53	31	na	na	na
Check-in/out	132	53	51	28	na	na	na
In-stay services	128	54	38	36	na	na	na
Marketing	129	49	41	39	na	na	
Brand name/reputation	136	54	42	40	na	113	na
Value-for-money	140	57	45	38	na	101	na
Communication with intermediaries	na	na	na	na	185	118	67
Deals and incentives	na	na	na	na	183	124	59
Meeting/convention facilities, design and accommodations	na	na	na	na	na	na	59
Meeting/convention services	na	na	na	na	na	na	57
Guestroom and nonmeeting/ convention services	na	na	na	na	na	na	54

Content Analysis

In data analysis, each interview protocol was divided into three types of information: hotel attributes, hotel practices, and customer benefits. Hotel attributes correspond to what elements of the hotel customers perceived. Hotel practices reflected customer perceptions of how the hotel was able to deliver on these attributes. Customer benefits were functional, emotional, and social consequences that respondents associated with a hotel featuring the various attributes.

The content of respondents' interviews pertaining to the overall champions was summarized from various angles: hotel attributes driving customer value at purchase and during the hotel experience, outlook on the champions' practices, and customer benefits. The customers' perspectives on the overall champions were presented within each individual case study. In the chapter on customer perspectives, we shifted the focus of the analysis toward a more global portrait of customers' perspectives on the best practices in the lodging industry. We first represent the various sources of value created by our portfolio of overall champions in terms of hotel attributes and the benefits these created for the customers. We then provide a similar industrywide description of customers' perspectives on functional practices by describing customer value created by what respondents had identified as the top performance in the lodging industry in a series of functional areas. Finally, we compare managers' perspectives as presented in the case studies to that of customers, as expressed in the survey, for both overall and functional practices.

Summary

In summary, the study involved three phases. The first phase relied on survey methodology to surface the best-practice champions as nominated by industry managers at both the corporate and property level. Phase II used in-depth interviews to capture the best practices of champions at the functional and overall level, and then the information was distilled into easy-to-read case formats. Finally, Phase III captured the perspectives of the end-users and intermediary customers of most of the overall champions. Customer perspectives have been incorporated into the overall cases, where applicable.

In the next two sections, we provide the individual case studies of the functional and overall best-practice champions. This large body of cases is then followed by a separate section on customers' perspectives of best practices. Finally, we provide conclusions regarding the findings of this study.

FUNCTIONAL BEST-PRACTICE CHAMPIONS

Introduction and Overview

A function-based orientation to best practices allows for the isolation of practices that are unique to specific disciplinary orientations. This approach to examining best practices is widely accepted and provides the advantage of helping professionals to focus on practices within their own departmental or discipline area of interest (Hiebeler, Kelly, & Ketteman, 1998).

We investigated practices by function to offer departmental managers, such as a director of sales and marketing, with the opportunity to concentrate their use of the study findings on their own area of influence regardless of the product segment in the industry in which the practice originated. The case listing by function provided later in this chapter is designed to help the reader locate cases in a specific functional area. Many of the cases in this report have activities, ideas, or practices that have applicability to several different functional areas, hence the listings by function may include the same case study in more than one functional category.

In our study the functional categories were identified for both corporate and property levels with the counsel of our industry experts. Since some functions differ between corporate and property levels, a distinction needed to be drawn between these two levels. Business development and design/architecture, for example, are often centralized areas of innovation that do not have property level counterparts. In other situations, like property level general management versus corporate level management, the activities and issues of concern are different and may elicit different types of practices. In summary, a total of six property level functions, and ten corporate level functions were identified as unique areas for best practices to emerge in this study. The functional areas are listed below in Table 1 for both corporate and property levels of operation. However, it should be noted that within the classification index of cases by functional area, we combined the corporate sales, marketing, and property sales & marketing functional areas into one section. In the original methodology and survey these functional areas were separate, but after reviewing the final case summaries of the best-practice champions from these three functional areas, it was determined that the activities represented by the cases were so diffused and blurred that one classification section representing all sales and marketing practices should be created.

Table 1: Functional Departments / Areas

Corporate Level Functions	Property Level Functions
Corporate Manager	General Manager
Controller	Controller
Food & Beverage	Food & Beverage
Information Technology	Information Technology
Human Resources	Human Resources
Operations / Rooms Mgt.	Operations / Rooms Mgt.
Sales	Sales & Marketing
Marketing	
Business Development	
Design / Architecture	

Critical activities within each functional area were devised and included in the Phase I nomination surveys as a guide to help the functional experts select champions within their own areas of expertise. Respondents, however, could nominate potential champions within the functional areas that did not relate to these critical activities. The key activities within each function are provided in Table 2 below. While these key activities were derived from previous research (Cline and Rach 1996; Enz and Corsun 1996; Renaghan and Green 1993; Roth, Chase and Voss 1997), they were substantially adapted for use in this study. After the data was collected, they were again useful as a guide for the construction of the classification of cases by functional area presented in the next section of this chapter.

Table 2: Functional Categories with Key Activities

Business Development
(Corporate Level Only)

Mergers / Acquisitions
Market Development Performance
Product Development Speed
Deal Making Skills / Shrewdness
Negotiating Skills / Closing Ability

Controller
(Corporate & Property Level)

Cash Flow Management
Integrating Accounting with Operations
Integrating Accounting with Marketing
Internal Control Systems
Capital Expenditure Planning Process

Corporate Level Management
(Corporate Level Only)

Vision / Mission Creation
Maintaining Quality / Developing Standards
Managing for Profitability
Managing for Customer Retention
Managing People / Fostering Teamwork / Growing the Potential of Your People

Design / Architecture
(Corporate Level Only)

Design Aesthetics / Functionality
Flexibility of Facilities and Diversity of Services
Relationships With Owners / Designers
Capital Expenditure Planning Process
New Product / Service Development

Food & Beverage Management
(Corporate & Property Level)

Distinctiveness / Diversity of F&B Services and Experiences
Profit Margin Management in Services
Maximizing Consistency and Clarity of F&B Service Standards
Cost Measurement and Inventory Monitoring
Purchasing / Inventory Management

General Management
(Property Level Only)

Managing People / Fostering Teamwork
Maintaining Quality / Developing Standards
Managing For Profitability
Managing the Owner Relationship
Adapting to Local Competitive Conditions with Speed / Flexibility

Human Resources Management
(Corporate & Property Level)

Measuring & Building Employee Satisfaction / Loyalty
Designing Selection and Retention Systems
Developing Employee Training and Development
Designing Employee Compensation and Rewards
Developing Employee Performance Standards & Appraisal Strategies
Diversity Management

Information Technology/Systems
(Corporate & Property Level)

Leveraging or Renovating Current Information Infrastructure
Integrating Technology with Operations
Integrating Property and Corporate Information Systems
Preparing and Training of People in the Use of Technology
Yield Management Systems
Reservation Systems

Marketing
(Corporate Level Only)

Brand / Image Management
Measuring / Managing / Building Customer Loyalty
Competitive Positioning
Long Term Market Development
Use of Multiple Distribution Channels

Rooms Division/Operation Management
(Corporate & Property Level)

Cleaning & Maintaining Physical Property
Managing Safety and Security
Guest Services & Relationship Management
Integration of Front-Office with Back-of-House
Managing Check-in / Check-out
Yield Management

Sales
(Corporate Level Only)

Managing Business Mix
Yield / Revenue Management
Sales Promotions
Building and Managing Long Term Relationships
Rewarding and Motivating the Sales Force

Sales & Marketing
(Property Level Only)

Managing Business Mix
Yield / Revenue Management
Sales Promotions
Building and Managing Long Term Relationships
Rewarding and Motivating the Sales Force

Functional Best-Practice Champions

Abbey Group Resorts ....Increasing Leisure Stays From Convention And Meetings Guests

Accor North America..Formalizing The Relationship Selling Process And Sales Team Activities

Accor North America..Internal Customer Satisfaction

AIMS Inc ....Making Unprofitable Hotels Profitable

AmericInn ....Solid Masonry Construction And Innovative Design

Ashley House Hotels-Keswick Hall ....Quality Service Management Program For Employees

The Balsams Grand Resort Hotel ....A Guest-History System

The Barbizon Hotel And Empire Hotel ....Standardized Recordkeeping For Operations And Guest Calls

The Boulders ....Food Forager To Improve Quality In F&B

The Boulders ....Self-Directed Housekeeping Teams

The Boulders ....Cornerstone Program: Developing A Service Culture

The Breakers Hotel ....Annual F&B Staff Reorganization And Single Theme Restaurant Concepts

Bristol Hotels & Resorts ....Streamlining The Operations Of Resource-Challenged Properties

Candlewood Hotel Company............................Designing An Extended-Stay Hotel For A Single-Niche Market

Candlewood Hotel Company............................Electronic Record Management

Carlson Hospitality Worldwide.........................World-Wide Reservation System

Carlson Hospitality Worldwide.........................Total Customer Satisfaction Via An On-Line Database And Employee Empowerment

Cendant Corporation..Comprehensive Diversity Initiative

Cendant Corporation..Developing Preferred Alliances With National Vendors

Cendant Corporation..Integration Of All Hotel MIS Functions

Choice Hotels International...............................In-House Executive Training And Development

Cincinnati Marriott Northeast ....Treating The Guest As Part Of The Family

Clarion Hotel-Comfort Inn & Suites.................Generating Sales Leads From Employees: A Contest Approach Program

Club Hotel By Doubletree ....Employee Care Committees

Coastal Hotel Group ....Employees On Loan For Training With The Buddy System

The Colony Hotel ....Guest-Friendly Environmental And Recycling Practices

Country Inns & Suites.......................................Successful Cobranding With Established Restaurant Concepts

Courtyard By Marriott.......................................Intranet Information Sharing

Dahlmann Properties..Improving The Work Environment And Decreasing Turnover

Day Hospitality Group.......................................Sabbatical Leave Program For General Managers

Days Inn Altoona ....Integrated, Community-Based Marketing Plan

Disney's Polynesian Resort...............................A Value-Based Process Of Training And Selection

Embassy Suites - Greater Minneapolis ....Consolidation And Centralization Of Reservations Sales Office

Essex Partners ....Achieving Greater Profitability Through Budgeting, Cost Controls, And Team Building

Fairmont Copley Plaza Hotel............................Using A Property Management System To Improve Concierge Desk Excellence

The Farmington Inn...Writing Historical Fiction Books To Enhance Marketing

Four Seasons & Regent Hotels & Resorts.........Designated Trainer Program For Front-Line Employees

Four Seasons & Regent Hotels & Resorts.........Developing A High Ratio Of Employees To Guests

Four Seasons & Regent Hotels & Resorts.........Ensuring A Luxury Hotel Experience

Four Seasons & Regent Hotels & Resorts.........Informal Dining Venue And Alternative Cuisine

Good Nite Inn ....Establishing Time Frames For Preventive Maintenance Tasks

Good Nite Inn ....Development Of Mobile Shop For Improved Guestroom Maintenance

Grand Theme Hotels ....The Creation Of A Process To Track And Control Labor Costs

The Greenbrier ....Programs Establishing The Resort As A Center For Culinary Excellence

Holiday Inn Express, Cripple Creek, CO ....Making Every Employee's Job A Sales Job

Holiday Inn Express, Helena, MT ....Achieving Quality Customer Service At An Economy Property

Holiday Inn SunSpree Resort............................Specialized Suites To Meet The Demands Of The Vacationing Family

Hotel Bel Air ....Comprehensive Environmental Management

Hotel Bel Air ....Proactive Property-Maintenance Program

Hotel Nikko At Beverly Hills ....Portable Telephone System Throughout Hotel

Hyatt Arlington Hotel ....Redesigning And Revitalizing A Food And Beverage Outlet

Hyatt Hotels Corporation ....Survey-Based Guest-Satisfaction Program

Hyatt Regency Chicago....................................Comprehensive Waste Reduction And Recycling Program

Hyatt Regency Scottsdale ....Developing An Environmental Recycling Program

Hyatt Regency Scottsdale ....Hospitality Training Program For High School Students

IMPAC Hotel Group ....A Lobby Kiosk Touch-Screen Guest Tracking System

The Inn At Essex ....Advertising On City Buses To Create Awareness

The Inn At Essex ....Providing Absolute Guest Satisfaction

Inn at the Market..Outsourced Human Resources To Professional HR Consultant

Inter-Continental Hotels & Resorts..................Building A Global Marketing Database

Kessler Enterprises...Development And Concept Of The Grand Theme Hotels

Kimpton Group and Outrigger Hotels..............Private Label Reservation System To Encourage Upselling

Knights Inn Summerton (Preea, Inc.)..............Creating Your Own Mailing Lists To Increase Business

Latham Hotel, Georgetown, Wash, DC..............Midscale Guestrooms Designed To Give An Upscale, Residential Feel

Marriott International ....Aligning Information Technology With Corporate Strategy

Marriott International ....Developing Products To Meet The Needs Of Targeted Market Segments

Marriott International ....Leveraging Leadership Capacity And Building Future Leaders

Marriott International ....Revenue Management Systems For Revenue Enhancement

Marriott International ....Sales Innovations Strategies

Marriott International ....Successful Creation Of New Brands

Marriott U.S. Postal Service
   Conference Center ....Express Check-In On Hotel Airport Shuttle Buses

Minneapolis-St. Paul Hilton ....Line Employee Empowerment

Motel 6..Developing A Memorable And Effective Advertising Message

Motel 6..Training Employees For General Management

Motel Properties Inc.......................................Employee Recognition Program

New York Marriott Financial Center.................Regular Status Meetings Between Executive And Department Staffs

Newark Gateway Hilton ....Guest Check-In On The Shuttle Bus

Omni Hotels...Integrated Property Management And Revenue Management System

Palisades Executive Conference Center ....Experience Engineering And Integrative Design

The Peninsula Beverly Hills Hotel ....24-Hour Check-In/Check-Out

The Pierre ....Implementing And Monitoring Cost-Plus Purchasing Agreements

The Pierre ....Maximizing Profitability By Managing The Sales Mix

Preferred Hotels & Resorts Worldwide ....Development Of Preferred Standards Of Excellence

Promus Hotel Corporation ....Guaranteed Customer Satisfaction

Promus Hotel Corporation ....On-Line Integrated Payroll/Benefit Accounting System

Radisson Worldwide.......................................Reward Program For Travel Agents

Ramada Franchise Systems.............................Employee Selection, Motivation, Training, And Satisfaction

Residence Inn By Marriott ....A Collaborative Approach To Quality Assurance In Extended Stay Hotels

Residence Inn By Marriott ....Sales Strategies For The Extended-Stay Market

The Ritz-Carlton Chicago ...."Compcierge" Position For Guests' Computer Problems

The Ritz-Carlton Dearborn ....Special Check-In Service For Frequent Guests

The Ritz-Carlton Hotel Co. ....Maximizing Guest Service

The Ritz-Carlton Tysons Corners ....Self-Directed Work Teams, Job Redesign, And Empowerment

Rodeway Inn International Orlando ....Rewarding Employee Performance In An Economy Hotel

Royal Palms Hotel & Casitas ....Restoration And Redesign Of Older Property For Residential Feel

SAI Luxury Hotels, Inc. ....Business Development/Renovation/Turnaround/Repositioning

Sheraton - Denver West Colorado ....Job Sharing Between Sales Managers

Sheraton Elk Grove...Annual Implementation Of A Broad-Based Best Practice

Simpson House Inn...Hospitality Training Curriculum With An Emphasis On Diversity

Sonesta Hotels ....Creating A Profit Center Training Operation

Sunstone Hotels..Focused Growth Of Hotel Company Utilizing A REIT

Swissôtel..Creation Of A Revenue Manager Position To Increase Room Sales Revenues

Swissôtel..Implementation Of A Global Sales Effort

Tamar Inns ....Implementation Of Self-Funded Health Insurance

Tishman Hotel Corporation ....Hotel Renovation: The Doral Park Avenue Hotel

Towneplace Suites By Marriott........................Cross-Trained Staffing Model As Driver Of Revenue

Travelodge ....Guest Loyalty At The Economy Level

US Franchise Systems, Inc...............................Franchising Agreements At USFS

The Waldorf-Astoria ....Gathering Customer Feedback And Coding Performances

The Waldorf-Astoria ....Revenue Maximization For The Food And Beverage Department

Walt Disney World Resorts And
    Theme Parks...Providing A "Touchable" Dining Experience

White Lodging Services ....Preshift Meetings For All Departments

Windsor Court Hotel ....Sophisticated Guest-Recognition Program

Winegardner & Hammons Inc. ....Pre-Opening Handbook For New Hotel Properties

Wyndham Hotels & Resorts ....An Integrated Approach To Food And Beverage

Accounting/Controller

Bristol Hotels & Resorts ....Streamlining The Operations Of Resource-Challenged Properties

Candlewood Hotel Company..........................Electronic Record Management

Essex Partners..Achieving Greater Profitability Through Budgeting, Cost Controls, And Team Building

New York Marriott Financial Center.................Regular Status Meetings Between Executive And Departments Staffs

Promus Hotels ....On-Line Integrated Payroll/Benefit Accounting System

Architecture/Design

AmericInn ....Solid Masonry Construction And Innovative Design

Candlewood Hotel Company..........................Designing An Extended Stay Hotel For A Single-Niche Market

Holiday Inn SunSpree.......................................Specialized Suites To Meet The Demands Of The Vacationing Family

Hyatt Arlington Hotel ....Redesigning And Revitalizing A Food And Beverage Outlet

Kessler Enterprises...Development And Concept Of The Grand Theme Hotels

Latham Hotel, Georgetown, Washington, DC...Mid-Scale Guestrooms Designed To Give An Upscale, Residential Feel

Marriott International.......................................Products To Meet The Needs Of Targeted Market Segments

Palisades Executive Conference Center ....Experience Engineering And Integrative Design

Royal Palms Hotel & Casitas ....Restoration And Redesign Of Older Property For Residential Feel

SAI Luxury Hotels, Inc. ....Business Development/Renovation/Turnaround/Repositioning

Tishman Hotel Corporation ....Hotel Renovation: The Doral Park Avenue Hotel

Business Development

AIMS Inc. ....Making Unprofitable Hotels Profitable

Cendant Corporation.......................................Comprehensive Diversity Initiative

Cendant Corporation.......................................Developing Preferred Alliances With National Vendors

Essex Partners ....Achieving Greater Profitability Through Budgeting, Cost Controls, And Team Building

Marriott International.......................................Developing Products To Meet The Needs Of Targeted Market Segments

Marriott International.......................................Successful Creation Of New Brands

Preferred Hotels & Resorts Worldwide.............Development Of The Preferred Standards Of Excellence

The Ritz-Carlton Hotel Co. ....Maximizing Guest Service

SAI Luxury Hotels, Inc. ....Business Development/Renovation/Turnaround/Repositioning

Sonesta Hotels ....Creating A Profit Center Training Operation

Sunstone Hotels..Focused Growth Of Hotel Company Utilizing A REIT

Tishman Hotel Corporation ....Hotel Renovation: The Doral Park Avenue Hotel

US Franchise Systems, Inc................................Franchising Agreements At USFS

Corporate Management

Accor North America.......................................Formalizing The Relationship Selling Process And Sales Team Activities

Accor North America.......................................Internal Customer Satisfaction

AIMS Inc. ....Making Unprofitable Hotels Profitable

AmericInn ....Solid Masonry Construction And Innovative Design

Bristol Hotels & Resorts ....Streamlining The Operations Of Resource-Challenged Properties

Carlson Hospitality Worldwide.........World-Wide Reservation System

Cendant Corporation........................Comprehensive Diversity Initiative

Choice Hotels International...............In-House Executive Training And Development

Coastal Hotel Group ....Employees On Loan For Training With The Buddy System

Country Inns & Suites ....Successful Co-Branding With Established Restaurant Concepts

Dahlmann Properties ....Improving The Work Environment And Decreasing Turnover

Day Hospitality Group ....Sabbatical Leave Program For General Managers

Embassy Suites - Greater Minneapolis ....Consolidation And Centralization Of Reservations Sales Office

Essex Partners ....Achieving Greater Profitability Through Budgeting, Cost Controls, And Team Building

Four Seasons & Regent Hotels & Resorts.........Ensuring A Luxury Hotel Experience

Four Seasons & Regent Hotels & Resorts.........Informal Dining Venues And Alternative Cuisine

Good Nite Inn ....Establishing Time Frames For Preventive Maintenance Tasks

Holiday Inn Sunspree Resort............Specialized Suites To Meet the Demands Of The Vacationing Family

Hyatt Hotels Corporation ....Survey Based Guest Satisfaction Program

Kessler Enterprises...........................Development And Concept Of The Grand Theme Hotels

Knights Inn Summerton (Preea, Inc.).............Creating Your Own Mailing Lists To Increase Business

Latham Hotel, Georgetown, Washington, DC ...Mid-Scale Guestrooms Designed To Give An Upscale, Residential Feel

Marriott International.......................Aligning Information Technology With Corporate Strategy

Marriott International.......................Developing Products To Meet The Needs Of Targeted Market Segments

Marriott International.......................Leveraging Leadership Capacity And Building Future Leaders

Marriott International.......................Sales Innovations Strategies

Marriott International.......................Successful Creation Of New Brands

Motel 6..Training Employees For General Management

Motel Properties Inc. ....Employee Recognition Program

Preferred Hotels & Resorts Worldwide.............Development Of Preferred Standards Of Excellence

Promus Hotel Corporation ....Guaranteed Customer Satisfaction

Promus Hotel Corporation ....On-Line Integrated Payroll/Benefit Accounting System

Radisson Worldwide...........................Reward Program For Travel Agents

Ramada Franchise Systems...............Employee Selection, Motivation, Training, And Satisfaction

Residence Inn By Marriott ....Sales Strategies For The Extended Stay Market

Residence Inn By Marriott ....A Collaborative Approach To Quality Assurance In Extended Stay Hotels

The Ritz-Carlton Hotel Co. ....Maximizing Guest Service

Sonesta Hotels ....Creating A Profit Center Training Operation

Sunstone Hotels ....Focused Growth Of Hotel Company Utilizing a REIT

Swissôtel ....Creation Of A Revenue Manager Position To Increase Room Sales Revenues

Swissôtel ....Implementing A Global Sales Effort

Tamar Inns ....Implementation Of Self-Funded Health Insurance

Travelodge ....Guest Loyalty At The Economy Level

US Franchise Systems, Inc.................................Franchising Agreements At USFS

Walt Disney World Resorts And Theme Parks ...Providing A "Touchable" Dining Experience

Wyndham Hotels & Resorts ....An Integrated Approach To Food And Beverage

Food & Beverage

The Boulders ....Food Forager To Improve Quality In F&B

The Breakers Hotel ....Annual F&B Staff Reorganization And Single Theme Restaurant Concepts

Country Inns & Suites ....Successful Co-Branding With Established Restaurant Concepts

Four Seasons & Regent Hotels & Resorts.........Informal Dining Venue And Alternative Cuisine

The Greenbrier ....Programs Establishing The Resort As A Center For Culinary Excellence

Hyatt Arlington Hotel ....Redesigning And Revitalizing A Food And Beverage Outlet

The Pierre ....Cost-Plus Purchasing Agreements With Food And Beverage Vendors

The Waldorf-Astoria ....Revenue Maximization For The Food And Beverage Department

Walt Disney World Resorts and Theme Parks.....Providing A "Touchable" Dining Experience

Winegardner & Hammons Inc. ....Pre-Opening Handbook For New Hotel Properties

Wyndham Hotels & Resorts ....An Integrated Approach To Food And Beverage

General Management

Ashley House Hotels-Keswick Hotel ....Quality Service Management Program For Employees

The Balsams Grand Resort Hotel ....A Guest-History System

The Barbizon Hotel and Empire Hotel ....Standardized Recordkeeping For Operations And Guest Calls

The Boulders ....Self-Directed Housekeeping Teams

Cincinnati Marriott Northeast ....Treating The Guest As Part Of The Family

Dahlmann Properties ....Improving The Work Environment And Decreasing Turnover

Days Inn Altoona ....Integrated, Community-Based Marketing Plan

Disney's Polynesian Resort...............................A Value-Based Process Of Training And Selection

The Farmington Inn..Writing Historical Fiction Books To Enhance Marketing

Good Nite Inn..Development Of Mobile Shop For Improved Guestroom Maintenance

The Greenbrier ....Programs Establishing The Resort As A Center For Culinary Excellence

Holiday Inn Express, Cripple Creek, CO ....Making Every Employee's Job A Sales Job

Holiday Inn Express, Helena, MT ....Achieving Quality Customer Service At An Economy Property

Hotel Bel Air ....Comprehensive Environmental Management

Hyatt Arlington Hotel ....Redesigning And Revitalizing A Food And Beverage Outlet

Hyatt Regency Chicago.....................................Comprehensive Waste Reduction And Recycling Program

Hyatt Regency Scottsdale ....Developing An Environmental Recycling Program

Hyatt Regency Scottsdale ....Hospitality Training Program For High School Students

IMPAC Hotel Group ....A Lobby Kiosk Touch-Screen Guest Tracking System

Inn at the Market..Outsourced Human Resources To Professional HR Consultant

Marriott U.S. Postal Service Conference Center ...Express Check-In On The Hotel Airport Shuttle Buses

Minneapolis-St. Paul Hilton ....Line Employee Empowerment

New York Marriott Financial Center................Regular Status Meetings Between Executive And Department Staffs

The Peninsula Beverly Hills Hotel ....24-Hour Check-In/Check-Out

The Pierre ....Maximizing Profitability By Managing The Sales Mix

The Ritz-Carlton Chicago ...."Compcierge" Position To Handle Guests' Computer Problems

Rodeway Inn International Orlando ....Rewarding Employee Performance In An Economy Hotel

Sheraton Elk Grove..Annual Implementation Of A Broad-Based Best Practice

Simpson House Inn...Hospitality Training Curriculum With An Emphasis On Diversity

The Waldorf-Astoria ....Gathering Customer Feedback And Coding Performances

White Lodging Services ....Preshift Meeting For All Departments

Winegardner & Hammons Inc. ....Pre-Opening Handbook For New Hotel Properties

Human Resources

Accor North America..Internal Customer Satisfaction

Ashley House Hotels-Keswick Hotel ....Quality Service Management Program For Employees

The Barbizon Hotel and Empire Hotel ....Standardized Recordkeeping For Operations And Guest Calls

The Boulders ....Self-Directed Housekeeping Teams

The Boulders ....Cornerstone Program: Developing A Service Culture

The Breakers Hotel ....Annual F&B Staff Reorganization And Single Theme Restaurant

Carlson Hospitality Worldwide........................Total Customer Satisfaction Via On-Line Database And Employee Empowerment

Cendant Corporation.......................................Comprehensive Diversity Initiative

Choice Hotels International..............................In-House Executive Training And Development

Cincinnati Marriott Northeast ....Treating The Guest As Part Of The Family

Clarion Hotel-Comfort Inn & Suites................Generating Sales Leads From Employees: A Contest Approach Program

Club Hotel By Doubletree ....Employee Care Committees

Coastal Hotel Group ....Employees On Loan For Training With The Buddy System

Courtyard By Marriott......................................Intranet Information Sharing

Dahlmann Properties ....Improving The Work Environment And Decreasing Turnover

Day Hospitality Group......................................Sabbatical Leave Program For General Managers

Disney's Polynesian Resort...............................A Value-Based Process Of Training And Selection

Four Seasons & Regent Hotels & Resorts.........Developing A High Ratio Of Employees To Guests

Four Seasons & Regent Hotels & Resorts.........Designated Trainer Program For Front-Line Employees

Four Seasons & Regent Hotels & Resorts.........Ensuring A Luxury Hotel Experience

Good Nite Inn...Establishing Time Frames For Preventative Maintenance Tasks

Grand Theme Hotels ....The Creation Of A Process To Track And Control Labor Costs

Holiday Inn Express, Cripple Creek, CO ....Making Every Employee's Job A Sales Job

Hyatt Regency Scottsdale ....Developing An Environmental Recycling Program

Hyatt Regency Scottsdale ....Hospitality Training Program For High School Students

The Inn at Essex ....Providing Absolute Guest Satisfaction

Inn at the Market..Outsourced Human Resources To Professional HR Consultant

Marriott International ....Leveraging Leadership Capacity And Building Future Leaders

Minneapolis-St. Paul Hilton ....Line Employee Empowerment

Motel 6...Training Employees For General Management

Motel Properties Inc......................................Employee Recognition Program

New York Marriott Financial Center.................Regular Status Meetings Between Executive And Department Staffs

Promus Hotel Corporation ....Guaranteed Customer Satisfaction

Ramada Franchise Systems, Inc......................Employee Selection, Motivation, Training, And Satisfaction

The Ritz-Carlton Dearborn ....Special Check-In Service For Frequent Guests

The Ritz-Carlton Hotel Company ....Maximizing Guest Service

The Ritz-Carlton Tysons Corner......................Self-Directed Work Teams, Job Redesign, And Employee Empowerment

Rodeway Inn International Orlando ....Rewarding Employee Performance In An Economy Hotel

Sheraton - Denver West Colorado ....Job Sharing Between Sales Managers

Sheraton Elk Grove.......................................Annual Implementation Of A Broad-Based Best Practice

Simpson House Inn ....Hospitality Training Curriculum With An Emphasis On Diversity

Sonesta Hotels ....Creating A Profit Center Training Operation

Swissôtel ....Creation Of A Revenue Manager Position To Increase Room Sales

Swissôtel ....Implementing A Global Sales Effort

Tamar Inns ....Implementation Of Self-Funded Health Insurance

Towneplace Suites by Marriott ....Cross-Trained Staffing Model As Driver Of Revenue

The Waldorf-Astoria ....Gathering Customer Feedback And Coding Performance

The Waldorf-Astoria ....Revenue Maximization For The Food And Beverage Department

White Lodging Services ....Preshift Meetings For All Departments

Windsor Court Hotel ....Sophisticated Guest-Recognition Program

Wyndham Hotels & Resorts ....An Integrated Approach To Food And Beverage

Information Technology

The Balsams Grand Resort Hotel ....A Guest-History System

The Barbizon Hotel and Empire Hotel ....Standardized Recordkeeping For Operations And Guest Calls

Candlewood Hotel Company...........................Electronic Record Management

Carlson Hospitality Worldwide........................Total Customer Satisfaction Via On-Line Database And Employee Empowerment

Cendant Corporation.....................................Integration Of All Hotel MIS Functions

Courtyard By Marriott....................................Intranet Information Sharing

Fairmont Copley Plaza Hotel...........................Using A Property Management System To Improve Concierge Desk Excellence

Hotel Nikko at Beverly Hills ....Portable Telephone System Throughout Hotel

IMPAC Hotel Group ....A Lobby Kiosk Touch-Screen Guest Tracking System

Inter-Continental Hotels & Resorts.................Building A Global Marketing Database

Kimpton Group and Outrigger Hotels..............Private Label Reservation System To Encourage Upselling

Marriott International ....Aligning Information Technology With Corporate Strategy

Marriott International ....Revenue Management Systems For Revenue Enhancement

Marriott International ....Sales Innovations Strategies

Newark Gateway Hilton ....Guest Check-In On The Shuttle Bus

Omni Hotels...Integrated Property Management And Revenue Management System

Promus Hotel Corporation ....On-Line Integrated Payroll/Benefit Accounting System

Radisson Worldwide...Reward Program For Travel Agents

The Ritz-Carlton Chicago ...."Compcierge" Position To Handle Guests' Computer Problems

Sheraton - Denver West Colorado ....Job Sharing Between Sales Managers

Swissôtel ....Implementation Of A Global Sales Effort

Operations

Accor North America...Internal Customer Satisfaction

The Balsams Grand Resort Hotel ....A Guest-History System

The Boulders ....Self-Directed Housekeeping Teams

The Boulders ....Food Forager To Improve Quality In F&B

Bristol Hotels & Resorts ....Streamlining The Operations Of Resource-Challenged Properties

Cendant Corporation...Integration Of All Hotel MIS Functions Into One System

Coastal Hotel Group ....Employees On Loan For Training With The Buddy System

The Colony Hotel ....Guest-Friendly Environmental And Recycling Practices

Courtyard By Marriott.......................................Intranet Information Sharing

Embassy Suites - Greater Minneapolis ....Consolidation And Centralization Of Reservations Sales Office

Fairmont Copley Plaza Hotel...........................Using A Property Management System To Improve Concierge Desk Excellence

Four Seasons & Regent Hotels & Resorts.........Developing A High Ratio Of Employees To Guests

Four Seasons & Regent Hotels & Resorts.........Ensuring A Luxury Hotel Experience

Good Nite Inn ....Creating Accountability For The Maintenance Staff

Good Nite Inn ....Development Of Mobile Shop For Improved Guestroom Maintenance

Grand Theme Hotels ....The Creation Of A Process To Track And Control Labor Costs

Holiday Inn Express, Helena, MT ....Achieving Quality Customer Service At An Economy Property

Hotel Bel Air ....Comprehensive Environmental Management

Hotel Bel Air ....Proactive Property-Maintenance Program

Hyatt Hotels Corporation ....Survey-Based Guest-Satisfaction Program

Hyatt Regency Chicago......................................Comprehensive Waste Reduction And Recycling Program

Hyatt Regency Scottsdale ....Developing An Environmental Recycling Program

IMPAC Hotel Group ....A Lobby Kiosk Touch-Screen Guest Tracking System

The Inn at Essex ....Providing Absolute Guest Satisfaction

Marriott U.S. Postal Service Conference

    Center ....Express Check-In On Hotel Airport Shuttle Buses

Minneapolis-St. Paul Hilton ....Line Employee Empowerment

New York Marriott Financial Center.................Regular Status Meetings Between Executive And Department Staffs

Newark Gateway Hilton ....Guest Check-In On The Shuttle Bus

The Peninsula Beverly Hills Hotel ....24-Hour Check-In/Check-Out

The Pierre ....Implementing And Monitoring Cost-Plus Purchasing Agreements

Promus Hotel Corporation ....Guaranteed Customer Satisfaction

Promus Hotel Corporation ....On-Line Integrated Payroll/Benefit Accounting System

Residence Inn By Marriott ....A Collaborative Approach To Quality Assurance In Extended Stay Hotels

The Ritz-Carlton Chicago ...."Compcierge" Position To Handle Guests' Computer Problems

The Ritz-Carlton Dearborn ....Special Check-In Service For Frequent Guests

The Ritz-Carlton Hotel Company ....Maximizing Guest Service

The Ritz-Carlton Tysons Corner ....Self-Directed Work Teams, Job Redesign, And Empowerment

Sheraton Elk Grove ....Annual Implementation Of A Broad-Based Best Practice

Towneplace Suites by Marriott ....Cross-Trained Staffing Model As Driver Of Revenue

The Waldorf-Astoria ....Gathering Customer Feedback And Coding Performance

White Lodging Services ....Pre-Shift Meetings For All Departments

Windsor Court Hotel ....Sophisticated Guest-Recognition Program

Winegardner & Hammons Inc. ....Pre-Opening Handbook For New Hotel Properties

Sales & Marketing

Abbey Group Resorts ....Increasing Leisure Stays From Convention And Meeting Guests

Accor North America...Formalizing The Relationship Selling Process And Sales Team Activities

The Balsams Grand Resort Hotel ....A Guest-History System

Candlewood Hotel Company.............................Extended-Stay Hotel For A Single-Niche Market

Carlson Hospitality Worldwide.........................Total Customer Satisfaction Via An On-Line Database And Employee Empowerment

Cendant Corporation..Developing Preferred Alliances With National Vendors

Cincinnati Marriott Northeast ....Treating The Guest As Part Of The Family

Clarion Hotel-Comfort Inn & Suites.................Generating Sales Leads From Employees

Club Hotel By Doubletree ....Employee Care Committees

The Colony Hotel ....Guest-Friendly Environmental And Recycling Practices

Country Inn & Suites..Successful Co-Branding With Established Restaurant Concepts

Days Inn Altoona ....Integrated, Community-Based Marketing Plan

Embassy Suites - Greater Minneapolis ....Consolidation And Centralization Of Reservations Sales Office

The Farmington Inn..Writing Historical Fiction Books To Enhance Marketing

Four Seasons & Regent Hotels & Resorts.........Developing A High Ratio Of Employees To Guests

The Greenbrier ....Programs Establishing The Resort As A Center For Culinary Excellence

Holiday Inn Express, Cripple Creek, CO ....Making Every Employee's Job A Sales Job

Holiday Inn SunSpree.......................................Specialized Suites To Meet the Demands Of The Vacationing Family

Hyatt Arlington Hotel ....Redesigning And Revitalizing A Food And Beverage Outlet

Hyatt Hotels Corporation ....Survey-Based Guest-Satisfaction Program

The Inn at Essex ....Advertising On City Buses To Create Awareness

Inter-Continental Hotels & Resorts.................Building A Global Marketing Database

Kimpton Group and Outrigger Hotels.............Private Label Reservation System To Encourage Upselling

Knights Inn Summerton (Preea, Inc.)..............Creating Your Own Mailing Lists To Increase Business

Marriott International......................................Developing Products To Meet The Needs Of Targeted Market Segments

Marriott International......................................Revenue Management Systems For Revenue Enhancement

Marriott International......................................Sales Innovations Strategies

Marriott International......................................Successful Creation Of New Brands

Motel 6...Developing A Memorable And Effective Advertising Message

Omni Hotels..Integrated Property Management And Revenue Management System

The Pierre ....Maximizing Profitability By Managing The Sales Mix

Radisson Worldwide...Reward Program For Travel Agents

Residence Inn By Marriott ....A Collaborative Approach To Quality Assurance In Extended Stay Hotels

Sheraton - Denver West Colorado ....Job Sharing Between Sales Managers

Swissôtel...Creation Of A Revenue Manager Position To Increase Room Sales

Swissôtel...Implementation Of A Global Sales Effort

Travelodge ....Guest Loyalty At The Economy Level

The Waldorf-Astoria ....Gathering Customer Feedback And Coding Performances

Windsor Court Hotel..Sophisticated Guest-Recognition Program

ABBEY GROUP RESORTS

Increasing Leisure Stays from Convention and Meeting Guests

Description

The Practice: The Return Special Value Program (RSVP) is a special promotion designed to provide an incentive to meeting planners and convention participants to return to Abbey Group Resorts as leisure guests. This incentive offers the meeting attendee a future leisure stay at the group rate in the Abbey Group property that hosted the group function. Abbey will honor the group rate for one year from the date of the group function, subject to availability, as long as the original group rate was not confidential, and except for certain holiday weekends, such as Memorial Day, Fourth of July, and Labor Day.

Why the Practice Was Developed: Being a seasonal resort operator, the Abbey Group has shoulder seasons from April to the first two weeks in May, as well as the latter part of September through October. Even during its busiest times, however, it has space available — especially early in the week — for individual reservations. The purpose of this practice is to increase overall resort occupancy and encourage group guests to become leisure guests. Large rate fluctuations between seasons are the norm. During the winter months, rooms will sell for $60 to $65, but this rate will increase as much as 300% during the peak season. So a participant in a group function in November can take advantage of the promotion to return with his or her family during the peak season at the group (slow-season) rate, provided space is available.

Execution

The Approach to Implementation: The Abbey resort development has been in operation for about 20 years on Lake Geneva, Wisconsin. Three hotels constitute the Abbey Group, the largest being the Abbey itself. Their mix of business is 60% group and 40% leisure customers.

Phillip Anderson, director of sales and marketing, sought to implement a plan to increase his occupancies. He developed the RSVP concept during spring and summer of 1998, and presented it to the Abbey president and the general managers. They gave him the go-ahead to market the plan, which was put in place during the summer. Now that the RSVP is included in the sales presentations to meeting planners, Abbey Group's sales specialists find the promotion engages buyers' attention because it serves the meeting planners' self-interests in three ways: (1) the meeting planners themselves can use the promotion for a later recreational stay, (2) the special incentive can be emphasized in the meeting literature to encourage greater meeting attendance, and (3) the promotion provides added value for client and participant at no cost.

Outcomes

Success of the Practice: The response from meeting planners has been favorable. While it is too early to draw significant conclusions, Mr. Anderson indicates that, as of December 1, 1998, he has had approximately 50 guests take advantage of the program. By summer 1999, he feels he will have a good handle on his results, and will be able to further define the best direction for the program to go.

Mr. Anderson anticipates that return business will accelerate as time goes on. Moreover, the additional business generated will help offset the cost of the 175-to-200 person cadre of full-time, year-round employees. This employee base swells to about 1,000 when the season is in full swing.

Insights

It is still too early to make a realistic appraisal of the success and profitability of this program. However, early indications from the sales staff and customers indicate a ready acceptance.

Contact

Phillip Anderson, Director of Sales and Marketing
Abbey Group Resorts
P.O. Box 20, Fontana WI 53125
Phone: 800-643-6382 Fax: 414-275-5910

ACCOR NORTH AMERICA

Formalizing the Relationship Selling Process and Sales Team Activities

Description

The Practice: Accor North America has developed a basic model of customer-relationship development. The six-stage process identifies customer expectations at each stage of relationship development, and the key activities that the sales team must conduct at each stage to meet customer expectations.

Why the Practice Was Developed: Accor North America has 18 hotels and 4,700 rooms under management, including Sofitel and Novotel. Robert Mackey, vice president of sales and marketing, felt Accor's sales practices failed to differentiate its properties from other similar competitive properties.

Execution

The Approach to Implementation: In 1995 Mr. Mackey established and led a cross-functional team of eight persons from different levels and backgrounds. Included on this team were the president of MasterConnect Associates, Accor North America's sales training vendor, and the director of research for Learning International. The Learning International affiliation provided access to research regarding customer preferences and best practices from other companies.

The team met every two months for a year and a half in two-day sessions. They studied other companies and looked at their own operations from a different perspective. The Learning International participation was vital, once LI adapted to hospitality culture and language. During the preparation of the program, an ongoing feedback process was maintained between the company and customers (both group decision-makers and individuals), as well as the company's employees. Employees consulted included a cross-section of both new and long-term employees. Many suggestions from these two sources were adapted for the program.

These meetings yielded a selection of new processes and a revision of old practices, culminating in a six-phase customer relationship program. Each phase analyzes customer expectations. Key sales activities are then established to meet customer expectations at each phase. To ensure that the focus remains on meeting or exceeding customer expectations, sales performance is measured in two ways: (1) completion of the key sales activities, and (2) customer perceptions of how well expectations have been met.

The six-phase model is as follows:

1 **Pre-sale research**
   a. Customer expectations – knowing their business and anticipating their needs
   b. Key sales activities
      1. Gathering information about their business
      2. Analyzing their sales potential
      3. Developing a strategic sales plan

2 **Probing and analyzing needs**
   a. Customer expectations – focusing on their specific needs, rather than asking fact-finding questions
   b. Key sales activities – use appointments to:
      1. Identify decision-making process
      2. Examine long-term partner potential
      3. Determine kind and scope of competition

3 **Presenting and recommending solutions**
   a. Customer expectations – submitting a clear contract tailored to their needs that is flexible enough to change if specifications change
   b. Key sales activities
      1. Internal team validates customer needs
      2. Solutions are cost-effective
      3. Use of third-party endorsements
      4. If business is lost, find out why

4 Implementing solutions – attempt to support value-added product that meets or exceeds customer needs

   a. Customer expectations – scheduling deadlines; specifying key hotel contact, time standards, and a communication process

   b. Key sales activities

      1. Introduction of operations group to client

      2. Internal accounting procedures

      3. Development of a thorough communication plan between hotel and client

5 Monitoring results – to ensure profitability and customer satisfaction

   a. Customer expectations – corrective action taken rapidly if need be; a high level of feedback and communication

   b. Key sales activities

      1. Compare actual business with committed business

      2. Continuous feedback and communications to maximize customer satisfaction

6 Maintaining and expanding the partnership – anticipating future needs and recommending new solutions

   a. Customer expectations – knowledgeable about their business to help them make better decisions

   b. Key sales activities

      1. Customer appointments to review results and ask for additional business

      2. Use outside services to keep up-to-date on customers' business

      3. Thank them for the business

Each of the six phases has a performance measure. A continuous internal and external analysis of the customer-relationship process provides sufficient information to enable an evaluation of each sales team's performance. An outside company randomly calls customers to assess how well the sales teams are meeting customer expectations. Each sales team receives a performance score each quarter; 25% of the team's sales incentive is based on this performance grade. The grading is completely objective, and each sales team has an assigned goal.

Costs: The 18-month process for preparing the six-phase plan cost approximately $75,000. The ongoing training and indoctrination of sales staff into the program is charged to the normal operating budget.

Outcomes

Success of the Practice: Sofitel's program began in June 1997, and the sales teams have increased their average performance score from 88% to 95%, exceeding the original goal of 91%. Novotel's program began in April 1998, and results are too premature to evaluate. Because there are too many other variables involved, no method has been found to accurately measure the effect of this program on increased hotel occupancy.

Insights

Advice and Observations: Mr. Mackey indicates that hard work is required for the implementation process of this practice. Progress and training audits encourage the continued use of the relationship-selling process. Mr. Mackey advises that while it is difficult to keep everyone on the same track, the process should be fully embedded in two or three years, and its use should be second nature to the sales staff.

Contact

Robert Mackey, Vice President of Sales and Marketing
Accor North America
245 Park Avenue, New York, NY 10167
Phone: 212-949-5700 Fax: 212-490-0499

Corporate Management

Human Resources

Operations

The Practice: Accor North America uses multiple practices to achieve high levels of motivation and retention of its employees. Those practices include (1) booster programs that empower employees; (2) GMs' bonuses linked to satisfaction scores and profitability; (3) a "270-degree" review process; (4) employee roundtables; and (5) meeting participants required to play specified roles.

Why the Practice Was Developed: When the hotel industry went through a major down cycle, Accor sought to reconfigure the way it was doing business. The founders and the president of Accor North America acquired additional training. The president then supplemented this training by attending an AMP course at Harvard. The president shared his new concepts and ideas with the top management team. Overall, a corporate philosophy of "autonomy" was embraced, meaning the goal was to avoid instituting practices whose purpose was to continuously check up on employees. The origin of this approach to running the company stems from the corporate founders' belief that "what leads to growth and profitability is managing people well."

From this philosophy, three broad strategies for developing and incorporating practices arose. As Timothy Barefield, vice president of human resources for Accor, explains, underlying the development of every practice are these three strategies: (1) "Don't say things; do them." Many companies "talk a lot about what they do, or what they wish they did, but in fact, the experience of employees is not consistent with what they hear their companies saying, so employees become cynical. Rather than talking about doing things, just go do them." Take action, and employee cynicism will be reduced. (2) "Don't do a lot of different things; just do a few things very well." Take one area where you can have the greatest impact and actually hit your goals. The worst thing for employees is when companies reengineer, "causing much pain and suffering," but then fail to achieve objectives at the end. This sequence of events results in a reduction in management credibility; however, if you do a few things very well, the employees will attribute greater credibility to management. (3) "Don't ask people to do things that you and your management aren't willing to do." Don't expect employees to do things to which you are not committed.

These strategies are the basis for every practice "from compensation to roundtable discussions by the executive team, so that all practices are consistent with the philosophy being espoused." As such, these strategies facilitate employee buy-in concerning organizational goals. The buy-in allows the company to eliminate audits and checks because the employees know what they are to do and they believe in the company. As a result, they perform at the expected level. In turn, the corporate philosophy of autonomy is supported.

The Approach to Implementation: The president of Accor North America, as well as outside consultants and the North American executive team, worked "every day" to develop practices that could reinvigorate Accor. Accor wanted improvement in all areas — customer satisfaction, employee satisfaction, and profit. Task forces were established at all levels, involving many individuals, to help develop practices that were consistent with the philosophy, and addressed customer, employee, and profit elements simultaneously. All employees were involved and affected.

Following the strategies outlined above, Accor developed several practices that were designed to improve customer satisfaction, employee satisfaction, and profitability:

1 A booster program for employee empowerment was developed to push decision-making down to a lower level. This program took approximately two years to implement.
2 Incentives for GMs were linked to the three goals, so 30% of GM bonuses are based on employee satisfaction, 30% of bonuses are tied to customer satisfaction, and 40% of bonuses are linked to profitability.

3 A 270-degree review process was put into place, in which managers in the company are evaluated by peers, subordinates, and superiors. This review process necessitated that select employees receive training to become review trainers; they then fanned out in the organization to train all employees because all managers undergo the 270-degree review. Initially, employees were uncomfortable with feedback on real performance that was required by the 270-degree review process, but they would now say it is well received.

4 At each hotel, employee roundtables were implemented so that all employees can discuss issues with the executive team.

5 At each meeting, employees must perform certain roles; that is, every meeting must have "a moderator, a scribe, a time-keeper, and a conscience." The sole purpose of the person who plays the role of the conscience is to end the meeting by looking each person in the eye and telling that person the one thing she or he did that hurt the progress or effectiveness of the meeting, or the thing he or she failed to do that would have helped the effectiveness of the meeting. At every meeting, each person gets or gives constructive feedback.

Operational Issues: Any new practice involves a task force and, typically, an outside consultant.

A Trial: Trials are conducted for each practice in one or two hotels. The trial period depends on the practice under consideration. Most trials have been successful and the practice has been incorporated throughout the company.

Costs: Mr. Barefield notes that costs have "not been that great in dollars." Most of it has been in "sweat equity." More training, better orientation, integrating people, and explaining the practices all take time. However, no additional time has been needed; time just had to be reallocated. Further, Mr. Barefield believes that the benefits of the practices far exceed any costs and effort.

Outcomes

Success of the Practice: Following the three-point strategy for the implementation of practices has resulted in success in all areas of the hotel and company. The results have been lower employee turnover, higher employee satisfaction scores, and "significantly better performance." People feel good about the company; they talk to others, both internally and externally. Employees have benefited through better career and personal development and increased responsibility.

Benefits for Customer: Customers perceive these practices in every interaction they have with an Accor employee. As a result, customers are likely to report a higher level of good experience and greater consistency in the Accor product and service. Customer satisfaction is determined by focus groups and targeted surveys.

Insights

Advice and Observations: Leadership must create a clear set of objectives. They must believe and commit to them. Autonomy, confrontation, and feedback must be lived and breathed. Consistency with each practice is mandatory.

Mr. Barefield believes that this three-point strategy is distinctive in the service industry. He further suggests that the strategies underlying the practices would not work with organizations that do not profess autonomy with their units; that is, it would be difficult to implement in a centralized organization.

Accor North America has 23,000 employees. Mr. Barefield believes incorporating the strategy would be easier to implement in a smaller organization. Furthermore, it would be difficult, but even more important, in a start-up company.

Contact

Timothy Barefield, Vice President of Human Relations
Accor North America
245 Park Avenue, New York, NY 10167
Phone: 212-949-5700 Fax: 212-490-0499

AIMS INC.

Making Unprofitable Hotels Profitable

Description

The Practice: Ashoka Investment and Management Services Inc. (AIMS Inc.) acquires bankrupt and/or dilapidated hotels and restores them to sound financial health. These turnarounds are accomplished primarily through careful negotiation, leasing food and beverage outlets, strict budgeting, and employee empowerment. One key to successful turnarounds is obtaining the hotels at sufficiently low prices to assure AIMS of a profit within one to three years. To date AIMS operates 24 hotels, all of which are now profitable.

Why the Practice Was Developed: Ashok Kumar is the president, owner, and operator of AIMS Inc., a privately held corporation. He was confident that he had the ability to turn around unprofitable hotel operations, even in cases where others had tried and failed. As a result, he originated the AIMS strategy.

Execution

The Approach to Implementation: Mr. Kumar utilizes the following approach in his turnaround strategy:

1 His first goal is to seek distressed hotels. Selection is based on Mr. Kumar's belief that he can turn the hotel around financially within one to three years.

2 He negotiates a lease based on 10-15% of the average gross room revenue realized during the last three years prior to his purchase. On particularly distressed properties, he requests a waiver on the first year's rent. The length of the lease may vary from five to 30 years, with allowance for renegotiation after 10 years.

3 If a food & beverage operation is a component of the hotel, he does not include it in the lease. Instead, it is leased to an outside operator.

4 He refurbishes the hotel at a fraction of the cost that other hotel operators spend by purchasing furnishings, fixtures, and equipment cast off by major chains that are refurbishing newly acquired properties.

5 He establishes a strict budget and financial forecast for management to follow.

6 He gives the GM full authority to run the hotel. Mr. Kumar does not believe GMs need to have extensive experience to run his properties, but they should have a mastery of front-office operations and the ability to identify problems in the day-to-day operation.

7 He advocates autonomy and trust of all hotel employees, and encourages employee feedback. This feedback provides him with many insights as to how the hotel is being operated. He seeks to develop a one-on-one relationship with all employees. Further, he provides pizza parties on special occasions, and gives employees an extra day off with pay when they receive special recognition by a guest.

8 He telephones each of his hotels seven days a week and speaks to the GM. He also receives a daily night report from the hotel auditor and a bank deposit report from the GM.

9 He or his associate, Mr. Timothy Whitehead, inspects each hotel at least once a month.

Outcomes

Success of the Practice: Mr. Kumar's 24 hotels range in size from 50 to 300 rooms with an average daily rate of $30-$90. The hotels average 60% occupancy rate, and all of them are profitable. However, Mr. Kumar recognizes that his ability to expand will largely be determined by the supply and demand for hotel rooms and how successful hotel operators are in retaining profitable operations.

Insights

Advice and Observations: Mr. Kumar's philosophy for success is, "Show a profit and you have a satisfied guest." Mr. Kumar is basically a one-man operation, although he does have one associate, Mr. Whitehead, who holds the title of CEO-consultant. Mr. Kumar believes this market offers the potential for anyone to enter without a major capital contribution — a $200,000-$300,000 investment can do the job in many cases.

Contact

Ashok Kumar, President
AIMS Inc.
608 Fillmore St., San Francisco, CA 94177
Phone: 415-215-7434 Fax: 415-552-4626

AMERICINN

Solid Masonry Construction and Innovative Design in a Limited-Service Product

Description

The Practice: AmericInn, a Midwest-based franchisor of limited-service hotels, uses unique construction standards to provide an innovative product to franchisees. These standards include solid-masonry construction, large guestrooms, and imaginative lobby and pool areas. Because of the concrete construction, the building is more stable than frame construction, so maintenance costs are lower than normal, producing savings that can be passed to the customer.

Why the Practice Was Developed: The practice of adhering to specific construction standards has been followed since the first development of the AmericInn product. According to Luke Fowler, president and chief executive officer, "Our construction standards have allowed us to achieve a low unit cost, which enables us to give the customer a good price value."

Execution

The Approach to Implementation: All AmericInn properties are newly built and consistent construction standards are followed throughout the chain. For example, solid concrete construction is used between the walls and precast flooring to reduce or eliminate the transmission of noise. The walls are finished with sheetrock, so there is no exposed masonry in the guestrooms. Another distinctive feature of the AmericInn product is a standard width of 14 feet for the guestroom; these "two extra feet" are believed to provide additional value and comfort to the customer.

Also required for all AmericInn properties are generous lobby and pool areas, which Mr. Fowler suggests are "generally larger than our competitors' by quite a bit." Every lobby has fireplaces and two-story vaulted ceilings. Each state-of-the-art pool is covered by a peaked roof composed of laminated beams with tongue and groove paneling made of cedar or fir. Both the pool and lobby areas are considered "signature items" of AmericInns. "The quality of these public areas justifies a higher yield on the room rate structure. Consumers feel much more pleased about their purchase when they have this type of environment," stated Mr. Fowler. "Typically you don't see this type of atmosphere in a limited-service product."

AmericInn also has its own in-house supply division, which allows the franchisee to customize the interior decor of the product, so that internally all the properties do not look the same. They work with the franchisee as much as possible within the standardized plans to provide a balance between the franchisee's wants and the needs of the chain. In addition, different prototypes are available based on the geographic location.

Outcomes

Success of the Practice: In a highly competitive environment, AmericInn has been able to continue to grow and compete within a somewhat saturated market. Mr. Fowler believes this success is a result of the quality and the content of the product; AmericInn takes great pride in the construction of its solid-concrete facilities.

The properties do well with business travelers during the week and, according to Mr. Fowler, "capture substantial weekend business because families love going there. It is a nice, comfortable place to be on a weekend."

Benefits for Customer: Mr. Fowler notes, "We have a remarkable pattern of excellent comments with very little negatives in our Guest Services Response program. We simply don't get complaints regarding the physical product."

Insights

Advice and Observations: Mr. Fowler believes that solid-masonry construction is the way hotels will be built in the future, and AmericInn is leading the way. He also suggests that customers will be demanding concrete guestrooms because the significant reduction in noise allows for a more restful stay.

Contact

Luke Fowler, President/CEO
AmericInn
18202 Minnetonka Blvd., Deep Haven, MN 55391
Phone: 612-476-9020 Fax: 612-476-7601

ASHLEY HOUSE HOTELS-KESWICK HALL

Quality Service Management Program for Employees

Description

The Practice: Ashley House Hotels-Keswick Hall incorporates a quality service management practice that is divided into three phases: (1) the Captain Quality program, in which an employee serves as a guest of the hotel for an evening and then spends the remainder of the week observing in every department; (2) the training program, which stresses communication skills; and (3) the Comfort Factor program, which alerts employees to hotel atmospherics.

Why the Practice Was Developed: Stephen Beaumont, general manager of Ashley House Hotels-Keswick Hall, originally developed his quality service management program at Haley's Hotel in Northern England, a hotel similar in size and quality to the Ashley House. He then instituted the same program at Ashley House when he arrived there in 1994. He believed that he had a very high-quality product in the Ashley House, but he wanted to ensure that he complemented the product with high-quality service.

Execution

The Approach to Implementation: While all three phases are important in developing a quality service management program, Mr. Beaumont says the Captain Quality program is the most important of the three phases. The phases are implemented as follows:

1 **Captain Quality** — All 55 employees participate, and the program operates 52 weeks a year. One employee is designated each week to be a guest of the hotel. The main purpose of this program is to orient each employee to the workings of every department in the hotel. The employee only spends one night as a guest of the hotel, which includes a complimentary dinner for two. After his/her week of observation in every department, the employee must submit a list of six points of needed improvement in the hotel. These six points are posted each week, and directed to the attention of the responsible department head. The responsible department responds to correct the problem. At the conclusion of his/her week as Captain Quality, the employee is presented with a company-logo T-shirt. The next Captain Quality is selected by drawing a name from a hat.

2 **Training Program** — The training program is conducted at a daylong meeting twice a year, usually during the January/February and July/August time periods. The program emphasizes communication skills, the responsibility of each employee to take the initiative in solving guest problems at the time that they happen, and the importance of every individual in determining the success of the hotel. Mr. Beaumont conducts the program himself with back-up support provided by department heads.

3 **Comfort Factor** — This facet of the quality service program is linked to the Captain Quality program. The purpose of this phase is to alert employees to the nuances that make up the atmosphere of the hotel; the noises, smells, lighting, and ambiance of the hotel must be conducive to providing a pleasant experience for the guest. This presentation on atmospherics is conducted on the day the new employee is oriented into the culture of the hotel, and then additional training sessions are presented two or three times a year to all employees to underscore the importance of atmospherics in the hotel.

Outcomes

Success of the Practice: As a result of Mr. Beaumont's quality service program, the employee turnover rate had dropped from 50% to 10%. Further, every employee has become aware of the functions and responsibilities of every department. As Captain Quality, the employee can personally observe the quality of service and facilities offered to the hotel guest.

Insights

Advice and Observations: Mr. Beaumont believes a similar program can be developed in any size hotel. What must be emphasized is the involvement of all employees, resulting in their providing personal input based upon their individual job positions.

Contact

Stephen Beaumont, General Manager
Ashley House Hotels-Keswick Hall
701 Club Drive, Keswick, VA 22947
Phone: 804-923-4340 Fax: 804-977-4171

THE BALSAMS GRAND RESORT HOTEL

A Guest-History System

Description

The Practice: The Balsams Grand Resort Hotel, a privately owned hotel that has been in continuous operation since 1866, has created a comprehensive guest-history program. The guest history indicates each guest's room, dining room, server, food and beverage, housekeeper, and activity preferences. If the guest likes to play golf, preferred tee times are noted; if the guest skis, preferred runs are recorded. In short, every single guest whim and wish gets entered into the guest-history system.

Why the Practice Was Developed: The Balsams is one of two surviving grand hotels in the White Mountains of northern New Hampshire. Because the resort is located far from most urban areas, "people don't just drop in off the road and ask for a room for the night," explained Steve Barba, president.

Management long ago recognized that the resort would need a high ratio of return guests if it were to be successful. Many other similar hotels in the area had failed. To entice guests back to The Balsams year after year, management chose to institute a guest-history program that would allow as much customization for each guest as possible.

Execution

The Approach to Implementation: The Balsams has always operated on the American meal plan. In the early 1970s a guest surmised that it must be a monumental task to keep track of all the meals and foods consumed in the main dining room and other food-service outlets. He approached the resort's management with the idea of creating a computer program that would do just that. Although management found the guest's proposition interesting, Mr. Barba concluded that where help was really needed was in the area of guest histories and reservations. Unfortunately, "there wasn't any system around in those days which could keep track of 209 individual rooms."

The former guest and Mr. Barba went to work to create such a system, "one of the first attempts at the use of artificial intelligence." Implementation started once the computer program was finished. The program has been a going concern ever since, and is still in use today.

Every time an individual telephones the property, that person is entered into the system. If the caller is a previous guest, that person's file is pulled up. Each file contains all the information that has been gathered about a guest during his or her previous stay. If the caller has not previously stayed at The Balsams, any information that can be gathered based on the caller's inquiries is entered. The information contained in the file is composed of the obvious, such as the dates of the guest's previous visits, his or her room number, type of accommodations, and rate paid. Also included, however, are such things as the guest's housekeeper and server team, choice of dining rooms, food and beverage selections, choice of activities and preferred tee times or ski runs, and of course, any special requests. The idea is to anticipate every wish on the part of the guest, and provide it prior to it being expressed.

Many of the repeat guests have come to think of the resort as "theirs," and of the guestrooms where they stay as "their" rooms. In fact, many guests rearrange the layout of the guestroom furniture. Even this preference for furniture arrangement is entered into the system, so that when the guests check in, the furniture is where they want it.

Today, the system is capable of not only tracking guests, but also inquiries, and is fully integrated with operations. The conversion rate (i.e., the rate at which inquiries become confirmed reservations) is approaching 50%.

Outcomes

Success of the Practice: The practice has been a tremendous success. Today, 85% of the occupancy consists of either former guests or first-time visitors who are there based on the recommendation of a former guest.

A novel "twist" has been the production of a video that is distributed to the guests. The video is a presentation of the resort from the guest's point of view. Guests show the video to their friends, in effect becoming part of the resort's sales force. Printed brochures are designed to achieve the same objective.

Insights

Advice and Observations: "The key to success is personal service and getting to know your guests. I or one of my partners are here in the lobby to greet each guest individually upon arrival," stated Mr. Barba. Further, each repeat guest is individually acknowledged with a handwritten note or a bottle of maple syrup.

A problem The Balsams currently faces is that the company that originally developed the program and system never grew into a major computer company. Consequently, few people in the computer industry are familiar with the system and its operational procedures.

Contact

Steve Barba, President
The Balsams Grand Resort Hotel
Route 26, Dixville Notch, NH 03576
Phone: 603-255-3400 Fax: 603-255-4221

THE BARBIZON HOTEL AND EMPIRE HOTEL NEW YORK

Standardized Record Keeping for Operations and Guest Calls

Description

The Practice: What started off as an idea to eliminate logbooks and standardize record keeping on one computerized form at The Barbizon Hotel and Empire Hotel New York has blossomed into what is now known as "HOTELEXPERT."

HOTELEXPERT, version 3.2, with "smartpaging," allows employees to activate calls from virtually anywhere in the hotel via telephone or a PC on a local area network (LAN). The system automatically assigns tasks and allows self-activation of pagers ensuring that calls go to the right employees. Tasks are transmitted to pagers with a "reminder" page sent within 15 minutes. If the task remains unresolved, "smartpaging" will then notify a manager-on-duty (MOD) or supervisor.

HOTELEXPERT's secondary function is tasking. Virtually all departments share one computerized form to order items in advance such as cribs, cots, room service amenities, and turn-down service. Tasks, with their countless revisions, are communicated via LAN, eliminating paper and meetings. Internal projects and preventive maintenance are efficiently administered.

The software's third function is its dynamic Query & Answer feature, which provides on-screen reports and graphs. Previously hard-to-retrieve information can be analyzed to measure quality. Researching guest requests, complaints, operations deficiencies, and employee productivity is made simple.

In 1998 some 180,000 tasks were expected to be logged at the Empire by over 100 employees in 14 hotel departments.

Why the Practice Was Developed: Val Reyes, general manager of both the Empire Hotel New York and Barbizon Hotel, set out to get operations data when he arrived in 1992. However, he was not satisfied with the information found in the traditional log books usually kept at the front desk in which guest comments, requests, and complaints were noted. In addition to the entries being undecipherable, there was no way to track the time required to fulfill each request, or to even know whether a request had been acted upon. To reconstruct the task fulfillment and average times was an onerous task, which simply did not get done. As a result, guest service and employee productivity suffered. Mr. Reyes set out to standardize record-keeping using one computerized form for all tasks, eventually branching through a LAN in 1993. All operations activity and guest calls were pooled into one central database.

Execution

The Approach to Implementation: A team comprising Mr. Reyes, his rooms division, engineering, housekeeping, and human resources managers worked with Metromedia Software Inc., a division of the hotel's conglomerate parent company, to develop the initial software programs, which were released in 1996. Then followed version 3.0, which included the telephone interface and Query & Answer features. The present form was completed in mid-1998.

Operational issues: In addition to monitoring guest requests, the system is also used for "tasking" in other departments of the hotel. Tasks can be inputted and scheduled in advance: food and beverage schedules, VIP amenities, delivery rates for room service, and tray pick-ups; engineering schedules, preventative maintenance, projects, and renovations management; housekeeping schedules, room tasks, lost and found, valet and laundry deliveries, and public space maintenance; and PBX schedules, mail, package and fax deliveries. The primary users of the system are the housekeeping and maintenance departments.

The general manager can display on his PC a series of reports showing the tasks scheduled, their status, time required to complete them, the employee responsible for completing the task, and the tasks requiring managerial or supervisory involvement.

43

The telephone interface, added to the system in Version 3.0, allows calls to be activated from anywhere in the hotel, and to institute a task and assign it via beepers to the pertinent employee.

Because each employee's productivity can be accurately tracked through the task database, the information is now used to determine employee bonuses on an objective rather than a subjective basis.

Outcomes

Success of the Practice: From the hotel standpoint, the repeat guest rate in both hotels (The Barbizon and Empire) has risen from 20% to 50%, and Mr. Reyes believes that the greatly improved quality of service is a major contributing factor to the increase.

It is estimated that increased productivity, the elimination of paperwork, and the ability to analyze trouble spots has saved both hotels a total of $750,000 over the last three years.

HOTELEXPERT was made available to the public in 1996 and is now in use in 25 hotels nationwide.

Benefits for Customer: The customer benefits from a higher, more efficient level of service, and a higher quality of the physical plant due to the rapid response to correct maintenance problems. Though the guest is most likely not aware of HOTELEXPERT'S existence, ongoing lobby interviews and comment cards have shown that, overall, the guests recognize and appreciate the level of service provided.

Insights

Advice and Observations: Mr. Reyes suggests that other hotels analyze their ability to know what their employee productivity is. He further adds that they should eliminate paper and reduce time for action.

Contact

Val Reyes, General Manager
(Prior to publication of this study,
Mr. Reyes left his position)
The Barbizon Hotel
140 E. 63rd St., New York, NY
Phone: 212-838-5700 Fax: 212-753-0360

THE BOULDERS

Food Forager to Improve Quality in F&B

Description

The Practice: The Boulders created the position of "food forager" to obtain the best fresh products — produce, meats, spices, seafood, and cheese — that can be found locally and nationally. The forager also works directly with local farmers to encourage them to grow specific produce for the resort. The resort's menus are designed around the products the forager finds, rather than the forager trying to find ingredients to fit the menu. The customer is made aware of this unusual practice by inserts in menus, resort displays, and wait-staff explanations.

Why the Practice Was Developed: The Boulders management was dissatisfied with the variety and quality of the produce being obtained for the resort's restaurants. Unfortunately, the purchasing agent did not have the time or expertise to procure a better product. As a result, the food and beverage department's passion for food seemed to be diminishing.

Gray Ferguson, food and beverage director, had seen a "forager" program practiced elsewhere, and believed it would benefit the resort. He presented the concept to the general manager, who favored the idea.

Execution

The Approach to Implementation: The executive chef embraced the idea of a food forager, and enthusiastically conveyed the concept to the chefs of all the resort's food outlets. The general manager promoted the practice to the media and to guests, while Mr. Ferguson sought support for the program with the resort purchasing agent and the local farmers.

The forager practice started small, but grew. At first, the forager just focused on buying the highest quality produce for the best price within the state of Arizona, where the resort is located. Later, as the forager became responsible for procuring spices, shellfish, cheeses, and meats, the forager's search broadened nationally.

Initially, the forager's reports advised of his progress, expenditures, delivery dates, and acceptance of products. Later, financial analyses were added to the reports. A forager hotline was installed to keep all restaurant outlets apprised of their incoming supplies. Ongoing chef's meetings, incorporating the forager's reports, stimulated the progress of the practice.

The chefs were able to react and adjust menus based on the products the forager found. The wait-staff focused on conveying the forager practice and promoting the distinctive menu items to the guests. Real acceptance of the forager concept occurred, however, when employees and guests tasted the food.

Operational Issues: Initially, the chefs were reluctant to accept a practice that required them to constantly restructure their menus around continuously varying products. The chefs did adjust, however, and came up with some dynamic responses.

Costs: Costs of the practice were minimal. The primary expense was the salary of the forager and the insurance on his personal vehicle. Other related costs included the promotional material to advertise the practice to guests, and the additional paper required for an expanded and ever-changing menu. Total costs since inception are approximately $45,000, which includes the forager's wages.

Outcomes

Success of the Practice: The forager practice has been successful. Food quality is higher, yet food costs are lower. Additionally, the distinctiveness of the menu offerings allows for an increase in pricing; consequently, profits are up.

The wait-staff gratuities have increased as a result of an increased average check. Additionally, the wait-staff feels a greater sense of pride in the restaurants' offerings because of their unusual nature and high quality. These two factors have reduced employee turnover.

Communication between the kitchens and the guests has been heightened, and greater rapport has been established with the back and front of the house due to menu meetings. The culinary preparers now have a greater sense of pride in their work, and a passion for food and its preparation has been fostered.

"The forager practice will be sustained and improved on," declares Mr. Ferguson.

Benefits for Customer: Customers are excited about the use of local and fresh foods, and the improved food quality. They also appreciate the presentations from the wait-staff explaining the program and the unusual menu choices. Guest comment cards have been positive. As part of the resort activities available to guests, invitations are extended to guests to attend forager meetings with local farmers; the guests enjoy the interaction with the food and beverage staff and with the farmers

Insights

Advice and Observations: Mr. Ferguson notes, "The key to successful implementation is enthusiasm and passion. If I were starting today, I wouldn't do anything different. I learned more about food and realized that with challenge comes growth. Better chefs were made."

In the future, Mr. Ferguson plans to revitalize the forager field trips with the guests, and establish a three-day food and wine event around the forager program.

Mr. Ferguson believes the practice should work at any property, unless there are no farmers nearby. However, he warns that a rigidly structured organization probably could not handle the practice.

Contact

Gary Ferguson, Director of Food and Beverage
(Prior to publication of this study,
Mr. Ferguson left his position)
The Boulders
P.O. Box 2090, Carefree, AZ 85377
Phone: 602-488-9009 Fax: 602-595-4664

THE BOULDERS

Self-Directed Housekeeping Teams

The Practice: The Boulders utilizes self-directed, three-person housekeeping teams. Each team divides and interchanges all room duties, chooses its own work areas, is responsible for room quality, and conducts its own room inspections. This practice, implemented in late 1998, also requires that each team be multi-cultural to assist staff members who are trying to learn English, and to encourage greater interaction among all employees.

Why the Practice Was Developed: As a deluxe resort, The Boulders requires a high level of service for each guestroom. However, guests frequently complained about too many housekeeping interruptions during the day. A reduction in room "entries" was necessary. In addition, housekeeping is perceived to be "the toughest job in the resort. It is boring." According to Linda Heyman, director of housekeeping, The Boulders wanted to find a better way to retain and motivate room attendants. There was also a need to make the housekeeping department more efficient, while simultaneously creating "a better place to work."

Housekeeping teams were not completely new to The Boulders. During big "turn" days when room cleaning bogged down, SWAT teams were used to expedite the cleaning process. Ms. Heyman proposed the team concept as a permanent solution; she had read about the team concept in other industries and believed it would work in hotel housekeeping. Ms. Heyman's boss, John Maddock, gave the go-ahead to try housekeeping teams.

The Approach to Implementation: The resort manager and the human resources director supported the team concept. Ms. Heyman actually implemented the practice, but the resort manager and human resources director provided her with moral support, payroll expense flexibility, and other necessary tools. The goals of the practice are to increase staff motivation, improve the working environment, upgrade guest service, and decrease guestroom disturbances. Ms. Heyman believes that accomplishing these objectives will eventually increase profits.

Ms. Heyman met with the housekeeping supervisors, and the structure of the practice was hammered out. Then the team concept was presented to all housekeeping staff. Implementation was accomplished in stages. First supervisors, then team leaders were trained in a series of meetings. Because of their "leadership" role, team leaders were given 50 cents more per hour.

A Trial: Team leaders created two test teams composed of the most enthusiastic employees. Slower staff members were teamed with faster ones. Feedback from the two teams was encouraged. Normally, a room attendant cleans 11 rooms per day (or 11 credits, depending on the size of the room). The two teams, on the other hand, initially were assigned 25 rooms (33 rooms did not work). At first, the teams were discouraged, as it was difficult to meet the 25-room standard. The three-

month test period produced many modifications based on the teams' feedback and ideas.

All employees were encouraged to help shape the practice. However, change was a problem with many employees. Initially, room attendants did not react well to the team concept; many preferred to work alone. Training was required, particularly with those who did not deal well with change. In addition, language and interpersonal skills training was implemented.

Currently, there are four teams; there will be 12 teams when the practice is fully implemented.

Operational Issues: Learning how to operate in self-directed teams has proven to take longer than anticipated. Consequently, additional payroll costs have been incurred, but it is expected that they will diminish. Equipment problems had to be resolved. In addition, there were personnel problems that had to be worked out through training. For example, housemen (who were one-third of the team) initially felt that it was not their job to do beds.

Costs: Start-up costs are higher as employees are allowed to be less efficient as they begin navigating the learning curve for this practice. Ms. Heyman believes that the benefits of the practice will eventually outweigh the costs.

Outcomes

Success of the Practice: The self-directed housekeeping teams have been very successful so far. Ms. Heyman notes that several of the objectives of the practices already have been achieved. Guests are happier, and the staff is more stable. Retention and morale of room attendants appear to have improved. Employees believe they have more control over their jobs. They do not have to work alone, and they have a more flexible schedule. At the outset, the staff has been less productive, but this is improving.

Once the practice is fully implemented, Ms. Heyman intends to assess the effectiveness of housekeeping teams by measuring time needed per occupied room.

Ms. Heyman feels that the work-team concept will spread to other departments, and certainly will be sustained in housekeeping.

Benefits to Customers: Because of the practice, rooms are readied for guest check-in faster, and guests have fewer intrusions on their privacy. Soon in-room minibar service will be incorporated into the team concept.

Insights

Advice and Observations: Ms. Heyman feels that much planning is necessary to implement a work-team practice. If she were doing it over again, Ms. Heyman would implement the practice at a slower pace. She also would assign fewer rooms to the team at first, and after learning how negatively some employees react to change, she would set more realistic goals.

Ms. Heyman believes that the practice would likely not work as well in a high-rise structure, but would be effective in a sprawling resort, and in hotels where there are large rooms. She states that the practice works very well with multicultural employees.

Contact

Linda Heyman, Director of Housekeeping
The Boulders
P.O. Box 2090, Carefree, AZ 85377
Phone: 602-488-7369 Fax: 602-488-6767

THE BOULDERS

Cornerstone Program: Developing a Service Culture

Description

The Practice: The Cornerstone Program comprises 10 principles by which employees at The Boulders will fulfill the vision of excellent guest service. Each employee carries a card with the 10 points, expressed as simple words and phrases.

The 10 cornerstones are expressed as follows:

The Zone (when anyone is within five feet of you, make eye contact, speak first, smile, and use the guest's name)

Own the request

Fiscal responsibility

Ambassador

Image

Phone etiquette

Cleanliness

Respect priorities

Personalize the experience

Have fun

Why the Practice Was Developed: As a luxury hotel, The Boulders sought ways to express how the resort is different from the average hotel. Managers also wanted to pinpoint what made its employees better than those of some competitors. They came up with the following vision statement: "Seek opportunities to create memories." While the first priority was to meet that vision, employee retention and dedication to training became paramount considerations. Unemployment in the Phoenix area is a minuscule 2.1%, and the resort is not served by public transit. With 180 positions open and a tight labor market, management was faced with hiring candidates who needed substantial training and orientation to a service position. The Cornerstone Program has been tremendous in dealing with this reality by helping to groom people for the level of service The Boulders wishes to offer, and thus maintaining a high degree of guest satisfaction.

Execution

The Approach to Implementation: The Cornerstone Program was formulated prior to the purchase of The Boulders by Patriot American Hospitality. The former owners and management spent a day to create the written vision for their organization that focused on why The Boulders is distinctive.

The team then developed the 10 cornerstones that would make the vision come alive. They determined that the cornerstones would be basic concepts that would apply to living in general. They wanted very simple words or phrases that would easily fit onto a commitment card that would reinforce employees' behavior. Not only would these cornerstones apply to the external guest, but also to the "internal guest" (i.e., the employees themselves).

Rather than bring in outside trainers who would then depart, management selected 15 managers from all the departments to be "Cornerstone Coaches." They teach, promote the program, and remind the staff of the cornerstones. The coaches were

trained in teaching the program. They then set up 15-minute sessions with different groups of employees to introduce the program, one cornerstone at a time. They explained the concept of the Zone for two weeks, and then moved on to another cornerstone. The process of explaining and embedding the cornerstones took a year.

Operational Issues: The initial coaches selected were dedicated, long-term employees, who showed leadership skills and who had integrity and the respect of the hourly staff. Although The Boulders originally selected Cornerstone Coaches only from among managers, three hourly personnel are now coaches.

Early critics of the practice came from both management and hourly ranks. Employees who felt that they already knew these principles thought they did not need a card to remind them. Reticent managers thought the program was silly and that it was just another of those management ideas that come and go. While the coach-managers bought into the practice, the other managers initially did not. Since part of the managers' annual evaluation turns on how they support the program, they are now working to support it.

A potential negative is the amount of time the coaches must spend both in preparation for and implementation of the training. Coaches spend an estimated five to six hours a week over and above their other property responsibilities. The coaches are currently not given additional compensation for time spent. Coaches also have a weekly planning session called the "coaches' huddle." Two executive committee members attend these meetings and act as advisors and monitors for the coaches. A similar program operates at other co-owned luxury properties. Coaches from the seven luxury properties spend three or four days at an annual retreat to discuss how things are done at the individual properties and to complete some additional training.

The coaches have put together manuals known collectively as "Focus". The manuals describe methods for teaching each cornerstone, including games that can be played, and training aids.

The coach's role has become a coveted position. The resort now holds tryouts to fill coaching vacancies. The tryout involves making a presentation on one of the cornerstones and writing an essay on why the person wants to be a Cornerstone Coach. Many Memory Makers want to become coaches. This is a real benefit because these are people that The Boulders are grooming to go somewhere in their organization.

Tactics for presenting the cornerstones have changed over time. New-employee orientation covers the cornerstones, and one month after starting employees go through Cornerstone College, an interactive half-day session put on by the coaches with group activities and role playing. After 90 days of employment, new workers are scheduled for Cornerstone Awareness Training, a refresher session geared for the new employees to have fun while learning.

Employee recognition has become a large element of the Cornerstone Program. Employees who do a particularly good job in carrying out the cornerstones can be nominated for the "Brag" program, and recognized in the resort's monthly newsletter. The resort rolled out a coin program in January 1999, in which employees are rewarded with specially struck coins for acts related to the cornerstones. Employees can redeem their coins for prizes and trips.

In place of the standard employee-of-the-month program, the resort has Memory Makers of the Month. In connection with the "creating memories" vision, The Boulders rewards a number of Memory Makers — at least one from the front and the back of the house — with a special lunch and prizes. The names of these employees are published in the monthly newsletter.

Outcomes

Success of the Practice: The Boulders has been able to retain employees even in a tight labor market. For 11 straight years, The Boulders has won the Andrew Harper Award for superior guest service. Judy Dewey, director of human resources, notes that the cornerstone concept seems to have extended to the employees' personal lives. They talk about being aware of the "zone" away from work and of picking up trash on the street. The practice has developed a camaraderie among employees.

Insights

Advice and Observations: To begin a project like this again, Ms. Dewey believes the resort would certainly want to give more consideration to the program's initial stages and to examine each step before rolling it out. In addition, the resort would have involved all the managers at the beginning, to achieve earlier support from them, and would have put the managers through the training first, instead of starting the program all at once.

All things considered, Ms. Dewey relates, this has developed into an innovative and positive practice for the retention and development of personnel — the key priority in a highly competitive environment.

Contact

Judy Dewey, Director of Human Resources
The Boulders
P.O. Box 2090, Carefree, AZ 85377
Phone: 602-488-9009 Fax: 602-488-7302

THE BREAKERS HOTEL

Annual Food and Beverage Staff Reorganization and Single-Theme Restaurant Concepts

Description

The Practices: After his arrival at The Breakers Hotel in Palm Beach, Kevin Walters began to review and revamp the existing food and beverage operation. As director of food and beverage, Mr. Walters instituted two major programs that have proven highly successful:

1 Complete reorganization of the staff each year involving promotions and lateral moves for over a dozen managers and supervisors to other positions within the operation to facilitate cross-training and upward mobility.
2 Replacement of the existing formal-dining and casual-dining restaurants and bars with single-theme food and beverage outlets, which gives the guest the choice of the cuisine desired rather than the choice dictated by guest attire.

Why the Practices Were Developed: Mr. Walters is a proponent of change for employees, especially in the food and beverage area. He wants to create a continuously stimulating environment for his young, dynamic, high-energy employees, so they will not become bored or leave for another property. Consequently, he intends to keep them learning, moving, progressing, and developing, so they will not be picked off by other companies. He also believes "people are at their best if they are a little bit over their head."

Mr. Walters believes the public has long had an aversion to hotel restaurants, probably going back to the days when most hotels tried to have some of every variety of food they thought a guest might desire — but none of it very good. He identified two ways to change the public's perception: Farm out the restaurants to name operators or create stronger hotel restaurant identities. Mr. Walters and The Breakers Hotel chose the latter approach.

Execution

The Approach to Implementation for the Staff Reorganization: Each spring for the past four years, Mr. Walters has reorganized his staff by moving between 12 and 18 managers and supervisors to lateral or advanced positions. All moves are performance based and voluntary; there is usually an increase in compensation. An employee may choose to remain in his or her current position without any repercussions.

Any department head or supervisor is eligible, both in the front and back of the house, and can move every year if desired. As an example, an assistant room service manager who has also been manager of the beach club restaurant, executive steward, beverage manager, and assistant food and beverage manager is now director of club operations.

After the first year, Mr. Walters began to see noticeable changes in his staff, and he believes the longer the program continues, the more benefits accrue. The annual staff reorganizations have encouraged the creation of a culture where every manager and supervisor perceives the opportunities offered by the property as being equal to or exceeding external opportunities.

The employees are gratified because they feel their careers are being advanced by the hotel. They recognize the cross-training is increasing their marketability and they appreciate the compensation increases that are linked to the program. Consequently, the program is increasing employee loyalty to the hotel.

The Approach to Implementation for the Theme Concepts: The conversion to the theme concept began with the transformation of the old-fashioned formal-dining room into a modern, stylish, Florentine restaurant with classic European cuisine complemented by an exhibition kitchen. The number of seats was reduced from 300 to 120, special European china was added, and the linen was upgraded. Everything was done to create the setting for a spectacular gourmet restaurant experience worthy of a five-star, five-diamond hotel.

Next, the former casual restaurant was converted to a top-caliber steak house called Flagler's Steakhouse. Red meat dominates the menu — only one chicken, one pasta, and one fish dish are listed. All ingredients are of the highest quality, and only USDA prime meat is used. This restaurant has a steak-house ambiance and its own tabletop.

Besides the main two restaurants, other outlets have also undergone conversions. The main bar, a 4,000 square foot room with a beautiful ocean view, had no business during the day. It was transformed into an oceanside seafood restaurant, with top quality ingredients, and its own tabletop and ambiance. In November 1998, the Victorian restaurant was changed to a southern Italian pasta house, with a special tabletop, pleasing ambiance, and top-quality ingredients. The latest entry, the Beach Club, opened on Christmas Eve 1998. It is in French Riviera style and serves quality, classic dishes in a distinctive way.

Mr. Walters is considering adding one more restaurant, an Asian Pacific Rim concept, which would bring the choices for dinner to five. He notes that five restaurants would be almost too many if it were not for the substantial amount of local business the theme outlets have attracted.

Outcomes

Success of the Practices: Mr. Walters believes the annual employee reorganization has been successful. Since his arrival four years ago, he has retained 80 percent of the food and beverage staff. Mr. Walters now uses the annual reorganization as a recruiting tool.

The cross-training has other benefits as well. In fall 1998 Mr. Walters took 12 of his department heads to San Francisco to attend the *Wine Spectator*'s California Wine Experience, and he did not have to worry about the hotel at all. He had full confidence his cross-trained staff could handle anything that might come up.

The theme restaurant outlets have also been effective. Food and beverage revenue has increased approximately 70% over the last four years. Mr. Walters attributes part of the increase to the theme concept along with a substantial increase in social catering and convention volume.

Benefits for Customer: Customers, both local and corporate, appreciate dealing with a seasoned, well-trained staff with a history of the hotel. Guests frequently comment they prefer the Breakers restaurants to competitive top restaurants in the area.

Insights

Advice and Observations: Mr. Walters has discovered that people love dining options and it is possible to move consumers past the stigma of a hotel restaurant, if you have a great product and the customers know exactly what they are going to get.

Contact

Joanne Schultz, Director of Food & Beverage
(Prior to publication of this study,
Mr. Walters left his position)
The Breakers Hotel
1 South County Road, Palm Beach, FL 33480
Phone: 561-659-8434 Fax: 561-659-8452

BRISTOL HOTELS & RESORTS

Streamlining the Operations of Resource-Challenged Properties

Description

The Practice: Bristol Hotels & Resorts has created a process for streamlining operations in "resource-challenged" hotels — defined as properties with fewer than seven managers, fewer than 60 employees, and/or fewer than 250 rooms. The central theme of this practice is to eliminate nonvalue-added activities to allow these hotels to focus on increasing perceptions of quality, and adding profit to the company.

Why the Practice Was Developed: In 1997, Bristol began the acquisition of approximately 20 economy and limited-service properties, and realized that some planning was required prior to the actual takeover. The idea was to make the acquisition as seamless as possible.

The properties were mostly smaller Holiday Inns with limited food and beverage service, and very limited staffing because they were running extremely low occupancies. All the properties were underperforming in their respective markets, and hotel general managers were stretched to their limits. They were conducting many functional tasks themselves including sales, and many of the accounting functions were being performed manually, with some using green bar paper.

According to Steve Boyle, regional director of accounting, Bristol determined that the most crucial needs for each property were up-to-date accounting systems and a strong sales effort. Bristol's task was to improve these functional areas, as well as others, for the newly acquired properties without burdening them with additional work and costs.

Execution

The Approach to Implementation: Corporate staff members from accounting, payroll, human resources, and operations departments were pulled together to develop a plan for assisting the properties in making the necessary improvements. The plan that evolved became known as "Bristol Lite," because the objective was to lighten the load of these hotels.

The implementation was conducted in three phases: (1) evaluation and modification of the new properties; (2) integration of new "Lite" processes into existing Bristol Hotels that qualify as resource challenged; and (3) implementation of any applicable Lite initiatives to all Bristol hotels in 1999.

Specific components of the plan for phase one included:

1 Employee hiring, orientation, and benefits enrollment conducted by the corporate office, thereby reducing workload and staffing requirements for the properties.

2 Elimination of duplicate forms and replacement of paper forms with electronic versions, where possible, to simplify processes and reduce costs.

3 Standardization of breakfast presentations.

4 Elimination of the newly acquired hotels from all e-mail groups to prevent initial information overload.

5 Reduction of the number of accounts from 761 to approximately 200. Mr. Boyle stated that "the acquired hotels didn't need all those accounts, detail upon detail, especially since they did not have the staff for it." Both the property and the corporate office benefited from this reduction because there was less confusion in coding AP invoices, and faster reviews of the P & L.

6 Reduction of payroll job codes from 119 to approximately 50. This reduction eased administrative woes, and as Mr. Boyle notes, "many employees in smaller properties work in various departments anyway."

7 Elimination of inventories for food, beverage, china, glass, and linen. Instead, these supplies were placed on a purchase-to-sale type of control; inventory adjustments were shown on the financial statements every six months. "The focus was on just-in-time purchasing to maintain pars, but the cost was entered as an expense, and all the time spent on inventories was saved," commented Mr. Boyle.

8 Elimination of the tracking for complimentary food and beverage functions, thereby removing the need for an income auditor to track these expenses. The corporate office made the decision to charge the expenses to food cost. According the Mr. Boyle, the objective was to "focus on issues that help the customers, and not fight over which department should be expensed."

9 Reduction of internal control checkups from 205 to 105 steps. An evaluation was done that compared the cost versus the benefit of each step in the internal control checkup, and when the cost-value relationship was not there, the step was eliminated.

10 Simplification of forecasting and budgeting resulting from the reduction of the number of job codes and the chart of accounts. This simplification means more time can be spent taking care of customers.

To ensure the successful implementation of this plan, information technology teams installed and tested computers at each of the properties four weeks before the close of the sale, so revenue numbers and other data could be transferred to the home office. Classes were conducted to assist the general managers and departmental managers in learning the Windows environment. Corporate staff members from the employee services department conducted training with the general managers, and oriented property employees to the Bristol way of doing business. Corporate accounting employees spent a week at each hotel to provide training in the various accounting procedures. Follow-up training was provided in each functional area a couple of weeks after the completion of the acquisition to provide assistance where needed.

Outcomes

Success of the Practice: The initiative for the new properties was very successful. In November of 1998, the Combined Quality Index (an index compiled by Holiday Inns for similar brands) goal was surpassed by approximately 10 points versus the overall combined Holiday Inn brand. This achievement was noteworthy since these properties were substantially below norm at the time of acquisition.

Overall, the Lite program was so successful that the practices were expanded to the rest of the organization, and the program continues to grow.

The acquired hotels have endured a significant cultural change from how things were done in the past, but they have been "pretty positive and happy" because of the commitment from Bristol. Technologically, the hotels have been "taken out of the dark ages," and they are now focusing on sales and quality.

Insights

In instituting such a process, Mr. Boyle suggests including as many people in the field as possible. "The more people are involved, the easier the process becomes, because you have more people taking ownership of the program."

Mr. Boyle also advises that because "the hotels were forced to start doing things a lot differently, they really need to be prepared for the change."

Contact

Steve Boyle, Regional Director of Accounting
Bristol Hotels & Resorts
14295 Midway Road, Dallas, TX 75224
Phone: 972-391-3106 Fax: 972-391-3798

CANDLEWOOD HOTEL COMPANY

Designing an Extended-Stay Hotel for a Single-Niche Market

Description

The Practice: Candlewood Suites is focused on a single business niche: the individual business traveler who requires seven or more nights of lodging. To fulfill the needs of this single target market, this mid-price extended-stay hotel chain has designed the guestroom for quality and comfort, and provided furnishings and equipment rarely found in a hotel. The design, furnishings, and equipment are intended to give the long-term guest a sense of being at home.

Why the Practice Was Developed: Jack DeBoer, chairman and chief executive officer of Candlewood Hotel Company, started his career by developing apartment houses. As he frequently received requests from potential tenants for short-term leases, he determined that there must be a market for this type of accommodation. The first hotel he built in Wichita, Kansas was called the Residence. The second hotel was called the Residence Inn. DeBoer built over 100 Residence Inns before selling them to Marriott Hotels. In 1988, Mr. DeBoer co-founded Summerfield Suites and built 16 properties. The profitability of extended-stay hotels was evident with the success of Residence Inns and Summerfield Suites. However, as these two brands were strictly targeted toward high-tier guests, Mr. DeBoer realized the need for another category of extended-stay hotels. Hence, he sold Summerfield Suites to the Summerfield Hotel Company, and in 1995, he founded Candlewood Hotel Company with partners Warren Fix and Doubletree Hotels, to satisfy the needs of the mid-tier guest. Specifically, Mr. DeBoer chose to focus on creating a marvelous experience for the lone traveler, a high-growth market segment.

Execution

The Approach to Implementation: "Candlewood does not try to be all things to all people. We try to do everything that we can to maximize the experience for the person who is traveling on business, particularly if he is traveling for an extended stay," explained Jeffrey Hitz, senior vice president of development. This focus allows them to concentrate on serving the needs of the niche guest.

The most significant difference between Candlewood and traditional hotels is the size of the guestroom. All studio rooms are 21.5 feet deep and 16 feet wide (vs. the traditional 11 or 12 feet). Thus, a typical studio contains about 350 square feet of living space. The one-bedroom unit contains 525 square feet (it is about 24 feet wide). The main difference between the two lodging options is that the one-bedroom unit is separated from the living area by a door; the living room contains a sleeper sofa, and there is a second TV in the bedroom.

The larger room size allows Candlewood to provide an oversized desk, a reclining lounge chair, 25-inch TV with a VCR, an oversized, high quality clock radio with a built in CD player, two phones with two lines each, voice mail, and desk height power and phone and data outlets. The kitchen contains a full-size refrigerator, full-size microwave, two-burner cook top, and a full-size dishwasher.

The "most impactful" amenity is the notion of the Candlewood Cupboard. The idea came from the basic philosophy of Candlewood: Keep operating costs low, so value can be provided to the guest. This goal necessitated the elimination of an on-site restaurant, and led Mr. DeBoer to suggest the "cupboard" concept. Mr. DeBoer felt that the traditional honor bars in most full-service hotels were a "rip-off," and he conceived the idea of a single, large, competitively priced honor bar. Thus, Candlewood Suites offers a large, fully stocked "mini-convenience store" located in its own room near the lobby, guest laundry, and exercise facility. The Cupboard is accessible to all guests. Guests pay for these products by either dropping cash into a slot, or filling out a slip to have the purchase charged to the folio. The signature item is soft drinks priced at $0.25, and no product is priced over $2.50. The strategy is to keep the Cupboard prices at or lower than the prices in a typical convenience store. "This has evolved into our 'wow factor'. We get feedback from customers telling us that they can't believe Candlewood does this," stated Mr. Hitz. "Our guests tell us that the real impact has been the trust factor that is communicated to them as to how we feel about them."

Other amenities offered by Candlewood Suites include free local phone calls, a long-distance rate of 25 cents per minute (with no surcharges), free guest laundry, fully equipped exercise facility, and an outdoor gazebo area with free use of barbecue grills.

Several changes have been made to the hotel design since the prototype was built, but no changes have been made to the room. "Someone going into the original building would have a difficult time noting any differences from the latest guest-room," asserted Mr. Hitz. The exteriors have changed, the gym has been slightly expanded, and other cosmetic changes have been made, but the basic layout and amenities have not been altered.

Candlewood Hotel Company relies heavily on guest feedback as a source for new ideas; consequently, Mr. DeBoer reads "each and every comment card." Candlewood has conducted some focus groups, which basically revalidated the Candlewood concept. The company also has an internal design review committee to which anyone in the company can submit an idea. The focus is on two goals: (1) improving the guest experience, and (2) reducing or better managing the costs put into the product.

Success of the Practice: The company is very successful and growing very fast. The first 11 months of 1998 yielded a pretax profit of $3.06 million for Candlewood Hotel Company. Currently, there are 54 company-owned properties, with nine more franchises. Eighteen properties are under construction, and two are franchised. Thirty-eight properties opened in 1998. As of October 1998, system-wide occupancy is 67.9%. Occupancy for properties opened prior to 1998 is running at 71.6%, and current ADR systemwide is about $54.

The simplicity and efficiency of the Candlewood Suites design allow Candlewood to keep operating costs low and to pass those savings on to guests in the form of competitive rates.

Benefits for Customer: The guest receives a superior product for a very reasonable price.

Advice and Observations: Mr. Hitz says it is important to figure out what the niche is and stay true to it. That kind of focus will create an outstanding experience. Mr. Hitz also advises not trying to be all things to all people. He notes that Candlewood "constantly" gets comments suggesting rooms with double doubles, a pool, king beds, and cribs. The response is, "You're right, we don't have it, and if that is what you need, we would be happy to refer you to a nearby competitor who offers those services because that is not what we are."

Mr. Hitz believes "the bigger box [i.e., room] and probably kitchens in rooms are the future of the hotel business."

Mr. DeBoer is a staunch opponent of "do-overs or conversion of old hotels." A completely new structure is the only way he will expand Candlewood. Mr. DeBoer believes the hospitality industry is not overbuilt but is under demolished. Painting and cleaning up a rundown, outmoded hotel and offering it to the public will no longer be an acceptable practice, he advises. Guests want and demand up-to-date services and facilities.

Jeffrey Hitz, Senior Vice President of Development
Candlewood Hotel Company
9342 East Central, Wichita, KS 67206
Phone: 316-630-5559 Fax: 316-630-5612

CANDLEWOOD HOTEL COMPANY

Electronic Record Management

Description

The Practice: Candlewood Hotels has developed an electronic system of recording and imaging virtually all accounting and construction records, thus eliminating the storage of nonessential hard-copy documents. Only those records that contain original signatures (e.g., contracts, leases, deeds) and those required by law are now stored as hard copies, although they are also included in the electronic system for information purposes.

The system utilizes two PCs, two high-speed scanners, and an optical disk "juke box." The information is stored on the optical disks, which are stacked in the juke box. Expansion of the storage capacity requires only the addition of more optical disks.

Why the Practice Was Developed: The conversion to computerized records was driven by three factors. First, the accounting personnel were spending valuable hours searching hundreds of boxes and file cabinets to find needed documents — and that cost money. Second, the document search time impeded responses to vendors, customers, and employees. Thus, the hotels could not resolve problems quickly and effectively. Third, the technology and software that would allow a conversion to electronic records management became readily available.

Execution

The Approach to Implementation: The idea and implementation of electronic records management was a joint effort between Pam Cloud, Candlewood's director of finance, and Lisa Penn, records management coordinator. The system took 18 months to research, design, and implement. Full implementation was achieved on October 7, 1998.

Development of the system involved researching software providers. Ms. Penn spent nine months contacting and researching 12 such companies prior to making a final selection. The product selected was DocuWare, developed by ALOS Micrographics and distributed by IKON Office Solutions.

Once installed, the actual use of the system is easy. Only one extra step is required in the normal document-processing procedure: scanning the document into the system. Two high-speed scanners and the system's user-friendly file index program make this step quick and easy. No additional employees were required, as the input time is much less than the time it formerly took to find documents.

Costs: The total cost of the system, including hardware and software, was $65,000. During her research, Ms. Penn had bids ranging from $30,000 to $250,000, and found that the adage "you get what you pay for" did *not* apply. Though the company selected was not the least expensive one, many of the more expensive systems were inferior in capability and service to the one selected.

Because the quantity of stored paper will be greatly reduced, the cost of storage space will decrease. The reduction in storage-space requirements results in a direct savings to Candlewood, as it will be able to better use leased floor space in its office building that was previously occupied by rows and rows of file cabinets.

Outcomes

Success of the Practice: In the first two months of operation, Ms. Penn saw a reduction of employees' search time. She expects the time savings to significantly increase as fewer documents are needed that are not in the system. Although labor savings are difficult to estimate, Ms. Penn expects to save approximately $90,000 per year.

Benefits for Customer: Vendors, guests (especially group master accounts), and all employees are positively affected because the time required to research and solve a problem or answer a question has been greatly reduced. This time savings has directly reduced labor costs for Candlewood's accounting personnel, and indirectly reduced similar costs for the vendor, customer, or employee seeking an answer from accounting. Because Candlewood Hotels constructs most of its own hotels, the system has been effective in handling numerous documents from contractors, subcontractors, and suppliers. In addition, the lower corporate operating costs translate into lower room rates for guests.

Insights

Advice and Observations: Ms. Penn advises doing extensive research to select the most cost-effective system provider. "The cost, time, and effort are well worth it."

Contact

Lisa Penn, Records Management Coordinator
Candlewood Hotel Company
9342 East Central, Witchita, KS 67206
Phone: 316-630-5500 Fax: 316-630-5588
Email: lpenn@candlewoodsuites.com

CARLSON HOSPITALITY WORLDWIDE

World-Wide Reservation System

Description

The Practice: Carlson has developed what it believes is the most extensive, efficient, and productive reservation system existing today. The system collects reservations from three sources: voice from 34 countries; GDS (global distribution system) from 140 countries; and the Internet worldwide.

Why the Practice Was Developed: Since Carlson's primary business is franchising and managing hotels worldwide (Radisson, Country Inns, Regent), a key competitive factor is its ability to provide marketing and reservations (room-nights) to its brands. Therefore, the firm realized that to be competitive, it must create and operate the most productive and cost-effective reservations system in the industry.

Execution

The Approach to Implementation: Scott Heintzeman, vice president of knowledge technology, led the development of the system, which was initiated 14 years ago. Carlson was the last major hotel company to develop an on-line, computerized reservation concept and decided against following the path others had taken, that of adapting existing airline reservation systems such as the Westron system. Instead, it started from scratch to develop its own system designed to provide more specific information on each property and more capabilities than the inflexible mainframe systems were capable of providing, while retaining the ability of interfacing with the airline systems. The initial cost of software development was $127,000, and hardware cost was "under a half million dollars." Six years ago it developed the seamless interface to GDS. Now all hotel systems are also developing seamless interfaces to GDS. Carlson has continued to upgrade the system since that time and will continue to do so as technology allows and the market demands.

Costs: The reservation system is the highest contributor at the lowest cost in terms of cost percentage per revenue sent to Radisson's hotels of any reservation system. Carlson's cost is 2% of revenue produced, whereas its five peers are 2.7%. The average cost of reservation systems for 21 industry leaders is 3.4%. Ten mid-price companies average 4.4%, and 10 mid-size companies average 2.5% (per Graycon 1997 Industry Analysis).

Outcomes

Success of the Practice: According to Graycon Co. (an independent research company), in 1997 Carlson's reservation system was number one in occupancy contribution. The average contribution of the top 21 industry leaders was 33.4%.

The Carlson reservation system (known as "Curtis-C") is also acknowledged worldwide for its patented "Look to Book" system that awards points to travel agents for booking hotel rooms via the GDS.

Benefits for Customer: For Radisson's franchisees, the benefit is the highest productivity and revenue production in the industry.

Insights

Advice and Observations: Presently 35% of all reservations are handled personally and 65% are handled electronically, with electronically processed reservations increasing by two percentage points annually for the foreseeable future. Mr. Heintzeman expects this trend to continue, and believes that "marketing through technology" is a necessity, not a luxury.

Contact

Scott Heintzeman, Vice President of Knowledge Technology
Carlson Hospitality Worldwide
Carlson Parkway, MN 55459
Phone: 612-449-3333 Fax: 612-449-1126

CARLSON HOSPITALITY WORLDWIDE

Total Customer Satisfaction Via an On-Line Database and Employee Empowerment

Description

The Practice: Carlson Hospitality Worldwide sought to establish a chainwide program in its Radisson Hotels Worldwide company of total customer satisfaction and a personalized relationship with all customers through the use of computer technology. The first step toward achieving this goal was to institute a 100% customer satisfaction policy in which all employees are empowered to handle customer complaints to the customers' satisfaction or refund their money. The second step, which is still under development, is a chainwide, interactive, on-line datatrust containing individual and group complaints, compliments, personal preferences, dietary needs, stays and location data, special requests, etc. This data will be immediately accessible to all guest service personnel for reference and input. The goal was to have this central nervous system operational by the first quarter of 1999.

Why the Practice Was Developed: Over the past several years, CEO/President Curtis Nelson believed that the industry was becoming increasingly inward-focused, and the trend was toward corporate consolidations and mergers with the emphasis on financial dealings and returns to investors to the detriment of creative methods of assuring customer satisfaction. These factors, coupled with the rapid advancement in communications technology, created "an opportunity [for Carlson] to create value for the customer and not be consumed by financially engineered values."

Execution

The Approach to Implementation: Between June and August 1997, the Carlson Hospitality staff conducted research on guarantees and closely examined the practices of competitors. Carlson's "100% Customer Satisfaction" program was then formulated. Three conditions for invoking the guarantee were delineated: (1) when the guest perceives a problem as "high in severity," (2) when the guest perceives that the hotel is responsible for the problem, and (3) when the hotel is unable to correct the problem in "any other way that will satisfy the guest." Moreover, all employees were expected to understand the guarantee, and were given the responsibility and authority to invoke the guarantee.

The 100% guarantee concept was then analyzed by several focus groups comprised of guests, employees, and operators. Subsequently, Carlson developed extensive training materials and programs necessary to convey the customer satisfaction concept to operators and hotel staff.

A Trial: From September to December 1997, Carlson conducted a pilot test at 28 Radisson hotels — 23 U.S. hotels, one Canadian hotel, two Latin American hotels, and two European SAS hotels — complemented by a Gallup study of guest response to the program. Results of the pilot test were later presented at regional meetings held in the first quarter of 1998. The findings indicated that the guarantee had been invoked 1,387 times by the guest or by a hotel employee on behalf of the guest, resulting in a cost of only 0.29% of room sales. Overall, the pilot test was an overwhelming success: The guarantee (1) defined a standard of service, (2) increased the guest's willingness to return, (3) increased occupancy rate, ADR, RevPAR and RSI, and (4) reduced customer complaints. Further, the results of the Gallup study indicated that the guests perceived a higher level of service, which produced a higher level of consumer confidence.

In January 1998, Carlson created a registration form for training operators and hotel staff, and began conducting guarantee workshops for the North American properties in the spring. The program was launched globally in September 1998. The training is conducted in two phases. First, Carlson requires that a fundamental training program titled "Yes, I Can! Making It Right" be in place prior to introducing the 100% guarantee. The "Making It Right" program is designed to help employees "use the appropriate judgement when choosing solutions to guest problems." The 100% guest satisfaction guarantee training explains the program, empowers the employee to act on the guarantee, and outlines the steps to take in invoking the guarantee. As of December 1998, 344 Carlson hotels have been trained. Two of the franchisees initially refused to implement the program, but have since changed their minds.

Eleven regional trainers, two of whom are based in Europe, conduct training. Furthermore, a full-time employee has been hired to help maintain the programs.

Operational Issues: By necessity, the development and implementation of the total customer satisfaction program has been a systemwide endeavor.

Costs: The cost of the first phase — "100% Customer Satisfaction" — is virtually zero, except for the guest refunds for unresolved complaints. The cost of development and operation of the central nervous system has not been determined, but will be "substantial."

Outcomes

Success of the Practice: There has been an increase in ADR and occupancies on a chainwide basis. This is not to say that all properties have shown increases, but the chain as a whole has. Thus, Mr. Nelson believes the program is profitable so far, in that the increases in ADR and occupancies far outweigh the amounts refunded. Additionally, market share is up, and customer retention rates have increased.

Guest feedback has been most positive and the vast majority of those customers whose money was refunded have returned to the same property or to other properties within the chain.

Benefits for Customer: Presently, the benefit for customers is the knowledge that problems will be handled quickly and/or their money will be refunded. With the implementation of the central nervous system, a much more individually personalized service will become evident.

Insights

Advice and Observations: Make sure the philosophy of "Total Customer Satisfaction" is fully understood and that the commitment is made at the top, i.e., owners and corporate officers. Train all employees and make sure they understand the philosophy. Create and provide the technology tools required. Most importantly, empower the employees to make decisions and to act on them.

In addition, Carlson Hospitality notes that if it were just instituting the 100% guarantee program, it would pick a test hotel in the Caribbean, and would form a global council to facilitate worldwide implementation.

Contact

Curtis Nelson, CEO/President
Carlson Hospitality Worldwide
P.O. Box 59159, Carlson Parkway, MN 55459
Phone: 612-449-1323 Fax: 612-449-1241

CENDANT CORPORATION

Comprehensive Diversity Initiative

Description

The Practice: Launched in November 1997, Cendant's comprehensive diversity initiative comprises the following five key elements:

1. Franchise development among minorities
2. Supplier and vendor development with minority vendors
3. Philanthropic giving
4. Career development and mentoring
5. Target marketing to minority audiences

The diversity initiative was instituted in Cendant's hotel division, which includes eight brands, and is being extended to the firm's other franchises.

Why the Practice Was Developed: The initiative started as a result of the NAACP Reciprocity Initiative. Several years ago the NAACP published a report card on minority progress in the hotel industry. Cendant received a C-minus, and none of the other dozen hotel chains surveyed fared much better. Cendant's director of diversity development, Donna Dozier Gordon, explained that the NAACP report was a "wake-up call" for the hotel industry, and the report caused a great deal of introspection among Cendant's executive leadership. They concluded that while they had not excluded anyone intentionally, they should take proactive steps to provide access for opportunities for African-Americans and other minorities. This motive formed the basis for the initiative.

Execution

The Approach to Implementation: To form the foundation of the initiative, Cendant convened a series of meetings with key opinion leaders in the African-American community. The first meeting, facilitated by the National Urban League, took place in October 1997, prior to the beginning of the initiative itself. Instrumental in developing the initiative was John Russell, the CEO and chairman of Cendant's hotel division at that time, and Tom Christopoul, executive vice president of human resources. An African-American director, Leonard Coleman, who is president of the National Baseball League and an Urban League director, also was an invaluable resource.

Franchise Development. As franchising is Cendant's core business, that domain became the first focus. At the October meeting with leaders in the African-American community, Cendant presented its franchise opportunities in limited-service hotel properties — a proposal that was well received. Six regional meetings — in Los Angeles, Atlanta, Chicago, Charlotte, North Carolina, Houston, and Washington, D.C — were similar to the first meeting, and also were facilitated by the Urban League. Each meeting drew about 40 people. To give the minority franchising program an extra boost, Cendant sponsored a financial incentive called "Keys to Success." The

incentive program entitled an approved licensee to receive a payment on opening a hotel of $1,000 per room for properties of up to 74 rooms and $1,500 per room for properties of 75 rooms or more (capped at $150,000). The payment is in the form of a loan that is forgiven if the franchisee remains in the system for a minimum 15 years, which is the life of a typical franchise agreement.

Supplier and Vendor Development. Hoping to identify minority-owned vendors, Cendant began this portion of the initiative by joining the National Minority Supplier Development Council, which is the country's preeminent minority-vendor advocacy organization. Additionally, the company's regional meetings helped locate potential suppliers. Two vendors had been approved as Cendant suppliers as of this writing — a California-based wall-furnishing supplier and an Orlando-based construction consultant. Next, Ms. Gordon plans to formalize an organizational goal for minority suppliers and establish a minority-supplier-development program.

Philanthropic Giving. Cendant contributed more than $1 million in 1998 to organizations that benefit minorities. Recipients included the NAACP, the National Urban League, the Jackie Robinson Foundation, and the Inter City Game Foundation, an organization that builds young people's self-esteem.

Career Development and Mentorship. Cendant has opened a reservation center in Orangeburg, South Carolina, a city that is home to two historically black colleges. The center's opening created an opportunity for Cendant to recruit minority students as employees. Not only was Cendant able to hire some 200 employees from the neighboring schools, but it established an ongoing mentoring program between the school and the reservation center. Additionally, Cendant developed a corporate-intern program in conjunction with Inroads, an organization that places talented minority students in internships in Fortune 500 companies. The students begin the program as freshmen and remain with the company until they complete their senior year. In the best case, the newly minted graduates will be employed by the company with which they have developed such a lengthy relationship.

Target Marketing. To fulfill a commitment to stepped-up target marketing, Cendant hired an African-American-owned advertising agency, Caroline Jones Incorporated. The agency developed a $2.5-million campaign that targeted African-American consumers, with ads to be placed with African-American media outlets. The agency developed a widely acclaimed commercial slogan, "Cendant: The name behind the name you trust."

Outcomes

Success of the Practice: Cendant received a B in the NAACP's 1998 grading — the highest grade awarded. Rolled out to the press and all the Cendant brands in January 1998, the program has been widely noted as a significant development by the franchisee community. Initially targeting a goal of 20 license agreements, Cendant executed franchise agreements that will result in more than 50 hotels during the first stage of the program. One franchisee is developing 30 Cendant properties. Prior to this effort, Cendant could only identify three African-Americans among its many licensees. The supplier program continues, and Cendant is searching for additional mentoring programs. Results from the advertising program are positive.

Insights

Advice and Observations: Ms. Gordon points out that minority consumers are becoming much more savvy about supporting companies they feel support them. Ms. Gordon suggests that the following elements are necessary for a diversity program to be successful: The director must be tenacious; senior management commitment must be strong; and internal training can make the case for diversity clear to existing employees. She concludes that people must realize that diversity requires an organizational shift. Not a project or a temporary effort, a commitment to diversity requires a new approach to conducting a business.

Contact

Donna Dozier Gordon
(Prior to publication of this study,
Ms. Gordon left her position)
Director of Diversity Development, Hotel Division
Cendant Corporation
6 Sylvan Way, Parsippany, NJ 07054
Phone: 973-496-8543 Fax: 973-496-7307

63

CENDANT CORPORATION

Developing "Preferred Alliances" with National Vendors

The Practice: Cendant Corporation negotiated preferred-alliance agreements with major U.S. corporations. Under these agreements, Cendant's various franchisees were given the opportunity to utilize these preferred vendors, resulting in substantial savings to the franchisee, and a revenue generator for Cendant. These "preferred alliances" serve as a major selling point for Cendant, the largest franchisor of rooms in the United States.

Why the Practice was Selected: Cendant's diversified portfolio includes eight franchise hotel systems — Ramada, Days Inn, Howard Johnson's, Super 8, Travelodge, Knights Inns, Villager, and Wingate Inns — as well as a rental car agency, —Avis — real estate companies — Century 21, Caldwell Banker, and ERA, — a relocation company, a mortgage company, and a tax preparation service, Jackson Hewitt. As a major franchisor, Cendant felt preferred alliances would not only increase the current franchisees' bottom lines, but would also enhance Cendant's ability to market its franchises. In addition, the alliances would provide some significant revenue opportunities for Cendant, and would benefit the other company divisions.

Execution

The Approach to Implementation: In 1994, Dan Tarantin was hired as vice president of preferred-alliance services to implement this program. Mr. Tarantin, along with Richard Smith, now chairman of Cendant's real estate division, decided to seek alliances with only the largest companies because they wanted vendors that could offer nationwide service to all their hotels. Mr. Tarantin went immediately to Coca-Cola and AT&T to negotiate national deals. Both vendors were excited about the opportunity Cendant presented. Other nationwide purveyors were contacted, but the most favorable initial deals were negotiated with Coca-Cola and AT&T. Eventually, other major deals were negotiated with Pizza Hut and EcoLab for the Travel Division, plus Airborne Express and AON Insurance for the other areas of Cendant. Overall, since 1994, Cendant has developed more than 110 preferred alliances.

Cendant's franchisor-franchisee agreement did not allow Cendant to dictate that the franchisee use any of the national vendors with which Cendant had developed an alliance. Consequently, Cendant had to present the alliance agreements as opportunities, leveraged by Cendant, that could increase the franchisee's bottom line.

Outcomes

Success of the Practice: There are a number of illustrations available to demonstrate Cendant's best-practice success. When this practice began, only 35% of Cendant's hotels were using AT&T, now more than 65% do. Mr. Tarantin estimates the savings to the franchisee runs from $3,000 to $7,000 annually. Cendant also generates a small percentage of revenue for itself.

All of the hotels have vending machines but the deal with Coca-Cola allowed the franchisee to increase profits from this. Since most of the hotels Cendant franchises do not have food operations, the deal negotiated with Pizza Hut placed the restaurant's tent cards in each hotel room. Each hotel receives $.75 for every order delivered to the hotel or its guests. Cendant, too, shared a small percentage of the Pizza Hut volume, which now totals close to a million orders a year.

Advice and Observations: When the Preferred Alliance program began, Mr. Tarantin and Mr. Smith were the only two persons involved. Now, there is a team of about 30, each of whom wears several different hats in expediting and promoting the program to franchisees. The program has been highly successful, and could be utilized by any hotel company having a sufficient number of properties to provide the leverage needed in negotiations with large corporations. A preferred-alliance program might also be useful to highly concentrated regional hotel chains which could negotiate agreements with regional vendors.

Contact

Dan Tarantin
c/o Jackson Hewitt
4575 Bonney Road, Virginia Beach, VA 23462
Phone: 757-687-8240   Fax: 757-973-8973

CENDANT CORPORATION

Integration of All Hotel MIS Functions

Description

The Practice: Cendant is a large multifaceted company that franchises 6,000 hotels under the following brands: Days Inn, Howard Johnson, Knights Inn, Ramada, Super 8, Travelodge, Villager, and Wingate. Project Power Up is a computerized system that integrates all hotel MIS functions into one system so that, through Cendant's huge database, all 6,000 of Cendant's franchised hotels can utilize the information contained in Cendant's huge database. The four main functions contained in the system are property management, central reservations, Internet communications, and direct marketing.

Why the Practice was Developed: Cendant believed that integrated technology is fundamental to the future success of the hospitality business. The company also wanted to give each owner and manager more control of each property, to make each hotel more efficient and profitable, to improve communications, and to bring local marketing efforts to a new level. Only 39% of Cendant's hotels were electronically abled and in some cases turned down more reservations than they booked; Cendant estimates $484 million in turndowns in 1997.

Execution

The Approach to Implementation: In-house development of the system started in June of 1997, and the first installations started in January of 1998. Two thousand hotels have been installed to date. They are presently installing 100 systems per week and will be finished with all hotels by October of 1999.

In the area of property management, Power Up provides:
- Inventory management and central reservations with a seamless interface
- Yield management to help charge full rates more often
- On-line credit card processing
- More efficient staff allocation
- Room maintenance management
- Functional interface options for all operating systems

The central reservation function is fully integrated with the property management system, so that manual input of reservations is eliminated. Furthermore, instead of a prospective guest dialing a franchise's 800 number, bookings can be done on-line directly and instantly.

The Internet function allows the hotel to stay in touch with its brand support team, with other franchises, and with the rest of the world. Prior to this system, each property was receiving at least 21 pieces of mail from corporate services each month; now this communication is done via the Internet or e-mail. By accessing a special, password-protected Web site, a general

manager can get all the information needed from the brand support team such as:
- Operating guidelines and standards
- Brand news
- Marketing information
- Research data
- Purchasing catalogs and pricing
- On-line ordering
- Training programs
- Quality assurance and other procedural updates

Marketing: Because of the vast amount of information contained in the database, individual hotels can access data to conduct targeted direct marketing. For instance, guests' special interests are noted in the database, and by accessing a particular special interest, a hotel can target market efforts directly to that group.

Through marketing templates and interactive training, managers with little marketing experience can be effective marketers in a very short time.

Operational issues: Installation and training consists of a one-day, off-site pre-installation seminar and seven-day (for most properties) on-site training at the time of installation. Ongoing training and assistance via the Internet, interactive training sessions on CD-ROM, and user-friendly system manuals are also included. A 24-hour assistance hot-line is maintained for properties to call.

Costs: Cendant has spent $75 million developing Project Power Up.

There is no cost to the property for the basic system. After the first year an annual service contract fee is charged, and the amount depends on the size and complexity of the property's system.

Success of the Practice: Cendant properties using the system report an average ADR increase of $8.00. Because Cendant receives royalties and a percentage of sales, the benefits of additional marketing, occupancies, and ADR are obvious.

Benefits for Customer: Because of the guest information contained in the database, returning guests can receive VIP treatment, such as pre-registration, and the fulfillment of special needs and preferences. Brand-sensitive data is available only within each brand and not shared with any other brand, including other Cendant hospitality brands.

Advice and Observations: Approach from the communications, rather than the property management, viewpoint and ensure that marketing and operations are involved in the project.

Scott Anderson, Executive VP - Sales & Marketing
Cendant Corporation
339 Jefferson Road, Parsippany, NJ 07054
Phone: 973-496-8655 Fax: 973-496-8445

CHOICE HOTELS INTERNATIONAL

In-House Executive Training and Development

The Practice: Choice Hotels has created an integrated executive training and development system designed to rate the overall performance level of its leadership team. The integrating mechanism for the system is a competency database that targets the core leadership and technical competencies required for effective performance.

Why the Practice Was Developed: Two years ago, Choice made the decision to move in a new business direction. It had been a hotel owner-manager-franchisee group as part of Manor Care, but now became strictly a franchisor. This change prompted recognition by the new CEO that the competencies needed to run the new business were probably different from those needed to run the previous business. The test of this theory was to do an assessment of the core competencies that were needed, and to structure an integrated model that would support the development of these core competencies.

The Approach to Implementation: In preparing for the development of its executive training and development system, Choice relied heavily on research prepared by the Corporate Leadership Council, a non-profit research group based in Washington, D.C. The council conducts long-range benchmarking studies in leadership capabilities, and HR best practices. One of its studies, "Forced-out Leadership Talent Sourcing and Retention," reviewed executive competency models in 50 companies, and concluded that the use of an integrated competency model constituted a best practice. Another competency development tool used by Choice was the Career Architect Portfolio Sort cards developed by Lominger Limited, Inc., a career counseling consulting firm.

Based on the research, Choice undertook the following steps to develop its system:

1 Identified business challenges facing the company in the future.
2 Identified competencies that would be absolutely "mission-critical" to achieve the goals set forth in their business plans.
3 Conducted focus groups at the director level, as well as the next level up.
4 Ranked identified competencies.
5 Received executive input via individual interviews. Critical questions asked: How might competencies be applied differently by level? What were the critical competencies for their function? What career derailers might there be: test case projects (used to quickly identify if new talent in the organization had the required competencies)?

6 Completed a composite model for distribution to the executive staff, who suggested refinements to the model.
7 Received approval to integrate the model into the executive staffing and development process.

The CEO and the senior vice president of administration, Tom Mirgon, were crucial in the development process noted above. The actual integration and execution of the model was left in the hands of Robert Barner, vice president of organizational development and learning, and Mindy Pruss, director of organizational development. They employed the following seven-step process to integrate the model into Choice's executive training and development:

1 Identified competencies needed at each of the top four levels of the organization: senior vice president, vice president, senior director, and director. They found, not surprisingly, that the competencies for success at the senior-vice-president level were similar to those needed at the vice-president level, and that the competencies required for a senior director were also similar to those needed for a director.
2 Assessed and compared competencies held by top executives to needed competencies, which necessitated a 180-degree evaluation of current and potential performance of the senior vice presidents, vice presidents, senior directors, and directors.
3 Conducted development planning and coaching.
4 Mapped potential career paths within the organization and based promotion decisions on the acquisition of competencies required for each level.

5 Identified high-potential talent and capabilities not only via direct supervisors but through a joint review and confirmation of those held competencies by Choice's entire leadership group.

6 Conducted an annual organizationwide talent review, which included a mapping of upcoming business initiatives against competency shortfalls by the senior executive staff. Choice now uses its competency base to perform an annual readiness assessment to determine current leadership capability to pursue new business initiatives.

7 Integrated competency models into all aspects of the human resources system.

Outcomes

Success of the Practice: The executive training and development system is considered very successful. The system is expected to save money because it promotes internal development, rather than external hiring; reduces employee attrition, by having a complete development plan in place as well as having highly competent leaders in the pipeline; and increases the ability to seize new opportunities in the marketplace as they arrive. Below the executive level, employees "are awaiting the building of competency models for their own level, as well as development tools to complement that identification," says Mr. Barner.

Since the integration of this system, Choice has introduced tighter brand standards; and strongly emphasized maintaining the integrity of the brand equity and raising brand standards. These improvements have been directly attributed to the competencies that have emerged as critical in the marketing arena.

Insights

Advice and Observations: Mr. Barner says that much of the success of the system is a result of initial sponsorship by the CEO.

Mr. Barner also reports that the senior staff has been surprised at the range of applicability in the model. Originally, it was thought of as a good development tool, but they have found it useful in selection, promotion, and assessment for succession planning. Consequently, the process now forms the basis of the succession planning process, promotional assessment process, and interviewing and selection processes (the latter currently under development.). However, before creating new uses for the model, Mr. Barner states that it is important to "have a clear line of sight of final application of the model, and get senior staff engaged as soon as possible, due to the automatic tendency to pigeonhole it into a development model and nothing more."

Regarding the identification of competencies, Mr. Barner notes that for each model, it is important to involve individuals at the same level of responsibility, as well as subordinates and superiors, to get a balanced view of competencies critical for performance at each management level. Furthermore, the "competency database should reflect changing business conditions and needs to be updated every two to three years in a fast-changing environment." He further states, "For this to work, data must be shared with people. Communicate like crazy to all management."

Contact

Robert Barner
Vice President of Organizational Development & Learning
Choice Hotels International
10750 Columbia Pike, Silver Spring, MD 20901
Phone: 301-592-6278   Fax: 301-592-6161

CINCINNATI MARRIOTT NORTHEAST

Treating the Guest as Part of the Family

The Practice: The Cincinnati Marriott Northeast has created a 12-point guest-service program designed to encourage the staff to treat each guest as if she or he were "part of the family and on a visit to your home." Continuous guest services training based on the 12-point program is conducted, and the 170 staff members are urged to go the "extra mile" in service so guests will repeatedly return to the hotel. Each employee is required to carry a pledge card identifying the following 12 points of guest service:

1   Address each guest by name, if possible.
2   Establish eye contact within 20 feet of guest.
3   Smile at a guest within 10 feet of guest.
4   Answer a guest with "it is my pleasure," rather than "you're welcome."
5   Escort a guest to his or her destination each time, rather than just pointing the way.
6   When a guest asks something of the employee, the employee should realize that he or she owns the request, rather than giving the request to some other employee.
7   Concentrate on what an employee will be "happy to do" rather than what the employee "can't do."
8   Always answer the phone on four rings or less.
9   Notify the department head of any accident.
10 Always wear the proper uniform and nametag, maintain a shoeshine, and carry the 12-point pledge card.
11 Arrive when scheduled and arrive on time.
12 Always show respect for other employees and work closely with them.

Why the Practice Was Developed: The original associate pledge was developed by the opening team of the hotel in May 1996. This pledge was intended to differentiate the hotel from competitors, and incorporated items that reflected the Winegardner and Hammons mission statement. The opening team did a good job in the initial pledge training, but during the first five months of operation, the focus on the original pledge began to wane. After arriving at the hotel in late 1996, Kent Bruggeman, the general manager, began an extensive campaign to refocus all the associates in the hotel on the pledge. However, Mr. Bruggeman's thoughts on managing customer service became better defined after hearing J. W. Marriott at the national conference in San Francisco describe his customer service philosophy as "always treat customers as part of the family." As a result, Mr. Bruggeman used this philosophy as the foundation for re-energizing the guest-service focus of the hotel.

The Approach to Implementation: Mr. Bruggeman reintroduced the pledge card with the 12-point guest service requirements that had been developed by Winegardner and Hammons' opening team. He mandated that the laminated pledge card is part of the associate's uniform and is to be carried with the associate at all times.

To create and reinforce an obsession with service to guests, Mr. Bruggeman discusses the importance of satisfying the guest in every daily meeting conducted with the hotel staff. At the weekly department head meetings, the first order of business is the pledge card, which describes how the Cincinnati Marriott Northeast is to achieve 100% guest satisfaction. Every

Friday afternoon Mr. Bruggeman invites all of the staff, and any guests who are available, to gather on the lobby terrace for a pep rally during which guest letters and cards are read. The associates yell the hotel's special cheer during the rally. The rally helps heighten the loyalty of the staff, and creates a spirit of family for associates and guests who are able to attend.

Mr. Bruggeman also introduces a discussion of "The Pledge" into special staff meetings several times a year, centering on the message conveyed to guests by employee performance of each of the 12 points. He explains, by example, why the guest return rate is so high at the Cinncinnati Marriott Northeast, and what this level of guest service means to the reputation of the Marriott image throughout the world. He clarifies what the guest-retention rate means to the hotel's owners and employees.

To further ensure adherence to the 12 points of the pledge, Mr. Bruggeman selects his job candidates based on his assessment of their willingness to provide superior guest service. At the start of the interview, he asks each applicant one very important question: "Are you willing to serve?" If the applicant responds, "Oh, yes, I am willing to serve food," Mr. Bruggeman automatically rejects this applicant. Mr. Bruggeman prefers to have a staff that has a proper understanding of what service is.

Finally, Mr. Bruggeman has instituted a number of staff-recognition programs for exceptional guest service. He awards breakfasts, lunches, and dinners; he bestows "Behind the Scenes" All-Star awards for the back-of-the-house staff; and he grants Employee-of-the-Year awards.

Outcomes

Success of the Practice: The 12-point guest-service pledge has resulted in numerous awards for the hotel, according to Mr. Bruggeman. The Cincinnati Marriott Northeast has received the number-one rating for the top Marriott suburban hotel in the country at least four times in the past 20 months. The hotel has had a number-one rating for the guest satisfaction survey four times in the last 18 months and has earned a 96% approval rating on the Marriott employee opinion survey for 1998. Mr. Bruggeman believes this latter achievement is because the pledge has provided the 170-member staff with intrinsic rewards, such as pride in their jobs and a commitment to providing excellent guest service.

Benefits for Customer: Guests have also benefited from the program, as illustrated through customer letters: After a maintenance employee performed a special service for a guest late one evening, the guest wrote, "This is the reason that I keep returning to your fine hotel because everyone is so kind, patient, helpful, and pleasant."

Insights

Advice and Observations: Mr. Bruggeman believes that it is essential to provide training to all staff members regarding the 12-point pledge. He also feels that it is important to have the support of the entire staff to produce the superior customer service that is crucial for success in the hospitality business. As Mr. Bruggeman notes, "Providing the guest with a superior experience is the only sustainable advantage that anybody has in our industry."

Contact

Kent Bruggeman, General Manager
Cincinnati Marriott Northeast
9664 Mason Montgomery Road, Mason, OH 45040
Phone: 513-459-9800 Fax: 513-459-9808

CLARION HOTEL -
COMFORT INN & SUITES

Generating Sales Leads from Employees: A Contest Approach Program

Description

The Practice: The Clarion Hotel and Comfort Inn & Suites hotel complex, which occupies 11 acres of land at Miami International Airport, initiated a program in which all employees were encouraged to become salespeople through the generation of leads. A contest was held in which each of the 80 staff members of the two hotels were encouraged to submit names, addresses, telephone numbers, and, if possible, the name of a principal of any company they came across in their travels. Any random meetings with business people were occasions when such leads might be generated. Additionally, leads could be obtained simply by spotting trucks with identification logos on them. Submission of all leads was encouraged, with no attempt made to isolate only those with strictly business potential. The contest was to be of specific duration and all employees who participated were to be given something, with winners of the four categories to be given cash prizes, and other participants being given certificates of appreciation.

Why the Practice Was Developed: As director of sales and marketing for both Clarion and Comfort Inn, Patricia Molina was aware of the seasonal nature of business in the greater Miami area, as well as the extremely competitive situation the hotels were in. Obviously, the winter months were not difficult for sales, but she wanted to develop the times between Easter and the October shoulder period.

While stopped at a traffic signal one day, Ms. Molina noticed a truck with business information on the side. As was her habit when on the road, she began writing down the information. Why, she thought to herself, don't we use our resource of 80 employees to do the same thing by making note of companies that they run across? Many of their employees have been with the hotels for a long time, morale was good, and the relationship between staff and management was so strong that she felt such a program would only have a positive effect.

Execution

The Approach to Implementation: Ms. Molina came up with a program for the contest. She discussed her plan with her assistant general manager, who was enthusiastic about the idea. The general manager of the properties also was supportive. Corporate was not involved in the planning or the implementing of the program, and Ms. Molina developed the program with the support of top management.

The contest was called "Hot Leads in Miami," and its implementation was simple. Each employee was to provide the sales office with leads from any source, and the sales department was to follow up on them via telemarketing initially, followed by personal sales calls from the two-person staff if the prospect seemed promising. Flyers were printed for all employees with spaces for lead names, addresses, phone numbers, contacts (if known), and sources of the lead. The program was discussed and explained at a department-head meeting, and then introduced to the entire staff at an employee meeting. The two-month parameters of the contest were explained, as well as the prize awards. A commitment of $500 allowed the following prizes to be offered:

- $200 First Prize — Employee whose leads produce the most revenue in a two-month period.
- $150 Second Prize — Employee providing the most leads with potential.
- $100 Third Prize — Employee whose leads produce the most new accounts.
- $50 Fourth Prize — Employee using the most creative way to find leads.

Costs: The costs of the program were minimal. Some printing expense for the certificates and flyers were involved, plus the cash outlay for prizes.

Success of the Practice: Ms. Molina considers the program an outstanding success. Thirty-eight employees supplied the sales office with 162 leads. A total of $10,749 in traceable revenue resulted over the two-month period. Overall, approximately 10% of the leads appear to have significant revenue possibilities, as determined by the telemarketing follow-up.

Ms. Molina notes that the meeting at which the prizes were awarded was a testimony of good fellowship and mutual success. Of special interest was the excitement generated in housekeeping and maintenance. The top prizes were awarded as follows:

First Prize – Night manager – Most revenue

Second Prize – Accounting clerk – Leads with potential

Third Prize – Front-desk clerk – Most new accounts

Fourth Prize – Reservations clerk – Most creative idea (She went to all the stores in a shopping mall and asked for the managers' business cards.)

Another similar contest is in the planning stage, and many employees are already asking when it will start.

Benefits for Customer: Some customers inquired as to why they were solicited, and were charmed at the idea of line employees being part of the sales force.

Advice and Observations: Next time, Ms. Molina will maintain and post a routinely updated record, so participants can be kept current during the two-month contest period.

Patricia Molina, Director of Sales and Marketing
Clarion Hotel-Comfort Inn & Suites
5301 NW 36 Street, Miami Springs, FL 33166
Phone: 305-871-6000, Ext. 7049 Fax: 305-871-4971

CLUB HOTEL BY DOUBLETREE

Employee Care Committees

Description

The Practice: Promus Hotels, parent company of Club Hotel by Doubletree, established "CARE Committees" to boost employee morale and thereby ensure excellent guest services. The concept is to involve everyone on all levels of the hotel operation, so that employees will have greater pride and feel that management is not only listening to them, but also willing to implement their valid suggestions and ideas.

Why the Practice Was Developed: Promus places a strong emphasis on being employee oriented. Established at all Promus Hotels, the CARE Committee's primary goal is to care for employees so they will provide top-notch service to guests and to their fellow team members.

Execution

The Approach to Implementation: To start the process, the human resources department actively seeks charter members for the committee. Every department is to be represented on the committee. The committee meets once a month for 30 to 60 minutes. The CARE Committee has two divisions, a subcommittee for guest relations and a subcommittee for employee relations. Employees on the committee may elect to be on the guest-relations or the employee-relations subcommittee.

The committee has a chairperson, president, vice president, secretary, and two co-chairpersons. The general manager is always the chairperson and attempts to be at every meeting. The vice president is always the human resources director, who monitors the committee's activities and acts as a resource. The president is elected for a one-year term, and oversees both subcommittees. The president's position has taken about five hours a week in preparation and implementation of the program. At the recent elections, this hotel has chose two presidents for the one-year term, so the responsibility would not be so overwhelming.

The Guest Relations Subcommittee:
- Monitors the guest index cards, also known as CARE Comment Cards. The committee considers what is and is not being done and what could be done better.
- Picks a guest each month or each quarter for a Mystery Guest Program. The hotel invites the individual to use all the facilities possible and to grade the hotel's performance. The mystery guests are given a free breakfast or a discount on their room.
- Monitors the guest CARE HotLine response log, which is kept at the front desk. Guests may call the hotline from their room to express any dissatisfaction with their room or the service they received.
- Monitors maintenance logs (known as CARE Repair) to be sure things are fixed in a timely manner.

The Employee Relations Subcommittee:
- Is in charge of audit service standards. The committee does an audit to ensure each department is taking care of employees and guests.
- Sets up a CARE Wheel, which is based upon a CARE Lotto Ticket concept. Employees who do something above and beyond the call of duty are given a portion of the CARE Lotto Ticket with a candy bar while the other portion gets put into that employee's department bucket. Everyone is allowed to give out a CARE Lotto Ticket. Once a month they go into each department and pull out two employee names from that particular department's bucket and those employees get to spin the CARE wheel and win a prize. The prizes are worth about $10.00.
- Operates the employee-of-the-month program. All employees vote for the employee of the month. In the monthly CARE Committee meeting, the human resources director identifies everyone who received nominations and the reasons why. The employee who gathered the most votes receives $100.00, plus a plaque to take home, as well as being featured on a plaque hung in the hotel lobby.

- Monitors the employee-of-the-year program. The hotel management chooses this employee of the year from the twelve monthly winners. The winner receives $500.00, plus a plaque to take home, as well as being featured on a plaque hung in the hotel for the next year.
- Monitors the Bright Ideas program. Employees submit ideas that may benefit the hotel to the human resources office. If the human resources director and general manager feel the idea is of value to the hotel, the individual may receive $25.00. If the idea is implemented system-wide, the individual may receive $500.00.
- Is in charge of throwing quarterly employee parties. The subcommittees are in charge of handling the decorations and menu.
- Is in charge of getting birthday cards signed by as many hotel employees as possible and sending them out to the employee's home on time. Employees also receive a bag of candy with a balloon attached and a cupcake on the day of their birthday.

Operational Issues: The initial concern was getting employees to buy into the program and assuring them that the program was based on an employee-oriented and friendly philosophy. Employees were initially hesitant to express themselves or suggest ideas for fear that they would be yelled at or, worse, ignored. The hotels conducted promotional campaigns to overcome this mindset.

To enable employees to attend scheduled meetings, the human resources office consistently holds CARE Committee meetings on the same day of the month and at the same time of day. The meeting is limited to no more than an hour, so it keeps things moving. The human resources office also provides snacks and beverages for each meeting and puts an emphasis on having fun.

Costs: HR budgets about $500.00 a month for the snacks, plaques, handbooks, paper supplies, decorations, and other items to keep the committee supplied.

Outcomes

Success of the Practice: Human Resources Manager Toni Spiziri has seen a tremendous improvement in employee morale since the CARE Committee has been in existence. Employee turnover has dropped substantially.

Benefits to the Customer: The CARE Comment Cards indicate that guest satisfaction has improved. The guests know that the hotel has a 100% Satisfaction Guarantee program in place. The employees are empowered to weigh the degree of the guest's concern or complaint, and make the decision on the spot to compensate the guest, or do what it takes to satisfy the guest within reason.

Insights

Advice and Observations: Ms. Spiziri states that Promus Corporation brought in a new management philosophy, more people- and employee-oriented than that of previous management firms. After so many years of little interaction between departments, it took employees a while to accept a program that says it is ok for departments to interact and to give input without being criticized or ignored.

To institute CARE Committees, Ms. Spiziri advises that commitment and active involvement from the top are essential. To overcome the potential barrier of getting employees involved, Human Resources may have to initiate a promotional campaign. Ms. Spiziri also believes it is important that the CARE Committee members see it as a fun experience. Additionally, the CARE Committee members need to see that the things they suggest are acted upon and management is listening to them. Finally, Ms. Spiziri notes that the CARE Committee has been a great learning and growing experience for the employees who are elected president.

Contact

Toni Spiziri, Human Resources Manager
Club Hotel by Doubletree
1450 East Touhy Avenue, Des Plaines, IL 60018
Phone: 847-296-8866 Fax: 847-296-7999

COASTAL HOTEL GROUP

Employees on Loan for Training with the Buddy System

Description

The Practice: The Coastal Hotel Group Buddy System was developed for training personnel in acquired properties. In a new twist on an existing hotel practice, skilled department heads in existing Coastal properties are identified by their general managers and loaned to the newly acquired properties to train their counterparts in the Coastal system.

Why the Practice Was Developed: As a small management company, Coastal could not afford the costs of a corporate training center. Coastal thus decided to send talent from its existing hotels to newly acquired properties. When proposing Coastal management services, the company now offers skilled talent to the proposed client as an incentive to use Coastal.

Execution

The Approach to Implementation: The Buddy System solved an immediate need for new properties to obtain individuals who have sufficient knowledge and skills to serve as trainers. The practice allows access to talent but does not require adding trainers to the corporate staff. Existing properties save labor costs during the slow season, as receiving hotels pay the salary and expenses of the trainer. All sides gain from this practice because the receiving hotel gains knowledge and insight, and the lending hotel reduces labor costs. Finally, the instructing employee (buddy) gains by sharing knowledge, building training skills, learning problem-solving techniques, and observing new operating scenarios.

In 1988, COO Graham Hershman started the practice, and the general managers have kept it alive. The COO and corporate staff inspired this concept. It took three to six months to implement. Mr. Hershman works with the human resources director, Susan Summers Evans, who with the general managers identifies the best buddies. Individual general managers are eager to champion their people as buddies, in part to lower payroll costs, but also to broaden the employees' experiences with different operations.

Corporate management determines the buddy needs of the acquired property and the training timetable. The COO gives an introduction to the acquisition personnel when the buddies arrive. Individual general managers and their executive committees are provided information regarding the training buddies.

The practice gives existing staff an opportunity to grow, and retention improves, therefore, as learning opportunities increase. Also motivating the use of the practice are improved profitability, lower labor costs, increased productivity, higher quality, and efficiency.

From the outset the practice has encountered little resistance. Before the Buddy System employees knew that things could be done better, but they were not seeing it happen. With the Buddy System someone is there to help.

Operational Issues: When the corporation was smaller, it was difficult to have the training resources available when needed. That is no longer a problem as the organization is now larger.

Costs: No real costs are involved. The providing hotel saves payroll costs when the buddy is away, and the new hotel pays payroll and living expenses.

Outcomes

Success of the Practice: Although success of the practice is not directly tracked, profits are up, turnover is down, and operations have been improved. When making a pitch to a potential customer, the corporate staff can provide talented resources and demonstrate profitable results.

Benefits for Customer: The practice is successful across the board. The customer is most likely to notice the practice at the front desk, but will enjoy a better overall experience.

Advice and Observations: The chain would do the same thing if it were starting today, as it believes that all parties benefit. Costs are minimal, if any, and the corporate office does not have to centralize training. In the future, Coastal plans to establish monitoring procedures for the practice.

The practice would work in all size properties — although possibly best in small properties.

Contact

Steven Brewster, Public Relations Manager
Coastal Hotel Group
Chicago, IL 60611
Phone: 312-654-2962 Fax: 312-988-9017

Susan Summers Evans, Corporate Human Resources Director
Coastal Hotel Group
Chicago, IL 60611
Phone: 312-654-2962 Fax: 312-988-9017

THE COLONY HOTEL

Guest-Friendly Environmental and Recycling Practices: Becoming a "Green" Hotel

Description

The Practice: The Colony Hotel, a seasonal resort in Kennebunkport, Maine, has a full-scale environmental program led by an environmental director. Guests are encouraged to participate in this program by using the recycling bins installed in each guestroom, conserving water in bathrooms, and reusing towels and sheets. Moreover, the three-diamond, 123-room property operates in an environmentally conscious manner.

Why the Practice Was Developed: The owner, a landscape architect, is an ardent environmentalist who makes environmental considerations an operational and marketing priority. Although the recycling practice may save money, that is not the main motivation. Rather, the owner believes that being environmentally conscious is the right thing to do. The recycling program began in 1989, the property created a formalized environmental position in 1994, and the program to involve the guest began in 1996.

Execution

The Approach to Implementation: Every guestroom has a rattan bin with four compartments labeled for cans, paper, glass, and other trash. Guests are informed about the recycling and environmental program in the "Guest Service Directory." To run the program, the property employs a recycling engineer (who also works six months at a co-owned Florida property). The hotel recycles kitchen waste and compost into its 11 acres of manicured, organic gardens. In addition, the property maintains an environmental bulletin board that incorporates seasonal topics that guests can apply at home. The bulletin board also features information about the hotel's recycling program.

In addition to recycling, the hotel adheres to a number of other environmental policies. To the extent possible, the hotel buys only recycled items, makes only double-sided photocopies, and grows its own flowers and herbs. It is in a three-year program to change over all lighting from incandescent to fluorescent and halogen and is also upgrading machinery in both kitchen and housekeeping. The current equipment is more than 40 years old and the new equipment will be much more energy efficient. For the upgrade program, the property uses only EPA Energy Star-compliant equipment. It sells and donates many of its cast-off products (e.g., furniture or equipment) instead of letting them go into landfills.

An ecology group, comprising members of all hotel departments, meets once a month for several hours. Meetings are always held on work time, and management encourages more than one person per department to attend the meetings. In the meetings, the committee works on creative brainstorming, researching new products, voting on ideas, and implementation of those ideas. One creative example of the environmental committee's work is its idea of converting wine-bottle corks into Christmas ornaments. Another idea was to convert old guestroom bed linens into baby crib sheets and blankets, potholders and aprons for the kitchen, and balsam-filled toys and dolls for sale in the gift shop. Since guests may bring their pet dogs, the committee arranged to have the housekeeping department make appliqued dog blankets that are waiting on the bed upon arrival.

All department heads are involved in the environmental program, and returning employees engender support among new employees by pointing out that they are personally working to save resources. In addition, part of the new-employee orientation that takes place in May at the beginning of each season has a strong environmental component.

Operational Issues: One particular operational issue is that the property comprises seven buildings: three guest buildings, three dormitories for staff, and a utility and maintenance building. The spread-out campus presents some operating challenges, but also offers opportunities for the enthusiastic employees, many of them college students.

Success of the Practice: While one may not be able to measure the program in terms of a cost-benefit ratio, the property benchmarks its criteria for success based on guest and employee reaction to the program. According to Janet Byrd, director of the environmental program, guest-comment cards are running 50% to 60% in favor, and a majority of guests participate in the environmental policies. Ms. Byrd attributes a significant increase in corporate business to the hotel's environmental program. In 1998, 10% more companies, over 1997 figures, asked for a green hotel for their meetings.

The property is the only one in Maine to be admitted into the Green Hotels Association, which Ms. Byrd definitely believes has marketing and advertising value. In 1998 the property also won the following awards: Maine Chamber and Business Alliance Recycling Hero Award; the Maine Development Foundation's Gold Star Award; and the National Trust for Historic Preservation's Historic Hotels of America program inclusion. The property has also gained certification by the National Wildlife Federation as a U.S. Backyard Wildlife Habitat, the only hotel in the Northeast so designated. Such awards are important to employee morale.

Benefits for Customer: One-third of guests in the hotel use the towel- and sheet-saver program. Meeting planners like the fact that the hotel makes double-sided copies. The property maintains a no-smoking policy because of its environmental focus. Because the hotel's environmental policy eliminated harsh chemical use, the facility is clean and nontoxic. The property serves healthful, locally grown products. The guest-room directory includes tips for saving water along with an explanation of the hotel's environmental policy. The hotel also has an educational component in which it offers guests the chance to tour the hotel's private beach with a wildlife biologist in July and August. A self-guided ecology scavenger hunt is available for family exploration throughout the season.

Ms. Byrd believes the environmental program makes the hotel more efficient in many ways. It is most successful in the use of recycled materials, she notes, both through purchasing and reuse.

Advice and Observations: Ms. Byrd suggests starting slow: "Define what you want to do. Start with your offices. Convene the staff. It's a good thing and should be talked up. You can move on from there to bigger projects. You must keep at it because eventually 'they will get it.'" Ultimately, the customer will "get it." In terms of renovating the hotel, she recommends using environmentally benign products. In sum, the program involves doing something they all feel good about rather than strictly focusing on saving dollars.

Janet Byrd, Director of Sales and Environmental Programs
The Colony Hotel
P.O. Box 511, Kennebunkport, ME 04046
Phone: 207-967-3331, Ext. 520 Fax: 207-967-5551
E-mail: info-me@thecolonyhotel.com
Web: www.thecolonyhotel.com/maine

COUNTRY INNS & SUITES

Successful Cobranding with Established Restaurant Concepts

Description

The Practice: Country Inns & Suites has developed a cobranding strategy with freestanding brand-name restaurants. Each hotel is situated adjacent to a T.G.I. Friday's or Italiani's. Hotel guests can charge restaurant checks to their hotel bills and obtain room service from the restaurants.

Why the Practice Was Developed: In the late 1980s, Country Inns was established as one of the three hotel brands owned by Carlson Hospitality. Jurgen Bartels, then chief executive officer of Carlson Hospitality, believed hotel guests were interested in obtaining breakfast in a facility in or near the hotel, but preferred to purchase lunch and dinner from off-site restaurants. As a result, Mr. Bartels conceived a strategy of adjoining Country Inns hotels and Country Kitchen restaurants. At first this strategy appeared sound, but over the course of development, the images of the two Carlson brands diverged. Country Inns matured into a midscale operation with a 50-50 mix of business and leisure travelers, while Country Kitchen restaurants evolved into an economy brand. The lack of synergy between the two brands encouraged Country Inns to examine other cobranding options.

Execution

The Approach to Implementation: Frank Steed, former president of Carlson Hospitality (parent of Country Kitchen and Country Inns & Suites), proposed developing future Country Inns adjacent to a T.G.I. Friday's. The Country Inns property in Minneapolis was the trial site for this plan. The immediate success of the property shaped the course of Country Inns' development. Country Inns & Suites are now cobranded with T.G.I. Friday's and Italiani's restaurants owned by Carlson Hospitality.

According to Paul Kirwin, current president of Country Inns & Suites, management has faced some difficulty in pursuing a cobranding strategy between a hotel and a restaurant because of site requirements. For its restaurants, Carlson seeks an "A" location that provides visibility, convenience, high traffic count, and proximity to dense residential areas. Retail and office space must be located nearby to drive the lunch business. However, the high price of an "A" location is prohibitive for the midscale Country Inns hotel. The challenge for Carlson has been to find a site that can support both facilities, but at a reasonable price. Fortunately, because the two operations require a much larger parcel than is necessary for the restaurant alone, the potential sale becomes especially attractive to the seller, thereby allowing for a mutually beneficial agreement to be reached. The development is designed so the restaurant is positioned at the forefront of the property, giving it the necessary visibility.

Outcomes

Success of the Practice: Both the hotel and restaurant benefit from this cobranding strategy. Room rate and occupancy are much higher at Country Inns cobranded with a T.G.I. Friday's or Italiani's. The restaurants benefit by gaining lunch and dinner business from the hotels. Approximately 15 to 20 percent of the restaurants' business is obtained from hotel guests. In addition, the brand-name restaurant satisfies the dining needs of the chain's hotel guests, and eliminates the capital costs of building a generic restaurant in the hotel.

Benefits for Customer: Guests perceive the brand-name restaurant as an amenity that makes Country Inns & Suites superior to comparable properties.

Advice and Observations: The cobranding strategy has worked particularly well for Carlson Hospitality since it has a food division with established restaurant concepts. Mr. Kirwin notes that despite the challenge of finding sites, the synergy has produced such dramatic results that Country Inns is committed to the strategy of cobranding its hotels with full-service restaurants.

Mr. Kirwin advises that cobranding works especially well for midmarket, limited-service hotels and midmarket, casual-theme restaurants because they serve a similar customer. In each case, these businesses provide complementary services needed and desired by the customer. Consequently, the revenues are incremental without significant added cost.

Contact

Paul Kirwin, President, Country Inns & Suites
Carlson Center
Carlson Parkway, P. O. Box 59159
Minneapolis, MN 55459-8203
Phone: 612-212-1344   Fax: 612-212-1338

COURTYARD BY MARRIOTT

Intranet Information Sharing

Description

The Practice: The SOURCE is an information resource to help Courtyard general managers and associates perform their jobs more effectively and efficiently. It organizes information into a single, easy to use property resource, using computer and electronic technology to replace manuals and other printed information. The information resource provides brand standards, answers operating questions, and assists users in expediting routine tasks. It provides timely and accurate information designed to solve hotel problems.

The initial content of the SOURCE includes:
- Brand system standards
- International sales and marketing
- Incentive marketing
- STAR training modules
- Accounting
- New-hire process
- Manager's guide to benefits

In the case of franchised properties, the manager's guide to benefits and accounting is not used, because the franchisees have their own standards in those areas.

Why the Practice Was Developed: Courtyard was expanding so rapidly that its ability to train and develop managers was being stretched to the limit. A communications tool that is fast, easy to distribute, and easy for managers and employees to use was required if Courtyard's quality standards were to be maintained.

Execution

The Approach to Implementation: When it was decided that an intranet system was not only feasible, but necessary, Brand Executive Kelly Vytlacil, who headed the development of the SOURCE, contacted two outside vendors to assist in designing the system. Imergy Inc. was retained to develop the technology, and Information Mapping Inc. was hired to develop the graphic and information content. The objective was to make acquiring the information as simple as possible, and to develop the content so that a maximum of four clicks would be required to access any topic or subtopic.

Input on the system was gathered through a series of focus groups comprising Courtyard general managers and staff. Essentially, the input was provided by the hotel staff and then collected by the corporate office.

A Trial: Three months prior to implementation, a trial was conducted in selected Courtyard hotels. As a result of the trial, several modifications and additions were made.

The development of the system took 18 months from conception to full implementation, and has now been in use for one year.

Operational Issues: To fully implement and expand the system, 20 "regional technology leaders" are employed nationwide to train Courtyard managers and key people.

A minimum of two computer stations are available in each hotel to allow immediate assess to the SOURCE. Input from the field is constantly gathered and, if pertinent, added to the information content. Information changes and additions are easily entered into the system, eliminating the need to print and mail to the properties. Furthermore, the system ensures that the information is distributed at the property level. The content also includes a section called "What's New," which flags and highlights the newest information.

Costs: The development cost was $400,000, which represents infrastructure for future development. Operating costs consist of intranet server space and three employees to maintain the software, and input changes and additions. These costs have been more than offset by the virtual elimination of hard-copy preparation and distribution, plus the intangible, but real, improvement in staff efficiency, training, and morale.

Success of the Practice: Feedback from the field has been tremendously positive. One of the most used, and therefore most successful, components is the "New Hire Process," which provides all hiring procedural forms (adapted to comply with each Courtyard state and local laws). It is conservatively estimated that the new-hire process saves a minimum of one hour per new hire. The 210 Courtyard hotels hired a total of 6,600 employees in 1998 (through September); thus the SOURCE provides the capability of redeploying 6,600 man-hours to other areas of the business needing attention.

Because the system contains up-to-date operating information, and is so easily accessible, the need for midlevel supervisors has been reduced, and consequently, so have their numbers, effecting further payroll reductions.

The usual voluminous loose-leaf binders containing standard operating procedures have been eliminated, thereby eliminating their production and distribution costs (and one more place for dust to collect).

Benefits for Customer: Though there are no direct benefits to Courtyard customers, indirectly they are the beneficiaries of hotel standards that are consistent, efficient, and timely. This is one of those best practices that is very effective, but one the guest does not even know exists.

Advice and Observations: According to Mr. Vytlacil, "The process for content owners to take responsibility for preparation and deployment represents a more complex cultural change than was anticipated."

The technological capability is available, but is only as effective as the information content available to the user. "Spend the time to research to find out the needs from the field personnel. Design the information around how users want to see it, rather than how content owners want to present it," suggests Mr. Vytlacil.

"Capital is negligible related to the return," states Mr. Vytlacil.

As technology allows, Courtyard's goal is to replace all paper processes with electronic processes.

Kelly Vytlacil, Brand Executive
Courtyard by Marriott
1 Marriott Drive, Washington, DC 20058
Phone: 301-380-8482 Fax: 301-380-1333

DAHLMANN PROPERTIES

Improving the Work Environment and Decreasing Turnover

The Practice: Dahlmann Properties developed a seven-part action plan, which Andy Dahlmann, director of acquisitions, calls "the Ritz-Carlton Action Plan." In 1993, after benchmarking Ritz-Carlton, Mr. Dahlmann organized and brainstormed with his mission statement development team to use the Ritz-Carlton plan as the key training aid for Dahlmann's lodging properties. The development team made adjustments to the Ritz-Carlton plan and tailored it to fit the specific needs, concerns, and physical layout of Dahlmann's "three diamond-plus" hotels. The ensuing plan was designed to implement Mr. Dahlmann's philosophy for considering employees as "internal guests" and be the principal guide for employee training.

Why the Practice Was Developed: Mr. Dahlmann joined the company in the late 1980s, with no previous background in hotel management. Initially, there was a one-year training program with the company in his position as assistant general manager, but he thought it was insufficient. Mr. Dahlmann wanted to learn the business from what he believed to be the best, the Ritz-Carlton Hotel Company, and then develop an action plan for the Dahlmann hotel properties.

During his initial years with the company, Mr. Dahlmann became concerned about the degree of personnel turnover and the extremely tight labor market in Ann Arbor, Michigan. He felt that employees were not being treated as well as they could have been. He also believed that the staff consisted of good people. If they were trained better, he reasoned, they would be better employees. He wanted to address these issues in his action plan.

Execution

The Approach to Implementation: Following a two-week benchmarking study of Ritz-Carlton, Mr. Dahlmann assembled his development team by selecting two department heads from each of the two hotel properties in Ann Arbor. To create a positive work-study environment, Mr. Dahlmann emphasized the team approach, encouraged input, was open to the ideas of all members, and displayed a synergistic management style. As part of the action plan, Mr. Dahlmann thought it was critical to create a friendly work environment for the employees and to improve the employee-selection and training processes.

When the development team concluded the action plan, it was presented to the other department heads and their input was requested. It was then taken down to the line employees and their input was requested. Mr. Dahlmann wanted to involve everyone in the plan and allow them to express their ideas. He believed that this was an excellent opportunity to empower his entire staff and to obtain participation in this project. The action plan that evolved from this process includes the following seven key points:

1 Develop the mission statement (three component parts).
   a. To provide outstanding guest services.
   b. To provide the finest service amenities.
   c. To create superior individual employees.
2 Develop a creed and the hotel basics (short version of the mission statement).
3 Create a friendly work environment.
   a. Consider the employees as "internal" guests.
   b. Examine the current work environment and discuss ways it could be improved.
   c. Make employees feel like "part of the family."
   d. Take employee concerns seriously.
   e. Maintain an open-door management policy.
   f. Obtain support for this program from department heads.
   g. Post thank-you cards on the bulletin board when someone helps out in another department.
   h. Establish a flash fund to provide an immediate financial reward for an employee who had done something exceptional.
   i. Establish a "Good Idea Board," the purpose of which is to track an idea so the employees do not feel it has simply been disregarded. Tracking categories are (1) suggestion/recommendation, (2) under study, (3) pilot,

(4) implemented, and (5) not implemented. Before an idea comes off the board, there is an agreement between the author and the manager. Bonuses of $25 are offered for the following idea categories:

    i. Improvement in guest services

    ii. Improvement in employee morale

    iii. Saves money

    iv. Improvement in safety

  j. Establish empowerment program.

  k. Establish lateral service, so anyone can be asked to help another department at any time. Everyone should know at least one item in another department.

  l. Create teamwork.

  m. Develop exit interviews.

4 Improve the selection process.

  a. Incorporate a job-preview session where the applicant is observed working in a department for half a day prior to a final job offer.

  b. Hire only those who smile. It is impossible to train one to smile.

  c. Verify that the interviewee understands the job description.

  d. Schedule an exit interview with terminated employees to understand what went wrong.

5 Improve the company's training process.

  a. Establish an orientation of each department during the initial week following the hire, so the individual will know a little about each department and the concept of "lateral service."

  b. Use quizzes and tests throughout the training period.

  c. Adhere to the training manual.

  d. Establish a half-day during initial training for the new hire to study the company's philosophies (e.g., the mission statement).

  e. Create a 21-day training process that includes various meetings with department heads and, on the 21st day, a meeting with the general manager to ensure everything is moving in the proper direction.

  f. Use videos and handouts.

  g. Create an ongoing and continuing education program.

6 Create a team concept.

  a. Emphasize employees being "selected," not "hired."

7 Improve guest services to the "external" guest. (Note: The "internal" guest is the employee.)

A Trial: Initially, the plan was put into effect at the Bell Tower, the smaller of the two hotels. When a department at the Bell Tower felt comfortable with the progress of the plan, its corresponding department at the other hotel, the Campus Inn, was notified and asked to review that section of the plan. The Campus Inn then had the option of proceeding with that part of the plan, backing off, or meeting for further discussion.

Cost: The costs of the practice, primarily management labor time, were never calculated. There simply were too many exterior factors — a better economy, more area conferences — to effectively measure a dollar figure for the benefits.

Outcomes

Success of the Practice: Subjectively, Mr. Dahlmann does feel his employees are more aware of the goals of the mission statement. He says their follow-through has led to a positive work environment and this, in turn, has improved guest services. The resulting lower personnel turnover means familiar faces for the guests to see, and guest exit interviews indicate a high satisfaction with the service.

Insights

Advice and Observations: Mr. Dahlmann believes it is important to involve everyone in the plan and to create a team concept. Change can be good, but it is important to review everything before changing. He believes in a synergistic management style, and advises it is easier to implement something if people feel involved and buy into the process.

Contact

Andy Dahlmann, Director of Acquisitions
Dahlmann Properties
300 South Thayer Street, Ann Arbor, MI 48104
Phone: 734-761-7600 Fax: 734-761-9178

DAY HOSPITALITY GROUP

Sabbatical Leave Program for General Managers with Experience

Description

The Practice: In 1998 Frederick Cerrone, president of Day Hospitality Group, instituted a mandatory 90-day paid sabbatical leave program for every general manager with five years' tenure. The GMs may do anything they desire with this time. Because the company is only four years old, the first GM will be eligible for this sabbatical in 1999, so the first test of this concept is still to come. The GMs will receive retroactive time worked to qualify.

Why the Practice Was Developed: Mr. Cerrone noticed that his general managers, whose average age is 28, value their free time a great deal. Their attitude is that "there is more to life than just work." Having seen many in his generation work long hours, year after year, and then not survive long after retirement, Mr. Cerrone states, "I'm not sure what they believe is all that bad; it is a fresh way of thinking."

In February 1998, Mr. Cerrone went on a mission trip to India. While he was there, he recognized that he was finally taking the time to do something that he had always wanted to do. He thought about all the years that he did not do things, specifically with his daughters when they were growing up, because he was committed to the workplace. He noted that these were times that one cannot recapture. This recognition served as a catalyst for the development of a sabbatical program for his relatively young group of general managers. Mr. Cerrone's sabbatical concept ties into one of the company's 17 value statements: "Believe in balanced living in all areas of life — career, family, spiritual, physical, financial, social, and educational."

Execution

The Approach to Implementation: As Mr. Cerrone mentally formulated the concept of a sabbatical, he identified several benefits that he wants this leave of absence to accomplish. He wants it to be meaningful and rewarding to the GMs — a time when his managers can "unplug," and do whatever they want to do. He wants the sabbatical to benefit not only his GMs, but also their families. He believes that it will provide the GMs with young children an opportunity to capture some very special times with their growing offspring. In turn, Mr. Cerrone also anticipates several benefits for the company. Mr. Cerrone believes the GMs will come back refreshed and replenished, in a new frame of mind with their creative juices flowing. He also thinks the sabbatical will provide an excellent opportunity for the junior managers to step forward, and "run the store," so they can be better evaluated for job promotions. Overall, Mr. Cerrone sees this as a win-win situation.

After mulling the idea, Mr. Cerrone approached his partner with the concept. He believed that 90 days was the right amount of time for the sabbatical. His partner countered with 30 days at first, and then 60 days; however, Mr. Cerrone would not compromise. He felt 90 days were necessary to allow the GMs to truly unwind and benefit from the experience. He sold his partner on the concept, and then bounced the idea off three of his senior managers, who were supportive. Mr. Cerrone then presented the program to his managers.

Outcomes

Success of the Practice: The company now uses the sabbatical as a recruiting tool and includes it in its hiring package. The company believes the practice has helped to retain managers; no managers have left since the plan was first presented.

Reflected in the potential success of the sabbatical concept and the success that comes with practicing the company's value statements are recent achievements that include:

- Number-one Fairfield Inn in the country in friendliness for December 1998.
- Number-one Fairfield Inn in the country in cleanliness for December 1998.
- Four of the six properties ranked in the top 10% for Marriott nationwide in guest tracking scores for December 1998.
- All six properties rank in the top 5%-6% for average rates for their Marriott class and brand type.

- Occupancy is well above the industry average and in the top 10% for Marriott brands.

Benefits for Customer: According to Mr. Cerrone, any time turnover is reduced, while training continues and morale is high, should be viewed as a benefit to customers. They will continue to see familiar faces that are making a sincere attempt to serve.

Insights

Advice and Observations: Mr. Cerrone believes the sabbatical leave program is a relatively inexpensive way to make a statement to managers that the company is committed to them in a way not typically found in the hospitality industry. "As owners and managers today," Mr. Cerrone states, "we must force ourselves to think 'outside the box' to provide these types of programs for our associates and managers." Mr. Cerrone also believes managers need to talk with their associates to see what makes them tick and what means the most to them. "Communicate with your managers and associates on a regular basis and in different ways. Be a teacher. Encourage them to have priorities in their lives and to put God first, family second, and their work and job third."

Mr. Cerrone notes that the Day Hospitality Group's vision statement is "Hospitality with Integrity." Integrity is defined as doing the right thing when no one is looking.

Contact

Frederick Cerrone, President
Day Hospitality Group
4725 Peachtree Corners Circle #300, Norcross, GA 30092
Phone: 770-446-1500 Fax: 770-604-9682

DAYS INN ALTOONA

Integrated, Community-Based Marketing Plan

Description

The Practice: The Days Inn Altoona has carefully cultivated the Altoona, Pennsylvania, market with a coordinated suite of development, marketing, and human resources practices.

Why the Practice Was Developed: Owner Gregory Sheehan grew up in the motel business and thus had the advantage of observing motels from an early age. He viewed ownership of his hotels, including the Days Inn Altoona, as an opportunity to put into practice a number of beliefs he had learned from his father, the Marine Corps, and his Christian upbringing concerning human resources management, customer service, and marketing.

Execution

The Approach for Implementation: Mr. Sheehan began his marketing and customer relations activities six months before the property opened. He canvassed the local businesses door-to-door; sent fliers to members of the local Chamber of Commerce; contacted military and government offices; and joined the tourist bureau, a stadium development committee, and the Chamber of Commerce. Among other promotional practices, the motel provides community-service and nonprofit organizations with free meeting space (subject to availability).

He carefully selected the hotel's location, and paid attention to details in construction, approving budget increases when they would result in improved guest perceptions or more durable equipment. He employed an interior designer to select the guest-room layout, colors, amenities, and furniture that would best satisfy the selected target markets: (1) businessmen and (2) women traveling with families. Thus, businessmen are pleased with the large desks, the 25-inch TVs, and the king-size beds; whereas, women with families respond well to the microwave ovens, refrigerators, irons, and ironing boards.

Mr. Sheehan set what he refers to as a "recession-proof rate." He believes that the room rate should "fall within the guests' comfort range" and should clearly establish in the eyes of the community that "the new property gives a product for a price the guest cannot beat."

Mr. Sheehan also selected his staff with great care, seeking "employees more qualified than myself" to perform the duties for which they were hired. He offered the best salary he could afford, medical and dental insurance, and a retirement plan. He also promised to train the employees to become seasoned professionals.

To mold his employees into a motivated, well organized, tightly knit staff, during the first six months, he held regular meetings with the staff to inculcate his operating philosophies and standards, and micro-managed their day-to-day operations. As the employees gained knowledge and confidence, however, he pulled back and let them make decisions — even when they made mistakes — so they would learn. He set up a system of recognition and rewards, was liberal with his praise, and sought their suggestions and opinions.

Finally, Mr. Sheehan developed the routine of conducting regular inspections of the building and grounds to discover anything that should be repaired or replaced. The goal is to correct maintenance and appearance problems before they come to the attention of the guest.

Outcomes

Success of the Practice: The Days Inn Altoona enjoys 70% repeat business and is the occupancy leader in Altoona. In 1997, the hotel was awarded the Days Inns of America, Inc.'s number one property in the world in the category of 75-150 rooms, and was one of only three motels in Pennsylvania to receive the Chairman's Award for Quality. The executive housekeeper ranked number two in Days Inn properties. The motel still has 30% of the staff that was hired in 1985. Although it is 13 years old, the property looks new and is in better shape than new competitors.

Benefits for Customer: Guests comment on their appreciation of the quality of service. Additionally, guests are surprised and pleased with the sophistication of the design and décor of the rooms, as well as with the number of amenities offered.

Advice and Observations: Mr. Sheehan believes that you should "treat people the way you want to be treated." He follows this philosophy with both guests and employees.

Mr. Sheehan notes that site selection is crucial; he points out that if one settles for a substandard location, the competition will build on the best site. He also believes that one should develop the "best motel money can buy" in terms of furniture, fixtures, and equipment. Furthermore, his focus is not on creating the greatest financial return, but on producing a quality product — although he admits his zero tolerance for "wear and tear" to his property seems extravagant to some.

Contact

Greg Sheehan, Owner
Days Inn Altoona
3306 Pleasant Valley Blvd., Altoona, PA 16602
Phone: 814-944-9661 Fax: 814-944-9557

DISNEY'S POLYNESIAN RESORT

A Value-Based Process of Training and Selection

Description

The Practice: Disney's Polynesian Resort uses "Leadership by Values" to increase employee motivation, to provide great service, to present an authentic vision of Polynesia, and to provide cultural and values education through entertainment. In other words, create a business environment or business culture more conducive for success. The cast members and management identified 11 shared values. The first four were theme values, which were part of the discussion of "what makes us Polynesian": (1) a sense of *Ohano*, or sense of family, which describes the way they would like their working relationships to be; (2) a spirit of *Aloha*, which means that the basis of their interactions is their desire to be caring and mindful of others; (3) a sense of *Kina'olea*, the desire to perform all interactions and services in a high quality way; and (4) a sense of *Mea Ho'okipa*, the desire to be the perfect host by "welcoming and entertaining guests and strangers with unconditional warmth and generosity." The remaining seven values were Walt Disney World core values (balance, courage, diversity, honesty, integrity, openness, and respect) and already formed the foundation of performance expectations at the resort.

An entire training program, "Magic of Polynesia," was designed to facilitate employee understanding and commitment to the business and values.

Why the Practice Was Developed: The resort, one of the originals opened at Walt Disney World, is a special-theme product. A goal was to emphasize and enhance the authenticity and distinctive atmosphere of current and proposed products and services. Additionally, improvements in cast morale was an objective; indeed, this area is where the Leadership by Values process had its greatest appeal and success. The value process involved talking about individual and personal commitment; identifying whether a person's life values were similar to the resort's 11 shared values; increasing awareness that Disney's Polynesian Resort was a great place to work; and providing orientation into the Polynesian culture. The idea was to find people who shared the values of Disney and Polynesia, so they could be themselves and act out of commitment instead of compliance.

Execution

The Approach to Implementation: Clyde Min, general manager, worked at a property in Hawaii with Dr. George Kanahele, an expert in management by values who has over 20 years of experience. When Mr. Min was recruited by Disney in Singapore three years ago, he brought in Dr. Kanahele as an external consultant. At the resort, other leading players included Mary Cooper, who developed and implemented the integration of the process; Shelly Randazzo, who as Polynesian show specialist provided the cultural expertise; and Stephen Hoel, who at that time was the human resource manager. These key individuals created three modules to assist employees with learning about Polynesia and to foster an alignment of personal and resort values. Cast members participated at every level.

Leadership by Values identifies and supports commonly shared values in three areas: the business, the product, and the behavior. The business of the resort is hospitality; the product is "a unique theme environment based on Polynesia"; the

behavior is the service performances by the cast members — how they demonstrate the 11 resort values with the guests and each other.

The management and cast members defined their business more specifically by using the following definition of hospitality: "to welcome and entertain guests *and strangers* with unconditional warmth and generosity." The result is that all cast members have a shared mission and vision.

Regarding the product, to the knowledge of Dr. Kanahele and Mr. Min, Disney's Polynesian Resort is the only resort that represents the 11 identified cultures of the Polynesian Triangle in the Pacific. Most resorts found in the Polynesian islands focus on sharing one culture. This concept is what makes the resort so unusual. This representation of the Polynesian Triangle is done through the story line, the performance theme, and the foods that are served, as well as allowing the cast members to study the differences among the islands and to greet guests with the salutations used in the different islands (from the Hawaiian *Aloha* to the Samoan *Tahofa*).

Module one was designed to provide three hours of instruction on the business of hospitality, and on the cultural elements of Polynesian hospitality and entertainment to be delivered as the product. Great emphasis is placed on the definition of welcoming guests, and the concept of strangers. This concept describes the feelings of anxiety or nervousness a person experiences when visiting a new place. The role of the host is to replace the anxiety of the stranger with unconditional and sincere care and concern. "At Disney not only do we expect the cast members to speak to the guests, but cast members are expected to welcome and share the spirit of Aloha with them," Mr. Minn says. Recognition and coaching is used to assist cast members in becoming the "perfect host" in sharing their aloha with the guests.

Module two focuses on the alignment of personal values with the resort values, and a commitment to display behavior demonstrating these values. The cast members are asked, "What are the key drivers in your life? What do you think you are all about? Who are you? What are the things that are important to you?" In most cases, their values are identical to the seven core values of Walt Disney World Resort. "Traditionally, Disney itself attracts great employees who are driven by a mission, and they find that Disney is a great employer that allows them to perform accordingly. We know and try to leverage this," stated Mr. Min.

Module three was focused on delivering "Kinaole" (flawless excellence in the highest degree) product and service to the guests. This concept represents the complete integration of the shared values-based behavior with the service standards of excellence. For example, why do we need to make eye contact? Why do we need to recognize a guest in a certain way and within a certain time frame? This module resulted in an efficient hospitality operation through which the culture of Polynesia was experienced by the guest.

The ability of the resort to get repeat guests depends on its ability to leave lasting lifelong memories with every guest. This can only be created and accomplished by the cast. "It's people who create those memories and relationships that guests can take away. If the memories are exceptional enough, those memories will bring them back for a repeat visit. People relate to people; they don't really relate to inanimate objects," stated Mr. Min. Management tries to convey to the cast members that "it is through them that the place or location is interpreted." It is through people that the sense of what Disney is all about is being experienced, and it is through the cast members that guests can experience the culture of Polynesia in some small way.

Costs: The three modules have been integrated into an eight-hour orientation and training class that all cast members attend within their first 30 days. The instructors are released from their areas to teach this class, which is scheduled twice a month.

Outcomes

Success of the Practice: The cast is performing better, with high morale and strong teamwork. The hotel is running better, as reinforced by guest letters and comments.

The property has also been recognized within Walt Disney World Resort in several ways. The R.A.V.E. award (Respect, Appreciate, Value Everyone) was awarded to the resort for its success in the area of diversity for two consecutive years. In 1998 the Diversity Spirit award was given to the resort for sharing continued passion of diversity awareness.

Benefits for the Customer: New, fun, and authentic traditions and opportunities have been created at the resort for both the cast and guests to participate in and learn about the Polynesian culture. The resort also achieved its fourth AAA diamond, 14 months ahead of the business plan.

Advice and Observations: Mr. Min says the Polynesian is "improving the program as we go along." It was "almost like a leap of faith in the beginning, because we didn't really know for sure that it would work, but we knew it was the right thing to do. There wasn't a clearly defined plan of action for us to follow, so we have had to create the next step as we go. This is an issue of personal commitment vs. compliance; without the commitment, it would never work. When the answers to *What does this company stand for?, Who am I?, and What are my values?* emerge, then you have attained Leadership by Values. The environment has to be created where a person wants to smile, not to do it because it is expected." The 11 resort values have been integrated into the reward, accountability, and coaching programs. A fourth module is currently under development.

Contact

Clyde Min, General Manager
Disney's Polynesian Resort
PO Box 1000, Lake Buena Vista, FL 32830-1000
Phone: 407-824-1232 Fax: 407-824-3174

EMBASSY SUITES - GREATER MINNEAPOLIS

Consolidation and Centralization of Reservations Sales Office

Description

The Practice: Three Embassy Suites properties in the Greater Minneapolis area have consolidated their reservations sales forces under one roof, effectively creating a centralized reservation system for the three, soon to be four, units. Previously, each of the three Embassy Suites properties had its own two-to-three-person reservations sales team located on the individual property.

Why the Practice Was Developed: Two years ago, Regional Director Tom Murray's research indicated that the individual reservation centers of the three Embassy Suites properties, all located within 15 to 20 minutes from one another, were not doing as well as they might in referring and capturing customers for sister properties. When one individual unit could no longer accommodate requests for space, these prospective guests were simply being lost to competitive properties due to the indifference of each property's sales force for its sister hotels, inadequate training, and other front-office responsibilities, which interfered with the room sales thrust. Mr. Murray determined that one reservation center for the three properties would likely result in conversions of room reservations from one unit to the other two properties.

Execution

The Approach to Implementation: Jane Serrano, general manager of the Minneapolis-St. Paul Airport Embassy Suites, was able to find space to accommodate the new central reservation system in her hotel by reshuffling offices and utilizing some extra space. Two to three months were required to renovate the space, install the upgraded computer system, and connect a sophisticated telephone system that would enable a reservations person to know which hotel was being called. The new computerized system provides instant inventory access to all three hotels as well as the Promus parent reservation system in Memphis. New responsibilities for the central reservations group were added during the consolidation, including revenue management, forecasting, and the preparation of rooming lists, all of which were previously done by the individual sales offices or the front desks.

Initially, the franchise owners were reluctant to accept this centralized reservation system, in part due to the capital expenses involved. The results of this practice have since eliminated that resistance.

Operational Issues: The staff of the reservation center consists of eight full-time personnel, including a manager and an assistant manager, and one part-time staff member. Robert Covey, a previous director of sales, was made reservations manager with the new title of director of revenue management, reporting directly to each of the three general managers. Mr. Covey, or his assistant, attends the weekly management meeting at each of the three hotels.

The reservation center opened in August 1997 and immediately provided an increase in staffing hours. Whereas previously, the staffing had been Monday through Friday, 8:00 a.m. to 4:30 p.m. in each of the three hotels, the new staffing procedure gave coverage from 7:00 a.m. to 9:00 p.m. Monday through Friday, and noon to 6:00 p.m. on Saturdays and Sundays.

The system was running smoothly within three months.

Costs: Ms. Serrano indicates the total capital costs to include the upgraded computer system, the additional phone commitment, and the physical renovation at the hotel to be less than $50,000. Costs for the ongoing system are allocated to each hotel based on their number of suites. This allocation method will continue when the new hotel opens, and the new property will be on-line immediately with the central reservation system.

Success of the Practice: Under the previous system, Embassy Suites properties were unable to keep track of lost room requests. Now they have that ability, and under the new system, have reduced lost business to a very small percentage. The conversion dollars, Ms. Serrano feels, are significant in enhancing all the hotels' revenues.

Occupancies are running in the mid-70s; average daily rate (ADR) at the Minneapolis-St. Paul Airport Embassy Suites has gone from $102 in 1995 to $138 in 1998, an increase that has delighted the owners. The other two units are running in the $115 range.

Ms. Serrano indicated that, as in many airport hotels, things can get "frantic" at the front desk. Since the central reservations system has been put into place, however, she and the other hotel general managers have noted a significant increase in the ability of the front desk to spend more time personalizing its guest services.

Specific cost savings on reservations centers were not initially a primary factor, but Ms. Serrano indicates there have been some savings, and that outcome will be greatly enhanced when the new hotel comes on-stream, as no additional personnel will be required to handle the fourth property.

Benefits for Customer: Each month Promus Hotels sends out 140 surveys per hotel to randomly selected guests to obtain a measure of customer satisfaction. In addition, a private company makes ten calls per month to each hotel to test the quality of the reservation service in speed, use of the caller's name, and length of time to make a reservation. The new reservation center has consistently scored in the top 10% of all hotels in both these surveys.

In the case of an oversell, there are four vehicles available to shuttle customers back and forth between hotels. They also run every half-hour to the airport and every hour to the mall.

Advice and Observations: Ms. Serrano regrets that they began the service in August, which is their busiest month. She thinks the properties would have been better served if the system had become operational in January. She also has found some difficulty in communicating with her department heads due to the reallocation of space necessary for the reservation center. However, she feels more than compensated for that inconvenience by having the reservation center on site, and by her front desk being able to deliver a better quality of service.

Jane Serrano, General Manager
Embassy Suites Airport
7901 34th Avenue South, Bloomington, MN 55425
Phone: 612-854-1000, ext. 250 Fax: 612-854-6557

ESSEX PARTNERS

Achieving Greater Profitability through Budgeting, Cost Controls, and Team Building

Description

The Practice: Essex Partners, an independent management company, has established a system of budgeting and cost controls that has allowed it to perform at a level that attracts the attention of both property owners and financial lenders. Part of this success is because it attempts to control costs that are usually not deemed the management company's responsibility, such as financing, insurance, legal, and audit expenses. It also has fostered a sense of *esprit de corps* among its managers, which has resulted in improved property performance.

Why the Practice Was Developed: Essex Partners specializes in the budget-hotel management contract business sector. It presently operates 16 hotels, primarily located in the Northeast, and the average size of its hotels is 100 rooms. Essex realized that, in order to compete in a very crowded and competitive market, it would have to prove that its operations were more efficient and produced a higher GOP than other comparable properties. If successful, it also would then be able to increase net profits for its owners by obtaining better financing and reducing other expenses usually not considered in management contracts, such as interest rates, insurance, legal, and audit costs.

Execution

The Approach to Implementation: The approach to making their operations more efficient and profitable consisted of three primary steps:

- Hire the best managers available.
- Create and maintain a budgeting process that assures the maximization of the property's potential and is *realistic*.
- Constantly review expenses, including those below the GOP line.

Essex utilizes two regional managers (eight properties each) to work directly with the property managers. The budget process begins with each manager projecting revenues for the coming year via telephone meetings. Subsequently, each manager, with the assistance of each department head, prepares the expense portion of the budget and submits the result to the regional manager. The regional manager then meets with each manager to review the entire budget on a line-by-line basis prior to final submission.

Regarding cost controls, the regional managers, Essex CEO John Mooney, COO Barbara Purvis, and development and purchasing personnel meet every Monday morning for 90 minutes to review possible areas of cost reduction for both corporate and property costs as well as other issues.

Operational Issues: The managers' bonuses are tied to performance relative to their budgets. In addition, each manager participates in a stock option program within Essex Partners. These stock options have produced an increased awareness and interest in corporate operating revenues and expenses as well as individual property issues. Because the managers realize that one or more nonperforming properties can affect the value of their stock options, an increased sense of teamwork has been created, wherein interproperty communications and assistance are prevalent.

Essex retains an industrial psychologist to work, as needed, with the regional and general managers. His primary objective is to foster team building and increase the interaction and communications among all the managers to exchange ideas and solve problems. When first initiated, there was some resistance with a few of the managers. Once the managers learned that the psychologist was a help and not a threat, they have become frequent users of his services. Interestingly, managers who resisted the most are no longer with the company. Their departure was not directly connected with the existence of a psychologist, but Essex believes that if had they utilized the service, they might still be with the company.

Success of the Practice: Because of the effectiveness of the practice, Essex has just completed the refinancing of 12 of its managed properties with an average reduction in interest rates of 2%, a direct benefit to the property owners.

It recently bid out the audit costs for its 16 hotels, and was able to reduce the combined cost of all properties from $150,000 in 1997 to $143,000 in 1998, an average savings of $6,700 per property. Savings of this sort positively and directly impact the bottom line.

Benefits for Customer: The customers in this case are the property owners with whom Essex has management contracts. Because of the sophisticated budgeting process and attention to costs, these owners are confident that their properties are being managed as well or better than their competition. Because of this efficiency, they have enjoyed direct savings in operating and ownership costs and an obvious increase in their return on investment.

Insights

Advice and Observations:

- Hire the best managers available and include them in all phases of the budgeting process and cost control decisions.
- Listen to the managers.
- Include in cost control analyses those costs usually considered the owner's costs, i.e., financing, insurance, etc.

Contact

John Mooney, Chief Executive Officer
Essex Partners
100 Corporate Woods, Suite 316, Rochester, NY 14623
Phone: 716-272-2315 Fax: 716-272-2396

Barbara Purvis, Chief Operating Officer
Essex Partners
100 Corporate Woods, Suite 316, Rochester, NY 14623
Phone: 716-272-2315 Fax: 716-272-2396

FAIRMONT COPLEY PLAZA HOTEL

Using a Property Management System to Improve Concierge Desk Excellence

Description

The Practice: The Fairmont Copley Plaza in Boston uses its Fidelio property management system to support its concierge services. In this regard, the system contains a database that puts essential guest information at the concierges' fingertips, thus freeing them for more direct guest contact. In addition, the system reduced the number of concierges required to fulfill guests' requests.

Why the Practice Was Developed: Wanting to provide the most consistent possible guest service, hotel management discovered that the concierge desk was overloaded with routine tasks, in part because a business center was located at the desk. The center involved sending and receiving faxes for the entire hotel. The concierge desk also had to deal with valet parking. With its new PMS, the hotel could streamline the concierge services.

Execution

The Approach to Implementation: In an effort to upgrade service, the hotel engaged an outside consulting company to survey employees regarding what was good and bad about the hotel. One outcome of the six-month process was installation of the Fidelio PMS. The system's functionality allowed Director of Concierge Services David Jamieson to build the database that allows him to expedite guest services and elevate service levels. Essentially, all guest needs are placed at his fingertips — an extremely important aspect of the job. Thus, the PMS records each guest's choice of newspaper, breakfast, and wake-up call preferences, and whether the guest likes overnight laundry service. The system reminds the concierge of guests who need special attention (e.g., an escort from the airport). He is also able, for instance, to prioritize dining choices for guests, and he maintains a listing of names of maitres d'hotel for all area restaurants, as well as a record of the restaurants' schedules and special attributes. He also has developed a list of top picks. Thus, the computer does not replace the core concierge service of interpreting guests' needs. For example, Mr. Jamieson says he will not recommend restaurants that he or his staff has not visited.

The system now contains details about every street in Boston, including how far it is from the hotel and the best way to get there. The concierge desk then can print cards with directions for guests.

Operational Issues: The new system allows Mr. Jamieson to handle guest needs with a staff of only five people instead of his former staff of seven to eight.

Outcomes

Success of the Practice: The Guest Satisfaction Index for the concierge department is high — in the 88% to 90% range. Mr. Jamieson has received complimentary letters from guests with positive referrals about his employees, and he has received many repeat guests. It is obvious from this program that Mr. Jamieson has created loyalty among a group of core guests who stay frequently at the hotel, as well as those who stay only occasionally.

Insights

Advice and Observations: Mr. Jamieson has served as a member of the local concierge association and is the regional director of the Clefs d'Or. He notes: "Ninety percent of the concierge's job is being nice to the guest. It's important to remember guests' names and to follow through with all requests. It's also important to communicate effectively." He says consistency in service and being positive every day is critical to benchmarking his performance. "This is a service business and you must be focused upon the guest," he explains. He does say that the computer is not a requirement but certainly facilitates enhanced guest services.

Contact

David Jamieson, Director of Concierge Services
Fairmont Copley Plaza Hotel
138 St. James Street, Boston, MA 02116
Phone: 617-267-5300 Fax: 617-267-7668

THE FARMINGTON INN

Writing Historical Fiction Books to Enhance Marketing

Description

The Practice: The Farmington Inn, in Farmington, Connecticut, produces a series of stories as a softcover book, which serve as an attractive promotional tool for the hotel and the surrounding area. The stories blend fact and fiction to introduce the reader to the inn and the history of the surrounding area. Indirectly, the stories serve as a guide to Farmington's tourist attractions.

Why the Practice Was Developed: Guests of the Farmington Inn frequently queried the staff about area attractions. The general manager suggested providing the guests with a one-page typed sheet with information about the community, so guests would have an idea of what was available for them to do while they were in Farmington. Richard Bremkamp, director of sales and marketing, wanted to do something a little more special for the guests; as a result, he developed the storybook idea.

Execution

The Approach to Implementation: Mr. Bremkamp first wrote *The Farmington Lady*. The story incorporates sights in the city of Farmington and the Farmington Inn, as a young girl repeatedly spies a ghost at various historical locations in the area. The story is "fiction based on historical fact and lore," states Mr. Bremkamp. At first, the owners of the inn were skeptical about using a book as a marketing tool; nevertheless, they gave approval for an initial printing of 1,000 copies. Since then the book has been reprinted several times for a total run of 10,000 copies.

The book, which takes 30 to 40 minutes to read, is placed on the pillow in each guestroom so the guest can read about the local area. Since guests are free to take the book with them, it has developed into a wonderful marketing tool, according to Mr. Bremkamp.

Outcome

Success of the Practice: *The Farmington Lady* has been so popular with guests that Mr. Bremkamp has written *The Spirit of Simsbury* for a sister property, and *Julia's Journey* for the Farmington Inn. The latter book is designed to complement *The Farmington Lady* and serves as a means of reenergizing repeat business. All books are written along the same lines of "fiction based on history," and have attracted favorable publicity. Indeed, the Farmington Inn gets requests for copies of the book from all over the world.

Mr. Bremkamp won the 1997 "Connecticut Innovative Business Award," a statewide Malcolm Baldridge-criteria award. The inn is the first (and so far only) hospitality business to win this award. Another award recently bestowed was the "Stars of the Industry" award, given by the Connecticut Lodging and Attractions Association. Mr. Bremkamp has also been contacted by other B&Bs asking him to write a story for them, but so far he has declined.

Insights

Advice and Observations: Mr. Bremkamp stated, "This is a marketing tool that could be used by any inn or hotel owner with a little imagination. This type of book requires a local character or characters. There has to be a thread running through the story. You need something logical to draw upon to connect your establishment with the community."

Mr. Bremkamp also considers his books great public-relations tools for the local area. It is "another opportunity to become a good community neighbor."

Contact

Richard Bremkamp, Director of Sales and Marketing
The Farmington Inn
827 Farmington Avenue, Farmington, CT 06032
Phone: 860-677-2821 Fax: 860-677-8332

FOUR SEASONS & REGENT HOTELS & RESORTS

"Designated Trainer" Program for Front-Line Employees

Description

The Practice: Four Seasons has created one or more "designated trainer" positions within each department as an approach to making front-line employee training as effective and consistent as possible. Each designated trainer is a line employee who holds a regular job assignment, but is specially selected for his or her job knowledge, standards adherence, patience, and communication skills. The designated trainer follows a carefully structured program (called the on-line training program or OLTP) in teaching and coaching new employees step-by-step on "how to achieve Four Seasons-defined standards of service with the right hospitality attitude." OLTP was the result of a joint development effort between the corporate office and the Four Seasons Seattle. The initial "standard" version of OLTP, consisting of more than 100 job-specific training manuals, was distributed in CD form to each hotel. Local operational management and training staff are responsible for its customization to suit local job descriptions and operating structures (e.g., different food and beverage concepts and service approaches).

Four Seasons operating and service standards are based on sound analysis of customer needs, and OLTP ensures a consistent definition of those standards and a close match between employee performance and customer expectations.

Why the Practice Was Developed: Early research found Four Seasons employees experienced inconsistent communication and training on Four Seasons standards, because of differing interpretations of those standards as the company grew rapidly. As managers were relocated within or recruited into the company, the risks of inconsistency became increasingly apparent. Also, with a tightening labor market, Four Seasons recognized the need to do a better job of training to retain current, experienced employees.

Execution

The Approach to Implementation: A temporary task force of four — composed of a corporate executive, the hotel's general manager, human resources director, and training manager — was established to develop the on-line training program, of which the designated trainer program became a key component. The training manager developed the content and structure of the program together with operating management in the Seattle hotel, while the general manager, human resources director, and corporate executive met regularly to refine and improve it.

After the on-line training program (with its designated-trainer concept) was fully evolved, it was then launched and promoted company-wide. Initially, some hotel managers balked at the amount of work required. In general, however, managers welcomed the plan because they saw it as filling a need for consistency of standards.

Five regional training coordinators, trained by the training manager, helped implement the program hotel-by-hotel for the first 18 months. OLTP is kept alive by training managers in almost every hotel and by regional vice presidents of operations, who review the effectiveness of the program during their regular hotel visits.

Development of the program from idea conception to the launch required approximately 12 months, with a further 18 months for full implementation in all hotels.

Operational Issues: No heavy investment in additional training is required to develop and implement the program. Designated trainers are selected and then groomed in a three-day workshop. The designated trainer is paid a premium rate for the time spent on training and is required to know each assignment in detail. Nothing is left to chance, as Four Seasons defined service and hospitality standards must be achieved. The employees' performance and progress during training and afterwards is measured against the standards that underlie the training program of which they are fully informed from the beginning of their training.

99

The Trial: The Four Seasons Seattle was the site of the three-month pilot test, which the original four-member task force thoroughly reviewed. The program was successfully implemented in food and beverage outlets, room service, and housekeeping. The pilot test proved positive from a standards point of view as well as from the perspectives of acceptance by managers and employees in the hotel. Only a limited amount of "fine-tuning" was needed.

Costs: Development costs were $75,000-$80,000, and the launch cost was $200,000 for a total of approximately 20 hotels. Aggregate costs over three years were approximately $300,000, or $15,000 per hotel. Ongoing costs are more than offset by shorter training times, greater efficiencies, and more consistent guest experience, according to John Young, executive vice president of human resources.

Success of the Practice: Mr. Young was a member of the original task force and views the practice as a success "without reservation." Whereas employee opinion surveys prior to the designated trainer program revealed a "lack of adequate training," employees now applaud the clarity of structure, the consistency of standards, and access to an informed and experienced designated trainer and department manager. Consequently, employee satisfaction is up, turnover is down, and retention has improved, so management spends less time on hiring and training. Labor costs have decreased, training time has been reduced, and quality has improved since the establishment of this program.

Almost 75% of all line employees promoted to supervisory positions have successfully filled designated trainer positions in their hotels.

There is a greater degree of perceived consistency from property to property now that the program is operating, while independent rating systems (e.g., *Conde Naste*, AAA, Mobil) have recognized Four Season Hotels with the highest awards for service in the industry.

Four Seasons attributes its rate leadership and highest RevPAR in part to its training programs, which represent a blueprint for each hotel concerning standards and training.

Insights

Advice and Observations: Mr. Young states, "If someone is already doing systematic training, they should look at our OLTP and designated trainer programs. Anyone not doing systematic training should be. If Four Seasons were faced with the same problem again, the main change we would make would be to start the OLTP sooner and finish it faster."

The designated trainer practice should be viable for firms with 15 employees or more.

Contact

John Young, Executive Vice President of Human Resources
Four Seasons & Regent Hotels & Resorts
1165 Leslie Street, Toronto, Ontario M3C 2K8, Canada
Phone: 416-449-1750 Fax: 416-441-4341

FOUR SEASONS & REGENT HOTELS & RESORTS

Developing a High Ratio of Well-Trained Employees to Guests

Description

The Practice: Four Seasons has developed a differential advantage by meticulously creating a deluxe customer service orientation designed to meet the needs of the luxury market for both business and leisure travelers. This orientation requires a higher ratio of thoroughly trained employees to guests.

Why the Practice Was Developed: To ensure the loyalty of its guests, and to warrant the five-star or five-diamond rating held by many of its hotels and resorts, Four Seasons believes it must maintain its service-oriented culture, which is facilitated by a high ratio of employees to guests.

Execution

The Approach to Implementation: According to Barbara Talbott, executive vice president of marketing, the success of the Four Seasons chain stems from the beliefs and principles that are part of the corporate culture. Four Seasons chooses to offer "only experiences of exceptional quality," and "properties of enduring value using superior design and finishes" supported by "a deeply instilled ethic of personal service." Four Seasons believes its greatest asset and key to its success lies with its employees and how they treat "guests, business associates, and colleagues." The current ratio of employees to guests in city hotels is approximately two to one, and in resorts, it is 2.5 to one or better.

Employees are carefully selected and trained, engendering a sincere attitude of caring about and anticipating customers' needs, so that guest satisfaction and successful financial results are consistently achieved. New recruits are carefully chosen; appropriate service attitude is considered significantly more important than prior hospitality experience. New hires are immediately oriented to the Four Seasons value system. Each new employee is interviewed by top management, and then participates in a seven-part orientation program spread over 12 weeks, culminating in an overnight stay in the hotel to experience all aspects of service just as a guest would. Mentoring relationships are developed formally and informally.

The important role employees play in the success of the chain is well recognized, and as a result, employee longevity is not unusual. For example, the typical tenure of a general manager is more than 12 years.

Outcomes

Success of the Practice: The Four Seasons stock is traded on the New York Stock Exchange, and is also listed on the Toronto and Montreal exchanges. Recent figures show a stunning growth pattern. For instance, net income rose from C$20.4 million in 1995 to C$52.8 million in 1997.

A recent *Fortune* magazine survey, for the second consecutive year, once again identified Four Seasons as one of the 100 best companies to work for, based on the result of an anonymous employee survey. Four Seasons is the only company headquartered outside the United States to be so recognized.

Insights

Advice and Observations: Isadore Sharp, chairman and chief executive officer, has stated on a number of occasions the factors shaping the company, not only at its inception, but as its continuing credo:
- To develop a group of medium-size hotels of exceptional quality.
- To make service its distinguishing edge.
- The Golden Rule: The company culture is to treat everyone as they would like to be treated themselves.
- To leverage Four Seasons' reputation by gradually divesting hotel real estate and investing that capital in management expertise.

Four Seasons is a chain focused on one niche. Further, "Four Seasons is constantly striving to maintain and improve the quality and scope of its services for the luxury market." As a result, the company will continue to be a "major innovator in the hospitality industry, developing services to make business travel more productive and efficient, and leisure travel hassle-free and more enjoyable," according to Ms. Talbott.

Contact

Barbara Talbott, Executive Vice President-Marketing
Four Seasons & Regent Hotels & Resorts
1165 Leslie Street, Toronto, Ontario M3C 2K8, Canada
Phone: 416-441-4395 Fax: 416-441-4414

FOUR SEASONS & REGENT HOTELS & RESORTS

Ensuring a Luxury Hotel Experience

Description

The Practice: The Four Seasons Hotel Company maintains a focus on quality operating and service standards to facilitate a luxury experience for all its hotel guests. These standards are consistent with the company's unwavering goal of providing the finest level of service and accommodations available in the international hotel industry.

Why the Practice Was Developed: Rather than compete in the vast mid-market, Isadore Sharp, founder, chairman, and CEO of the Four Seasons Hotel Company, decided to establish a hotel company that would be an exemplar of service. Mr. Sharp believed that he could attain financial success by providing guests with the finest of services, the best accommodations, up-to-date amenities, and most of all, consistent quality standards.

Execution

The Approach to Implementation: Mr. Sharp established the high-quality operating and service standards for his hotels and employees. That quality image is sustained by President and COO John Sharpe, Executive Vice President Wolf Hengst, and other members of top management, who travel frequently to maintain checks on standards. These executives require total commitment from the chain's 26,000 employees to provide superior services, and to maintain the furnishings, which must be in keeping with a luxury hotel property. Nothing else is acceptable. To ensure compliance, each hotel is routinely inspected by divisional vice presidents, and an outside consulting firm inspects each property twice a year.

Operating standards are updated by a committee that meets quarterly. The standards committee, comprised of senior vice presidents, regional vice presidents, and some general managers, reviews all of the present operating and service standards. The committee obtains input and suggestions from focus groups, guests, and general managers, and makes modifications as needed. There are no compromises in the quality of the established standards, which are designed to meet guests' demands and preferences.

Operational Issues: Training is very important in maintaining standards, and the company uses a vast array of training methods and devices. The basic defined standards are very clearly defined and written for all employees to review; these standards are pursued relentlessly. New employees go through an intensive orientation for two days at a time to learn the basics of Four Seasons' philosophy and culture. Continuing employees participate in an ongoing training process with departmental managers. The company retains training professionals who schedule training classes for the employees at each hotel. Moreover, in some countries, the company has developed its own learning centers to teach employees to speak languages appropriate for local and international hotel guests.

The company is keenly aware that the attitude of its employees is reflected in guest attitudes. Therefore, the firm holds regular employee meetings to review philosophy and standards. Principles are discussed in weekly department-head meetings, weekly planning-review meetings, and daily operating-review meetings. The daily meetings also cover, for example, which VIPs are expected, special dinners to prepare, special catering events and meetings to come, and guest complaints (when they occur).

General staff meetings occur once or twice a year. Also, several times each year the president, executive vice president, or senior vice president will call for a meeting with 30 to 50 department heads and their assistants. The meeting ensures that all of the department heads and their assistants know what is transpiring within the company.

A longstanding policy requires most promotions to come from within the existing staff. The result is a low turnover rate in the staff. Longevity is also encouraged by an awards program. Awards are given to the Employee of the Month and the Employee of the Year. The Employee of the Year wins a five-day stay at one of the Four Seasons Hotels for the employee and his or her spouse.

Success of the Practice: The chain has received a number of quality awards from various travel magazines and ratings services. Mobil has awarded each Four Seasons Hotel either a four- or five-star designation. In *Travel and Leisure* magazine's "World's Best Awards," Four Seasons and Regent hotels captured 18 slots among the "Top 100 Hotels." Zagat Publications, which rates U.S. properties, gave Four Seasons properties an average rating of 27 points out of 30. Sixteen Four Seasons properties ranked among the "Top 100" in Institutional Investor's "World's Best Hotels" survey. In addition, Andrew Harper's *Hideaway Report* has given a first-rate designation to various Four Seasons Hotels, and the AAA has awarded its five-diamond designation to most Four Seasons Hotels. Recently, Four Seasons was chosen for the second year in a row by *Fortune* magazine as "one of the top 100 employers" in the United States. Only two of the 100 companies were hotel companies; Four Seasons was the only non-American hotel company.

Mr. Sharp's philosophy is, "You can't play tennis by watching the scoreboard." Thus, he believes that if you have the right product, the profit will follow. Indeed, in every city where the Four Seasons Hotel is located, its average room rate is among the highest.

Wolf Hengst, Executive Vice President
Four Seasons & Regent Hotels & Resorts
1165 Leslie Street, Toronto, Ontario M3C 2K8, Canada
Phone: 416-441-4353 Fax: 416-441-4381

Insights

Advice and Observations: Appropriate image is important to the Four Seasons brand; and so quality standards must be maintained. There is concern among management that if any Four Seasons Hotel does not live up to the standards of excellence, then the image of the entire chain will be damaged. Thus, the company stays focused on quality.

Additionally, the company tries to capture the local feeling of any community in which it manages a hotel, especially outside of North America.

FOUR SEASONS & REGENT HOTELS & RESORTS

Informal Dining Venue and Alternative Cuisine

Description

The Practices: Four Seasons Hotels & Resorts' guiding principle within food and beverage (F&B) operations is to stay progressive and always remain sensitive to the guests' needs. This tenet has manifested itself into two different practices for Four Seasons F&B operations. The first is the strategic use of only one F&B outlet within a majority of Four Seasons' hotels, rather than the traditional strategy of multiple venues with varying degrees of service and quality as seen in other hotel chains. The second is a concept of cuisine choices in which Four Seasons has added trademarked, nutritionally balanced Alternative Cuisine, homestyle, and vegetarian options to its main F&B and room service menus.

Why the Practices Were Developed: Four Seasons' goal is to have its hotel F&B outlet rated one of the top three restaurants in any city where Four Seasons is located. A single outlet supports this objective because it allows for a more focused approach to satisfying the needs of the guest — better attention to food quality and presentation, better understanding of small details, and higher service levels delivered through a smaller but better qualified staff. At the same time, Four Seasons recognized that guests were moving away from various tiers of dining and were more interested in high-quality food with timely and efficient service. The development of broader cuisine choices evolved as more and more customers were looking for healthier meals and frequent travelers wanted more of a "homestyle" menu instead of traditional restaurant menu items.

Execution

The Approach to Implementation for Single F&B Outlets: When examining the success factors of independent restaurants, Four Seasons realized that it was an independent restaurant's ability to narrowly focus quality and service into one outlet rather than diffuse resources among many that led to independent restaurants' competitive edge over hotel restaurants. Thus, Four Seasons decided to design only one F&B outlet into a majority of its hotels and began this practice over 20 years ago with the Four Seasons Hotel in Washington, D.C.

The creation of the initial restaurant concept is driven by three factors: the location of the hotel, the anticipated market mix, and the competitive environment formed by local hotels and restaurants. Rejecting the idea of different tiers of quality and venues between volume outlets and formal dining restaurants, Four Seasons has opted for an integrated informal/formal dining strategy. One main dining outlet is created with a smaller venue adjoined or nearby. Both venues share the same menu, staff, chefs, and kitchens. The main venue provides more of a table service atmosphere and dining experience. The smaller venue is more informal, provides quicker service, and has extended hours. However, the difference between the two venues is one of design functionality, not of quality of food or service. The room service menu is also developed from the main F&B outlet menu as well.

In addition, the main venue is not an old-fashioned hotel dining room experience. Four Seasons believes customers have moved away from ritual table service and a formal atmosphere, and instead prefer elegant yet informal and relaxed environments where they can converse more readily but still enjoy a high quality menu. This type of venue also lends itself to capturing the local market from outside the hotel. Four Seasons may vary the degree of informality with the meal as well, having no tablecloth and an informal place setting for breakfast and lunch, but for dinner, enhancing the elegance of the surroundings somewhat with a tablecloth, candle, and new place setting. In recent years, to augment the single F&B outlet, Four Seasons has added some limited menus to its bars and lounges. It has upgraded these areas with small satellite kitchens or small buffets for light informal meals or cook-to-order requests.

The Approach to Implementation for Broader Cuisine Choices: The second practice that Four Seasons has introduced over the last few years is the concept of "broader cuisine choices." The concept first began about 15 years ago when guests started to become increasingly more health conscious. At that time, fitness was becoming more popular, especially among the public who frequented Four Seasons hotels. Four Seasons restaurants began to notice an increase in requests for specially cooked food and healthier menu items. In response, Four Seasons created a series of nutritionally balanced items called Alternative Cuisine that were considered low fat, low cholesterol, low sodium, and low calorie. Four Seasons hired a dietary consultant to develop an initial list of 100 core "healthy" recipes to be used for the new menu options. The cuisine is offered at all Four Seasons restaurants as either part of the main menu, on which it is marked as an Alternative Cuisine item, or on a separate small menu.

After the initial core set of recipes was developed, Four Seasons allowed the individual restaurants to create and promote their own Alternative Cuisine dishes to add variety to the menu. Each hotel takes potential recipes to a local registered dietician to be analyzed and certified as nutritionally balanced. Although there is no specific chainwide dietary criteria for the recipes, the general rule is that the menu item must fit within the food style and concept of the restaurant, and visually look no different from a main menu item either in portion or presentation.

The second set of recipes added to the Four Seasons broader cuisine choice concept was "homestyle." This set of menu items was introduced approximately two years ago after Four Seasons received significant feedback from frequent travelers. These guests were tired of traditional "restaurant" food and wanted something simpler, easier on the palate, and similar to home cooking. In response, each hotel developed a set of recipes taken from favorite recipes of the chef's family or relatives. The menu items were first introduced in the room service menu and have since moved to the lunch menus of the restaurants. Recently, Four Seasons has added another set of core recipes to its restaurant menu — "vegetarian." This menu addition was also based on feedback from customers, as well as an increased trend of vegetarianism among its guests.

The chefs and sous chefs have reacted favorably to the evolving concepts. They have challenged themselves to develop recipes that demonstrate the same level of imagination, food quality, and presentation as other items on the menu. Serving staff and other restaurant personnel realized the value of responding to customer feedback and providing the guests with what they truly wanted.

Costs: The strategy of having only one main venue for F&B has saved costs for Four Seasons. The savings on labor costs due to a smaller staff concentrated in one venue have been substantial, especially for hotels in tight labor markets. The cost of the Alternative Cuisine, homestyle, and vegetarian cuisine has been negligible with most of it composed of additional training for the chefs and kitchen staff.

Outcomes

Success of the Practices: Four Seasons believes its dining strategy has been very successful. Its hotels' restaurants capture roughly 80% of their guests for breakfast, with the remainder using room service. For lunch, about 75% of covers come from the local market. Monday through Thursday the dinner covers are split 50/50 between guests and local residents; the percentage of covers on the weekend from local residents is much higher.

The broader cuisine choices have been successful as well. The popularity of certain menu items does vary depending on season and locale, but in general the Alternative Cuisine items account for 20-30% of lunch orders and 10-12% of dinner. However, in some locales, such as California, the items account for almost 50% of the items ordered. The homestyle recipes are also popular. At the Four Seasons Hotel Chicago, the meatloaf sandwich has replaced the club sandwich in popularity, and homestyle menu items account for a third of room service sales.

Benefits for Customer: Four Seasons has remained attuned to its guests' needs and thus its customers have greatly benefited from the F&B program. Four Seasons provides an F&B outlet that maintains a high quality of food and at the same time provides an elegant yet relaxed environment for dining. The addition of the smaller venue allows access to the main menu, but with faster service and more hours of availability. The broader cuisine choices provide food more tailored to individual tastes and needs, without sacrificing quality or increasing cost.

Advice and Observations: Alfons Konrad, senior vice president of food and beverage, provides the following insights on F&B operations: "Food is a living thing ... food can only be better when one is totally immersed and evaluating techniques and balances of flavor on a continuous basis ... one must always stay progressive ... once your program becomes routine or habitual, the customer loses interest. The challenge is to deliver a high quality product in an atmosphere that respects and reflects the customers' needs — how much time they have, what the purpose of the meal is, what their dietary preferences are, and the manner in which they prefer to entertain."

Contact

Alfons Konrad, Senior Vice President, Food and Beverage
Four Seasons & Regent Hotels & Resorts
1165 Leslie Street, Toronto, Ontario M3C 2K8, Canada
Phone: 416-441-4306 Fax: 416-441-4381

GOOD NITE INN

Establishing Time Frames for Preventive Maintenance Tasks

Description

The Practice: Good Nite Inn has established standard time frames for the completion of all property maintenance tasks to allow for proper scheduling and staffing of guestroom maintenance. The practice, based on a time and labor study, requires that the maintenance staff be accountable for completing specific quantities of work within a set time interval.

Why the Practice Was Developed: Skip Hall, vice president of operations for Good Nite Inn, believed guestroom repair and maintenance defects as reported by guests were at unacceptable levels — four repair and maintenance defects were reported for every one housekeeping defect. Mr. Hall intuitively figured that if he could control and harness the time it took to complete specific maintenance tasks, then he could establish accountability for the maintenance staff. In turn, the maintenance staff would be more productive and guest-reported defects would decrease.

Execution

The Approach to Implementation: A task force was established comprising a rooms quality manager, general manager, training manager, regional manager, and Mr. Hall. Over time, the task force determined the specific daily, weekly, monthly, and quarterly time requirements for every maintenance task (e.g., window washing, carpet cleaning, changing air filters), for every piece of equipment, furnishing, or fixture. Included in the time specification were set-up, break-down, cleanup, and break periods. The task-force study revealed that the time required for the execution of regular preventive maintenance duties still yielded 2 1/2 hours per maintenance shift for the performance of specific guestroom maintenance, as well as emergency maintenance. At the conclusion of the study, the task force presented its findings to the general managers. After four to five months of design, the program was implemented in late 1997.

Based on the task-force recommendations, the rooms quality manager, with input from the general manager, became responsible for creating a schedule of maintenance duties to be performed and the standard times attached to each task. This scheduling calendar, prepared only one or two days in advance, requires approximately 30 minutes a day to complete. Consequently, on any particular day, a maintenance engineer knows exactly which maintenance tasks are to be completed for which guestrooms and the time frame in which they are to be done.

Costs: To fully implement the program required the services of two key maintenance engineers, who devoted approximately 100 extra hours (estimated to be worth $2,000) to assemble the program. The books delineating the task-force findings and specifications were supplied to each hotel at an additional expense. However, the only ongoing expense for the program is the time required by the rooms quality manager and general manager to complete the maintenance schedule.

Outcomes

Success of the Practice: The practice has proven to provide many benefits. First, the rooms quality manager's scheduling efficiency has improved. Second, morale and retention of maintenance workers has increased, even in areas with many labor issues. Indeed, turnover has fallen from 150% to 50% in the repair and maintenance department, thus saving the company money. Mr. Hall credits this improvement to greater job clarity for the maintenance staff. Workers now know what is expected of them. Third, workers' compensation claims have decreased. Good Nite Inn saved approximately $50,000-$100,000 in compensation claims that were directly attributable to the repair and maintenance department, partially because of the lower turnover. Fourth, hotel and guestroom maintenance has improved and is more consistent. Other departments have noticed the improvements because guest complaints have dropped.

Benefits for Customer: Based on comment cards, guest satisfaction has greatly improved, which Mr. Hall believes is the bottom line.

Advice and Observations: Mr. Hall notes it is critical that the correct timing be specified for each task. Consequently, time specifications should be validated and confirmed by different parties. He also believes the rooms quality manager should check the work of the maintenance engineers. Finally, Mr. Hall suggests placing notes in the guestroom that inform the guest of the preventative maintenance that is scheduled for the room. Doing so allows the repair and maintenance department to handle tasks as scheduled preventive maintenance rather than as future emergency maintenance.

Contact

Skip Hall, Vice President of Operations
Good Nite Inn
18859 Wilshire Blvd., Suite 400, Los Angeles, CA 90025
Phone: 310-268-7772, Ext. 412 Fax: 310-268-9172

GOOD NITE INN

Development of Mobile Shop for Improved Guestroom Maintenance

Description

The Practice: Good Nite Inn developed the concept of a mobile maintenance shop using a converted housekeeping cart. The cart is inventoried with all types of repair components for guestroom maintenance and is used by the maintenance staff to provide outstanding guestroom upkeep.

Why the Practice Was Developed: Trent Selbrede, the present general manager of the Good Nite Inn in Ontario, California, was formerly the general manager at the Good Nite Inn in Fremont, California, when he conceived the idea for a mobile maintenance shop. At the time, repair items were scattered around the maintenance room and throughout the property, so locating needed items was time consuming. Furthermore, this disorganization produced an inadequate inventory of required repair items. As a result, the maintenance staff was traveling to Home Depot at least four times a week to pick up items.

Because the Fremont property ran a 95% annualized occupancy, Mr. Selbrede could not afford out-of-order rooms, which further added to his concern about the disorder and inefficiency in the maintenance and repairs department. Mr. Selbrede figured if he could place an appropriate inventory level of repair items on one cart for use by an engineer each day, maintenance personnel could be more efficient and productive.

Execution

The Approach to Implementation: Suggestions regarding the mobile maintenance cart and its inventory were obtained from the director of operations, the maintenance staff, head housekeeper, and director of training. Mr. Selbrede and the rooms quality manager spent approximately two months configuring and reconfiguring the cart inventory before determining exactly which items should be carried and in what quantities. The cart is now part of the daily maintenance routine. The maintenance cart has everything from pull chains for lamps to porcelain and wood touch-up kits. A maintenance engineer can complete nearly any type of guestroom repair by using this cart. The cart also assists the maintenance and repairs department in maintaining an adequate inventory of repair items, provided they spend 15 minutes each morning replenishing the cart.

Outcomes

Success of the Practice: After the program had been in place a few weeks, it was clear to the entire hotel staff that the mobile maintenance cart improved the efficiency of the maintenance and repairs department. For example, without a maintenance cart, a typical guestroom check took 15 to 20 minutes including repairs and re-check. With the maintenance cart, the room check takes approximately three to five minutes. With the maintenance cart, a complete room "detailing," which is performed on each guestroom three to four times a month, requires only two to five minutes. As a result, there is less room down-time. In addition, the practice has resulted in fewer trips to Home Depot for the maintenance workers, as they now have the lead time needed to place catalog orders.

After the implementation of the mobile maintenance cart, the regional office's monthly property inspection ratings rose from 85% to 99%. In terms of profitability, Mr. Selbrede quantified the savings at two hours per day in labor cost. Last, employee satisfaction, especially in housekeeping and front desk, has improved. The front-desk staff is happier and more confident about selling the product because guest complaints have decreased.

Based on the success of the program at the Fremont property, the director of operations touted the practice to the general managers at the other Good Nite Inn properties.

Benefits for Customer: Mr. Selbrede's informal lobby survey of departing guests indicates that most people are extremely happy with the hotel and the better room quality. Furthermore, guests are quite impressed by how much maintenance and repair work is accomplished while they are out for a few hours during the day. As a result, the property is receiving three to four additional excellent comment cards each week.

Advice and Observations: Mr. Selbrede believes a major part of the program's success is based on the inventory part of the program and the 15 minutes each morning spent restocking the cart. He emphasizes that it is important to have a good inventory program so there is enough supply on the cart at all times. He also notes the maintenance staff must believe that the practice will make their jobs easier, although he indicates that after six to eight weeks the maintenance workers will wonder how they ever lived without it. Finally, Mr. Selbrede says it is important to follow up and to ensure the maintenance workers have the tools they need to complete the job.

Contact

Trent Selbrede, General Manager
Good Nite Inn
1801 East G Street, Ontario, CA 91764
Phone: 909-983-3604, Ext. 305 Fax: 909-986-4724

GRAND THEME HOTELS

The Creation of a Process to Track and Control Labor Costs

Description

The Practice: Grand Theme Hotels conducted a series of "time and motion" studies for most of the hourly positions in the company's four properties to determine exactly how long each task (e.g., check in, check out, cleaning an occupied room, cleaning a check-out room, serving a meal) required. Supervisors and managers prepare schedules according to those targets.

Why the Practice Was Developed: According to Mark Kane, general manager, the purpose of identifying time requirements for each operational task was to reduce labor costs in a tight labor market.

Execution

The Approach to Implementation: Once Grand Theme made the decision to initiate a time and motion study, an outside organization, Synchronamics, was hired to measure the time required to perform each aspect of a specific job. For example, in the bathroom, Synchronamics observed how long it took to change towels and to clean the bathtub/shower, toilet, countertop, and floor. Many measurements were taken of the same tasks, using different housekeepers on different days in different areas of the hotel, to derive an average number of minutes for the total job of cleaning a guestroom. Nearly all operational tasks underwent the same careful scrutiny to derive an average time for completing each task in the hotel.

The hourly employees affected by the study were involved in each step of the process from the beginning. Meetings were held to explain the what, why, and how of the process. The employees were told that they would share in whatever savings the company realized as a result of this practice. Task times were discussed with the employees, and they were given the opportunity to voice any disagreement. When the disagreements were justified, adjustments in the times were made.

The time and motion study provided some surprising results. For example, Grand Theme Hotels discovered that the average number of minutes required by a housekeeper to clean a room is about 20 minutes, including travel time, rather than the "standard" 30 minutes. Grand Theme Hotels adjusts this average time requirement up and down depending on the type of hotel (three-star versus four-star), and the amount and style of furniture in the room. Housekeepers were rewarded $75 for the first month of the program for meeting their production quotas; now they are awarded $50 per quarter. All rooms are inspected periodically to make sure the quality does not suffer,

and some housekeepers have more rooms inspected than others. All, however, have at least two rooms inspected. In addition to the above, housekeepers are allowed to "buy" rooms when the need arises.

The process is closely tracked. In housekeeping, for instance, a report is generated that shows cost per room, hours per room, and dollars per hour for each different level of the department, which makes it easy to spot when actual labor costs vary from targeted labor costs. Variances in these expenses are discussed immediately.

Labor costs are also reduced by the environmentally sound practice of changing sheets every third day, and changing only those towels left on the floor of the bathroom. A brochure in the room explains how many thousands of gallons of water are saved, as well as how many hundreds of pounds of detergent do not enter water reserves.

Outcomes

Success of the Practice: Grand Theme Hotels has achieved the productivity standard (or better) since implementing the program. In addition there is greater consistency in the performance of tasks.

Benefits for Customer: For guests, the quality and consistency of standards are now better. Mr. Kane explained that in the two years that he has been with Grand Theme Hotels, he has received only one letter from an unhappy guest related to the program.

Advice and Observations: Mr. Kane advises involving all the employees in the entire process, making sure they are heard, and including their input in the program. He also suggests sharing the benefits with the employees. He notes that upkeep and tracking are essential, team meetings need to be held every day, and feedback needs to be given daily. Individuals who need retraining should get it as soon as possible.

Contact

Mark Kane, General Manager
Grand Theme Hotels
5905 International Drive, Orlando, FL 32819
Phone: 407-351-2100 Fax: 407-345-5249

THE GREENBRIER

Programs Establishing the Resort as a Center for Culinary Excellence

Description

The Practice: The Greenbrier has established a reputation for culinary excellence by instituting several practices. The center-piece of these practices is a formal, three-year culinary apprentice program. Related practices include a culinary school for guests during the off-season; conferences and seminars with food critics and writers as guest speakers; an active partnership with the local high school culinary training program; newsletters to 600,000 of the resort's guests; and the publication of *The Greenbrier Cookbook*. In turn, these practices have increased resort occupancy year-round.

Why the Practice Was Developed: The resort is in a remote location and lacks proximity to a pool of experienced culinary person-nel. For years, The Greenbrier depended upon seasonal European chefs, a policy that required constant recruitment and training, as personnel changed from season to season. Management thought the kitchen staff needed to be stabilized. In addition, the resort was not being well-utilized during the slow seasons and needed promotional efforts to improve occupancy during these periods.

Execution

The Approach to Implementation: The Greenbrier culinary apprenticeship program, the first of its type founded in the United States, was developed by the resort's food director in 1957. The hotel made contact and established relationships with the principal culinary schools in the United States. The three-year, formal apprentice program is open to graduates of a two-year culinary school, or individuals with equivalent experience. Candidates are carefully selected based on recom-mendations. They must spend several days at the hotel working with the hotel's kitchen staff and getting acquainted with the town as part of the selection process. The successful candidates are paid in the range of $9.50 per hour, and must find their own housing. During the three years, the apprentices work in all areas of the hotel's kitchens. Their presence helps stabilize the kitchen staff. They attend a formal class four hours per week where issues not related to the hands-on kitchen activities are taught. The program graduates six or seven individuals per year.

In 1993 a culinary arts program was developed in partnership with the local high school. This program promises permanent employment with The Greenbrier to interested applicants, further stabilizing kitchen personnel. This program is aligned with a national program called "Pro Start," which is endorsed by the National Restaurant Association with support from the state of West Virginia and its hospitality educational programs. The hotel employs 90% of its workforce from the local area, and this educational partnership underscores the significant community presence of The Greenbrier. The association with

the local high school continues as part of the hotel's commit-ment to educating young people interested in culinary careers, and to being a responsible member of the local community.

The cooking skills class for guests, the food critics' and writers' symposiums, and the newsletters have been part of the promotional effort dedicated to maintaining The Greenbrier's reputation as a culinary center of excellence, and increasing business during the slow season. The newsletters, distributed quarterly, have proven to be the most effective direct-marketing tool for the hotel. All of the culinary activities, as well as other features of the hotel, are communicated to The Greenbrier's target market through this promotional tool.

Outcomes

Success of the Practice: The Greenbrier's continued high occupancy and excellent reputation are the final judge of the success of the programs.

The Greenbrier apprentice program and the high school culinary arts partnership have resulted in the retention of a highly skilled kitchen staff. The conferences and symposiums for food critics and writers have been particularly effective in establishing the reputation of The Greenbrier as a culinary center, bolstering the standing of the resort throughout the industry. Further, the subsequent publicity from the conferences has increased guest attendance at the cooking schools that are conducted for eight weeks in the slow winter season.

Benefits for Customer: There are many reasons why guests at The Greenbrier are drawn there, but its reputation as a culinary center has become an important variable in the guests' decision-making process. The management of the hotel further believes that the apprenticeship program and the high school partnership program have resulted in the hotel guest receiving quality and consistency in the food and beverage service.

Insights

Advice and Observations: The most important ingredients in the successful mix of The Greenbrier's culinary programs are the involvement and enthusiasm of the employees, according to Rod Stoner, vice president of food and beverage. To maintain this spirit, management must keep the staff challenged.

Mr. Stoner also believes that managers must stay abreast of industry trends, study the programs of other properties, and seek distinctive ideas for adaptation to their own hotels.

Contact

Rod Stoner, Vice President of Food and Beverage
The Greenbrier
300 W. Main Street, White Sulphur Springs, WV 24980
Phone: 304-536-1110 Fax: 304-536-7860

HOLIDAY INN EXPRESS, CRIPPLE CREEK, CO

Making Every Employee's Job a Sales Job with Sales Responsibilities

Description

The Practice: Every employee at the Holiday Inn Express in Cripple Creek, Colorado, is a sales associate. All employees, from the night auditor to the front-office staff, contact guests and follow up on leads. The practice necessitates establishing a mindset among all employees that promoting sales is the most important part of their jobs regardless of the positions they hold in the hotel. Management sets the precedent by providing employees with information about all operating aspects of the business (occupancy, costs, and operating profit) and the importance of interacting with guests on a one-on-one basis.

Why the Practice Was Developed: This practice was put into effect when Chris Mauter, owner and general manager, took over the hotel in 1994. He required that the first item on the job descriptions for every hotel position be "every employee must be sales-promotion minded." When some existing and new staff (especially housekeepers) questioned how this policy could possibly apply to them (given their limited guest contact), Mr. Mauter explained the importance of every employee being a salesperson and contributing to the profitability of the hotel.

Execution

The Approach to Implementation: The staff is trained to "sell" hotel guests by striving to interact with each guest. To reinforce this goal, the hotel holds a special promotion twice a year whereby any guest, who is not first greeted by a hotel employee with whom the guest has come into contact, may lay claim to a free night at the hotel. The purpose of the promotion is to encourage all employees to initiate conversations with the guests. The promotion is advertised on flyers and in the guest-rooms.

Not only do customer-contact employees work on sales to guests staying in the hotel ("interior sales"), but auditing and front-desk personnel also perform sales tasks on potential guests ("exterior sales"). During the graveyard shift, the auditing department sends fax messages to a list of leads (e.g., chamber of commerce contacts, former guests with future business potential, local business leads) expressing the hotel's interest in accommodating them. Sales associates (i.e., front-office employees) follow the fax with a personal call or a telephone call; the hotel expects each front-office staff member to make 10 sales calls per day. This exterior sales program is supervised by a guest-service manager who is attached to the front office.

Employee recognition is also important in encouraging good guest relations. Mr. Mauter believes that if you take good care of your employees, your employees will take good care of your guests. Consequently, employees providing extraordinary service, as determined by their appropriate peer groups, are rewarded as follows:

- Employee of the Month Award: a plaque and $50
- Employee of the Year Award: a plaque and $100, plus a dinner for two
- Manager of the Year: $500
- Innovative Manager of the Year: $200
- Other awards include an extra day off given to employees because of special performance.

Outcomes

Success of the Practice: When Mr. Mauter arrived at the hotel, occupancy hovered between 55% and 60%. Since then the hotel's occupancy has grown to an average of 76% to 80%. The hotel has among the highest ADRs of all Holiday Inn Express hotels. During the four-year period that Mr. Mauter has operated the hotel, it has received the Holiday Torchbearer Award (highest award) and the Quality Excellence Award (second highest) three times. In addition, it has received the Cripple Creek award for the best hotel operation for the past four years.

Advice and Observations: Every hotel must go back to the basics — service to the guest. Any hotel large or small can put the principles of this program into effect. Every employee can be a salesperson, provided he or she realizes that everyone plays an important role in having a satisfied guest.

Contact

Chris Mauter, Owner/General Manager
Holiday Inn Express, Cripple Creek
P.O. Box 1329, Cripple Creek, CO 80813
Phone: 719-689-2600 Fax: 719-689-3426

HOLIDAY INN EXPRESS, HELENA, MT

Achieving Quality Customer Service at an Economy Property

Description

The Practice: The Holiday Inn Express in Helena, Montana, successfully exceeds customer expectations through numerous practices including employee training and rewards, extra amenities, a smoke-free environment, personalized welcoming letters to guests, and a focus on surpassing corporate standards.

Why the Practice Was Selected: The owner of this property is BDR Inc. of Albuquerque, New Mexico. BDR Inc. is a family enterprise that is focused on providing a quality experience for the hotel's guests.

Execution

The Approach to Implementation: Betsy Baumgart, general manager, opened the hotel in 1995. Employees are extensively trained. In addition to receiving training manuals from the Holiday Inn Company, Ms. Baumgart or the housekeeper will instruct a maid for five days before they give the new hire an assignment; front desk employees are trained for 10 days. Ms. Baumgart has also developed a bonus program for all employees which is based on the quarterly profits of the hotel. This program has been quite successful because the hotel has regularly increased in profitability since its opening.

Ms. Baumgart has continued to add amenities to the property. Although Holiday Inn Express is a mid-market hotel, guestroom amenities include: an iron, ironing board, and hair dryer; coffee maker and coffee; 25-inch screen television; computer data port; and free local telephone calls. The hotel also offers a fitness center and a business center with Internet access.

The hotel was made smoke-free to keep it fresher, and to attract the health-conscious guest. Ms. Baumgart initially worried about this decision, but guests appreciated the decision because they are guaranteed a smoke-free environment. This Holiday Inn Express has marketed itself as a healthy choice.

Ms. Baumgart dictates and prints a welcoming letter to each guest and places it in the guestroom. The letter advises the guests that they can call her about any of their needs and she will take care of them.

At this property, there is a strong emphasis on quality at all times. Although corporate inspections are made every six months, Ms. Baumgart inspects guestrooms at least three days a week; the chief housekeeper inspects all guestrooms every day. These inspections are designed to ensure the guest receives the highest quality stay possible.

Outcomes

Success of the Practice: To date, the hotel has received two quality excellence awards, and in 1998 it received the Torch Bearer Award, the highest award Holiday Inn grants for guest satisfaction. Only 78 properties among Holiday Inn's 2,600 franchises have been the recipients of this prestigious award. Furthermore, employee turnover is low, and there is a definite pride on the part of the employees concerning the quality product and service they offer.

Insights

Advice and Observations: In spite of franchise competition in this area, the friendly management and staff have shown that a continuing emphasis on a quality product results in success.

Contact

Betsy Baumgart, General Manager
Holiday Inn Express
701 Washington Avenue, Helena, MT 59601
Phone: 406-449-4000 Fax: 406-449-4522

HOLIDAY INN SUNSPREE RESORT LAKE BUENA VISTA HOLIDAY INN HOTEL & SUITES MAIN GATE EAST

Specialized Suites to Meet the Demands of the Vacationing Family

Description

The Practice: The Kidsuites concept was initially developed at Holiday Inn SunSpree Resort Lake Buena Vista and Holiday Inn Hotel & Suites Main Gate East in Orlando, Florida. Kidsuites configure a room within a room, so that both vacationing parents and accompanying children have privacy, space, entertainment, and bedding.

Why the Practice Was Developed: In 1995, Terry Whaples, then operating partner of the SunSpree Resort in Orlando, was vacationing in Texas with her husband and seven-year-old daughter. The Texas resort's accommodation was a three-room cabin designed like a jailhouse with two bedrooms and a third room not much larger than a closet with a door. In this tiny space was a twin bed. Her daughter squealed with delight when she saw it, saying, "Wow, my own space." Her daughter's excitement over her "own room" planted an idea with Ms. Whaples.

Execution

The Approach to Implementation: Several months later, Ms. Whaples and her general manager, Jim Olson, were exploring ways of better using their hotels. Part of their discussion centered on the typical family vacation in a standard hotel room with two double beds; that is, Mom sleeps with daughter, Dad sleeps with son. They wondered how to make the time spent in the guestroom more pleasurable for the whole family. Ms. Whaples recounted her Texas experience, and they decided to create a room within a room.

A Trial: The first experiment was a life-size dollhouse, which occupied about 80 square feet of the guestroom. The dollhouse had Dalmations on the wall and other exciting décor to enchant both boys and girls, and included a trundle bed. Guests were asked to rate this experimental concept. Parental response was overwhelmingly favorable, and the children were delighted because they had their own space and entertainment spot. The dollhouse allowed replacement of the two double beds with a king-size bed for the parents. Ms. Whaples felt the Kidsuites concept was a winner and proceeded to the next step.

The Kidsuites had to be planned so that they complied with building, sprinkler, and life safety codes. In addition, when bunk beds were selected for use in the Kidsuites, child safety and insurance issues had to be addressed. Consequently, parents were required to sign a liability form waiving the hotel's responsibility for injuries sustained as a result of using the

bunk beds, and a set of rules had to be developed (e.g., no rough play, no children under six in the top bunk).

In December 1995, Ms. Whaples presented her Kidsuites concept to the executives of Holiday Inn Worldwide, including John Sweetwood, now president of Holiday Inn Express, and Craig Hunt, president of Holiday Inn Hotels & Resorts. They gave an enthusiastic "go" to her plan.

Ms. Whaples enlisted creative ideas from the catalogue department of J.C. Penney and a core group of sponsors, such as Coca Cola, Little Caesar's, Sea World, U.S. Space Camp, and Kiwi Airlines, to help develop the Kidsuites themes. The companies were given complimentary room nights in return for their sponsorship.

The hotel developed 31 Kidsuites. In 1996 Ms. Whaples hosted a full-scale media party to publicize the Kidsuites program. Deemed a "press conference for kids," 60 reporters and their families, as well as travel agents and corporate sponsors, attended. However, the *children* of the reporters were the ones seated, and given hats, pens, and small pads of paper. The adult reporters were asked to step to the side of the room, and the children were given free reign to ask questions. The parents of these miniature reporters made certain the event and Kidsuites received a wide range of publicity. Between 1996 and 1997, Ms. Whaples added 100 more Kidsuites at the SunSpree Resort.

Costs: The initial cost for the Kidsuite conversion began at $15,000 per unit. With experience, the subsequent conversion costs dropped to around $5,000 per unit. However, Ms. Whaples was able to increase her room rate from $70 to $105, and customers willingly paid the new rate. Ms. Whaples estimates that the return on investment required only four to six months. Depreciation was planned for seven years. Overall, Ms. Whaples believes it was a great investment.

Outcomes

Success of the Practice: Kidsuites was a huge success for Ms. Whaples, so much so that she has since sold the SunSpree Resort to fund her new project, the Holiday Inn Family Suites Resort at Lake Buena Vista, to open in phases beginning in summer 1999. This new project will be an 800-suite property. Each 485-square-foot suite will feature a king or queen bed, pull-out sleeper sofa, two to three TVs, rocking chair, paddle fan, iron, and ironing board. Projected ADR is $129; guests will receive a full, all-you-can-eat American breakfast buffet. There will be seven different types of specialized suites:

1 Kidsuites — 474 units, accommodating up to seven people, with a private king bedroom for the parents and fun-theme bedroom for the kids.

2 Cinema Suites —12 units for up to four people featuring a 60-inch TV, surround sound system, and dual rocker-recliner with footrests.

3 Sweetheart Suites — 18 units that will accommodate four, with amenities including a heart-shaped whirlpool tub, 50-inch TV, and remote-controlled sound system.

4 Classic 2-Bedroom Suites — 212 inexpensive units will accommodate up to six guests with two queen size beds, one in a private adult bedroom and one in a semi-private bedroom.

5 Residential Suites — 74 units, each with a full-service kitchen. Designed for much of the international business, 80% of these suites connect to Kidsuites.

6 Business Suites — five units consisting of a separate bedroom and conference room, with a four-seat, 42-inch conference table, television, VCR, and work station with separate modem line.

7 Fitness Suites by Nautilus — five units consisting of a separate bedroom and fitness room. The fitness room will be equipped with a recumbent cycle, adjustable abdominal bench, floor mats, free weights, and television and VCR for fitness tapes.

A voucher system entitles each sponsor to a fixed number of rooms per year in exchange for its assistance in planning and design. The sponsors also benefit from the in-room advertisement resulting from the use of their logos in the suites' décor.

Benefits for Customer: A trip to Orlando with children is now a vacation in a suite that provides a residential feel that helps lessen the stress of "doing the theme-park shuffle."

Insights

Advice and Observations: Ms. Whaples believes those who neglect the opportunity to think in terms of a total vacation "miss the boat." Vacations should consist of a total package — the great experience sought by the vacationing family should not happen only outside the hotel room. Further, Ms. Whaples says the experience provided by Kidsuites encourages children to "beg" Mom and Dad to stay at her property. Thus, Mom and Dad's decision-making process becomes heavily influenced by the children's preference in lodging options.

Contact

Terry Whaples, President and Operating Partner
Holiday Inn Family Suites, Inc.
5678 Irlo Bronson Memorial Highway, Kissimmee, FL 34746
Phone: 407-828-8940 or 407-396-4488 Fax: 407-396-8915

HOTEL BEL AIR

Comprehensive Environmental Management

Description

The Practice: The Hotel Bel Air in Los Angeles has developed a comprehensive environmental program that includes a reduction in natural gas and electrical energy usage, a reduction of water and sewer usage, and a recycling program to reduce waste of paper, plastic, cans, and glass.

Why the Practice Was Developed: In California, state law mandates a certain amount of recycling. The hotel developed this environmental program in part to comply with this law, but primarily to maintain the beauty of the hotel property while instilling an environmental consciousness in daily operations.

The idea for the environmental program came from Anthony McHale, the hotel manager, and Walter Avelar, the kitchen manager. Many portions of the program developed were based on Mr. Avelar's and Mr. McHale's employment experiences in other hotels. The program was designed so that all of the hotel department heads and divisions would want to keep the idea alive and prospering.

Execution

The Approach to Implementation: Mr. Avelar and Mr. McHale formed a special committee comprised of the key departmental managers plus one employee from every area. Each departmental employee was to communicate the ideas of the committee to the rest of his or her department. This communication process was critical, as all employees needed to be involved in the training and educational portion of the program. The special committee was named "Guardians of the Grounds," a designation selected from a competition awarding $100 to the employee who entered the winning name. The committee spent one year developing a comprehensive environmental program for the hotel.

The "Guardians of the Grounds" first set goals that included an energy reduction of 10%, a recycling program to reduce landfill deposits by 25%, and lastly, the establishment of a communication program to help attain the first two objectives. The human resources staff was extremely helpful in achieving the latter goal, as they recorded meeting minutes, and then distributed these notes to all departments and to the employee cafeteria, where the notes were posted. The individual team members appointed to attend the "Guardians of the Grounds" monthly meetings became ambassadors and enthusiastic supporters of the program.

Employees were encouraged to adhere to the program through incentives they could earn. For example, they received a gift certificate and/or a "Guardian" T-shirt when observed following the environmental program.

Many suggestions were generated to help the hotel reach the goals the "Guardians of the Grounds" had established. Some of these ideas included changing regular light bulbs to higher-efficiency, longer-lasting bulbs; installing timers for electrical systems; installing plastic strips and other insulating material on doors; installing timers on the irrigation systems to reduce water usage on the 11 acres of grounds; and implementing a manual energy management system in which lights and air conditioning are turned off in unoccupied rooms. The manual energy management system is handled very carefully to prevent upsetting guests; hence, incredibly good communication between the front desk, security, and housekeeping is required for implementation.

Costs: The hotel spent $9,500 for a bailing machine and approximately $1,000 to purchase some small recycling containers.

Outcomes

Success of the Practice: Mr. Avelar compared actual garbage removal and energy costs against the same period of the previous year, before the program was put into effect. This comparison showed a $10,000 savings in 10 months of the program; for example, $250 was saved each week ($13,000 per year) because the hotel was able to reduce garbage pickups from four to three. In addition, $1,500 of revenue was received from the sale of cardboard. These savings and revenues more than offset the $10,500 cost of implementing the program. In fact, Mr. Avelar estimates the entire investment was recovered in the first nine months of the program. Best of all, the savings resulting from the program do not negatively impact guest service, yet they do increase the pride all employees feel in helping to improve the environment.

Benefits for Customer: While the customer does not directly benefit from the program, two evident benefits were the switch from paper cocktail napkins to linen cocktail napkins, and paper washroom towels to terry washroom towels, which improved guest service.

Contact

Walter Avelar, Kitchen Manager
Hotel Bel Air
702 Stone Canyon Road, Los Angeles, CA 90077
Phone: 310-472-1211   Fax: 310-440-5865

Insights

Advice and Observations: Mr. Avelar says it is important to get more people involved in the program in less time. That is, more information must be disseminated to all employees at every level to get a faster reaction to the program. He says it is important to keep the program growing and to have more conscious involvement by the staff; there must be 100% involvement at every level. It is also critical to have the support and enthusiasm of senior management.

"It is most difficult to make this program work in the house-keeping department," Mr. Avelar notes, "as the sorting process for recycling is quite difficult." He did say, however, that house-keeping did an excellent job in turning off lights and monitoring the HVAC system.

"This is a great opportunity that is good for everyone — there are cost savings, the employees feel great, and it is good for the environment. A real win/win scenario," states Mr. Avelar.

Mr. Avelar would like to see customers become more aware of the program by having some type of recognition system at that level. He warns, however, that program awareness must not be obtrusive as customers do not want to be inconvenienced.

HOTEL BEL AIR

Proactive Property-Maintenance Program

Description

The Practice: Members of the engineering department are empowered to make decisions to solve maintenance problems as soon as any problem is found — no traditional work tickets are used. In addition, one engineer is assigned to check rooms for problems before they develop.

Why the Practice Was Developed: Chief Engineer George Edwards put this program into effect in December 1997. The idea for this practice came from the engineers themselves at an engineering department meeting. A primary reason for establishing this proactive maintenance program is that the engineers wanted to eliminate or reduce the time guests have to wait to have maintenance problems corrected.

Execution

The Approach to Implementation: The system works as follows: When a problem occurs in the housekeeping department, it is phoned into a dispatcher in housekeeping or the PBX department. The dispatcher, in turn, calls in the request to the engineering department. An engineer immediately responds to the request, logging the trouble request only if it requires entering an occupied room. The work accomplished is then verified by the floor's room-inspection staff. No written work order is required, although the dispatcher keeps a log of repair requests.

The other essential part of this program is a proactive preventative maintenance program. One engineer is given the ongoing daily responsibility of checking the rooms that will be vacated that day. As the hotel is more than 50 years old, such an ongoing program is essential to help maintain its deluxe status. The engineer gears his workday to this process. Consequently, in many cases, any problems are resolved before the room attendant makes up the room for the next guest. The room-check engineer can handle most of the minor problems, and calls on others for assistance if necessary. He does not hesitate to put the room out of order if repairs will be time consuming.

Operating Considerations: The hotel employs a total of 12 engineers, of whom five per day are on duty to service 60 suites and 32 guestrooms. To supplement the preventative maintenance program, the hotel added two painters to the staff.

The major change in operating procedures was in the manner of communication between the engineering department and the other operating departments of the hotel.

Outcomes

Success of the Practice: The hotel is being maintained better than it ever was in the past. Work requests are handled promptly and efficiently. Most important, there are few guest complaints as maintenance problems are identified and corrected before the guest settles into the room. If a problem develops after the guest occupies the room, the engineers are able to handle it more promptly.

Insights

Advice and Observations: Mr. Edwards believes that this practice demonstrated that the engineering department is an integral part of operations. It also restored confidence in the department, and reduced friction between housekeeping and engineering.

According to Mr. Edwards, anyone can put a similar program into effect. It is not a complex program; it simply requires eliminating paperwork and empowering employees to take action when needed.

Contact

George Edwards, Chief Engineer
Hotel Bel Air
701 Stone Canyon Road, Los Angeles, CA 90077
Phone: 310-472-1211 Fax: 310-440-5860

HOTEL NIKKO AT BEVERLY HILLS

Portable Telephone System throughout Hotel

Description

The Practice: The Hotel Nikko at Beverly Hills has installed a portable (not cellular) telephone system throughout the hotel, including all guestrooms and meeting rooms and for selected hotel staff. These phones have the capability of receiving incoming calls and making outgoing calls, including long-distance calls, although the phones operate only within the confines of the hotel. The system went on-line in August 1998. In addition to portable phones in each guestroom, employees use them in such areas as housekeeping, the bell stand, convention services, maintenance, security, food & beverage, and the front desk. Thirty extra phones are available for guest use in meeting and banquet rooms or guestrooms. These extra phones can easily be programmed to relate to a specific guestroom or group master charge.

Why the Practice Was Developed: The Nikko is a 300-room upscale hotel located in Beverly Hills, catering primarily to the business and entertainment markets. Each guestroom had two phone lines available, one for data and one for voice. Through guest comment cards and personal contacts at the front desk, it became clear that many guests desired better communication capability in the form of a third phone line, so they could simultaneously handle multiple data and voice functions. A study indicated that the cost of installing a third wire to each guestroom would be prohibitive. While on a personal trip to the local Home Depot, Max Malek, systems manager, noticed several employees carrying and using portable phones to make calls and announcements over the store's PA system. Hence, Mr. Malek's visit to Home Depot was the source of the idea for using portable rather than hard-wired phones.

At the time the only other similar installation was being tested at the Westin St. Francis in San Francisco. Mr. Malek and Bradford Rice, front-office manager, conducted research and learned that the St. Francis had only two floors operable. To the best of Mr. Malek's and Mr. Rice's knowledge, the Nikko is one of the few hotels on the West Coast with a fully operational system at this time.

Execution

The Approach to Implementation: Mr. Malek researched the feasibility of the portable system, and contacted three communications companies. Two of the three recommended cellular phones. However, it was determined that the reliability of cellular phones in the Los Angeles area was not good enough for this application. The third company, Freepoint, Inc., was selected because it had the most expertise in portable-phone technology and offered a revenue-sharing plan to offset costs. Lucent Technologies was selected to provide the phones and switch gear because its switch gear and hardware were capable of interfacing with the hotel's existing switch gear, which was made by Hitachi. Moreover, the Hitachi switches could be expanded to accommodate the additional traffic from the portable system.

Operational Issues: The implementation, from inception to operation, took 14 months. Because the system could not be phased in slowly or in stages, the actual implementation was conducted in a short time with a minimum of telephone-system interruptions. The interruptions were scheduled at night and were usually of one hour or less duration. The system has proven to be popular with staff members, especially housekeeping and convention services, because of the ease of communication between departments.

Costs: The entire system cost approximately $1 million. Through the revenue-sharing plan with Freepoint, guests pay a charge of $9.95 per day for use of the portable phone. This charge is passed on to Freepoint to offset the installation cost.

Outcomes

Success of the Practice: Prior to the installation of the system, an average of two guest comment cards per month indicated that guests would like more phone lines. Now comment cards are complimentary regarding the portable phone service.

Hotel telephone use has increased by 6.5%, and telephone revenues have increased by $2.00 per occupied room night since the installation.

Benefits for Customer: Guests now have the capability of calling anywhere from any location within the hotel. They also can receive incoming calls no matter where they are in the hotel. Guests are more inclined to use the portable phones instead of their cellular phones because of the ease of contacting another guest or department within the hotel directly (especially useful for corporate meetings), and because incoming calls will automatically be routed to their portable phones.

Advice and Observations: Those wishing to install such a system should make sure there is a staff person on site who is well versed in telephone technology, or hire a consultant to follow the selection and installation process through to completion.

If at all possible, use a company that has a local office. In Nikko's case, Lucent's staff was located in Denver, which made accessibility and communication more difficult.

Make sure the hotel staff is informed and trained about all operational aspects of the system prior to going on-line with it.

Future plans are to expand the system to interface with cellular capability when reliable technology becomes available.

Contacts

Bradford Rice, Front Office Manager
Hotel Nikko at Beverly Hills
465 S. La Cienega Boulevard, Los Angeles, CA 90048
Phone: 310-247-0400 Fax: 310-247-0315

Max Malek, Systems Manager
Hotel Nikko at Beverly Hills
465 S. La Cienega Boulevard, Los Angeles, CA 90048
Phone: 310-247-0400 Fax: 310-247-0315

HYATT ARLINGTON HOTEL

Redesigning and Revitalizing a Food and Beverage Outlet

Description

The Practice: At the Hyatt Arlington, a dated dining room, sports bar, and lobby lounge were completely reconceptualized into venues having new, vibrant, and energetic tones that, with their transformation, had an enormous impact on the entire hotel and its image in the community.

Why the Practice Was Developed: The three food and beverage outlets of the hotel were dated in concept and design, and had lost their customer appeal. The owner, having discriminating (California) tastes, had a strong desire for a product that was contemporary and did not resemble a typical hotel dining venue. The volume of restaurant business also was significantly off from desirable levels.

Execution

The Approach to Implementation: The owner of the property requested from Hyatt a seasoned veteran who would be able to obtain the desired results from the F&B outlets. Hyatt Hotels sent George Vizer as the new general manager to take on this formidable task.

After comprehensive market research and analysis, Mr. Vizer selected a fusion of contemporary and Mediterranean concepts. This direction was taken for several reasons: (1) the Mediterranean approach to cooking has healthy connotations; (2) the concept has enduring appeal; and (3) the concept's ability to provide cuisine that appealed both to the local community and the traveling in-house guests. This concept was selected prior to the seemingly endless wave of Mediterranean restaurants that followed suit.

The concept was one year in the making, going through numerous revisions. Major changes were needed to create the desired effect. Mr. Vizer, Lori Crowley, director of operations, and Chris Savage, executive chef, decided to tear into the side of the building and put floor-to-ceiling windows into the old restaurant space, which was dark and unimaginative. This move helped to transform the space into a sun-drenched lively venue splashed with vivid colors of the Mediterranean. The restaurant became Mezza 9 (a play on words — the restaurant is on the mezzanine level and also offers nine Mezze items daily — small, shareable plates, "Mediterranean Dim Sum"), a whimsical, imaginative concept and an innovative culinary approach.

The restaurant took four months to construct. Brennan, Beer, Gorman and Monk was the interior design company that collaborated with the Hyatt Arlington pre-opening team.

The Olive Press Bar on the lobby level was also "born," a quintessential martini bar that complements the efforts of Mezza 9.

Outcomes

Success of the Practice: Mezza 9 and Olive Press opened in May 1998. Revenues and cover counts have doubled from those before the renovations and Mezza 9 has received continuous rave reviews. The restaurant is always noted as anything but a typical hotel restaurant and is always compared to California restaurants with cutting edge concepts.

Insights

Advice and Observations: Mr. Vizer advises, "Today's traveling and local dining public are more sophisticated than ever. Therefore, if one endeavors to reconceptualize an outlet within a hotel, a venue must be created which can compete with the freestanding restaurants and bars of the 1990s. You must dedicate resources (i.e., a dedicated chef who 'breaks the mold'; a maître d' who will become a 'fixture, a known commodity' of the dining room), and maintain an unrelenting commitment to consistency, even when business is slow. Don't close the restaurant, cut staffing, or skimp on quality if you want to build a loyal following."

Contact

George Vizer, General Manager
Hyatt Arlington Hotel
1325 Wilson Boulevard, Arlington, VA 22099
Phone: 703-525-1234 Fax: 703-875-3298

HYATT HOTELS CORPORATION

Survey-Based Guest Satisfaction Program

Description

The Practice: Hyatt Hotels has contracted the Gallup Organization to conduct ongoing random phone surveys to measure guest satisfaction within two weeks of a guest's stay. Results of this measurement, subsequent analyses, training, and integrated compensation plans are enabling Hyatt to take a holistic approach towards continuously increasing guest loyalty.

Why the Practice Was Developed: Hyatt Hotels wanted to have an objective and accurate measurement of guest satisfaction. This issue was particularly important following its HyPerformance Management initiatives to enhance operating efficiency. Hyatt Hotels wanted to ensure that service and quality remained the priority and were not being compromised at any of the hotels.

Execution

The Approach to Implementation: Hyatt Hotels utilized a three-tiered approach to implementing its guest satisfaction and loyalty survey. First, the company set out to determine which method of surveying would yield the greatest response rate. Phone interviews, Interactive Voice Response/Voice Response Unit, and mailed and written surveys were tested on one control group that received an incentive for participation and another that did not. This test yielded results overwhelmingly in favor of the phone methodology, with a response rate of nearly 90%. So as not to bias the results, Hyatt elected not to provide any type of incentive to its guests who voluntarily complete the interview. Second, Hyatt undertook an extensive qualitative study to determine which items to include on the survey. This phase of the process included personally interviewing more than 100 general managers and corporate executives and 200 guests in an effort to determine what is important to both commercial and resort travelers. After reviewing the results, a 60-question survey was developed. This survey was then used in the quantitative phase of the project where a baseline study of 1,100 guests was conducted. Following the baseline study, statistical analyses were performed to distill the 60 questions down to 15. The survey rolled out in November 1995. Hyatt's goal was to have a survey that would not be burdensome to its guests and one that would be meaningful and actionable at the hotel level.

This survey takes under four minutes to complete and assesses overall satisfaction, likelihood to return to Hyatt, and key drivers to satisfaction such as the room, customer service, check-in, if the guest experienced a problem, and (if so) the associated level of service recovery.

To assure that the data are collected in a timely fashion, Hyatt provides Gallup a weekly electronic file containing information on guests who stayed the previous week. This file contains data on the hotel and the guest's name, address, phone number, checkout date, Gold Passport status, and total spending.

Twice a week, the hotel general managers receive from Gallup, via facsimile, action sheets containing information regarding specific guest complaints. The hotel general manager then follows up with the guest by phone. For Gold Passport members who participate in the interview, the company adds a thank-you message on its account statement mailing.

The hotel general managers also receive detailed reports monthly, quarterly, and year-to-date. The report divides the various types of hotels into buckets and the best bucket score is included for each question for benchmarking purposes. Use of this data has become widespread throughout the company. This has stimulated a heightened awareness of the importance of customer service and has driven a positive cultural change in the attitude toward quality.

To date, nearly 90% of the guests contacted complete the survey. One of the major advantages of this program is that the company receives information from a much broader cross-section of guests. Guests are often reluctant or unwilling to provide the hotel with their complaints, but this program encourages guests to be more forthright with their comments.

Gallup's services cost Hyatt in excess of $1 million annually to interview guests at 104 hotels. Gallup selects guests to be interviewed at random, and completes around 800 interviews per hotel per year. This number yields a margin of error of +3.5%. Clearly, this is a more accurate and objective gauge of guest satisfaction and loyalty than the traditional comment cards and video guest surveys.

To assure actionability of the data, hotels are provided with various analyses that help them identify their properties' strengths and weaknesses. A highly successful tool that has been used by Hyatt is the leverage analysis or quadrant map. This map helps each individual hotel identify the target areas that are most important to the guest. To support improvement in the various areas, a cross-functional best-practices team at the corporate office has been deployed. On a monthly basis, this team focuses on an area most in need of improvement and publishes a best practice to assist the hotels in addressing the area. Hyatt is also using survey results in setting yearly incentive compensation goals and management objectives for the hotels.

Outcome

Success of the Practice: Since beginning the Gallup Guest Satisfaction and Loyalty study in November 1995, over 200,000 guests have provided feedback regarding their stays at Hyatt Hotels. This valuable feedback has led to statistically significant improvements in almost every measured department and area over the past three years. The percentage of guests who experienced a problem with their stay has decreased 30%. Also, guest ratings on overall satisfaction with their stay has increased significantly with an 8% increase in the percentage of guests that provided a "top box" or 5 rating.

In addition to improvement in the top-line numbers, analysis of the data has led to a better understanding of which areas are most important to guests. In many ways, Hyatt has been able to determine actionable steps for improving the level of customer service provided, most of which costs Hyatt little or nothing in terms of expendable resources.

Insights

Advice and Observations: David Kong, general manager of sales and marketing, says the large investment of $10,000 per year per hotel is more than justified by the guest satisfaction results obtained. He points out that any hotel not able to make such an expenditure can still have an effective guest satisfaction program by proactively soliciting guest feedback and documenting all guest complaints. Using analyses and problem-solving methods, the root causes of the problems can be surfaced and corrective actions can be determined and implemented.

Contact

David Kong, General Manager, Sales & Marketing
Hyatt Hotels Corporation
200 W. Madison, Chicago, IL 60606
Phone: 312-750-8511 Fax: 312-920-2351

HYATT REGENCY CHICAGO

Comprehensive Waste Reduction and Recycling Program

Description

The Practice: In spring 1989 the Hyatt Regency in Chicago implemented a comprehensive waste reduction and recycling program, the first program of its type in Chicago. The hotel has a recycling department with a manager and a full-time staff of eight, and all hotel departments and employees participate in the recycling program. The entire hotel is equipped with efficient recycling bins and containers.

Why the Practice Was Developed: Bill Clark, the chief engineer, had a growing concern about the diminishing space in landfills. Consequently, he wanted to reduce the waste generated by the hotel.

Execution

The Approach to Implementation: A college intern was involved with shaping the environmental program — a significant task given that the Hyatt Regency in Chicago is the largest property in the Hyatt chain. It took approximately six months to get the program running. Since then, the Hyatt Regency in Chicago has been a model hotel in recycling.

The fully staffed, state-of-the-art recycling department is located in the East Tower of the hotel. Its employees sift through tons of trash each year, and all employees participate in the recycling effort by separating trash into special blue bins. A 40-yard container is used for different types of glass — brown, green, and clear — and each office has two garbage containers — one for paper, and the other for nonrecyclable items. Overall, the hotel recycles cardboard, newspaper, glass, aluminum, office paper, computer paper, styrofoam, and magazines.

The hotel employees along with meeting planners are encouraged to use glass instead of styrofoam, paper instead of plastic, and cloth instead of paper napkins. Soft drinks are dispensed from a fountain instead of bottles or cans. All soap containers are returned to the supplier for reuse, and water treatment chemicals are placed in storage tanks instead of disposable 55-gallon drums.

Costs: The recycling set-up cost $55,000 for two cardboard-bailing machines, an aluminum crusher, a mixed-paper bailer, and a huge box for glass. A recycling truck was also purchased.

Outcomes

Success of the Practice: According to Fayaz Fes Ahmed, recycling manager, the endeavor by the Hyatt Regency and its employees has paid off. Annually, the hotel recovers approxi-

mately 70 percent of recyclable materials from over six million pounds of garbage, preventing one million pounds of refuse from being deposited into Chicago's landfills each year. Since the program began, the hotel has recycled 1,400 tons of cardboard, 896 tons of glass, 630 tons of newspaper, 329 tons of magazines, and 33 tons of aluminum cans. The hotel has halved hauling costs to $100,000.

The recycling program has also had an unexpected benefit. Sorting the trash has resulted in salvaging silverware, towels, dishes, coffee servers, and key cards, which has had a considerable economic impact at the hotel. The hotel has currently recovered $120,000 in hotel items, including $5,000 worth of silverware.

Benefits for Customer: Although the customers are not directly involved, they are aware that they are staying in an environmentally friendly hotel, and that in itself shows that the customer is also committed to the environment.

Insights

Advice and Observations: Mr. Ahmed advises that "all hotels meet and discuss how they can get involved. With the Illinois state law demanding that all hotels participate in a recycling program, perhaps they could use the Hyatt as a model in developing their own programs."

Contact

Fayaz Fes Ahmed, Recycling Manager
Hyatt Regency Chicago
151 Wacker Drive, Chicago, IL 60601
Phone: 312-616-6804 Fax: 312-565-4344

129

HYATT REGENCY SCOTTSDALE

Developing an Environmental Recycling Program

The Practice: The Hyatt Regency Scottsdale maintains a strong environmental program that involves every individual at the resort. The program's latest goal is to have 90% of all materials used at the resort be made with recycled content or be recycled when they leave the property. The property also urges other area hotels to follow similar practices.

Why the Practice Was Developed: Environmental Program Manager Paul Hayes believes the environmental program constitutes "the right thing to do," particularly since the resort sits on the north edge of the delicate Sonoran Desert ecosystem. Additionally, the program ties into the area's Native American history, which demonstrates a long-term concern about resource use. Finally, the resort is helping to educate tomorrow's leaders in environmental issues.

The Approach to Implementation: Various ideas were implemented to initiate an environmental program at the resort. Originally, interns were responsible for implementing the program, but they struggled because they did not know the resort business. Management understood the need for consistent efforts to make the environmental practice successful; they therefore created an environmental program manager position, in which Mr. Hayes was placed. Second, the resort impaneled a "Green Team," comprised of one employee from every department, that meets monthly or bimonthly. The team has a "Green Book" that discusses the environmental program for team member education. Environmental program information is posted on bulletin boards for employees. Important components along with the Green Book and the Green Team are employee orientation and an employee newsletter.

Many staff members and vendors were initially resistant to change and to adoption of environmental initiatives. To help offset the resistance, the resort developed a tournament, "Eco-Golf," in which departments play one hole per week against each other in an 18-week tournament. The game involves environmental facts as well as golf. The resort gave employees an Eco-Golf Competition memo with information on such issues as air quality, recycling, and energy reduction. For example, Americans annually throw away enough paper plates and picnic items to serve six meals to everyone on earth. During the week, Mr. Hayes visits departments to ask questions regarding the Eco-Golf Competition memo. The departments get golf points for answering the questions correctly and for low levels of departmental contamination. The winning department can choose its own award (e.g., dinner, video

coupons, a massage, or a round of golf). Mr. Hayes notes that employees now understand that the environmental program is their responsibility.

Operational Issues: The resort was constructed originally with a lush, Hawaiian-style landscape, not conducive to environmental protection. To integrate the resort with its Arizona environment, the property has taken steps to conserve water and energy. Irrigation, for instance, which used to be above ground, has now been largely converted to an underground system to reduce water evaporation.

The resort has color-coded bins in all areas to make it easier for the staff to recycle. Mr. Hayes educates buyers and managers to look at all alternatives for purchasing and resource reuse. For example, six-pack soda rings are recycled. Broken china is turned into mosaic tile, and denim uniforms are made into pencils. The resort is still using small shampoo bottles that are not recycled — except that the bottles still containing shampoo and conditioner are sent to various charities.

Customers have little direct involvement in the program. A brochure in the guestroom explains the program, but the recycling bin in the guestroom is used infrequently. Management has heretofore been hesitant to involve the customer in environmental practices, but it is starting to do this now.

Success of the Practice: According to Mr. Hayes, the program has been successful. For one thing, the program attracts eco-related transient and group business. Mr. Hayes receives calls every day from other hotels about the Hyatt Regency Scottsdale's program. Employees, working hard to fulfill their environmental responsibilities, regularly call him for information on where to dump recyclables.

Insights

According to Mr. Hayes, the Hyatt Regency Scottsdale has made excellent use of its program for the betterment of the community and the entire lodging industry in Arizona. The resort has put together a wonderful book of environmental initiatives that now serves as a blueprint for the Arizona Hotel & Motel Association.

Advice and Observations: Mr. Hayes suggests that it is important to use visual aids in executing the strategy. One visual aid shows the 200 tons of coal that are not burned each year due to the resort's energy-conservation system.

It is also important to have one or two cheerleaders for this program, Mr. Hayes advises. Make sure the program starts slow and makes steady, but measurable progress. Keep the bar moving and raise your expectations — raise the benchmark. If something is not working, don't let it get you down. The program does add to employee satisfaction and does create unity among employees. Mr. Hayes says this is a profitable practice — trying to run a profitable business that is not in conflict with the environment is a challenge but also a great opportunity.

Lastly, senior management has to be committed to investing in the program, even in the absence of government mandates.

Paul Hayes, Environmental Program Manager
Hyatt Regency Scottsdale
7500 East Doubletree Rack Road, Scottsdale, AZ 85258
Phone: 480-991-3388 Fax: 480-483-5573

HYATT REGENCY SCOTTSDALE

A Community-Based Hospitality Training Program for High School Students

The Practice: The Hyatt Regency in Scottsdale, Arizona, has created an unusual educational outreach program. The Hyatt Regency sponsors classes in hotel management to junior- and senior-level students at the local high schools. A Hyatt Regency training manager conducts the college-level course at the high schools, using the same textbook college students use, as well as materials from the Educational Institute of the American Hotel & Motel Association. The classes meet five days per week, and cover skills that are needed in the hospitality field, such as leadership, communication, public speaking, and interviewing. Students take field trips so that they are exposed to many different aspects of the hospitality industry. In the second year of the course, students are eligible to intern at local establishments.

Students who enter at the junior class level begin the first phase of the "two-plus-two-plus-two" hospitality career program. The class curriculum leads directly into a two-year associate degree program at Scottsdale Community College, which transfers to the School of Hotel and Restaurant Management at Northern Arizona University. Students also have the option of going directly into the four-year hospitality program at Northern Arizona University.

Why the Practice Was Developed: The rapid growth of tourism in Scottsdale resulted in a shortage in qualified hospitality employees. As a result, Northern Arizona University, Scottsdale Community College, Scottsdale School District, and the City of Scottsdale approached the Hyatt Regency about developing an educational program that could be instituted at the high school level. The goal was to develop student interest in the industry at a relatively early stage.

The Approach to Implementation: Denise Pruitt, training manager of the Hyatt Regency Scottsdale, was approached by the general manager of the resort about the idea. The GM actively supports opportunities for education. A partnership was formed between the Hyatt and the other participants. Ms. Pruitt was selected to be the classes' instructor. Although Ms. Pruitt continued to be employed by Hyatt, she also taught the classes in hotel management at the local high schools. The vice president supported her in the implementation of the program, which she designed and wrote.

During the planning stages different managers at the Hyatt saw the benefits of these classes and contributed their guidance and support. Many hotel professionals in the area were guest speakers in Ms. Pruitt's classrooms. The most supportive constituents were the parents of the students, as they recognized that proper education and training would lead to many possible career opportunities in the hospitality industry.

Operational Issues: The program required between six and seven months to plan. Curriculum development started in March, and classes began in the fall with the start of the school year. Ms. Pruitt worked closely with the school district to develop materials and with Hyatt for support and feedback as she sought to implement the program. It was a challenging time, since the coalition between the corporate world and academe produced much red tape. Ms. Pruitt worked with the director of development at Northern Arizona University, the superintendent of the school district, the dean of students and the chairman of the hospitality department from the community college, and the department of economic development for the City of Scottsdale. Four times a year Ms. Pruitt and the four major participants hold meetings at which recommendations are made, changes are discussed, and projections are established with a fresh sense of direction.

The marketing of the program began in the hospitality industry and the school district, and networking for the program was started in the community. Some educators had concerns that opportunities might be taken from others; however, the academics began to see that the hospitality industry can also provide a valuable form of education.

After months of planning, the class started at one of the local high schools. Students from five different high schools were allowed to enroll in the class. Because of increasing student enrollment, the class is now being held at two high school campuses. One of the classes has 15 students and the other has 20 students. All enrolled students are treated like adults, creating a great target for behavior.

Costs: Because the salary of Denise Pruitt was split five different ways, with Hyatt donating its part, the cost of the instructor was nominal.

Outcomes

Success of the Practice: Ms. Pruitt believes the program has been beneficial to the young people of Scottsdale, as any interested student was able to enroll in the course. The program has provided the Scottsdale hospitality industry with qualified and skilled workers. Many students went to work at the Hyatt, and others went to work in different hospitality firms. The graduating students have received great reviews; not one bad experience has been reported. Some graduating students who have continued their education in this field have been recipients of scholarships from Northern Arizona University, the Arizona Hotel Foundation of the Arizona Hotel & Motel Association, and the Valley Hotel & Resort Association. The program is currently in its third year of operation, and Ms. Pruitt is training another instructor to take her place.

In addition, Ms. Pruitt has provided implementation guidelines to instructors in local Native American communities who have expressed interest in offering a similar program. She has also offered technical support and made the Hyatt Regency Scottsdale available as a resource for guest speakers and field trip experiences.

Benefits for Customer: The practice has benefited the customer by providing him or her with better trained service providers. Unknowingly, the customer was a secondary recipient of a community-based project.

Insights

Advice and Observations: According to Ms. Pruitt, a joint partnership among a community college, city government, school district, university, and hotel is an optimum way of facilitating a practice such as this one. While there is no wide scale push for this educational program on the national level, it could be easily replicated.

In implementing this program, Ms. Pruitt went from recruitment manager to teacher. She says trained and qualified hospitality personnel make a difference in the workplace. In addition, she believes the teacher really can make a difference, but must love what he or she does in the classroom.

Contact

Denise Pruitt, Training Manager
Hyatt Regency Scottsdale
7500 East Doubletree Rack Road, Scottsdale, AZ 85258
Phone: 602-991-3388 Fax: 602-483-5573

IMPAC HOTEL GROUP

A Lobby Kiosk Touch-Screen Guest-Tracking System

General Management

Information Technology

Operations

Description

The Practice: In the lobby area of each IMPAC property is a kiosk containing a touch-screen monitor on which the guests can answer a series of questions regarding their stay. The guest-tracking questions are designed to obtain comments and allow the guest to rate all hotel departments. The data are downloaded each night, and then distributed daily to the property's general manager and the corporate office in Atlanta. Data are available at any time during the day, providing the opportunity to immediately address any problems. Sometimes a problem is corrected before the guest checks out.

Additionally, once each month the kiosk is rolled into a more private location and guests are invited to participate in an "Associate Satisfaction Survey." This survey is more extensive and allows for much more input by the guest. These data are also sent to the GM and corporate office at the end of the day.

Why the Practice Was Developed: The system was begun five years ago, because IMPAC's president, Robert Cole, was dissatisfied with the existing guest-feedback program, which primarily consisted of the traditional in-room guest-survey cards. Mr. Cole felt the time lapse from data collection to compilation and reporting was too long. Consequently, the information became more of a historic review and was not usable for immediate action. Also, the old system did not provide any sense of urgency.

Execution

The Approach to Implementation: IMPAC's Chief Information Officer Nancy Wolff, the vice president of human resources, and an information technologist designed the system and worked with a third-party software graphics-design company to complete the system. Thirty-five standardized kiosks were then built, and one was placed in each property. The design stage took six months to complete.

Today, the system averages 35 responses per day per property. Collected data are also used as a factor in the determination of employee bonuses, which, according to Ms. Wolff, has been universally accepted by the employees.

Operational Issues: The system is presently being converted from the use of individual PCs in each location to a network system whereby the kiosks will contain a work station connected to a mainframe computer in Atlanta via T-1 phone lines. This modification will eliminate the reliance on and cost of individual PCs, and provide even faster data collection and dissemination. It will also allow the use of more kiosks within the properties that can be tailored to specific functions (e.g., food and beverage, guest services). The new system will be completed and installed during the third quarter of 1999.

Costs: Each kiosk costs between $5,000 and $7,000, which is built into the hotel acquisition cost. Operating costs are negligible and consist only of electricity, telephone, and hardware-maintenance expenses.

Operating costs of the new system will probably be the same as the present system. Although the cost of T-1 phone lines is high and the mainframe computer costs more than PCs, the cost will be offset by the elimination of PCs in favor of less-expensive work stations. The intangible cost savings are the increased speed of data handling, the ability to easily change the software, and the ability to use more kiosks at very little additional cost.

Outcomes

Success of the Practice: Though obviously not a profit center, the system has improved maintenance, improved employee productivity, and improved the overall quality and image of the properties, Ms. Wolff says. IMPAC managers have also found the data to be useful in the preparation of capital budgets, in that they can pinpoint and justify capital expenditure requests.

Benefits for Customer: The customer feels that the hotel cares enough to ask for immediate feedback. Moreover, customers have more confidence in the reliability of the information being used than they do in the cards left in the room or mailed to some obscure address.

Insights

Advice and Observations: Ms. Wolff suggests that anyone incorporating this idea would be wise to use more kiosks in each property to individualize questions by department, and to use network architecture instead of PCs.

Contact

Nancy Wolff, Chief Information Officer
IMPAC Hotel Group
3445 Peachtree Road, Suite 7000, Atlanta, GA 30376
Phone: 404-365-3830 Fax: 404-364-0088

THE INN AT ESSEX

Advertising on City Buses To Create Awareness

The Practice: The Inn at Essex, in cooperation with the City of Burlington, Vermont, wrapped a city bus in a huge vinyl picture of the hotel stating various points on why one should stay there. These featured items included the hotel's meeting and convention space, as well as fine dining facilities.

Why the Practice Was Developed: The use of this guerrilla-marketing tactic was deemed necessary at a time when the hotel was just coming out of a difficult economic period. The Inn was a new property in a location that was being developed next to a highway and near a major corporation purchasing 11,000 room nights per year. Unfortunately, when the hotel opened, the highway's completion was delayed, the recession started, and the large corporate client stopped all travel purchases. Consequently, the hotel was placed in a critical condition for approximately three years and neared failure until it was placed under new ownership.

Besides facing a poor economic climate, the hotel also lacked visibility. It is not located in a high-traffic area (e.g., downtown area); thus it suffered from out-of-sight, out-of-mind syndrome. Unfortunately, there was *no* marketing budget, and standard billboards are not allowed in Vermont, so creativity was required. Hence, a "moving billboard" was developed.

Execution

The Approach to Implementation: Linda Seville, director of marketing at The Inn at Essex, developed the "moving billboard" idea and brought it to the attention of the joint marketing committee, composed of The Inn at Essex and the New England Culinary Institute, which loved the idea. A sub-committee worked out the details of what hotel features to promote. Ms. Seville had heard about a company that could print photographs on a vinyl wrap material, which would allow The Inn at Essex to showcase its best feature — its architectural style. The other option was to paint the ad directly on the bus. However, this latter option would require repainting the bus periodically to keep the ad looking "fresh," and the painting would likely not convey the vibrant, "lifelike" image that a photograph would. The committee decided to use the vinyl wrap.

Since the chosen vehicle for the "moving billboard" is a city bus, it stops outside the competitors' hotel properties as well as at all other downtown areas. This factor provided the Inn with considerable visibility among area residents and tourists. Not only did the bus advertising receive lots of attention and garner press coverage, but motor coaches traveling in the area wrote down the number from the advertisement and called the Inn for information.

This promotional medium was a first-time effort, not only for the Inn, but also for the City of Burlington. After some time, the Inn committed to a second bus. As the bus was driven around town, the Inn passed out cider and cookies to passengers and distributed hotel brochures and coupons for eating in the restaurant.

The general manager and food and beverage director of the Inn were on the joint marketing committee and were both supportive of Ms. Seville's efforts. While the committee members feared the advertising would be too expensive, they also realized the costs of not doing it. The bus traveled hundreds of miles per week, and the Inn received much more exposure than it would have from any other form of advertising for this type of market. The concept was developed with the Chittenden County Transportation Authority marketing department and was well received by the CCTA general manager. Everyone was excited about this new marketing opportunity.

Operational Issues: The only operational issues brought up by Ms. Seville were the difficulty in budgeting this line item and tracking the success of the program. Given the acclaim received, those factors were not offsetting negatives.

Costs: The cost to implement the program was $13,000 per year per bus ($15,000 per year if only one bus was contracted), and $12,000 per bus for design and installation. Ms. Seville feels that the benefits far outweigh the costs.

Linda Seville, Director of Marketing
The Inn at Essex
70 Essex Way, Essex, VT 05452
Phone: 802-764-1444 Fax: 802-878-0063

Outcomes

Success of the Practice: The Inn's management heard many positive comments from people who saw the bus and enjoyed the cider and cookies. Additional positive remarks were received from meeting planners and travel agents. Ms. Seville indicates that the volume of meetings and conferences as well as restaurant business has increased, with group business increasing approximately 20% and restaurant business increasing 15% to 20%. In her view, these results indicate an extremely successful advertisement campaign. As an added benefit, staff morale improved with "ownership" of the bus.

Insights

Ms. Seville believes that the bus wrap would be a great marketing tool for independent properties, but not as much for chains unless their location is difficult and they have something distinctive to sell. Ms. Seville does not believe this advertising medium works as well for a service business unless it is related to a destination or something that provides a strong visual image. Part of Ms. Seville's success was based on a strong photograph with a romantic and quintessential Vermont country hotel feel that was placed on the bus. In other words, it was not just a hotel but an experience that was conveyed. In fact, the bus itself took on a life of its own, as it was rented out for functions and special events!

Advice and Observations: If starting over, Ms. Seville would make certain the bus was better maintained, and she would have conducted research on more vinyl companies. Further, Ms. Seville felt that, in retrospect, she would have created benchmarks and had better tracking of the results of this program. She also advised those hotels considering a similar type of promotion to keep in mind the "40-foot rule": you must decide what message you can get across on a 40-foot bus traveling at 40 miles per hour.

THE INN AT ESSEX

Providing Absolute Guest Satisfaction

The Practice: The Inn at Essex maintains a practice of accommodating all guest requests. Employees are instructed to always say "yes." Consequently, no detailed policy manual for this property exists as there are no "dos and don'ts" as to how it operates.

Why the Practice Was Developed: Jim Lamberti, owner-manager, was employed for more than 20 years in the customer service division of the electronics industry. This experience helped him recognize the importance of saying yes to his customers, and Mr. Lamberti developed a philosophy of always responding positively to any request from a customer — as long as it was not immoral or illegal. Mr. Lamberti believed this philosophy could be adapted to the hotel industry. Hence, when he opened The Inn at Essex in 1989, he instituted this philosophy as hotel policy.

Execution

The Approach to Implementation: Mr. Lamberti believes that a detailed policy manual simply exists as an "excuse to say no to guests." Therefore, the policy manual utilized and distributed to all new Inn employees is a one-page document, which states the following:

1 The hotel has had a four-star rating since its opening in 1989.
2 Be proactively friendly.
3 Always find a way to say yes.
4 When faced with a situation, if you make a decision for the benefit of the guest, 90% of the time you will be right and management will back you 100% of the time.

Mr. Lamberti orients his employees to this policy during the interview process. New hires are told they will have to memorize the "policy manual" by the end of the interview and then they are presented with the one-page document.

To further encourage employees to act and behave in a warm, friendly manner consistent with the homespun atmosphere of a country inn, several tactics are used:

1 Employees' uniforms are casual, which fits the atmosphere of the hotel. For example, bellmen wear a white shirt and dark trousers; front-office staff wear ties but not formal dark suits, which is a departure from the structured uniforms of most hotels. As long as employees are dressed properly and fittingly, they may wear whatever clothing they deem appropriate.

2 Supervisory personnel are nearly always promoted from within. For example, the current assistant general manager started as a room clerk when the hotel opened.
3 There is no detailed job description of any position in the hotel. New employees are assisted in learning a specific position by their supervisor. Employees in one department help others outside their department, including Mr. Lamberti and his wife. Every action is geared to taking care of the guests' needs.
4 Employees are rewarded for helping the hotel maintain its four-star rating. Upon annual notification that the hotel has maintained its rating, each first-year employee receives a bonus of $50-$100; for each additional year of employment, each employee receives an additional $50, plus an additional $100 if his or her department did not receive any complaints during the year.
5 An exchange program has been developed with a nucleus of other New England hotels to provide Inn employees with insight as to how other hotels operate. This program has the added benefit of allowing employees to stay at another property for free.

Success of the Practice: The Inn at Essex has maintained its four-star rating from its opening day. Employee satisfaction is high, although the Inn is not the highest-paying property in the area, and employee retention is high despite overtures from other properties. The employee exchange program is particularly popular with employees. Finally, repeat guest business is strong. Mr. Lamberti attributes a great deal of the hotel's success to the manner in which the staff is treated and appreciated by management.

Mr. Lamberti's hotel has the distinction of having the second longest tenure as a four-star hotel in the state of Vermont. He believes this distinction will be maintained as long as he operates this hotel by taking care of the guests.

Insights

Advice and Observations: According to Mr. Lamberti, "The guest may not always be right, but they are always the guest. If we try to say yes, more often than not, we will have a satisfied customer at the end of the day."

Contact

Jim Lamberti, Owner-Manager
The Inn at Essex
70 Essex Way, Essex Junction, VT 05452
Phone: 802-764-1432 Fax: 802-878-0063

INN AT THE MARKET

Outsourced Human Resources to Professional HR Consultant

Description

The Practice: A small hotel with only 57 employees, Inn at the Market has added a part-time human resources manager through outsourcing, thus providing its employees with the same human resources services that are provided in larger hotels. The human resources manager's responsibilities include employee relations, workers' compensation, and equal employment opportunities. The cost for this consultant position is $1,000 per month.

Why the Practice Was Developed: Joyce Woodard, general manager, wanted to make it easier for employees to go to someone other than their supervisor for personal or job problems that could not be solved by the supervisor. Ms. Woodard could not justify a full-time human resources manager, however, and sought to provide this resource on a part-time basis.

Execution

The Approach to Implementation: Ms. Woodard remembered a friend and colleague, Audrey McCombs, with whom she had worked before. Ms. McCombs had been the human resources manager with Sheraton in Tacoma, Washington, but had resigned to raise a family. With approval from the hotel's owners, Ms. Woodard persuaded Ms. McCombs to accept the position of human resources manager as a part-time consultant.

To implement this practice, Ms. McCombs, in conjunction with Ms. Woodard, first developed an employee's handbook and job description for each job category. Subsequently, Ms. McCombs' activities and routine were defined. She visits the hotel three times a month. She attends staff meetings with the six supervisory personnel, and meets individually with supervisors to review any employee problems and to provide an update on human resources developments. She prepares a monthly fact sheet presenting the dates of hire, salary changes, and performance evaluations for all employees. This fact sheet is reviewed with each supervisor, and Ms. McCombs is involved in all employee wage reviews. She also coaches new supervisors in proper hiring procedures, and provides new employee orientation each month.

During each visit, Ms. McCombs conducts a walk-through of the hotel, completing a cycle in each department at least monthly. Employee complaints and questions are addressed at that time. To ensure that every employee is aware of when Ms. McCombs will be in the hotel, the dates of her scheduled visits are enclosed in the employees' monthly paychecks.

Some initial resentment towards Ms. McCombs was encountered from the maintenance engineer, who resented some of Ms. McCombs' recommendations. Eventually these issues were worked out. The housekeeping department, being the largest department in the hotel, was especially receptive to assistance from a human resources specialist.

Outcomes

Success of the Practice: Ms. Woodard believes this practice has produced better-qualified and satisfied employees, which are the main ingredients in creating satisfied customers. Additionally, managers are better informed and well trained. The availability of the human resources manager provides the employees with a confidential and impartial representative, and the additional guidance serves as an impetus for employee improvement.

Benefits for Customer: Guest questionnaire forms are generally all positive.

Insights

Advice and Observations: Ms. Woodard says a similar program could be established in other hotels. The services of a human resources consultant could be retained by a group of two or three hotels, thereby sharing payroll expenses.

Contact

Joyce Woodard, General Manager
Inn at the Market
86 Pine Street, Seattle, WA 98101
Phone: 206-443-3600 Fax: 206-728-1955

INTER-CONTINENTAL HOTELS & RESORTS

Building a Global Marketing Database

Description

The Practice: Inter-Continental Hotels & Resorts has created a global strategic marketing database, called Global 2000, which contains detailed and extensive guest history and consumption patterns for guest stays worldwide. Inter-Continental collects the data from over 100 hotels out of 160 within the chain, representing over 90% of its worldwide rooms revenue. The database currently contains data on over 13 million guest stays and 9 million guest profiles. The system has three important features: Data are collected from all customers staying at participating hotels, not just frequent travelers or members of a guest loyalty program; the data are collected at the time of departure instead of at the time of reservation, capturing the consumption behavior of the guest; and the system is worldwide and designed to interact with a wide range of reservation and property management systems.

Why the Practice Was Developed: Information regarding total stays, room-nights, and other basic information was routinely available, but the marketing department found it was unable to answer some senior management inquiries, such as, "How many guests do we have on a worldwide basis?" and "How many consolidated room-nights did this corporate client provide last year?" The marketing department decided to create a centralized system of guest data collection and warehousing to better track guest stays, travel patterns, and consumption behavior. Inter-Continental decided to use existing guest databases from within the airline and casino industries as its model.

Execution

The Approach to Implementation: Senior management decided that the rooms department and the information technology (IT) department would jointly create the database based upon the marketing department's communicated needs. Annette Kissinger, director of rooms and database marketing, coordinated the project. The rooms and IT departments then selected a few outside vendors to aid in the creation of the system. The following chart demonstrates the coordination required among the various parties to create the database:

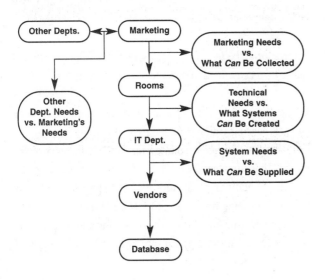

The various relationships offered different challenges to planning the database. The marketing department had to thoroughly define and document its needs. The rooms department had to effectively understand the marketing department's needs and determine how to integrate the needs with hotel operations by answering such questions as what kind of data can be collected, from whom should it be collected, how should it be collected, and when should it be collected. The IT department had to interpret these parameters and design a method to collect the data that could easily be integrated with existing operations and then design a system to warehouse and analyze the data once collected. In addition, other departments within Inter-Continental saw the development of this database for marketing as an opportunity to assert their own needs, especially in the area of financial data collection. However, to create an effective marketing decision support system, Inter-Continental was careful not to diffuse the focus by also trying to achieve additional operational goals. Lastly, the IT department was quite skeptical of the overall effort as it perceived this project as possibly too grand in scope and draining needed resources from other initiatives. Once the system parameters were developed the IT department had to select vendors who could supply the needed technology and who had the skills needed to complete the project.

After defining and developing the technology for the system, Inter-Continental moved ahead with the creation of the overall system in several distinct steps. The first step was the development of the standards and training needed to implement the system. The international nature of the data collection presented several challenges from negotiating various regional legal perspectives to creating standardized coding for data collected from around the world. However, the biggest operational challenge was the data collection at the property level. Because the overall system is only as good as the data collected at the property level, Inter-Continental first standardized procedures for data collection, and then embarked on a worldwide training program. Videos, games, and other training materials were created and distributed to commence a series of two-day training workshops conducted at each property. Finally, managers had to be encouraged to schedule adequate front desk staff to ensure the data were collected properly and in a timely fashion. This hindrance was overcome once general managers were persuaded that the information collected could be used to help fill low-demand periods and to reduce unsold rooms through eventual direct-mail campaigns.

The second step involved the technical aspects of the data collection and the central data warehouse. A standardized format was created to accommodate several different front-office systems and a way to summarize revenue information into different source categories (e.g., rooms, food and beverage, etc.). Initially, the properties sent weekly uploads on diskette, which then had to be manually inputted into the central database. However, the recent development of an intranet allows each property to e-mail the data directly to the central warehouse for uploading. The development of the central warehouse presented more difficulties as well. Currency converters and a decimal locator had to be developed to handle the multiple currencies found in each region. A method had to be developed to merge multiple stays, provide feedback on data quality, and notify hotels if data were missing or inadequate. Since data were collected at the time of departure, the central warehouse not only had to contain basic guest stay information, but also accommodate a wealth of data on guest consumption and behavior that were consolidated into individual profiles.

After the data were collected and warehoused, the third step was to determine their use and format for distribution. Inter-Continental had to answer such questions as: Who needs information on a hotel, regional, or global basis? How frequently? In what format will that information be distributed? Based on Inter-Continental's response to these questions, standardized reports then had to be developed quickly to demonstrate the advantages of the Global 2000 database to the senior management and to encourage general managers to have their hotels participate in the data collection.

The fourth step in the development of Global 2000 was the direct-marketing applications. Addresses had to be updated, verified, and cleaned by an "address hygiene" application for direct mailing. Procedures were created to use the database to target customized "marketing messages" and promotions to various customer groups based on the profile information.

The fifth step was the development of a "user friendly" interface for data retrieval from the data warehouse. Inter-Continental wanted to be able to do quick "counts" for mailings, identify target markets, provide detailed analysis of guest behavior, and do guest profiling for acquisition. A graphical user interface was developed for the central corporate offices and the four regional offices. Currently, individual properties do not possess direct access to Global 2000 and have to obtain data from the regional or central office.

A Trial: Inter-Continental began the Global 2000 initiative in 1993 and developed the technology, standards, and training strategy through 1994. In late 1994, a trial was started with approximately 20 hotels. The trial was successful, and Inter-Continental began full data collection in January 1995 with more than 40 hotels participating in the program. Since January 1995, Inter-Continental has enrolled more than 100 of its properties in the initiative.

Operational Issues: Once the system was fully operational the IT data center had to move to a 24-hour shift.

Costs: The primary cost of the initiative was labor and training costs. Preparing training materials and conducting training workshops worldwide accounted for most of the cost of the project. Unfortunately, the rooms and IT departments were not able to add additional staff to work on the project and had to reallocate existing resources and rely on outside consultants. Hence, another major cost was the consulting and development costs of the software and hardware by the outside vendors. IT was able to cut some costs by developing the graphical user interface in conjunction with a start-up software developer who had done previous work in the the airline industry. The overall costs of the project were primarily carried by the rooms and IT departments.

Outcomes

Success of the Practice: Inter-Continental has been pleased with the development of the Global 2000 database. Since 1995 the data quality indexes have steadily improved, and there is currently over 95% compliance with the use of the standardized codes. Ms. Kissinger believes there have been many foreseen and unforeseen advantages to the new system such as:

- Target mailings are now more effective using the new system. Response rates vary from 3% to 22% depending on the mailing. Using the system, the marketing department "can reach 5,000 targeted customers with a customized message for under $10,000," according to Ms. Kissinger. The reduced marketing costs and an increase in sales were originally the primary goals behind the project.

- Inter-Continental can now effectively measure advertising campaigns by tracking the trends of new customer acquisition and noting any spikes. This allows a better allocation of advertising resources and the development of better media strategies.

- The Global 2000 database has evolved into a tool for finding creative solutions to operational issues by looking at data patterns. For example, the rooms department used the database to help with some problems regarding the booking of reservations and telephone procedures at the front desk of the properties. First, the rooms department identified which market segments were using the phone to book reservations and then designed more effective procedures to increase productivity and better suit guests' needs.

- A new series of management and benchmarking reports were developed based on the data for individual hotels, regional sales offices, and the marketing department.

- Owners and managing partners view the Global 2000 as a major asset of their affiliation with Inter-Continental and the database aids in the attraction of new business partners for the company.

- Inter-Continental has greatly increased participation in its guest loyalty program by targeting previously unenrolled frequent travelers with special promotions and reduced membership fees. This focus on the loyalty program reduced the need to seek outside partners for frequent travel promotions and marketing. Furthermore, the guest loyalty data can also be used to cross-sell between properties within the same city.

- There was a major shift in the decision-making of senior management. Basic assumptions about operations, which previously did not have data supporting or refuting their validity, were challenged by the data being collected in the Global 2000 database. Senior management had to adjust to different decision-making processes based upon analyzing and querying the newly available data.

Benefits for Customer: Customers have benefited from the target marketing by receiving promotional material tailored to their specific needs. Customers have actually welcomed receiving material from Inter-Continental, according to Ms. Kissinger, because they find it useful and appropriate. Inter-Continental also conducted research on check-in practices in which guests indicated that once they check-in at one Inter-Continental property, they should not have to provide personal information again at another property. This has become a major future goal for the Global 2000 database called "Global Guest History."

Insights

Advice and Observations: Ms. Kissinger identified several "pitfalls" and problems encountered in the development of a database of this nature:

- Data quality was an important challenge. International addresses were frequently of low quality and reliability, and yet it was expensive to employ data-hygiene procedures on international addresses. Global differences in address formats also had to be resolved. The key ingredient was improving the quality of data collection at the individual properties without delaying check-in time.

- The timeliness of the information was another factor. Managers and departments wanted data processed quickly and returned promptly. Consequently, standard reports that could be quickly created and easily understood had to be designed.

- Other departments tried to co-opt the database for their own needs. "Do not let others convince you the marketing database can be used for operations or accounting functions," asserts Ms. Kissinger.

- Legal requirements regarding data privacy varied from country to country and had to be resolved. Guest information had to be handled carefully and guests' concerns about selling the information to outside vendors had to be addressed. Any marketing partnerships had to be prudently considered.

- The development of a data warehouse vs. a traditional marketing database was an issue. It was determined that the data warehouse would contain sales and customer data only, and the customer data would be maintained, as summary tables were not enough for relationship marketing. The marketing department needed the "ability to drill down" and analyze the data components. The customer file needed to be flexible enough to add research responses, appended data, RFM codes, and no-mail codes.

- Senior management had to be educated on the long-term benefits and the eventual cost savings of such an endeavor. It is necessary to "show incremental profit and revenue" and "reinforce that retaining customer loyalty is important," says Ms. Kissinger.

- The selection of outside technology and marketing consultants posed some complications. Inter-Continental had difficulty locating vendors who adequately understood the specific needs of the hospitality industry. They also had to make certain the technology was state of the art and could grow with additional applications and over time. Ms. Kissinger laments not being able to add additional training and database management staff to handle certain needs internally vs. going to outside consultants, as she believes using more internal resources would have aided the overall project.

- Inter-Continental tried to grow Global 2000 too quickly. The number of participating hotels jumped from 43 to over 100 between 1995 and 1998. This rapid growth burdened the training staff and created difficulties in maintaining data standards and integrity. If Ms. Kissinger had to do it again, given the same limited resources, she would start with a smaller group of hotels in a single region and expand more slowly.

- Training costs and time were greatly underestimated. The single largest investment was in the initial training. Training of new hires continues to be expensive, as is the continuous updating of standards.

- A more systematic approach to gaining input from the marketing department on its needs should have been established. The input from marketing was not focused or defined enough. In retrospect a permanent advisory board should have been created to provide consistent input on the project and give the marketing department a better sense of ownership of the project.

- Advances in technology need to be considered. Planning should project three to five years into the future. Be prepared to "reinvent the wheel again" to keep the database current.

Contact

Annette Kissinger
Director of Rooms and Database Marketing
Inter-Continental Hotels & Resorts
P.O. Box 4590, Stamford, CT 06907
Phone: 203-351-8240

KESSLER ENTERPRISES, INC.

Development and Concept of the Grand Theme Hotels

Description

The Practice: Innovation is the key to Kessler Enterprises' successful business development in the specialty area of theme hotels. Richard Kessler, president and chief executive officer, states that "It is one thing to have a clever or creative idea; it is another to make sure we can develop it fully so that we provide a complete experience for our guests and a profitable one for our company." To that end, Kessler Enterprises searches for a location that people yearn to visit. Kessler considers all elements of a total sensory and entertaining experience, and carefully analyzes the market to make sure the project is financially sound. Kessler then makes use of the talents of the whole organization to develop the theme hotel concept from beginning to end.

Why the Practice Was Developed: Mr. Kessler believes the future of the lodging industry lies in providing for the total experience of the guest — a guest who is becoming more and more sophisticated in "shopping and buying" habits. This sophistication comes from highly creative, energetic marketing techniques, high-design product packaging, and increased levels of "magical" expectations generated by the entertainment giants, such as Disney and Universal Studios. In addition, today's lodging guest has more discretionary income than in the past and is willing to spend it on exciting and pleasurable experiences. Thus, after 29 years in the lodging industry, Mr. Kessler directed his company toward becoming a lodging experience enterprise.

Execution

The Approach to Implementation: The successful development of Kessler Enterprises' theme hotels requires a comprehensive design process. First, Kessler researches the anticipated location for the hotel seeking its history and any significant experience or event in the area. A market analysis is conducted that then dictates the price level and thus the product level that is appropriate for the area. Generally, Kessler's goal is to find areas that need and can sustain $2^{1}/_{2}$- to four-star hotels. Any of the historic structures in and around the area are photographed, from which a theme emerges. Further development of the theme around the history of the location continues. Architects and designers use this information and Kessler's market conclusions to create the first draft of the form and style of the facility. Kessler's internal team of operations, finance, and construction people then contribute their perspectives in the planning and decision-making process. The design process continues throughout the development and construction of the Grand Theme Hotel.

Before the hotel opens, Kessler gives careful consideration to the selection of personnel for the hotel. The general manager and his or her staff must reflect the entire ambiance of the hotel. In addition, Kessler designs and selects collateral, furnishings, custom music, and all other elements and details with the theme and "sense of being" in mind. Elements of education, history, personality of the area, and art are intertwined into the hotel. All of these elements, combined with the outstanding customer service rendered by tastefully costumed personnel, must create a truly unusual and memorable experience for the guest. The goal is to make staying in a Grand Theme Hotel a total sensory experience.

A visit to the Doubletree Castle, for example, engages guests completely, according to Mr. Kessler. The color, sounds, artwork, and excitement imprint on children. For the sophisticated collector or historian, the art and variety of antique collections intrigue and entertain. Grandparents can sit by the pool while the grandchildren participate in a theme scavenger hunt. Older teens can walk safely to Point Orlando, while convention goers can easily walk to the convention center. All guests fully experience the "essence of the locale" where they visit. Most cities or even areas surrounding the hotels have a colorful history that can fascinate a visitor.

Costs: Additional costs related to the creation of a theme are primarily in the selection and purchase of the artwork necessary to create a realistic theme. Although the initial cost of quality artwork is high, the fact that it is of collectible grade makes the expense an investment, because the artwork will appreciate in value.

As an example, Kessler has purchased one of only two existing Imperial Grand Bosendorfer pianos for the soon-to-be constructed Grand Bohemian Hotel in Orlando. Built for the 1,000th anniversary of Vienna, the piano will be the centerpiece of a music room and lounge. It has a value of approximately $250,000.

Outcomes

Success of the Practice: Mr. Kessler states: "Our guests return, and their comments clearly confirm their delight. This is our measure of success. And, yes, every theme hotel we have created has been profitable beyond normal expectations."

"We believe the theme concept adds a minimum of 10% to the ADR, compared to competition."

Benefits for Customer: Mr. Kessler believes the customers are the beneficiaries of this most distinctive experience that is designed with their pleasure in mind. "Once they enter our hotels, they are immersed in the experience. They see, feel, and appreciate the painstaking detail that has been created for their delight and pleasure. On another level, we find that people realize we have designed something special with them in mind. We get thousands of comment cards and letters of appreciation for creating a total experience for their travel or vacation enjoyment."

Insights

Advice and Observations: Theme hotels are "what guests want today and will continue to prefer in the future," states Mr. Kessler. Hotel companies must be prepared to provide a total entertainment experience for guests if the companies are to remain competitive.

Contact

Richard Kessler, President/CEO
Kessler Enterprises, Inc.
7380 Sand Lake Road., Suite 120, Orlando, FL 32819
Phone: 407-996-9999 Fax: 407-996-9998

KIMPTON GROUP HOTELS AND RESTAURANTS AND OUTRIGGER HOTELS AND RESORTS

Private-Label Reservation System to Encourage Upselling

Description

The Practice: Kimpton Group Hotels and Restaurants uses a private-label central reservation service provided by Outrigger Marketing Incorporated (OMI). Both Outrigger Hotels and Resorts and Kimpton Group Hotels use the central reservations system (CRS). Kimpton and Outrigger find the cross-selling capability of the system a powerful tool that contributes to improved occupancy and rate. This affects all 24 Kimpton properties and 21 Outrigger Hotels located in Waikiki. Another distinctive feature of the system is that it provides different quotes for accommodations for a specific date. Attached to each quote is an on-line incentive that serves to encourage the hotel reservation agent to upsell the customer.

Why the Practice Was Developed: The Kimpton Group has a high concentration of properties — 15 hotels in San Francisco alone with an inventory of approximately 3,200 rooms. Under the old decentralized reservation system, each hotel had its own three-to-four person reservation department. However, such a system made it difficult to cross-sell other Kimpton Group properties. Another factor that helped to drive changes in the reservation system: According to the director of reservations, Dean Di Lullo, as the Kimpton Group has grown it has become the boutique hotel leader in its markets, even though it competes against the offerings of large hotel chains. To maintain its role as market leader, the Kimpton Group wanted an equal or better level of technology.

Execution

The Approach to Implementation: Development of the implementation plan and specifications for enhancements to OMI's existing central reservations system were the joint efforts of Kimpton Group and Outrigger's marketing, information and technology, and reservations departments. Outrigger has been developing the system software for several years in conjunction with OPUS 2 Revenue Technologies and Enterprise Hospitality Solutions. Mr. Di Lullo and Ken Taylor, the vice president of information systems for Outrigger, served as the driving forces behind the adoption of the new system. Kimpton Group conducted customer focus groups with its most loyal, frequent guests, meeting planners, and travel agents to determine how the system should be configured to meet their needs. In January 1997, Outrigger began customizing the Stellex 2.0 CRS program to fit Kimpton Group's needs. Nine months later Stellex 2.5 was ready to implement at the first Kimpton Group pilot hotel.

The system was designed so that when a central reservation agent selects a property and accommodation combination for a hotel for a particular date, the system provides the agent with three initial quotes. Each quote has an on-line incentive-point value assigned to it. This incentive induces the agent to sell the most attractive accommodations (e.g., suite vs. regular room). As a result, the hotel reservation agent selling the desirable booking accumulates more incentive points than a person selling the lower-rated booking. "What is nice about the system is that it provides the agent the ability to sell versus being an order taker," states Mr. Di Lullo. "Most central reservation applications just give the ability to sell an accommodation for a hotel for a date, but don't give a listing of all the possibilities and combinations for that hotel. If you enter a sell request for a room at a Marriott Hotel for the corporate rate, the system will come back with a display of only corporate rates. That is, either the display reads not available or it comes back with a display that says it is available and here is what the rate is. Our system actually lists available accommodations not just for the corporate rate but any rate and room-type combination available to the general public that meets or exceeds the revenue-management target. So this gives the hotel reservation agent the opportunity to sell to the customer without having to enter multiple requests."

In addition to encouraging upselling, the system gives reservation agents the ability to cross-sell their properties more effectively. The agent can search for a rate category or special package across all Kimpton Group hotels with one search. Hence, the system allows for maximum yield management.

The system is being installed at all Kimpton Group properties using a graduated rollout. About 50% of the Kimpton Group hotels are now online with Stellex 2.5. Rollout of the system is to be completed by the end of 1999.

Cost: Development and customization of the system cost $1.2 million. Kimpton Group's share of the costs are being recouped over a five-year period from the properties based on a per-reservation basis. Kimpton Group's reservation cost is only 2% of revenue, partly because of the increase in revenue Kimpton Group is enjoying; industry reservation costs average 3% of revenue.

Outcomes

Success of Practice: The use of the system has improved profits because ADR has increased 8-11% without a negative impact on occupancy. In addition, the centralization of the reservation system has allowed each property to reduce its reservation staff from 4 or 4 1/2 to 1 1/2, consisting of a revenue manager and one other part-time employee.

Front-office staffs have enjoyed the central reservation system because the guest services staff can be more attentive to guests and not jockey registering guests with answering reservation calls. Revenue managers like the system because they can ensure availability for business that is willing to pay a higher rate — that is, quote "the right rate for the right date."

Benefits for Customer: The system provides meeting planners and travel agents with the ability to book any Kimpton Group hotel with a single phone call. Individual customers are able to make one phone call and obtain rates and availability for any Kimpton Group property — no more redialing of numerous 800 numbers. Thus, the system provides the customer with one-stop shopping.

Other benefits for the customer have also occurred. Under the decentralized reservation environment, Kimpton Group was abandoning 8-10% of calls and providing a 60% service level. Under the centralized reservation environment, Kimpton Group properties are abandoning fewer than 2% of calls and providing a 90% service level, meaning 90% of the calls are answered within the first 20 seconds. Kimpton Group has had positive feedback from its customers on this improved level of service.

Insights

Advice and Observations: Mr. Di Lullo offers this advice, "Don't skimp on ensuring people in the organization understand the application and how to be successful with it. Provide training, and make sure people understand revenue-management concepts. If the people in your organization understand the big picture and why the organization is using the system, revenue improvements will occur more rapidly."

Mr. Di Lullo also suggests that anyone undertaking a similar project should gain the understanding and support of key executives before going to the individual properties. "It is also important to convey that technology doesn't detract from personal service, but instead allows the staff to spend more time concentrating on their guests."

Contacts

Dean Di Lullo, Director of Reservations
Kimpton Group Hotels and Restaurants
222 Kearny Street, Suite 200, San Francisco, CA 94108
Phone: 415-955-5433 Fax: 415-296-8031

Ken Taylor, Vice President, Information Systems
Outrigger Hotels and Resorts
2375 Kuhio Avenue, Honolulu, HI 96815
Phone: 808-921-6701 Fax: 808-921-6715

KNIGHTS INN SUMMERTON (PREEA, INC.)

Creating Your Own Mailing Lists to Increase Business

Description

The Practice: The Knights Inn in Summerton, South Carolina, has developed its own mailing lists and targeted its budget services to local fishing and golf attractions to create demand in an impoverished geographic market. The hotel has used billboard advertising to create product awareness and offer a no-nonsense price structure. It is also active in organizing fishing tournaments and golf packages. By creating niche products for the regional golfing and fishing enthusiasts, CEO Arun Bivek has been able to add new business in an otherwise sleepy town.

Why the Practice Was Selected: The Knights Inn and two other properties (Econo Lodge and Travelodge) owned and operated by Mr. Bivek are located in a county with a population of 500 residents. The hotels are in a pass-through town with no fast-food restaurants and no gas stations open past 9:00 p.m. Over 10 years ago, a local bank that had repossessed the hotel property asked Mr. Bivek to get it operating so the bank could liquidate. Instead of spending the six weeks required to improve the operation, Mr. Bivek bought it.

Mr. Bivek said the only way he could entice traveling customers to stay at the hotel was to advertise a guaranteed rate on highway billboards up to 90 miles away. His advertising promised no hidden charges and, moreover, when the customers drive up they can see the rooms before making the decision to stay. He believed that one stay at his hotel would create loyal customers, and he expected every satisfied guest to refer 10 new guests to him. Unfortunately, his transient guests stay just one night as there is no local industry and no tourist attraction in Summerton, except golfing or fishing, to encourage lengthier visits. Mr. Bivek wanted to devise a means for prolonging the average stay of his hotel guests.

Execution

The Approach to Implementation: Mr. Bivek conducted market research by going to the area golf courses where he saw many out-of-state license plates. Unable to obtain the names and addresses of the owners of these vehicles, he hired a golfer who had recently retired as a timeshare salesman to compile a mailing list of golfers playing at these local courses. Mr. Bivek merged this mailing list with his hotel's guest-history database, and supplemented that with names from local newspaper advertising. In his search for the golf-outing business, Mr. Bivek mailed 10,000 advertising pieces to golfers in 11 states in the Southeast region of the United States. The promotion was successful, and because of the volume of golf business he generated, Mr. Bivek was able to negotiate better rates and preferred tee times with the local courses.

To lure the fishing business, Mr. Bivek invited the four local fishing guides to see his three properties and printed brochures featuring the hotels for these guides to hand to their clients. He learned from the guides that the sports enthusiasts liked to leave early in the morning so he started opening his restaurant at 5:00 a.m.

Operational Issues: The chief operating change was opening up the restaurant for breakfast at 5:00, which required only one additional waitress, as his cooks were already in at that time.

Costs: The only costs besides the waitress were the costs of the fishing brochure and the commission for the two salespeople. The commissions became so large for the original salesman that his daughter quit a job in a neighboring state and came to work with her father in this business.

Outcomes

Success of the Practice: Mr. Bivek's strategy was not to be greedy when he was just getting these practices up and running. His initial package prices were just a few dollars above his cost, and he lost $20,000 in the first year (1996) because of his initial investment in advertising. He did, however, put heads in beds and increase occupancy. The second year he generated $180,000 in new revenue. In 1998 (the third year) it is a profitable program. The fishing business books approximately 10 rooms per night during the October-to-May season. The owner has also been involved with the Chamber of Commerce and is always the host hotel for fishing tournaments that are sponsored by Mercury Engine and other major companies. To become the exclusive hotel, he gave 10 complimentary rooms to the Chamber of Commerce. Based on the success of this particular practice for the tournaments, he is also working on complimentary meeting space for county meetings, school board meetings, and the like. This is leading to more paid business for groups, weddings, and other function business.

Mr. Bivek also believes that he is now breaking even on his food service, because his restaurant is capturing additional customers such as the fishing groups, which in the past would have had to skip breakfast because no restaurant in town was open early enough.

Last, employee morale and job security have improved. Mr. Bivek's three budget hotels employ over 80 people. Mr. Bivek deals with the staff as a team and as a family-owned operation. Employees may work in rotation at the Knights Inn or at the Econo Lodge next door — "a flexible procedure."

Insights

Advice and Observations: Mr. Bivek suggests looking for business in one's own backyard. Learn from the successes of other hotels in the community. Learn, as well, from your own mistakes. Mr. Bivek said he would not do anything differently if he were starting over, since he believes this has been a successful program. In particular, he has developed his own mailing list and would not consider purchasing mailing lists as he believes there is a lot of waste in using that approach.

Contact

Arun Bivek, Chief Executive Officer
Knights Inn Summerton (Preea, Inc.)
P.O. Box 68, Summerton, SC 29148
Phone: 803-485-2895   Fax: 803-485-2895, Ext. 161

LATHAM HOTEL, GEORGETOWN, WASHINGTON, D.C.

Midscale Guestrooms Designed to Give an Upscale, Residential Feel

The Practice: Drawing in part from designs and techniques at 12 deluxe hotels in New York City, the Latham Hotel in Georgetown has developed an award-winning room design.

Why the Practice Was Developed: A 1996 decision to renovate the property became a full-scale research project on the best designs in hotel rooms. Formerly known as the Georgetown Marbury Hotel, the property name was changed to the Latham, partly in tribute to the excellent Latham Hotel in Philadelphia. Owner Paul Whetsell worked to upgrade the Georgetown Latham, improving both the occupancy and average room rate. In 1996, when Mr. Whetsell and CapStar Hotel Company obtained full ownership and decided to completely renovate the property, they installed a new general manager, Dixie Eng. Mr. Whetsell sought a team of his own choosing to inspect 12 hotels in New York City.

The Approach to Implementation: A team of experienced hotel executives from the management firm MeriStar Hotels & Resorts inspected 12 New York City hotels that were similar to the Latham. This team consisted of the following MeriStar executives: general manager, director of sales, director of operations, food and beverage director, executive chef of the Citronelle Restaurant, vice president of sales, and vice president of operations. The team inspected the following hotels: the Doral Court, the Doral Tuscany, the Gorham, the Lowell, the Mansfield, Morgans, the Paramount, the Plaza Athenée, the Royalton, the Shoreham, the Stanhope, and the Wales.

Team members concentrated on the products and the techniques used by the operators of these 12 hotels. They inspected room design, bars and lounges, restaurants, the quality and type of fabrics, room amenities, the service culture, lobby designs, meeting rooms, and public-area carpeting. They also studied who was patronizing these properties. The team spent two days and nights inspecting these 12 properties and then used the data collected to develop a plan to renovate the Latham Hotel. To start, the hotel needed a decorator of good repute who could give the Latham Hotel a residential look, while selecting materials that would wear well. After an in-depth study the team selected Duncan and Miller Design from Dallas.

As desired, Duncan and Miller designed the guestrooms with a residential atmosphere, which extends throughout the hotel, making the rooms atypical. Bathrooms feature an Italian marble floor with wallpaper typical of home designs. The marble sink has storage underneath, and an adjustable towel warmer holds four towels.

The bedrooms have been renovated to accommodate the residential atmosphere of this hotel. The rooms include love seats with two pillows covered by a tapestry fabric facing glass-and-brass tables. Carpeting is similar to what one would find at home. The armoires, containing a television set and four drawers, have four mirrors on the front panels. The desks are topped by marble. In addition to offering two data ports and two-line telephones, the hotel has placed Hewlett-Packard faxes and printers in the rooms. Covered by down comforters, the beds stand high on risers, creating a European feel. Two-step wooden stairs at the end of the beds allow the guests to climb in. Two paintings of Washington, D.C., history hang above the beds. Three feet from the beds are small, marble-top dressers with five drawers. Windows are trimmed by sheer drapes of Irish linen covered by a blackout drape. All guestrooms have an ironing board and iron, and upgraded rooms have a dressing robe also hanging in each closet.

Success of the Practice: The Latham was a finalist in the 1998 *Lodging Hospitality* awards for best guestroom design. The hotel's occupancy and ADR have substantially improved as a result of the redesign, with revenue per available room increasing by double-digit percentages in the past two years. The hotel has a high return clientele that is pleasantly surprised at the architecture of the guestrooms, the well-designed lobby, the selective meeting rooms, the excellence of the restaurant, and the superior service of the staff.

Insights

Advice and Observations: Mr. Whetsell, the founder of this company, believes that a hotel will be successful if it is well designed and well matched to the market that the hotel wants to attract. An owner must establish what the market needs in terms of its possible clientele and then follow through with sales and marketing.

Contact

Dixie Eng, General Manager
Latham Hotel - Georgetown
3000 M Street, N.W., Washington, DC 20007
Phone: 202-726-5000 Fax: 202-337-4250

MARRIOTT INTERNATIONAL

Aligning Information Technology with Corporate Strategy

Description

The Practice: Marriott International's Information Resources Strategy and Planning process aligns information systems and technology with business strategy. The process produces a vision for future systems and technologies that align with and support the business strategy, and a set of plans to guide the portfolio of projects that must be executed to deliver these capabilities to the business. A key benefit of this process is a comprehensive strategic enterprise architecture that lays the foundation for Marriott to quickly and effectively alter its systems and technologies in the future in response to changes in business needs and the competitive climate. Nimbleness and speed of change are the competitive advantages that Marriott enjoys as a result.

Why the Practice Was Developed: Marriott's Information Resources division uses this information technology strategy and architecture development process because it places the strategic needs of the business at its core. The process drives all aspects of the Information Resources organization to deliver products and services that are aligned with where the business processes of the future will be, not just where they are today. Also, the methodology yields opportunities for economies of scale through reduction of technology diversity and the elimination of data and functional redundancy. The result is a dramatically reduced total cost of ownership with a concurrent significant increase in functionality directly aligned with Marriott's business processes of the future.

Execution

The Approach to Implementation: Marriott's Information Resources Strategy and Planning process has three steps: Baseline Assessment, Strategy Development, and Plan Formulation. Each of the three phases of the process examines the use of information technology throughout the organization, both within and outside of Information Resources. Areas covered include:

- technology infrastructure (e.g., computing and communications platforms),
- application systems (e.g., the business-specific functionality required within business processes, such as the Reservation System and Customer Information System),
- human resources (e.g., sourcing strategies, how many are required, what skills are required, the roles they play, etc.)
- management controls (i.e., the way the Information Resources function will be organized to deliver services, and the principles, policies, standards, and other governance that will guide its efforts),
- investment (i.e., the funding and recovery programs that will allow the Information Resources efforts to succeed), and
- business user preparedness (i.e., the ability and readiness of the organization to learn and change; to absorb and leverage the information systems and technology in the context of the business processes of the future).

During the Baseline Assessment phase, the current level of support that Information Resources provides for Marriott International is assessed. The goal is to determine strengths and weaknesses of the Information Resources organization, and the systems and technology it has provided to support the business to date.

During the most recent assessment, the Information Resources team facilitated workshops with senior managers from the business (e.g., marketing, food and beverage, sales, rooms operations) to assess how well the current set of application systems supports the operation of the business and how this support could be improved. Benchmarking (i.e., comparison to similar companies) was used to assess the relative strength of the technology infrastructure, human resources skills, the effectiveness of management procedures, the level of spending on technology, and other key indicators of IT efficiency and effectiveness.

Business and Information Resources management and associates enthusiastically received the Baseline Assessment portion of the planning process. From the baseline assessment, Information Resources developed a list of "Quick Hits" (i.e., short-term projects) that would improve Information Resources' support for business operations immediately. For example, several different user help desks from various brands and departments were consolidated into one help desk for all

Marriott International end users. Also, the decision was quickly made to standardize one single suite of office automation and messaging software across all business units and functional areas, guaranteeing (among other benefits) that attachments to e-mail messages could be opened, read, and edited by anyone in the company.

During the second step, Strategy Development, the vision of the hotel of the future from a systems and technology perspective was constructed. To create this vision, Information Resources managers worked with senior managers from the business (e.g., marketing, food and beverage, sales, rooms operations) to envision and document their future business processes. These process models depict the organizational components of Marriott and the interrelationships of these parts over time in providing hospitality services.

As these process models were being created, the IR senior management team spent considerable time and effort developing and agreeing to a comprehensive set of Information Resources Principles. These principles form the "rules of the road" for systems and technology procurement, development, integration, and deployment. They can be described as the fundamental beliefs of the organization in each of the dimensions of the strategy that were outlined earlier. The principles allowed the rest of the strategy and architecture to be developed much more effectively because they represented "pre-made" decisions. The teams were able to more quickly resolve differences during points of disagreement by falling back on the framework provided by the principles.

The business process models of the future formed the context for determining information needs of the future. Once the Business and Information Resources teams were satisfied that all information had been planned for the future, a data-driven analytical approach was used to derive a strategic application systems architecture. This future application systems architecture for Marriott is a loosely coupled, message-oriented, component-based model. This gives maximum flexibility for implementation and future modification as business requirements and strategies change. It also promotes a high degree of data integrity, responsiveness, and simplicity of development and integration.

Once the application and information architectures were formulated and characterized, the underlying technology infrastructure strategy and architecture were developed. This was accomplished by applying a number of methods, practices, and "rules of thumb" evolved over years of work in developing and delivering enterprise information technology architectures in other organizations. Refinements resulted in a solidified, integrated enterprise architecture that, by virtue of the modeling technique used, was directly aligned to and linked with Marriott's strategic business processes of the future. Strategies were also developed for the other dimensions as well, including management controls, human resources, investment, and business user preparedness.

In the third phase, Plan Formulation, the Information Resources team created a framework for how it will move from the current state documented in the Baseline Assessment to the strategic vision described in the strategic architecture. What emerges is a three-year plan that identifies all projects required to implement as much of the strategic architecture as possible within that interval. It also contains an extended vision for four to five years, bringing the planning horizon to five years.

The plan describes implementation priorities and timing, staffing requirements and sourcing strategies, costs and benefits, required training, and other projects that make up a comprehensive program to deliver on the strategic vision. Within the program of activity, dependencies emerge across the systems development and integration projects, and existing legacy systems and technologies must be "bridged" to one or more of the target applications and technologies. The number of combinations and permutations of projects to deliver future capabilities while retiring old ones is staggering. To isolate the best combinations of projects, the planning process relies heavily on the technique of scenario planning. Scenario analysis with robust modeling techniques and tools allowed Marriott to analyze the many possibilities to arrive at a few permissible scenarios, with associated costs and benefits. From these few, a preferred scenario was selected to form the foundation for final IR.

The Plan. The entire plan to move Marriott steadily toward the future state is reviewed annually and adjusted as the needs of the business change, as technology advances, and as business environmental factors and external agents change the environment within which Marriott International must operate. The IR plan forms the basis for the systems and technology portion of the annual budget process in Marriott International. It also allows Marriott to prioritize and manage its projects at an enterprise level, avoiding the probable sub-optimization of resources that individual, unlinked business unit and functional area plans would generate.

Outcomes

Success of the Practice:

- The Information Resources Strategy and Planning process enables Marriott's business strategy.
- The Information Resources division has solidified its relationship with the business units and functional areas and has become a partner at the "business strategy table."
- The identification and execution of "Quick Hit" actions discovered in the assessment phase have already yielded significant benefits in operational efficiency and reduced costs.
- A framework for annual review and updating of the technology plan and strategy allows it to remain aligned with Marriott's business strategy and to stay abreast of important systems and technology trends. Marriott has a clear "roadmap" for the future, and the principles and architectural models to guide its activities and investment. The process is efficient. Guesswork is eliminated.

Insights

Advice and Observations: The critical success factors of the project were:

- The commitment of senior Information Resources management to the process of aligning the Information Resources division's planning and resources with Marriott's business strategy.
- The involvement of senior-level management from each operational department (e.g., non-Information Resources) from the beginning of the process.
- Cultural change was (and remains) the biggest challenge to integrated planning.
- Consensus was difficult, and at times impossible to attain. However, "alignment" (i.e., those few who could not reach consensus with the larger group agreed to support the decision of the group wholeheartedly, despite their opposition during the debate) was possible. The agreement to strive for "alignment" allowed the process to move forward steadily.

Contact

Barry L. Shuler, Senior Vice President
Information Resources Strategy and Planning
Marriott International
One Marriott Drive, Dept. 996.08
Washington, DC 20058
Phone: 301-380-6586   Fax: 301-380-3801

MARRIOTT INTERNATIONAL

Developing Products to Meet the Needs of Targeted Market Segments

Description

The Practice: Employing feasibility and trend studies to identify market segments, Marriott selects the most viable segments to target, and then designs a product around the needs of that market. For example, Marriott decided to design a lodging product targeted at midscale business travelers, a market segment whose needs were not being adequately met by full-service products. "The need was to create a guestroom and guestroom building that could be developed and built in an efficient construction fashion. The need for construction efficiency was critical to the product's success since construction costs had to be low enough to allow a rate that would meet the customer's budget," explained John Fetty, senior design manager. The result was Courtyard by Marriott.

Why the Practice Was Developed: The customer is defined as the guest, the franchisee, and Marriott's own corporate development division. The three "customers" influence product design. Thus, Courtyard was designed because customer research indicated that the existing moderate-segment hotels were not meeting the needs of many business travelers.

Execution

The Approach to Implementation: In designing Courtyard, the needs of all three customers — guest, franchisees, and corporate development — were considered. The ultimate goal was to create a product that would provide the paying customer with a good night's rest, as well as desired amenities, such as a restaurant and lounge, quality check-in, and excellent service.

Courtyard could not include all of the amenities of a full-service hotel because room rates would be too high. Consequently, the amenities package was pared down to features perceived as most important by guests. Because it was created for suburban markets, Courtyard was also clearly packaged in low-rise construction, rather than as a high-rise. In addition, the construction techniques had to be streamlined to remain within tight budgetary constraints.

Certain spaces within the building block had to be aligned to facilitate a leaner operation from a staffing standpoint. "Design has to synthesize how the operation functions. The arrangement of internal space is just as important as external space because it all influences how a product is rolled out. A lot of consideration was given to the mistakes and errors of design in existing properties, so as not to repeat them. The result was the creation of a product which eliminated a lot of that," noted Mr. Fetty.

When Courtyard was ready to be franchised in the early '90s, Marriott met the needs of these customers by developing a hotel that was useful to franchisees, particularly in small markets. The focus for this model was on quality control and focusing on elements that benefited the guest. According to Mr. Fetty, "The structure became a lot leaner than it was before, but yet retained the spirit of the spaces and services."

Operational Issues: Marriott continues to solicit feedback from numerous sources as a means of ensuring its products meet the needs of the targeted market segments. Customer focus groups meet at different geographic locations at different times of the year to provide direct feedback on a variety of topics including guestrooms and public spaces. The information gathered here is analyzed and studied; the better ideas are incorporated into the next design generation. Mr. Fetty attends many of the focus group meetings. "If we have a good idea, we want to hear from the customer what they feel will perfect it. As a designer, you rely on the feedback from the end user," he said.

Other mechanisms are also used to obtain customer feedback. Information is received monthly from frequent travelers, and then filtered upwards through the operations network. Product-development committees, management advisory councils, and design and development committees are all used as sources of information. "These are all vehicles that branch out to the marketplace, to the ownership body, and really capture things from a grass roots level," Mr. Fetty stated.

Outcomes

Success of the Practice: Marriott continues to produce successful products. In the case of Courtyard, the brand has grown steadily, and occupancy and ADR have increased over the past several years.

Insights

Advice and Observations: Mr. Fetty suggests, "Don't try to complicate the design; facilitate what is needed all within one room. Not an easy project, but simplistic. Don't get too specialized. Keep it fairly simple. The guest is the most influential person of all those that have input into the design process." Mr. Fetty also advises the designer to correct mistakes as quickly as possible.

Marriott is now studying the customers of the future to determine where the customer base will come from and what its wants, wishes, and desires will be in the next millennium. Based on these studies, plans are being made as to what the product of the future will look like.

Contact

John Fetty, Senior Design Manager
Marriott International
One Marriott Drive, Dept. 70/1-3.01, Washington, DC 20058
Phone: 301-380-8793   Fax: 301-380-8063

MARRIOTT INTERNATIONAL

Leveraging Leadership Capacity and Building Future Leaders

Description

The Practice: Marriott International has embarked on a leadership development initiative to ensure continuity of world-class management talent now and in the future. One element of the leadership development initiative is the creation of a Benchstrength Management System, which consists of the tools and metrics used by current senior management to build leadership capacity. Senior management is responsible for identifying potential leaders and then ensuring that these future leaders develop the skills and competencies needed to carry the company forward. The goal is to raise the level of current leadership performance through staffing decisions and other development actions and to maintain a strong pipeline of future leaders.

Why the Practice Was Developed: As Marriott flourished into a global organization, it needed to ensure that the necessary managerial talent was in place to maintain this growth. The leadership development program ensures that Marriott will have the leaders to drive that growth — in terms of quantity, capability, and vision. "We want to have a high level of predictability in both the amount and quality of leaders we produce in the future," commented Dr. David Rodriguez, senior vice president of staffing and development. "If we do this well, we will continue to grow the business and generate profits for our shareholders."

Execution

The Approach to Implementation: The program creates a management framework for senior managers to develop future talent. Senior managers address issues such as: What should leadership requirements at different levels of the organization look like in the future? What competencies do we want leaders to possess? How does the senior team work together to develop future leaders? What specific staffing and development actions will get us there?

Drawing from external and internal research and best practices across industries, Marriott developed a system for identifying and developing future leaders. Utilizing the leadership development process, senior managers assess junior managers' performance and potential to determine what specific skills or competencies they need to develop. This information is used to construct targeted development plans and to guide the staffing of mission-critical positions that can also serve as challenging "stretch" assignments for high-potential managers. The premise is to raise the level of leadership benchstrength for the company, while at the same time optimizing the pursuit of current market objectives.

In addition to the leadership development program, Marriott is seeking to attract the top talent available from the marketplace and campuses by raising the quality of its employment marketing. The goal is to continuously tailor "employment value propositions" to targeted talent pools in the marketplace and to ensure that internal processes (e.g., career development) deliver on the "promise."

Outcomes

Success of the Practice: For a large and increasingly global organization like Marriott, having a consistent framework for assessing and developing leadership capacity is an invaluable tool. The firm now has one platform for looking consistently at talent across brands, businesses, and functions, and assessing leadership potential against the requirements of different levels of management. Moreover, the Benchstrength Management System ensures that the company focuses on core capabilities that are keys to future success (e.g., building a global management-capable leadership team).

Benefits for Customer: While the process has been in place for less than a year, its effect on the customer should be substantial, partly because the process "puts rigor into how the senior-most jobs in the company get staffed," said Dr. Rodriguez. "The belief is that if you have world-class leaders at each management level, they will attract and develop higher-caliber talent throughout the organization. The anticipated result is that customers will experience a higher level of service, and this in turn will contribute to profitable, loyal relationships with them."

Advice and Observations: "Don't spend an excessive amount of time planning it," advised Dr. Rodriguez. "The most important thing you can do is get senior management involved and working together to 'know the people' and to have a rigorous staffing process. It's essential that the organization develop the discipline required to make informed staffing and development decisions that place the right people in the right jobs at the right time. This not only builds the pipeline, but also ensures that the very best occupy the most critical jobs in the company."

Contact

David Rodriguez, Ph.D.
Senior Vice President, Staffing & Development
Marriott International
One Marriott Drive, Washington, DC 20058
Phone: 301-380-8886 Fax: 301-380-4229

MARRIOTT INTERNATIONAL

Revenue Management Systems for Revenue Enhancement

Description

The Practice: Marriott International has a history of success developing and enhancing systems that use existing market data to create forecasts for bookings for its properties. The system isolates the different market segments that use Marriott properties and provides a comprehensive understanding of those segments' reservations behavior, price sensitivity, and stay patterns. This information has enabled Marriott to optimize room revenue by increasing room sales.

Why the Practice Was Developed: Over the years, Marriott has been good at controlling costs. However, profits from the fixed inventory of hotel rooms can only gain so much through efficiency and cost control. Thus, Marriott chose to focus on maximizing top-line revenues — room sales — as a means to improve profits. The ability to successfully increase room sales, though, required a method of revealing meaningful patterns in the data.

Execution

The Approach to Implementation: In 1984, the company began by capturing room demand data concerning various market segments and invested in yield-management systems the following year. The proprietary software was jointly developed by the Marriott systems and Aeronomics Inc. (now part of Talus). Early yield-management approaches were simple, providing recommendations to open and close rates. Nevertheless, Marriott learned booking and stay patterns (e.g., the weekend getaway tends to be booked two to three weeks in advance, while the business traveler tends to book five to ten days in advance). The company gained greater control of inventory, and in 1991, the current yield-management system was developed. Fully integrated with the reservation system, it creates arrival demand forecasts and provides sophisticated inventory restriction recommendations.

An important aspect of the system is that guests will find no variation among distribution channels, for the system offers the same inventory and rate structure to all outlets. The system also produces overbooking recommendations for each property, factoring in cancellations, early departures and stay-overs. One system supports Marriott, Ritz-Carlton, and Renaissance properties, while a separate system serves Courtyard and Residence Inns and will extend to Fairfield Inns and TownePlace Suites properties.

The combined systems allow reservation and yield-management revenue to be maximized on each room sold, and provides the ability for Marriott to cross-sell its properties on a referral basis to both location-driven and tier-driven clientele.

Operational Issues: With the increased complexity of the revenue management systems, the reservations manager required additional training. The position, which has been upgraded to the equivalent of a director of sales, reports to the sales and marketing director.

Outcomes

Success of the Practice: The success of the practice is monumental. David Babich, vice president of revenue management, talks in terms of "hundreds of millions of dollars" in additional revenue that has resulted. Marriott anticipates increased revenues of 1% to 3%.

Other benefits include providing the properties with a better profile of the expected guests, and identifying weak occupancy periods for additional promotional efforts.

Benefits for Customer: Customers have benefited from Marriott's yield management, due to effective inventory control and pricing. Through the management of demand patterns, customers are more likely to find a room when they need it, and customers who are price sensitive can be accommodated on certain days when they might otherwise have been turned away.

Advice and Observations: Marriott is moving toward applying yield management in all areas. Mr. Babich indicates that revenue management is counter to the traditional hotel strategy, and requires a cultural change. Strong leadership from top management and extensive communication and education are required when adopting revenue management practices. Begin by valuing data on customer demand and segmentation, and use these data to improve inventory management and pricing.

Contact

David Babich, Vice President, Revenue Management
Marriott International
One Marriott Drive, Washington, DC 20058
Phone: 301-380-1517 Fax: 301-380-5728

MARRIOTT INTERNATIONAL

Sales Innovations Strategies

Description

The Practice: The Marriott International sales team has developed several innovative ways to make it easier, faster, simpler, and cheaper to book Marriott brands. Innovations include a customer-centric sales force, the ability to sell multiple brands, Event Booking Centers, the cross-selling of transient reservations, single-image inventory, on-line marketing, and linkages with travel agencies.

Why the Practice Was Developed: Marriott asked its customers what changes they would like to see in the way their business was transacted. At the same time, Marriott had recruited a number of sales and strategy professionals with experience in other industries, including Richard D. Hanks, executive vice president of sales. Together, this led Marriott to reevaluate the traditional industry approaches to sales, and to find new and better ways to approach sales in the lodging industry.

Execution

The Approach to Implementation: In the hotel industry, salespeople are customarily based in the hotel (hotel-centric) and they fly to customer locations to try and drive business into their hotels. Mr. Hanks points out that only in the hotel industry do the salespeople work in the "factory." Most other industries are customer-centric; that is, they attach a salesperson to a customer. Marriott is rapidly moving to complete the positioning of much of its sales force as customer-centric. In addition, another part of the sales force cross-sells Marriott's 11 brands in selling centers, which frees the salespeople from routine duties and allows them to concentrate on selling based on need and usage segmentation. Mr. Hanks notes, "Marriott has advanced market segmentation and occasion-driven use by providing different hotel experiences for the traveler." Marriott began the customer-centric practice by taking its top 30 accounts across all of its business, group and transient, and assigning them a specialty sales force that is focused on a stronger customer relationship than is customary. The goal of the sales force is not just to bring in additional room-nights, but to work with customers to help solve all of their business needs.

Marriott has sales forces representing the company around the world. These employees are also account based, sell all the brands, and have the ability to represent all 1,700 hotels. This group is able to penetrate both the association and the corporate markets. In addition, Marriott has a network of general sales agents (GSAs) who are not Marriott employees but represent Marriott in areas where it has not yet opened an office. Marriott has 39 sales and satellite locations around the world and 45 GSAs in countries in which it does not yet have an office.

One of the latest of Marriott's innovations is the creation of Event Booking Centers (EBCs). By the end of 1998, Marriott had opened 45 of these centers. These are small-meeting reservation centers used for booking 50 rooms or less. The customer telephone call goes to the booking center, not the hotel. Each center handles between 5 and 20 hotels of all brands to provide the customer with one-stop shopping. The center primarily offers meeting packages, but if the customer wants to negotiate each and every item, the center personnel will provide that service. If the requested property is unavailable, the center will pick another. Mr. Hanks says the goal of these centers is to handle 80% of the transactions that are small and routine; thereby freeing up the rest of the sales force to be account managers, proactively selling rather than sitting back and being order takers over the phone.

Marriott also just instituted cross-selling for transient guests, which is an important business segment for most locations. Similar to the EBCs, the sales force tries to find space with the brand requested within a 50-mile radius. If nothing is available, the sales force tries to satisfy the guest's need with another Marriott brand.

Marriott has "single-image inventory," meaning a customer who calls a reservation agent or a travel agent, uses the Internet, or calls the hotel directly will find the same inventory and the same rates. Marriott has used single-image inventory since 1984, whereas some of its competitors have announced the development of similar systems as recently as 1998.

Marriott has an interactive sales and marketing department that is primarily aimed at the GDSs. Marriott captures about 20% of the room-nights through the GDS, although it has only a 6% share of the rooms available on the system. In addition, Marriott maintains an Internet site that is currently growing about 12% a month in terms of reservations booked. The site will generate over $50 million for 1998.

Marriott also has a keen interest in the travel industry sales market. The firm participates in about 200 trade shows a year and is continually involved with travel agencies. As part of this involvement, Marriott has created the "Hotel Excellence" program, which is a comprehensive travel agent training course on how to effectively sell a hotel. The course incorporates Marriott brands in demonstrating the effectiveness of segmentation and occasion-driven use in determining the right hotel to meet the customer's needs.

Outcomes

Success of the Practice: The Marriott sales force has been ranked as the only lodging chain to appear in the top 25 by *Sales and Marketing* magazine for the past two years. American Society of Travel Agents recognizes Marriott as number one for best payment of commissions, and it ranked number one for responsiveness and helpfulness in the industry.

Benefits for Customer: The benefits to the customer are speed, convenience, availability, and trusted relationships.

Insights

Advice and Observations: Mr. Hanks notes, "Many times hoteliers forget they are doing the bidding of customers." Hotel companies often start with what they have and try to sell that to the customer, rather than selling what the customer wants to buy. "Some customers want speed and convenience; others want high-touch, low-tech; while others want a consultative sales approach." Sales and marketing must determine what customers want, and then fulfill that want.

Hotel salespeople must be "customer- and solutions-oriented business people, instead of Willie Loman commission closers," states Mr. Hanks. Furthermore, salespeople should not be based in the hotels, but based where the customers are. The industry needs to become customer-centric versus hotel-centric.

Regarding future directions, Mr. Hanks believes the industry will have to continue "upskilling" its sales force to compete for the best employees in the worldwide labor market.

Contact

Richard Hanks, Executive Vice President of Sales
Marriott International
Marriott Drive, Washington, DC 20058
Phone: 301-380-6734   Fax: 301-380-2237

MARRIOTT INTERNATIONAL

Successful Creation of New Brands

Description

The Practice: Marriott International is the recognized leader in the creation, development, and marketing of brand names of properties within the hospitality industry. Its success has been fueled in part by the process used to determine the desirability and feasibility of creating a new brand of hotels.

Why the Practice Was Developed: Marriott defined a process for creating new brands because it recognizes that the type of hotel used by a customer is often occasion driven. Hence, Marriott wants to have a strong presence in most hotel segments. Achievement of this objective is facilitated by Marriott's marketing strength, arguably the strongest in the industry, which is capable of introducing and sustaining new brands better than its competition.

Execution

The Approach to Implementation: Marriott uses an integrated approach led by multiple disciplines yielding a well-rounded perspective. At Marriott, this includes the following constituencies: brand management, franchising, development, finance, market management, architecture, and construction. This leads not only to the best answer for the customer and the portfolio, but also the franchise and financial community. At first glance, Marriott's approach to creating a new brand appears to be simplistic, but it is actually a complex process involving many interrelated factors and processes. They are:

- Define and research the competition within the appropriate segment. What is Marriott's segment market share? Which chains are aging and vulnerable? What are Marriott's competitors' strategies and focus, likelihood of success, development activity, possible acquisition candidates, positioning, and product features?
- Define and categorize existing and future market segments and the demographics of those segments. Study future customer trends to identify unanswered gaps or needs not currently being addressed in the marketplace. Examples: full service, limited service, business vs. leisure, female travelers, suites (full and limited in-room amenities), short-term vs. long-term stays.
- Identify the market segments that are aging and vulnerable (i.e., the segments that have the oldest and lowest valued properties).
- Determine how the new brand fits into Marriott's marketing structure and imaging.

- Conduct focus groups with consumers for suggestions and reactions.
- Determine interest in the new brand by existing and possible future franchisees. They are included in the creative process not only to generate enthusiasm for the end product but also because of franchisees' ability to identify and react to change in consumer behavior, bringing fresh insights to Marriott.
- Determine rates of return through various indices used by investment constituencies. Compare potential returns to other Marriott International brands and those of competitors.
- Determine the acceptance of the new brand by the financial community, such as Wall Street, REITs, lenders, institutional investors, and individual investors. If the brand or its market position is perceived unfavorably, as the economy segment presently is (either rightly or wrongly), the brand will not succeed because of a lack of available funds to develop the properties.
- Estimate potential market demand and share at different price points, determine the sources of business, and evaluate interaction with existing Marriott brands.
- Estimate eventual number of units and impact on earnings per share.
- Consider international growth potential.
- Consider how the new brand would fit into and affect future lodging products being contemplated by Marriott.
- Determine the appropriate image of the new brand, including name, logo, and color scheme.

Success of the Practice: This process has resulted in the creation of successful brands, including Courtyard, Fairfield Inns, and TownePlace Suites by Marriott.

More recently, Marriott has applied this process to a rebranding strategy. Fairfield Suites was introduced as a brand extension of Fairfield Inns in 1996. By 1998 there had been significant changes in the industry and competitive environment. Marriott had seven Fairfield Suites hotels open, with commensurate franchisee feedback, performance numbers, and consumer reaction available.

Based on this information, it appeared that the concept might be better positioned in the moderate tier to maximize its potential for all stakeholders. Accordingly, Marriott undertook the process just described to determine whether this was an appropriate strategy. Specifically, it found the following:

- The product was already solidly positioned in the moderate tier, based on ADR ($75), customer profile, and source of business.
- The "all-suite" market had a demographically different target audience than the traditional "room" segment. The customer composition is younger, more female, more leisure-oriented, and more likely to travel with children. This is a market where Marriott was underrepresented.
- There is an upside average rate potential with a different name (which would connote a moderate-tier position) attached to the suites modifier.
- The moderate tier is sizable, populated with older hotels and vulnerable to a well-conceived all-suite product.
- There was no clear leader in the moderate-tier all-suite segment; it is a market in which Marriott should capture significant share with a distinct brand.
- Franchisees indicated strong support for pursuing a new Marriott brand in the segment.

Therefore, Marriott made the decision to undertake a new Marriott-endorsed brand in the moderate-tier all-suite segment. The new brand, SpringHill Suites by Marriott, was introduced in November 1998. There are now 17 properties open and 51 under development, as of January 1999.

Benefits for Customer: New Marriott brands provide properties catering to demographic markets not previously served by Marriott, thereby creating an opportunity for the traveler to stay at a Marriott property.

For franchisees, there are more brands through which to grow their Marriott portfolio and leverage existing market penetration.

Finally, this practice serves Marriott International and shareholders by providing incremental EPS growth through additional units that otherwise would have been developed under a competitive flag.

Insights

Advice and Observations: Joe Lavin, senior vice president of franchising, had this advice to offer: Ensure that all the implementation steps are complete and that franchisee and customer support is in place. Think outside the box; do not be constrained by old paradigms: Nothing is impossible. Recognize the delicate balance between guest satisfaction and investment in the product.

Contacts

Joe Lavin
Senior Vice President, Franchising
Marriott International, Marriott Drive, Dept. 944.52
Washington, DC 20058
Phone: 301-380-4026 Fax: 301-380-2225

Kathy Townsend, Brand Vice President
SpringHill Suites by Marriott
Marriott International, Marriott Drive, Dept. 955.74
Washington, DC 20058
Phone: 301-380-3775 Fax: 301-380-8668

MARRIOTT U.S. POSTAL SERVICE CONFERENCE CENTER

Express Check-in on Hotel Airport Shuttle Buses

Description

The Practice: To expedite check-ins and avoid delays at the airport, the Marriott U.S. Postal Service Conference Center in Norman, Oklahoma, has instituted a practice that allows guests to complete their hotel check-in procedure when they board the shuttle bus going from the airport to the hotel. This practice reduces the number of "waits" the guest might otherwise encounter.

Why the Practice Was Developed: Two factors triggered the institution of this practice. First, the hotel is located some 23 miles from the airport requiring a 30-minute ride. Second, shuttle buses wait at the airport for 30 minutes before departing for the hotel. Therefore, some guests, who arrive at the bus stop at the same time the bus arrives at the airport, could possibly wait a half-hour on the bus before getting underway for the 30-minute trip to the hotel. At which point, guests would then have to "waste" additional time registering at the front desk. The goal of this practice was to reduce the amount of time guests expended from the time of their arrival at the airport until they were able to enter their rooms.

Execution

Implementation of Practice: Dan Gallant, director of rooms and reservations, the general manager, and the night manager were primarily responsible for implementing the bus check-in service. Prior to instituting this practice, arriving guests were personally interviewed about hotel registration procedures, and a Guest Service Index (GSI), placed in each guestroom, also queried respondents about the conference center's check-in process. With 950 available guestrooms and average check-ins running between 250 and 600 rooms per day, an improved check-in procedure was determined a must for this property.

To enable the guest to register in the bus, the driver is supplied with a canvas bag that contains a voucher imprinter for credit cards and room keys for the guestrooms. These rooms have been pre-blocked by the front office staff. The guest can go directly to the assigned room upon arrival; the identity of the guest in each room is eventually obtained from the credit card imprint made at the airport. Periodically, management makes trips to the airport to personally review the bus check-in procedure and to ensure it is properly carried out.

Outcomes

Success of the Practice: The results of this program have all been positive, as indicated by GSI scores that run between 94 and 96. The conference center is limited to accepting postal employees, with very few isolated exceptions. Consequently, postal employees make up 98% of the guests. Occupancy averages 70% on weekdays and 45% on weekends.

Insights

Advice and Observations: Mr. Gallant is not sure this practice would be beneficial to all airport facilities. He felt that a hotel would have to have a large number of arrivals each day. Furthermore, some hotels may not approve such a practice because the identity of the guest in each room is not immediately known.

Mr. Gallant further suggests that the vehicles used for transportation should have a minimum capacity of 24-25 people.

Contact

Dan Gallant, Director of Rooms and Reservations
Marriott U.S. Postal Service Conference Center
2801 East State Highway 9, Norman, OK 73071-1104
Phone: 405-447-9100 Fax: 405-366-1865

MINNEAPOLIS-ST. PAUL HILTON

Line Employee Empowerment

Description

The Practice: The Minneapolis-St. Paul Hilton allows its line employees to make any decision involving guest satisfaction. Whenever there is any problem, question, or complaint from a guest, the practice empowers the employee confronted with the problem to do whatever has to be done to resolve the situation to the complete satisfaction of the guest. While this practice began at the front desk, it has spread to all of the guest contact areas including bar, restaurant, housekeeping, and maintenance.

Why the Practice Was Developed: When he came to the hotel some 14 months ago as front-office manager, Patrick Simpson found that, as a matter of policy, any problems that were brought to the attention of a front-desk contact person by a guest had to be referred to the shift supervisor. In many cases, further referral to the department head was pursued, causing unseemly delay and further guest irritation. Even a small problem, such as a request for a late checkout, had to follow this procedure. Invariably, solutions to guest problems, minor as they may be, could take 10 minutes or more. Guest dissatisfaction with these procedures was evident in guest comments, both written and oral. Mr. Simpson noted that the general manager, being of the old school, liked the going-through-channels procedure and saw no reason to change.

Execution

The Approach to Implementation: Upon the departure of this general manager, Mr. Simpson, the current director of front-office operations, discussed the concept of empowering employees to achieve greater customer satisfaction with the department heads and line supervisors. A "few" of the department heads, of which there are 13, as well as some of the supervisors were reluctant to endorse this practice, as they felt their authority might be compromised. On the other hand, the guest service staff, numbering about 50, was enthusiastic about being given the responsibility and right to solve situations immediately.

Implementation was begun at a 20-minute meeting of the front-office staff in which the practice was described and discussed. Of concern to the staff were repercussions from the management resulting from a staff decision that might cause an internal problem. The staff was absolutely assured that no employee would ever be criticized or condemned for solving any problem immediately to the satisfaction of the guest. Other departments took from four to six months to adopt the practice.

No trial time or test period specifics were considered. Further, no customers or owners of the franchise operation were involved in either the planning or execution of this practice. Mr. Simpson's practice was unconditionally adopted with, as he says, "both feet first." Not surprisingly, in its initial execution,

the staff members exhibited some hesitancy until they were sure that the "no criticism" promise was being carried out.

A new general manager was brought in two months after the previous one left. He immediately and wholeheartedly endorsed Mr. Simpson's practice, which had been adopted one month earlier.

Operational Issues: Several specific applications of this policy serve as examples to further explain the extent to which empowerment has been carried out, but these examples also illustrate how operational issues must be coordinated to provide the desired level of customer satisfaction:

1 In the case of a "walk," traditional industry policy has been to provide transportation to another property, one night's lodging, and phone calls for the unfortunate guest. Mr. Simpson's employees have further empowerment to authorize a second night's payment at the referred hotel if the guest so desires. Mr. Simpson follows that up with a letter guaranteeing a free night at his hotel the next time the guest is in town.

2 Any problem with a guestroom is immediately handled through a "Priority Card," either given to a maid or dropped at the desk. These cards must be the maintenance department's highest priority, so much so that they guarantee the problem will be handled within thirty minutes. Once the problem is taken care of, maintenance leaves a note for the guest saying "we came running as soon as we heard."

3 Dining room and beverage servers are now authorized on their own to comp food and/or beverages that are not to the guest's satisfaction. Mr. Simpson adds that guest abuses of such largesse are nonexistent, and reaction to this empowerment is extremely positive.

A final operational issue involved staffing. Mr. Simpson had noticed that his staff tended to be very similar to each other in age, ethnicity, and social status — almost clones, as he perceived it. He felt that staff changes, as they became necessary as a result of routine attrition, would be best served by a more diverse group with dissimilar backgrounds and thinking, thus enabling them to react better to more unusual guest problems. This proved to be the case.

Costs: The costs have been small. Any lost revenue (extra room night, comped food) has been more than covered by increased guest satisfaction and the resultant sales.

Outcomes

There are no changes planned in this program, nor have there been any since its inception and development. "It has worked and continues to do so," says Mr. Simpson.

Success of the Practice: Within two months of the program's inception, the results began to come in. Guest comment cards began to show dramatic positive results and that trend has continued. Since Mr. Simpson's arrival, occupancy on the executive level has gone from 83% to 89% and the ADR from $89 to $101. He and his general manager estimate savings of "thousands of dollars" in advertising, training, and other expenses. New employees of the diverse backgrounds mentioned earlier are staying longer, which has curtailed the necessity for recruiting, advertising, and training. Expenses have been decreased since employee retention has been at a high level.

While it is difficult to be specific, Mr. Simpson indicates morale among his departments is at an all-time high. He has "sporadically" been asked to consult with others of his franchise group regarding this practice, and has spoken at the University of Wisconsin's School of Hospitality Management.

Benefits for Customer: Guests now expect an immediate solution to any problem. Their experiences elsewhere have programmed their thinking into expecting hassles and delays. This practice eliminates those. For example, Mr. Simpson tells of one case when a guest approached him seeking a late check-out privilege. Mr. Simpson advised the guest that the room clerk would take care of it. The guest's response of, "Won't she have to check with someone?" was met by Mr. Simpson's response of, "Not in this hotel!"

Insights

Advice and Observations: Mr. Simpson believes empowerment makes an employee more aware of his or her own worth. The trust between staff and management towards the goal of superior guest service unites them in what might otherwise be an adversarial relationship.

The confidence of the employee so empowered radiates in his or her guest contact ability, which in turn gives the guest confidence that his or her stay will be a rewarding experience.

Contact

Patrick Simpson, Director of Front Office Operations
(Prior to publication of this study, Mr. Simpson
left his position at the property.)
Minneapolis-St. Paul Hilton Airport
3800 E. 80th Street, Bloomington, MN 55425
Phone: 800-637-7453 or 612-854-2100   Fax: 612-854-8002

MOTEL 6

Developing a Memorable and Effective Advertising Message

The Practice: More than a decade ago, Motel 6 introduced its "we'll leave the light on for you" advertising campaign. The theme of the campaign was to emphasize Motels 6's low prices and value in a down-home, friendly, hospitable, no-frills presentation that would clearly identify Motel 6 as a major player in the budget market. Many years later, this advertising campaign is still helping Motel 6 maintain a high occupancy rate within the budget segment.

Why the Practice Was Developed: In 1986 the Motel 6 advertising agency, The Richards Group from Dallas, was instructed to come up with a national advertising campaign to reverse declining occupancy by creating an appealing brand image for value. Prior to the inception of the program, whatever advertising existed was planned and executed on the local level at each individual property. There was no attempt being made to have a cohesive chainwide presentation.

Execution

The Approach to Implementation: The Richards Group believed a spokesperson would have to be selected whose voice could carry the folksy image it wished to project on radio. Radio was to be the sole carrier of the spots, as Motel 6 did not begin television advertising until 1996. Richards retained Tom Bodett, a resident of Homer, Alaska, who was a writer and radio personality in his own right. At the same time, the concept of "we'll leave the light on for you" was developed as a theme to emphasize the unpretentious value of the product, as well as the homespun theme. The Richards Group worked with the Motel 6 marketing department to develop a media plan.

The original spots were designed to focus only on value. The bold statement of a clean room at the lowest price was emphasized in the first phase of the radio promotion. In the early 1990s, a second phase took shape. The spots began to feature the addition of some basic amenities, including the acceptance of credit cards and televisions and telephones in the room. Other amenities have since been added such as dataports, guest laundry, HBO and ESPN, free morning coffee, pools, and fax machine availability.

A third phase took place in the mid-'90s as an extensive room renovation program was begun. Scripts and tone were altered to stress these new features, always keeping in mind that the folksy theme was to be a watchword for the continuous image as well as a unified consistent strategy of keeping current without losing the down-home appeal.

Costs: Motel 6 is now spending close to $30 million on media, marketing, advertising, reservations, and collateral. Most spots are purchased for national radio and TV, with costs varying from city to city. Market buys change constantly and are updated as need dictates. The chain's 50 franchise holders are assessed 3% of rooms sales for the advertising programs, and the balance of the funds comes from general revenue.

Outcomes

Success of the Practice: On a scale of 1 to 10, Carol Kirby, executive vice president of marketing and sales, rates the program as a 10. When the advertising campaign was originally introduced, occupancy went up 8 points in 18 months. Motel 6 still outperforms its competition in occupancy. Current occupancy is 66.5% with an ADR of $37.50. Customer acceptance has been monumental, as "we'll leave the light on for you" has become a catch phrase.

The advertising campaign has provided a sometimes funny but always consistent message. Mr. Bodett still does the voice-over for the spots. The ad campaign has won seven CLIO awards, plus more than 100 other honors, including Mercury and Galaxy, making it the most decorated campaign in lodging history. Television now consumes 65% of the media budget, with radio making up the remainder.

Benefits for Customer: Those customers seeking value at a budget price recognize Motel 6 as the leading candidate for their business.

Advice and Observations: Most hotel chain advertising is fairly generic, Ms. Kirby states. She observes that hotel advertising, as a rule, does not engender thoughts of a specific hotel company. The typical presentation with the smiling couple in the guestroom or around the pool generally applies to any and all hospitality companies. Motel 6's approach, on the other hand, is objective with a specific factual statement that it is the lowest-price national chain.

Contact

Carol Kirby, Executive Vice President of Marketing and Sales
Motel 6
14651 Dallas Parkway, Ste. 500, Dallas, TX 75240
Phone: 972-702-6990   Fax: 972-386-4017

MOTEL 6

Training Employees for General Management

The Practice: Motel 6 established an employee-development program that makes every employee eligible for consideration as a general manager. This program consists of three phases: cross-training, manager-on-duty, and general management training. It works as follows:

Phase 1: Cross-Training Program. Every employee of the hotel, whether in housekeeping, laundry, maintenance, or front office, is made aware of his or her potential to be a general manager. A booklet has been printed and is distributed to every employee describing in a pie chart each operating department's function and importance to the success of the hotel's operation. By showing an interest in and becoming cross-trained to work in all other departments, employees can be considered for promotion and become qualified as candidates for the manager-on-duty (MOD) program.

Phase 2: Manager-on-Duty Program. Fully cross-trained employees who show the potential for and interest in general management are selected for the MOD program. First, the employees are given a training manual to learn all facets of a general manager's duties and responsibilities. After a self-study period, a general manager from another Motel 6 in the area tests the employees, who become certified as managers-on-duty if they pass. They are qualified to be acting manager for a day or an extended period of several days at the discretion of the general manager. During this period as interim manager, they are compensated at a higher rate.

Phase 3: General Manager Assignment. If employees successfully complete phases 1 and 2, they can be appointed to full-time general-manager positions. Prior to taking over a hotel, potential general managers receive an in-depth, five-week training program in one of Motel 6's regional training offices, as well as in the assigned hotel.

Why the Practice Was Developed: Joe Eulberg, senior vice president of human resources, joined the Motel 6 chain in 1992. At the time, the hotels were managed by teams (most often, husbands and wives). Indeed, the general manager's position was advertised as, "Management team wanted, includes one-bedroom apartment." This approach did not obtain the type of qualified manager needed to manage these hotels into the future. Issues of nepotism arose when one spouse worked for the other, and the image of "Ma and Pa Kettle" managing a hotel was out of date. Mr. Eulberg believed that a "qualified" manager, rather than a management team, was a better model for managing Motel 6 hotels. To help fill the need for such qualified managers, the employee-development program was begun.

The Approach to Implementation: Prior to implementation, the human resources team gained the complete backing of Motel 6's president and executive officers. The actual implementation of this program was "evolutionary rather than revolutionary." The transition or gradual replacement of management couples was based on natural attrition, not outright termination (absent a justifiable cause). By spring 1998, employees who had come up from the ranks were managing over 300 of Motel 6's 760 hotels. Fewer than 70 hotels are still being managed by couples, while the balance are being directed by managers hired from outside sources.

One of the major keys to the success of this program is the five regional offices located near major metropolitan areas (i.e., San Francisco, Dallas, Phoenix, Atlanta, and Chicago). Each corporate office is located in close proximity to a Motel 6 hotel and is staffed by a regional vice president, training manager, and human resources manager. The training manager is directly involved in employee development, especially in the first phases of the program.

Operational Issues: One of the major issues was the transition from a Mom-and-Pop team management concept to professional management. Even though only 60 to 70 couples remain as managers, Mr. Eulberg maintains there were no unusual repercussions from the departure of so many management couples, especially since the attrition occurred over a five-year period.

Outcomes

Success of the Practice: The benefits achieved from promotion from within can be contrasted with the $6,000-$10,000 cost involved in bringing a new manager from the outside. Further, this program has created a pool of available management personnel who otherwise might not have the opportunity to be considered for a management position. The program also creates a new incentive for hotel employees to get ahead, and it improves the diversity of the general manager population. Finally, there has been a 10% drop in employee turnover since this program started.

Benefits for Customer: Motel 6 conducts an annual market-research program, usually during the summer months, that asks 1,000 guests key questions about their hotel stays. The research emphasis is on quality of service and product. There is also a program of systematic quality measurement conducted by "anonymous" inspectors. As Motel 6 has provided the guest with more professional management practices over the past few years, positive responses have increased from 62% to 90%.

Insights

Advice and Observations: Mr. Eulberg offers this advice for others who are implementing similar promotion-from-within programs: First, be willing to hire better people — even those who are "overqualified." The goal is to obtain employees who are promotable. Second, ask and encourage all employees to participate in the development program. Many employees may be "diamonds in the rough," who just have not applied for training simply because they have not been asked to do so. Third, be ferocious about consistent cross-training of employees. To achieve this goal, Motel 6 assesses its property managers on their willingness and ability to train their staff. In addition, the bonuses of managers are held until they complete reviews on all their employees.

Contact

Joe Eulberg, Senior Vice President
Motel 6
14651 Dallas Parkway, Dallas, TX 75240
Phone: 972-702-6801 Fax: 972-702-5996

MOTEL PROPERTIES INC.

Employee Recognition Program

Description

The Practice: Motel Properties, Inc., of Jekyll Island, Georgia, provides each employee with recognition from the time of the initial interview and throughout his or her employment. Examples of recognition include free dinners for the employee and a companion at one of the company restaurants, cards sent to the homes of employees after hiring, birthday cards sent to employees' homes, Employee-of-the-Month awards, newspaper ads plus $50, and Certificates of Honor.

Why the Practice Was Developed: The recognition practice originated as a means of increasing employee retention. The unemployment rate in the area is less than 3%, and there is a shortage of available applicants for job openings. The focus on employee recognition was designed to curb turnover, while increasing employee satisfaction and, in turn, increasing customer satisfaction.

Execution

The Approach to Implementation: Mike Akers, vice president of operations, was the catalyst for the program. He created the management team — consisting of the directors of resort properties, interstate properties, operations, sales, marketing, accounting, facilities, and human resources — which then developed and implemented the recognition concept. The management team formulated the practice, then discussed changes and made additions. The department of human resources is the working force behind the concept, but it is the management team that selects the Employee of the Month.

Each time a new idea emerges, the human resources department analyzes and implements it, and then drops any idea that has proven to be ineffective. The management team has sustained the recognition program by consistently integrating it into the company's operations, structure, and culture.

Operational Issues: Initially, the managers of many properties resisted the idea; they did not want to spend the time and money that was involved. Initial concerns also occurred in the food and beverage departments, although these departments have had the most success with the recognition program.

In addition to the recognition program, Motel Properties, Inc., sought to increase employee retention by creating job security. On Jekyll Island, where several of its properties are located, employee layoffs in the hospitality industry are common due to the seasonality of tourism. Motel Properties, Inc., however, made a decision not to follow this trend, but to retain its employees even during the low season.

Costs: The cost of implementing the recognition program has not been established, but there are obvious positive returns, according to Janice Cook, director of human resources. The additional resources that have been needed are time, meals, awards, mailings, and other minor things.

Outcomes

Success of the Practice: Ms. Cook notes that the recognition program has been a great success. Employee retention has increased, revenues are higher, and the bottom line is greatly improved. A competitive advantage has been established, as image, efficiency, and quality are now evident at the properties. Employees are pleased with the practice, yet the cost to the company has been minimal. All sides have benefited from the recognition program.

Benefits for Customer: Although the impact on customers has not been directly measured, customers are happier. They have communicated their positive impressions about the properties, particularly in regard to the front desk, the food outlets, and housekeeping.

Insights

Advice and Observations: Ms. Cook recommends more measurement of the program's effectiveness be undertaken. Further, she notes that the practice must be continually managed; in addition, employees must be treated consistently and equally.

173

Ms. Cook reports that the recognition program did not work for Manager of the Year. Some managers felt the program was only a popularity contest and they were not happy with it.

Finally, Ms. Cook states that it is important to continually add to, perfect, and monitor the recognition program. She says, "If we were starting now, we would not do anything different or change the process."

Contact

Janice Cook, Director of Human Resources
Motel Properties, Inc.
85 Bendview Drive, Jekyll Island, GA 31527
Phone: 912-635-4715 Fax: 912-635-3230

NEW YORK MARRIOTT FINANCIAL CENTER

Regular Status Meetings Between the Hotel Executive Committee and Department Management Teams

Description

The Practice: The New York Marriott Financial Center organized a program in which one day per month is reserved for the executive committee members to meet with department management teams on their financial status and current month's results. Each department team is responsible for its department's results and prepares for the monthly interviews with the executive committee by graphing results. The purpose of this program is to make department teams accountable for their own departmental results. If all departments improve, there should be an overall improvement for the hotel. This format also facilitates recognition of team improvements.

Why the Practice Was Developed: In 1995 Dan Flannery, hotel manager, attended a two-day re-engineering forum which included a presentation by New York Police Commissioner William Bratton. The purpose of his presentation was to discuss the police department's approach to managing the various internal departments and to ensuring the accountability of the staff. After attending this two-day forum, Mr. Flannery came to the conclusion that this process could be adapted and made workable in the hotel industry.

Commissioner Bratton established a practice in which each of the 72 precincts was responsible for its own results. To increase accountability for each precinct, Commissioner Bratton instituted COMSTAT (communicate status) meetings. During monthly meetings, the top brass of the police department interviews the senior officers of the individual precincts to determine how successful each precinct has been in reducing crime in New York in three focus areas: (1) reduction of overall crime, (2) reduction of violent crime, and (3) reduction of fear crime. Each precinct tracks its progress in each area, which allows the police staff to determine whether the crime rate is increasing or decreasing in their precincts. When the crime rate is increasing in any precinct, the department staff tries to find out why it is increasing and take the proper steps to reverse this trend. In recent years the crime rate has dropped dramatically in New York, and Commissioner Bratton attributes much of this success to the focus and accountability of the COMSTAT process.

Execution

The Approach to Implementation: Mr. Flannery was so impressed with what was being done in the New York Police Department that he decided to use this practice in his hotel. He discussed the plan with his executive committee. The program was adapted to focus on three strategic areas in the hospitality industry: (1) associate (employee) morale, (2) guest satisfaction, and (3) financial results.

A Trial: The sales, engineering, front office, housekeeping, kitchen, restaurant, room service, and banquet departments were selected to implement the program. At the end of the six-month trial period, the executive committee felt that these departments had responded positively to this strategic approach. After the practice had been in effect for one year, the Financial Center and World Trade Center Marriott hotels merged management teams and now this program is used in both hotels.

Both hotels now set aside a day for the executive committee to meet with each department team concerning the month's results, and to compare current results to last year's outcomes. The executive committee first and foremost reviews the financial results for each department, a process known as a critique meeting. The department head is responsible for the budget in his or her department and has to present an exceptional reason for failing to achieve budgeted results. Each department head develops a graph for his or her department and brings the graph up to date before each monthly meeting. Currently, the graphs each department head presents to the executive committee indicate a successful trend. In addition to financial results, the department heads are questioned about what they have accomplished to improve guest satisfaction and employee morale. Normally, an hour is sufficient for each department head to meet with the executive committee, except the food and beverage department, which meets for $1^1/_2$ hours because of its greater complexity. Commitments made to action steps are documented and followed up in the next COMSTAT meeting.

Costs: There is no cost to this practice, except that it requires computers to complete the reports and graphs.

Outcomes

Success of the Practice: Establishing greater departmental accountability and responsibility has been so successful for this hotel that the Marriott Marquis Hotel in midtown Manhattan and the Marriott World Trade Center have started to use the same practice. Additionally, the Marriott Financial Center has received numerous company awards over the past three years, including national awards for team initiatives and highest associate opinion surveys.

Benefits for Customer: There are 51 scores for quality assurance ratings from the guests; over 43 of the 51 possible scores improved in 1998.

Insights

Advice and Observations: Mr. Flannery states that if he established the practice again, he would set aside a longer time for the executive committee's monthly interview of the department heads. He believes the department heads receive valuable experience in the operation of the hotel during this interview, and that one hour was insufficient for them to attain a comprehensive understanding of some of the operational procedures. Mr. Flannery suggests that department heads be able to review departmental capital expenditures during the meeting to update their progress on these initiatives.

Contact

Dan Flannery, Hotel Manager
New York Marriott Financial Center
85 West Street, New York, NY 10006
Phone: 212-385-4900   Fax: 212-266-6118

NEWARK GATEWAY HILTON

Guest Check-in on the Shuttle Bus

Description

The Practice: The Newark Gateway Hilton currently offers *Mobile Zip-in Check-in* for its hotel guests. When guests arrive at the airport and board the shuttle bus, they are automatically checked into the hotel via their credit card or Hilton HHonors card. Each shuttle bus carries a global positioning device, which tracks the location of the van, and a card reader, which tracks the guest's arrival via wireless communication with the front desk. This practice expedites the check-in process by eliminating the need to stop at the front desk upon arrival at the hotel.

Why the Practice Was Developed: Consumer research conducted by Hilton Hotels indicated a need to facilitate the check-in process for the guest. Further, improved check-in procedures represented an opportunity to incrementally increase the level of service quality Hilton offers.

Execution

The Approach to Implementation: The idea for an express check-in service originated with the president of Hilton Hotels. Acting upon this suggestion, the Newark Gateway Hilton formed a cross-functional team representing front office, security, housekeeping, finance, sales and marketing, and reservations. John Luke, vice president of front-office operations and systems, remarked that it was important to involve these departments in particular, so that each area affected by the decision would have some input into the process. After brainstorming for approximately one month, the team developed the *Mobile Zip-in Check-in* program. The program was implemented in February 1998.

Operational Issues: When boarding any of the hotel's airport buses, the guest presents a credit card or Hilton HHonors card. This information is relayed via wireless communication to a specific workstation at the hotel's front desk, where the guest's name and credit card are displayed on the computer monitor. At this time, the guest's pre-prepared key packet is retrieved. The guest is then greeted at the hotel's front door by a hotel team member and handed his/her key packet. The guest can then continue straight to his or her room, bypassing the front desk completely.

Outcomes

Success of the Practice: With the implementation of this process, overall guest satisfaction has improved, as indicated by guest comment cards. Further, the practice sets a tone of operational efficiency from the outset of the guest's stay at the hotel.

Benefits for Customer: Fifty percent of the guests do not stop by the front desk; thus, the check-in process is much easier and less time-consuming.

Insights

Advice and Observations: Mr. Luke notes that this practice was a response to a customer need, as identified in Hilton's research; consequently, customers have supported the project from day one. Based on the praise guests have given the service, Hilton is in the process of expanding this service to its other airport sites.

Not only has the incoming guest benefited from this practice, but departing park-n-fly guests have also been better served. The card reader aboard the shuttle identifies guests on the shuttle to the parking attendant back at the hotel garage, so that the guests' cars are ready to go when they arrive at the parking area. Additionally, the global positioning device identifies the exact location of the shuttle. Team members can then determine the exact arrival time of the shuttle to the hotel and be in position to greet the guests as they depart the shuttle.

Contact

John Luke
Vice President of Front Office Operations & Systems
Hilton Hotels Corporation
9336 Civic Center, Beverly Hills, CA 90210
Phone: 310-205-4452 Fax: 310-205-4437

OMNI HOTELS

Integrated Property Management and Revenue Management System

Description

The Practice: Omni Hotels is in the process of integrating a company-wide property management system (PMS) in its Omaha-based reservations system to produce a fully integrated, highly efficient reservations system that also includes a state-of-the-art revenue management system (RMS). The RMS, also known as OmniCHARM (centralized hotel automated revenue management), was especially designed to work with Omni Hotels' new PMS and reservations center.

Each night, all Omni Hotels properties feed their reservations data into OmniCHARM via the central reservation information system. OmniCHARM then formulates length-of-stay restrictions to help Omni Hotels maximize rooms availability and revenue. The data are computer analyzed to determine selling strategies for each of the hotels regarding rates, length of stay, and weekdays vs. weekends. This information can be projected into the future as far as Omni Hotels wishes.

Why the Practice Was Developed: The primary reason for developing the practice was to maximize company-wide rooms revenue by improving efficiencies and, in the process, Omni Hotels' return on investment. Taking advantage of new technology allowed Omni Hotels the opportunity to develop this practice at an affordable rate. (Heretofore, handling and analyzing large amounts of reservations and forecasting data on a daily basis were impossible. If done on a weekly or monthly basis, the data were of little value by the time they became available.) Other benefits from the practice include significantly improved customer-service levels.

Execution

The Approach to Implementation: The installation of the new PMS and the development of OmniCHARM began in 1996 when the company was acquired by Texas-based TRT Holdings. Recognizing the importance of investing in technology to maximize overall company efficiency levels, Omni Hotels' new ownership and management set out on a course to create a PMS/RMS that would be the benchmark for and the envy of the hotel industry. The development team was headed by a newly created, corporate-appointed revenue management team located at the company's reservations center in Omaha. Over the next year, the revenue management team worked closely with property general managers, rooms division managers, sales managers, and PMS and RMS creators (MAI Systems and Talus Corporation, respectively). Based on property feedback, Talus created a system using user-friendly, Windows NT-based software — a significant improvement from the complicated RMS currently in use by the industry. In addition to creating a user-friendly system on which it would be easy to train people, Omni Hotels made the decision to conduct beta testing of the system before installing it company-wide, thereby avoiding many of the pitfalls experienced by some of its competitors. Omni Hotels installed the system for

test purposes at two hotels in Dallas and Chicago. These installations were completed in June and September 1998. Following successful test runs, the systems will be installed at all Omni Hotels beginning first with those properties that will benefit from it most.

According to Dennis Hulsing, senior vice president for sales and marketing, Omni Hotels expects to have the new PMS/RMS fully integrated throughout the company by the fourth quarter of 1999.

Operational Issues: Because the new PMS/RMS replaces each property's existing PMS, a corporate installer and MAI Systems representative will need to spend approximately two weeks on-site installing the PMS and conducting the necessary staff training, followed by a week of installation and training on the RMS by a Talus representative and corporate revenue management director.

Costs: The development and installation of the new PMS/RMS has cost Omni Hotels between $4 and $5 million.

Success of the Practice: Omni Hotels anticipates revenue increases from 3% to 7% once the new PMS/RMS is in place.

Benefits for Customer: Because of the company-wide room data that will be funneled into the central reservations center database each day, Omni Hotels expects guest service levels to increase. This way, a guest who stays at the Omni Hotel in Houston on a Monday night and then checks in at the Omni Hotel in Dallas the next night can expect to automatically receive the same special requests or services he or she requested the night before. Because guest information is processed nightly in the system database, specific customer information becomes available to all Omni Hotels reservations agents and front desk operators. This database allows Omni Hotels to better serve its customers by staying current on what its customers want and expect from Omni Hotels.

Other benefits from the installation of the new PMS/RMS include significant reductions in hotel overbookings. As a result, hotels will be able to minimize having to "walk" guests to other hotels due to lack of availability, thereby inconveniencing fewer guests.

Dennis Hulsing, Senior Vice President for Sales & Marketing
Omni Hotels
420 Decker Drive, Suite 200, Irving, TX 75062
Phone: 972-871-5624   Fax: 972-871-5667
Email: dhulsing@omnihotels.com

Insights

Advice and Observations: For companies considering developing and installing similar systems, Mr. Hulsing advises:

- Go into it with the mindset that the process is a long-term investment and recognize the probable need for improvements and changes in technology down the road
- Devise systems that work with your company's own nuances and be sure to leave room for the ability to tweak information manually
- Create user-friendly systems on which people can be easily trained
- Hire analytical and business management-minded people to oversee the PMS/RMS at the property level
- Be prepared to review current business processes and make changes
- Also, be prepared to develop a business transition plan to implement business process changes.

PALISADES EXECUTIVE CONFERENCE CENTER

Experience Engineering and Integrative Design

Description

The Practice: The IBM Palisades Advanced Business Institute in Palisades, New York, uses experience engineering and mingles architecture with landscaping until the separation between the two is comfortably blurred (see www.ibm.com/abi). Experience engineering is a psychological approach to shaping and directing behavior. The concept of integrating design and the environment extends to the exterior trim, which is unfinished so it will weather and blend with the surroundings, and to the landscaping, which has no formal hedges or plantings. The Palisades Executive Conference Center was also built to take advantage of several existing ponds.

Why the Practice Was Developed: IBM designed these buildings to "blend into the surrounding area and not be intrusive to the community." The object is to design a facility that does not damage the area's scenic potential, a practice that IBM follows in designing all of its buildings.

Execution

The Approach to Implementation: Five parcels of land were purchased to put together the conference center. Opened in 1989, the facility consists of two main wings — the classroom wing and the living or hotel wing — interconnected by a long hallway. In the center of this long hallway, a three-story building contains the lobby, reception, and food service areas. Although the reception and dining areas are glass-enclosed to give a full view of the trees and ponds, the classrooms are windowless to reduce distractions. The facility was designed to be as unobtrusive as possible. IBM manager Dan Gassert explains that "even in the fall, when all the trees are losing their leaves, you still can't see the facility from the roadside."

All the guestrooms are identical by design, and each is equipped with IBM workstations, Internet access, and common workstation applications so guests can be productive.

The facility incorporates the new concepts in the area of "experience engineering," which can best be described as a positive way of directing experiences. For example, instead of placing a sign in front of a coffee break that reads "XYZ Company Only," the preferred wording is "XYZ Company, this is your coffee break." The first version sends a negative clue, which is perceived as undesirable. Some of the facility's other experience engineering techniques are:

- Playing music in the hallway between the living and learning buildings, so as to distract the visitor from the fact that it is a long corridor

- Placing the key for the guestroom's lockable drawer in the drawer (rather than in the lock) to avoid giving an impression of a security problem

Outcomes

Success of the Practice: IBM, in the past, has had its own internal version of the Malcolm Baldrige award for excellence, and the facility has won both the silver and gold prizes for internal quality.

Benefits for Customer: Guests are asked to fill out a 45-question survey. The current index indicates that 99.7% of the guests are satisfied, and 61% of the guests rate the total experience as excellent. Management receives about 7,000 questionnaires every year, for a response rate of 30%.

Insights

Advice and Observations: Because the market changes so fast, the center is trying to develop ways to sense what the customer wants and to respond quickly with changes.

Contact

Daniel F. Gassert, IBM Manager
IBM Advanced Business Institute
Palisades Executive Conference Center
Route 9W, Palisades, NY 10964-8001
Phone: 914-732-6100 Fax: 914-732-6119

THE PENINSULA BEVERLY HILLS HOTEL

"24-Hour" Check-in and Check-out

Description

The Practice: The Peninsula Beverly Hills offers 24-hour check-in and check-out with no additional surcharge to the guest. Guests may check in as early as 5:30 a.m. and check out as late as 11:30 p.m. on any given day without additional charges. The practice requires that a few housekeepers be assigned to an early morning shift that begins at 5:00. Using a few modifications in the usual cleaning operation to avoid waking guests, the early-shift housekeepers clean, self-inspect, and release to the front desk an inventory of cleaned rooms. Guests arriving in the morning never have to wait for a room to be readied and can check out as late as they like.

Why the Practice Was Selected: The general manager, Ali Kasikci, identified three events that led him to formulate and promote the idea of a 24-hour check-in and check-out: (1) in 1996, he attended an executive education course in which he was exposed to the idea and a book that discussed it, (2) a few months later, he read an article that again identified the check-in and check-out failures of hotels, and (3) his own frustrations when traveling and being unable to check in to his hotel in the morning prior to a business meeting unless he had paid for the room for the night before.

He noted, "If the day is 24 hours long, guests should be able to check in and check out at any time they like." Hotels should not force guests to adapt to the hotel's time frame. Instead, operations should accommodate guests according to guests' wishes.

The practice began as an idea in January 1996, was tested in the summer, and was fully implemented by the staff of the hotel in January 1997.

Execution

The Approach to Implementation: It was important to gain customer feedback first to be sure that this practice would be of sufficient importance to the Peninsula's guests to merit any changes it would require in housekeeping operations. Mr. Kasikci began by discussing the idea with his marketing director, sales managers, and front-office manager. Each of these managers informally collected feedback from customers about the concept, and "talked it up" to other managers in the hotel. Customers were very responsive to the idea — especially those from Australia and New Zealand whose 14-to-17-hour flights generally arrive in the early morning hours and depart late in the evening, as well as frequent business travelers from the East Coast who routinely caught the red-eye into Los Angeles and then caught it out again the very next evening. These guests did not want to wait six or seven hours to get into their rooms after such arduous flights.

Armed with the support of guests and various managers, the next step was to determine whether it was operationally feasible. Mr. Kasikci asked his executive housekeeper and her staff to determine whether the rooms could be ready at all times for early arrivals. To assist in this determination, the housekeeping staff collected data for two months regarding how many guests checked in or checked out during each time period, and how many guests requested late departures and for what time. These data were further broken down by high vs. low season, and by day of the week. This information enabled the Peninsula staff to examine patterns to determine how many rooms were really needed and by what time the rooms would have to be ready for occupancy. They found that by 8:00 a.m., regardless of occupancy rate, they comfortably had seven to ten rooms that had been vacated by early departures. Thus, it was feasible to consider the idea.

Prior to implementing the practice, Mr. Kasikci also discussed the idea with competitor hotels in his market. These competitors were the biggest critics; they said the idea would never work, and that the Peninsula would be quickly forced to give up the practice. The Peninsula's housekeeping staff was also hesitant. However, their attitudes changed after extensive discussions and efforts to focus on the positive implications for the hotel.

Operational Issues: Of concern in implementing the practice was the possibility of creating an annoyance for sleeping guests while vacated rooms were cleaned (e.g., talking in the hallways, doors slamming, vacuum cleaner noise). To reduce vacuum cleaner noise, the standard upright vacuum was replaced with a small, battery-operated Dustbuster-type vacuum.

A Trial: Six months after formulating the idea of a 24-hour check in and check out, the hotel tested the practice with two of the most experienced and autonomous housekeepers. They were instructed not to converse in the hallways and to quietly open and close room doors. Housekeeping inspections were eliminated for the rooms done in the early morning. The pre-dawn cleaning involved the use of much dimmer electric lighting (instead of the bright California sun) — something to which the housekeepers had to adjust. In addition, the house-keepers selected had to be proficient in English since they were required to telephone the front desk each time they completed a room.

Now housekeepers are assigned to the early morning shift on a voluntary basis. The hotel recognizes that it is important that the work pattern suit the individual. In addition, housekeepers who volunteer are given a dollar ($1.00) an hour in incremental pay, the same incentive given to those housekeepers working the graveyard shift. The early shift attracts those who want to have the opportunity to spend their afternoons involved in other activities, such as family time or coursework.

Costs: The cost of implementing this practice was "minute," chiefly the cost of purchasing the Dustbuster-type vacuums. Had the experiment failed, those vacuums could have still been used in the restaurant area. Revenues from late departure and early arrival charges have been lost, but Mr. Kasikci has viewed these lost funds as an investment toward long-term revenue stemming from customer loyalty.

Outcomes

Success of the Practice: This practice was easy and it aston-ishes the guest. Mr. Kasikci views the ultimate benefit of the practice to be the customer loyalty and repeat business that has been generated. The hotel has a 68% guest return, and the highest market share ("head and shoulders above the nearest competitor") in its competitive market. In addition, the practice has had the benefit of creating more flexible work schedules for the housekeeping staff. The elimination of room inspections has presented no problem.

Benefits for Customer: Twenty-four hour check-in and check-out has made the guests' lives better. Guests are "astonished and their eyes sparkle" when informed that they can check-in and-out at any time. Mr. Kasikci notes, "We've raised the bar in terms of customer service."

Insights

Mr. Kasikci notes that a lot of great ideas are never put into practice because "we always make excuses that operationally it is not possible." Instead he argues that we should look at the benefit we can acquire from the long-term loyalty and relationship of customers.

Advice and Observations: This practice is not for everyone. If you are in a monopolistic situation, and few of us are, then do not do it. If he were to do it over again, Mr. Kasikci states that he would have implemented the practice sooner and would never have presented it as being something different. He believes he has done something that should have been adopted by the industry long ago.

Contact

Ali Kasikci, General Manager
The Peninsula Beverly Hills Hotel
9882 Little Santa Monica Blvd., Beverly Hills, CA 90212
Phone: 310-551-2888   Fax: 310-788-2319

THE PIERRE

Cost-Plus F&B Purchasing Agreements Monitored by Independent Consultants

Description

The Practice: The Pierre, a Four Seasons property in New York City, has given financial responsibility for food purchasing to an independent consultant. The consultant, with the assistance of the executive chef, writes specifications for all food products and negotiates contracts with a single vendor in each food category. The result is lower food costs and reduced kitchen labor expenses.

Why the Practice Was Developed: The proper execution of the purchasing functions for restaurants requires setting specifications, selecting vendors, obtaining best pricing, and monitoring receiving to ensure adherence to specifications and quantities. Although the profitability of the food and beverage department depends upon the skillful execution of these tasks, The Pierre's management believed the excellence demanded in these purchasing activities could not be achieved without diverting the main efforts of the executive chef away from the kitchen's culinary creations. Consequently, The Pierre chose to hire a consulting firm to assist with food and beverage purchases.

Execution

The Approach to Implementation: The Pierre hired Sherman Associates to set up a purchasing program. The consultants initially spent several weeks observing the kitchen's operations and writing specifications for all food products. They made recommendations to the executive chef to change specifications when a less expensive item could be substituted without compromising quality. Decisions were also made to modify specifications to better use or, in some cases, eliminate preparation personnel if offsite preparation could be achieved less expensively. Additionally, the consulting firm trained the kitchen staff on the receiving function: to check incoming products for adherence to specifications, and to verify quantity and weight. The next phase of the project required negotiating contracts with the hotel's vendors that specified a percentage profit over the tax cost to the vendors. If a vendor was unwilling to enter into the agreement, the consulting firm found another vendor.

The consultant now receives a monthly inventory list, from each of the vendors, except for the produce list which is obtained weekly. These lists itemize all products purchased by the hotel, and specify the vendor's true cost. The hotel also forwards a list of every purchased item and the price paid to the consultant. These corresponding lists are compared and monitored for adherence to the agreement, and checks are made against a database for most items. Once a year, the consulting firm checks the total bookkeeping function of the vendor to ensure that the stated cost of each item is accurate. This auditing function must cover the entire accounting system of the vendor — not just vendor invoices from suppliers — to take into account all deals, rebates, and other financial arrangements between vendors and their suppliers that may affect the price to the hotel.

Operational Issues: Initially, according to Franz Klampfer, executive chef of The Pierre, the cost-plus purchasing program was received with some hesitation. The vendors were unhappy with the cost-plus contract, but in most cases agreed to the plan to retain the hotel's business. They also had reservations about opening their books to the auditors of the consulting firm. Similarly, the kitchen staff was concerned about compromising on product specifications. However, management prevailed and the program moved forward.

Outcomes

Success of the Practice: Cost-plus purchasing has been beneficial. Food costs have been reduced by approximately 5%, and kitchen labor costs have decreased by 2%. The program has reduced the number of vendors, which results in greater efficiency for the hotel, but in most cases, the selected vendors had to agree to carry additional items to eliminate the need for multiple vendors for a few specialty items.

Advice and Observations: This practice is not likely to be warmly received by either a hotel's staff or its vendors, since it substantially changes the way business has previously been conducted, Mr. Klampfer warns. However, the benefits of the program are worth the effort.

According to Mr. Klampfer, this practice can be effective only if the property is able to meet all of the credit terms of the vendors. Furthermore, the quantity of purchases made by the hotel must be sufficient to guarantee economies of scale to the vendors before they will agree to the limited profit percentage and the consultant's audit.

Contact

Franz Klampfer, Executive Chef
The Pierre
2 East 61st St., New York, NY 10021
Phone: 212-838-8000   Fax: 212-826-0319

THE PIERRE

Maximizing Profitability by Managing the Sales Mix

Description

The Practice: The Pierre instituted a sales program focusing on maximizing profitability by realigning the sales mix. Consequently, group sales efforts were reduced and a greater focus was placed on obtaining individual sales — both domestic and foreign — because of their willingness to pay higher rates than groups.

Why the Practice Was Developed: The Pierre is a luxury hotel in New York City that enjoys the enviable mix of high demand and limited availability. However, after examining the way the sales department was handling business, it was determined that gross operating profit was not achieving full potential because the hotel was too aggressive with group sales. Groups occupied rooms at discounted rates during peak periods, and the hotel had to turn away new rack rate business. This situation was especially problematic because the hotel management wanted to attract new clients.

Execution

The Approach to Implementation: The Pierre managers calculated that The Pierre is sold out at least 100 days each year, for which it could obtain rack rate. This strategy meant refocusing the sales managers towards filling shoulder and soft periods with group sales. Using the Delphi property sales system and the selective sell targets, Didier Le Calvez, general manager, and the sales department set a limitation on the number of group rooms that would be allocated for each day of the year. Any deviation from the selected group mix required the personal approval of the director of marketing. A maximum 10% group business is allowed during high-pressure periods.

After reducing group sales, The Pierre management focused on introducing new clients into the hotel. Domestically, the hotel had relied heavily on Wall Street business, a tactic that was detrimental to the hotel during weak economic periods. In an effort to bring in new business, the sales department is now seeking both entertainment and fashion industry business. Specifically, The Pierre has chosen to target more of the Los Angeles market, so the hotel promotes a residential profile with the travel agent market and through frequent sales visits to the L.A. area.

The Pierre also wanted to increase business from overseas markets. The hotel management realized that average rates in foreign countries (especially in major cities like London and Paris) are high. Overseas customers are more accustomed to paying high room rates, making it possible for The Pierre to be more aggressive in rates for this market. As a result, The Pierre has added a sales manager for the Japanese market.

There has been strong support for this remix of business from the director of marketing; the entire planning committee, comprised of all division heads in the hotel; and the regional vice presidents of marketing and operations.

Operational Issues: Mr. Le Calvez notes that the higher the rate, the more services clients demand. Thus, he cannot raise the rate without improving the quality of service from the entire staff. To reach the desired level of service, The Pierre has added a full-time position of training manager with another half-time position beginning this coming year. The Four Seasons process of four levels of pre-hire screening is maintained and attitude is the number-one criterion for most job positions.

Outcomes

Success of the Practice: The remix of business at The Pierre has resulted in greater profitability and higher ADR. Gross operating profit has tripled. Guest retention is now 65%, and many of these repeat customers are from overseas. The hotel management has successfully leveraged the brand name of The Pierre and used the best resources of Four Seasons Hotels and Resorts.

Additionally, the lower selective sell target for groups has put more upward pressure on group rates. As a result, these room rates are now approaching $500 during peak demand periods. Rack rate now comprises 31% of total rooms revenue during the year because The Pierre has inventory available when the demand is there.

RevPAR has improved substantially with an annual ADR increase of 7% to 11.5% over each of the past three years, and occupancy has increased from 70% to 81% since 1995. Because the return on investment has grown dramatically for the owners, they are more receptive to putting dollars back into the hotel through capital improvements. In turn, management has more leeway to improve the product. The hotel has also been able to put more money into employee relations, and because of the increased volume of business throughout the year, seasonal layoffs have been minimal.

Benefits for Customer: The physical product for the customer has been improved. The Pierre has spent $67 million in improvements since taking over the hotel from Trusthouse Forte.

Insights

Advice and Observations: To bring in new business, Diana Adamson, director of marketing, says that major press tours in Europe, including visible road shows with slides, are very important. Personal invitations of bonafide FAM tours for journalists and travel agents are key. Mr. Le Calvez personally extended these invitations in Europe, while his director of marketing did the same in South America. The press tours not only promote the hotel, but the city at the same time. The Los Angeles media show is also crucial for that market. The Pierre believes it is more important to do these road shows than to spend money on advertising.

The Pierre advises that it is critical not to do what other hotels have done, which is to live off their reputation. The Pierre also finds it important not to have a specified group sales manager. Now every sales manager performs total account management for both individual and group sales.

Finally, The Pierre notes that 15 years ago selling the hotel and managing the inventory was the responsibility of the reservations manager. This is no longer acceptable. Now, senior management must be more on top of things. They must understand and keep their fingers tightly on the pulse of room sales. Yield and RevPAR is top management's business! Mr. Le Calvez says it is important to analyze historical data of one's own hotel for the past five years before making any decisions. He also says it is important to understand your city's demand factors.

Contact

Didier Le Calvez, General Manager
The Pierre
795 5th Avenue, New York, NY 10021
Phone: 212-838-8000   Fax: 212-826-0319

PREFERRED HOTELS & RESORTS WORLDWIDE, INC.

Development of the Preferred Standards of Excellence

Description

The Practice: Preferred Hotels & Resorts Worldwide, Inc., a luxury brand of 120 hotels and resorts in 25 countries, has refined and developed one of the most comprehensive and detailed quality assurance programs in the industry. Preferred's brand has grown around its trademarked *Standards of Excellence* quality assurance program. The program has more than 1,500 standards and practices, and is updated as new standards, practices, and technology develop. In order to become and remain a member of Preferred, a property must meet these quality standards and practices. To ensure compliance, annual unannounced inspections are conducted by an independent third-party auditor.

Why the Practice Was Developed: Preferred Hotels & Resorts Worldwide, Inc., started as a referral service in 1968 organized by six independent hoteliers; it has grown to represent a membership of 120 independent luxury hotels and resorts operating in 25 countries. The quality assurance program was started about 20 years ago as a means to build and integrate the brand with the various independent members of the organization. Preferred has since evolved into a global shareholder-owned hotel marketing and distribution company that represents a "global standard of quality worldwide — whether in Indianapolis or London," stated Peter Cass, president and chief executive officer. The quality program has become key to Preferred operations for determining membership, maintaining quality, and marketing and building the brand image.

Execution

The Approach to Implementation: The *Standards of Excellence* quality assurance program is focused on two categories: service and facility. There are currently about 1,500 distinct standards and practices on which a property is evaluated. A Quality Assurance Committee within Preferred, using a "best practices" approach, developed the initial set of standards and practices. As technology, customer requirements, and new innovations emerged, Preferred, along with member participation, added new criteria. To assure objectivity and consistency, an independent third-party auditor evaluates quality levels.

To continue Preferred membership, a property must meet and maintain the established standards and practices; a member's commitment to quality is what creates the Preferred brand standard. Membership is quite selective and only one in ten properties is ultimately chosen. Sizes of member hotels vary widely — the largest is over 1,000 rooms, the smallest has 60 rooms, and the average is about 200 rooms.

When a hotel applies for membership, Preferred's auditor conducts an unannounced inspection of the property. To maintain anonymity, the inspector uses a fictitious name and credit cards. The audit is conducted over the course of two days, and points are awarded on the basis of the standards and practices. Two checklists are utilized — one for resorts and one for business/city hotels. There are approximately 6,000 total points to be awarded for facility and service. The property must attain a passing score in each category. This unannounced inspection process continues on an annual basis once the property becomes a member of Preferred. Full-time inspectors include men, women, couples, and families who assume the roles of typical guests.

At the end of the audit, the inspector asks to meet with the general manager (and/or the senior staff) to review critical facility or service areas on which the inspector would like to comment. The intent is to communicate, to the GM, major concerns that the inspector may have so corrective action can begin immediately.

The computerized report is sent to Preferred for processing the data, scoring, and returning the completed report to the property. The scores are also entered into a database at Preferred's headquarters to track how well the hotels are performing in different categories to analyze trends or spot potential problems.

The report is an objective, comprehensive third-party review of the hotel. Reports include photographs as well as detailed, handwritten notes from the auditor notating exactly what he did, to whom he talked, and the services that he encountered. "This provides the GM a fantastic training tool because it is an objective, third-party evaluation from someone who has no axe to grind," notes Mr. Cass.

Hotels are provided with comparative data of unnamed member hotels, so the GM can see how his or her property compares with other members in quality levels, by operating department, as well as by size and type of hotel or resort. The inspector is encouraged to make notations of innovations he notices; these are included in the report. This, in turn, encourages further innovation, which is reviewed by Preferred's Quality Assurance Committee, in a continuing cycle of improvement.

Operational Issues: To maintain objectivity, third-party auditors must represent both sexes, come from various parts of the world, and have different nationalities. A record is kept of the individual auditor's scores in order to track any biases.

If a property fails in either category, it is placed on probation for six months, and at the end of the probationary period, re-inspected by a different auditor to ensure objectivity. If the property meets the minimum passing requirement, probation is lifted. If it fails the reinspection, the hotel is subject to termination from Preferred membership.

As part of the ongoing evolution of the *Standards of Excellence* program, Preferred is announcing a major enhancement: the inclusion of guest evaluations. Starting in February 1999, three alternative ways for gathering consumer data are to be tested for six months, and the most effective one will be adopted.

Outcomes

Success of the Practice: The *Standards of Excellence* quality program has the following benefits:

- Creates "best practices" models for the general manager.
- Stimulates the general manager to improve standards and quality vis-à-vis other Preferred hotels and resorts.
- Creates an overall increase of quality standards.
- Increases innovation through the sharing of practices.

- Demonstrates how these service standards are actually applied in the descriptions of the auditor's service encounters; the auditor report becomes a training tool.

The program has integrated the quality and practices of the Preferred brand while allowing the various member properties to still provide their "individual" services and guest experiences. The individual member hotels and resorts maintain their distinctive quality yet are united in a conscious commitment to standards and practices.

More than 40% of Preferred's hotels and resorts schedule additional inspections to make sure they are prepared for their annual "official" audit. The inspection process is so successful that many owners ask Preferred to inspect the property soon after they hire a new GM.

Benefits for Customer: The guest is assured of a certain standard of quality in the facility and level of service when he or she visits a Preferred hotel or resort. Since all the facilities are different from each other, there is no "cookie-cutter" effect.

Insights

Mr. Cass believes Preferred Hotels & Resorts Worldwide, Inc. has a very unique system; the process can be emulated and duplicated under a "best practices" model, but the unique standards and practices requirements and the commitment to innovation, personal service, and quality standards must be developed over time. Mr. Cass also believes that the documentation for the program lends itself to effective employee training and motivational programs.

Advice and Observations: One of the key elements of success and development of the program has been the continuous updating and refining of standards over the last 10-15 years as new technology and practices have emerged, says Mr. Cass. This update and refinement also presents one of the greatest challenges.

Contact

Robert Cornell, Senior Vice President of Development
Preferred Hotels & Resorts Worldwide, Inc.
311 South Wacker Drive, Suite 1900, Chicago, IL 60606
Phone: 312-913-0400   Fax: 312-913-0444

PROMUS HOTEL CORPORATION

Guaranteed Customer Satisfaction

The Practice: The Promus Hotel Corporation guarantees 100% complete satisfaction for any guest who stays at any one of its hotels. In the event a guest is not completely satisfied with the hotel service or facility for any reason, the guest will incur no charges of any kind, and the hotel will ask no questions.

Why the Practice Was Developed: The Promus Hotel Corporation franchises the following hotel brands: Hampton Inns, Hampton Inns and Suites, Embassy Suites, Homewood Suites, and most recently, Doubletree Hotels, Resorts, and Guest Suites. Thus, the corporate portfolio now boasts 1,300 hotels.

In 1988 President Raymond Schultz expressed his concern that the owners of the franchised hotels would let their hotels' maintenance be downgraded after a few years due to age and cost. He did not want that condition to affect the image of the Promus Hotel Corporation, then known as Holiday Corporation. Although Promus has 20 inspectors who examine all its properties at least twice each year, the possibility exists that guests may experience a hotel that is not well maintained before the inspectors realize that a property needs upgrading. Consequently, Promus's chairman, Mike Rose, and Mr. Schultz decided to do two things to maintain a quality enterprise:

- Require a franchisee to keep its hotels in spotless condition, guarantee that the service is outstanding, and ensure that the property is well maintained.
- Provide Promus employees with a positive incentive to give exceptional service and ensure that any other request for service will be delivered in a manner satisfactory to the guest.

As a means of achieving these objectives, Mr. Schultz originated a guaranteed-satisfaction concept. Mr. Rose, Mr. Schultz, and Mark Wells, senior vice president for marketing at Hampton Inns, researched the possibility of guaranteeing the satisfactory outcome of each guest's stay at any one of their hotels. They found that no other hotel or chain of hotels had established this practice.

The Approach to Implementation: The administrators of Promus shared their research and discussed the possibility of guaranteeing each guest's stay with the employees of their company. Critics of the proposed practice included some department heads who thought that it would not work for their properties. Others felt that a few guests would take advantage of this plan and would stay at many of their hotels for free. Some employees felt that they could not maintain the hotels to be able to guarantee complete satisfaction for all of their hotel properties. Some managers predicted the employees would "give the store away" under this system, while others thought they would lose control of staff supervision. A few managers felt that they would have a difficult time training the staff to reach the required levels of service and maintenance. Even outside critics believed that Promus might try the guarantee for a few years, but would eventually have to abandon it. On the other hand, since no other hotel chain had this guarantee

in place at the time, some managers favored giving the practice a trial.

The research on guaranteed satisfaction was also systematically shared with and reviewed by hotel guests. The guests were positive about the proposed practice. They seemed to appreciate what Promus was trying to do to improve service and maintenance. The guests seemed to believe that the guarantee provided a real incentive for the company to improve the operation of each property to avoid the problems associated with an unsatisfied guest.

A Trial: The pilot program for this practice began in 1988 and took 12 months to complete. To begin the trial, 30 hotel managers visited the corporate office for a review of this proposed practice. They were asked to consider using this practice in their hotels, and were trained to become "leaders" rather than

189

just general managers. They were also trained to train the employees for this new concept. Mr. Schultz wanted employees to be trained and empowered to fix problems on the spot, rather than waiting to see what a supervisor would do. Having the problem resolved immediately would make the guest happier. In addition, if an employee solved the problem, the employee would build confidence in his or her ability to handle guests' problems.

The pilot program also contained a component for determining customer needs. After questioning many hotel guests, Promus found that most guests desired spotlessly clean rooms, a friendly staff, and efficient service. They also wanted to deal with a company that manages with integrity. Finally, guests valued risk-free service that is focused on quality. However, some owners of franchised properties derided the satisfaction-guarantee plan because they were worried some guests would attempt to use the guarantee to defraud the hotel owners.

By October 1989, Mr. Schultz believed it was time to put the guarantee into place organizationwide. Since implementation, this 100% guaranteed-satisfaction plan has been promoted in the following manner:

1 Internal advertising,
2 Explanations by front-desk receptionists upon every guest check-in,
3 In-room material,
4 Lobby billboards,
5 Print media (i.e., newspapers and magazines),
6 Memos to travel agencies, and
7 Broadcast media (i.e., radio and television).

Now that the practice has been in place for several years, the guests know what to expect with regard to clean accommodations, the level of service, and the friendliness of the staff. When a problem does arise, the company has found that guests do not want their money returned to them, but they want the problem to go away as rapidly as possible. Moreover, the company has learned that most people are basically honest and have a sense of integrity when dealing with other people.

The company considers this guarantee one of the cornerstones of its culture, which is taking care of hotel guests.

Outcomes

Success of Practice: The satisfaction guarantee has been most successful for property operations and management. Further, Promus has trained its managers to lead by example rather than attempting to drive their staff, and to celebrate their employees' successes when they go out of their way to do a good job for a guest.

Promus administrators discuss the satisfaction guarantee each day. Financially, this practice has been successful. Return intentions for guests "saved" by the guarantee exceed all expectations.

Insights

Advice and Observations: Promus's philosophy of treating employees like part of a family, its belief in the honesty and integrity of the traveling public, its ability to foster loyalty in customers, and its ability to empower and train its employees to satisfy customers have led to long-term successes.

In the future, the Promus Hotel Corporation will continue with the same practice. Promus believes it is living proof that if you treat your employees well, the loyalty of your staff increases, and if you provide clean accommodations and excellent service to the guests, customer loyalty results.

Contact

Jim Hartigan
Senior Director, Quality Assurance/Guest Satisfaction
Promus Hotel Corporation
1755 Crossover Lane, Memphis, TN 38117
Phone: 901-374-5998 Fax: 901-374-5976

PROMUS HOTEL CORPORATION

On-Line Integrated Payroll/Benefit Accounting System

Description

The Practice: Promus Hotels has developed a computerized, integrated payroll- and benefit-accounting system that is accessible on-line. Using a customized Windows program, the system displays the various benefit options available to an employee. After the employee makes his or her selections, the employee's choices are automatically forwarded to the corporate headquarters for payroll information and deductions. The system is paperless and seamless.

Why the Practice Was Developed: The traditional paper forms that Promus used for benefit selection were difficult for employees, causing many mistakes to be made. Additionally, much time was expended before the forms arrived at corporate headquarters and the appropriate information could be entered into the company system. Furthermore, the opening of Promus' multi-site River Boat division created a greater volume of work for the corporate benefits department. This growth spurred the need to improve the efficiency of the payroll/benefit system, but at a reasonable cost. Unfortunately, no existing technology was appropriate.

Execution

The Approach to Implementation: In 1994, Promus's corporate benefits and human resources department turned to the technology department for formulation of the program. The technology department created a workable system, which was tested in the field at several representative hotels in each lodging segment. Adjustments to the technology and a few edits (i.e., HMO registration) were made to the system during the trial period. Technology instructions and support systems were evaluated; human resource managers, general managers, and corporate human resources and technology departments were involved. The system was then progressively rolled out to all hotels. Memos, manuals, instructions, and technological support to the hotels were provided. Implementation of this system required approximately 1 to 1 1/2 years, including the test period.

The program was instantly successful and was used in all departments of every hotel. The employees liked the on-line program, as the benefits selection process was quicker, easier, and more accurate than the paper forms. Very few new employee skills were needed, although computer literacy, Windows knowledge, and program understanding are necessary. The system replaced paper reference manuals and forms with on-line communications.

Operational Issues: Some initial opposition to the on-line system was offered by field locations as a result of inadequate information and because of a resistance to "something new." Once the benefits of the program were discerned, resistance dissolved.

Costs: Costs have not been assessed but are minimal. The program has resulted in greater efficiency, theoretically reduced costs, and improved employee satisfaction and morale.

Outcomes

Success of the Practice: The payroll- and benefit-accounting system means virtually no errors in the selection of benefits, and speed of response has been gained. Human resources employees can now devote their efforts to other pressing issues, both at the corporate and field levels. Corporate and property managers have a general feeling of "taking care of their employees." Maintenance of the program is minimal, and additional properties easily enter into the system.

Benefits have far exceeded any time and costs involved. When managers are asked whether the program should be continued, they reply, "Absolutely! We would do it again tomorrow. We couldn't function without it." Indeed, general managers are now asking for additional technology.

Advice and Observations: To initiate this program, the human resources department must have a strong relationship with the technology department. Strong communications, support, and training are important in the implementation of a payroll- and benefit-accounting system.

The system would not work well where there are multiple payroll operations. Additionally, the system probably would not be successful in international programs because of communication technology variances, languages, and cultures.

This program should be established in other multiple-unit operations that have a central payroll and benefit system. It saves much time, decreases chance of human error, and minimizes hard costs.

Contact

Kelly Jenkins, Vice President of Corporate Compensation, Benefits and HR Information Systems
Promus Hotel Corporation
755 Crossover Lane, Memphis, TN 38117
Phone: 901-374-5510   Fax: 901-374-5509

RADISSON WORLDWIDE

Reward Program for Travel Agents

Description

The Practice: The "Look to Book" program rewards travel agents with points that can be redeemed for travel or gifts based on the number of reservations they book on-line with Radisson. This "frequent booker" program, similar to frequent-flyer programs, is intended to produce and reward brand loyalty.

Why the Practice Was Developed: Radisson is owned by Carlson Companies, which also owns some of the largest travel businesses in the world. As a result, Carlson is firmly committed to relationships with the travel industry. The Look to Book program is a logical blending of Carlson's travel and hotel businesses. Furthermore, the frequent-booker program provides a competitive advantage over other hotel companies that do not have such a close relationship with travel agents.

Execution

The Approach to Implementation: Radisson's objectives were to:

1. Implement a loyalty-point program that functioned with no paperwork and no manual processing
2. Implement a program that rewarded the leveraged audience of travel agents
3. Implement a system that worked on all GDS systems worldwide
4. Implement a system that allowed Radisson to instantly recognize and award each travel agent booking

The first technical obstacle was to upgrade Radisson's systems and data network to communicate with travel agents in a three-to-seven-second time frame. Next, it was necessary to design a bank that could securely manage the rapid deposit and withdrawal of Look to Book points. After all the technical and programming work was completed, a training and support system was developed to advise travel agents on how to participate in this new award system. This system was also designed to handle problems and questions from the participants.

Radisson believed that the GDS channel was poorly used and wanted to retain market leadership in the GDS, so time was of the essence. Radisson also knew that the quality of data on the GDS needed improvement. To support the strategy, Radisson created a seamless interface between its host systems and those of the GDSs. This allowed travel agents to bypass the GDS database and view full English-text room descriptions directly from Radisson's own database. Radisson's design for this process has since become an industry standard.

Additionally, Radisson knew that travel agents needed much more training to use the GDSs correctly and that numerous enhancements were needed in the GDSs to make them agent friendly. Therefore, Radisson initiated the creation of HEDNA and held the organizational position of president for the first four years. Today, the association of electronic reservations executives continues to expand in its worldwide efforts to improve the use of the GDS.

The seamless interfaces that Radisson designed provide travel agents with access to the Radisson reservations system, making it easier for travel agents to sell Radisson rooms and support the notion of rate integrity, meaning that the consumer gets the same rate from the travel agent, Radisson reservations, or a specific Radisson property. This rate integrity is essential to the success of the program.

Upon successful implementation of the Look to Book program, Radisson was awarded Patent No. 5,483,444 for creating a "system for awarding credits to persons who book travel-related reservations." This patent has since been registered worldwide.

The Look to Book program creates an award for the individual travel agent (as opposed to the travel agency) who books Radisson reservations on-line. Each travel agent can earn points redeemable for hotel stays, travel, and gifts. The appeal to agency managers and owners is that the agent now has a personal economic incentive for adding to the total transaction, thus benefiting the agency and the individual travel agent. The idea is to encourage travel agents to do more than make an airline reservation, especially appealing during a time of airline commission caps.

After every transaction, an electronic notice is immediately sent to the individual agent, showing the number of points that have just been earned, as well as giving the status of the total current redeemable points, and the additional pending points (i.e., points not yet earned because the reservation has not been consumed).

Operational Issues: The idea for the frequent-booker program originally was quite controversial because of its novelty: "It just had not been done," President Brian Stage explains. The alternative was to devote the dedicated monies to more traditional marketing methods, but that option appeared less promising.

Costs: The application of electronic seamless interfacing has low administrative costs, which allows for a richer reward structure without burdening the hotels, which ultimately pay for the program.

Outcomes

Success of the Practice: Mr. Stage is pleased with the results of the Look to Book program. Of the 400,000 or so travel agents worldwide, approximately 200,000 participate in the program; and of those about 125,000 are active, meaning they have booked multiple reservations in the past year. Look to Book members work in over 90 countries, even in countries in which Radisson does not have a hotel presence.

The practice has also been profitable: "It is an important way to add value to the hotels that come into the system. It enables them to grow the system. It is hard to quantify the benefit, but Radisson is doing about $1 billion in travel agency business on a global basis annually," Mr. Stage states. Moreover, in the United States, almost 60% of room revenue generated by the company's hotels comes from Radisson's reservations system, and of that, almost 60% is through the GDS, "most" of which is from travel agencies.

Benefits for Customers: The impact on the customer is that the travel agents have sought to examine and satisfy customers' needs in a more comprehensive manner than done formerly.

Insights

Advice and Observations: Mr. Stage would not do anything differently from what has been done. He also makes these observations: "Significant leverage can be gained by working through the travel agency companies. Radisson does not see the travel agent commission line on the hotel's profit and loss statements as an expense; we think it is an investment in business. Further, Radisson sees travel agents as part of the sales force, as opposed to people who are nibbling at our bottom line."

Contact

Brian Stage, President
Radisson Worldwide
P.O. Box 59159, Carlson Parkway
Minneapolis, MN 55459-8204
Phone: 612-449-3443 Fax: 612-449-3401

RAMADA FRANCHISE SYSTEMS, INC.

Employee Selection, Motivation, Training, and Satisfaction

Description

The Practice: The Ramada Franchise Systems has created a comprehensive, integrated initiative for the employees of all U.S.-based Ramada licensees called Personal Best Hospitality. This program, unique in the mid-scale hotel market, uses sophisticated tools in a four-prong approach to improve employee acquisition, training, motivation, and satisfaction. The four major components of this initiative are:

- A prescreening predictive test for prospective and current employees to identify strengths and aptitudes
- A stimulating training program using interactive CDs that ensures employee participation
- An employee loyalty program established to increase motivation and satisfaction
- Guest satisfaction with employee service surveyed on a monthly basis by an independent outside firm

Why the Practice Was Developed: Steve Belmonte, president and chief executive officer of Ramada Franchise Systems, originated the idea of the employee initiative at a time when most other mid-scale chains were concentrating on product and amenities; he believed focusing on employees would keep Ramada one step ahead of the competition.

Execution

The Approach to Implementation: The employee initiative was developed during the summer of 1996. Eighteen months were required to lay the foundation and put the pieces together. Ramada's 12 regional directors of marketing and 12 regional training managers were the first to be trained. During the first four months of 1997 each hotel was visited, and the acquisition and training segments were installed.

Ramada began by concentrating on getting the right person in the right position, as there has always been a problem in hiring for hotels, especially in tight labor markets. It contracted with Praendex, an Arizona company, to provide its licensees with a pre-screening test called the Predictive Index, a simple five-to-seven-minute test of words the respondent selects to describe himself or herself. The questionnaire is faxed back to Praendex for scoring and within 24 hours a detailed motivational analysis of the candidate who applied for the position is faxed to the hotel. Tim Pigsley, the corporate director of Personal Best Hospitality and one of the creators of this initiative, reports the Predictive Index is an "amazing success" countrywide, not only in making the right hiring decision but also in looking at the available pool of candidates. It has definitely helped in retention, which has been a long-standing, "horrendous" problem in the hotel industry.

After successfully placing employees in the proper positions, the corporate office turned its attention to supplying employees with the best possible training tools. Ramada provides each franchisee with an interactive CD player and customized CD training programs. The programs are self-paced and participants must answer questions to progress through the interactive CD; these programs differ significantly from the typical passive training system. The subject matter in these CDs includes hospitality skills and Ramada's core belief that the hotel business is a service industry. The focus of the training is on satisfying the guest, not just checking guests in and out. In addition to these interactive CDs in both English and Spanish, Ramada provides the franchisees with the normal training videos and printed material.

Ramada also strongly promotes another tool — formal education. Once the employee has been placed in the right position, Ramada provides tuition reimbursement for employees who take courses in the hospitality industry to further their careers. The employees are able to pick any accredited school of higher learning; Ramada bases reimbursement on the courses selected and the grades of the employee. It has funded a variety of courses including computer classes and an HVAC repair course, and has just finished sponsoring an employee who graduated with a degree in hotel management.

As part of its educational initiative, Ramada also provides funding for obtaining a CHA or any of the other industry certified designations. In addition, Ramada saw the need for a certification program for line employees. This program specifies study requirements and an exam. Employees who complete this certification are rewarded with a certificate, a pin, and a letter from the president.

Thirty days after the training and acquisition programs were put into place, the employee motivation component was initiated. Ramada has developed a loyalty program for employees in which employees earn points by participating in training, by performing a special service, or by performing unusual services for certain frequent guests. For example, an employee is able to earn $5.00 in points the first day on the job. Employees can redeem points for gift certificates at places like the Gap, Shell Oil, Footlocker, Target, Chili's, and Macaroni Grill. Each month, general managers nominate an employee or "star" of the month from his or her property. All nominees receive generous extra points; the "star" also receives a nice watch, additional points, and special recognition from the president of the company. Every three months Ramada picks three of its "stars" for its *USA Today* advertising campaign. Each "star" is featured in an ad along with his or her story taken from the Ramada guest log. The three employees are flown to New York, taken to dinner at Mr. Belmonte's home, driven around in a chauffeured limousine, featured in a photo shoot, and given a grand tour of the city ending with dinner at the top of the World Trade Center. The ads featuring employees appear in 2.2 million copies of *USA Today* a few weeks later. This system makes the employee more interested in what service or training might be needed to reach "star" level.

After a six-month "shake-down" period for the training, acquisition, and motivation segments, the guest survey was added. Ramada contracted with a survey company, Customer Survey Technology, to provide information on the results of the employee initiative on guest service. Twenty-second surveys on service are conducted at random in the lobby as the guest checks out. Once a month, the survey company provides each licensee with a detailed analysis of the service level. This information helps the hotel stay focused on guest service goals.

Operational Issues: The initiative was designed to be very flexible. The franchisees are able to choose the pieces they want from an "a la carte" menu to fit the needs of their market place and employee base. Mr. Pigsley has a headquarters staff that monitors the progress of each hotel. Ramada also maintains a "hot line" to assist the licensees with any problems that might occur and work with individual properties to customize the initiative for a smooth fit into daily operations.

Outcomes

Success of the Program: The program has been very successful in the eyes of all involved. Some of the Ramada licensees who own properties with other mid-market franchises have declared it the "best thing they have ever seen come out of a franchiser company." The employee acquisition program has increased retention and job satisfaction. More employees are looking at the hospitality industry as a career and taking advantage of the training and educational opportunities, resulting in a better trained staff. The motivational programs are popular with the employees, and the franchisees are happy with the guest survey results.

Insights

Advice and Observations: Mr. Pigsley advises anyone interested in instituting a similar program to focus on covering the four components: employee acquisition, training, motivation, and satisfaction. The tools used are not as important as making sure all four points are covered.

Contact

Tim Pigsley, Corporate Director of Personal Best Hospitality
Ramada Franchise Systems, Inc.
339 Jefferson Road, Parsippany, NJ 07054
Phone: 973-496-1568   Fax: 973-496-0322

RESIDENCE INN

A Collaborative Approach to Quality Assurance in Extended-Stay Hotels

Description

The Practice: Residence Inn utilizes a collaborative approach in its quality assurance program. The goal is to provide assistance to properties rather than criticism and, in the process, improve employee performance.

Why the Practice Was Developed: In her study, Pat Adams, senior vice president of quality assurance, found that hotel inspections followed punitive approaches to taking care of a quality violation. She felt that this approach only served to encourage hotel staff to hide problems from the inspectors. As a result, some problems might go unresolved and would then impact the guest's hotel experience. Residence Inn did not want these type of occurrences to negatively influence the brand image it had worked so hard to build. Ms. Adams decided to develop a different approach to hotel inspections to ensure that Residence Inn quality was up to par at all properties.

Execution

The Approach to Implementation: Utilizing Ritz-Carlton Hotel Company and Walt Disney Resorts as benchmarks, Ms. Adams began formulating a different procedure for quality inspections. She believed that most employees want to do a good job, and those employees not performing at the expected level lacked sufficient training. Ms. Adams developed a quality assurance program with a much more positive approach.

Unlike other programs, Ms. Adams' quality assurance initiative does not only utilize checklists, and employees are not punished for quality infractions. Basically, an employee cannot fail an inspection. Instead, the underperforming employee is advised how to correct the quality problem. Thus, the quality assurance program emphasizes teaching rather than punishment. This redirected emphasis facilitates the development of trust between an employee and a supervisor, and a supervisor and a manager. As a result, the employees are more likely to call attention to safety and security issues, as well as other quality issues.

To implement the program, Ms. Adams, along with a Quality Assurance Team composed of former general managers, visited each Residence Inn and thoroughly inspected each hotel. The team examined continuing maintenance, guestrooms, dining rooms, lobbies, services and safety processes, fabrics, parking, and local reputations. The team also investigated the overall quality trends each hotel was experiencing. After these initial inspections, the team returned to the hotels to train the general managers about the quality assurance process that was being implemented. The idea was to teach the general managers to conduct their own inspections and, in turn, to teach the staff, as a means of ensuring the guest has a good hotel experience.

Ms. Adams also believed that it was important for each property to understand the value drivers of guests as revealed by the negative and positive letters they sent. Consequently, the Quality Assurance Team reviews hundreds of letters from guests and analyzes all of them. In conjunction with other customer research programs, the analyses of the letters are used to advise the general managers of problems that customers have encountered.

Outcomes

Success of the Practice: The overall guest satisfaction has been around 83% for the past several years.

Insights

Advice and Observations: Ms. Adams says she ultimately realized that superior quality is never attained because it is an ongoing perception that is never completed. However, she believes that providing the employee with a helping solution brings a hotel closer to attaining superior quality than criticizing the employee.

Contact

Pat Adams, Senior Vice President of Quality Assurance
Residence Inn
One Marriott Drive, Washington, DC 20058
Phone: 301-380-4502 Fax: 301-380-7507

RESIDENCE INN BY MARRIOTT

Sales Strategies for the Extended-Stay Market

Description

The Practice: Residence Inn has trained its sales force to go directly to the decision makers who commit themselves and others to extended stays. Consequently, the training provides direction regarding specific divisions within corporations to investigate for extended-stay sales opportunities. It also provides guidance by not relying on traditional departments, such as corporate travel offices, which generally do not yield extended-stay lodging business. Every one of the company's properties has at least one on-site salesperson, and in some cases three or four, who are trained to ferret out qualified prospects and examine how their long-term lodging needs can be met by Residence Inn options.

Why the Practice Was Developed: Although extended-stay clients, defined as those who need five or more room-nights, have been a segment of the lodging market for many years, the segment was not specifically targeted for sales efforts until Residence Inn entered the market 20 years ago. According to Stacey Milne, brand team vice president, Marriott has sought to redefine extended-stay lodging through assiduous research and diligent attention to the needs and wants of the market segment.

Execution

The Approach to Implementation: All Residence Inn salespeople are required to spend one week in entry-level training, called the "sales edge," provided by the Marriott training department. The salespeople are taught to research the area in which they are located to pinpoint opportunities for their product. They are trained to go into the various divisions of a company to ascertain prospects' needs. Specifically, the salespeople are educated to investigate the following divisions:

1 Training departments of any company: They may offer two- to three-week classes.
2 Human resources departments: The relocation of business associates and their families can be a major source of business.
3 Project assignments, especially in the information data area: Programmers, engineers, and system installers frequently have to be on-site for lengthy periods of time.

After locating prospects, the salespeople are trained to discern how the needs of the client can be met by the lodging options — studios, one-bedroom suites, two-bedroom suites, and penthouses — that Residence Inn offers. After finding the best "fit" for the client, the salesperson explains the benefits of lodging with Residence Inn to the customer. The benefits may be derived from the amenities offered, such as a free extended continental breakfast, full daily housekeeping, complimentary social hour, weekly complimentary dinner, and free grocery-shopping service. Last, the decision maker is invited to visit the property.

Outcomes

Success of the Practice: Residence Inn has been able to maintain an occupancy rate in the mid-80s. For the first three quarters of 1998, notes Ms. Milne, the occupancy rate was 84.7% and RevPAR was up 4%.

Insights

Advice and Observations: According to Ms. Milne, business people requiring five or more nights of lodging remain the primary target markets of Residence Inn. To supplement the sales effort, the chain places television advertising — specifically, on ESPN college football and news channels. By considering the viewing habits of the target market, Residence Inn believes it can best get the message to the extended-stay traveler.

Contact

Stacey Fell Milne, Brand Team Vice President
Residence Inn by Marriott
One Marriott Drive, Department 955.07,
Washington, DC 20058
Phone: 800-638-8106, ext. 82397 Fax: 301-380-6197

THE RITZ-CARLTON CHICAGO

"Compcierge" Position to Handle Guests' Computer-Related Problems

Description

The Practice: To efficiently and quickly respond to the increasing number of guest requests for assistance concerning computer-related problems, The Ritz-Carlton Chicago created a new staff position within the MIS department. The "Compcierge," as the position is known, serves guests who are experiencing technological difficulties (e.g., printing failures, Internet disconnectivity, disk errors, or dataport incompatibility) and provides computer equipment on a loaner basis (e.g., surge protectors, universal power converters, desk-height power plugs, and a "personal computer connectivity kit"). There is no charge for the Compcierge's service or equipment. The Compcierge can be found at the Concierge desk, located just in front of the Business Center, from 9 a.m. to 6 p.m., Monday through Friday.

Why the Practice Was Developed: The Concierge and Business Center personnel were increasingly being asked computer-related questions for which they did not have answers. In some cases, the Concierge personnel did not have the technological knowledge and skills necessary to assist guests. In other cases, the software required by guests was not available in the Business Center.

Execution

The Approach to Implementation: When management determined that the hotel's MIS department was capable of handling most of the guests' computer-related problems, the decision was made to utilize the expertise of the MIS personnel to provide an additional service to the guests. In a series of meetings, the Concierge, MIS, and Business Center personnel discussed solutions to common computer-related guest problems. These meetings also revealed that some additional hardware and software were necessary to maintain the desired level of guest service. According to Tom Kelly, general manager, the hotel purchased this technology for $13,000.

The Compcierge service was first offered in April 1998 and was promoted to hotel guests via the Concierge desk, the in-room guest directory, and the Business Center.

Operational Issues: The Compcierge service is provided by MIS personnel who are on-call by the Concierge. Because the hotel has three MIS people already on staff, additional staff was not required. MIS staff conducted on-going training for the Concierge and Business Center personnel, so that guest computer problems can be resolved quickly. Because of the proliferation of new software, the Concierge staff advises MIS when requests are made for software that the hotel does not have, and MIS immediately investigates the software, and, if feasible, buys and installs it.

Costs: Because there was no need to add personnel, no additional payroll cost was associated with this service. In addition to the $13,000 originally spent on upgrades, the hotel incurs minor ongoing hardware and software expenses.

Outcomes

Success of the Practice: The number of guest requests for computer assistance has increased from two to five per day, and the guest-comment cards have been most complimentary regarding this service. A side benefit of the practice has been increased morale among the Concierge, Business Center, and MIS personnel.

Benefits for Customer: Most of the hotel's market are business travelers. Consequently, there is a high degree of computer technology usage by guests. This use frequently translates into a need for technical assistance. For example, the Compcierge has helped several guests make needed changes to the content of disk-based presentations — a service for which these guests are extremely grateful.

Advice and Observations: Mr. Kelly advises making a commitment to providing the Compcierge service by training a sufficient number of personnel. Additionally, he suggests that hotels adopting this practice maintain awareness of new technology-related guest problems, stay up to date with new software, and expand computer capabilities.

Contact

Tom Kelly, General Manager
The Ritz-Carlton Chicago
160 East Pearson Street, Chicago, IL 60601
Phone: 312-573-5001 Fax: 312-266-9498

THE RITZ-CARLTON DEARBORN

Special Check-in Service for Frequent Guests

The Practice: The Ritz-Carlton Dearborn offers one-stop check-in and registration (OSCAR), a guest-recognition program that permits frequent guests to bypass the traditional check-in at the front desk. These frequent guests have been identified by The Ritz-Carlton's guest tracking system, CLASS (Customer Loyalty Anticipation Satisfaction System), which was implemented in March 1998. CLASS enables The Ritz-Carlton to record its guests' stays and frequency, as well as their preferences.

Why the Practice Was Developed: As a result of the data gathered through CLASS, The Ritz-Carlton confirmed that it has a large number of repeat customers globally. Since The Ritz-Carlton Dearborn, like all Ritz-Carlton properties, focuses on anticipating guest needs, it did not want guests, particularly loyal customers, to be inconvenienced in any way that could be avoided. A speedier check-in process for these frequent guests was one way of anticipating their needs and reducing inconveniences. This process also was feasible since the installation of the CLASS system provides the hotel with all the check-in information needed on these guests. Hence, the OSCAR initiative was developed to improve guest recognition, to anticipate guests' needs, and to build a long-lasting relationship with guests.

Execution

The Approach to Implementation: Sven Girelinger, former front-of-the-house manager (since promoted to the Pentagon City property); Michael Fernandez, former rooms manager (since promoted to the Rancho Mirage property); and Lisa Rezin, guest recognition manager, were primarily responsible for the development and implementation of the OSCAR program at the Dearborn property. The program works only with repeat guests of the property, since it depends on the guests being visually recognized.

A list of OSCAR members arriving on a given day is prepared. A key packet is readied, and a room assigned, based on the guests' known preferences. The list of all OSCAR arrivals is distributed to all departments and discussed at the daily five-minute line-up meetings.

Coordination with other departments is critical. For example, because the guest is checked in early in the morning, but has not arrived physically on property, PBX must be informed so that phone calls and faxes received are hand delivered.

The front desk executes the normal preregistration process for the arriving OSCAR guests, and a VIP packet is typed and placed in the OSCAR book, a cobalt-blue leather binder that is given to the doorman.

The doorman or valet parker (who is most likely to recognize frequent visitors) receives the OSCAR notebook with the list, as well as all the key packets for the day. (This notebook is passed from shift to shift, as needed.)

Upon the guest's arrival at the hotel, the doorman or valet parker is able to say to the guest, "Mrs. Andrews, welcome back to The Ritz-Carlton! Here is the key to your room. Will you be needing any assistance?" If assistance is needed, the guest is introduced to the bell captain. The guest then proceeds directly to his or her room, bypassing check-in procedures and any possible delays and inconveniences. Once the doorman hands the key to the guest, he informs the front desk, so that all departments are aware that the guest is in-house.

The OSCAR notebook contains a checklist of items to be verified by the doorman: the name of the guest, who handled check-in, the room occupied, who handled preregistration, and the time the guest received the keys. The doorman, in effect, becomes an extension of the front desk.

If the guest does not arrive due to bad weather or cancels the reservation, the OSCAR guest is checked out of the system, and the room is made available for another guest. This last step is particularly crucial during sold-out nights.

Only those who are frequent visitors to the specific property are enrolled in OSCAR. The exceptions, of course, are VIPs, such as nationally known celebrities or entertainers. "Membership" in OSCAR is strictly based on frequency of visits and "is a luxury extended to our most frequent and valued customers," states Ms. Rezin. There is no minimum number of stays required before a guest becomes eligible for membership; all he or she needs to do is be a frequent enough visitor that he or she is recognized by the staff. Although membership is voluntary, there are several administrative steps to be taken, such as getting the guest to sign an "application" that allows the hotel to bill the expenses incurred during the visit directly to the guest's credit card. Approximately 50% of the individual travelers of the Dearborn property's guests are considered repeat guests, and roughly 10% of daily arrivals are in OSCAR.

The doorman or valet parker is key to the success of the program, and they are long-term employees of the hotel. They have taken ownership of the program and, in fact, are encouraged to "nominate" guests for membership in the program.

Outcomes

Success of the Practice: OSCAR is successful. The program is currently in force at two Ritz-Carlton properties, but all other properties throughout The Ritz-Carlton system have been directed to implement a guest-recognition program of a similar nature. Of course, a guest can be a member of OSCAR in one property and not in another, depending on where his travels take him.

Benefits for Customer: The customer has been very receptive to the practice — "They love it! It's a welcome back home feeling." Ms. Rezin believes, "There is no greater benefit to our guests than our anticipation of their needs and our ability to recognize them. The guests also enjoy the payment convenience and check-in speed of OSCAR."

Insights

Advice and Observations: Ms. Rezin believes the program is successful as designed, and there is nothing that should have been done differently. She suggests that it is necessary to get the guest to establish credit and make him or her aware of the program. A warm welcome is critical, as is the anticipation of guests' needs. Ms. Rezin notes, "The sensitivity of the need to visually recognize our guests has been heightened with the guest services employees. They now actively engage guests they have seen to connect a name with their visual recognition." As a result, OSCAR is an "evolutionary program with daily growth as more regular guests gain recognition." Ms. Rezin advises, "Know your guest: who he is, what he wants, and how he wants it." She also suggests that the doorman's buy-in to the program is critical.

Contact

Lisa Rezin, Guest Recognition Manager
The Ritz-Carlton Dearborn
300 Towncenter Drive, Dearborn, MI 48126
Phone: 313-441-2000 Fax: 313-441-2121

THE RITZ-CARLTON HOTEL CO.

Maximizing Guest Service

The Practice: The Ritz-Carlton's credo of "Ladies and Gentlemen Serving Ladies and Gentlemen" is the basis of a sophisticated and unique method of attaining the maximum level of guest service in all areas and departments of its hotels. Patrick Mene, vice president of quality, identifies two strategies The Ritz-Carlton uses for delivering superior customer service: (1) the selection of the right person for the job, and (2) the training and constant reaffirmation of The Ritz-Carlton principles.

Why the Practice Was Developed: In many guest surveys that were carried out over the years, friendly, efficient and professional service was consistently the top requirement of hotel guests. As a means of achieving excellence in customer service and creating a competitive advantage, the ideology of "Ladies and Gentlemen Serving Ladies and Gentlemen" was espoused by President Horst Schulze when the present-day Ritz-Carlton chain was started in 1983. This credo has since undergone constant reinforcement and improvement.

The Approach to Implementation: Though the basic concept is formulated at the corporate level, the implementation takes place at the property level using two fundamental practices: proper selection and training.

At The Ritz-Carlton, each employee is *selected*, not hired. Each applicant is subject to a structured interview that is empirically scored. Applicants are selected only when their score is in an acceptable range. Consequently, people are hired who share The Ritz-Carlton values. In addition to the use of standard evaluation tests, an unusual method of personnel selection is employed, especially in new or takeover property situations. A reception or series of receptions is held to which prospective employees are invited. These receptions provide management and the department heads the opportunity to observe the prospects in social situations and face-to-face communications.

In opening situations, Mr. Schulze conducts a half-day seminar with all employees — usually seven days prior to opening — to explain The Ritz-Carlton's operating principles and management style. After opening, this responsibility is delegated to the property manager.

In accordance with the Deming principle of management, managers and workers assemble in project teams to determine operating methods, interdepartmental problems, and solutions. This team practice results from corporate management's belief that employees have greater pride and joy in their work when they are involved in the planning and standards of their job functions. For example, employees are empowered to "leave the system and spend up to $2,000 to solve a guest problem."

Success of the Practice: The Ritz-Carlton's superior guest service has yielded several benefits. First, midlevel supervisory personnel have been reduced by approximately 30% due to the success of team concepts. Second, employee turnover has been reduced. The amount of reduction due to the best practice is difficult to quantify, but Mr. Mene considers it a significant factor. Finally, Mr. Mene says greater customer loyalty has been cultivated, which has a major effect on RevPAR.

Benefits for Customer: Mr. Mene believes that the true benefit for customers is "the knowledge that service at The Ritz-Carlton will always be of the highest standard."

Advice and Observations: First, recognize that rigid job delineation is over, so companies must be prepared to empower employees so they have the freedom to excel in their jobs. Second, concepts and principles must emanate and be constantly reinforced by the top.

Patrick Mene, Vice President of Quality
The Ritz-Carlton Hotel Co.
3414 Peachtree Road - Suite 300, Atlanta, GA 30326
Phone: 404-237-5500 Fax: 404-261-0119

THE RITZ-CARLTON TYSONS CORNER

Self-Directed Work Teams, Job Redesign, and Employee Empowerment

Description

The Practice: The Ritz-Carlton Tysons Corner established an innovative pilot program to shift as much decision-making responsibility as possible from management to the hourly staff. This program involved a detailed examination of current practices in each department and resulted in the elimination of certain management positions (by attrition; no one was fired), the creation of new titles for remaining executives, and the empowerment of hourly staff.

Why the Practice Was Developed: After The Ritz-Carlton Company won the Malcolm Baldrige Award for excellence in 1992, the president of the chain became interested in adapting some concepts from manufacturing to hospitality, especially in the area of self-directed work teams. The basis for this action was the strong belief on the part of several Ritz-Carlton executives that greater employee empowerment would help to expand "the Ritz-Carlton culture," appeal to the staff, and result in even more outstanding customer service. In accordance with this objective, the general manager of the Tysons Corner property persuaded a former colleague, Marie Minarich, to move from Chicago to explore and institute new human resources concepts.

Execution

The Approach to Implementation: Ms. Minarich and the general manager began by meeting with the executive committee to enlist its assistance in developing the steps necessary to empower the hourly staff to assume many of the duties and responsibilities of management. A mandate was issued to "think out of the box" with the realization that this would require a drastic change in the operating policies and procedures of the hotel. The executive committee's first decision was to change its name to the "guidance team," to help set the tone for what it hoped to achieve.

As any proposed changes would require the active participation of all employees, the group immediately began a campaign to generate interest and enthusiasm. The project was given a name, "The Tysons Corner Project," and a mission statement was created and signed by all employees. Special attention was given to keeping all employees, especially the hourly workers, fully informed and consulted every step of the way.

After considerable discussion the group identified a number of management tasks for possible transfer to the hourly staff. These included work schedules, payroll information, interviewing and selecting team members, and forecasting budgets. Department head titles were changed to better reflect their new responsibilities. For example, the front-office manager became the front-office team leader, the sales and marketing manager became the pre-arrival team leader.

Operational Issues: The company offered a transfer to any of the management staff not comfortable with the changes. The food and beverage manager and the chef were the only ones who chose to leave.

A Trial: The front office was selected to inaugurate the year-long trial run because it was a small group and the staff already enjoyed a moderate degree of empowerment. The tasks proposed for transfer were discussed in detail, and the hourly front-desk employees were asked whether they as a group would be willing to take over these tasks. Managers pointed out that this change would give them a high degree of autonomy and more control over their work. As an added incentive the hotel offered half of the savings from eliminating the front-office manager position, which worked out to about $1.00 more per hour for each member of the group. The initial success of the program in the front office encouraged management to expand the trial by transferring decision-making responsibilities to several different teams throughout the hotel. The trial was so successful at the Tysons Corner property that the practice was rolled out to the entire hotel company in June 1995.

A key component to the success of this program is the Ritz-Carlton policy of emphasizing employee selection. Candidates are carefully screened to ensure they have the talent for the service industry. Prior hospitality experience is of little importance since job tasks can be taught.

Success of the Practice: The program has been a resounding success by almost any measure. At The Ritz-Carlson Tysons Corner, employee turnover dropped from 56% in 1993 to 34% at the end of 1994 and an estimated 25% in 1998. Payroll costs were significantly lowered as the managerial staff went from a ratio of about 1 for every 15 employees to 1 for every 50, and in some cases 1 manager for every 75 employees. Employees at all levels have acquired additional skills, and managers have become seasoned executives faster. Two already have been promoted to general managers. The hotel's employee-satisfaction ratings moved from the second lowest in the chain at the end of 1993 to the second highest in June 1995.

Benefits for Customer: Monthly guest satisfaction surveys of meeting planners and individual travelers indicated that the Tysons Corner project had significantly increased guest satisfaction ratings.

Observations and Suggestions: Ms. Minarich thought it essential to "create a purpose and then find the road map to get there." Also crucial was the support of the president of the Ritz-Carlton chain, which encouraged the Tysons Corner staff to spend the time and effort necessary to develop procedures never before tried in the hotel industry, especially in a deluxe chain noted for personal service. Last, Ms. Minarich emphasized the importance of the early involvement of the staff in the development of a new project.

Marie Minarich, Director of Human Resources
The Ritz-Carlton Tysons Corner
1700 Tysons Boulevard, McLean, VA 22102
Phone: 703-506-4300 Fax: 703-917-6509

RODEWAY INN INTERNATIONAL ORLANDO

Rewarding Employee Performance in an Economy Hotel

Description

The Practice: Rodeway Inn International Orlando has developed an employee satisfaction program that rewards excellent performance. The program is designed to enhance the morale, efficiency, performance, and satisfaction of every hotel employee.

Why the Practice Was Developed: The general manager, Nicholas La Falce, instituted the employee satisfaction program because he reasoned that guest satisfaction could only happen if employees were satisfied.

Execution

The Approach to Implementation: For the program to be successful, Mr. La Falce required the complete support of his supervisory staff. They provided 100% support, as the employee satisfaction program not only improved morale but performance as well.

The employee reward program currently includes the following components:

1 An immediate "thank you" is given for any good deed by an employee.
2 Special inexpensive gifts (e.g., candy, plastic champagne glass filled with jellybeans, cupcakes or cookies, flowers) are given to all employees on holidays: Christmas, New Year's, Mother's Day, 4th of July.
3 Star award pins (embossed with the name Rodeway) are given for any special singular or group performance.
4 English classes are conducted for all employees. The majority of the employees are Hispanic/Creole, and English is actually a second language.
5 The Employee of the Month and Employee of the Year are selected and announced at a luncheon for all employees. Prizes include radios and TVs. Other prizes are raffled. Two Employees of the Month are selected — one from the back of the house and one from the front of the house. Selection in both categories is determined by:
   a Supervisory personnel
   b Department heads
   c Guest comment questionnaires
Each of the two Employee-of-the-Month winners receives a $50 check, tickets to a local attraction, complimentary dinner for two in the hotel's main dining room, and a complimentary day of salary compensation.

Each of the two winners of the Employee-of-the-Year award receives a $100 check, dinner for four in the main dining room, and two or three nights of complimentary hotel accommodations at a designated hotel in the area.
6 Employees are given free passes to Disney World. (These passes are gifts from Disney because the hotel is involved in a number of Disney World packages.)

Costs: A monthly budget of $100 to $150 was established for this program.

Outcomes

Success of the Practice: Each facet of this program was successful from its inception. Every level of employee has benefited from the program because improved morale went hand in hand with improved job performance. Additionally, Mr. La Falce believes that the program has played a major role in helping reach the hotel's 99% occupancy rate. The moral here is "have a satisfied employee and you have a satisfied guest."

The practice also has helped the hotel gain industry recognition. The Rodeway Inn International Orlando is the first Rodeway hotel to receive Choice Hotels' President's Award. The award was based on the quality of guest services (based on guest comment questionnaires) and the general condition and cleanliness of guestrooms and public areas.

Advice and Observations: Mr. La Falce's formula for success is, "Keep an open mind, take the time to visit your staff, and operate on the same level as your staff."

Mr. La Falce believes his employee satisfaction program is applicable to any size or type of hotel in the country. He emphasized again the simple credo, "Have a satisfied employee and you will have a satisfied guest."

Contact

Nicholas La Falce, General Manager
Rodeway Inn International Orlando
6327 International Drive, Orlando, FL 32819
Phone: 407-996-4444 Fax: 407-352-5806

ROYAL PALMS HOTEL AND CASITAS

Restoration and Redesign of Older Property for Residential Feel

Description

The Practice: Fred Unger, owner, undertook a two-year restoration of the Royal Palms Hotel and Casitas to return it to its former 1929 elegance. As part of this extensive renovation, Mr. Unger had 20 interior design teams provide 20 different design schemes. Each design team was assigned a different section or set of rooms at the estate and was allowed to use its own creativity as long as the design matched the overall theme. The design teams donated their time, and, in exchange, the Royal Palms Hotel and Casitas held a three-week, pre-opening showcase open house from which all proceeds were donated to the Phoenix Symphony.

Why the Practice Was Developed: Mr. Unger wanted to restore the hotel property to the elegance of the original structure when it was built as a private residence in 1929. The key goal was to recreate as much of a residential feel as possible while maintaining the historical Spanish Mediterranean theme of the property.

Execution

The Approach to Implementation: Mr. Unger, with the assistance of architect Don Ziebel, developed the basic concept for the renovation program, which involved three elements of building design — the two-story hotel comprised of 68 units (34 single rooms and 34 suites), 44 casitas (single rooms located in several clusters of buildings), and four deluxe villas comprised of three one-bedroom suites and one two-bedroom suite.

To ensure that the renovation project would have a variety of design ideas while adhering to the ambiance and charm of the original structure, Mr. Unger and Mr. Ziebel contacted the American Society of Interior Designers to find the 20 design teams and to encourage the use of the hotel as a showcase house. The design teams were successful in perpetuating the theme of the original estate, and used the hotel as a show house because the hotel was intended to have a residential, versus commercial, feel. The proceeds from the showcase open house were donated to the Phoenix Symphony.

In order to enhance the historical Spanish Mediterranean theme, various materials and features were purchased and added to the property to create an aged feel. An entire stone road from an old church in Mexico was transported to the property to act as a drive. Old railroad trusses were purchased to use as beams throughout the property. An antique fountain was bought and fully restored. Hammocks and antique benches were placed around the property. The finish on the property is all mustard tone in order for it to look weathered and aged.

Property signage is kept to a bare minimum in order to maintain the residential ambiance.

Outcomes

Success of the Practice: The restoration has resulted in higher occupancy and average room rate. The current owner, Destination Hotels and Resorts, projects average rates of $225 per night with 70% occupancy rate in 1999.

Insights

Advice and Observations: General Manager Greg Miller warns those who are undertaking restorations of this size to "expect the unexpected." Restoration of old facilities offers many surprises regarding structural integrity, plumbing, wiring, etc.; consequently, many field changes will likely be required. Mr. Miller found this to be especially true with the Royal Palms Hotel due to the uniqueness of design and the effort to make a commercial property feel residential. According to Mr. Miller, the tactic of using numerous design teams to create a hotel "show house" was very successful; the grandeur and elegance of the hotel are much greater than Mr. Unger or the designers originally had visualized.

Contact

Greg Miller, General Manager
Royal Palms Hotel and Casitas
5200 East Camelback Rd., Phoenix, AZ 85108
Phone: 602-840-3610 Fax: 602-840-0233

SAI LUXURY HOTELS, INC.

Business Development/Renovation/Turnaround/Repositioning

Description

The Practice: SAI Luxury Hotels, Inc., identifies and purchases distressed properties, improves the physical property and management structure, then sells the hotel for a profit.

Why the Practice Was Developed: Some time in the early 1980s, Dr. Devendra Sharma concluded that profits could be made in the hospitality industry from buying, renovating, and selling properties, without actually becoming a long-term holder. In late 1982, he invested in a Holiday Inn in Salem, North Carolina, and, after renovating it, sold it for a profit 14 months later. Based on that success, he and a group of investors formed SAI Luxury Hotels, Inc., in 1992.

Execution

The Approach to Implementation: A set of criteria was developed to be followed in determining whether a property had sufficient potential to warrant investment:

- Good location, preferably downtown in a metropolitan area
- Midscale to upscale property
- Franchised (or independent only if eligible for a chain's flag)
- Relatively old facility in dire need of renovation
- Potential of becoming an upscale product
- Owner motivated to sell
- Third-party management company in place
- Minimum base for room revenue
- Significant potential to increase net operating income

SAI performs due diligence in determining an appropriate offer price, estimating renovation costs, and establishing a funding basis. Before an offer is made, SAI projects monthly cash flows, including all expenses, so there are no surprises. "There are no unknowns after we buy the property," stated Dr. Sharma.

Once the purchase is complete, SAI requires substantive information from the management company, including the daily revenue reports, accounts payable, accounts receivable, cash-flow projections, monthly competition survey, sales analysis, monthly financial statements, weekly manager reports, sales reports, reservation system contributions, maintenance and renovation reports, and the daily deposit records.

In addition, each property is required to report its marketing efforts in each of the following areas:

- Contacts with tourism offices
- Contacts with travel agents
- Sales calls
- Clients actively solicited
- Contacts with top accounts
- Contacts with major corporations in the area
- Contacts with groups and associations
- Contacts with the franchise reservations system
- Parties, promotions, and flyers

Outcomes

Success of the Practice: As measured by the return SAI has obtained from its investment, the practice has been successful. In 1993, SAI purchased a Sheraton Hotel in Lowell, Massachusetts, for $2.5 million. The property was renovated and sold for $5.8 million in 1997. A similar success occurred with a Sheraton Hotel in Greensboro, North Carolina, that SAI purchased for $5.2 million. After investing approximately $2 million in renovations, changing the management company, and franchising with Hilton, SAI sold the property for $16.2 million. SAI then purchased a Sheraton in Hartford, Connecticut, for $11.5 million; it invested about $2 million in upscale renovations, resolved labor problems, significantly improved operations, and sold the hotel for $28 million. Currently, SAI has two properties in the South Florida area and one in Montvale, New Jersey. As soon as the improvements are complete, and the properties' net operating incomes are high enough, SAI will sell them.

Advice and Observations: Dr. Sharma offered the following points of advice: Spend time on due diligence. Do not short-change the renovation. Work closely with the management company, but do not leave everything up to the management company. Do not be an absentee owner, but instead visit on a regular basis. Take care of the guest. The quality of the product and the quality of the service determine guest retention rates.

Contact

Devendra Sharma, Ph.D., Chief Operating Officer
SAI Luxury Hotels, Inc.
11608 Appaloosa Run West, Raleigh, NC 27613
Phone: 919-846-8959 Fax: 919-847-3995

SHERATON - DENVER WEST COLORADO

Job Sharing between Sales Managers

Description

The Practice: The Sheraton-Denver West has instituted the practice of job sharing within the sales department by authorizing two sales managers to share one full-time sales position. Although the practice requires that they have close communication with one another, this interaction is accomplished via a sophisticated computer system and a 15- to 30-minute meeting each week.

Why the Practice Was Developed: Changing family circumstances required that a sales manager alter her work status. The sales manager indicated she would be disappointed to leave her job, but felt that any full-time position in the near future would be out of the question. Because this sales manager was highly experienced and valued, William Walp, director of sales & marketing, sought other options to retain the sales manager in some capacity.

Execution

The Approach to Implementation: During a brainstorming session concerning employment options, the sales manager broached the subject of sharing the sales job with a former Sheraton sales associate who was looking to return to the work force part-time. Because Mr. Walp did not know the former sales associate, he suggested she come in and discuss sharing the job. After determining that job sharing might work for the hotel, Mr. Walp asked the two women to prepare a report that included a detailed description of the manner in which they envisioned sharing a single sales position.

While this task was in process, Mr. Walp gathered data from the Internet on job sharing. He was most concerned with the ability of the two sales managers to communicate effectively with the client and to assure clients that they were, in essence, dealing with one person.

The job description prepared by the two women thoroughly addressed Mr. Walp's specific concerns. The description incorporated all the duties and responsibilities of a regular salesperson, but emphasized the necessity of entering into the computer each client contact and its result. Call reporting and communication had to be the watchwords. Further, clients had to have assurances that each of the two sales managers would have a thorough knowledge of each account. The two sales managers' area of responsibility was to include corporate and SMERF sales.

Mr. Walp forwarded the proposal to his general manager, who knew both sales managers. The general manager liked the fit, and obtained approval from the vice president of franchise operations.

Operational Issues: A common hourly pay rate was agreed upon, but the fringe benefit package for each sales manager is yet to be resolved. As of this writing, the corporate office is working on the legalities of dividing a benefit package.

A Trial: During a 90-day trial period the two women alternated between two days on and three days off each week. Coordination was facilitated by some direct communication between the two women each week. Beyond that, both sales managers had to enter every sales contact and topic of client discussion on the call reports, as a means of providing a seamless "connection" with the client.

Costs: The only cost associated with the program was the printing of one business card with both names. The cost of recruiting, soliciting, and training a new employee did not have to be borne because the two employees already were knowledgeable and oriented to the hotel.

Outcomes

Success of the Practice: Mr. Walp is delighted with the program, and his concern about the ability of the client to understand job sharing has abated, largely due to the careful documentation of both sales managers. Too, their enthusiasm for the program and their part-time schedules give them a high energy level that infuses their workdays.

Benefits to Customer: Because one of the sales managers is always available during regular business hours, the customer has not had to wait for a follow-up call to be returned, as might occur when dealing with a part-time representative. Further, while the two sales managers work separately, they always introduce themselves as a duo, and provide proper assurances to the client.

Insights

Advice and Observations: Mr. Walp says he is fortunate to have two compatible people who understand what is required to make job sharing successful. He wishes he had thought through the fringe benefit problem more thoroughly, but expects a resolution of this issue soon. With other departments, part-time workers present fewer potential problems than are likely in a two-in-one sales position. However, for the time being, this practice is working admirably.

Contact

William Walp, Director of Sales & Marketing
(Prior to publication of this study,
Mr. Walp left his position at the property)
Sheraton - Denver West
360 Union Boulevard, Lakewood, CO 86228
Phone: 303-987-2000 Fax: 303-985-7545

SHERATON ELK GROVE

Annual Implementation of a Broad-Based Best Practice

Description

The Practice: Each year the executive committee of the Sheraton Elk Grove identifies and selects a practice that is considered the best method by which to improve financial viability, as well as guest and employee satisfaction. The chosen practice must exemplify a "Hotel of the Year" practice. This practice is then conveyed to all hotel employees, who receive incentives based on the financial and satisfaction improvements resulting from the practice. Because the selected practice is broad-based and not isolated to any one department, the implementation of the practice gives the entire team the ability to see how each one contributes to the overall goals of the hotel.

Why the Practice Was Developed: When General Manager Mike Escalante arrived at the Sheraton Elk Grove, the hotel was in poor financial shape, and guest and employee satisfaction was very low. He felt the hotel was in dire need of improvement. Feeling that the hotel had to be more productive and efficient, Mr. Escalante initiated this "best practice" program after examining Sheraton's "Total Quality" program.

Execution

The Approach to Implementation: The executive committee utilizes "Malcolm Baldrige" criteria to select a practice to implement. The practice must transcend defined departments; that is, it must be sufficiently broad to impact the entire hotel.

Information about the practice is communicated at a meeting of all employees as a "State-of-the-Union" address. Explanations are provided to demonstrate how the hotel, employees, and guests will benefit. The practice is then implemented into the business plan of the hotel. Key processes of the selected practice are identified, and each executive committee member is assigned a key process and goal. Each committee member, in turn, sets up a subcommittee of line employees who are actually responsible for implementing the assigned component. The executive committee members provide weekly reports on their subcommittees' progress and problems.

An incentive program for the line staff is tied to the improvements that result from the implementation of the practice. This incentive program encourages employees to buy into the "best practice" program because they see benefits for themselves, as well as improvements in the hotel. In the initial stages, though, there was some resistance to the program, especially from midlevel managers and the line staff who simply resisted "something new" or who felt the "process takes too much time to implement."

Operational Issues: Mr. Escalante notes that it takes approximately four to six months to implement the program. His initial trial period, accomplished at a previous hotel, lasted 1 1/2

years, and resulted in modifications to the laundry process, the check-in process, and the food-ordering process.

To facilitate the type of decision making required by this program, Mr. Escalante first conducted one-on-one training in "fact-based decision making" with all members of the executive committee. Line employees also are slated to receive this training; in the meantime, the information has been made available to them.

Costs: Mr. Escalante finds it difficult to quantify the costs of the program. The meetings do take time, but no new resources have been needed. The benefits of the program have outweighed any time requirements "many times over."

Outcomes

Success of the Practice: The "best practice" program has been quite successful. Employee satisfaction scores and profitability have significantly increased. The best-practice process is now a part of the core ideology and culture of the hotel. The success of the program has encouraged Mr. Escalante to continue the program indefinitely.

Benefits for Customer: Guests have noted many changes in the hotel and in their interactions with employees. Customers have reported enhanced service, a better physical product, and a perception of better value. Indeed, guest satisfaction surveys, in particular, are "record-breaking."

Advice and Observations: Next time around, Mr. Escalante states that he would probably implement the program a little slower, as some employees found it difficult to align with the practice process. They did not understand it and resisted.

Further, Mr. Escalante notes that methodology, effects, and facts must be documented; consequently, training in software is essential. The executive committee must meet weekly to monitor progress.

Mr. Escalante would delegate more of the tasks involved in the program, as it is "too much for the GM." He also notes that the "best practice" program is ongoing, but in three to five years, he believes the program will become part of the culture to enhance guest and employee satisfaction and, ultimately, financial results. However, patience is critical: "I'm not where I want to be, yet," says Mr. Escalante.

Finally, Mr. Escalante believes his "best practice" program should work in all properties, regardless of size, although it would not work in a "close-minded" organization.

Contact

Mike Escalante, General Manager
(Prior to publication of this study,
Mr. Escalante left his position)
Sheraton Elk Grove
121 NW Point Blvd.
Elk Grove Village, IL 60007
Phone: 847-290-1600   Fax: 847-290-1744

SIMPSON HOUSE INN

Hospitality Training Curriculum with an Emphasis on Respecting Diversity

Description

The Practice: Simpson House Inn offers hospitality training, with a strong emphasis on respect for diversity, among all its managers and staff. Dixie Adair Budke, general manager, identifies the program as "Simpson House University." As part of the training curriculum, she introduced a module labeled "Getting to Know You," which used Myers-Briggs testing to illustrate how everyone has different communication styles. In the "Language Bridge Program," Ms. Budke teaches both English and Spanish as second languages. During the "All-Staff Pow-Wow," the employees unite to celebrate "fabled service" and discuss common issues.

Why the Practice Was Developed: Ms. Budke was hired to move the property from a four-diamond to a five-diamond rating. Initially, Ms. Budke visited five-diamond properties to see what they "looked like, smelled like, and felt like." She then studied her staff and found a diverse group: young people, retired people, and five separate cultures and languages spoken. One-third spoke only Spanish, one-third spoke only English, and a third were either "bi" or "poly" lingual. There was a vast continuum of education, from marginal to highly skilled, and the staff was made up of a cross-section of different dispositions and temperaments. Ms. Budke also recognized that many of the staff had never had the opportunity to stay at a five-diamond property, so they had to trust the standards she set as appropriate to the level. Some were new to the world of work and were learning for the first time how work environments function. She established an interactive performance review process that clearly focuses on standards, expectations, and ongoing personal and professional development.

Ms. Budke, who is currently working on her doctorate in human and organizational development and systems, states, "Seamless, flawless, gracious service can only be given by people who feel good about themselves and what they are doing, and are motivated intrinsically by their own competence and sense of personal mission. I emphasize our opportunity to exercise our service ethic. Those who have such an ethic thrive in this industry, while those who don't struggle greatly. Gracious hospitality is about serving from the heart."

Execution

The Approach to Implementation: Ms. Budke realized that she needed to develop basic training programs. Her initial focal point was the development of entry-level personnel; her targeted individual was "the weakest link on the property."

Currently, Ms. Budke's training addresses issues frequently found in most hospitality programs. She discusses objective measures, including occupancy rates, the AAA standards, profit and loss, and holding people to standards. She teaches her managers about management practices, business procedures, and guest psychology. However, she also includes a number of distinctive programs to promote understanding and self-esteem among the diverse staff.

All-Staff Pow-Wows, conducted in English and Spanish, give the staff an opportunity to discuss issues. The meetings, held in a training room of a nearby church, start at 8:00 p.m., after the beds for the guests have been turned down. Each Pow-Wow lasts three hours, with one hour for housekeeping, one hour for

celebrating, and one hour for innkeeping. Ms. Budke calls the meetings mandatory, but she believes in the theory "feed them and they will come," so she always provides food and music.

To further improve staff communication, Ms. Budke designed "Language Bridge," which teaches both English and Spanish to the staff. This training module includes different activities to help with the language barrier. For example, at the December meeting, each of the Spanish-speaking personnel wrote a Christmas card in English to an English-speaking staff member, and English-speaking staff members reciprocated with holiday greetings in Spanish.

To help employees understand themselves and their co-workers, Ms. Budke developed the "Getting to Know You" training module. As part of this module, Ms. Budke administers the Myers-Briggs temperament indicator test to all employees. The test is given in both English and Spanish. She then promotes the idea that there is no right or wrong way to communicate; each person just has a preferred communication style. After this discussion, she brings the English-speaking and the Spanish-speaking employees from the same departments together, so they are able to see how much they have in common in the way that they view the world — whether they were outgoing or reserved, more comfortable with paperwork or with greeting people.

To further diminish conflict, Ms. Budke instituted a no-tipping policy. When she first arrived, staff members were accusing other employees of stealing tips. Furthermore, big tippers received better service than those who did not tip well. As a result, tipping prohibited a team effort. Ms. Budke believes, "If you hire people you respect, grow them like professionals, and pay them more than they would make at any other property, at the same level, tipping does not become an issue."

There was high turnover and tremendous resistance from the staff when Ms. Budke instituted extraordinarily high performance standards and training programs. Some of the turnover was voluntary and some was not. Resistance came primarily because not everyone wanted to work at the expected level. "That's not necessarily good or bad, but if you want to be on the varsity team, you have to be willing to get up at 6 o'clock and go to practice every morning. You can't be a Friday player."

Success of the Practice: Simpson House Inn operates in a year-round market, and occupancy averages 86%. The Inn is 100% full on the weekends and in the summer. "The next goal is to get to 89% occupancy and maintain a 'zero defect' culture."

Ms. Budke primarily measures success by morale, and by how many people attend the language classes and staff meetings. Today, she believes that the "Simpson House Way" is embedded in her staff's culture, and that even if she left next week, the "Simpson House Way" would sustain itself.

In 1997, Simpson House Inn became the first bed-and-breakfast to be awarded the AAA's five-diamond designation, and it has since maintained that designation level. Ms. Budke believes this achievement is largely a result of the programs she has successfully implemented as part of Simpson House University.

Benefit for the Customer: Excellent customer feedback about the staff indicates that the level of service continues to rise.

Insights

Advice and Observations: Ms. Budke believes that all employees can be motivated by their own competence, if they are trained. She suggests that all employees want to do meaningful work and want to be in an environment that respects their ability to do so. Her challenge was to see whether what she believed was really true, so she established Simpson House University from the ground up. She wanted to provide an environment where people could grow, and even if they left, she wanted it to be a positive termination. One of her goals is to promote the "double bottom line," in which the human factor, productivity, and success are considered equally important. She realizes that it will not happen overnight; it may take a year or more. It will come when it is embedded in the culture.

For this type of diversity training to work, Ms. Budke believes the company must be fully committed to a long-term strategy. The training is not a "silver bullet." She suggests that companies "take the long-term view of success and look at it through different lenses — first people, then productivity. If the first two elements are working solidly together in an environment of respect and creativity, profits will come."

Contact

Dixie Adair Budke, General Manager
The Simpson House Inn
121 East Arrellage Street, Santa Barbara, CA 93101
Phone: 805-963-7067 Fax: 805-564-4811
E-mail: simpsonhouse@compuserve.com

SONESTA HOTELS

Creating a Profit-Center Training Operation

Description

The Practice: Sonesta Hotels offers two innovations in human resources training. The first practice was to create a wholly owned Sonesta subsidiary, Training by Design, that provides staff, management, and executive training for Sonesta and 50 or so other companies. This program has allowed human resources to become a revenue-producing department rather than a cost center.

The second practice is the creation and use of "Personal Service," a board game, the objective of which is to get individuals to think creatively about how to solve a guest problem.

Why the Practices Were Developed: Sonesta is a small, privately held company with 16 properties spread throughout the world in disparate, often exotic, locations. Regarding guests, "location gets them there the first time, but it is the service which brings them back," states Jackie Sonnabend, executive vice president. Consequently, Sonesta has had to become innovative in developing training programs that will provide the desired level of service. Ms. Sonnabend recognized that training should be interesting: "People learn only when they are engaged. Everything is designed to create interest and involvement on the part of the participants." Furthermore, training needs to be creative, as exemplified by Ms. Sonnabend's invention of Personal Service, a game that won the AH&MA Gold Key Award.

Execution

The Approach to Implementation for "Training by Design": In the 1980s Sonesta began a personalized service class for the hourly staff. This initial class blossomed to include training managers, supervisory staff, and eventually upper-level executives. Training is used as a vehicle to communicate and reestablish the Sonesta culture. The philosophy of the training department is to think of employees as clients, and therefore the training department must customize the programs to meet client needs. Location can determine what some of the needs are. The corporate training department spends a lot of time with the general managers and the human resources department developing a training plan for the year, customizing it, and then delivering it.

In the early development stages the company insisted that GMs attend the management training, so they could see its value. Once the GMs participated, they became believers and supporters of the training program.

Former operations managers are used as trainers. This gives them credibility in the eyes of hourly and management staff "because they have been there." Sonesta's training staff numbers eight, led by Grace Andrews, director of training. Some trainers are based at corporate headquarters; some are based at the properties. All managers are trained in English. Trainers travel to the hotels for the sessions so managers at a specific property get the same training at the same time and learn the same skills.

Training is built into the budget. The minimum "suggested" number of hours of training for the clients is two weeks of training per group, spread throughout the year. Training is done on a departmental basis for the hourly staff, whereas managers are trained as a group, across department lines. The Sonesta executive committee receives its training at the annual retreat.

After a decade of fine-tuning its training, Sonesta began getting requests from other companies to conduct their training. At first they rejected the idea, but slowly started to say "yes," and eventually realized they had a business. "Training by Design" was then developed as a wholly owned subsidiary of Sonesta. Currently, about 60% of Training by Design's clients are outside of the hospitality industry.

"Training by Design" uses the same approach with external clients as it does with internal ones. The trainers spend time with clients to find out what their culture is and how the training can be used to reinforce that culture.

The Approach to Implementation for "Personal Service":
As Sonesta built its training program during the '80s, Ms. Sonnabend created "Personal Service." In developing the prototype of the "Personal Service" training game, Ms. Sonnabend played it with 50 managers and traveled to five different hotels. She asked managers to write the scenarios and tested it by playing it with GMs at the annual meeting. This process improved the development of the game.

The game is played as follows: Four two-person teams are given a board token. When a team rolls a die, it moves the token the required number of spaces, landing on a square. The team to the right picks a service card, which contains a service scenario. The idea is that the team that rolled the die has to design a way to respond to the scenario described on the service card.

The team that has read the scenario from the card then judges whether the answer is a good one or not, and how many points that team will receive. Because there are no right or wrong answers, often the teams disagree, resulting in discussions involving all eight players. The game was designed to create this time of "dissension" to get people to discuss service. The game takes about 90 minutes to play. Sometimes tournaments are held between departments.

Operational Issues: The first and foremost hurdle that had to be overcome within the Sonesta organization was the bottom-line orientation of operations. When they were having a month with good revenues, employees did not have the time to attend training classes. On the other hand, when occupancy was low, staff hours were reduced, and therefore the staff was not on-site for training. The solution to this difficulty was to place the training budget in the HR department, not in the operating departments, "so it could no longer be used as a reason not to train."

As Training by Design started to take off, there were naysayers who questioned the need to train other companies. "Why do we want to do this outside business? Why spend money to hire new trainers?" asked some. However, those opinions changed when the revenue dollars began flowing in.

Success of the Practice: Ms. Sonnabend stated that overall the training program has been successful in every hotel, but not every program is successful at every property. "What works in Boston does not always work in Florida," she noted.

One of the benefits of having a high-caliber training staff was exemplified as follows: Trainers were conducting an empowerment class in Bermuda, and as they got into the training, they discovered that middle managers felt disempowered. "We were able to switch gears in the middle of the program because the trainers themselves are also training designers. They can shift and recover in the middle of the session. The customized approach really works."

It is perceived that the clients (i.e., the employees of Sonesta) are able to grow to their full potential. The training is a tool to help them get there.

Benefits for Customer: There are large numbers of guest comment cards commenting on how friendly and helpful the employees are. "In fact, Training by Design has attracted clients because they stayed at a Sonesta hotel, inquired as to who did the training of the staff, and hired us to do their training," commented Ms. Sonnabend.

Advice and Observations: If she could have done something differently, Ms. Sonnabend would have tried to develop Training by Design as a business entity sooner than she did. She wishes she had seen the value of this line of business earlier. Training by Design has enabled the company to hire more trainers for Sonesta hotels, so it has enriched the pool of trainers.

"Spend a lot of time in learning the culture so you can customize the training to the local needs," Ms. Sonnabend suggests.

Advises Ms. Sonnabend: "You have to be able to generate support, to be creative in getting that support." Some of the things she did were to invite the GMs to come to the training sessions, or to give them a role to play in the training. She offered to run training sessions at corporate meetings to get people engaged and interested.

"Don't be shy about involving the decision makers, help them get excited about what you do, and then the road becomes easier," Ms. Sonnabend concluded.

Contacts

Jackie Sonnabend, Executive Vice President
Sonesta Hotels
John Hancock Tower
200 Clarendon Street, Boston, MA 02116
Phone: 617-421-5400 Fax: 617-421-5402

Grace Andrews, Director of Training, Sonesta Hotels,
and President, Training by Design
John Hancock Tower
200 Clarendon Street, Boston, MA 02116
Phone: 617-421-5486 Fax: 617-927-7686

SUNSTONE HOTELS

Focused Growth of Hotel Company Utilizing a REIT

Description

The Practice: Robert Alter, chief executive officer and chairman, has developed Sunstone Hotels through a Real Estate Investment Trust (REIT) and has expanded its ownership of hotels through a focused policy of hotel size, type, and geographic location. By staying within the policy guidelines, the company is better able to maintain control over its operations and produce a more consistent profitability than if it were to be more broad-based and less operationally minded than it is. The practice is designed to acquire hotels that are producing substandard profits, are perhaps not in acceptable physical shape, and are available at a low cost-per-room price in strong markets with barriers to new competition. Sunstone Hotels has elected to confine its geographic base to the West Coast, Mountain states, and Rochester, Minnesota. Once a hotel has been acquired and restored, it is then rebranded based on its size, type, area market, and competition. Thirty-four percent of the hotels are now Marriotts, with the rest branded as Sheraton, Radisson, Holiday Inn, Doubletree, Hilton, Hampton Inns, Hawthorne Suites, and others.

The company's portfolio is 70.1% full-service hotels, 12.5% extended-stay properties, and 17.4% limited-service inns.

Why the Practice Was Developed: To expand the company through the purchase of additional hotels, the obvious capital acquisition requirements had to be met. The formation of a publicly traded REIT was the best method available and provided the most flexibility of any financing method available at the time.

Execution

The Approach to Implementation: Sunstone owned 10 hotels in 1995 when it formed a REIT and went public. Sunstone contributed its hotels for its equity portion of the REIT. Sunstone's approach is to acquire "broken" hotels, fix them up, and rebrand them. Its employees call themselves "hotel doctors." Unlike most other REITs, Sunstone manages all its hotels through its operating company.

Sunstone is comprised of two entities: Sunstone Hotel Investors and Sunstone Hotel Properties. The former is the owning and REIT company, and the latter is the operating and management company that operates all Sunstone hotels. Mr. Alter believes strongly that Sunstone's hotels be operated by Sunstone management.

Costs: The major cost of any REIT is its leverage. Sunstone has been able to keep its leverage to 42% of its asset base, while other REITs have higher leverage. Sunstone has spent $100 million refurbishing 30 of its hotels.

Outcomes

Success of the Practice: Sunstone has grown from 10 hotels in 1994 to 60 today. Average size of the hotels has grown from 130 rooms to 200 rooms per hotel. RevPAR from operations (cash flow) has grown from $1.05 per share to $1.51 per share. Total revenues have grown from $30 million in 1995 to $330 million in 1998.

In December 1998, Sunstone was named Developer of the Year by Marriott Hotels, Resorts and Suites at Marriott's 1998 National Franchise Conference. Sunstone owns 17 Marriott-branded hotels, including six Marriott full-service hotels, six Residence Inns, four Courtyards, and one Fairfield Inn.

Benefits for Customer: Because of Sunstone's strategy, the customer gains the benefit of the availability of lodging that was not attractive or desirable in the past.

Advice and Observations: Mr. Alter has these suggestions for others who would like pursue a similar strategy:

- Stay focused, stay in a consistent class of asset, and stay within a specific geographic area.
- Manage your own hotels.
- Keep debt leverage to a manageable and realistic level.

Contact

Robert Alter, CEO/Chairman
Sunstone Hotels
P.O. Box 4240, 115 Calle de Industrias, Suite 201
San Clemente, CA 92674
Phone: 949-361-3900 Fax: 949-361-5196

SWISSÔTEL

Creation of a Revenue Manager Position to Increase Room Sales Revenues

Description

The Practice: Swissôtel created a revenue manager position to help maximize revenue in room sales. The revenue manager, stationed at the highest level of the hotel property, decides the best price that may be obtained for the product, using the date, the season, the day of the week, the competitive situation, and other factors that enter into establishing a price structure.

Why the Practice Was Developed: Carl Kortum, senior vice president of operations, joined Swissôtel three years ago after a stint in Puerto Rico and was immediately struck by the fact that Swissôtel was operating in a seller's market. He recognized a need for a system that could readily adjust rates to weekly and seasonal demand for the various market segments — commercial, group, and leisure — that Swissôtel served. However, he believed the person or system that was pricing the room should not be the one selling the room. Selling rooms is not difficult if one's rates go low enough, according to Mr. Kortum. The challenge was in developing a system that could provide the optimum rate for maximization of room revenue.

Execution

The Approach to Implementation: Mr. Kortum first convinced the skeptical executive committee of his headquarters hotel in Chicago that the revenue manager should be on the same level as the assistant manager, the controller, and the director of sales. Mr. Kortum had to be persuasive before his proposal was reluctantly adopted.

In filling the position of revenue manager, the individual selected, as a rule, has experience in reservations and front desk, and is math- and detail-oriented. Positioned as an executive, the revenue manager is expected to make decisions, take some chances, be willing to stand by those decisions, and adjust to the inevitable mistakes. The revenue manager, working closely with the director of sales, sets the room rates for as long as several years into the future. The revenue manager's decision can only be overruled by the general manager, which, Mr. Kortum notes, rarely happens.

Costs: Beyond the training of the revenue managers and their subsequent salaries, the cost for this program has been negligible, but the results have been significant.

Outcomes

Success of the Practice: Swissôtel has been able to raise occupancies to approximately 80-85%, with an ADR of $210 in season and $160 in soft periods. This lower rate is offered for weekend specials, which have resulted in strong Saturday nights. Fridays, too, have become much better, but Sundays, as in most commercial hotels, are still tough to merchandise.

Benefits for Customer: Mr. Kortum is convinced the customer, through some ingrained process, expects "value." If he or she perceives the rate is too high, the customer will go elsewhere. If the rate is too low, hotel revenue is lost. The revenue manager, through his tools, experience, and knowledge of the competitive market, can enhance the "value" perception, by having available rooms during peak demand, and by appealing to a broader market by decreasing rates in lower demand times. Ultimately, the customer sets the room rate, and the revenue manager's job is to ensure the rate provides intrinsic value to the customer and dollar maximization to the hotel.

Insights

Advice and Observations: Mr. Kortum believes the emphasis on ADR that many general managers have should be revised to emphasize RevPAR, which is the issue the revenue manager addresses. Initial concerns that the revenue manager might be perceived as "gouging" have proven to be without basis, as the revenue manager's job is to increase *and decrease* rates when the situation warrants. Mr. Kortum further notes that a state-of-the-art computer system is a principal and vital part of the revenue manager's decision-making process.

Contact

Carl Kortum, Senior Vice President of Operations
Swissôtel
323 Wacker Drive, Chicago, IL 60601
Phone: 312-565-8240 Fax: 312-565-4382

SWISSÔTEL

Implementing a Global Sales Effort

Description

The Practice: Swissôtel has established a global sales effort for key accounts, facilitated by a proprietary, computerized global sales data system. This practice places a global team leader in the area from which the bulk of the key account's business is generated; regional team leaders for the same key account are located in other geographic sectors. This sales team cross-sells the key account to drive account sales by using the information on the key account contained in the global sales system.

Why the Practice Was Developed: Shortly after Steve Houser accepted the position of vice president of sales and marketing - The Americas, he learned that North American salespeople were selling only North American properties. He and the senior vice president of sales and marketing initiated a needs assessment program. The findings revealed that no cross-selling was being done anywhere in the organization. That is, key accounts were handled strictly in the region where they were located. In addition, the study indicated a strong need for an integrated global sales system. This need was dramatically evident based on Swissôtel's plan to more than double in size by the end of the year 2000.

Execution

The Approach to Implementation: In April and May 1998, the sales staffs worked on acquiring information about their various accounts to ascertain:

1 Whether the account was a potential key account. (To be eligible for key-account status, the customer must provide Swissôtel with 300 room-nights per year in at least two or more locations.)
2 The currency of the information available on the account.
3 The decision makers within the account at both corporate and local levels.

This information was then fed into the new proprietary data system. Full use of this system will be available by June 1999, when the system is scheduled for completion. The system ensures that the key accounts and their Swissôtel use are fully quantified, and the value of any additional new accounts can be readily determined.

Swissôtel also initiated a global sales team effort for qualified key accounts that designates a global team leader and regional team leaders for each account. For example, a multinational company, XYZ Corporation, is "owned" by the northeast sales division, where the majority of the business originates. Consequently, the global team leader is in the northeast division, and regional team leaders are assigned to the other geographic areas in which the XYZ Corporation has a presence. This strategy means that a sales manager may be a global team leader for one key account and a regional leader on another

key account. The global and team leader's sole responsibility is selling; approximately 35% of their time is spent on the road. As a result of this initiative, the sales organization has become an account-driven agency rather than an occupancy-driven one. The new data system provides full information on the key accounts to facilitate the sales task.

Operational Issues: Mr. Houser's sales budget is 8% of total revenue, and he must preapprove all sales trips. The sales force is evaluated by their contributions to operating goals.

Outcomes

Success of the Practice: The global sales effort for key accounts has been very successful, garnering a 25% revenue increase totaling $9 million from 150 accounts since the program's inception. The Americas division, for which Mr. Houser is responsible, represents 35% of the global account responsibility. Mr. Houser anticipates that the future growth rate will be enhanced by the new data system and the additional key accounts that will be identified.

Benefits for Customer: Swissôtel has a "Swiss Elite" program for key accounts that guarantees availability for up to five rooms at any property worldwide, regardless of the hotel's other commitments. Thus far, this guarantee has met with no problems. The key accounts are keenly aware of their leverage and respond to Swissôtel's efforts.

Insights

Advice and Observations: Mr. Houser believes that others wishing to attempt such a program must be willing to do their homework along with lots of analysis. They must be prepared for cultural resistance in the hotel company. Mr. Houser also notes that clear communication throughout the properties can turn into high expectations and high results in both new accounts and repeat business.

Contact

Steve Houser
Vice President of Sales and Marketing - The Americas
Swissôtel
323 Wacker Drive, Chicago, IL 60601
Phone: 312-565-7919 Fax: 312-565-4382

TAMAR INNS

Implementation of Self-Funded Health Insurance

Description

The Practice: Tamar Inns has implemented a self-funded health insurance plan for employees and their families at its six properties, and opened its own medical office, staffed with a doctor, nurse practitioners, and medical assistants. Tamar implemented cost controls for primary care in its medical office and negotiated "capitated" rates for both in-hospital care and specialist care needs. Dental, prescription, and psychiatric counseling plans also have been implemented. Tamar Inns has been able to realistically budget and effectively manage costs in these areas while offering enhanced services for its employees. Ten years after implementing its self-funded plan, the "cost per covered life" remains well below the cost of when it last opted for an outside insurer in 1988.

Why the Practice Was Developed: Insurance costs throughout the industry were escalating at a double-digit rate throughout the 1980s and early 1990s. After failing to gain a realistic "loss" history from its outside insurer while requesting competitive bids from selected insurance companies, Tamar decided to implement a self-funded insurance plan.

Tamar Inns also felt that if it ran its own primary-care medical office, it could provide better and more responsive care for its employees' medical needs at a lower cost to the company. An extremely tight labor market in the greater Orlando area found the hospitality and lodging industries hiring many people from different cultures and ethnic backgrounds. There were some significant language challenges, and doctors in the area lacked personnel who could effectively communicate in the native tongues of Tamar's employees. As a result management believed that a percentage of Tamar employees were not receiving adequate care. With its own medical office staffed with personnel fluent in Creole, Spanish, and English, Tamar felt the communication barriers would be broken down, and in turn, morale would rise and turnover would decrease.

Execution

The Approach to Implementation: Bob Cox, risk manager, Harris Rosen, president, and Frank Santos, chief financial officer, collectively made the decision to implement a self-funded insurance plan in 1989. To achieve their goals, they knew that they would have to first dedicate the time to learn the medical end of the business and then implement programs to achieve realistic cost controls within three key areas of health care — primary care, in-hospital care, and specialist care. After an initial one-year experience with an inclusive preferred provider organization (PPO) offered by an Orlando-based hospital system, they felt that they had to come up with better ways to control the continually spiraling health-care costs.

The team noted that in the Orlando area hospitals were running an average occupancy of 65%. In a brainstorming meeting, a suggestion was made to approach the hospitals to have them quote to Tamar a capitated rate for in-hospital care for the Inns' covered life employees based upon the average 35% unused beds in their facilities. The concept was to rent the rooms that no one else was using. The second part of this proposal was to guarantee the selected hospital payment on the tenth of every month for the agreed-upon capitated rate. That is, Tamar offered the awarded hospital a guaranteed monthly check calculated on a negotiated rate and based upon the use of a percentage of the hospital's unused beds. This gave Tamar a controlled cost for in-hospital care.

At the same time Tamar decided to operate its own primary-care medical office, which allowed it to control the costs of patients' procedures, costs that had varied widely when the employees selected their own doctors. Some employees did express a concern that the company might begin to know too much about their personal lives. These employees proved to be a small percentage, however, and it grew even smaller when employees calculated their savings by joining this plan. The primary-care office staffs 18 employees under the leadership of Nancy Littleton, office administrator, and Miriam Finegold, M.D. The medical staff is fluent in several languages, which has improved communications with employees. Tamar initially spent $175,000 to renovate and expand the physical facility to meet the needs of the medical office. The medical office, with an annual budget of $550,000, now covers 1,800 square feet.

225

The third key area Tamar's management team had to address was the costs for specialists. Garritt Toohey, vice president, spearheaded the negotiations for a flat rate with four dental offices in the greater Orlando area. Prior to this, Tamar employees were seeking dental attention from nearly 85 separate dentists in the area, and rates varied widely. After completing a "zip code match," the company selected four dental offices and negotiated flat rates for a guaranteed monthly fee from the dentists. For other specialists, such as gynecologists and pediatricians, Tamar partnered with its selected hospital to set up capitated specialists' rates. This was finalized in May 1995.

During this same period, Tamar negotiated a prescription plan with Walgreen's drugstore.

Coverage is available for all employees whose work week exceeds 30 hours, after an initial 30-day post-hire period.

Employees not in the plan, primarily part-time employees, may use the primary-care facility for $15 per visit. Employees may use the medical office during work time and do not have to clock out to do this. All employees are seen within 24 hours of when they request an appointment. Nationally, the average wait for a doctor's appointment within a health maintenance organization (HMO) is estimated at approximately 14 days.

Costs: Currently, the cost of this insurance plan for the covered employee is:

- $5.50 per week, per covered employee.
- Zero deductible for the primary care.
- $10.00 deductible to see a specialist, per incident.
- Zero copay for generic prescriptions.
- $3.00 copay for nongeneric prescriptions.
- $200.00 copay per hospital visit, per incident.

Outcomes

Success of the Practice: With control of primary-care costs and negotiated capitated rates for both in-hospital care and specialist care, Tamar's cost per covered employee has remained substantially below the national per-covered-life cost, resulting in a 10-year savings exceeding $37 million.

Furthermore, Mr. Cox notes that while Tamar Inns' health-care costs are substantially lower than the health-care costs of the competition, Tamar offers better medical service and expanded coverage. At the same time, employee morale is higher, and sick time and turnover have been reduced. Jonni Kimberly,

Year	Number of Covered Lives	Tamar Cost Per Covered Life	National Cost Per Covered Life	Tamar Total Cumulative Savings	Savings Percentage
1989	436	$ 936	$2,700	$ 769,104	65%
1990	435	1,720	3,040	574,200	43%
1991	524	2,223	3,425	629,848	35%
1992	1,014	745	3,710	3,006,510	80%
1993	1,240	871	3,784	3,612,703	77%
1994	1,382	1,384	3,383	2,762,894	59%
1995	1,513	1,256	3,533	3,445,752	64%
1996	2,301	913	3,897	6,865,632	77%
1997	2,471	1,033	3,924	7,143,760	74%
1998	2,830	1,080	4,315	9,155,050	75%
Total	14,146	$12,161	$35,711	$37,965,453	66%

human resources director, has played a major role in communicating benefit information to the employees while keeping the company updated on all federal, state, and local issues, laws, and human resource regulations.

Benefits for Customer: The customers have benefited because good training techniques are not interrupted by continuous high turnover. This practice has resulted in the customers' seeing familiar faces and receiving better service.

Insights

Advice and Observations: Mr. Cox notes that this was not an overnight automatic success. Hundreds of hours of study and fine-tuning were required to achieve the efficiency and cost savings that have been realized. Tamar had to learn about the best software to use and how to hire qualified, patient-friendly doctors and nurse practitioners.

Mr. Cox also warns that this practice makes the company subject to more criticism from employees because the company is not only the administrator of the health plan, but the health provider as well. As a result, the company has to be prepared to respond directly to employees who may be unhappy with a service. "It is Tamar's philosophy to treat our employees (associates) as we would our hotel guests," notes Mr. Cox.

To institute this practice, "it is essential that a company have a strong commitment from the top," states Mr. Cox. Management must devote the time and be given the tools to learn the medical end of the business. Too, there must be enough employees within a concentrated area to justify the fixed expenses. Finally, the company must be able to partner with a hospital to develop some sort of capitated arrangement.

Contact

Bob Cox, Risk Manager
Tamar Inns (RSC Insurance, Inc.)
7345 Sand Lake Road, Suite 402, Orlando, FL 32819
Phone: 407-370-0776 Fax: 407-370-0931

TISHMAN HOTEL CORPORATION

Hotel Renovation: The Doral Park Avenue Hotel

Description

The Practice: Tishman excels at hotel renovations because its three divisions — Tishman Hotel Corporation, Tishman Construction, and Tishman Real Estate — are able to interweave their talents and abilities. The result is what Rob Manning, project manager, calls the "Tishman Edge." The knowledge and expertise that Tishman pulls from its three divisions enables it to yield a highly successful product — as was the case with the renovation of the Doral Park Avenue.

Why the Practice Was Developed: "Tishman is able to draw on expertise from their own estimating, scheduling, contracting, construction management, and hotel operating groups," explained Mr. Manning. "This enables Tishman to provide what the guest actually requires and expects, 'plus one,' as well as what the employees actually require to service the guest." Thus, Tishman knows it can produce a superior product within ownership's overall strategy.

Execution

The Approach to Implementation: The Doral Park Avenue is a 188 room property that has narrow guest corridors, limited vertical transportation, and no loading dock. The original structure was built in 1926, and the most recent renovation of the property had occurred in the late 1980s. The owner had received the property as a foreclosure, and called on Tishman Real Estate to broker the sale of the property. To help establish the pricing, the brokerage assignment involved Tishman's hotel, design, construction, and mechanical divisions to determine the level of investment a potential buyer would expect to invest. The assessment provided the owner with a more realistic and practical understanding of what the asset required.

When the owner decided to hold the property, Tishman Hotel Corporation was contracted to manage the property and Tishman Interiors (construction) was contracted to manage the renovation. Because Tishman had provided the cost estimates, Mr. Manning noted, "we were held to the budgets we had developed for the owner in the sell analysis."

The budget for the renovation included mechanical, plumbing and electrical, some elevator work, new roofing, guestroom and lobby work, as well as some minor structural work. Three-quarters of the budget went into "aesthetic" upgrades. Little to no structural changes were made, other than the addition of three ADA rooms.

The Gettys Group from Chicago was retained to handle interior design. There were two different types of case goods in the guestrooms, and through the excellent efforts of Gettys, both

types were salvaged. The interior soft goods package, which Gettys selected, complements both types of case goods. "They did a very good job within budget parameters," stated Mr. Manning.

The property was open during renovation, and three floors at a time were put out of service. Total renovation time of the guestroom areas was about 3 1/2 months. Several challenges had to be overcome during renovation. The hotel has no loading dock, so all the loading and unloading had to be done curbside. There are only three elevators in the hotel, two guest elevators and one service elevator. The guest elevators were limited to guest use during peak hours. Use of the service elevator also was limited due to use by housekeeping, room service, and mini-bar attendants. Consequently, new furniture, fixtures and equipment had to be delivered between 2 a.m. and 6 a.m., placed on the floors, and then distributed during the day.

There are on average about 13 rooms per floor, and due to the restrictions imposed by the building and hotel operations, during any given week half the rooms on a floor were being stripped of furnishings, which were stored in the balance of the rooms on the same floor. These rooms then had the carpet removed, painting done, and new vinyl and carpeting installed. The following week the same process was done on the second half of the rooms. On the third week, the new FF&E was put into place. This required precision timing and teamwork from all involved — housekeeping, movers, liquidators, and tradespeople.

Success of the Practice: The project was completed under budget and on time. There has been a significant improvement in the product and increased value of the asset. As a result, the hotel has been able to change some of its client base and yield a significant increase in the ADR.

Benefits for Customer: There have been very positive reactions from the guests.

Rob Manning, Project Manager
Tishman Hotel Corporation
666 Fifth Avenue, New York, NY 10103
Phone: 212-399-3600 Fax: 212-262-0037

Insights

Advice and Observations: Mr. Manning offers these suggestions for others undertaking similar renovations: Understand the owner's intent. Maintain an up-to-date budget and schedule. Work with the hotel operations team, keeping it apprised of what to expect. Coordinate with all the hotel departments; maintain constant communication. Understand what can and cannot be done. Know what the operations team is expecting and what it can lend to the process. Anticipate what temporary hindrances will be placed on operations, and let them know.

TOWNEPLACE SUITES BY MARRIOTT

Cross-Trained Staffing Model as Driver of Revenue

Description

The Practice: Towneplace Suites has developed a staffing model that is the driving source of revenue behind the concept of the brand. Towneplace Suites has been able to position itself as an affordable extended-stay brand by reducing staffing costs. The typical Towneplace property, which contains 95 suites, has a service team of 10 to 12 associates with a high degree of accountability and responsibility for all members. The general manager has an expanded role with direct responsibility for sales and other operations. However, even with reduced staffing, Towneplace Suites is able to deliver a high level of service due to its cross-training program.

Why the Practice Was Developed: Towneplace Suites was designed to appeal to the extended-stay traveler (i.e., traveling for five or more consecutive nights) in search of a moderate-priced accommodation. To be successful in the highly competitive extended-stay lodging market, Towneplace Suites needed a more economical yet functional staffing model capable of maintaining the high level of service that is associated with the Marriott image. Using Dr. Len Berry's "On Great Service" as a resource, Tim Sheldon, senior vice president of the brand, and his team envisioned and developed a unique service philosophy and staffing model that maintained the Marriott standards yet minimized labor costs.

Execution

The Approach to Implementation: The staffing, training, and service models were developed as an integral part of the brand concept. The first step was communicating the high service expectations to the prospective franchisees, who represent 70% of the ownership, and reinforcing the idea that service would not be compromised due to a smaller staffing model and a lower price point. The second step was the development of the actual training and service tools. Mr. Sheldon and his team benchmarked activities at Residence Inn and Courtyard by Marriott to develop a matrix of different service encounters. This matrix of approximately 20 activities became the basis for the cross-training of Towneplace Suites' general managers and staff. Various role-plays and training tools were created for each aspect of the matrix, and a four-point ranking was used to evaluate managers' and employees' abilities in each function.

Next, Towneplace needed to select prospective general managers for the new properties. Strong leadership skills were deemed a must. In addition, a screening tool called the SRI Assessment, created for Marriott by Gallup, was used to assess the entrepreneurial skills, multitasking abilities, and degree of service orientation held by general manager candidates. Those who demonstrated the greatest leadership skills in conjunction with the highest compatible SRI scores were the top candidates. Once hired, all new general managers attended a four-week training course, of which three weeks focused on service delivery, including the cross-training matrix, and one week focused on sales.

After the general managers were trained, the fourth step was the training of their newly hired service team members. A regional leader, the new general manager, and the new service team spent three days together training and reviewing the various functions of the service-delivery matrix. During training, each member of the team was rated on each function within the matrix. Employees were then empowered to train other members of their team in the skills for which they were highly rated to increase the overall skills of the team and spread functionality. The training also focused on encouraging aggressive problem solving, and working as a service-delivery team. The goal was to create a small, highly motivated team with an integrated service culture and high degree of independent problem solving skills.

One of the methods used to achieve this objective was an emphasis on role-playing. All members of the brand team (both property and corporate) have little red role badges. Any time a brand team member places the red badge over his or her nametag, employees on-hand immediately have to enter a role-play in which the brand team member is treated as a guest. Role-playing gives the employees an opportunity to demonstrate and improve their service-delivery skills.

Another effective method has been the sharing of service anecdotes with the entire organization. Each property shares service stories and examples of how service team members have handled various situations and met individual guests' needs, via the company intranet and through daily meetings held at every property. This information sharing has aided in increasing skills, capturing new ideas, and actively demonstrating the various aspects of the service-delivery matrix. It also has helped to create an organizational model in which the focus is on constant cross-training designed to continuously improve the service to guests.

Operational Issues: Towneplace Suites has had to face the operational challenge of providing training in a multilingual environment. The teams at each property are so small that it is difficult to provide specialized language training, and thus communication was sometimes problematic.

A second challenge has been the transition from pre-opening to operation. As a new brand, Towneplace Suites has limited resources. Training and hiring of the general managers and their staffs occurred during pre-opening when each property's staff could be trained as a whole. Now that the brand is operating, Towneplace has to handle issues of turnover and new hires. Consequently, Towneplace has had to adjust its initial training techniques, and examine how to reinforce its service message for new hires. A team of general managers is currently examining options.

Outcomes

Success of the Practice: Towneplace Suites has been pleased with its financial performance. The model of reduced labor costs coupled with high service delivery has been successful in the 17 properties opened to date. In addition, the employees benefit through greater job satisfaction due to: (1) a high level of decision-making responsibility, (2) their ability to improve/increase their skill base with cross-training, (3) the team environment (vs. hierarchy), (4) the continuous improvement process (vs. the general manager making decisions and requiring the staff to implement), and (5) the high degree of accountability.

Benefits for Customer: The cross-trained staff increases the level of guest service for the following reasons:

- Problems are solved more quickly because any team member is capable of responding to any guest request.
- Because the team member to whom the problem is handed is responsible for solving it, guests receive faster resolution to their problems.
- The overall property environment is much more relaxed as guests are able to create "relationships" with service team members with whom they have direct interaction.

Insights

Advice and Observations: The ability to deliver against the TPS staffing and service model is dependent on:

- Hiring the right people, with strong leadership skills and a true commitment to service.
- Providing the necessary tools to allow property teams to focus on continuous improvement.
- Creating accountability for all team members.
- Establishing measurements so all team members know for what they are accountable.

Committing to such a practice (i.e., cross-training) also requires an acknowledgement that it will be necessary to expend resources — financial and human — to develop processes for which results may not be obvious in the short term, but will create value for the brand in the long term.

Contact

Erica Alexander
Towneplace Suites by Marriott
One Marriott Drive, Washington, DC 20058
Phone: 301-380-3019 Fax: 301-380-3802

TRAVELODGE

Guest Loyalty Program at the Economy Level

Description

The Practice: Travelodge has created a guest loyalty program called Travelodge Miles that is similar to airline programs and awards points for room-nights, which can be redeemed for travel awards or merchandise items found in the Travelodge catalog. The program is easy to operate at the property level and has a lower threshold for guest participation than other guest loyalty programs. Guests receive VIP status, a gold credit card, and surprise gifts at various levels. Employees also are rewarded.

Why the Practice Was Developed: Travelodge chose to upgrade its guest loyalty program as part of its strategic plan to grow the Travelodge brand. Focus groups had shown the previous loyalty program had mainly benefited the "road warrior" and the threshold for wider guest participation was too high — especially for two important market segments Travelodge wanted to attract, leisure guests and the senior market. Travelodge also was committed to enhancing the value of the brand to the franchisees and increasing the perceived value to both existing and potential guests.

Execution

The Approach to Implementation: Dorothy Dowling, vice president of marketing, and her staff began by creating an application form to be distributed at the property level. This form contained a plastic credit card that could be detached, easily completed, and used immediately. The balance of the form could be filled out at the guest's leisure and given to the front desk or forwarded by fax or the Internet. This eliminated a common complaint — that it takes six to eight weeks in most programs to be able to use the card.

A catalog of gifts was created to appeal to the guests. Each year previous gift selections are reviewed and the catalog is revised, reflecting previous selections and latest trends, to keep the catalog current and fresh.

The first Travelodge Miles award level was set at a low 250 points, which requires anywhere from a three- to seven-night stay depending on the property. The top award is 3,750 miles, which entitles the guest to a weekend at a resort, or such merchandise as a mountain bike, a barbecue, or a Eureka vacuum cleaner.

When a guest reaches 750 miles, anywhere from 8 to 15 nights depending on the type of hotel, Travelodge mails a membership card with the guest's name embossed in gold, which recognizes the guest as a Travelodge VIP. When the card is presented at the property, the guest receives VIP treatment, which includes free local calls. The guest also is authorized to use a special VIP reservation line. Travelodge maintains a guest history file on the VIP guests; this information is passed to the property along with the reservation.

The Travelodge Miles program was inaugurated in July 1997 with a huge media blitz. A newsletter announcing the new benefits was sent to all members of the previous program. The franchisees were given colorful promotional tools to interest the guests. All franchisees received detailed instructions on how to administer the program. Within a 60-day window an incredible 94% of the franchisees were participating in the program. There are currently 104,000 members, many of them very active with stays of 80 to 100 room-nights a year. Travelodge Miles awarded 25,000,000 miles during its first year of operation.

As part of its effort to grow the Travelodge brand, retain existing guests, bring in new business, and deliver value to the franchisees, the Travelodge marketing department created strong marketing programs and used the guest loyalty program as the cornerstone. Three times a year — spring, summer, and fall — Travelodge offers special promotions where it rewards guests with double miles as an extra incentive to encourage them to come into the properties, learn more about Travelodge, and experience the product.

During the spring promotion, when customers reached 750 miles, they automatically received a 30-minute prepaid phone card as a thank you for their business. During the summer promotion Travelodge affiliated with Dream Works to provide tickets to the movie *Small Soldiers* and sent customers with 750 miles four tickets to the movie. In the fall promotion, the gift for 750 miles was a customized Sleepy Bear and Rand-McNally road atlas. These are gifts and do not require a guest to redeem his or her miles, although the gifts can be acquired by guests for 250 points each, if the guest so chooses.

When Travelodge started the Travelodge Miles program it also built a communications system, including video training programs, to communicate with the franchisees on how to use the program. This system also provided the property with daily figures to create awareness of the benefits for the franchisee in creating revenue.

Franchisees, eager to enhance the program and make it even more successful, suggested an employee reward be built in for generating new members in the program. Last spring, employees who signed up 10 new members received the prepaid card; in the summer program they received the free movie tickets. Travelodge wants to reward employees as they know the employees are the most important factor in securing new members.

Outcomes

Success of the Practice: The guest loyalty program has been a success from the standpoint of all the interested parties. The marketing program with the guest loyalty program as its cornerstone has undoubtedly helped Travelodge become one of the fastest growing Cendant brands. The franchisees have benefited significantly as Travelodge Miles members stay longer — 2.1 nights compared to 1.7 — and the average room rate for the members is $5.00 higher, proving the loyal guest is the best guest.

Benefits for Customer: The guests benefit because the lower thresholds allow more guests to participate in Travelodge Miles. The guests value their gold credit cards and VIP status, which are rare at the economy level. The merchandise selections and travel rewards can be enjoyed not only by the guests, but also shared with their families. Last year one guest did all his Christmas shopping from the catalog.

Insights

Advice and Observations: Ms. Dowling advises anyone considering a guest loyalty program to build compliance at the property level by creating revenue increases for the franchisee and constantly communicating this information to the property. Furthermore, the program must be easy to administer at the property level and not interfere with the guest's desire for a speedy checkout.

Contact

Dorothy Dowling, Vice President of Marketing
Travelodge
339 Jefferson Road, P.O. Box 278, Parsippany, NJ 07054-0278
Phone: 973-496-8913 Fax: 973-496-2284

US FRANCHISE SYSTEMS, INC.

Franchising Agreements at USFS

Description

The Practice: Mike Leven, the founder and president of US Franchise Systems, Inc., and his partner, Neal Aronson, developed what they consider to be "a fair and reasonable franchise agreement." Since beginning USFS, the backbone of the organization has been franchisee relations. The goal has been to treat franchisees honorably and reasonably, and the franchise agreement reflects that philosophy. Agreements are based on Mr. Leven's philosophy of, "We are here to share ideas, wisdom, and expertise with franchisees, co-workers, and the industry, along with the promise that we can be a franchise business that makes guests happy, makes a fair profit, and can be a light in the corporate world for others to emulate ... I want to honor the risk taker and to satisfy the customer, so that all three parties of the play win — franchisee, guest, and USFS."

Execution

The Approach to Implementation: The franchise agreements developed by USFS are far less one-sided than many others are. For example, any substantial change in standards requires approval of a two-thirds majority of franchisees in the system, while in a traditional franchise agreement such changes are normally at the licensor's discretion. If a franchisee's property is performing at an occupancy of 50% or less after two years of operation, he or she may leave without payment of liquidated damages, contrary to traditional agreements. Other terms in the franchise agreement contribute to building good faith and good relationships, such as no unreasonable upgrade requirements and impact policies, and no hidden fees. In addition, areas of exclusivity are offered for the term of the contract and determined by the franchisee and USFS together on a case-by-case basis to logically address such factors as market size, hotel size, proximity to competing lodging facilities, and other demand generators. In the case of a transfer, while most companies charge full application fees (which can amount to well over $50,000), USFS's fee is only $5,000. When an agreement is transferred, if the previous hotel has maintained a quality score, there is no property improvement plan, which helps to encourage good quality in the system.

The table at the end of this case illustrates key areas of differentiation between a USFS franchise agreement and a traditional license agreement.

Operational Issues: One operational issue was the communication and reservation system. USFS was the first company to develop a reservation system that handles all reservations via the Internet — "total communications." Reservations at local properties are communicated entirely to CRS through the Internet. Recently the company also unveiled full Internet booking capabilities down to last-room availability.

Outcomes

Success of the Practice: The phenomenal growth of USFS is offered as evidence of the success of treating franchisees as partners. As of September 30, 1998, systemwide, there was a total of 902 properties open or under development in 49 states, South and Central America, Canada, the Caribbean, Israel, and South Africa, a 20-fold increase from the 45 hotels open or under development when the company began. This figure represents 518 Microtel Inn & Suites, 222 Hawthorn Suites, and 162 Best Inn properties.

Benefits for Customer: Many of the franchisees have told Mr. Leven that the key reason they went with US Franchise Systems, over the many competitors, was its user-friendly franchise agreement.

Insights

Advice and Observations: Mr. Leven "does not want a franchise business that talks down to [the franchisee], but one that talks with [the franchisee], where people feel free to take advantage of what our economic system has to offer them, not at others' expense, but from their own skill." Further, Mr. Leven notes, "I want our company to be an example for others to follow, that it can be done the right way."

Franchise Agreement Type	US Franchise Systems	Traditional
Protected Territory	Life of agreement negotiated with each deal	None, or formula that is generally not reflective of individual deal
Transfer Fee	$5,000	Full application fees that can run $50,000 and higher
Liquidated Damages	Tied to property performance: Occ.<50% — No fee Occ. 50-59.9% — One year notice Occ. 60-69.9% — Two years' royalty fees Occ.≥ 70% — Three years' royalty fees	Three years of royalty and marketing and reservation fees under any circumstances, or full fees for remaining term of contract
Mandatory Major Upgrades to Hotel	Based on quality scores for previous five years	At licensor's discretion
Change in Manual or Standards	Changes requiring substantial investment require approval of 66% of the hotels in the system	At licensor's discretion

Mike Leven, President & CEO
US Franchise Systems, Inc.
13 Corporate Square, Suite 250, Atlanta, GA 30329
Phone: 404-321-4045 Fax: 404-321-4482

THE WALDORF-ASTORIA

Gathering Customer Feedback and Coding Performances

Human Resources

Operations

Sales & Marketing

Description

The Practice: The Waldorf-Astoria uses an innovative practice to maintain and improve quality and service while measuring hotel performance. A "quality quiz" is given to guests at every service contact point. A coding scheme was developed to track the results of the quiz and indicate any actions needed to improve operations. The coding scheme was so successful in helping to improve performance it has been expanded to all hotel measurement devices.

Why the Practice Was Developed: The development of the "quality quiz" and the coding scheme was a partnership between Hilton and J. D. Power. The original idea was to create a breakthrough in the level of satisfaction of Hilton's customers throughout the entire company. Observing that customer-satisfaction indices had plateaued, Hilton was looking for something to stimulate response.

Execution

The Approach to Implementation: According to Eric Long, general manager, most customer comment cards are never completed by guests because they are relatively lengthy. Thus, response rate is not satisfactory. To counter that problem, Hilton developed a 30-second quality quiz that is administered at check-out, in the restaurants, and at virtually every customer contact point. The feedback is immediate, and a great return rate is achieved since it is such a short survey. Similar surveys were developed by the Waldorf-Astoria to measure customer satisfaction following a catering or meeting event.

Each quality quiz comprises only five or six questions with a scale of one to seven, and the customers check off where they perceive the property to be in relation to the question asked. There are nine different cards, each with different questions, and they are randomly sorted. These cards measure only critical "care abouts" ("care abouts" were defined in a separate study by Hilton).

Approximately 100 to 125 surveys are received and scored daily. The results go to Mr. Long, who circles the low scores and the customer comments that require follow-up. The more serious concerns are immediately flagged for a personal follow-up phone call or written letter, as may be appropriate.

J. D. Power and Hilton have partnered in the measurement criteria for customer satisfaction data gathered from the quality quizzes: red, yellow, and green zones. Green is "good"; yellow is "you're making progress, but there is still work to do here"; and red is "we're really below the expected performance." The results of the quality quizzes are placed in month-end summaries, which indicate to the hotel employees exactly where they are, and how they are doing, by department, discipline, and as a whole. "It is absolutely amazing to see the reaction when a particular team sees its performance is in the red zone. We could have the same score without the red designation and the team will be thoughtful. But add the red coloration, and it is like lightning," claims Mr. Long. The color scheme has been so successful the hotel has expanded it to encompass virtually all of the hotel measurement devices.

Outcomes

Success of the Practice: "Our financial targets are exceptionally high, and yet our customer satisfaction index is at an all-time high," according to Mr. Long. The Waldorf Towers recently was named one of the top 25 luxury hotels in North America during the last survey conducted by *Condé Nast Traveler* magazine.

This program is a corporate-wide program, and takes time to implement, but the effect on the hotel has been significant. The intention is to drive the program all the way down the organization, even to a specific section of a housekeeping floor.

Benefits for Customer: This quality quiz program "has really knocked down the rate of complaints by a sizable percentage," asserts Mr. Long. This reduction in dissatisfaction is due to the fact that the vast majority of guests have any complaints resolved while they are still at the property. Since the start of the quality quizzes, the Customer Satisfaction Index has reached a new historical high for the property by a wide margin, while the hotel has attained the highest room rate ever.

Insights

Advice and Observations: Mr. Long suggests that companies attempting to implement a similar program need to spend as much time developing and involving the nonexempt management as the exempt teams. Not doing so is a mistake; it is necessary to make the time. "You must have a totally connected leadership team."

Contact

Eric Long, General Manager
The Waldorf-Astoria
301 Park Avenue, New York, NY 10022
Phone: 212-355-3000 Fax: 212-371-3510

THE WALDORF-ASTORIA

Revenue Maximization for the Food and Beverage Department

Description

The Practice: The Waldorf-Astoria instituted revenue management for all food and beverage outlets, resulting in a number of actions. Instead of focusing only on cost-cutting measures (potentially reducing food and labor cost percentages), a plan was developed to increase revenue for each food and beverage outlet. Besides advancing ideas on how to increase revenue, chefs were trained in how to schedule staff more efficiently, thus saving labor costs. To maximize revenue and compensate for a decrease of "in-house capture rates," food and beverage outlets were repositioned to attract nonhotel markets. A food and beverage marketing position was created to coordinate food and beverage marketing efforts of all units and to help implement revenue-maximization efforts. Service-recovery systems were improved. A training program on wines for line staff was implemented so that they would feel more confident selling and serving wines. A new restaurant reservations system was introduced, helping to improve dining room use, cut telephone use in restaurants, and improve communication between guests and each food and beverage operation.

Why the Practice Was Developed: Although the hotel's food and beverage department was generating a significant amount of revenue and showed good profitability, management felt that the food service operations' potential for revenue was not fully realized. Managers wanted to increase departmental profitability and improve service standards. The flagship restaurant, in particular, had the potential to either make contributions to departmental profit or at least not produce losses. Instead of competing with each other, food and beverage units within the hotel needed to coordinate advertising efforts, presenting a clear understanding to the outside customer of the different products and services the Waldorf-Astoria offers.

Execution

The Approach to Implementation: Instead of a top-down management approach, Christophe Le Chatton, director of food and beverage, and his predecessor involved unit managers and head chefs of all food and beverage outlets in evaluating each food service operation by identifying areas for improvement pertaining to quality standards, revenue maximization, communication, operational effectiveness, and technology. Five different teams were formed, each one assigned the task of identifying potential problems and developing suggestions on how, for example, revenue could be maximized, or communication or technology improved. A set of comprehensive objectives was developed through an interdepartmental approach involving the food and beverage director and executive chef, as well as a food and beverage analyst, the catering director, and the room-service director.

Initial skepticism by the staff that the best practice might represent "a typical management cost-cutting effort, especially reducing labor cost," was overcome through the involvement of all key players in brainstorming ideas and developing business plans for the food and beverage outlets. According to Mr. Le Chatton, "fear about negative consequences of the revenue

maximization effort and the relative lack of knowledge about the practice could have stymied the success of the practice had the key players not been involved in the development of this best practice."

Each unit developed a business plan to bring about an increase in revenues and profitability for the unit. Through this approach all team members became stakeholders in the success of the revenue and profit maximization effort. Special attention was given to reducing labor cost. However, instead of a directive to unit managers and head chefs to cut labor cost across the board, top-level culinary staff was trained in effective labor scheduling, resulting in a significant decrease of labor cost. Weekly forecasts were reviewed with each food and beverage outlet's chef, and methods were developed to match appropriate staffing levels with the expected volume of business. Line staff, especially in the area of dining room service, received additional training (aside from the customary training new employees receive), so that the highest level of service could be offered consistently. A dining-out program, allowing wait and kitchen staff to be a dining guest in other Waldorf-Astoria restaurants and restaurants outside the hotel, made each culinary and service team member "the toughest critic," generating many ideas for improvement and an increased awareness of food and service quality.

Costs: The overall costs of this practice were relatively small. The largest cost is represented in the newly created food and beverage marketing position. Being able to spread these costs among 36 outlets reduced the burden for each facility significantly. Expenditures for the "dining out" program are relatively small. All costs were easily offset by the increase in revenue and improved departmental profits.

Outcomes

Success of the Practice: Throughout all the dining rooms, cover count rose by 100%. Restaurants previously losing money could either be turned into profitable operations or at least losses could be reduced by more than 80%. An improved reservation system allowed for consolidation of marketing and advertising activities, thus increasing effectiveness of food and beverage marketing efforts. An improved level of dining-room service, a newly installed restaurant-reservation system, and changing menus to attract local markets led to higher customer satisfaction, as measured through guest satisfaction surveys, administered and analyzed through an outside firm. The dining-out program has enabled managers and line staff to develop a clear understanding of Waldorf-Astoria's service standards. Training in the area of dining room service and wine appreciation increased the service staff's comfort level merchandising wines, which in turn improved guest satisfaction and added significantly to beverage sales throughout the various restaurants.

Benefits for Customer: Among the most notable benefits are the improvements in the service-recovery system and dining-room service, especially in luxury restaurants, through increased awareness of quality standards. An improved, more user-friendly restaurant reservation system benefits guests as well, as they can call one restaurant and are able to receive information on other restaurants and their menus or special events from one source.

Insights

Involve everybody who plays a role in the success of this practice, notes Mr. Le Chatton. A vision that can be shared by line staff and management is a key ingredient for success. Staff members working at the front line often bring good ideas forward.

Advice and Observations: Provide the necessary tools to achieve the objectives, for example, training in the area of staff scheduling, suggests Mr. Le Chatton. The dining-out program also has helped the line-level management and staff to gain a better understanding of quality standards. Attempt to communicate clearly with all the players and make everybody a stakeholder.

Contact

Christophe Le Chatton, Director of Food and Beverage
The Waldorf-Astoria
301 Park Ave., New York, NY 10022
Phone: 212-355-3000, Ext. 4804 Fax: 212-872-7272

WALT DISNEY WORLD RESORTS AND THEME PARKS

Providing a "Touchable" Dining Experience

Description

The Practice: Each of the more than 500 theme food and beverage outlets of Walt Disney World Resorts and Theme Parks provide a "touchable experience," delivered to the guest via the atmosphere and the food. According to Dieter Hannig, vice president of food and beverage operations, "dining has to be a complete experience, satisfying the palate, the need to be pampered, and the need for entertainment. Guests want to be transported to another setting, another country, or another culture while they dine."

Why the Practice Was Developed: Mr. Hannig remarks, "Fifteen or 20 years ago it was acceptable to place a gourmet restaurant, a coffee shop, and a snack bar in a hotel. Menus were selected and prices were set, and the customer would come and make the food and beverage operation successful. This is not the case anymore. People are much more sophisticated, expecting more than sustenance when visiting restaurants. Disney Corporation wants to offer an experience that is touchable — food, service, ambiance, and entertainment — each time a guest visits one of their food-service outlets."

Mr. Hannig goes on to say, "People coming to WDW expect magic, not only in the theme park, but also in the hotels and, last but not least, the food and beverage operations. If you are in the Magic Kingdom you don't expect anything to go wrong. Our guests expect perfection, every time."

Execution

The Approach to Implementation: The design of the restaurant is a crucial element of the guest's experience. Walt Disney World strives to make each restaurant as authentic as possible, including the service, the menu, the beverage list, and the décor, to assure that each guest's dining experience brings the highest level of satisfaction. For example, a restaurant in Disney World with a Northwestern theme offers food from Seattle, wine from Oregon, and a log cabin décor, creating an experience as close as possible to being in Oregon or Seattle itself.

Access to restaurants is easy, uncomplicated, and, most important, nonintimidating. "It is important to remember that many restaurant patrons do not feel comfortable walking through long hotel corridors and big lobbies to enter a restaurant; therefore, we have located some of our restaurants so that they feel like a free-standing food-service operation," says Mr. Hannig.

After many long hours or days of travel to WDW, the arriving guests are often tired and need a stress-relieving environment. Through personal service in its restaurants, WDW helps its guests to relieve that stress and to have a carefree and memorable stay. To ensure topnotch guest service, training is conducted for both managerial and line staff to foster an understanding and commitment to the mission of the food-service operation. Line-level employees are empowered to make decisions with respect to service recovery and to ensure that each guest has an excellent dining experience, without having to confer with management. Managers are trained to check on each guest's table during their restaurant visit allowing for maximum guest contact and immediate feedback. A bottom-up approach to management is practiced and includes line-staff evaluation of top management's performance.

Outcomes

Success of the Practice: Each of WDW's food-service operations makes significant contributions to the profitability of the resort and theme park. According to Mr. Hannig, the rate of returning guests is also high and customer satisfaction is high, as measured through surveys administered at the location and through outside research firms.

Thanks to outstanding food-service operations, several WDW restaurants have won prestigious awards in recent years.

Advice and Observations: When planning dining operations, keep the total experience of the patron in mind. All team members, be they managers or line staff, are equally important to the success of each food-service operation. Provide ongoing training to all staff — managerial and line — to enable them to contribute to the success of the business to their fullest extent.

Contact

Dieter Hannig, Vice President of Food and Beverage
Walt Disney World Resorts and Theme Parks
P. O. Box 10000, Lake Buena Vista, FL 32830
Phone: 407-560-4520 Fax: 407-560-9131

WHITE LODGING SERVICES

Preshift Meetings for All Departments

General Management

Human Resources

Operations

Description

The Practice: White Lodging Services has instituted 15-minute preshift meetings for line employees in all departments as a mechanism for improving communication, goal setting, training, employee recognition, and corporate policy. The guidelines for each departmental preshift meeting are determined by the corporate office, and different topics are introduced each day. Seventy-five percent of the meeting time is devoted to listening to the line staff's suggestions, criticisms, concerns, and ideas. Employees are paid for the 15-minute preshift meetings.

Why the Practice Was Developed: Chairman and CEO Bruce White believes that managing a department or hotel shift-to-shift is the best way to achieve extraordinary success. This derives from benchmarking efforts by Mr. White. He found examples of companies that were effectively using this idea, and drew on their practices as the foundation for the White Lodging Services preshift meeting. The common goal is guest service.

Execution

The Approach to Implementation: Although Mr. White conceived the practice of preshift meetings, the key to its success can be attributed to the alignment of all levels of management in embracing the concept. The long-term goal was to improve guest satisfaction both internally (the employee) and externally (the customer). Roger Aufieri, executive vice president of operations, brought the concept to reality. Mary Jo Dolasinski, director of training and career development, was charged with rolling out the practice to the properties. It was introduced at the annual managers' meeting. In subsequent weeks, a "Passport to Excellence" — listing the hotel mission, three steps to service, critical success factors, and 22 basic standards of operation — was issued to every employee. Also, each hotel celebrated the advent of preshift meetings with a big party, the theme of which was "Beginning a Journey to Excellence."

Initially, some line-staff members resisted the practice. For example, the housekeeping attendants felt they needed to get their rooms cleaned, but after realizing the benefits of the meeting, they now look forward to the preshift. Some managers also disliked the idea of the preshift meeting at first because it required an additional 15 minutes of their time.

Facilitated by Ms. Dolasinski and the regional managers, implementation required six months. The preshift meetings are designed to improve two-way communication between the line staff and managers, establish a forum for recognizing the line staff, improve service quality, and increase profitability.

Over time, the preshift has evolved so Wednesday meetings also include a "Training Moment." Additionally, the preshift includes a "Corporate Topic of the Week," so that all the staff is kept "in the loop." Classes, too, have been integrated into the preshift so that Spanish/English and other languages are taught.

Operational Issues: To increase the productivity of the preshift, managers are trained in listening skills, because 75% of the meeting requires listening to employees, while only 25% of the meeting involves managerial presentations.

Costs: The cost of implementing the practice has been minimal, primarily consisting of printing Passport Cards and developing training grids. The benefits of the preshift have surpassed any costs by "20-fold."

Outcomes

Success of the Practice: The preshift meetings have been a resounding success, as measured in four ways:

1 Guest satisfaction comment cards and surveys.
2 Employee turnover statistics.
3 Financial results.
4 Internal audits.

The preshift meetings have facilitated open communications at all levels. Additionally, the preshift provides the means for directing all activities each day and reducing response time.

Line-staff feedback has been positive, and employee retention has improved. Employees now have a continuous learning process in place. Furthermore, they can network with each other and their supervisors, and they have an opportunity to provide feedback to the company on a daily basis. The practice of preshift meetings has been most successful in housekeeping, laundry, maintenance, and front desk.

White Lodging Services consistently performs above brand averages within all the brands that it manages. Radisson has awarded White Lodging the Presidential Award for four years running. Marriott has recognized the company and many of its leaders with various awards and honors. Other company recognitions have come from Hampton Inn, Sleep Inn, and Holiday Inn.

The belief within White Lodging Services is that the preshift meetings have played a strategic role in keeping alignment and focus through all levels of the organization. White Lodging Services further contends that it is this alignment and focus that has allowed the company to grow from 13 hotels in 1993 to its current 56 hotels, an addition of 43 hotels in five years.

Ms. Dolasinski notes that preshift has been a very powerful tool within the company and has become one of the cornerstones of company culture. Since its inception, many companies have observed the practice, have embraced its basic tenets, and are now implementing the practice in their own organizations.

Insights

Advice and Observations: Topics and length of time for the preshifts may vary in the future as the needs of the organization change, but the meetings always will play a vital role in the company. Ms. Dolasinski states that "in implementing preshift meetings, one of the keys to success is in the rollout, or kickoff. The company needs to inject excitement and pizzazz. It also has to show the benefits to its employees of having preshift meetings."

Ms. Dolasinski suggests that all companies seeking to implement this practice be completely committed to the preshift meeting. Otherwise, it is difficult to execute. Ms. Dolasinski believes the practice will work in all types of entities — hotels, large or small; departments of 2 or 20; restaurants; and theaters. Indeed, Ms. Dolasinski states that she "can't think of where the practice would not work."

Contact

Mary Jo Dolasinski, Director of Training and Development
White Lodging Services
1000 East 80th Place, Merrilville, IN 46410
Phone: 219-769-3267, Ext. 4347 Fax: 219-756-2902

WINDSOR COURT HOTEL

Sophisticated Guest-Recognition Program

Description

The Practice: The Windsor Court Hotel in New Orleans conducts a strong guest-recognition program and solicits comments from guests on checkout to ensure they are satisfied with their stay and to field any complaints. Employees are empowered to immediately resolve guest complaints or problems. Additionally, the general manager or a guest-relations manager greets every repeat guest on arrival and departure.

Why the Practice Was Developed: The purpose of the practice is to provide the guest with the best possible service and facilities available in a hotel. Managing Director Hans Maissen noted that about 20 percent of the program was in place when he took over the property four years ago. He initiated a change in guest-service policies to ensure that the hotel delivered five-star service.

Execution

Approach to Implementation: The program involves strong guest feedback and personal interaction. For the first part, each guest receives a questionnaire with a self-addressed envelope at checkout. Also upon checkout, the cashier asks the guests if they incurred any problems during their stay, and asks whether they might offer one recommendation to the hotel. If the front-office staffer receives a complaint, it is recorded on a guest-incident form together with the action taken to rectify the problem. Management then follows up with a letter or phone call. Every employee has the authority to act on the spot to resolve a guest complaint. Every month all the complaints are tabulated in a computer, and each one is reviewed and any necessary additional action is taken at that time.

Employees who exemplify the service standards of the hotel are recognized in several ways. The hotel has a "Kudos" program, which gives an award to any employee who is recognized by a guest as providing some special or friendly service. Each Kudo has a $5 value and can be exchanged at the gift shop for merchandise. The hotel also honors an employee of the month and an employee of the year. The yearly winner receives a round-trip ticket to London for two with seven days of hotel accommodations, plus $1,000 pocket money.

Mr. Maissen makes it a point to have each repeat guest personally greeted at arrival and departure. While Mr. Maissen cannot do this 100 percent of the time, he sets a personal goal of greeting at least 25 percent to 30 percent of guests. Two guest-relations managers, whose office is located in the lobby, greet the remainder of the guests. They ensure that newly arrived guests have the right room assigned to them, that appropriate amenities are placed in the guest room, and that any additional guest requests are fulfilled.

Operational Issues: To ensure that the guest-recognition program operates continuously, Mr. Maissen established a hotel executive committee (composed of the hotel manager, director of sales and marketing, comptroller, human resources, and public relations director).

Repeat guests are given small gifts that vary according to how often they have stayed. The program begins with fruit, flowers, and candy, and each succeeding stay brings a larger gift. Once guests reach the 20th return visit, they are given a monogrammed bathrobe to use in the guestroom during each subsequent visit.

Outcomes

Success of the Practice: The Windsor Court was rated the number-one hotel in the world in 1998 by readers of *Condé Nast Traveler*, outranking many prestigious hotels in major markets.

Insights

Advice and Observations: Mr. Maissen is a firm believer that management must be personally involved in ensuring that the guest receives the very best in care. He believes that this philosophy is lacking in many hotels today — and too much time is spent in the office rather than around the hotel/guests. "Inspect, don't expect."

He considers that the premise for a successful hotel is to focus on the basics of ensuring that guests are given the attention and service they deserve. A hotel manager must be visible and aware of the guests. What separates hotels is the difference in service and attitude of the hotel staff.

Contact

Hansjörg Maissen, Managing Director
Windsor Court Hotel
300 Gravier Street, New Orleans, LA 70130
Phone: 504-596-4780 Fax: 504-596-4754

WINEGARDNER & HAMMONS INC.

Pre-Opening Handbook for New Hotel Properties

Description

The Practice: Winegardner & Hammons Incorporated (WHI) uses a comprehensive hotel pre-opening assignment book, ensuring that each new hotel can be successfully operated at all phases. Maximum customer satisfaction and maximum return on investment from the outset are prime motivators for this practice. From the hotel's mission to the comprehensive budget (pro forma), all tasks and objectives are clearly delineated. Among the 35 areas covered in the pre-opening handbook are the costs of small wares, marketing and advertising activities, sales targets for rooms and catering departments, staffing levels and hiring dates for all departments, and training of new staff. Payroll costs and pre-opening inventory costs also are predetermined, based on previous experiences in hotels with similar structures and market areas. The pre-opening book has been developed over many years of practice and is constantly being refined from the opening of one hotel to the next.

Why the Practice Was Developed: Several years ago WHI opened a new property for a hotel company. This function had not previously been part of WHI's portfolio. To ensure optimum success for this new hotel, the president, senior vice presidents, and other executive-level managers consolidated and expanded previous pre-opening manuals into a comprehensive handbook.

Execution

The Approach to Implementation: The pre-opening handbook evolved over a period of 12 years. Through coordinated efforts across all departmental lines, corporate managers involved in pre-openings shared the goals and visions, and communicated them via the pre-opening handbook.

With this handbook, WHI has been successful in opening many new hotels, avoiding the pitfalls of cost over-runs and delayed opening dates often associated with hotel openings. Even though each hotel property has its own idiosyncrasies, many of the pre-opening tasks are the same. Hence, standardization by means of a pre-opening "bible" increases communication among corporate and property-based management and staff, reduces stress and budgetary uncertainties, and ensures that new properties open on time and with appropriate efforts.

Outcomes

Success of the Practice: The pre-opening handbook has helped to improve productivity during the pre-opening and opening phases of new hotel properties. Other measurable effects include staying at or under budget, opening new properties on time, and achieving desired returns on investment. As a result, WHI has received Marriott Corporation's best opening practice reward.

Benefits for Customer: The most important factor in the success of a newly opened hotel is guest satisfaction, leading to repeat business. Dennis Lanners, vice president of food and

beverage, stated: "Guests of newly opened properties expect the same level of service, type of amenities, state-of-the-art facilities, and competent staff as can be found in hotels that have been in operation for years." Well-managed pre-opening activities ensure that hotel guests have the same experience as if the hotel had been open for months, if not years. Guest-satisfaction surveys consistently indicate high ratings even during the soft openings and the period immediately following the hotels' grand openings.

Insights

Advice and Observations: Mr. Lanners suggests that in developing such a handbook it is important to involve all affected players; work from both directions, top to bottom and bottom to top; and learn from each new opening. Understand the long-term implication of a well-managed pre-opening phase. Besides the clear delineation of tasks for all pre-opening team members, staff training is another key factor for Winegardner & Hammons's success in hotel openings.

Contact

Dennis Lanners, Vice President of Food and Beverage
Winegardner & Hammons Incorporated
4243 Hunt Road, Cincinnati, OH 45242
Phone: 513-891-1066, Ext. 454 Fax: 513-794-2590

WYNDHAM HOTELS AND RESORTS

An Integrated Approach to Food and Beverage

Description

The Practice: Wyndham Hotels has reengineered its food and beverage program to upgrade the food and beverage culture within the organization. To instill the new culture, Wyndham's "Best of Class" program has required the following major changes:

- Reengineering of menus and recipes.
- Reconceptualization of the hotels' restaurants.
- Modification of dining rooms and introduction of display exhibition kitchens.
- Upgrade of table tops and wait-staff uniforms.
- Upgrade of china, glass, silver, and specialty merchandising pieces.
- Development of seasonal food festivals and beverage promotions.
- Promotion of F&B products within the hotels, using high-quality graphics and unique signage, including two-sided banners.
- Recruitment and hiring of outstanding culinary talent.
- Collaboration with food vendors to obtain unique products, and with wine vendors to determine wine lists and tastings.
- Implementation of a wine-by-the-glass program using premium varietal wines with high brand awareness.
- Development of a server training program that emphasizes product knowledge and upselling techniques.
- Implementation of incentive programs designed to motivate servers to become better educated about the food and wine products they serve.
- Reinvention of room-service standard operating procedures and in-house marketing materials (training video, manuals, menus, in-room directory, equipment, and proper service etiquette).

Why the Practice Was Developed: Patrick Colombo, vice president of food and beverage concepts, wanted Wyndham Hotels to become a leader in food and beverage innovation, quality, and service. The primary desired outcome of these strategies was to position Wyndham Hotels as the consumer's preferred hotel brand. Wyndham also has achieved higher check averages, improved product and service quality, increased unit sales volume, increased in-house guest capture ratio and outlet cover counts, and attracted and retained quality personnel through increased pride and financial rewards.

Execution

The Approach to Implementation: In January 1998, a core group of food and beverage executives and chefs was assembled under Mr. Colombo's direction. This group designed the "Best of Class" program and created training materials over a period of four to five months. They had five primary strategies for reengineering Wyndham's F&B program:

- Differentiating and enhancing a unified Wyndham brand.
- Establishing quality and service standards that exceed guest expectations.
- Increasing product and service consistency.
- Enhancing revenue through marketing programs and product merchandising.
- Maximizing food-service purchasing leverage and economies of scale.

The core group then worked with the staff of each of the hotels to implement the program over a period of several months. Implementation involved adding quality staff, and educating and training employees to instill the "Best of Class" culture among the food and beverage staff of each hotel. By the middle of 1998, approximately 125 hotels managed under the Wyndham Hotels brand had implemented the "Best of Class" program.

Operational Issues: The first task was the creation of the internal communications campaign. Following this step, four new regional culinary directors and eight regional food and beverage directors were put in place. In addition, new room-service products and service standards were established, and new, high-quality staff employed. Quarterly food festivals and beverage promotions were designed, and new wedding marketing packages were prepared. To support these special promotions, in-house merchandising and signage were designed, and staff training manuals and videos were developed.

Many aspects of the staff training were conducted by food and beverage vendor-partners. At first, property managers were reluctant to turn any portion of the training over to outsiders, but resistance waned as they recognized the educational benefits. As a result, the training was conducted in a timely, consistent manner, while local managers were able to devote their attention to other management functions.

Outcomes

Success of the Practice: Initial results are showing a 15% unit increase in total sales, a 40% increase in wine sales, and a 55% profit flow-through on new revenue generated. The perception of increased customer value has allowed higher check averages, which in turn has increased staff earnings and improved staff retention. In addition, the perception of quality food and beverage has positively influenced the overall image of the hotels.

In continuing to "grow" the practice, the development of a "food culture" within the Wyndham Hotel organization will be further enhanced by the creation of three new restaurant concepts: (1) Caliterra (California/Italian bar and grill), (2) Lune di Mare (Italian Riviera cuisine), and (3) Tutta Manza (Italian steakhouse). These concepts will be located in selected resort and luxury properties in the system.

As a result of the success of this practice, the "Best of Class" program will expand first to banquet services and then to the rooms side of the hotels, with an emphasis on customer service.

Benefits for Customer: Customers now perceive the food and beverage products of Wyndham Hotels to be better than those of competitive hotels.

Insights

Advice and Observations: Mr. Colombo believes the "Best of Class" program has been successful because substantial efforts were made to gain the commitment of upper management at both the corporate and property levels. This essential support was garnered by carefully planning each phase of the program, and then fully showcasing it at every hotel prior to its rollout.

Contact

Patrick Colombo
Vice President of Food and Beverage Concepts
Wyndham Hotels and Resorts
1950 Stemmens Freeway #6001, Dallas, TX 75207
Phone: 214-863-1000 Fax: 214-863-1665

OVERALL BEST-PRACTICE CHAMPIONS

Introduction and Overview

In this study overall best-practice champions are those individual managers, individual hotels, or brands of hotels that, beyond performance in specific areas, succeed in making hotels better places for guests to stay, for employees to work, and from which investors and owners may profit. Many of our overall best-practice champions were excellent in several functional best practices such that they deserved the designation as an overall champion. Overall champions were identified for each product segment and five key competency categories.

Overall champions were selected in all of the product segments of the industry, because it was reasoned that practices that have benefits for one product segment, such as budget hotels, may not be appropriate for hotels in a different segment, like luxury hotels. The champion in the budget segment declined to participate in the study; therefore an overall best-practice champion does not represent that product segment. Overall champions were also selected in key competency areas. These competency areas are central to the overall operation of hotels and deserve attention because they are critical factors for success in competitive terms.

Key Competency Areas

Key competency areas are the areas within an industry that are considered essential to producing results. In our study five key competency areas were repeatedly identified in the two phase I pilot tests by industry nominators, and hence they were placed in the phase I nomination survey as critical areas for identifying best-practice champions. The key competency categories include customer service, physical property, employee retention and loyalty, quality standards, and profitability.

Key Competency Areas

Customer Service
Physical Property
Employee Retention & Loyalty
Quality Standards
Profitability

The definition of product category was adapted from the Bear Stearns Financial Services Company's United States lodging industry categorization scheme, coupled with the addition of casino hotels and resorts, a product type not included in the Bear Stearns' scheme (Adler and Lafleur 1997). We chose this industry categorization scheme with the counsel of our industry experts because it allows us to compare and recognize the success of firms and individuals operating in similar competitive and operational contexts with similar resources. In Table 1 are the definitions of each product category as defined for our phase I nominating survey.

Table 1: Product Segments (Based on Bear Stearns Industry Classification Scheme)

Deluxe Hotels — elegant, distinctive, highest-quality décor; upscale restaurants, full range of first-class amenities and customized services

Upscale Hotels — well-integrated décor; quality furnishings; premium guest room amenities and facilities; high staff-to-guest ratio

Mid-scale Hotels, with or without F&B — nicely appointed rooms; range of facilities may be limited; good quality amenities; some special services available

Economy Hotels — clean and comfortable; functional, limited range of amenities; some services offered

Budget Hotels — clean, well-maintained; offers a minimum of service and amenities; price-sensitive guests

Extended-Stay Hotels, Upper Tier — large suite units with separate living and sleeping areas; complete kitchen; personalized service; plush, comfortable rooms

Extended-Stay Hotels, Lower Tier — functional suite unit with small living and small sleeping areas; kitchen area

Casinos — hotels whose focus is on gaming

Phase III Data Integration

The 29 overall best-practice champions cases presented in this section are the final product of the phase II interviews and the phase III market-based customer interviews. The overall best-practice case studies reflect the business approaches the champions utilized to make their hotels compelling for the guests, the employees, and the investors. These cases contain decisions and actions regarding real estate investment, property design and management, the organizational development of managers and employees, and the processes to organize, manage, and improve upon their operations.

In each overall best-practice case study for which significant customer information was collected, the data from the phase III market interviews are integrated into the summary. The Guest Perspective presents the various hotel attributes driving customer decisions to stay at the champion hotel or brand (under the sub-heading Value Drivers in the Purchase Decision), as well as those aspects customers liked at their last stay at the champion hotel or brand (under the sub-heading Value Drivers in the Hotel Experience). A third sub-section is the Benefits to the Customer that describes the end-users' perspective regarding the customer benefits (e.g., a worry-free stay, feeling at home, etc.) that dominate the hotel's or brand's image in the respondents' minds. Lastly, in this section we explore those managerial and operational practices that were most visible to customers and that they cited as the reasons why the champion was able to deliver value. These are presented in the sub-section designated Outlook on Management Practices. The second main section of phase III findings is entitled Intermediary Perspective. This section highlights the intermediaries' (travel agents and meeting planners) motives to do business with the champion and what they believe are the most valuable attributes of the champion's products and services.

Overall Best-Practice Champions

| Bristol Hotels & Resorts | Overall Best-Practice Corporate Champion In Profitability | Create A Culture Of Results, Not Of Trappings |

| Caesars Palace Hotel & Casino | Overall Best-Practice Property Champion In Casino Segment | Building A Hotel That Has…Mystique |

| Cincinnati Marriott Northeast | Overall Best-Practice Property Champion In Customer Service | We Are…Northeast |

| Courtyard By Marriott | Overall Best-Practice Corporate Champion In Midscale Segment | An Unfailing Desire To Listen To Our Guests |

| Days Inn Altoona | Overall Best-Practice Property Champion In Economy Segment | Professional Pride And Personal Values |

| Disney's Polynesian Resort | Overall Best-Practice Property Champion In Upscale Segment | Creating And Delivering A Magical Experience |

| Embassy Suites | Overall Best-Practice Corporate Champion In Upscale Segment | When The Operating Strategy Is The Brand Strategy |

| Extended StayAmerica | Overall Best-Practice Corporate Champion In Extended-Stay Lower-Tier Segment | To Be The Leaders In A New Industry Segment, Build Market Share Faster And Deliver Quality |

| Fairfield Inn By Marriott | Overall Best-Practice Corporate Champion In Economy Segment | Impress More Guests, Sell More Rooms, Have More Fun |

| Four Seasons Hotel New York | Overall Best-Practice Property Champion In Physical Property | The Most Beautiful Stage Ever Performed Upon |

| Four Seasons And Regent Hotels & Resorts | Overall Best-Practice Corporate Champion In Deluxe Segment | Consistency Over Time |

| Four Seasons Hotel Washington, D.C. | Overall Best-Practice Property Champion Industry-Wide | A Passion To Serve |

| Hampton Inn | Overall Best-Practice Corporate Champion In Quality | The Unconditional Guarantee As A Cultural Belief |

| Holiday Inn Cincinnati Airport | Overall Best-Practice Property Champion In Midscale Segment | The Smartest Investment You Can Ever Make—The People |

| Homewood Suites Alexandria | Overall Best-Practice Property Champion In Extended-Stay Upper-Tier Segment | On Being A "Yes" Hotel… |

The Houstonian Hotel, Club, And Spa	Overall Best-Practice Property Champion In Employee Satisfaction	A Humanistic Approach To Profitability
The Kimpton Group	Overall Best-Practice Corporate Champion In Physical Property	Differentiation To The Extreme
The Mansion on Turtle Creek	Overall Best-Practice Property Champion In Deluxe Segment	Staffing Up To Customer Needs
Marriott International, Inc./ J.W. Marriott, Jr.	Overall Best-Practice Individual Champion In Corporate Management	Success Is Never Final
Marriott Hotels & Resorts	Overall Best-Practice Corporate Champion In Employee Satisfaction	It's A Marathon, Not A Sprint!
Mirage Resorts	Overall Best-Practice Corporate Champion In Casino Segment	Creating Artistically Pleasing Hotels For Guests And Employees
Mohonk Mountain House	Overall Best-Practice Property Champion In Profitability	Creating Profits By Not Focusing On The GOP
The Peninsula Beverly Hills Hotel/Ali Kasikci	Overall Best-Practice Individual Champion In Property Management	Every Day You Have To Re-Invent Yourself
Residence Inn By Marriott	Overall Best-Practice Corporate Champion In Extended-Stay Upper-Tier Segment	A Relentless Focus On Extended-Stay
The Ritz-Carlton Hotel Co.	Overall Best-Practice Corporate Champion Industry-Wide	Lead People, Manage Processes
The Ritz-Carlton Naples	Overall Best-Practice Property Champion In Quality	Quality… A Different Way To Manage
Sleep Inn	Overall Best-Practice Corporate Champion In Customer Service	Customer Service Is The Wild Card
Super 8 Motel, Inc.	Overall Best-Practice Corporate Champion In Budget Segment	A Focus On Hospitality
Towneplace Suites By Marriott-Brookfield, Wisconsin	Overall Best-Practice Property Champion In Extended-Stay Lower-Tier Segment	Remodeling The Property Hierarchical Structure

Overall Best-Practice Champions — Corporate

Bristol Hotels & Resorts	Overall Best-Practice Corporate Champion In Profitablity	Create A Culture Of Results, Not Of Trappings
Courtyard By Marriott	Overall Best-Practice Corporate Champion In Midscale Segment	An Unfailing Desire To Listen To Our Guests
Embassy Suites	Overall Best-Practice Corporate Champion In Upscale Segment	When The Operating Strategy Is The Brand Strategy
Extended Stay America	Overall Best-Practice Corporate Champion In Extended-Stay Lower Tier Segment	To Be The Leaders In A New Industry Segment, Build Market Share Faster And Deliver Quality
Fairfield Inn by Marriott	Overall Best-Practice Corporate Champion In Economy Segment	Impress More Guests, Sell More Rooms, Have More Fun
Four Seasons and Regent Hotels & Resorts	Overall Best-Practice Corporate Champion In Deluxe Segment	Consistency Over Time
Hampton Inn	Overall Best-Practice Corporate Champion In Quality	The Unconditional Guarantee As A Cultural Belief
The Kimpton Group	Overall Best-Practice Corporate Champion In Physical Property	Differentiation To The Extreme
Marriott Hotels and Resorts	Overall Best-Practice Corporate Champion In Employee Satisfaction	It's A Marathon, Not A Sprint!
J.W. Marriott, Jr./ Marriott International, Inc.	Overall Best-Practice Individual Champion In Corporate Management	Success Is Never Final
Mirage Resorts	Overall Best-Practice Corporate Champion In Casino Segment	Creating Artistically Pleasing Hotels For Guests And Employees
Residence Inn By Marriott	Overall Best-Practice Corporate Champion In Extended-Stay Upper-Tier Segment	A Relentless Focus On Extended-Stay
The Ritz-Carlton Hotel Co.	Overall Best-Practice Corporate Champion Industry-Wide	Lead People, Manage Processes
Sleep Inn	Overall Best-Practice Corporate Champion In Customer Service	Customer Service Is The Wild Card
Super 8 Motel, Inc.	Overall Best-Practice Corporate Champion In Budget Segment	A Focus On Hospitality

Overall Best-Practice Champions — Property

Caesars Palace Hotel & Casino	Overall Best-Practice Property Champion In Casino Segment	Building A Hotel That Has…Mystique
Cincinnati Marriott Northeast	Overall Best-Practice Property Champion In Customer Service	We Are…Northeast
Days Inn Altoona	Overall Best-Practice Property Champion In Economy Segment	Professional Pride And Personal Values
Disney's Polynesian Resort	Overall Best-Practice Property Champion In Upscale Segment	Creating And Delivering A Magical Experience
Four Seasons Hotel New York	Overall Best-Practice Property Champion In Physical Property	The Most Beautiful Stage Ever Performed Upon
Four Seasons Hotel Washington, DC	Overall Best-Practice Property Champion Industry-Wide	A Passion To Serve
Holiday Inn Cincinnati Airport	Overall Best-Practice Property Champion In Midscale Segment	The Smartest Investment You Can Ever Make — The People
Homewood Suites, Alexandria	Overall Best-Practice Property Champion In Extended-Stay Upper-Tier Segment	On Being A "Yes" Hotel…
The Houstonian Hotel, Club, and Spa	Overall Best-Practice Property Champion In Employee Satisfaction	A Humanistic Approach To Profitability
The Mansion On Turtle Creek	Overall Best-Practice Property Champion in Deluxe Segment	Staffing Up To Customer Needs
Mohonk Mountain House	Overall Best-Practice Property Champion In Profitability	Creating Profits By Not Focusing On The GOP
Ali Kasikci/The Peninsula Beverly Hills Hotel	Overall Best-Practice Individual Champion In Property Management	Every Day You Have To Re-Invent Yourself
The Ritz-Carlton Naples	Overall Best-Practice Property Champion In Quality	Quality…A Different Way To Manage
Townplace Suites By Marriott - Brookfield, Wisconsin	Overall Best-Practice Property Champion In Extended-Stay Lower-Tier Segment	Remodeling The Property Hierarchical Structure

BRISTOL HOTELS & RESORTS

Overall Best-Practice Corporate Champion in Profitability
"Create A Culture of Results, Not of Trappings"

The Driving Source Of Excellence

In 1988 Bristol Hotels was a small, privately held company with eight hotels, a two million dollar cash loss, and on the verge of bankruptcy. A three-day meeting assembled Bristol's corporate executives and the general managers of the hotels to decide on a survival strategy. Their past strategy had been primarily based on matching competition in terms of customer value. Both corporate executives and managers came to realize, as did many other companies within the lodging industry at that time, that they were doing things because their competitors were doing them. With no change, the company would "go broke" in the very near future. At this meeting, a consensus was reached which called for a dramatic shift in operations and management to a strong customer orientation. This shift translated into a $3 million turnaround in 1989. In 1998, Bristol Hotels and Resorts operated over 120 hotels, under various brands nationwide, and with a GOP margin for same-unit sales of 37.1 percent.

The Delivery of Excellence

Shifting to a Bottom Line Mindset: According to Peter Kline, Chairman/CEO of Bristol Hotels & Resorts, managers of individual properties in the 1980s were focused on generating more revenues. The belief was that an increase in revenue automatically led to profitability. The route to revenue was to give the customer more, whether or not he asked for it. In fact, afraid to lose sales to a competitor, any new services or amenities offered were almost immediately matched. An important aspect of the turnaround was to establish a different mind-set, along the lines of, in the words of Mr. Kline, "If it's the popular thing to do, we're not going to do it," or at least not before having assessed both sides of the profit equation.

Searching for Value for which the Customer Is Willing to Pay: In the dissection of the business that followed the 1988 meeting, management sought ways to eliminate waste, those things that did not serve as determinants of the customers' purchase decision, or those things for which customers did not care about enough to pay. Many opportunities were found. For example, over $100,000 was spent annually on newspapers, over half of which were never read. This figure does not even include the cost of disposal of all those newspapers. Now, guests are offered newspapers at the front desk, restaurants, and from room service in the hotels. The savings are significant and customer value is unchanged.

Another area in which significant savings were made is room amenities. As colorfully noted by Mr. Kline, in 1989, Bristol Hotels & Resorts stopped participating in the "amenities creep" game that was prevalent in the hotel industry at that time. The bathrooms in a Bristol Hotel were beginning to resemble a drugstore in the number of different items offered to the guest. A limited assortment of top-quality amenities is now offered.

A search for profitable sources of customer value was also made at structural levels. Hotel cocktail lounges and the entertainment that was part of them were eliminated and replaced by lobby bars. In most cases, lounges were converted to banquet and meeting space that was much more profitable and in higher demand with their clientele.

Bristol Hotels & Resorts saw significant opportunity in its food and beverage operations, in particular the banquets. Banquets are profitable and utilize the meeting space but they require a costly, quality kitchen. Bristol avoided the "ego" restaurants. Instead, it developed and executed simpler restaurant concepts that were acceptable to the hotel guests, and concentrated resources to support the quality and expense of the kitchens that were necessary for the banquets.

Delivering Efficiently on Customer Value: Changes in staffing and human resource management strategies were critical to Bristol Hotels & Resorts' success in delivering customer value in a cost-effective way. Staffing was reorganized in all hotels. Bristol shifted from a fixed to a variable payroll so that management in the hotels could better adapt staffing costs to variations in customer demand. Middle management and many supervisory positions were eliminated to enrich the content, responsibilities and salaries of those positions that were deemed keys to creating customer value. Others were made hourly positions. For example, housekeeping inspectors were eliminated. Instead, a housekeeper self-inspection program on guestrooms was instituted. In an unorthodox move, Bristol defined job descriptions and reporting relationships around the individual occupying that position and not the other way around. This increased the productivity of the individual and the flexibility of the organization, which enhanced Bristol's ability to make changes and respond to competitor strategies and other events. The result was that they had "fewer people working in the hotels, each making more money."

Streamlining was made to various internal processes as well. For instance, all hotels centralized their purchasing. In addition to increasing efficiency, this change consolidated Bristol Hotels & Resorts' purchasing power, giving them leverage with suppliers for better prices and terms.

Finally, the top-line was carefully monitored, deploying sales assets more aggressively than they ever had before. More sales representatives were trained and they were better utilized. As a result, Bristol Hotels & Resorts developed a better street presence than their competitors in various markets. They focused not only on meetings business, but also on the banquets, weddings, and bar mitzvahs that are so profitable to a hotel.

Redefining the Meaning of Growth: For most companies, growth means an increase in the number of hotels or in the amount of sales they make. In their transformation from a top-line to a bottom-line mind-set, Bristol Hotels & Resorts shifted to a system whereby growth was assessed in terms of profitability at each hotel and for the company. They shifted from a top-line focus to a bottom-line focus; that shift led to a number of changes in the way they managed the properties.

Bristol Hotels & Resorts' solid financial health in the last few years has allowed them to make some major strategic acquisitions. They continue to operate in the "mid-market with food and beverage" segment of the hotel industry even though they believe most hotel companies have written this segment off. They think mid-scale with f&b is "fun." That means opportunity. This hotel segment has 45 percent of the total rooms in the United States, yet is the product segment with the fewest competitors doing a great job. For Bristol, that means more customers for them. Bristol Hotels & Resorts have chosen food and beverage as one element that provides them the opportunity to differentiate themselves from the competitors and make a difference in the customers' minds. Their goal is to be the number one independent management company in the hotel business.

Insights

Mr. Kline has definite suggestions for any organization trying to change. He firmly states that "you can't create change from the middle of the organization down. It has to start at the top. And you've got to live your goals and aspirations at the top." At Bristol, they have created a culture of results, not of trappings. There are no private offices. There are no reserved parking spaces. The entire company is on a first-name basis. It is a culture that emphasizes a teamwork approach to focusing on the customers. It is not perfect. Like in any organization, there are politics. But unlike other organizations, their politics are created from the bottom-up and not the top-down.

Contact

Peter Kline, Chairman & CEO
Bristol Hotels & Resorts
14295 Midway Road, Addison, TX 75001
Phone: 972-391-3000 Fax: 972-391-1500

CAESARS PALACE HOTEL AND CASINO

Overall Best-Practice Property Champion in Casino Segment
"Building a Hotel that Has...Mystique"

The Driving Source of Excellence

Caesars Palace was the first theme resort on the Las Vegas strip and it has become legendary for events and the antics of celebrities such as Frank Sinatra and his cronies. In its 33-year history, it has developed an aura and a mystique that has given Caesars Palace a unique image and high name recognition around the world. Caesars Palace is the third best-known brand name in the world. The management's ability to keep the history and recognition alive seems to be what has kept Caesars Palace so successful.

The Delivery of Excellence

A Unique Hotel Concept: There is only one Caesars Palace. The size of the hotel is considerable: originally built with 850 rooms, 1,200 rooms have been recently added for a total of 2,550 rooms. Everything in the place possesses a Roman theme, such as employees in costumes from the era of Caesar and lots of marble surroundings and columns as in the emperor's palace. There is a mixture of "fiction and fantasy" to the property that gives the hotel a "mystique" and a "vibrancy," 24 hours a day. The Roman theme lends an air of decadence. People are there to live their fantasies and have fun. The high-end slot machine area, for example, attracts spectators just to watch individuals take a chance on the high-end slot machines at $1,000.00 dollars a pull. What a memory, even better if you risk the money!

A Place for Champions: Caesars Palace has always been known to offer the highest limits (bets) on any casino game in Las Vegas. Thus, it attracts the big players, the "whales," who are the individuals whose bets are in the seven-figure range. In addition to hosting aspiring gambling champions, Caesars Palace considers itself the "Home of Champions" at a more general level. They were the first to stage sporting championships and events (spectacles) in Las Vegas. When people remember the Muhammed Ali fight or the Evel Knievel jump, they remember Caesars and the mystique grows. Caesars Palace is fantasy. Innovative, unique ideas are constantly searched for to attract attention, to create legends, to get people to talk about them forever. This is the Caesars Palace way of continually polishing the brand, living up to the promise of fantasy, fun and excitement. Or at least, part of the strategy. Of significant importance is the actual delivery on the brand promise on a day-to-day basis.

Service Quality as a Source of Customer Value: George Martkantonis, vice president — hotel operations, believes that 50 percent of what customers like in Caesars Palace comes from the excitement of the experience but that the other 50 percent is the service they receive. That quality service is often defined by the personal recognition of the guest. The hotel has been there long enough to have many traditions. It is not uncommon for the third and fourth generation of a family to now be regular guests. And those regular guests ask for certain employees to serve them. Thus, management recognizes that longevity of employees is as important to profitability as new and exciting facilities.

The Employees at the Core of the Caesars Experience: Managers recognize the importance of the employee in building the mystique of the hotel. Employees not only deliver the service, they also make the fantasy real. Employees remain with Caesars Palace because of the excitement and the pride of working for one of the best-known brand names. Of the 5,500 hotel employees, 250 have been there from opening day. Employees are offered outstanding work conditions: Caesars Palace is one of the top five hotels in Las Vegas in terms of employee compensation. The benefits are excellent, including the quality of food and ambiance in the employee cafeteria. Caesars is presently investigating on-site day-care, recognizing that employee needs are changing.

Mr. Martkantonis believes you must have trust between employees and managers and that this trust must be earned in several ways. Of particular interest is the 360-degree evaluation: an employee/associate survey is performed every nine months and the feedback is used to solve the issues surfaced in the traditional way. In addition, though, every employee does an upward evaluation of his superior. This upward evaluation shows the respect for employees by management. Furthermore, in every department in the hotel, promotion is done from within. This reflects the importance Caesars places on employees in the delivery of excellence. The result: it pays!

257

Coaching and Building the Team: The management style that makes Caesars work is that of a coach, a coach of the team that builds and preserves the Caesars Palace mystique. Throughout the hotel, the culture is one of collaboration between management and employees. Caesars has been there long enough that the major problems in the various aspects of the operations have been solved. Management's job is to remind everyone of what the brand stands for and not to make drastic changes. A "tweak" is quite enough, thank you. Have fun! The hotel works and day-by-day the mystique of the hotel is built. In addition, to develop new management talent, the hotel works very closely with the University of Las Vegas' Hotel School. Managers from Caesars lecture in many of the classes and try to recruit the best of the graduates for Caesars.

Outstanding Occupancy: Between 1997 and 1998, occupancy increased from 91 to 95.1 percent. Hard to imagine, but what makes it stupendous is that during this period the hotel added 1,200 rooms. Caesars Palace receives between three and seven thousand reservation calls per day. And regrets over 2000 of them. They have broken occupancy records every month for the past seven months. Clearly, people recognize the quality of the brand and the consistent delivery on the promise of fantasy, fun and excitement.

Guest Perspective

Reflecting the hybrid nature of customer value recognized by the general manager, the interviewed guests mentioned, with relatively equal frequency, various aspects of the physical property and customer service as primary sources of value in driving their decision to go to Caesars for the first time and to return again. Physical property and service attributes both contributed to create this unique "atmosphere" that was highly valued by most of the customers we interviewed. Mentions were made of the comfort and aesthetics of the guestroom, the majesty of the lobby, the unique way in which personal needs were treated, the friendliness of the staff, and the food quality, etc. Respondents who were more serious gamblers valued the various complimentary benefits they received and the smoothness and efficiency of various hotel procedures such as check-in/check-out. Regular guests also appreciated the personal recognition they received.

Insights

To create a success story similar to Caesars Palace takes time. The stories must become legends, and the myths evolve over time. The mystique builds. The key to success, according to Mr. Martkantonis, is to focus on building the team that will get the job done. You must build a team that is not only competent but one that will get along, that will help each other. Then you have a chance. And along the way, you will have fun, too.

Contact

George Martkantonis, Vice President — Hotel Operations
Caesars Palace Hotel and Casino
3570 Las Vegas Blvd. South, Las Vegas, Nevada 89109
Ph: 702-731-7308   Fax: 702-731-7172

CINCINNATI MARRIOTT NORTHEAST

Overall Best-Practice Property Champion in Customer Service
"We Are...Northeast"

The Driving Source of Excellence

The Cincinnati Marriott Northeast in suburban Cincinnati has been open almost three years. In that short period, management has been able to grow an organization built around and focused on customer service; the kind of great service that, according to Kent Bruggeman, general manager, is talked about so easily in hotel ads, but is so challenging to deliver in practice; the kind of customer service that in a competitive market translates into yield premiums and high profitability. This case is about an employee motivation program directed toward customer satisfaction that became an organizational culture.

The Delivery of Excellence

The Pledge to the Guest: When Mr. Bruggeman arrived at the Cincinnati property two years ago, the hotel had already begun to "drift." The excitement of the opening in early 1996 was gone. Guest satisfaction scores had drifted downward and management turnover was high. The owners decided that focusing on the customer was the only way to remain profitable for the long term. Not long into his new job, looking around for something that could differentiate Cincinnati Marriott Northeast from nearby competitors, Mr. Bruggeman came upon the associate (employee) pledge to the guest. This pledge was a 12-point program devised by the opening team of the hotel to motivate employees and build esprit de corps. The pledge included items like: "I pledge to follow the 20-10 rule by making eye contact with any customer within 20 feet, and acknowledging the customer verbally and with a smile once they are within 10 feet; to always escort guests rather than pointing out directions to another area of the hotel; and to wear the proper uniform at all times including nametag, proper shoes (clean and polished) and to take pride in my personal appearance." In making the pledge, employees agreed to observe certain standards and policies in their interaction with guests. The basis of the pledge was a belief that focusing on the quality of employee-guest encounters would improve customer satisfaction.

What Mr. Bruggeman understood from his years as a general manager is "this (the pledge and the resulting behaviors) makes a difference." But he also had enough experience to understand that starting an employee program — or any program, for that matter — in a hotel is not difficult. But all programs lose their effectiveness, their ability to motivate, over time. He and the management team had to come up with new ways to keep the program going, to keep it fresh for employees. That meant employees had to understand it, to see the results of their behaviors on guest satisfaction and to feel proud of their accomplishments. As he expected, the staff of the hotel, especially the 43 "Plankholders" (employees there since opening day), committed themselves to the program. However, challenges awaited in making the pledge program part of the daily hotel life of every employee in the hotel.

The Pep Rallies to Keep the Pledge Alive: Making the pledge part of the day-to-day life at Cincinnati Marriott Northeast started with the orientation program. Then, all department meetings started with the pledge. One of the most innovative ideas was the weekly pep rally held in the lobby of the hotel in the middle of the day. These are just like the pep rallies that you remember from school. During the rally (led by the general manager), the GM reads the name of every employee whom a guest has complimented, along with the compliment. He asks the question: "Why address a guest by name?" and the employees respond in unison, "Guests like it." And, of course, what would a pep rally be like without a cheer? Theirs is, "We are...Northeast." "How much...this much." Laugh if you like but it works. "This is how we do business here," says Mr. Bruggeman. Because of the program and the link to the celebrations, "the associates are driving the bus."

The Build-up of a Service Culture: The program is more than pep rallies. As the program took hold, employees were given more responsibility. A program called "The Ambassadors" was started composed of employees who managed the hotel's interactions with the community. When The Ambassadors were recently given the management of the United Way campaign, they decided to run a bingo game and sold 6,000 tickets in 13 days.

The employee selection process became another key aspect of Mr. Bruggeman's strategy to develop a successful service culture, as not every applicant wants to serve. Mr. Bruggeman interviews every applicant that has made it to the end of the selection process. He is the final arbiter, the last hurdle before employment. For him there is only one issue: is the candidate an individual who wants to serve others? As Mr. Bruggeman says, "The Cincinnati Marriott Northeast is a place for people [guests] to go, away from home and still feel like they are with family." The technical skills can be taught, but the ability to live the associate pledge in dealing with guests requires a certain attitude. So he asks variations of the same question: "Are you prepared to serve?" "What do I mean by that question?" "What makes you think you can do that?" The correct answer is some variation of "I like making people happy," or "Making people happy makes me feel good." Not every candidate will pass the test. In a tight labor market such as the one this hotel operates in, the temptation is to lower the selection standard. That is why Mr. Bruggeman conducts the final interview. "You have to have the nerve to reject someone," he says. Perhaps that is the difference between a motivational program and a true culture of service.

This program has to be "lived" by every manager and supervisor every day. It is not easy to get supervisors to buy into the program, but once they do, the difficult part begins — that of motivating the employees. Managers lead the employees by also living the pledge. The hotel has a formal "lobby lizard" program in which all managers, including the general manager, are scheduled during the heavy check-in and check-out periods each day to spend time conversing with guests in the lobby. This lobby session is when the managers learn the guests' perspective of what is happening in the hotel. The lobby sessions also demonstrate leadership, illustrate the importance of guest interaction, and assist managers in learning the things the employees are doing right. Employee turnover is approximately 60 percent, which is excellent for this tight labor market. Last year, of the 26 managers in the hotel, only one left, and three are slated for promotion. Clearly, they are learning something important about management.

Finally, the management of the hotel cannot do it alone. The co-owners, Western Southern Life Insurance Company and Winegardner & Hammons management company, have supported the service culture program with extra capital and encouragement. They understand it and they believe in it.

Winegardner & Hammons is also the operator of the hotel, and the company tangibly supports the operational policy changes.

Pay-off for the Employees, the Guests, and the Investors: In the most recent employee/associate survey, 96 percent of the employees rated the hotel as an excellent place to work. Many comments expressed variations of "This is about the best place we've ever worked." According to internal information, the guest has also responded to the service culture. Comparing the hotel to other full-service suburban Marriott hotels, the Cincinnati Marriott Northeast hotel ranked number four in guest satisfaction in the United States. In the guest "intent to return" category, against the same set of hotels, it ranked number one in the United States. According to the Smith Travel Research (STR) Report, the competitive set for the hotel decreased 1.4 percent in occupancy this past year. This hotel was up 6.4 percent. REVPAR growth for the competitive set was down 1.8 percent. For the Cincinnati Marriott Northeast it was up 13.6 percent. Guests want to stay there. They are "zealots." Twice in one week the hotel was told by corporate guests to bill them personally for the difference between the hotel corporate rate and what their company authorizes.

The program also translates into profit for the owners. The hotel has never been behind its budget. Operating margins have increased every year in every department in the hotel since opening. Both revenue and profit experienced double-digit growth last year. The profit before rent, interest and depreciation was 35 percent last year. As Mr. Bruggeman says, "In a 60 percent hotel market, we sold 3,000 room nights in the corporate market at a $30 premium over the competitive set, strictly because the customer likes the service." This kind of passionate loyalty also protects the hotel against recessions and new competitor openings.

Guest Perspective

Value Driver in the Purchase Decision: "We are… Northeast" works for the customers we independently interviewed. Service (be it in terms of its overall quality or, more specifically, for its friendliness and attentiveness) headed the list of hotel attributes driving customers' purchase decisions, with a comfortable lead over convenient location. Customers' membership in the frequent-stay program came in third, followed by the guests' familiarity with the Marriott brand for some, and with the Northeast property itself for others. Various attributes related to the physical property (overall quality and cleanliness) and to the guestroom, in particular the work equipment, were also mentioned with some frequency. One hundred percent of the customers we interviewed said that the Cincinnati Marriott Northeast delivered on the attributes that drove their purchase decision.

Value Drivers in the Hotel Experience: Customer service also emerged as the primary hotel attribute creating unique value during the hotel stay. Guests also mentioned service friendliness, genuineness, and promptness. The physical aspects of the property were also powerful sources of unique value, especially public spaces, landscape, and various qualities of the guestroom (overall lighting, work equipment, comfort, and aesthetics).

Customer Benefits and Outlook on Management Practices: An enjoyable experience, a relaxing stay, comfort, convenience, as well as a sense of being at home are the many benefits customers derived from their stays at the Cincinnati Marriott Northeast. In terms of management practices, customers noticed various aspects of human resources management, including employee selection and training, and the staff's willingness to go beyond the call of duty. Mention was also made of the quality of the communication systems and the promptness of message delivery.

Insights

Mr. Bruggeman is the "coach" of this team. That's the most important role that he plays, to not let people get off the path of customer service and associate service, to keep them fired up and not lose the "focus." For any other hotel that wants to focus on customer service, his advice is to make sure the company has the right management team that will work with the employees. Nobody does it alone. And the company should remember that it is in business to make the customer feel like family. If the company works at it diligently, then it will eventually say, as Mr. Bruggeman does, "This is the best staff of people I've ever worked with." And understand that, "there's no real secret to delivering the best customer service."

Contact

Kent Bruggeman, General Manager
Cincinnati Marriott Northeast Hotel
9664 Mason Montgomery Road, Mason, OH 45040
Phone: 513-459-9800   Fax: 513-459-9808

COURTYARD BY MARRIOTT

Overall Best-Practice Corporate Champion in Midscale Segment
"An Unfailing Desire to Listen to Our Guests"

The Driving Source of Excellence

Craig Lambert, senior vice president and brand manager, says a relentless focus on the customer led Courtyard by Marriott toward this award as overall best-practice corporate champion in the mid-scale hotel category. Courtyard by Marriott, launched in the early 1980s, was the first hotel concept to be completely designed on the basis of comprehensive and sophisticated consumer research. From this research Marriott learned the drivers of value for its customers: a clean, functional room delivered in a friendly, comfortable and consistent environment, which had to be translated into operational and service practices. This objective was achieved through three key competencies:

- Listening to and considering the views of guests in all decision-making.
- Combining the primacy of the guests' satisfaction with the importance of associates (employees) as individuals in delivering that satisfaction via a service culture based on the Marriott philosophy.
- Leveraging industry demand for hotels into different tiers of services and prices, via the Marriott distribution system, thereby increasing revenue and profit. For example, Marriott entered the mid-tier lodging segment where it did not previously have a product offering.

The Delivery of Excellence

Listening to the Guest: It is this focus on listening that makes it "easy to stay in a Courtyard," as their current advertising slogan proclaims.

Management's efforts are intended to make the "customer's voice" a critical component in all operational and strategic decisions. To capture the customer's voice, Courtyard spends more money on customer and consumer research than any of its competitors. The initial research, which was instrumental in the design of the Courtyard concept, consisted of three comprehensive and sophisticated research pieces, two major segmentation studies and one conjoint analysis study of customer trade-off behavior. Since the inception of Courtyard in the early 1980s, this research has been repeated three times — representing an enormous investment — to monitor the customer's changing values. This ongoing customer research provided Courtyard with information on what and when to change. Courtyard spends almost $1.5 million annually conducting monthly traveler tracking studies. Finally, it purchases syndicated tracking studies, which cost approximately $100,000 to 150,000 per year. For Courtyard, these expenditures are readily justified to ensure the customer's voice is heard.

Courtyard has learned from its research that the customer's definition of value has changed since the chain began. Quality-level expectations have increased, and the competition has gotten better at delivering it. As a result, customer expectations

for hotel performance have risen. Courtyard has learned other important facts contributing to understanding the customers' value perceptions. For example, customers are placing increasing value on their time. The challenge for management is to understand and act on this knowledge.

Combining Guest and Employee Satisfaction: "The product might represent 50 to 60 percent of the guest purchase decision, but it is the employees that make it or break it for the guest experience," says Mr. Lambert. "And that drives the repeat business. Satisfied associates take care of the guests and the guests' satisfaction produces the financial results."

A service culture permeates the Marriott organization and was inculcated into the Courtyard concept. That culture has a theme that the guest is primary in all decisions. Yet, Courtyard recognizes that satisfied employee associates are critical to guest satisfaction. That is, if Courtyard has satisfied associates, those associates will willingly take care of the guests; in turn, those satisfied guests will make Courtyard their hotel of choice; and, with proper management, excellent financial results will be achieved.

In selecting employees at Courtyard, the personality profile of the candidate is more important than the skill profile. Courtyard believes that the candidate can be trained in skills, but must bring to the job the type of personality that is willing to serve the customer. Courtyards are small hotels (25 to 40 FTE), so employees act as a team. They voice their opinions, give their ideas and are listened to. They are close to their managers. The organizational surveys indicate that associates believe they can make a difference in the work environment and the guest experience. The size of the organization also means that change can and does occur at a much faster pace. Given the employee-management relationship, associates are less resistant to rapid change, since they are part of the decision-making process.

That Marriott service culture also provides Courtyard with a tremendous source of talent, fueled by an active inter-Marriott transfer program. Approximately 20 percent of all Courtyard managers come from the hourly ranks of Marriott employees. Thus, Courtyard is provided with an important and distinctive pool of talent already living the service culture philosophy.

Leveraging Demand: The final key competency critical to the success of Courtyard is its ability to leverage the demand generated by the perceived value of the customer orientation and focus, and to offer different tiers of services and prices from the entire Marriott brand. This capability is facilitated by the inclusion of Courtyard in the Marriott lodging reservation and sales distribution system.

Delivering Financial Performance: From an owner perspective, Courtyard is an excellent investment; it gets 90 percent of its revenues from guestroom sales (high margin), minimizes staffing, and maximizes the rate potential. That is, Courtyard gets most of the rate of a full-service hotel and has much less cost.

Studies show that owners are satisfied with the performance of the brand. They also like the fact that it is the top chain in delivering demand to a hotel. Courtyard gets more reservation calls per room and has the highest contribution to occupancy from central reservations of any hotel chain.

Value Drivers in the Purchase Decision: In an independent survey, we found Courtyard guests are motivated to purchase a room at this hotel chain based on the following top ten factors: convenient location, consistent availability of room, familiarity with the brand, brand image in the mid-scale market, friendliness of the staff, aesthetics of the property in general, atmosphere in the food and beverage facilities, service quality in general, frequent-stay program, and reasonable price. The guest's perception that price is less important than the other value drivers helps explain how this mid-scale concept obtains almost the same rate as a full-service hotel. Although not in the top ten, guestroom design (e.g., size, working equipment, kitchenette) was also mentioned frequently as an important determinant of the purchase decision for leisure and business customers alike. For 80% of the customers interviewed, Courtyard by Marriott delivered on these value drivers perfectly.

Value Drivers in the Hotel Experience: Consistent with Mr. Lambert's view, the results of our study of Courtyard customers indicate that service determines the guests' satisfaction with their Courtyard by Marriott experience. Customers identified the following eight attributes, presented here in the order of most to least frequently mentioned, as having the greatest impact on their hotel experience: friendliness of the staff, cleanliness of the property, convenience of the location in moving around, aesthetics of the property, quality of room service, efficiency of the service, quality of food and beverage, and aspects of the guestroom (i.e., furniture comfort, HVAC, work equipment, bathroom fixtures). However, leisure and business guests differed in their selected value drivers. For leisure guests, the top five mentions all related to the physical product; for business guests, service was more predominant.

Benefits to Customer: In our market research for this study, the benefits guests believe they derived from Courtyard by Marriott are consistent with those promised in the brand positioning: feelings of security, comfort, worry-free stay, saving time, and providing a home away from home.

Outlook on Management Practices: Customers identified those practices they believe Courtyard by Marriott uses to create these critical value drivers, presented here in the order of the most to least frequently mentioned: the staff offers beyond-the-call-of-duty service; the properties are well maintained; Courtyard caters to the market; a hot, complete breakfast is provided at reasonable prices; the operations are efficient; selling points are offered; and the advertisements are well done.

Intermediary Perspective

Value Drivers for Travel Agents: Travel agents we surveyed recommend Courtyard by Marriott to their customers, first, for its low prices, and then, with equal frequency, for the convenient locations and the quality and cleanliness of its properties. In their own experiences with Courtyard, travel agents like, particularly, the consistency of the service they receive, and the willingness and effort the reservation staff put forth to ensure room availability. They also are pleased with the computer systems for reservations, and the attractiveness of the travel agent incentives Courtyard provides.

Insights

The development and continued success of Courtyard are not the result of one person's efforts. Central to the success has been the relationship of the brand to the key competencies of the Marriott organization. Hence, the brand team plays an important role by providing the framework of what is important for the organization — to keep it focused and going in the right direction today and tomorrow. Mr. Lambert serves in the role of historian. Since he's been with the concept from the beginning, Mr. Lambert has an understanding of what can be learned from the past. Such knowledge is not used to say, "no, we already tried that!" but instead, to explain what was tried and how it might be built upon with new ideas.

Others have had a role in Courtyard's success. The advertising agency of Lowe and Partners challenged Courtyard's beliefs about consumer thinking, based upon their experience with other products and services outside of the hospitality mindset. Doug Schifflet has been instrumental in providing the industry and custom-research studies, and assisting in their interpretation and recommendations for action. Additionally, Yankelovich Partners has provided the latest consumer trends in travel and their potential impact upon Courtyard.

Advice and Observations: Given the proliferation of new hotel product types introduced in the last 10 years, Mr. Lambert has some humble advice to those who wish to succeed with a new introduction. Most of the new introductions have been by entrepreneurs willing to take the necessary risk. "Great entrepreneurs have this great gut," says Lambert. But the trick will be to balance this "gut" with the voice of the customer when making strategic and operational decisions. Customers will continue to have lots of choices, and their needs and expectations will change over time, perhaps often and dramatically. A great "gut" will not be enough to sustain success throughout the life of the concept.

His second piece of advice is to build a good product that creates value for the customer, both through the quality of the offering and through the prices charged. That requires giving the customer a strong reason to buy in a world of many choices, and managing the costs of the business to continue to offer a "fair" price in a world of deals. Finally, you need good people at all levels to execute. Nobody does it alone. Find them and nurture them.

Contact

Craig Lambert, Senior Vice President and Brand Manager
Courtyard by Marriott
One Marriott Drive, Washington, DC 20058
Phone: 301-380-1658   Fax: 301-380-2680

DAYS INN ALTOONA

Overall Best-Practice Property Champion in Economy Segment
"Professional Pride and Personal Values"

The Driving Source of Excellence

Greg Sheehan, owner of the Days Inn in Altoona, Pennsylvania, believes the pride of owning and managing his hotel is responsible for the success of his property. Rather than a boast, this is the expression of a philosophy of life and work, according to which (1) running a hotel is a most honorable profession; (2) a hotel is a part of the community and thus a long-term business providing jobs for those in the community; and (3) a hotel is not an investment bought and sold for a quick return but is instead a reflection of the owner's values and self-respect. Mr. Sheehan is an owner, but he is also a hotelier in the traditional and respected meaning of the term.

Mr. Sheehan's philosophy has evolved from growing up in the family's 40-room hotel, which provided numerous opportunities to develop common sense, customer empathy, and the ability to run a profitable business with loyal customers. The owner's job, he learned, is to set the standards for the property, standards that favor the guest and show visible pride of ownership and respect for the business. Only then, he believes, can you convince your management and employees to take pride in the property and in what they do. Hotels should not waver in their standards. They should set them at the appropriate level and reinforce them by putting in place consistent delivery systems. For this to happen, owners play a key role. Too often, according to Mr. Sheehan, owners perceive the hotel as an investment, a stream of revenues, and not as businesses they personally identify with or operate. From this perspective, reinvestment is often not part of their success equation, which can result in a slow drift to mediocrity.

The Delivery of Excellence

Basic Sources of Customer Value: Mr. Sheehan's experience has taught him that customers have definite expectations. The business traveler wants a property with a "nice feel" to it and a functional, comfortable room. The family customer — wherein the wife/mother is typically the key decision-maker — wants a clean hotel that smells and feels like home; that is, the hotel feels warm and comfortable. All guests need to feel relaxed, so the property must be operated to give off "good vibes."

Visible Customer Value: For Mr. Sheehan, delivering on the guests' expectations is not sufficient. He believes the exceptional hotelier must offer "visible value." Customers have to perceive that their hotel experience at the Days Inn Altoona exceeds the offerings of competitive properties. Consequently, Mr. Sheehan tries to "WOW" the customer. This operating strategy means that the property is kept fresh and up-to-date, and FF&E is replaced before the guest notices a problem. Although an expensive strategy, Mr. Sheehan believes it is important for long-term success. "WOW" efforts are extended in other areas. For example, the guest's check-in at the front desk is always professional and accommodating, crafted to make the customer feel important and respected. Locks and lighting are well maintained to give the guest a safe and secure experience. The property performs "professionally," and decisions are always made in the best interest of the

guests. There are no New Year's Eve parties, for example, because they might interfere with the guest's comfort.

Visible Employee Value: Employees must also perceive that working for Days Inn Altoona provides them with greater value than what would be obtained by working at a competitive property. Mr. Sheehan cultivates this employee perception of visible value by demonstrating respect toward his staff, and conveying his pride in the hotel business and the property. As a result, Mr. Sheehan fosters pride in his employees.

Moreover, working conditions, salaries, and other incentives also present visible value for employees: "Salaries are above competitor's." The health-care plan for all employees includes medical, dental, and eye coverage. There is a 401K plan and a vacation policy. Besides these economic incentives, the owner makes sure that employees have the best tools for the job and that those tools are always in working order. Long-term employees get "ownership" of their tools. For example, housekeepers with long job tenure get top-of-the-line vacuum cleaners, and only they may use them.

Employee input is constantly sought to determine if there is something that could make the job better. Mr. Sheehan listens and is willing to try new ideas. He understands that not all of those ideas will work, but believes all are deserving of study.

Visible Performance: The hotel operates at 180% of fair market share. A recent feasibility study for a convention center in Altoona estimated that hotels in the area operated at an average occupancy rate of 64 percent. Days Inn Altoona operates at 79 percent occupancy.

Perhaps more important than the financial success, Mr. Sheehan is gratified to be a valued individual in the community. Because he takes such pride in his business, others in the community believe he shows respect for them as citizens and neighbors. The community also values Mr. Sheehan's business philosophy and acumen; thus, they seek his opinion on a variety of matters.

Guest Perspective

Value Drivers in the Purchase Decision: A small number of Days Inn Altoona business customers were interviewed. The value drivers that motivated their decision to stay at the hotel were, in decreasing order, the convenient location of the hotel, their familiarity with the place, the service friendliness, the cleanliness of the guestroom and of the property in general, and guestroom comfort. Not too far from Sheehan's basic customer values! All nine business customers said the Days Inn Altoona delivered this value.

Benefits to Customer: The customers' derived benefits are much in line with Mr. Sheehan's take on guest expectations: "feels comfortable," "at home," and "provides a convenient, non-complicated place to stay."

Outlook on Management Practices: When asked about possible practices that enable the hotel to create these benefits, customers noted consistency in the delivery of various services; the way the hotel provides personal recognition; and the well-trained and knowledgeable staff that ensures the guests' messages are delivered efficiently.

Insights

Advice and Observations: Mr. Sheehan's advice to others who want to be successful with their own business is, not surprisingly, to start with themselves. An owner must establish a core of beliefs, a set of values that will define personal behavior and provide the foundation for business decisions. To succeed, owners must actively seek and listen to advice from superiors and subordinates, but owners must also learn to separate the "wheat from the chaff." Mr. Sheehan suggests making a plan and then implementing it. Owners must give their best to the plan and their employees. Success, however defined, will follow.

Contact

Greg Sheehan, Owner
Days Inn
3306 Pleasant Valley Blvd., Altoona, PA
Phone: 814-944-9661   Fax: 814-944-9557

DISNEY'S POLYNESIAN RESORT

Overall Best-Practice Property Champion in Upscale Segment
"Creating and Delivering a Magical Experience"

The Driving Source of Excellence

Disney's Polynesian Resort was built in 1971 as one of the first themed resorts at Walt Disney World. The promise made by Clyde Min, the general manager, and his team to the customer is that of a magical experience with an authentic Polynesian flavor. Creating and delivering this "Magic of Polynesia" is the challenge faced by Disney's Polynesian Resort. Successfully meeting that challenge has garnered the resort the overall best-practice property champion award among upscale hotel properties. This challenge has many facets: The complex details underlying magic have to operate so smoothly that they become imperceptible; an experience is not something that can be faked, the place has to have a "soul"; authenticity in what the staff does and what the guest feels is the rule; whatever is needed to create and deliver the magic experience has to be organized in an efficient and profitable way. According to Mr. Min, three strategies are the core of the Disney's Polynesian Resort's accomplishment. First, a leadership philosophy based on a careful alignment of the employees' personal values and those of the resort. Second, a comprehensive training program, Magic of Polynesia, to articulate this leadership-by-values philosophy. (Note that the Disney's Polynesian Resort has received a best functional practice award in human resources management.) Finally, a performance management system that monitors the precious but fragile balance between what is profitable, good for the guest and good for the employees.

The Delivery of Excellence

Leadership by Values: When Mr. Min came to the property several years ago as general manager, he was faced with the challenge of developing a system that can not only deliver "excellent service" to the guests but that can also create and deliver on a day-to-day basis the magic, authentic, Polynesian experience promised in the hotel positioning. At the time, the resort was experiencing high employee turnover and an inability to deliver services that were up to expectations. If such problems are of significance in all hotels, they are especially serious when the core of the product being sold is authenticity in service and soul in the experience. Mr. Min recognized that creating and delivering such a product could only be done on a day-to-day basis if he was able to get employees' commitment. Otherwise, service would never be perceived as sincere and authentic. But how do you get the front-line employees to want to smile and give great service? How do you teach the "dignity of work?"

Mr. Min decided that the only way to go was to establish a leadership philosophy based on a careful alignment of the corporate values of the Walt Disney Company, the property values of Disney's Polynesian Resort and the employees' personal values. This alignment of values would guide the planning and management of all operations on the property and guide all decision-making. It would also guide a behavior of respect, dignity and integrity of all individuals operating in a way consistent with the personal value of the people who were

creating the guest experience. It might also require showing employees how they can be happy in that environment in their specific job: by bringing happiness to others, they bring happiness to themselves.

The leadership-by-values program, initiated in January of 1996, was developed with the assistance of Dr. George Kanahele of Hawaii, a consultant and teacher who specializes in management by values. Mr. Min referred to Disney's Polynesian Resort as an aloha-driven organization, with, at its core, the universal message of aloha. The set of values underlying the leadership philosophy are: aloha (unconditional love and care), balance, courage, diversity, flawlessness (service execution), ideal host, family, openness and respect. These values are carefully integrated into all aspects of management: mission statement, training modules, cast involvement opportunities and design of guest interactions. An important step in this long journey was the articulation of the leadership-by-value philosophy into a comprehensive training program.

The Magic of Polynesia: The goal was to create a resort with "soul." The Magic of Polynesia is a comprehensive training program. It facilitates employees' understanding of the business, the company, and the distinctive nature of the Polynesian magical experience and of its underlying values, and of the behaviors required to deliver such an experience on a day-to-day basis. The details of the program have been presented in the functional practice case study. This idea is to help employees understand that the way they live their personal lives need not be different from their work lives. If they are in the right business, and in the right place, with their values aligned to those of their workplace, what they live and believe at home is what they can believe and live at work. The process of and commitment to this "values alignment" by the property and employees, leads to employee understanding of and commitment to the business, to the satisfaction of the guest. When that understanding is translated into the hospitality context — service standards, creating guest memories, being a good host, creating family — the authentic service experience is created. With the program, the employees study the Polynesian culture(s) and the spirit of aloha. They then compare it with their own personal values and those of the property. They then have the choice to commit to the organization, to live those values in their work lives in creating experiences and memories for the guests. It is truly putting the soul into an organization. And according to internal data, customer satisfaction soars! The guests are treated like family: there is a warm welcome; a sincere and consistently caring experience while at the Resort; and the opportunity to authentically explore and experience Polynesian culture.

Monitoring Performance for Commitment and Balance: Creating and delivering a magical and authentic experience relies upon a precious, but fragile, balance between what is profitable, good for the guest, and good for the employees. Thus, the system in place to measure and monitor performance at Disney's Polynesian Resort must account for such balance among the key aspects of management roles. Disney's Polynesian Resort uses a scorecard for management performance that reflects the commitment, not compliance, of the leader to managing by values. Managers are evaluated on the balance they maintain among many dimensions: financial performance, guest satisfaction, cast (employee) service excellence (measured through quarterly surveys and monthly focus groups with customers), criteria set to assess how well they manage by values, and, finally, their personal development program (how well they have improved certain leadership competencies and behaviors).

Financial Performance: The Disney's Polynesian Resort has a high guest repeat-business percentage which has increased over the last two years. What is more dramatic is that this increase has taken place during a time period when four new properties opened at Walt Disney World. Departmental profits, gross operating profits and net revenue from property operations have all grown significantly. Expenses have decreased and productivity has increased. All in all, the resort is achieving higher levels of revenue with less operating costs. At the same time, it is reducing expenses by achieving efficiencies throughout the operation. Through managing by values, it has created a positive environment where employees feel more involved and have a sense of ownership of their destiny. The result is high motivation and greater profitability for the operation.

Guest Perspective

Does Disney's Polynesian Resort deliver the magical and authentic Polynesian experience promised to the guests? Comments from the interviewed guests are telling in this regard: "I love the way they treat me, like a god"; "It seemed like it was constructed to be true to form, not just a plastic image"; "I am going to the Polynesian on a regular basis because it has a Polynesian atmosphere"; "Absolutely breathtaking — it's as nice as Hawaii"; "We generally stay there, my wife likes the flavor of that hotel"; "You have to give high marks to Disney people who pull off the atmosphere." In addition to such comments pertaining directly to the guest's experience, a large number of functional attributes were mentioned as a purchase motive and unique source of customer value created during the hotel experience: the "smoothness" of the service and the attention to details; the convenience provided by a location close to the Magic Kingdom and by the Monorail; the cleanliness of the property. For 93% of the respondents, Disney's Polynesian Resort delivered on the hotel attributes that had motivated the guest purchase. The variety and quality of food served at the restaurants also emerged as a significant source of customer value.

Insights

Mr. Min sees his role of general manager as being focused on cast (employee) development. He is the coach. He presents the vision over and over and over again and mentors the staff. With the high level of cast participation and involvement engendered in the program, he needs to coach. It sounds tedious but it's not. He "couldn't think of anything better to do than make people happy." He believes other hotels and resorts could copy his resort's success. But he warns that "it's really a leap of faith. It's difficult to see at first how his approach will overcome the low morale, the service gaps, the turnover." He states that it takes courage and feeling your way to the next step. It is really managing by your own personal values.

Contact

Clyde Min, General Manager
Disney's Polynesian Resort
P.O. Box 1000, Lake Buena Vista, FL 32830
Ph: 407-824-1232   Fax: 407-824-2388

EMBASSY SUITES

Overall Best-Practice Corporate Champion in Upscale Segment
"When the Operating Strategy Is the Brand Strategy"

For Steve Porter, executive vice president of operations for Promus Hotel Corporation, the success of Embassy Suites in the upscale market is simple: "The operating strategy is the brand strategy." In other words, the driving source of excellence at Embassy Suites lies in the development of a unique, well-focused brand positioning strategy that is operationalized into key activities, systems, and processes that make a difference both to guest experience and profitability.

Embassy Suites' branding strategy is centered on those customers who like to mingle with other guests and employees when they stay in a hotel. At Embassy Suites, market researchers call such customers "downstairs stayers" (part of the action downstairs in the hotel) as opposed to "upstairs stayers" (who go up to their room and shut the door). Complimentary, full American breakfast in the morning and cocktails in the evening are served in the atrium lobby. Such features provide the guests not only with a bolstered opportunity for social exchanges, but also convenience and control in the various details of their hotel stay. No need to wait for early room service: the breakfast is served downstairs. Various features of the product and service experience offer maximum convenience to the guests, be they businesspersons or families: a two-room suite with separate living and sleeping areas, two phone lines, two televisions, a large work space, microwave oven, and pullout sofa bed. What Embassy Suites offers does appear simple, but it is powerfully perceived by the guest.

Social interaction, convenience, and control are at the core of the Embassy Suites' promise to its target customers. As passionately expounded by Mr. Porter, these promises made by the brand become the prescriptions for the "whats" and the "hows" of operations and management in every hotel. This strategy has resulted in a system-wide 52 percent gross operating profit and 35 percent net operating income.

At Embassy Suites, the operating strategy, in line with the brand strategy, is to deliver on the brand promises of social interaction, convenience, and control with the objective of maximizing the revenue premiums. There are four major components to the operating strategy: (1) team member satisfaction; (2) guest satisfaction; (3) yield premium; and, (4) profitability.

Team Member Satisfaction and Trust: Embassy Suites strongly believes that for the employees to be able to "make magic" for the guests, each employee on the team has to be satisfied with his/her work and trust the organization. The mechanisms to evaluate employee satisfaction are designed to reinforce the focus on trust. For instance, when Embassy Suites does twice-annual employee surveys, monitoring is made not only of the actual score but also of the participation rate. Management believes that if employees trust the organization they will feel confident enough to share their thoughts, feelings and ideas. Anything less than a 90 percent participation rate by employees in a property is cause for

follow-up analysis. In addition, employee performance evaluations are done "up" the organization by the employee on his/her direct supervisor. If there is trust, then the supervisor will want and need to hear the feedback in order to be effective. Clearly, there must be enormous self-confidence throughout the organization if this process is to work. At Embassy Suites that trust in employees is made tangible in the authority they have to invoke the 100 percent unconditional guest satisfaction guarantee. If the guest is unhappy for any reason, the guest does not pay. This policy is not only part of the brand promise, it is a powerful tool to assist employees in creating magic for the guests, and it is also a powerful tool in building that trust in the organization.

Guest Satisfaction: Embassy Suites routinely monitors guest satisfaction, but here also, in a very focused way. Every month, nearly 100 guests are asked to express their satisfaction with their stays at Embassy Suites on an A (excellent) to F (fail) scale. This survey yields a minimum of 30 responses per hotel per month. Managers are trained to earn high "A" scores from guests. Embassy Suites' managers believe that those individuals who are satisfied enough to give an "A" grade are the "zealots" for the brand. These zealots provide Embassy Suites with all or the majority of their business and offer word-of-mouth recommendations to their friends and colleagues. These are the loyal customers that every hotel wants. "B" stayers are not zealots and are just as likely to go to the competition on subsequent visits as return to Embassy Suites. What Embassy Suites has learned in studying the difference between the A and B stayer is that only minor things cause the lower score, things that are not expensive to fix, such as staff interaction. Obviously a C, D, or F score, fortunately almost non-existent, is immediately explored and solutions identified.

Presently, Embassy Suites is achieving A scores from 61.5 percent of its guests, surpassing the guest satisfaction goal, in terms of the combined product/service, of 60 percent. To focus everyone's attention on the target goal of 60 percent, Embassy Suites provides bonuses to employees at every level of the hotel. The bonuses are paid every quarter. Sub-goals are also developed in each department on the aspects of operations that are deemed most critical to guest satisfaction. This approach also emphasizes the team culture so that nobody wins at the expense of co-workers.

Yield Premium in RevPAR Management: Hotels only have a finite amount of capacity to sell and do not have the luxury of inventory to buffer changing patterns of demand. The challenge facing management every day is not to sell all the rooms but to sell all the rooms at the highest possible price. That requires both rate and occupancy strategies and the decision-making ability to know when each strategy is appropriate and how to execute it effectively. Embassy Suites has an objective to deliver a 20-point yield premium; that is, to operate at 20 percent above weighted fair share. It presently operates at 115-117 percent, which represents excellent performance. The first aspect of its strategy for achieving the yield premium consists of a pricing strategy that is simple to understand and simple to execute: rooms are offered at one of five rates and these prices are constant across distribution channels. The customer is not quoted one price when calling the hotel and a different price when going through a travel agent.

The second aspect of the yield premium strategy is to set the goal for the ADR at the published rate, which means that there is little discounting. This requires the general manager and

salespeople to price aggressively, using the techniques they have been taught. Moreover, the company has developed a proprietary pricing-decision support software program to assist salespeople and managers in making pricing decisions. This software models the competitive environment and factors in the hotel's historical performance to take a 90-day "forward look," assessing demand and the hotel's projected business mix to determine the hotel's optimal pricing strategy. The hotel can accept the recommendation or over ride it. The system can also do occupancy/rate trade-off analysis so the general manager can immediately "see" the impact on his profit objective from any contemplated change in rate or occupancy in response to environmental or competitive factors. The pricing strategy and the revenue performance of the property are constantly evaluated with site visits to provide assistance for future decisions and to identify and correct errors. The goal is not to make decisions for the management of the hotel. Rather, it is to "make leaders, not managers." As the hotels learn how to make good pricing decisions, their confidence grows and they learn when and how to be more aggressive in their pricing. Of course, with highly satisfied guests, one is much more willing to price aggressively.

Profitability: The business planning and budgeting document for each hotel can be no longer than 15 pages to force managers to think in clear, succinct terms regarding the strategies, actions and budget necessary to deliver the profit objective. Again, to assist the general manager, the company has developed a proprietary method that uses a sophisticated mathematical analysis, based on forecasted demand and the historical performance of each competitor in the set, to predict performance for each competitor and establish the RevPAR targets for Embassy Suites. As any manager knows, revenue budgeting is an area that is fraught with uncertainty and number manipulation. For example, adding one more hotel to the competitive set always lowers the definition of fair share. And there is always room for honest disagreement as to what revenue figure is achievable against the competition. This method reduces that uncertainty and makes the process more objective. The hotel can adjust the target based upon any unique local conditions or environmental factors. Once the revenue (RevPAR) target is agreed upon, the system computes the expense portion of the budget, again based upon historical operating assumptions and known inflationary increases. The end result of all this effort is a profit goal for the hotel. If circumstances change during the year, the general manager can adjust the rate or occupancy strategies while still focusing on the ultimate profit objective.

Guest Perspective

Value Drivers in the Purchase Decision: Based on our independent survey, Embassy Suites' alignment of branding and operating strategy appears to work. After location, the top four most powerful sources of customer value driving the purchase decision are tightly linked to Embassy Suites' operating strategy: large-size rooms, low/good prices, food and beverage (primarily breakfast), and a sense of familiarity with the place. These value drivers were common across all market segments. The next most frequently mentioned value drivers pertained to the constant availability of rooms and the variety of services offered. Hotel attributes also frequently mentioned as value drivers at purchase bore on service quality, on aspects of the room other than size (cleanliness, furniture comfort, kitchenettes), of the physical property (in general and its aesthetics), and on the efficiency at check-in and check-out. Of the customers interviewed, 94 percent of them reported that Embassy Suites delivered on their value drivers.

Value Drivers in the Hotel Experience: Customers appeared to value the ability to deliver on the brand's promises in their actual experience at an Embassy Suites hotel. The three aspects of the hotel experiences most frequently mentioned as value drivers were all related to the core of the brand concept: the size of the room, the quality of service (in general, as well as attentiveness, speed and friendliness) and the quality of their food and beverage (overwhelmingly, breakfast). The only brand promise not reflected in customer perception of value was social interaction. Cleanliness of the property, comfort of room furniture, quality of meeting rooms, and the health club were the other aspects of the hotel experience to be most frequently mentioned as value drivers. Differences among market segments emerged in terms of their respective dominating value drivers: Both transient and meeting/convention business customers valued most the room size; whereas for leisure customers, the cleanliness of the property was the most frequently mentioned source of value during the hotel experience.

Benefits to Customer: Comfort emerged most clearly as the benefit most successfully created for the Embassy Suites' guest. The list of benefits most often reported by the guests also included relaxation, a sense of overall satisfaction, a pleasurable experience and security.

Outlook on Management Practices: The practice of providing a complimentary breakfast clearly topped the list of practices viewed by the guest as critical in delivering value. In fact, breakfast was mentioned by guests one out of three times. Other complimentary services (in particular the cocktails) and the consistency in services came in second. Mentions were also made of the satisfaction guarantee, the quality of the room communication system, the staff selection and training, and the staff going beyond the call of duty, with a specific reference to their prompt message delivery.

Intermediary Perspective

Value Drivers for Travel Agents and Meeting Planners: For both travel agents and meeting planners, convenient location was the primary value driving their decision for sending guests to Embassy Suites. The two intermediaries, though, differed in terms of their second and third value drivers. For travel agents, the size of the room and the brand name and reputation were powerful value drivers. For meeting planners, their decision to buy Embassy Suites hotels was based on low/good prices and meeting room size. Turning to their actual experiences as intermediaries with Embassy Suites, meeting planners were much more verbal than travel agents in listing things they liked. These pertained to the overall quality of the physical property, the rooms (meeting rooms and guestrooms), and the quality of the food and beverage in the various functions. The travel agents appeared more sensitive to the sales representative and to the quality of the package deals.

Insights

Any company that wants to create a tighter alignment between its brand strategy and operating strategy needs to do a number of things. Mr. Porter says the company first needs to create a "team of equals," as no one individual knows everything necessary to succeed in this endeavor. That group then needs to determine the key issues, to create the solutions, activities, systems, processes and the like, and then, execute. He cautions to be "real deliberate" about the measurement systems and criteria used to measure performance in each area. The company is going to manage what is measured, so the company must be confident that it is measuring the right things correctly. Build in milestones along the way to help people stop and celebrate both the successes and the failures on the journey. Not everything will work as planned but it is important to acknowledge the effort of all those involved. Also, success, when it comes, needs to be shared.

Contact

Steve Porter, Executive Vice President, Operations
Promus Hotel Corporation
755 Crossover Lane, Memphis, TN 38117
Phone: 901-374-5428   Fax: 901-374-5521

EXTENDED STAYAMERICA, INC.

Overall Best-Practice Corporate Champion in the Extended-Stay Lower-Tier Segment
"To Be the Leaders in a New Industry Segment, Build Market Share Faster and Deliver Quality"

The Driving Source of Excellence

The extended-stay lower-tier is a young segment of the lodging industry. To become the leader in this segment, Extended StayAmerica (ESA) recognized a great opportunity, and turned it into three hotel products that win for the guests, the employees, the owners, and management. And, in the best spirit of capitalism, the company rapidly rolled them out to "build market share quicker" and control the "high ground."

When a new niche develops in the lodging industry, having a strong hotel concept is just the beginning. Any hint of success draws competitors out of nowhere, financially ready and willing to copy your great product. Competitive advantage in the lodging industry, regardless of the segment, is always short-lived. ESA recognizes this truism and is determined not to let competitors catch them.

To win, when challenged by a growing number of quality competitors, requires finding and building on the finite number of good sites available and developing the operating muscle before competitors can. Speed is a key to dominating in the eventual market share battle. In 1995, there were only two ESA properties. At the end of 1998 there were over 305; and in 1999, ESA intends to open approximately 60 more properties. Here is how ESA is doing it.

The Delivery of Excellence

A Compelling Place to Invest: ESA is a public company traded on the New York Stock Exchange. Approximately 30 percent of the shares are held by the management of the company and by the founders, George D. Johnson and H. Wayne Huizenga, who invested the initial capital. Fifty percent is owned by institutional investors, and the remainder by the public.

ESA believes that a large part of its success is due to its willingness to invest in ownership of the brand. The company buys the real estate on which the hotels are built, and it owns and operates all its hotels. This requires an enormous amount of development capital but it allows the company to move quickly and to obtain the sites it wants. ESA believes ownership control is just as important. Having a branded product with high operational standards and minimal staffing and management, the company believes it must "inspect what it expects" to ensure a satisfactory guest experience.

ESA continues to invest in and grow its regional operating infrastructure to manage the business. It now has six regions across the United States that encompass 60 districts. The regional offices have a director of real estate, which decentralizes the development function and allows it to happen more quickly. Depending on each region's level of activity, each director has several real estate managers working on property acquisitions. Similarly, each region has a complement of construction professionals to assure that new construction is on-time and within budget.

A regional director of operations manages the district managers. Each of these district managers is responsible for six to eight hotels. This infrastructure is extensive and expensive, but has been important in the national roll-out of the brand. It leads to quicker development and ensures that properties, once opened, do not get lost in the rush to grow and also ensures that their performance is maximized. ESA recognizes a significant portion of the long-term value of the brand comes from the operation of the properties, and that the guest experience must be monitored. This commitment to operating structure also means there are significant opportunities for managers to be promoted. Currently, it takes approximately 12 to 18 months for promotion to general manager of a property, and another 12 to 18 months for promotion to district manager. Extended StayAmerica capitalizes on its extensive pool of talent by promoting from within.

ESA's ability to raise capital has been critical in fueling the rapid rollout. At a time when the availability of development capital is decreasing, ESA will invest approximately $350 million in development during 1999. The majority of this funding will be from internal cash flow, but with some limited debt financing.

ESA's return on investment is 17 percent; the current operating margin is 58 percent. The company continues to reinvest its cash flow in the development of new properties, and with a senior management team that is experienced and credible, ESA continues to grow quickly.

A Compelling Place to Stay: The ability to build market share quickly would be wasted without being able to provide a compelling place to stay for the guest. ESA believes its three hotel concepts are winners. The company has three brands competing at different price points that meet the needs of the extended-stay customer, usually an individual who is relocating, undergoing training, or performing a special assignment. StudioPlus Deluxe Studios offer well-furnished studios in the 400-square-feet range and are priced at $300-400 per week. Crossland Economy Studios offer smaller 227-square-feet studios with the same core features served up in a smaller portion. These studios are priced at $159-199 per week. With over 190 properties, Extended StayAmerica Efficiency Studios is the largest brand in the ESA portfolio. Each studio is a roomy 300 square feet and is separated into a living area with a work desk and a reclining easy chair, a sleeping area with a queen-size bed and a complete kitchen area with a refrigerator, microwave, and cooktop, as well as plates, silverware and utensils.

All hotels offer two service levels. For the nightly or short-term guest, there is a traditional hotel service with cleaning and linen change daily. For the extended-stay guest (seven days or more), there is linen and housekeeping service once weekly and towel service twice weekly. The price for a week's stay at Extended StayAmerica Efficiency Studios is approximately $200 to $300, which is generally 60 to 70 percent of the competitors' prices in a given market area. ESA believes a significant portion of its value equation is giving "seven nights of product for five nights of price."

According to ESA's internal data, this value model is working: Customers are very satisfied and they come in large numbers. The "overall guest satisfaction" scores, as measured quarterly by The Gallup Organization, have averaged 4.1 out of 5.0 for the last two years. The "likelihood to recommend" scores average 4.4 out of 5.0. Finally, "the cost of staying at ESA for the value received" scores averaged 4.5 out of 5.0. In spite of the stress imposed on the organization by the rapid rollout and the inherent problems associated with growth, ESA is presently performing at 117 percent of its fair market share; its ambitious goal is 120 percent.

An Innovative Place to Work: The staffing model applied at ESA is different from that of a traditional hotel. For instance, the optimum size of an Extended StayAmerica Efficiency Studios property is approximately 100 studios, and there are only five to eight full-time employees; the balance of each hotel's 12 to 15 people are part-timers. There is also less management, although there is 24-hour staff coverage at each property. Laundry is done at night, and the individual responsible is available to respond to guests as needed. This staffing pattern results in a significant saving in operating costs.

Since guests are staying for a long period, the emphasis is on building customer relationships rather than completing transactions. The staff has more time to get to know and to interact with guests and a sense of family often develops. Thus, the human resources model emphasizes motivating employees to build these relationships. In the lobby of each property is the ESA creed, which clarifies what is expected of each employee. It reads:

- Treat each guest as you would want to be treated.
- Treat fellow employees with the respect they deserve.
- Be a good steward of all that is entrusted to you.
- Use good judgment at all times.

All of the staff training and motivation is designed to translate this creed into action. An acronym ESA uses to frame the training and the service it strives for between employee and guest is F.A.R.E.: Friendliness, Attentiveness, Responsiveness, and Empathy. Employees are trained to deliver these attributes and to understand how they make a difference in each guest's experience.

The job of senior management also has to be innovative to provide the strategic leadership necessary to keep the brand growing quickly. The company's style is to push decision-making down as close to the property as possible while maintaining a high "standards umbrella" that is uniformly administered from property to property; hence, the importance of and investment in the regional operating structure. Regional and property management executes the product and service delivery processes — the what, why, how, when, and where of managing for the guest. The high guest satisfaction scores and employee satisfaction scores tell senior managers that they are "doing the right things." Senior management can thus focus its efforts on growing the brand, knowing a positive guest experience, "the family feeling," is consistently being offered.

Value Drivers in the Purchase Decision: Based upon a survey of ESA Efficiency Studios' guests, conducted by Cornell University, ESA's assumptions about what customers value in this industry segment appear to be appropriate. Both leisure and business guests identify three primary reasons for staying at ESA: convenient location, guestroom kitchenette, and low prices. Other value drivers in the purchase decision that were frequently mentioned include: bathroom size, familiarity with the brand, cleanliness of the property, guest room size, bathroom amenities, and overall quality of service. One hundred percent of interviewed guests believed ESA delivered on these value drivers.

Value Drivers in the Hotel Experience: The guest's appreciation of the guest room kitchenette tops the list of value drivers emerging for the actual hotel experience. Apparently responding to ESA's four-point creed and its F.A.R.E. service philosophy, customers also valued various aspects of the service, such as overall service quality and friendliness and attentiveness of the staff. Service was a central value driver particularly for the leisure customers. Other aspects of the physical product also contributed to value: overall liking for the guest room, cleanliness, and bathroom size, as well as guestroom entertainment and work equipment.

Benefits to Customers: The benefits derived from ESA most frequently mentioned by guests are, in decreasing frequency: providing a home away from home, comfort, and privacy.

Outlook on Management Practices: Customers identified those practices they believe ESA uses to create these value drivers: the best properties, beyond-the-call-of-duty service, good management, cater to the market, and knowledgeable staff.

Value Drivers for Travel Agents: Travel agents we surveyed first noted that ESA is often requested by the customers themselves. The reasons travel agents recommend ESA center on functional value drivers, specifically room cleanliness, efficiency, low price, and availability.

Advice and Observations: Jay Witzel, the ESA's chief operating officer and president, believes that all businesses succeed from the outside in. Not only does the business need a great idea, but there has to be a large enough market to support it. The business model needs to emphasize value for the guest and for the owner. Then, given the competitive intensity that is a part of the industry, the business organization must be able to move quickly and sustain that speed.

Jay S. Witzel, Chief Operating Officer & President
ESA Management, Inc.
450 E. Las Olas Blvd., Suite 1100, Fort Lauderdale, FL 33301
Phone: 954-713-1805   Fax: 954-713-1695

FAIRFIELD INN BY MARRIOTT

Overall Best-Practice Corporate Champion in Economy Segment
"Impress More Guests, Sell More Rooms, Have More Fun"

The Driving Source of Excellence

A major driver behind Marriott's success with Fairfield Inn has been its ability to redefine what an "upper" economy hotel chain is in the mind of the customer. After all, an economy hotel is a simple concept, and there are few attributes that can be manipulated to create a difference in the customer's mind. For Fairfield Inn, an economy hotel does not mean "cheap prices and a cheap hotel." Instead, it redefined this product segment by developing a concept on the basis of customer value, emphasizing customer satisfaction with both the room *and* with the overall experience at a price competitive with other economy brands and independents. What Fairfield does on a consistent basis and what it believes makes Fairfield successful is this experience of the guest at the property level; that is, the interaction with the staff; the "feel" of the property; and the clean, functional, comfortable room all combine to provide a positive experience noticed and remembered by the guest.

The Delivery of Excellence

Impress More Guests: Bruce Bloom, senior vice president and brand manager for Fairfield Inn, believes managers and associates working within the Fairfield Inn's culture together provide the consistency to create a different guest experience at the property level. The culture of Fairfield Inn is simple: "Impress more guests, sell more rooms, have more fun." All efforts, all policies, all corporate support are to live and reinforce that culture. The people of Fairfield Inn believe the credo, and it guides their behavior. The culture allows the right things to happen to and for the guest.

Customer value in the Fairfield Inn equation is computed by dividing the guest experience by the price. That guest experience is composed of three key beliefs. The first belief is that the guest expects to be treated with respect. Employees are more willing to provide that respect because they are treated with respect. The second belief is that the guest wants a clean room in a pleasant environment; every hotel brand in this product segment offers this component with varying degrees of consistency. Finally, the third belief is that the guest wants friendly interaction with the staff; the customer wants to feel good. And, of course, the price must be competitive with other alternatives. The difference, though, is the experience. Fairfield Inn believes that if it executes properly each time on those beliefs, the customer will choose Fairfield Inn.

To execute properly requires constant feedback from the guests. Fairfield does that both informally and formally. It conducts a monthly, random telephone guest satisfaction survey of check-outs to monitor the property's performance in delivering the experience. It practices a "Lounge Lizard"

program where every morning the general manager is out front talking to guests, usually at the continental breakfast, monitoring guest experiences and ensuring their satisfaction. Finally, in those instances of service delivery failure, representatives are empowered to go to great lengths to resolve a customer's problem.

Fairfield Inn claims its guest satisfaction surveys constantly praise the experience received by guests on property. As telling is Fairfield Inn's 15 percent RevPAR premium over the competitive set.

Fun and Success for Associates and Managers: Fairfield Inn works to create an environment in which the general manager of the property can succeed with associates and guests. Since the majority of properties are franchised, the associates are not employees of Marriott. Thus, it is with the general manager that Fairfield believes it can make a difference. The general manager is the leader of the property. These general managers are young and relatively inexperienced. For most, this is their first posting as a general manager. The culture is one of helping them to succeed with the associates and ultimately, the guests. Impress more guests, sell more rooms, have more fun.

To help the general managers succeed, Fairfield Inn, as do all Marriott brands, uses an extensive, scientific selection process for managers as well as for employees. It matches the personality attributes of the candidate against the attributes of successful holders of that position. This is information Fairfield has collected through research and stored in a database. The key is to match the right person for the job requirements/attributes. Fairfield believes the technical and administrative skills can be taught, but the attitudes that fit the culture, that assist in success, are those the individual brings to the job. These attitudes cannot be taught.

After selection, new managers participate in a four-week training program. This program focuses on the mechanics of the position and also the culture of Fairfield Inn and the Marriott Company. The training emphasizes respect for the individual and managing through praise and recognition for accomplishment.

Fairfield has high standards for its managers and associates. In order to "win" in this product segment, Fairfield believes it must "out-execute the competition." Thus, high standards are necessary. The best way to get people to meet those standards is to ensure they have the tools to do the job and to reward them. The wages Fairfield Inn pays associates are competitive but it is the non-wage compensation that retains them and gets them to execute every day for every guest stay. That is where the culture of respect becomes so important; it is the atmosphere in which the associates perform their daily work. The way in which they are treated by management is the way they will treat the guests and be treated by them in kind. Respect, reinforce, reward the behaviors that are important to success. Have more fun! It sounds easy but it's not. "It's damn hard to execute properly. It means hiring and retaining the right people and getting them to execute," Bloom says. That is why Fairfield emphasizes people and corporate culture.

The third pillar to assist the general managers and the properties to succeed are the regional and annual meetings, held to recognize, reinforce and reward the successes of managers and associates. Fairfield purposely has many rewards meetings and many awards and ways to recognize the accomplishments of their people. They refer to these ceremonies as "bleeding blue" (the roof color of Fairfield Inns). Have more fun.

With a Fair Share of All for the Franchisees: Critical execution could be hampered by the fact that 85 percent of Fairfield Inns are franchised. Conventional wisdom holds that franchisees are difficult to control and to motivate to maintain standards. This is not the case with Fairfield Inns. The franchisees must believe in the system because they are making

it happen. While Marriott utilizes a quality assurance program, it does not have a quantitative score attached to it. Instead, the franchisees and customers are paramount in ensuring quality standards are maintained.

From the franchisee's perspective, Fairfield maximizes the REVPAR premium. It is run by a franchisor (Marriott International) that is a hotel operator (Marriott owns approximately 50 percent of its properties) and which understands the issues an operator faces. It is a brand that has longevity (14 years) and proven success with customers. Franchisees know that if they execute properly, they will be financially successful. Thus, the royalty fee of 4.5 percent, which is a 1 to 2 percent premium over other economy brands, is one the franchisees willingly pay to be associated with this brand. A typical franchisee owns more than one Fairfield Inn. One franchisee owns a portfolio of 280 hotels encompassing a variety of brands—100 of those hotels are Fairfield Inns.

Guest Perspective

Value Drivers in the Purchase Decision: Consistent with the brand positioning, the customers' key purchase motives (besides the highest priority of convenient location) did reflect a balance between price, friendly service, and clean, comfortable rooms. Familiarity with the brand, quality of the brand image, advertising, as well as recommendation by friends completed the list of top value drivers. Interestingly, the marketing-effort drivers were much more influential for leisure customers than they were for business guests. Note, however, that these drivers still come after convenient location, which accounts for the purchase decision of a large majority of leisure guests. For business guests, location lost its powerful hegemony, being mentioned equally as often as low price, followed by cleanliness of the property, and appreciation of the guestroom, the furniture in particular. For 83 percent of the customers interviewed, Fairfield Inn delivered on these value drivers perfectly.

Value Drivers in the Hotel Experience: Confirming that Fairfield Inn can deliver on its promises, the two dominant attributes customers particularly liked from their hotel experiences were the staff's friendliness and the cleanliness of the property. Staff friendliness was particularly salient for leisure guests, ranking only fourth for business guests. Other key drivers of the hotel experiences were: the ability to deliver quality consistent with the brand name, convenience of the location in moving around, and guestroom size and cleanliness.

Benefits to Customers: The benefits derived from Fairfield Inn by Marriott are consistent with those promised in the brand positioning, i.e., an enjoyable experience combined with more functional benefits, such as security and convenience.

Outlook on Management Practices: Confirming the staff and management's focus on the customer, mention of staff going beyond the call of duty to please the guest was mentioned first by a wide range of customers, followed by: "they do good maintenance of their properties," "the free continental breakfast," "they train their personnel well," and "they have more staff than usual in that type of hotel."

Intermediary Perspective

Value Drivers for Intermediary Customers: Travel agents surveyed recommended Fairfield Inn by Marriott to their customers first for its low prices, and then, with equal frequency, convenient location, constant availability of rooms, and service quality. The travel agents' perceptions of high service quality persists in their assessment of what they liked the most in their relationship with Fairfield Inn. They also mentioned their ability to rely on the brand reputation, the quality of management and the promptness with which incentives are paid.

Insights

Mr. Bloom sees his role of brand manager as that of a "champion for the brand." He and his team maintain the brand integrity, develop the systems, and formulate and provide tactics that will maintain the brand's success. But without the knowledge, experience and support of the Marriott organization, Fairfield would not be the success it is today. Nor would it be successful without the performance of the franchisees. It is the franchisees' interest and involvement in growing the brand and executing it properly that also contributes greatly to its success.

Fairfield Inn believes it has the opportunity to double the size of its system in the United States; there are also international opportunities. Fairfield Inn believes there are better ways to leverage the brand flag and use the Marriott system to produce

additional revenues, such as Marriott's Sales 2000 effort. Another opportunity is to become more proactive in sales to increase the number of customers and to increase frequency of purchase both in the business and in the leisure segments.

Advice and Observations: The advice Mr. Bloom offers to others that would emulate the success of Fairfield Inn is simple: "listen to your customers and meet and exceed their expectations, and remember that you're only as strong as your people."

Contact

Bruce Bloom, Senior Vice President and Brand Manager
Fairfield Inn by Marriott
One Marriott Drive, Washington, DC 20058
Phone: 301-380-4514   Fax: 301-380-5470

FOUR SEASONS HOTEL NEW YORK

Overall Best-Practice Property Champion in Physical Property
"The Most Beautiful Stage Ever Performed Upon"

The Driving Source of Excellence

The hotel industry learned from John Portman many years ago that a visually stimulating building in its own right can differentiate a property in the customers' minds and substantially contribute to increased revenues for a property. A quintessential case in point: The Four Seasons Hotel in New York City, the industry-wide overall best-practice property champion for physical property. The Four Seasons Hotel, New York City is a beautiful hotel that perfectly fits the image of the Four Seasons' brand. The exterior does not displace its location or brashly announce its presence. It fits into the neighborhood, having enough self-confidence not to draw undue attention to itself. The design inside is dramatic and unique. The philosophy of the design joins "beauty" to "simple convenience."

The Delivery of Excellence

The Architect's Vision: The vision of I.M. Pei in his visual use of space creates a sense of wonderment and awe in the viewer as he enters the building. The view is clean, uncluttered and futuristic, all lines and angles with height and breadth. At the same time, as the viewer interacts with the space, it calms and soothes him. The angles and lines are like soft strokes on the anxious ego, they do not jar but instead relax. The windows in the public spaces and the guestrooms are large, for the views are dramatic. They perfectly complement the interior design of the building. The guestrooms are large. The color scheme is soothing and the furniture is light-colored. There is a separate tub, shower and dressing area. The guest feels comfortable. The public space is beautiful but functional. There are no corridors. There is no search of where to go and what to do. There is nothing confusing. The furniture, the layout, the process of service, it all fits from a design point of view and has been made for the convenience and comfort of the customer. You feel as a customer very comfortable and well-taken care of. The customer is often not even aware of the design but responds to it. And isn't that the definition of good design?

Design Impact on Guests: The customers of the Four Seasons Hotel "live" design. They are aware of it through the various ways in which fashion pervades their life-style, their own living spaces. "The hotel lobby scene" has a number of sitting areas and is perfect for "people-watching" and of course to be "seen." The customers of this hotel want to be part of the design, part of the drama being performed every day at this hotel, and they want to do so on a regular basis. More than 50 percent of the guests are repeat customers!

Design Impact on Employees: Good design also impacts employees in a very positive way. They feel very good about working in such surroundings. There is a cachet to working at the Four Seasons New York. Employees comment that they get immediate respect when people learn where they work. They are aware of the importance of design as they get the immediate feedback from the customers. It fits very well with the Four Seasons' philosophy of service, refined and attuned to the customers' needs just like the design of the hotel. In this environment, employees love to give good service and to anticipate the guest's needs. The design, furthermore, does not get in the way of delivering that service consistently. There are no obstacles in the physical environment that get between the employee and the guest. The design of this hotel "is the most beautiful stage they've ever performed upon. They feel great," says Herbert Pliessnig, general manager.

Financial Performance: Mr. Pliessnig is convinced there is money in beauty. The hotel has one of the highest average daily rates in the city of New York and he believes that perhaps 10 to 20 percent of the rate is for beauty. And the high rate does not discourage customers: Occupancy is in the high 80's.

What is the barrier to wider use of design as a competitive strategy in the lodging industry? Why do we not get better design of properties in the hotel industry? Except for a few celebrated exceptions, such as the Four Seasons New York and Ian Schrager's hotels, the use of design as a competitive strategy remains extremely scant, in spite of its potential profitability. Mr. Pliessnig suggests two reasons. The first is money: good design costs more. Plus, it requires thought, effort and creativity, and takes time. All of those factors add up to money. The second reason is taste. It's difficult to find someone who can create good design. And who is even to say what is good hotel design? Design, like art, will evoke a response from the customer. Some responses will be positive and some will be negative. Many people in the industry may find it safe to stay in the middle and, as Joe Baum, the famous restaurant concept designer once said of new restaurant concepts, "it's the bland leading the bland."

Contact

Herbert Pliessnig, General Manager
Four Seasons Hotel New York
57 East 57th Street, New York, NY 10022
Ph: 212-350-6601   Fax: 212-350-6665

Insights

Mr. Pliessnig believes that putting money into good design is worth it. Good design is timeless. Customers identify with and respond to it. But a design has to work operationally. You have to know what makes the customer comfortable and how to deliver excellent service in an environment. It is not a goal made up of two separate functions performed independently by architects and the hotel management. It is a partnership that has to meld to satisfy the needs of the guests. And "if we're not doing all this for the guest, then for whom?"

FOUR SEASONS AND REGENT HOTELS & RESORTS

Overall Best-Practice Corporate Champion in Deluxe Segment
"Consistency Over Time"

The Driving Source of Excellence

John Sharpe, president and COO, says consistency over time is the key factor responsible for the success of Four Seasons and Regent Hotels & Resorts.

Four Seasons and Regent Hotels & Resorts, in the business of operating deluxe hotels and resorts, manages 42 hotels and will add an additional 15 over the next two years. The company only owns three of those properties, and has a small equity position in a fourth hotel; it is not playing in the hotel real estate game. Furthermore, Four Seasons is not in the short-term stock market wealth game, nor has it been bought and sold a number of times.

Four Seasons and Regent Hotels & Resorts is a "pure" hotel operator which has chosen to take the time to develop consistent excellence. The average remaining life of its Four Seasons' management contracts is 56 years, and the average remaining life of its Regent Hotels' management contracts is 10 years. Almost all its contracts have non-disturbance clauses that enhance Four Seasons' management security significantly.

The Delivery of Excellence

It Starts at the Top: Four Seasons and Regent Hotels & Resorts was founded in 1960 and is still led by the same individual, Isadore Sharp. Over the years, ownership has remained with individuals legally and passionately committed to the long-term continuing success of the company as an operator of deluxe hotels. Four Seasons may be one of the few hotel companies in North America not susceptible to takeover due to the unique share structure of the company. Mr. Sharp maintains control through multiple voting shares.

Mr. Sharp was trained as an architect but operated in the construction industry most of his career. The stability enjoyed by the company to a great degree is provided by the thread of consistency of Mr. Sharp's vision and has resulted in a management philosophy that translates into strategic decisions that lead to success.

Furthermore, Four Seasons' senior managers have been around for a long time and they intend to remain for a long time. Their ethics, attitude and professional diligence set the example for others in the company to follow. They "walk the talk." Each member of the group is focused and consistent in managing for the long-term. The result of that management philosophy and focus, and company stability is a sense of clarity and security for all constituents.

In turn, general managers of the hotels are able to make clear to the employees what Four Seasons is today and what it will be tomorrow. Management is also able to clarify for the owners of the properties what Four Seasons will be in the future, and, to investors, what they are buying into. Part of everything Four Seasons does, every decision it makes is with the long-term in mind. The company creates value, not short-term increases in the stock price. This manner of doing business overflows into the human resources strategy and the guest experiences created.

It Happens with the People: Four Seasons believes that the only control it has on the guest's experience (i.e., the product) is the motivation and attitude of the employee. Since Four Seasons manages properties for long periods of time, it can justify the time and effort required to obtain the right people. A case in point is the hiring strategy used to open the Four Seasons Hotel in New York. Management wanted to maximize the pool of applicants for the 525 positions available. They ended up with 32,000 applicants. The larger the pool, the greater the probability of finding the best. Screening this sea of individuals was just the first step. Those candidates that passed the initial screen went through five interviews. Four Seasons wanted to hire nice people, those with personalities that would be motivated to serve the guest. Eighty percent of the jobs went to individuals with no previous hotel experience. John Sharpe argues that the needed skills can be taught, but without the right employee attitude and motivation the guest will not be satisfied. The hiring process was long and tedious, and absorbed a lot of time and effort on the part of many individuals in the company, but when a company's management is thinking long-term, they have the luxury of taking the time to do it right.

Besides formal training, employees learn by example from management and by observing management behavior. Management development is to build a consistent attitude and manner of behavior that over time builds confidence and comfort in each employee. The goal of management is to lead by example, showing respect for employees and guests. This is the Four Seasons' difference — the ability to develop an environment built on respect and leadership that allows the employee to take care of the guest. It doesn't cost more to do it that way but it takes more time. Taking the time to do it right provides the Four Seasons edge. In a Four Seasons' hotel, the back of the house is treated with the same respect as the front of the house. Attention is paid to cleanliness, orderliness and the health and well-being of all employees. In a recent issue of *Forbes* magazine, Four Seasons and Regent Hotels & Resorts was again listed as one of the 100 best companies to work for in North America.

The Guest Is the Center of All: Everything Four Seasons does is for the convenience of the guest, with a relentless search for more sources of value to the hotel experience. Four Seasons has been constantly innovating and introducing new products and services that will make the returning guest's experience even more comfortable and convenient. For instance, Four Seasons was the first hotel chain to introduce no-smoking rooms in hotels. This was an operational nightmare at the time. It did it anyway because it believed it would convenience and comfort the guest. Today, 70 percent of rooms are no-smoking. It was the first hotel chain to introduce overnight pressing, laundry, and dry-cleaning. It was the first with the overnight shoeshine. It does not put a chocolate on the pillow at turn-down service, believing it's the last thing guests need before they go to bed.

Obviously, the Guests Perceive the Difference: 15 of the hotels are AAA five-diamond award winners. The RevPAR for the chain is $176, a 36 percent premium over Four Seasons' major competitor. Its analysis of guest histories shows that its regular customers are using them for all occasions, not just for business or leisure.

The Support of a Strong Brand Image: A number of years ago, Four Seasons realized that creating individual hotels with a great reputation was not enough. Much leverage could result if the Four Seasons' experience could be conveyed by a strong, yet unique, brand image. Using marketing executives with a consumer product background, not traditionally found in the hotel industry, it developed a more effective marketing program more precisely targeted to its clientele. As a result, Four Seasons is now a well-established global brand, which leverages the sales and marketing efforts of each of its hotels around the world. The equity of its brand has also created unique growth opportunities, including attractive mixed-use residential developments, such as found in Boston, Massachusetts, where a Four Seasons' hotel has been paired with a condominium development making the entire offering more attractive.

A Strong Presence in the Most Important Markets: With complete coverage in major cities in the United States, Four Seasons can afford the luxury of waiting and growing where it makes sense economically. Management does not have to do a set number of deals each year; it can take its time. And in the present markets, Four Seasons' properties are all extremely well located. New competitors would have great difficulty matching quality of location. The cost to a competitor of acquiring locations, building to the same standards and making a profit would be impossible.

Guest Perspective

Value Drivers in the Purchase Decision: Consistent with the Four Seasons' strategy, our independent study found service (whether mentioned in general, or specifically, for the staff friendliness and attentiveness) and brand image (both general or differentiated for a market segment in particular) are respectively the first and second reasons guests elect to stay at a Four Seasons' hotel. Other frequently mentioned value drivers in purchase decisions were: convenient locations, overall liking for the room, quality of food and beverage, aesthetics and cleanliness of the properties, and value for money. Interestingly, service is a particularly powerful value driver for the transient and meeting/convention business customers. In contrast, for the leisure customers, the brand reputation and various aspects of the physical properties appeared to contribute most to the purchase decision. For 97 percent of the customers we interviewed, the actual hotel experience delivered upon their value drivers.

Value Drivers in the Hotel Experience: Customers identified the following attributes, presented here in decreasing frequency of mention, as the aspects of their hotel experience at Four Seasons and Regent Hotels & Resorts that they liked: overall service quality, convenience of the location in moving around, friendliness of the staff, quality of food and beverage, variety of services offered to the guest, room entertainment system, and various aspects of the physical facilities. For leisure customers, even though they purchased primarily on the basis of the brand reputation and the physical product, the overall service quality and the quality of food and beverage were most frequently mentioned as value drivers during the hotel experience. For the business markets, service retains its predominance in the guest's appreciation during the hotel experience as well.

Benefits to Customers: The list of experiential benefits the guests derived from their experience with a Four Seasons' hotel included comfort; a sense of pure enjoyment; and feeling pampered, relaxed and at home. These benefits combine to provide a worry-free and convenient hotel stay. Experiential benefits, versus functional aspects, are most frequently mentioned by guests. Very much in line with the brand positioning for business travelers, the benefits of feeling pampered and at home were mentioned most often by guests in the two business segments. For leisure customers, the primary experiential benefits were comfort, a sense of pure enjoyment, and feeling relaxed.

Outlook on Management Practices: As if the guests could read John Sharpe's mind, "consistency in what they do" topped the list of management practices viewed as those that were critical in delivering value drivers. Second came the staff going above and beyond the call of duty, followed by specific aspects of human resources management, i.e., staff selection and hiring, the quality of staff training, and the number of employees. The presence of knowledgeable and helpful concierges was also among the most frequently mentioned practices.

Intermediary Perspective

Value Drivers for Travel Agents and Meeting Planners: Travel agents and meeting planners differed in terms of rationale for sending guests to Four Seasons and Regent Hotels & Resorts. For travel agents, the three most significant reasons to recommend Four Seasons were convenient loca-

tion, the brand reputation, and simply because the guest had already chosen Four Seasons. For meeting planners, primary value drivers were the overall service quality and the convenient locations. In terms of their own experiences as intermediaries with Four Seasons and Regent Hotels & Resorts, both travel agents and meeting planners liked, in particular, the friendliness and efficiency of the staff with whom they dealt, and the quality of the follow-up information they received upon any request. They also were pleased with the sales incentives.

Insights

John Sharpe sees his role as that of custodian of the brand. His job is to keep that sense of stability, to keep the company on "an even keel." He wants to ensure that people do not get carried away with all the changes going on in the hotel industry, or the success Four Seasons has enjoyed to date. Mr. Sharpe also expects his employees to follow Four Seasons' basic principles every day: serve the guests, make them comfortable, and treat them and colleagues with respect. His advice to others that would create a similar success is: Make your first hotel a success. Take the time to get it right. Stay close, play in your own backyard, and build the company one step at a time.

Contact

John Sharpe, President and COO
Four Seasons and Regent Hotels & Resorts
1165 Leslie St., Toronto, Ontario M3C 2K8, Canada
Phone: 416-441-4318   Fax: 416-441-4381

FOUR SEASONS HOTEL, WASHINGTON, D.C.

Overall Best-Practice Property Champion Industry-Wide
"A Passion to Serve"

The Driving Source of Excellence

Stan Bromley, the general manager of the Four Seasons Hotel in Washington D.C., freely admits that the physical property of the hotel, opened in 1979, does not have the "sizzle" that newer hotels have. Thus, the reason for the recent $24 million renovation of the hotel and its 13,000-square-foot fitness club and day spa. As he sees it, the Four Seasons Washington was selected as the best hotel property on an industry-wide basis because of its "software" — the quality of its service, and the precision and passion with which it is delivered by its staff and managers. The key to achieving this kind of excellence seems to be the Four Seasons' ability to gain the trust and respect of its managers and its line staff to "walk the talk" to instill a passion to serve, and reinforce their willingness to continually go back and make sure the product is uncompromising.

The Delivery of Excellence

Asking and Answering Two Basic Questions: For Mr. Bromley, success for any business begins with asking two fundamental questions: Where can I make a difference for customers and staff, and where can this difference make a profit? The Four Seasons Hotel, Washington, recognized that its physical plant was limited, and offered fewer opportunities to excel compared with newer hotels. But the Four Seasons' brand stands for unswerving excellence in service and attitude, and that provided the opportunity for the hotel to overcome its "average" physical plant.

The Key Role of the General Manager: If the brand is crucially important in hotel positioning, the general manager is the key player for building service excellence at a particular property. He/she must have the deep understanding of the business and know how to get the job done on a day-to-day basis by continually proving himself/herself to the staff and managers. Every employee must be convinced to carry the torch for what the hotel stands for. Second, the general manager has to understand the financial side of the business — how a hotel makes a profit. This means knowing when to spend money for guest satisfaction and revenue increases and when to cut costs. Finally, the general manager has to encourage the owner to take an interest in the business. Otherwise, the hotel will never get the necessary capital to achieve physical plant excellence. To do that, the general manager has to "adapt" to the owner. The owner has to trust him/her. Only then can there exist a partnership for excellence. For those in the industry who know Stan Bromley and those who work him, he excels in all of the above.

In addition, Mr. Bromley sees developing the next generation of leaders as another very important part of his role as general manager. New managers need to be trained to lead. Four Seasons and Regent Hotels & Resorts hires for attitude, looking for management recruits who are "bright, sharp and intelligent," have the ability to fit in and adapt, and most definitely have a sense of humor. According to Mr. Bromley, three out of ten recruits will automatically succeed; they have the right stuff. Five out of ten need some form of support and the remaining two will seek their careers elsewhere. This is where a general manager can make the difference; giving time, support and interest to the new assistant manager, as he/she acquires the needed experience. Mr. Bromley is adamant that "you must know how to do it technically in order to lead," and that, "you need to prevent a culture clash between the well-traveled customer and the new right-out-of-school assistant managers, who may not be exposed to, nor aware of, the lifestyle and habits of the luxury traveler." Fields in which experience is to be acquired are comprehensive, covering nine specific leadership and management disciplines at all Four Seasons hotels. In order to succeed and learn to lead, the general manager has to be willing to let the new recruits experience the "not-so-good" times as well, when things go wrong.

A Culture of Excellence: Service excellence requires the development of a culture at the hotel that makes it easy for employees and managers to live that philosophy every day. The bibles for that culture are the policies and procedures and the operating standards of the hotel and the brand. But

285

these standards must be matched with people who have a passion to execute. This means hiring the right people and instilling this passion in them.

The employee selection process at Four Seasons Washington is time-consuming and precise. Only one of eleven applicants makes it through the process. There is a 90-day probation period and approximately 10 percent of new hires leave. The hotel hires for attitude before technical ability. It believes that you "cannot teach people to be nice, to care." Turning to human resources management, training soon gives way to the "reality" of the operations. That's where the attitude of the employee becomes important and makes a difference. Finally, at the Four Seasons Washington, managers recognize that you cannot make employees do anything anymore. You can, however, make them want to do things. You must focus on both the "human" and technical aspects of service delivery, instilling and nurturing in employees the passion to serve. That only happens if management recognizes that it serves the employees and guests as well, and not the other way around. The incentive for the employees is the way they are treated. Since they are the customers of management, their respect needs to be earned every day. The internal "dignity areas" of the hotel are those affecting the lives and human aspect of the staff, such as: the locker rooms must be clean, well lighted and maintained; the cafeteria must offer the best food of any hotel cafeteria in town; there must be enough uniforms and they must fit well; and employee nametags must show the right name and must be replaced quickly when lost. When done well and consistently, these dignity areas show the respect of management for the employee. They are treated as individuals with trust, faith and respect. The manager is the "coach," constantly showing employees how to earn their stripes with the guests.

The Guest's Perception of Excellence: Only when guests perceive excellence of service does the hotel know it has reached the "finish line" of service excellence. According to Mr. Bromley, the general manager must also play a key role here in making this perception one of excellence. He must be visible and "be around" in order to make sure that the managers and employees are delivering service that is perceived by the guest as excellent. The general manager has to have an eye for detail, a sufficiently inquiring mind and the reputation of a trainer/coach/enforcer. As Stan Bromley says, "As general manager, what I and the management team do every day is taste and test it. Everything I come in contact with is either hot or cold, slow or fast, rude or friendly, clean or dirty, painted or chipped." In a way, this provides a safety net for the operation and the employee. Management and employees go back and look for their own mistakes, correct them, and learn from them. As Mr. Bromley says, "who better to complain about us than us."

According to internal data, the guest is clearly satisfied. The hotel has high repeat business. The "stock ticker" for the general manager is talking to employees and guests. Given the culture of excellence of this hotel, they are willing to share their positive and negative experiences. This enables management to monitor how customer attitudes, opinions and expectations change, and to keep raising the bar of service excellence. The customer in this market has become smarter and savvier about great service and is more demanding than ever before. The speed with which customers expect their requests to be met has increased. They expect top value for the money they pay. At a Four Seasons Hotel that means: guest privacy is protected, a spotless room, great service, things done right the first time, individual recognition, sincerely friendly employees, and urgent recovery both technically and attitudinally when mistakes are made.

Financial Performance: The bottom-line report card for the general manager is the monthly profit and loss statement. He "scours" it looking for unanticipated variances in both the financial performance compared to the annual budget, and to last year. The quoted rates at the Four Seasons are approximately $100 higher than their competitive set, with a gross operating profit margin in the mid to high 30 percent range. The general manager meets monthly with the owners to discuss financial results and to plan future projects. The owners understand the operation. They are partners with the Four Seasons' corporate office and local hotel management to maintain the success of the hotel. It is only when management is a trusting partner with the employees and the owners that you can truly achieve both long-term service excellence and financial success.

Insights

Mr. Bromley believes that other hotels can achieve excellence in service just as the Four Seasons Washington has done. But you first have to know yourself as a manager and continually prove yourself to your people and the guests. It is about leadership, not management. And, of course, you must have "a natural never-ending passion to serve."

Contact

Stan Bromley, General Manager
Four Seasons Hotel, Washington, D.C.
2800 Pennsylvania Avenue, NW, Washington, DC 20007
Ph. 202-342-0444   Fax: 202-342-1673

HAMPTON INN

Overall Best-Practice Corporate Champion in Quality
"The Unconditional Guarantee as a Cultural Belief"

Driving Source of Excellence

Hampton Inn, a midscale hotel chain of more than 827 properties owned by Promus Hotels, is recognized as the industry leader for quality. At the core of its relentless quest for quality lies the unconditional guarantee. Not only was Hampton Inn the first company in the hotel industry to make such an offer, the unconditional guarantee has remained the focal point of all that management does, it drives all the decisions. The company's goal is to keep the business simple and it doesn't get much simpler than this guarantee: if the guest is not satisfied for any reason, he doesn't pay. Making that guest satisfied so that he does not invoke the guarantee is what leads to higher quality at Hampton Inn. Since Hampton Inn has offered this guarantee for more than 10 years, the guarantee has evolved into the cornerstone of the corporate culture.

The Delivery of Excellence

The Foundations: The architect of Hampton Inn's quality strategy was Ray Schultz, the founder of Hampton Inn. He believed in the concept and risked offering the guarantee to back up that belief in the product. It was a gamble unheard of in the hotel industry. Offering an unconditional guarantee requires a passionate belief in the consistency of your product and management. Yet, at the same time, the guarantee is a dominant force in driving quality. Chris Hart, a former professor at the Harvard Business School, was the founder of the guarantee. He developed the idea, brought it to Hampton Inn, and assisted in its implementation. Today, the new senior management team at Promus Corporation continues to support the brand and the strategy. They understand it and fully support it.

The Core: According to Rick Schultz, vice president operations, quality at Hampton Inn begins with the product. The customer is guaranteed a clean, comfortable room with great service at a good price. To deliver the great service, the focus is on the employees, or team members. Hampton Inn believes, even with a great product, the employee "makes you or breaks you" with the customer. The unconditional guarantee allows employees to feel the pride of ownership, since they can decide to refund the customer's money.

To Deliver on the Core: To "energize" the employees so they are motivated to give great service, the company has a mandatory training program entitled "We Care Guaranteed" that all employees must complete. This program explains the guarantee and the employee's role, and ensures consistency across all hotels in the delivery of service. As the employees learn, the guarantee is not about giving the customers their

money back, it is about doing things right. Customers do not want their money back, they want things done right. Since the invocation of the guarantee is low, approximately 0.4 percent, the lesson has been learned and is being practiced by the employees. To monitor employee satisfaction, Hampton Inns conducts a satisfaction survey two times per year. The results are "consistently good," showing that employee pride is there. Although the majority of properties are franchised and figures are not available, the employee turnover in company-owned hotels is under 60 percent.

To Control the Delivery of Quality: Quality must be reflected in guest satisfaction. Hampton Inn has two methods for ensuring guests are satisfied. First, the Quality Assessment Evaluation Program requires all properties to be inspected annually by a Promus inspector. As Rick Schultz says, "we measure ourselves up one side and down another." The company also conducts monthly mailout surveys with a random number of check-outs. Guests are asked to express their overall satisfaction with their stay at Hampton Inn on an A (excellent) to F (fail) scale. Hampton Inn sets high expectations for itself by setting its satisfaction goals only on the basis of the A scores. These are the most important customers, for not only are they the most loyal but they are also the zealots who will praise Hampton Inn to their friends and colleagues. To achieve these A ratings, a hotel must focus on quality and provide the guest with a perfect experience. Setting these high standards only makes good business sense. Presently, 65 percent of their guests score the overall experience as an A.

The Backbone for Quality in Growth: Franchisees are the backbone of the growth of Hampton Inn; they believe in the brand. The management of Hampton Inn understands franchisees are buying faith and trust in those who hold and manage the brand. The job of Hampton Inns' managers is to deliver the Hampton Inn guest promise consistently to justify that faith and trust, and they do that by focusing on quality, driven by the unconditional guarantee. The gross operating profit is in the mid-50 percent range, and franchisees know there is a premium in owning the Hampton Inn flag. "Quality" is the reason they give for owning the brand. They know the standards are tighter than at other hotel brands. First is the unconditional guarantee. Next is the guest satisfaction monitoring system. Then comes the quality assurance evaluation system. Finally, a large corporate support apparatus is available to help the properties when requested. Hampton Inn believes it needs to "watch out for the franchisees."

The Return on Quality: Service quality and customer satisfaction at Hampton Inn translates into a yield premium. The REVPAR for Hampton Inn is $48.79, significantly above its competitors. A look at the history of the brand also shows the relationship of quality, guest satisfaction, and brand profitability. The growth in the number of hotels has been excellent. More importantly, it has evolved from an economy lodging brand priced at $28 into a midscale without food and beverage lodging brand priced at $65. Hampton Inn has stuck to its core competencies in the product and the service, all wrapped in the unconditional guarantee.

Guest Perspective

Value Drivers in the Purchase Decision: Based on our independent guest survey, Hampton Inn's focus on quality is noted by its customers. Hampton Inn is one of the few chains for which convenient location did not distance all other hotel attributes as a source of value driving the purchase. Service quality (overall, and friendliness in particular) tied with convenient location as the first motive driving customers' purchase decisions. The three other value drivers that place in second position are also at the core of Hampton Inn's strategy: overall quality of the physical property, cleanliness, and low/good prices. Other most frequently mentioned sources of value driving customer purchase decisions were: familiarity with the brand, free breakfast, word-of-mouth from friends/relatives, and the consistent availability of rooms. Interestingly, while leisure customers derived value primarily from location, low-price, and familiarity with the brand, the core components of Hampton Inn's quality strategy, i.e., the quality of the property and of the service, were primarily

sources of value for the two business customer segments. For 93 percent of customers interviewed, Hampton Inn delivered on these value drivers perfectly.

Value Drivers in the Hotel Experience: Service (overall quality and friendliness) and cleanliness (property in general and room in particular) head the list of hotel attributes that created unique value for the customers during their stays. Other frequently mentioned sources of values were: convenience of the location when customers must move around, free breakfasts, the landscape of some properties, the low prices of various services during the stay, and the health club. Various aspects of the guestrooms were also mentioned. Value drivers were similar across market segments. Service emerged as a powerful source of customer value during the hotel experience, particularly for the meeting/convention segments.

Benefits to Customers: The benefits guests derived from Hampton Inn are consistent with its promises: a convenient, comfortable, relaxing place to stay, a hotel that offers good value-for-money.

Outlook on Management Practices: Customers identified those practices they believe Hampton Inn uses to create these critical value drivers: the free breakfast, beyond-the-call-of duty staff service, well-maintained properties, good management, well-trained staff, and consistent service.

Intermediary Perspective

Value Drivers for Travel Agents: Travel agents we surveyed recommend Hampton Inn to their customers equally for its low prices as for its brand name/reputation, before convenient locations. For meeting planners, convenient locations and low prices are the two primary motives driving their purchase decisions. In their own experiences with Hampton Inn, both types of intermediaries valued most highly service quality, whether at the overall level or in terms of its specific qualities (friendliness, professionalism, attentiveness). Among the practices intermediaries believed were keys to Hampton Inn's ability to create value for them, the most frequently mentioned were: first, computer systems for reservations, and tied for second, the quality of its sales representatives and the attractiveness of the intermediary incentives.

Insights

Mr. Schultz advises any new brand that wishes to emulate Hampton Inn's success to keep things as simple as possible. Do not try to be all things to all people. Focus. And keep the decision-making in the hands of the people taking care of the customer. Do that and you cannot fail.

Contact

Rick Schultz, Vice President Operations
Hampton Inn
Promus Corporation
755 Crossover Lane, Memphis, TN 38117
Phone: 901-374-5523   Fax: 901-374-5521

HOLIDAY INN CINCINNATI AIRPORT

Overall Best-Practice Property Champion in Midscale Segment
"The Smartest Investment You Can Ever Make — The People"

The Driving Source of Excellence

For the fifth consecutive year, the Holiday Inn Cincinnati Airport was recently presented Bass Hotels and Resorts' Torchbearer award, the company's most prestigious award for quality service. The hotel is one of only 78 properties recognized among Bass Hotels and Resorts' more than 2,800 hotels for maintaining the highest standards of excellence in product quality, hotel operations, guest services, and profitability. David Bowles, the general manager of the Holiday Inn Cincinnati Airport, passionately explains that the excellence of the property is due to the employee associates. He believes the hotel's human resources management system has resulted in a team committed to service excellence, which in turn creates value to the guest and high profit to the owners.

The Delivery of Excellence

Beginning with Employee Selection: At the Holiday Inn Cincinnati Airport, "management set its sights to look for the best to be the best." Not an easy task as the unemployment rate in the Cincinnati area is only 2.5 percent. The temptation is always to hire a warm body if for no other reason than to relieve the workload of other employees; but the hotel resists. A position will not be filled unless the right individual is available. The selection process consists of three formal interviews, with the general manager always being part of the final interview. Criteria are set for each line position. In addition, individuals are assessed for the right attitude and chemistry, qualities that help to deliver excellence in a simple, natural manner. Candidates with the right "attitude" are out-going, self-organized, have a good appearance, and they think on their feet during the interview. As can be imagined, finding such job candidates requires substantial effort, but management believes the endeavor is worth it, for these are the employees that will provide the service that will generate repeat business from customers. To settle for employees who are not the best means that the property becomes just another airport hotel fighting for fair share, and that is clearly not the road to profitability.

Orientation and Training: Once hired, all new employees receive an extensive orientation. Besides the standard benefits and life-safety lectures, employees receive an extensive introduction to the culture of service at the hotel. They are also introduced to the service pledge, a simple seven-item credo that explains the hotel's way of doing business to ensure guest satisfaction. Items in the pledge include: always focusing on what I "can do" for the guest versus what I "cannot do," addressing the guest by name whenever possible, "owning"

customer requests and complaints and following up to ensure 100 percent satisfaction, never handing off unresolved issues, taking pride in personal appearance at all times including nametag and proper shoes, and arriving at work on time and when scheduled. While these are simple objectives, they set the expectations for employee behavior right at the beginning of employment. Further, the consistency with which the pledge is followed clearly has a dramatic impact on customer satisfaction.

The training that follows the initial orientation is reflective of guest service. The employees learn the technical aspects of the position, but more importantly, how those features contribute to excellent customer service and satisfaction. Training is continued on-the-job. For each position in the hotel, an experienced employee serves as a formal trainer and acts as an ambassador to help the new employee learn the job. Each new employee must pass a validation exam with a score of 100 percent, thereby indicating he or she has mastered the job. Management believes that the hotel's standards must be sustained at a high level to deliver the desired excellence in customer service.

The Rest Is Management: At the Holiday Inn Cincinnati Airport, managers believe if they take care of their "own people," then the employees will take care of the guests. Dialogue with employees and the celebration of their accomplishments is important. "You can shower people with memos, but one-on-one gets things done," Mr. Bowles says. Consequently, employee evaluations are conducted at the end of one month, three months, and annually thereafter to give the employee feedback on performance. Managers also believe in rewards for a job well done. Thus, managers constantly search for acts of superior employee performance and reward these employees with "you've done an excellent job." The managers back it up by rewarding the employees with a crisp $2 bill. As a result, when somebody asks about the $2 bill, the employee can say it was a reward for a job well done, which means a lot to the employee.

Each department in the hotel holds a monthly meeting and at least two of the items relate to guest satisfaction. The general manager attends each of these meetings to listen to the ideas and feedback, and to share items on guest satisfaction, be it the latest scores or a comment card received from a guest. For those people who do not like to speak up at meetings, a suggestion box program effectively allows them to get their ideas before management. A quality committee evaluates the suggestions and awards a $25 prize for the two best ideas received each month. The MVP (most valuable player) award is given to any employee who is complimented by name in a guest letter. The employee receives a cash award and a certificate that is hung in the back of the house. They are also acknowledged at the quarterly award meeting.

The general manager also holds a "coffee talk" each month attended by the employee of the month from each department. The objective for the meeting is to discuss ways to improve the hotel to better serve the guest. There are other meetings as well, during which employees are encouraged to "think out of the box, to get new ideas and suggestions onto the table to be considered." All of this results in "positive, open communication." Finally, an associate-driven quality committee meets monthly. This committee selects and undertakes any project to create a better work environment that will help the employees help the guest. While these ideas are pretty basic, says Mr. Bowles, they are the key to good employee relations.

Investing in people is a long-term investment. Employee turnover in 1998 was 93 percent; approximately two-thirds of the turnover was voluntary and due to wages. In a tight labor market, the best individuals leave for better compensation — a fact of life in any industry. The real achievement is that the hotel maintains its quality service even with this turnover, which speaks highly of their human resources management system. As a means of combating high turnover, the hotel is instituting a new incentive program tied to the guest satisfaction scores. Bonuses will be approximately $100 per person.

Return in Guest Satisfaction: The hotel guest satisfaction scores are extraordinary. Within the Holiday Inn grading system, the hotel received 931 points out of a possible 1,000 in the CQI (combined quality index). The hotel's product score was 85 percent, the service score was 89 percent, and the overall satisfaction score was 86 percent. For 1998, the RevPAR score was 123 percent. The hotel receives 12 to 18 comment cards a day, mostly positive.

Return in Franchise Fees: In mid-1998, Bass Hotels and Resorts began using a Quality Failure Index to focus the hotels on achieving zero defects. To emphasize the importance of the Index, the monthly franchise fee is determined by the score received. Those hotels that have fewer defects have a reduction in fees. The owners of the Holiday Inn Cincinnati Airport will be making extra profit.

Guest Perspective

Based on the interviews we conducted with guests, the Holiday Inn Cincinnati Airport's strong emphasis on employees pays off. After location, service was second as a primary purchase motive, ahead of price and brand name. In this industry segment, the power of customer service to influence the consumer decision is the exception rather than the rule. Customers commented on the service quality in general, the friendliness of the staff, and the sense of personal recognition these attributes were able to create. Cleanliness, various qualities of the guestroom (i.e., the furniture), and the comfort and convenience of the amenities were also important as sources of value for the customers. The guests identified practices the hotel specifically used to create value as employee acknowledgement of guests, the efficiency of message delivery, and the consistency with which the various services were delivered from one stay to the next. The primary benefits that the interviewed customers derived from their hotel experiences included a worry-free stay, a sense of comfort, convenience, and a familiarity that met their expectations.

Insights

Mr. Bowles believes other hotels can achieve the financial success of the Holiday Inn Cincinnati Airport. "It's all about taking care of your people. It's the most important thing you do." If other hotels emulate this behavior, they will get to a great bottom line. But the managers have to lead by example. Employees need to see that the managers "walk the talk." The general manager sets the example, the tone for the property. Mr. Bowles is a never-ending cheerleader for his property. He's proud of it, and believes it is the smartest business investment he has ever made!

Contact

David Bowles, General Manager
Holiday Inn Cincinnati Airport
1717 Airport Exchange Blvd., Erlanger, KY 41018
Phone: 606-371-2233   Fax: 606-371-4308

HOMEWOOD SUITES ALEXANDRIA

Overall Best-Practice Property Champion in Extended-Stay Upper-Tier Segment
"On Being a 'Yes' Hotel…"

The Driving Source of Excellence

Any seasoned traveler will tell you that he or she can walk into a hotel and tell within the first 30 seconds whether the experience will be positive or negative. Charles Gellad, the general manager of the Homewood Suites in Alexandria, Virginia, tells the story of the guest who explained to him one day that he usually stayed at a nearby hotel on his frequent trips to the area. But after staying at the Homewood Suites he would now characterize the other hotel as a "No" hotel for a myriad of reasons, especially because of the "No" hotel's rules or policies that never allowed the hotel to fully accommodate his requests, modest though they were. On the other hand, having experienced the Homewood Suites Alexandria, he would characterize it as a "Yes" hotel for its emphasis on making the guest feel at home. According to Mr. Gellad, there is no magic formula for success. The key, however, to making it happen is the staff. Success takes a lot of common sense and "treating the guest the way you want to be treated." That's the definition of this "Yes" hotel.

The Delivery of Excellence

The Homewood Suites' Concept: Homewood Suites is a relatively new upscale extended-stay brand from the Promus Hotels Corporation. Presently, there are approximately 100 properties. Each property is approximately 105 units. Their value proposition is a full-size two-room suite, an expanded continental breakfast and a complimentary social hour in the evening. Since this is a Promus brand there is the unconditional service guarantee. The price point is approximately $92.00 dollars.

Guests perceive the Homewood Suites Alexandria as "clean, friendly and service-oriented." It recently won an award from Promus corporation for its friendliness. It is a great value. Guests get a two-room suite that gives them maximum privacy, the 100-percent satisfaction guarantee which assures that things will be done right, and caring, friendly employees who will try to meet their requests — to create a "Yes" hotel.

Employees Are the Key: Homewood Suites Alexandria wants the employees to view the job as "fun, friendly and fair." If they feel this way they will be motivated to give the guest great service. The process starts with employee selection. The hotel looks for candidates who are upbeat and who have stable work histories. Managers want an employee who "portrays happiness." They are not worried about a lack of technical skills if a candidate has the right attitude. "We can train on systems, we can't train on personality," asserts Mr. Gellad. Employees are also empowered to satisfy the guest through the unconditional service guarantee. If the guest is not happy for any reason, any employee is empowered to refund the cost of the stay. For employees, this authority and responsibility adds to their self-confidence. They know the

responsibility for the guest's happiness is in their hands and they go the extra mile to make it happen. Employees enjoy working at the Homewood Suites Alexandria and are willing to go the extra mile for the guest. Because they are treated fairly there is a lot of consistency in employee-guest interactions. Guests see the same faces on each visit. Employee turnover is a phenomenal 8 percent. The average length of experience for the front desk is three years, for housekeeping eight years.

Management Style: Mr. Gellad believes that his job is to create the climate that allows the employees to do the job. He believes you lead by example. He does that by trusting his employees, giving them an assignment and leaving them alone. Communication is also important. That means not only talking to your employees but, more importantly, listening to their ideas. The trust and the communication create a culture of openness. People feel good about themselves and that's what leads to great service.

Customer Satisfaction: According to internal market research, customer satisfaction scores are very high at Homewood Suites Alexandria. Guests grade on an A–F basis: 81 percent of the guests last year gave the hotel an "A" for service. For the Homewood system the average was 69 percent. Eighty-four percent of the guests graded the hotel "A" for the combined product plus service score. Again, the system average was 69 percent. The hotel's intent to return score was a fantastic 97 percent. That is what leads to loyalty.

Financial Performance: The Homewood Suites Alexandria delivers a $20.00 RevPAR premium over the Homewood system, which, according to Mr. Gellad, is primarily due to the emphasis on service. The hotel also enjoys a $10.00 rate premium over its competitive set, which translates into an additional $300,000 per year. The hotel's yield is at 111 percent and penetration is 101 percent. All in all, it competes very successfully against the competition, and, with a high GOP of 55 percent and an NOI of 38 percent, the owner is very happy.

Guest Perspective

Not surprisingly, service (overall quality and friendliness) was tied with location as primary sources of customer value driving purchase decisions for Homewood Suites Alexandria guests. Services also clearly emerge as the most significant sources of unique value being created during the hotel stay. Here, references were made to friendliness, attentiveness, and genuineness, as well as to overall service quality. Various aspects of the physical property were also important purchase motives, namely the aesthetics and the comfort of the room, the kitchenettes, and the meeting rooms. Customers' familiarity with the hotel was also frequently mentioned as a purchase motive. In addition to services, hotel attributes that created the most unique customer value during the stay were the health club and the guestroom entertainment unit. Customers felt they were at home, pampered, and in a place they knew well and that met their expectations.

Insights

For anyone who wants to create a similar success story as the Homewood Suites Alexandria, the answer is obvious. "Take care of your people," says Mr. Gellad. When you do that, then you can fine-tune the operation and take care of the details. And it's in the details that a satisfied guest experience is made. The guest notices the details. If you put an elephant and an ant in the lobby of the hotel, the guest will notice the ant. You can't do it the other way around. You can't take care of the details without taking care of the employees, for they are the ones that make the decision whether to do those "little" things. And they only go the extra step for the organization that takes care of them.

Contact

Charles Gellad, General Manager
Homewood Suites Alexandria
4850 Leesburg Pike, Alexandria, VA 22302-1102
Ph: 703-671-6500   Fax: 703-671-9322

THE HOUSTONIAN HOTEL, CLUB, AND SPA

Overall Best-Practice Property Champion in Employee Satisfaction
"A Humanistic Approach to Profitability"

The Driving Source of Excellence

According to Gina Allen, human resources director, the Houstonian's selection as the overall best-practice property champion in employee satisfaction is due to one unique aspect of its business strategy: managerial decisions and profit maximization is built around respect and dignity for all employees. According to Ms. Allen and the leadership team, this is the reason why the property has been extraordinarily profitable.

The Delivery of Excellence

Improving Lives: The mission statement at the Houstonian Hotel, Club, and Spa reads "Making People's Lives Better Through Business." Such a statement reflects not only the deeply held, humanistic, personal values of the managers and owners, but also the precise alignment of the business strategy with these timeless principles. They believe company success in a people-intensive business is dependent on the success of each individual in the organization. Profit cannot be achieved unequally, on the backs of others. Thus, management has designed a business strategy based on what it calls the Houstonian Triangle.

The Houstonian Triangle: Management believes that three stakeholders must win if there is to be profit, and if everybody's lives are to be improved. These stakeholders are customers, employees and shareholders. It is an equilateral triangle, no one stakeholder is more important than the others. Business is conducted to balance the often-competing requirements of all three groups. For example, in making the wage decision, the shareholders' needs of long-term stability and profitability vis-à-vis alternative uses of their capital is balanced against competitive wage rates and prices needed to arrive at a wage increase. The question for Houstonian managers is not how little can we pay our employees, but how much can we pay balanced against the other stakeholder requirements. A constant effort is devoted to recognize and grant equality to the needs and values of employees, and to celebrate their continuing contribution to the success of the business.

This strategy works because everyone in the organization buys into this humanistic approach to business. It is an inside-out approach in that it begins with the individual and the understanding of one's own beliefs and needs. As convincingly argued by Ms. Allen, "You can only know others if you know yourself." The managers at the Houstonian know their people because they know themselves. All employees have taken the Stephen Covey course on "The Seven Habits of Highly Effective People."

Human Resources Management Strategies: The process begins with employee selection, with the character and competence of the candidate being paramount. Screening is an extensive process, with job candidates going through at least five interviews, two by the human resources department, one by the department head, one by co-workers, and finally one by the general manager. Once selected, the training program begins with an extensive orientation to the vision, values and mission of the Houstonian, followed by the technical training required for the position.

Employee retention is a key to the success of the Houstonian's philosophy. Given the time and effort required to find employees with the right ability and values, the Houstonian does not want to lose them. Management does not believe that money will motivate people, especially if they do not want to do something. But as part of living the values and balancing the stakeholders' needs, management believes that employees must be compensated fairly and share in the success of the organization. The wage rates are standardized for the vast majority of employees and they all receive the same wage. The Houstonian believes that no one person is worth more than another, and the contribution of each is important and necessary to the success of the organization. Raises are given to non-exempt employees at the end of three months, twelve months, and annually thereafter on the employee's anniversary date. Everyone receives the same percentage increase. There are no merit raises. Individual respect and recognition comes to employees in other ways, not from unequal compensation increases. Managers recognize employees for a job well done, and those who excel are picked for special projects and promotion.

While there is no merit raise, there is an extensive bonus program paid quarterly to share the success of the organization with employees. The program emphasizes the team and the property; consequently, there is no reward for individuals at the expense of others. The program keeps people focused on the triangle — everybody wins or nobody wins. The total bonus for a regular full-time employee in 1998 was $746 dollars.

In addition to fair compensation, the benefits program is also excellent. All employees receive full medical, dental and eye care for which they pay only $32.00 dollars a month. They have a 401(k) plan and a credit union. The health club is open to employees during non-busy periods. Finally, the employees receive discounts at the spa and pro shop. The company's benefit rate is 38 percent, a testament to sharing to succeed.

The Houstonian Hotel, Club, and Spa also creates a pleasant social environment for the employees. Picnics and parties for the staff and their families are organized regularly. A free one-week camp is provided for employees' children in the summer. Health fairs and pot-luck dinners are held. Coupons for turkeys are distributed to all employees at Thanksgiving. A 1998 holiday bonus of $450 was given to each employee as a thank-you for a job well done. Employees and managers alike believe in laughter. However, everybody knows where to draw the line.

The Return-on-Investment for the Stakeholders: Such a humanistic approach seems to pay for everyone. The employee turnover is 20.1% annually, which is exceptionally low. Guests are extremely pleased by the great service they receive, as indicated by the overwhelmingly positive comment cards. Retention of club members is over 95% at a time when existing city clubs are at 60 to 65%. And on the financial side, profits have nearly quadrupled since Redstone purchased the property in 1992.

Never Resting on Past Accomplishments: Recently, the Houstonian Hotel, Club, and Spa began a program called "Quantum Leap," to take the organization to the next level. In this program, managers have formed employee teams to improve the operations in key areas. The goal is to cut costs, improve revenues, be more consistent in service delivery and make the organization a better place for everyone to work. The areas of focus are: revenue, expense/margins, physical improvements, safety, co-worker, customer service, culinary, club programming, grounds, environmental, public relations, and unique features. Each of these teams are charged with taking a long-term view of the "What is possible?" for their particular piece of the business.

Insights

Ms. Allen is convinced that other organizations can accomplish as much as the Houstonian, but these firms must recognize that employee satisfaction starts inside-out and top-down. The firm has to identify and live its own values and celebrate the accomplishments of the employees. All stakeholders in the triangle have to win. Finally, firms must realize that it is not one thing that they do that produces the success, it is many things. And they "gotta keep at it, every day."

Contact

Gina Allen, Human Resources Director
Houstonian Hotel, Club, and Spa
111 North Post Oak Lane, Houston, TX 77024
Ph: 713-680-2626   Fax: 713-685-6853

THE KIMPTON GROUP

Overall Best-Practice Corporate Champion in Physical Property
"Differentiation to the Extreme"

The Kimpton Group is a small chain of 23 boutique hotels. The chain, which began in 1981, is headquartered in San Francisco and until recently operated mostly on the West Coast. After having fine-tuned its formula as a niche operator, the Kimpton Group is now expanding into the Midwest and East Coast with an aggressive growth plan. Kimpton's formula for success is called "adaptive use," the conversion of buildings originally constructed and operated for purposes other than hotels. This practice has allowed Kimpton to create hotels that are "always warm and comfortable, but also bold and vibrant," thus enabling Kimpton to be spectacularly successful in "doing it their way." Kimpton offers a lodging "experience," something its baby-boomer customers want but cannot get from the large, gray hotel chains. Each project is different. Empty office buildings have been converted into hotels, a department store in Portland, Oregon, was turned into a suites hotel, and even an empty telephone switching station in Seattle is now a Kimpton hotel.

The Kimpton Group is successful for two reasons, according to Tom LaTour, president. First, the company constantly challenges itself. The corporate culture is to keep improving, to learn from each project, and not copy a past success. Second, Kimpton listens to the customer. Kimpton constantly improves on the hotel product, and on the physical product, the building acquired and adapted. Kimpton wants each hotel to be perceived as unique. In operations management parlance, Kimpton is a "job shop." In each project it is building its "first hotel." The goal is to take differentiation to the extreme.

The Delivery of Excellence

Top Management: At the core of the Kimpton Group's success are the two top managers: Bill Kimpton and Tom LaTour. Bill Kimpton is not only the chairman but the soul of and inspiration for the company. Formally an investment banker, Mr. Kimpton's non-hotel approach has provided the foundation for the corporate philosophy. The president, Tom LaTour, leads the organization and executes the growth strategy. He provides the corporate environment that supports the personal growth of the many people who contribute to the success of the organization. Kimpton is a team of individuals.

Adaptive Use as a Strategy: To make an adaptive use project financially feasible and able to offer value to the guests, the strategy begins with seeking under-valued building assets in urban central business districts and acquiring them at attractive prices. Before acquiring any site for reuse, Kimpton Group studies the lodging market carefully; citywide occupancy and rates must be healthy.

The second step of the adaptive-use strategy is to understand the building in its context. "The building speaks to you," says Tom LaTour. They review the building's layout, infrastructure, and HVAC, as well as historic preservation issues and other regulations. The key is to match the building's opportunity with the market. The puzzle is in calculating the cost per room

for the hotel. How do you "fit" the hotel in the building so that it works properly in the most efficient and effective way? To solve that problem requires thinking "outside the box," which takes years of business experience and many successful projects. But most importantly, it takes creativity. The management at Kimpton Hotel has both experience and creativity.

One of the keys to the "fit" is the orientation of the guestroom in the hotel. In adaptive use, the result may be strange-looking rooms of odd sizes that may not work for the guest or for the operation. In Kimpton's thinking, the guestroom must look like home for the guest, while still being perceived as unique, exciting, and interesting. Over time, the Kimpton Group has learned to partner with a small group of designers that understands and complements the Kimpton creative philosophy.

To ensure the guestroom works, Kimpton Group constructs model guestrooms to test assumptions made in terms of effectiveness for the guest, efficiency for the operations, and financial feasibility for the company. Purchasing costs are calculated and reworked under different assumptions. Throughout the whole planning process, feedback is gathered from customers, contractors, and sub-contractors. Kimpton's management listens closely and has become adept at assessing risks. It wants no financial or construction surprises as it moves forward on a project.

The same development strategy is also applied to restaurants. Most of the Kimpton hotels have restaurants adjacent to but not part of the hotel. Hotel restaurants are not usually profitable, but guests still have food and beverage needs. By putting independent restaurants in the reused building, Kimpton maximizes the square footage potential of the building, but provides the restaurants with their own identities. As with the hotels, the restaurant concepts are creative and exciting, and the quality of the food is excellent. They're profitable because the "locals" as well as the hotel guests use them. According to current operators, they are also "fun" to manage.

Service Strategy at Kimpton Hotels: Success in the hotel industry is not solely dependent on the physical building or the guestroom. A hotel must compete on service. For the Kimpton Group, the key is its excellent employee retention; turnover averages approximately 20 percent per year. Employees remain because they like to work with a leader, and because the success of the company provides opportunity for capable and ambitious individuals. This attitude is reinforced by a strong strategy for promotion from within. The company's goal is to have three out of four jobs filled internally. Employee surveys reveal that 75 percent of the respondents are satisfied with the organization and their jobs.

The Kimpton Group works hard to foster managers' competencies and confidence as well. It believes that if managers understand their own potential, they will be better supervisors and managers overall. An intensive self-awareness program is offered to all managers in the company to help them understand and work on hindrances to their success.

Market Performance: Guests respond positively to Kimpton's offerings. Chainwide, average annual occupancy is 85 percent. In addition, the feedback Kimpton receives via customer surveys is first about the "energized people service," and then about the neat, exciting product. Kimpton's strategy is to price the experience below the competition which, given the quality and excitement of the experience offered, clearly denotes value for the customer. Such a pricing strategy is driven by Kimpton's decision to compete against the large chains, offering more of clearer, more visible benefits at lower prices.

Kimpton's management is not worried about someone attempting to copy its success. For one thing, it is a small

company and therefore not visible. Second, Kimpton relies on its ability to creatively differentiate each property — without a large advertising budget. Third, the management of Kimpton is small; there are few managers and they have the courage of their convictions. They know how to assess risks and are not afraid to take them. Kimpton believes that as long as the large competitors have committees to make decisions, serious competition from that side will remain elusive. "They all create beige," Mr. LaTour says.

Financial Performance: The financial track record proves the success of the formula. In 17 years, Kimpton has never had a project failure, providing investors with returns of above 15 percent on each project. Kimpton has no secret formula. Its buildings have been acquired at the right price, and have been adapted creatively for both efficiency and effectiveness. Kimpton has been able to offer an exciting product with energized service, all at a price below the competition.

Guest Perspective

Value Drivers in the Purchase Decision: One of the guests we interviewed epitomizes, from the customers' perspective, what Mr. Kimpton and his people attempt to create: "They try to be different in the decor and the overall look. They make it warm, inviting and fun at the same time. They don't sacrifice one for the other." In fact, the hotel attributes driving customer purchases were equally distributed among the location, the property, the service, and, to a slightly lesser extent, the "reasonable price for excellent quality."

Value Drivers During the Hotel Experience: The physical attributes of Kimpton hotels appear to be the most significant source of unique customer value during the hotel stay. The overall quality of the properties, their small size, the aesthetics, the innovative design in the lobby and in the guestrooms, and the room entertainment system were all mentioned as important value drivers during the hotel experience. Friendly and attentive service also added unique value to the guest's experience, and the restaurants were also sources of customer value.

Customer Benefits and Outlook on Management Practices: Customers reported that the benefits created by Kimpton hotels included fun, privacy, and excitement. The hotels also made customers feel good, with no worries. Among the management practices customers valued most were, not surprisingly, the ability to acquire top properties, and the various efforts of the staff to deliver good service. Mention was also made of innovative treatments offered to the guests such as wine being served in the lobby, or some "speciality" breakfast in one property or another.

Intermediary Perspective

Value Drivers for Travel Agents and Meeting Planners: Two attributes of Kimpton Group hotels provided the primary basis as to why travel agents and meeting planners recommended Kimpton hotels to their customers: the reputation and image as unique boutique hotels, and their physical property, primarily because of the small size and various aesthetic qualities. In the words of one meeting planner, "they are just more detailed since they are small. It seems that each hotel has its own philosophy." The physical property was particularly important for meeting planners. Convenient location, good prices, and familiarity with the brand also mattered but to a lesser extent. In their own dealings with Kimpton, the attributes that intermediaries mentioned most often were the quality of service provided by the staff and sales representatives, with both being willing to go beyond the call of duty. Meeting planners also valued Kimpton's flexibility, while both intermediaries appreciated the quality of the incentives.

Insights

Others can succeed with the adaptive-use concept, Tom LaTour believes. A good market must be selected and then patience is required until the right asset is found. Then a chance must be taken. Kimpton takes prudent chances. It succeeds because it is good at assessing risks, so there are no surprises in the middle of a project. Kimpton is also excellent at balancing efficiency with creating value for guests and owners. The business is still all about the people: the customers, employees, investors, and local community. Kimpton must win in every project.

Contact

Tom LaTour, President
The Kimpton Group
222 Kearny, Suite 200, San Francisco, CA 94108
Phone: 415-955-5401   Fax: 415-296-8031

THE MANSION ON TURTLE CREEK

Overall Best-Practice Property Champion in Deluxe Segment
"Staffing Up to Customer Needs"

The Driving Source of Excellence

The Mansion on Turtle Creek is a five-diamond, five-star hotel. The *Zagat Guide* has selected it as America's Best Hotel the last six years. *Institutional Investor* magazine has voted it the Best Hotel in the World. Its restaurant has won many prestigious awards. Therefore, it is not surprising to see the Mansion on Turtle Creek selected as the best hotel property in the deluxe category. Jeffrey Trigger, the general manager of the Mansion, says there are no secrets to creating the perfect deluxe hotel. It is all about execution in the delivery of hospitality. To achieve this level of success, you first must believe in a level of perfection, believe that it is financially worth it, and be ready to work hard at reaching that excellence. You also must focus not solely on immediate financial and operational results, but understand that long-term investment is necessary before a profitable return can be achieved. These are, in a nutshell, the driving sources of The Mansion on Turtle Creek's excellence.

The Delivery of Excellence

Management and Ownership: Success starts with assembling a core group of experienced managers who know how to operate hotels. Rosewood Hotels & Resorts, which operates the Mansion on Turtle Creek, has a style of management that emphasizes "leading by example." The organizational structure is flat. Managers do not sit in big offices and they do not have lots of meetings. They practice "managing by walking around." They are there to help the employees deliver satisfaction to the guests. The general manager plays various roles in orchestrating the dynamics: At various times, he/she is the visionary, the style-setter, the mother/father, or the bully. He/she needs to balance the owner's, guests', and employees' needs to see that everyone wins.

Another key success factor at the Mansion on Turtle Creek is the alignment of ownership and management. Both believe in the same things and are going in the same direction. In more concrete terms, to create the perfect deluxe hotel, there is willingness on the part of the owners to pay for a guest/staff ratio that is aligned with guest expectations. At the Mansion "we don't staff down, we staff up to customer interaction needs," Mr. Trigger says.

Human Resources Management: The final block in building for success is to employ the right people and give them the freedom to make the guest happy. The human resource management strategy is based on a policy of trust rather than a list of rules. The Mansion hires people who genuinely want to serve. Those who don't would not be happy at the Mansion anyway. The policy of the place is "never say no to a guest, there are too many ways to say yes." Skills and personality are both important but it is the "genuineness" of the candidate that determines selection.

At all Rosewood Hotels & Resorts, training for services is not based on "heavy scripting." Management wants employees to "be themselves" because it is the emotional authenticity of the interaction with the guest that comes through and makes the service be perceived as great. Instead, each department has a set of core standards that frame what should happen in the various functional areas so that they play their respective parts in the creation of the guest experience. Similar standards, developed at a more general level, apply to every employee in the hotel and define the culture of the property. These standards cover the following areas: positive encounters; never say no; first impressions; listen to the guest; can we talk (telephone skills); know your guest; and we are family. Management focuses on each for a month with the employees. This set of core and general standards ties everybody together in the quest to satisfy guests.

Work conditions compare favorably to competitors. Compensation is excellent, both wages and benefits. Finally, employees know management cares about them. The managers are there beside them: leading, coaching, and setting the example for everyone. As Mr. Trigger states, "You can't care about the guest if you don't care about the employees." In addition, the systems in place are carefully designed to allow employees to satisfy guests. Thus, the positive feedback from these interactions add to the work benefits. For all these reasons, employee turnover is low — 3.3 percent YTD in 1999.

Creating Guest Advocates: At the Mansion on Turtle Creek, the goal is not only to satisfy the guests, but to transform them into advocates for the hotel. Not only do the Mansion's managers want more customers, but they want 100 percent of the business of the customers they currently have. Only

301

advocates will give that kind of loyalty. Advocates are more profitable as they are not looking for the cheapest rate and they forgive the hotel when a mistake is made. It is not a philosophy of average daily rate but one of "revenue per stay." Such an extreme customer loyalty, or advocacy, if you will, has another benefit. The *cachet* is that the developed brand has helped the company in securing other projects, some of them on an international basis. Owners and developers recognize the operating excellence of the Mansion on Turtle Creek and want to be part of the family.

Financial Performance: Creating customer advocacy translates directly and indirectly into revenue and profit. The REVPAR for the hotel is the highest in the state of Texas. Its yield is 122.5 percent. In addition to the rooms, even more revenues come from food and beverage, which has a gross operating profit of over 30 percent. Such a margin is over two-and-one-half times the normal food and beverage profit for a luxury hotel.

Mr. Trigger believes that other hotels can achieve the success of the Mansion on Turtle Creek. It is not easy and it doesn't happen quickly. "You have to set goals, ones that are measurable and consequential," he says. Those goals have to show that your organization stands for something important. Finally, you, the leader, must be passionate about what you're doing. Then you can create the perfect deluxe hotel.

Contact

Jeffery Trigger, General Manager
(Prior to publication of this study,
Mr. Trigger left his position)
The Mansion on Turtle Creek
2821 Turtle Creek Blvd., Dallas, TX 75219
Ph: 214-559-2100   Fax: 214-528-4187

J.W. MARRIOTT, JR., MARRIOTT INTERNATIONAL, INC.

Overall Best-Practice Individual Champion in Corporate Management
"Success Is Never Final"

The Driving Source of Excellence

J.W. "Bill" Marriott, Jr., is chairman of the board and chief executive officer of Marriott International, Inc. He is the overall best-practice individual champion in corporate management. According to Bill Shaw, the president and chief operating officer of Marriott International, Inc., Bill Marriott is the most knowledgeable hotelier in the lodging industry. His passion for understanding and meeting customer needs and his extensive knowledge of hotel operations and the hotel industry have provided the focus and the guidance that have driven the growth and financial success of Marriott International. A leading hospitality company, Marriott International has operations in 50 states and 53 countries and territories. In 1998, the company's system-wide sales topped $16.0 billion and it employs approximately 133,000 associates. Its operations include three major businesses: Marriott Lodging; Marriott Senior Living Services; and Marriott Distribution Services. The lodging group operates or franchises over 1,600 hotels and 37 timeshare resorts totaling approximately 325,000 rooms and 3,900 timeshare villas worldwide.

The Delivery of Excellence

The Care of the Guest First: The care of guests is the most important asset of Marriott International. It is what makes Marriott International different from other hotel companies. It's not some gigantic company formed as part of the current hotel industry consolidation. It is also not an innovative financial entity created on Wall Street to generate profits through complex financial maneuvers. Marriott International is a hotel operating company with superior knowledge of customer needs and of the operational activities necessary to consistently satisfy those needs. Its mission is to be the global leader in hospitality lodging and to operate the preferred brand in every lodging category, with a strong bias for quality in everything it does.

For Mr. Shaw, the person within Marriott International who best understands customer needs and what is necessary to meet them is Bill Marriott himself. In 1957, Marriott opened his first hotel, The Twin Bridges Motor Hotel, in Arlington, Virginia. Bill Marriott was involved and has been involved ever since, constantly preaching the credo of quality products and services and operational excellence. Those are what lead to customer loyalty and long-term profitability. He is the customers' champion. In his day-to-day corporate life, he continually stresses three things. The first is the constant need to improve, to always try to get better. As he says, "Success is never final." Second is the sharing of best practices across brands. Practices that are invented by one person in one part of the company should be shared with everyone in the company. Finally, to always be looking for new ideas. Customer needs change and competitors improve.

Reflecting on today's success blinds you to the pitfalls awaiting tomorrow.

The Care for the Employees: The second major asset of Marriott International is its employees. To be the global leader and the preferred brand in every category requires employees capable of delivering those services. "We don't produce anything, we provide service," says Bill Marriott. He learned the importance of motivated employees from his father. Employees are the first points of contact with the guest. Bill's father taught him to hire people with the right attitude: warm, friendly, and with service excellence in their heart. And to communicate and listen to them and celebrate their successes alongside them. It's a lesson he took to heart. In his frequent visits to Marriott hotels, Bill Marriott always walks the property with the general manager. His concern: Is the general manager involved? Does he know his employees' names? If the answer is affirmative, he's pretty sure the customer is being cared for.

Good Owner, Developer, and Franchise Relationships: To be the preferred lodging company means you must be the first choice with the best of owners, developers, and franchise partners. These constitute another important customer group to Marriott International. Bill Marriott wants to make sure the company understands and satisfies the needs of this group. "Marriott has to provide the support they need," he says. That means providing them with competitive advantages in each of the Marriott lodging brands and, most importantly, making it easier for them to do business with Marriott International.

Management Style: Among his colleagues at the company, Bill Marriott is known for being very involved in the business on a daily basis. With over 40 years' experience in the hotel business, he's seen it all in the industry. He not only provides the vision for the company, he gets into the details of the business planning. He believes in "seeing and being seen." He actively practices "management by walking around." He is visible and accessible. He also wants the right people running the company. These are individuals who are energetic, committed to the team and who genuinely care about people. Managers are proactive and decisive. Bill Marriott cares about them, celebrating their successes but constantly challenging them to be better. Success is never final.

Vision on the Future: What does Bill Marriott see as the challenges for the company in the future? He wants the company to be the world's leading provider of hospitality services for his lodging customers, residents that select his senior living communities, and food service customers who rely on the company's food distribution services. Not surprisingly, the first priority is developing greater consistency in service delivery, with the goal of building customer loyalty. The second priority is to build operational excellence. The use of technology, especially information technology, is a key in this regard. There is a wealth of customer information available and the challenge is to capture it and use it to improve customer satisfaction. Finally, to improve service, quality and consistency at the hotels, so as to raise the bar against the competition. With Bill Marriott's hotel industry knowledge and experience guiding the company, there can be no doubt Marriott International will succeed in achieving its ambitious goals.

Guest Perspective

In phase III of the study, we interviewed customers and intermediaries of all brands included in the Marriott portfolio, many of them being overall best-practice champions in other categories. Across all industry segments, and for both types of customers, respondents perceived the value created by the Marriott brands as being a balanced and consistent mixture of convenience and, service friendliness, as well as comfortable and functional physical properties, all wrapped in the reassuring familiarity of the Marriott brand name. These attributes influenced customer purchase decisions and were sources of unique value during the hotel experience proper. What differed across brands were the precise ways in which the hotel concepts had been carved and were being delivered upon as a function of each specific target market. The managerial practices that respondents frequently identified as the reasons why Marriott creates customer value in 1998 are still basically those learned years ago by Bill Marriott from his father: hire employees who go beyond the call of duty to satisfy the guest; acquire the best properties and maintain them; and build efficiency and consistency into the operations.

Insights

A final comment from Mr. Shaw on Bill Marriott: "He has a unique ability for challenging everybody. He is very grateful of what everybody does, very appreciative and he tells them. But, he always finishes with 'we have to do better.'" Success is never final.

Contact

Nick Hill, Director, Communications
Marriott International, Inc.
One Marriott Drive, Washington, DC 20058
Ph: 301-380-7484   Fax: 301-987-9014

MARRIOTT HOTELS AND RESORTS

Overall Best-Practice Corporate Champion in Employee Satisfaction
"It's a Marathon, Not a Sprint!"

The Driving Source of Excellence

Marriott Hotels and Resorts was selected on an industry-wide basis as the best hotel chain for employee satisfaction. As the first, and still the flagship hotel brand in the Marriott Corporation, Marriott Hotels and Resorts believes employee satisfaction is critical to its long-term success and has chosen to put employee satisfaction at the core of its business strategy. This strategy prevails in Marriott Corporation as well. The Marriott Corporation has more than 200,000 employees and has worked hard to develop a very strong, consistent, enduring organizational culture with respect to how all employees should be treated. That cultural value can be stated as follows: "If you take great care of your people, they will take great care of your customers and will earn your owners great financial results." This 70-year-old culture evolved from the values, the thinking and the business practices of the Marriott family. This culture has been maintained through employee selection, training, and evaluation, and has translated into financial results.

The Delivery of Excellence

The Selection: Employee satisfaction at Marriott Hotels and Resorts starts with the process of selection. The Marriott process is comprehensive and goes well beyond that of interviews matched to job descriptions. For virtually every position in the company, from guest contact at the property level through senior executive positions at corporate, a profile of excellence, i.e., the ingredients necessary to be successful in that position, has been developed. This excellence profile encompasses both the profile of the position, enumerating the necessary skills and degree of experience for success, and a personality profile, i.e., the personality attributes also necessary for success in that position. The personality profile of the candidate is determined through a paper and pencil test designed for Marriott by SRI International.

In addition to the assessment of fit to the excellence profile, the candidate for a position at Marriott Hotels and Resorts also has to submit to peer interviewing and drug testing as part of the selection process. Although it requires a great deal of time and expense, Mike Jannini, brand vice president for Marriott Hotels and Resorts, insists that it is one of the keys to success. So much time, energy and money is wasted by selecting the wrong employee. As he is fond of saying, "You can train a dog to climb a tree, but you're better off hiring a squirrel." According to Mr. Jannini, if you hire the right person you can clean up 50 percent of the problems commonly found in human resources management. Employee selection is an investment, not an expense at Marriott.

The Training: Training provides the second step in the development of satisfied employees. All new employees go through an orientation process, part of which covers the values of the Marriott organization. During orientation, the employee learns what the organization is and what it is not. New employees learn of two Marriott beliefs: (1) it is "an honor to be of service to others" and (2) "the boss is of service to employees." These beliefs underlie a culture that is clearly not for everyone. Consequently, if employees do not or cannot buy into the philosophy, they are offered the opportunity to leave. Those who stay know that part of their routine performance evaluations will be based on their ability to live these beliefs.

The objective of the next step in the training process is to assist an employee in becoming productive. Marriott Hotels and Resorts does not define hotel productivity in terms of the number of employees or the hours worked per room. Productivity is thought of in terms of how to get an individual employee to execute at more than 85 percent of his or her potential. Of course, if you've selected correctly, based upon an understanding of the personal and technical requirements for the position, then the potential will be very high and the motivation to excel will be there.

It is noteworthy that at Marriott Hotels and Resorts, the philosophy of training is not to practice on the customer. Customer-contact employees are trained off-line in the basic skills for the position, then certified. They must pass a test showing they have mastered all the necessary elements to be successful in that position. Marriott sees this approach to training as simply protecting the brand equity of the company.

Employee Performance Evaluation: Another aspect of Marriott Hotels and Resorts' employee satisfaction strategy bears on performance evaluation, which emphasizes the developmental or "upside" aspects of the assessment exercise. Less emphasis is placed on what employees have done wrong during the performance measurement period and more on what they can do better and, most importantly, on precise ways in which they can improve to reach their individual potential. Thus, there is not a lot of blame placed on the employee in a performance review. It is a critique of performance, not a criticism of the employee. Managers show employees the obstacles between themselves and what they are trying to accomplish. Managers see their job as assisting in this development.

Manager Performance Evaluation: Since 1995, Marriott Hotels and Resorts has used a "Balanced Scorecard" for the assessment of its hotel general managers. Thus, the ability of a hotel general manager to make his/her "numbers" is necessary but insufficient to be judged successful. Instead, a manager must succeed equally well in a number of dimensions — financial performance, customer satisfaction, employee associate satisfaction and competitive performance (price premium and market share) — all of which have proven to be important contributors to the long-term well-being and profitability of the firm. Note that a general manager can perform well financially, but if the score on associate performance, for example, is low, he/she could be terminated.

Based on the scores earned, a hotel is placed in the green zone, yellow zone or red zone for follow-up monitoring and assistance. These performance numbers are not confidential; everyone sees everyone's numbers, which results in tremendous peer pressure. At the annual general managers' meeting, over 150 awards are made to celebrate the achievements of successful individuals in front of his/her peers and to provide the incentive and motivation to improve. Amazingly, over 75 percent of the franchisees are using the scorecard to assess general manager performance in their hotels. Marriott will soon make it a requirement of all franchisees.

Employee Satisfaction and Turnover: Marriott Hotels and Resorts conducts a yearly employee satisfaction survey by telephone. Questions cover the perception of the individual in areas such as hygiene, training, work environment, and accessibility of the supervisor. This study allows Marriott to determine the degree to which the organizational culture and management are working to create employee satisfaction. Front-line employee turnover at Marriott Hotels and Resorts is less than 40 percent annually.

Growth from Within: Marriott Hotels and Resorts is continually working to improve the employee/associate assessment system, to assist individuals throughout the organization to achieve their potential and thereby maximize the pool of talent available to the organization. The objective is to develop "bench strength," so that those individuals who already live the Marriott philosophy can be promoted and can respond to any plans for market expansion. The result of this approach is the creation of a "spirit" in the organization, derived from Marriott's celebration of individual contributions and accomplishments, and Marriott's efforts to show the individual team members how to improve and move to a higher level of accomplishment.

To improve the ability to develop the growth potential of its front-line employees, Marriott Hotels and Resorts is considering the adoption of a Balanced Scorecard approach at this level as well. Presently, managers utilize only one score and believe they need three to six different assessments to develop a scorecard for employee associates. Their goal is to measure the value that an individual or team creates and contributes in pursuit of the organization's business strategy. With such an index, executed right down to the line level in a property, the company can better manage costs and increase revenues. It can then share the value created by the employees with the employees. Although this is an ambitious approach to human resources accounting, Marriott believes it is the next logical step in its human resources development strategy.

Guest Perspective

Value Drivers in the Purchase Decision: The rationale of placing employee satisfaction at the core of the Marriott Hotels and Resorts' business strategy is that satisfied employees at all levels in the operation will perform better on the constellations of details that drive customer value. This rationale appears justified, as our independent survey indicates the role of employees' performance in shaping customers' purchase decisions ranks second as a value driver in customer purchase decisions. Excellence of employee performance is also reflected in cleanliness, a pervasive task in which all employees are involved, which ranks fourth in driving customer purchase.

The first and third value drivers were respectively convenience and the brand image and reputation. It is important to note that numerous physical property aspects of Marriott Hotels and Resorts are also frequently mentioned as sources of value motivating customer purchase; in particular, the aesthetic aspects of the property, and the size of and the furniture in the room. Frequent-guest memberships was also a noticeable value driver. It is interesting to note that, except for location, the dominating value driver varied by market segment. Leisure guests primarily valued the brand image and reputation. For the business guests, it was their membership in a frequent-guest program that drove purchase decisions, whereas the meeting/convention markets were mostly sensitive to service quality. Ninety-four percent of the customers interviewed said Marriott delivered on the value drivers that were of importance to them.

Value Drivers in the Hotel Experience: Not surprisingly, the two hotel attributes mentioned most frequently as sources of customer value during the hotel experience are both tied directly to the day-to-day employees' performance: cleanliness (property in general, and rooms) and service quality (friendliness and attentiveness). Other attributes most frequently mentioned by the guests as aspects of their hotel experience that they liked were the guestroom (size, furniture, as well as overall liking), and architecture and aesthetics of the property. Here again, the meeting/convention customers were more sensitive to service quality as a source of value. Business customers primarily derived value from the guestroom size and other aspects of the physical property. Finally, cleanliness appears to be what leisure customers valued most as contributing to a positive hotel experience.

Benefits to Customers: The list of benefits the guests derived from their stay at a Marriott Hotels and Resort's property includes a sense of overall satisfaction, comfort, a pleasurable experience, as well as a feeling of security and relaxation. To this list, members of frequent-guest programs added the pride of personal recognition.

Outlook on Management Practices: Practices related to the staff performances topped the list of practices viewed as those that were critical in delivering the value drivers. These practices were, in order of frequency: the staff goes beyond the call of duty, the properties are well-maintained, and the services are delivered with a high degree of consistency. Guests also mentioned the staff's special ability to deal with the convention/meeting customers, employee training, and security measures as factors that helped create customer value.

Intermediary Perspective

Value Drivers for Travel Agents and Meeting Planners: For both travel agents and meeting planners, three sources of value drove their decision for sending guests to Marriott Hotels and Resorts: the convenience of Marriott's location, the overall service quality, and Marriott's low/good prices. For meeting planners, value at purchase was also derived from Marriott's brand name and reputation, as well as the size of the property. Interestingly, the intermediaries all ranked service quality as the aspect they most liked in their own experiences with Marriott Hotels and Resorts; however, beyond that, travel agents and meeting planners differed in their perceptions of service attributes that drive value. While travel agents primarily value the low/good prices, meeting planners valued the quality of the follow-up information they received, and the efficiency of check-in and check-out, with price trailing as a distant third. Meeting planners also mentioned the cleanliness of the property, professionalism of the staff, and Marriott's ability to customize services as sources of value. In terms of hotel practices that benefit intermediaries, travel agents appeared more sensitive to Marriott's promptness in paying commissions, while meeting planners maintained their emphasis on various aspects of the follow-up information and, in addition, highlighted the practice of both sales representatives and hotel staff going beyond the call of duty.

Insights

As can be seen, Marriott Hotels and Resorts' approach to employee satisfaction is more than building and reinforcing a culture, it is a policy of the company that has proven to contribute to outstanding financial performance. Mr. Jannini has some sobering advice for any organization that wishes to focus on employee development and satisfaction as a business strategy. "Before you open the door, check your conscience level on a human level." Focusing on employees, he believes, is not a tune-up for any organization; it is a Pandora's Box. If a company opens this door, it cannot be closed again. Understand that by following this strategy, a company is inviting all of society's problems to its doorstep and making itself responsible for them. As a business strategy for a company, "it's a marathon, not a sprint."

Contact

Mike Jannini, Brand Vice President
Marriott Hotels and Resorts
One Marriott Drive, Washington, DC 20058
Phone: 301-380-8210   Fax: 301-380-3120

MIRAGE RESORTS

Overall Best-Practice Corporate Champion in Casino Segment
"Creating Artistically Pleasing Hotels for Guests and Employees"

The Driving Source of Excellence

Mirage Resorts describes itself as a "hotel company that has some casinos." Fifty percent of its revenues is non-gaming. Mirage Resorts is an extremely successful company with some very well known brand names that exhibit excitement, creativity and wonderment. Its properties include Bellagio, Mirage, Treasure Island, Golden Nugget-Las Vegas, Golden Nugget-Laughlin, and Beau Rivage. As Steve Wynn, chairman and chief executive officer, states in the introduction to the company's 1997 annual report: "When an artist paints a picture, the intent is to provoke a reaction in the viewer. Every brush stroke, every choice of color and texture is designed to stimulate and entertain. A great painting draws the observer into being a participant, to interact with the art and to realize the emotions it is creating. Great hotels are similar to great pieces of art. They stimulate, provoke and entertain the guest. They draw the guests into the experience and enhance their lives, making the world a better place." Mirage Resorts believes that this mindset underlies its success in developing and operating great hotels. Everything Mirage Resorts does is about being receptive to change, learning new ways to do things, and putting everything together in a way that creates a unique experience for the customer.

The Delivery of Excellence

Organizing for Creativity: Mirage Resorts is intensely focused on being the best. According to Arte Nathan, vice president of human resources at Bellagio, it does this by creating an organization in which managers and employees have the freedom to create. At Mirage Resorts, the individual freedom given to managers is believed to eliminate barriers to creating great resorts or developing the systems necessary for their successful operation.

To avoid obstacles on this creative route to success, Mirage Resorts has taken away the corporate organization and the bureaucracy associated with it. No job descriptions exist for senior management; individuals are hired to achieve a goal, not to perform a specific set of tasks. By the same token, Mirage Resorts has also taken away the excuses for failure.

This philosophy is not anarchy, but the expression of a strong will, from Mirage Resorts' leaders, to keep the thinking and the organization fresh. They want managers and executives to come up with a running stream of good ideas and to execute them. In fact, as explicitly stated when someone joins the company, creativity is required, as is the ability to make a good business case for the great idea. Although corporate obstacles have been removed, there are also checks and balances to the development and execution of creative ideas to ensure that business potential is developed.

Management Philosophy: The visionary driving Mirage Resorts' success is Mr. Wynn. He is focused and attentive to detail. He is constantly walking the properties, seeing them in action, talking to employees, checking, asking questions, and making suggestions. He wants to make each building, each resort so captivating that the guest and employees will stop in wonder. Mr. Wynn's management philosophy is to ensure that the operators keep the "promise" of the buildings. He is the artist. Managers manage. They have made managing by walking around (MBWA) a philosophy. Managers do not sit in their offices, away from the guests, away from where the money is being made. They are constantly in the field, inspecting the properties, asking questions, coming up with new ideas, testing systems and procedures, reflecting on their feelings and observations, and checking details. Mirage Resorts' managers believe that in this way, problems don't remain hidden long. "It's the only way you find something out."

Searching for and Nurturing New Ideas: As mentioned earlier, the organization at Mirage Resorts is about good ideas and their development. No bureaucracy, no egos, no budgets, no policies are allowed to be an obstacle to the surfacing and nurturing of those ideas. Mirage Resorts' managers are driven to continuously change and improve the operations for employees and customers. Everybody in the organization has the right and the responsibility to bring up a good idea when appropriate. Managers are required to listen to those ideas and consider them. Feedback is provided on each new idea.

A manager at Mirage Resorts has maximum authority, maximum responsibility not to fail, and maximum accountability. It is a high-anxiety organization and it takes "guts" to work there. It is clearly not for everybody. But for those who want to succeed, to work hard, and who enjoy change, then Mirage Resorts is the right organization. It is free enterprise in action.

Within the Mirage Resorts' context, a manager becomes a razor-sharp businessman. He/she can call on all the support and the resources the organization has to offer for assistance. But it is his/her responsibility to help the organization succeed.

Customer Service: According to Mr. Nathan, Mirage Resorts is all about service and the guests love it and come back. The comments received from guests are 90 percent compliments about employees and 10 percent about issues requiring resolution. "The guest forgives everything with a smile," says Mr. Nathan. "It's the way you would run your own little hardware store."

Organizational Climate: How does the system feel to employees? Mirage Resorts characterizes its employee relations policy as "firm and fair." Managers listen to employees and try to do what is right and fair. They spend a lot of time and effort on employee communications and satisfaction. In every Mirage Resort, managers are as proud of the back of the house as they are of the front of the house. At the recently opened Bellagio Resort, the rumor is that the best restaurant in the building is the staff dining room. The employee areas are carpeted throughout. There are live trees and a stained glass dome ceiling in the employee entrance. Mr. Nathan sees the employees as the guests of the management. "If we don't treat them right, they won't treat the guests right."

Since there is no corporate entity or bureaucracy, no mission statement or policy guides exist for employees. There are no performance evaluations. Evolving in such a creativity-driven organization requires lots of hand-holding as well as a good balance of rewards and criticisms built into the system. Managers and employees alike practice the "Golden Rule," and the behaviors that are consistent with these values are reinforced by the corporation. Mirage Resorts believes in "catching people doing things right."

The work climate at Mirage Resorts seems to please present and potential employees alike. For the opening of Bellagio Resort, 99 percent of the applicants who were offered jobs accepted. They have not had a grievance or an employee lawsuit in 10 years. Equally impressive is the corporate-wide employee turnover rate of only 12 percent in 1998.

Creativity Pays: Mirage Resorts' chain-wide occupancy is 98.7 percent. Its hotels also have the highest ADR (average

daily rate) in their markets in Las Vegas. Profitability is also excellent. Mirage Resorts outperforms its competitors in terms of earnings, the value of the assets, and the revenue per square foot, as well as on any measure of financial profitability commonly utilized in the industry. In turn, Mirage Resorts invests it all.

Guest Perspective

Value Drivers in the Purchase Decision: Mr. Nathan may be right when he says that Mirage Resorts is all about service. In our independent survey of Mirage Resorts customers, service (friendliness and overall service quality) ranked first as the hotel attribute with the largest influence on motivating purchase. Following at some distance was convenient location, and familiarity with the brand image and reputation. Good prices and recommendations by travel agents followed as drivers of the purchase decision. The aesthetics of the properties and their cleanliness were also mentioned by a certain number of respondents. Although the customers interviewed were primarily leisure customers, the limited number of transient and meeting/convention business customers did not give sign of strong variations across segments, except for good prices, which appeared more powerful drivers of purchase decisions for leisure than for business customers.

Value Drivers in the Hotel Experience: During the hotel stay, food and beverage service was the strongest attribute in creating value for customers, particularly for the leisure segment. In this regard, customers valued both food and beverage quality and variety. Service was also a powerful source of unique customer value during the hotel stay, coming in second. The other important sources of unique customer value during the hotel experience pertained to the aesthetics of the property and security.

Customer Benefits and Outlook on Management Practices: An "enjoyable" experience, comfort and relaxation appear to be the key benefits that drive customers to Mirage Resorts. A good number of respondents also mentioned a general sense of satisfaction with their hotel stays. In deriving these benefits, customers cited a rich diversity of management practices as possible sources of Mirage Resorts' ability to deliver value. Three practices dominate the list: having very high-caliber interior designers, an in-depth knowledge of their target market, and a high employee-to-guest ratio.

Respondents also mentioned Mirage Resorts' ability to create a unique, exciting atmosphere; the consistency in operations; and the well-trained, knowledgeable staff that is willing to go beyond the call of duty. All of these attributes are likely a result of the many strokes in the piece of art created by Steve Wynn and his team.

Intermediary Perspective

Value Drivers for Intermediaries: The first motive driving intermediaries' recommendation of Mirage Resorts to their clients is the brand name and reputation, followed by convenient location. Both travel agents and meeting planners gave the same priority to these two attributes. Two hotel attributes shared the third position: the overall quality of service and value-for-money. Physical aspects of the property, including its overall quality, and the quality and size of the meeting rooms were also mentioned as important value drivers for intermediaries. When intermediaries noted comments made by satisfied customers after a stay at a Mirage Resorts' property, these customer remarks pertained to service, physical aspects of the property in general, and the guestrooms and the meeting rooms. In their own dealing with Mirage Resorts, travel agents valued a rich diversity of qualities of Mirage Resorts' service: friendliness, professionalism, attentiveness, and efficiency. In terms of benefits, both types of intermediaries value, for themselves as much as for their customers, the worry-free yet productive quality of their experience with Mirage Resorts.

Insights

Mr. Nathan believes other companies can "create" the success of Mirage Resorts, but only those who are not willing to follow the crowd. Mr. Nathan advises that companies focus on the work, not on jobs. He also suggests that companies not build in obstacles or impediments to the goal. He believes that beating up employees and managers is the biggest mistake management makes in the hospitality industry, while the creation of bureaucracies is the biggest mistake made in building organizations. As Mr. Nathan points out, the hotel industry is a service business, and no one can be allowed to get between the individual employee and the customer. At Mirage Resorts there are no obstacles to success.

Contact

Arte Nathan, Vice President Human Resources
Bellagio Resort
Mirage Resorts
3600 Las Vegas Blvd., Las Vegas, NV 89109
Phone: 702-693-8212   Fax: 702-693-8579

MOHONK MOUNTAIN HOUSE

Overall Best-Practice Property Champion in Profitability
"Creating Profits by Not Focusing on the GOP"

The Driving Source of Excellence

Mohonk Mountain House is one of the oldest continuously operating resorts in the United States. Opened in 1869 by Albert Smiley and still operated today by a fourth-generation family member, Bert Smiley, Mohonk is a place that, as the mission states, "provides opportunities for the re-creation and renewal of body, mind and spirit in a beautiful, natural setting." The resort includes 2,200 acres of woodlands with many trails and observation points for the enjoyment of hikers and nature-lovers. Adjacent to the property is the 6,400-acre Mohonk Preserve for further enjoyment and spiritual renewal.

In the late 1980s the resort, although profitable, was not generating sufficient income for required capital improvements and for the development of new projects. Bert Smiley became president and, with the assistance of his wife Nina as marketing director and a dedicated group of managers and employees, he set about the task of "renewing" Mohonk for the next 100 years and generating the level of profits needed to sustain Mohonk's historic success.

Mr. Smiley and his team of employees enhanced profit, but not by focusing on gross operating profit, a short-term perspective usually applied to difficult financial situations. Instead, they chose to focus on the long-term, on the strengths and beliefs that had helped Mohonk succeed for well over 100 years. In other words, they reinforced the sources of customer value that Mohonk had traditionally created for the guest, and made these sources more visible and appealing to a larger number of people willing to pay for them.

Mohonk is again financially secure and ready for the next 100 years. From 1990 to 1998, guest nights increased by 18.4 percent and revenues by 95 percent. During that same time period, its gross operating profit increased by 244 percent, pre-tax profit increased ninefold, shareholder equity more than quadrupled, and the debt-equity ratio fell by 45 percent of its initial value.

The Delivery of Excellence

The Mohonk Guest: Mohonk focuses on the family market. It develops and maintains repeat business by creating traditions for families. The entire environment in and around the hotel is kid-friendly, as are the various resort activities. Mohonk emphasizes nature programming and making nature accessible to the entire family. It wants all the family guests to "relax and feel it." Mohonk is definitely not a theme park, though. As explained by Mr. Smiley, "to understand Mohonk is to recognize that it is a thinking person's resort."

The Mohonk Guest Experience: For more than 100 years, the guest experience at Mohonk has remained relatively the same, designed around a basic set of core values. These values include: the integration of the physical, mental, and spiritual well-being of the guest; the guest perception of Mohonk as a second "home;" the conservation of the surrounding natural resources for the future enjoyment of guests; the maintenance of an atmosphere of serenity; and the maintenance of the beauty of the gardens and grounds.

When asked about Mohonk in internal surveys, guests mentioned most frequently the "home-like" atmosphere, the beauty of the surroundings, and the emphasis on nature and the serene atmosphere. In addition to the surrounding natural environment, various aspects of the physical and social environment create the unique Mohonk experience. For example, there is no cocktail lounge (but you may certainly order a drink); there is a comfortable, well-stocked library, but no televisions in the guestrooms; there is a professional naturalist on staff; there are extensive flower gardens; and there are frequent musical events. There are even non-denominational morning prayers held daily during the summer season.

In addition to the basics offered by the hotel and the environment, Mohonk offers more than 40 theme programs per year which are extremely popular with couples and families. These programs range from the "Tower of Babble," which offers opportunities to learn a language, to a program exploring the winter woods, to another immersing oneself in a weekend of science fiction movies.

To make the stay "hassle-free" for all guests, so they can "relax and feel it," the pricing strategy is Full American Plan: all meals and almost all activities and programs are included. For instance, there is not a separate fee for weekday golf or for the kids' program.

Focusing on the Long-Term to Increase Profitability: For Mohonk, focusing on the long-term to increase profitability meant producing and marketing the guest experience more effectively. To maintain and enhance the quality of the guest experience, significant resources were deployed in the restoration and improvement of the physical facilities and human resources management. One hundred percent of the profit each year was reinvested into capital improvements to buildings and grounds, a decision made possible by private ownership. In addition, every employee and manager was encouraged to focus upon the factors that had sustained Mohonk's success as a means of improving the effectiveness of the operations while providing the expected, unique guest experience.

Turning to marketing, various successful efforts were undertaken. In the early 1990s, when Mohonk was financially challenged, rates were not cut to drive more business. With a long-term focus and belief in the unique offering, the management team took a chance and actually increased the rates approximately 9 percent per year from 1990 to 1992, right in the teeth of the recession. It was a courageous move, and it worked. Significant efforts were also made in promotion so the customer could see more "visible value" at Mohonk.

The Unique Role of the Employees: Mohonk's employees are one of the keys to the continuing success at Mohonk. Management's goal is to create a positive working environment by fostering morale and building a team spirit. Relationships with people are important throughout the organization. Management tries to create an environment where each employee feels part of the Mohonk family. It is striving for a sense of shared goals and a commitment to excellence among all employees and managers. The Quaker spirit, a legacy of the first generation of Smileys, is evident in the collegial decision-making practiced by management. In addition, owners, managers, and employees celebrate together on a number of occasions: Christmas, beginnings and ends of seasons, and the employee golf tournaments. Families are invited to the staff Christmas party and employees are encouraged to use the resort's recreational facilities with their families when not on duty. The concept of family is taken seriously at Mohonk.

This spirit is reflected in various human resource management strategies. Employee training begins with a long orientation to the history and meaning of Mohonk. There is little formal scripting or training on how to interact with guests. The goal in everything that happens at Mohonk is to establish an environment where employees can be spontaneous and authentic in their interactions with guests. A key focus for management is to manage turnover so guests will see the same employee "family" faces each year. Management turnover averages 15 percent per year and staff turnover is approximately 30 percent per year.

Mohonk has always paid employees competitive wages. As part of additional attempts to retain employees during the profit-enhancing efforts of the early 1990s, Mohonk has succeeded in avoiding unscheduled layoffs. Since 1993, bonuses have been paid yearly to all full-time employees. Mohonk also provides special holiday gift certificates, redeemable at local merchants, to all employees. In the spirit of egalitarianism prevailing in the family, management gives an identical amount of gift certificates to each employee. The program has an added benefit in that it shows support for the local community.

Guest Perspective

The image portrayed by the Mohonk's guests we interviewed reflects, almost perfectly, the management's perspective described above. What customers value the most from the Mohonk experience is its uniqueness, and its ability to produce familiar and "close to home" feelings. In the words of a repeat guest, "my kids have grown up here… it's part of the family." Most of the cited purchase motives or unique sources of value during the stay referred to the physical surroundings: the outdoors, as well as the Victorian style of the building and various features that create a unique atmosphere. Respondents also mentioned the rich diversity of activities and the service quality. In terms of the benefits most immediately identified with the Mohonk experience, guests mentioned relaxation, change of pace, sense of wonder, and feeling safe and at home. The owners' investment in maintaining the facility and improving promotional material appears to have been returned in terms of customer value, since these factors were mentioned as management practices underlying Mohonk's success. The all-inclusive pricing is also highly valued by customers.

Insights

Mohonk Mountain House has a distinct niche, opines Mr. Smiley. It is not for everyone. The focus on nature and "encouraging the contemplative faculty" may not have mass appeal. But for those who respond to it, there is a clear offering of value. Management's job is to align all the activities and systems needed to deliver on the promise that has kept Mohonk alive for 130 years. This job requires a lot of thought and reflection.

Contact

Bert Smiley, President
Mohonk Mountain House
1000 Mountainrest Road
New Paltz, NY 12561
Phone: 914-255-1000   Fax: 914-256-2161

THE PENINSULA BEVERLY HILLS,
ALI KASIKCI

Overall Best-Practice Individual Champion in Property Management
"Every Day You Have to Re-Invent Yourself"

The Driving Source of Excellence

Ali Kasikci has been the general manager of the Peninsula Hotel in Beverly Hills for the last seven years and was nominated by managers industry-wide as the overall best-practice individual champion in property management. According to his close colleagues with whom we interviewed, Mr. Kasikci is clearly a leader, setting the tone for the property and constantly challenging the staff and himself to create the perfect experience for the guest. Comments from his colleagues on the operations committee of the hotel are telling: "Great vision. A hotelier through and through;" "Tough, unrelenting, challenging, direct. He will never compromise any service standards;" "He operates as if he were the producer and the director of a film;" "Unrelenting dedication and commitment to quality;" "Full of fun, organized, inventive, and energetic;" "A good mentor." Under such leadership, it is therefore not surprising to learn that the Peninsula Beverly Hills has a 68-percent return clientele and is financially highly successful: occupancy at 82 percent, the highest in the competitive set; average daily rate at $387.00; gross operating profit margin at 37 percent. The hotel is a five-diamond, five-star award winner and is on virtually every list of top ten hotels in the world.

The Delivery of Excellence

The Relentless Quest for Unique Customer Value: The core value that Mr. Kasikci has instilled at the Peninsula Beverly Hills is this relentless quest for new, innovative ways to do something special for the guest, something that is perceived as unique. For example, the hotel monograms the pillowcases in the guestrooms with the guest's initials. It's difficult, it's time-consuming, but it's also special and unique in the eyes of the guest. It is a signal to the guest that the hotel is willing to go the extra step to satisfy him or her. Another case in point that was recognized as a functional best practice: the 24-hour check-in. The decision to offer this innovative service option was made after analyzing guest travel patterns and recognizing that many guests were connecting to or from international airline flights. No longer do the guests of the Peninsula Beverly Hills adapt their travel schedules to the standard hotel day of in after 3 p.m. and out by noon or beg for early check-in or late check-out. The hotel adapts to them. They may check-in at any time and the room is theirs for 24 hours. Risk is involved in such a decision: Will the return for the guest be worth the trouble it represents for operations? Mr. Kasikci is not afraid to fail, he recognizes that not every new idea will work.

Becoming the Preferred "Global Innkeepers": Underlying the impressive loyalty rate mentioned above lies a strategic decision to do for global travelers what innkeepers have been doing for their guests since the beginning of time: taking responsibility for their key guests' travel needs, inside and outside the hotel. Staff at the Peninsula Beverly Hills act as the personal travel agent for these key guests, making reservations, solving travel problems, doing whatever is necessary to make things more comfortable for these individuals. Inside the hotel, Mr. Kasikci convincingly states that his job is to make the hotel function for the guest. Anybody can provide good service in a hotel. But that is not enough for the Peninsula. It is trying to stimulate that elusive "sixth sense" in the guest for great service. Guests cannot describe it but they know when they experience it. They feel it but they don't know exactly what it is. That is a difficult task, to make the entire experience for the guest greater than the sum of the individual interactions with the hotel and, at the same time, prevent any inconvenience that can happen so easily when multiple details have to be assembled in creating this experience. Under such conditions, when travel needs are fulfilled in such a unique way — both inside and outside the hotel — one thinks twice before knocking at the next hotel's door.

Leading Within an Unorthodox Structure: When the purpose of a hotel is to anticipate the guest's needs and to satisfy them in an exceptionally innovative way, the place has to be organized in nontraditional ways. Over time, Mr. Kasikci has surrounded himself with strong members in the operations committee, to whom the staff reports directly. There is a weekly operations committee meeting normally lasting one-and-one-half to two hours. There is no agenda other than whatever issues surrounding guest services have come up, and how the hotel could do things better. Mr. Kasikci believes that these unstructured meetings are important. "It takes time for things to unfold, for good ideas to surface," he says. "Good ideas come from the heart and mind." For them to surface in a group, the relationships among the members must be strong and positive. The meetings strengthen those relationships. The ideas which surface can then be discussed at length, thought about, and challenged. The good ideas will solidify and become appreciated by everybody. Those are the ones that get implemented.

Ali Kasikci's Message to the Employees Is Simple: "We are the trustees of income received from the guest. The guest pays the employee's salary. There are no ranks, only responsibilities at this hotel. In the eyes of the guest we are all equal." These are simple homilies but, coupled with visible leadership, they clearly state what is important at this property. And the employees believe and act upon them. With over 300 staff members, employee turnover is only 21 percent. Twenty percent of the staff has been there since pre-opening, and over 50 percent of the staff has been with the hotel five or more years. That is a phenomenal accomplishment.

Unorthodox organizational structure also prevails in the Peninsula Group, with ownership of each of the hotels in the chain being local. The owners of the Peninsula Beverly Hills are actively involved in guiding the success of the hotel and they meet with the general manager weekly. The owners have very high financial expectations for the property and they expect the general manager to lead in a way that creates value for the customers, the employees, and for them as well. They challenge him constantly with their questions and requests. They don't accept the status quo or the standard answer of "this is how it's done in the hotel industry." Mr. Kasikci says that they are "reasonably unreasonable." Leaders need challenges.

Vision of the Future: Mr. Kasikci believes the hotel industry is different today than it was years ago and will keep changing. There are so many changes taking place in society, to which hotels must react. Ours is clearly a knowledge society and hotel guests are well-educated and very sophisticated. Hotels must constantly find new ways of doing things, they must anticipate the changing needs of guests or they will quickly find themselves outdated and pre-empted by more aggressive and contemporary competitors. Many hotels and general managers talk about satisfying guest needs but their actions contradict it. The philosophy of the management and staff in hotels should not

be to talk about guest needs but to anticipate them and respond in a positive manner, trying to solve the problems of their guests before they have even thought of them. In the present and in the future as well, to lead an organization that is committed to satisfying these sophisticated and demanding guests requires a willingness to constantly question one's present behavior and adapt and change as necessary. "Every day you have to re-invent yourself," says Mr. Kasikci.

Insights

When asked if other hotels could achieve the level of perfection and success enjoyed by the Peninsula Beverly Hills, Mr. Kasikci answered affirmatively. You not only must focus on the customer with dedication and passion but you must re-invent the hotel industry. It is a very sophisticated business. "Don't accept the conventional wisdom of how the business operates." Re-invent!

Contact

Ali Kasikci, General Manager
The Peninsula Beverly Hills Hotel
9882 Little Santa Monica Blvd.
Beverly Hills, CA 90212
Ph: 310-551-2888   Fax: 310-788-2309

RESIDENCE INN BY MARRIOTT

Overall Best-Practice Corporate Champion in Extended-Stay Upper-Tier Segment
"A Relentless Focus on Extended-Stay"

The Driving Source of Excellence

Thirteen years ago when Marriott acquired Residence Inn there were 62 hotels in the Residence Inn chain. Today there are over 300 hotels. That growth and success is the result of a relentless focus on understanding the extended-stay hotel business — to learn what this non-traditional guest wants; to develop and execute the systems, processes, and programs necessary to reach this customer; and to satisfy his/her needs in all their details.

As Tim Sheldon, senior vice president and brand manager for Residence Inn, asserts, it is simple! Everything flows from the vision and the mission of the company, which has not changed much over the 22 years of existence of Residence Inn. The vision: "Residence Inn will be number one in extended-stay lodging. It will provide great hotels where talented people deliver service so memorable our guests tell stories about it." The mission: "We are the leading extended-stay hotel where people away from home feel they are among friends. We will do whatever it takes to satisfy every guest, every day, every stay." Later, these were translated into a set of guiding principles for franchisees, management and employees.

The Delivery of Excellence

Understanding and Serving the Extended-Stay Guest: The extended-stay customer is a guest who stays longer than five nights on a given trip, most often due to relocation, a project assignment, or a training course. His or her needs are different from the traditional hotel guest's. Often, the customer is unfamiliar with the area and therefore the staff acts as his or her concierge. With a longer stay, the hotel becomes home, the place one lives. The room at Residence Inn is 40-50 percent larger than a traditional hotel room and has distinct living, sleeping and kitchen areas.

To further differentiate the brand, Residence Inn has been focusing on all the detailed services that are necessary to meet customer needs on every day of every extended stay: free breakfast and complimentary newspaper in the morning; at night, a hospitality hour which turns into a light dinner or a weekly BBQ. Most properties have an exercise room, and provide both valet and guest laundry services. Residence Inn also offers a grocery shopping service whereby the guest puts in an order in the morning, and it will be in place in the kitchen by the end of the day. As much as possible is done to help the guest maintain the lifestyle he or she has at home.

Residence Inn carefully monitors how the needs of the extended-stay customer are changing. The "voice of the customer," as Mr. Sheldon says, prescribes the changes to be made to improve upon any aspect of the guest experience. For instance, ongoing customer research caused changes in the original room layout, which had no desk, to the present prototype which features a large desk, a worklight and two phone lines. Residence Inn is presently looking at ways to make more business services, such as fax machines and printers, available to guests. Other changes it is considering as a result of the research include more hot items at breakfast, a larger exercise room and express check-in/check-out.

The Key Role of the Franchisees: One of the keys to Residence Inn's ability to deliver excellence for the extended-stay guest is the relationship with the franchisee. Nearly 60 percent of the properties are franchised. The goal of the Residence Inn brand management team is to provide the franchisee with the information and the training necessary to succeed. Nothing is taken for granted. A franchisee may own other, traditional properties and be successful, but Residence Inn believes the same methods will not work in extended stay; hence, Residence Inn teaches him/her the business.

Residence Inn believes the extended-stay hotel business is different than the traditional hotel business and operates on that basis. For a new property, the training begins with the owner. He/she receives an executive orientation to understand the extended-stay guest and his/her needs, and how Residence Inn operates to satisfy and succeed with that guest. For the general manager there is a two-week course called "Goldmine" which teaches him/her the standards of Residence Inn and how to manage the property.

The Joint Effort of Sales and Service: Each property has between one and three salespeople, which might seem unnecessary for a property that averages 120 rooms. Yet again, the understanding and the detail come into play. Since the extended-stay customer is difficult to find, advertising and other forms of communication will not bring him/her to the front door. The extended-stay customer is located in every department in a company and thus he/she must be found "one customer at a time." Direct sales are necessary and the sales team at any given property will attempt to reach all the companies that are likely to relocate employees, or to organize corporate meetings or training seminars. Complete saturation of the area and penetration of each department of each company is a golden rule, and appropriate support is provided to salespeople, employees and management. For the salespeople on property, a one-week course, "The Edge," teaches them how to represent the brand in their sales activities and how to find and service the extended-stay customer.

Turning to staff and management, Residence Inn is defining the specific behaviors it wants them to exhibit, what it calls the "touchpoints," with the guest, e.g., taking a reservation, cleaning a room, handling mail, or interacting with the guest at breakfast. Behavioral standards are being developed by the general managers and employees, and will be made available throughout the system on CD-ROM.

Moreover, to ensure that a property's ability to satisfy the guest is sustained long after opening, there is an ongoing effort to continually "re-energize" the property and the system through awards, refresher courses and a host of activities to keep the properties focused on finding and satisfying the extended-stay guest. In a two-and-a-half day refresher course, "Mission Possible," attendees focus on how Residence Inn sells and why it does it that way. There is annual fall sales training for the general manager and the director of sales, which provides the newest tools on how to sell the extended-stay product. Each property participates annually in a week of activities entitled "True North," focusing everyone in the system on selling and servicing the extended-stay customer. There is also an annual sales conference in which participating properties send a salesperson and an operations person to learn how to work together to sell. Along with these training/reminder tools are the hundreds of minor celebrations, the awards and recognitions, to the many individuals for a job well done.

Sales management at Residence Inn also involves a careful monitoring of the short-stay guests, who are necessary to smooth the traditional peaks and valleys of demand over the whole week. Residence Inn seems to be successful in attracting both extended-stay and short-stay guests; its RevPAR Index for 1998 was 124 percent, the highest of any Marriott lodging brand. The operating margins are also much higher, since it is less costly to service a long-stay guest. As one owner of 30 Marriott hotels distributed across a variety of their brands remarked, "Residence Inn is the prettiest girl on the beach."

Guest Perspective

Value Drivers in the Purchase Decision: In addition to the convenience of the location, our independent study indicates there are a variety of reasons why customers choose to stay at Residence Inn. In decreasing order of frequency, those that were mentioned most often were: the value for money, the cleanliness of the properties, their liking of the properties in general, the overall service quality, the constant availability of rooms, the brand reputation, the aesthetics of the properties, their liking of the room and its furniture, and the friendliness and efficiency of the staff. Differences emerged across customer segments. For Residence Inn's core transient business customers, the four most significant drivers were location, cleanliness, service efficiency, and travel agent recommendation. For the meeting/convention customers, the top five drivers, except for convenient locations, were all related to physical aspects of the hotel. Finally, for leisure customers, convenient locations and value for money were the two clearly dominant value drivers at purchase. Of the customers interviewed, 91% of them reported that Residence Inn delivered on its value drivers.

Value Drivers in the Hotel Experience: Reflecting the relevance of Residence Inn's service strategy, it is the service — either general liking or staff friendliness — and not the physical properties that dominated the list of what attracted the guests' attention during their stays. Among the physical attributes that were liked the most, guests mentioned most frequently cleanliness, room size and room work equipment. Whereas service was absent from the leisure customers' value driver at purchase, it is precisely this attribute that they liked the most during the actual stay. The two attributes enjoyed the most by transient business customers during their stays were the health club and the size of various segments of the room.

Meeting/convention customers mentioned a rich variety of attributes they appreciated during their stays: staff friendliness, size of the room, room work equipment, breakfast, and location.

Benefits to Customers: Comfort, convenience and a worry-free stay are the three benefits that clearly dominate for Residence Inn's customers. For a good number of respondents, Residence Inn also provided them with "a home away from home," a place to relax.

Outlook on Management Practices: Residence Inn's customers had a rich diversity of management practices to mention as the means for the delivery of their value drivers and benefits. The following practices, presented in decreasing order, were those most frequently cited: good selection of furniture, providing free extras (breakfast, in particular), providing consistent service from one visit to the next, staff who do more than necessary, and good maintenance of the properties.

Intermediary Perspective

Value Drivers for Travel Agents and Meeting Planners: Except for the perennial "convenient location," travel agents and meeting planners cited different reasons for recommending Residence Inn to their clients. Travel agents' motives pertained primarily to the brand reputation and the physical property, whereas for meeting planners, service quality and value for money were driving their purchase decisions. Differences also emerged in the salience of Residence Inn's practices for these two intermediaries: Travel agents most appreciated the reservation system and the incentives; while meeting planners, possibly reflecting the effectiveness of property-level sales efforts, highlighted primarily human-resources-related practices tied to service quality.

Insights

Mr. Sheldon sees his role as that of making sure that the positioning and execution meet the needs of the customer. He keeps the organization focused on achieving the vision and represents the voice of the customer as the organization goes forward. To accomplish these tasks, he heads a brand team made up of a number of directors who oversee marketing, sales, operations, and overall support for the brand. His advice to others who would build a successful brand is to have a vision of what the business will be someday, then articulate all the functions in detail, especially how these functions interact with one another. Next, focus the organization and execute "one customer at a time, every day, every stay."

Contact

Tim Sheldon, Senior Vice President and Brand Manager
Residence Inn by Marriott
One Marriott Drive, Washington, DC 20058
Phone: 301-380-3000   Fax: 301-380-3802

THE RITZ-CARLTON HOTEL COMPANY

Overall Best-Practice Corporate Champion Industry-Wide
"Lead People, Manage Processes"

The Driving Source of Excellence

The Ritz-Carlton Hotel Company successfully manages 34 hotels around the world. Asked about the driving source of Ritz-Carlton's excellence, that enabled it to be chosen as the overall best brand, Patrick Mene, vice president of quality for more than eight years and one of the key artisans of the Ritz-Carlton quality approach, provides a four-word answer: "Lead people, manage processes."

The Delivery of Excellence

Lead People: At The Ritz-Carlton, leadership means joint planning and action. It eschews the adage "managers plan—workers do." It involves every individual in the work that affects him or her, throughout the organization. Both managers and workers plan and do together, with a common purpose. As Mr. Mene puts it, both managers and employees, or any human being for that matter, may "work for money, but they die for causes." The cause in which everybody feels pride and joy is the work they perform every day, which aims at providing every guest with The Ritz-Carlton experience, in the most effective and profitable way.

At The Ritz-Carlton, strategic decisions are made only after thorough consideration of all possible implications has been done both at the corporate level and across all areas involved at different levels in the organization. Ritz-Carlton does an extraordinary amount of planning, according to Mr. Mene. It does not subscribe to the philosophy of "fire, ready, aim."

When leadership is based on such a thoughtful, cross-functional review of all-important decisions, then the alignment of decision and execution comes naturally. A common thread runs through the organizational pyramid, from the company mission to corporate goals to key initiatives and finally to strategies and their implementation in daily hotel life. As a result, corporate staff and operating management know where they want to go and everybody understands their individual roles and how to perform them. Everyone is involved, everyone understands where the company is going, and, because everyone has had input, they are committed in the execution of their individual piece in the creation of the Ritz-Carlton guest experience.

Manage Processes: In 1992, The Ritz-Carlton Hotel Company won the Malcolm Baldrige quality award, being one of few service companies to have won this most prestigious prize. This achievement, as well as this current selection as industrywide overall best-practice corporate champion, may rest mostly on the effectiveness of its business management systems which tightly integrate strategic planning and operational planning with the development and execution of a set of key processes that create the Ritz-Carlton guest experience.

The strategic planning system, centered on new and more effective ways to serve the guest better, begins with the detailed review of trends in worldwide customer markets and of the various practices in place in the hotel industry in general and with key competitors. Current, past, and potential customer groups are scrutinized alike. What are the priorities of customers and how are they changing? What are the priorities of non-customers and what would we have to do to make them a Ritz-Carlton customer? New product opportunities are all carefully scrutinized in terms of their costs, their contribution to the guest experience and their impact on profitability. Management carefully studies the relationship between revenue and quality. The Ritz-Carlton past guest satisfaction experience and performance data is also duly analyzed. Finally, various special studies are commissioned to gain a fuller understanding of the issue under consideration. Management believes it not only knows its customers well but it also knows "potential" customers well.

At the operational level, The Ritz-Carlton's relentless focus on process management, centered on customers, has no equivalent in the rest of the lodging industry. A deluxe hotel like a Ritz-Carlton can be broken down into roughly 30 key processes, some designated for the core production of the hotel experience, some for support services, Mr. Mene says. Production processes include: recognition and greeting of regular guests; cleaning and re-stocking a guestroom; conveying the set of needs of a client's meeting or convention throughout the hotel; performing preventive maintenance on a guestroom; and providing lateral service across departments in a hotel. The support processes relate, for example, to doing rational pricing or deploying the sales force.

By focusing on managing the processes rather than managing the people, the organization is constantly learning how to get better. And this strategy pays financial dividends. Ritz-Carlton has calculated the return on investment from its efforts on a project by project basis; every dollar invested in projects results in a $6.00 return on the investment.

When you focus all your attention on managing the people in the organization, you end up stuck in the status quo. Moreover, by focusing on the customer, Ritz-Carlton can pinpoint carefully those processes that are keys to creating value, satisfaction, and loyalty, thereby setting priorities for resource allocation and action more effectively. People who execute those key processes are also involved in the development and fine-tuning of the processes. This day-to-day integration of its "leadership by action" into the ways hotel processes are designed and delivered to create "The Ritz-Carlton" guest experience is at the core of The Ritz-Carlton's superior performance.

Monitoring the Return on Investment in the Guest Experience: In a nutshell, the experience the Ritz-Carlton brand sells to its guest can be summarized in three features: recognition of regular guests, beauty of the surroundings, and a genuinely caring attitude. Such attributes of the guest stay create value for the guests and, as a result, their long-term loyalty is among the highest in the industry. Here again, in measuring and managing loyalty, one can recognize the systemic and systematic approach that characterizes the Ritz-Carlton way.

For measurement and monitoring purposes, Ritz-Carlton managers measure loyalty as a function of the value attained by the guest, divided by the cost. Value is defined as both the actual aspects of the hotel experience that present a benefit (what The Ritz-Carlton does for me) and the ultimate consequences that such benefits create for the guest (what I can do because of The Ritz-Carlton). Specifically, the guest-value side of the loyalty equation is measured by the guest-satisfaction scores on the key processes, multiplied by the importance scores to the guests of that segment for each

process. The cost side of the loyalty equation is measured by the hotel's price-value gap (the ideal price value minus the actual premium price value) multiplied by the percentage of difficulties encountered by the guests during their stays (percentage of customers who remember one or more difficulties during their stays).

If the loyalty score is above one, then the guest is receiving more than he/she gives up and therefore should come back. The greater the number of customers with such loyalty scores, the greater the likelihood the hotel will keep its customers. If the percentage of loyal customers goes up, the hotel will be more profitable, as loyal customers use the hotel more often for a broad variety of reasons, are willing to pay a premium price and use more hotels in the brand. To increase loyalty, you must increase the benefits to the customer and minimize the difficulties encountered in the experience, and you can only do that by managing the processes and leading the people. And the end result of all this effort is increased revenue and profitability. According to the company's calculations, a 1 percent increase in guest satisfaction results in a $2.50 increase in RevPAR. Also, not only is the guest satisfaction higher, but The Ritz-Carlton's profit is 3 to 4 percent higher than its major competitor.

Guest Perspective

Value Drivers in the Purchase Decision: Of all hotel chains we covered in our independent study, Ritz-Carlton is the one for whom service presents the most distinctive competitive advantage in influencing customer purchase decisions. One out of four respondents' value drivers at purchase pertained to service (whether mentioned in general, or specifically for staff friendliness and attentiveness). The Ritz-Carlton brand name and reputation comes in second as a value driver at purchase. Convenient locations were a third important source of value for The Ritz-Carlton's customers. Other value drivers in purchase decisions frequently mentioned were various aspects of the physical properties (specifically, aesthetics, cleanliness, and bathroom amenities), food and beverage quality, room comfort and efficient check-in/out. For 93 percent of the customers we interviewed, the actual hotel experience delivered upon their value drivers. Note that service was a particularly powerful value driver at purchase for Ritz-Carlton leisure and convention/meeting customers. For business customers, service as a value driver followed the travel agent's recommendation and convenient location.

Value Drivers in the Hotel Experience: Heading the list of value drivers in the hotel experience, the quality of service retained the same power as it had in the purchase decision. Physical quality of the room, and quality of food and beverage services became more powerful value drivers during the hotel experience, respectively occupying the second and third rank among the most frequently mentioned hotel attributes. Other most frequently mentioned aspects of "The Ritz-Carlton hotel experience" that the guests liked, in particular, related to beautiful landscapes, cleanliness of the property and the guestrooms, aesthetics of the properties, and the health clubs. Respondents also mentioned the quality of room service and the efficiency of check-in/out. Interestingly, the primary source of value varied from one market segment to the next. For the leisure market, the quality of food and beverages emerged as the most important value driver. For transient business customers, service was most frequently mentioned. Finally, for the convention/meeting guest, physical aspects of the hotel (primarily the room, but also the property in general and landscaping) were the most powerful value drivers.

Benefits to Customers: The most frequent benefit that the guests derived from the Ritz-Carlton hotel experience was that of having a "worry-free stay." Other benefits are presented here in decreasing order of mention: convenience, comfort, an enjoyable experience, and feeling pampered and at home.

Outlook on Management Practices: A staff that "goes beyond the call of duty" topped the list of management practices viewed as critical in delivering the value drivers. Second came consistency in what The Ritz-Carlton does, followed by efficient service processes, having good interior design, and providing free extras. The staff's personal recognition of regular guests, the Ritz-Carlton communication system, and the presence of knowledgeable concierges were also mentioned.

Intermediary Perspective

Value Drivers for Travel Agents and Meeting Planners: Both travel agents and meeting planners selected or recommended Ritz-Carlton for the same top three reasons: Ritz-Carlton's reputation as a luxury hotel, the convenience of the locations, and the overall service quality. Both intermediaries also mentioned the aesthetics of the properties and the landscape as sources of value driving their purchase

decision. In terms of what they liked in particular in their dealings with Ritz-Carlton, more than 60 percent of intermediaries mentioned service quality, be it overall or for the staff's professionalism, friendliness, and attentiveness. The aesthetics of the properties, and the brand name and reputation tied for second. Interestingly, the primary benefit derived from Ritz-Carlton services varied between the two types of intermediaries: Travel agents valued a worry-free recommendation to their clients, while for meeting planners, the Ritz-Carlton experience appeared to boost their own professional image.

Insights

Mr. Mene believes a systematic approach to hotel management, such as the Ritz-Carlton system, is available to any company that wants to take the time to develop it. The focus must be on quality and the company must benchmark against well-recognized standards, such as those applied in the Malcolm Baldrige quality award, or in companies that have successfully focused on quality and customer-service excellence. The current philosophy in the hotel industry focuses exclusively on how to manage people, managers, and employees. Insufficient search is made for innovative methods to improve processes and service delivery systems in ways that relentlessly help staff and managers organize their work more productively.

Contact

Patrick Mene, Vice President Quality
The Ritz-Carlton Hotel Company
3414 Peachtree Road, Suite 300, Atlanta, GA 30326
Phone: 404-237-5500   Fax: 404-261-0119

THE RITZ-CARLTON NAPLES

Overall Best-Practice Property Champion in Quality
"Quality… A Different Way To Manage"

The Driving Source of Excellence

At the Ritz-Carlton Naples, excellent quality is having the features that customers want in a hotel — most importantly "genuine, caring personalized service" — and delivering consistently on those features. Most hotel companies rely on slogans, cheerleaders and mottoes to drive the quality philosophy through the properties. It doesn't work in the long-term. The Ritz-Carlton Hotel Company takes an organized, systematic approach to managing quality, a system developed around standard quality principles. The Ritz-Carlton Naples is a prime example of this systematic approach to quality improvement in action. Brian Bennett, the Director of Quality, sees hotel management philosophies as a continuum with traditional hierarchical management at one end of the continuum and quality management at the other end. He believes that the hotel industry is moving from traditional management to quality management and that Ritz-Carlton is farther ahead on that journey. At the Ritz-Carlton Naples, "we're at 6 out of 10 and have a long way to go," he says, "but the competition is only at 3."

The Delivery of Excellence

Quality at the Corporate Level: At The Ritz-Carlton Hotel Company, quality starts with Horst Schulze, the president. Because of his commitment and that of senior management to quality, there is "real alignment" at all levels of the organization. Systems are designed so that there are no strategic or organizational obstacles on the route followed by hotels and individual contact employees to satisfy the guest. The quality system is thus a framework of objectives and standards of how the hotel will function and the manner in which each employee is to perform his or her tasks in a way that lead to satisfaction, for the guest and for him/herself. Satisfaction of the guest and the employee is the source of profit and the long-term company success. This over-arching principle defining the quality approach at The Ritz-Carlton Hotel Company is captured in the well-known motto: "We are ladies and gentlemen serving ladies and gentlemen."

The motto is translated into the credo, the promise made to every guest of the hotel. This is what the company believes and what drives the daily life of the hotel. It is worth repeating: "The Ritz-Carlton Hotel is a place where the genuine care and comfort of our guests is our highest mission. We pledge to provide the finest personal service and facilities for our guests who will always enjoy a warm, relaxed yet refined ambiance. The Ritz-Carlton experience enlivens the senses, instills well-being and fulfills even the unexpected wishes and needs of our guests."

This credo is translated into the three steps of service that provides the model for any employee-guest interaction. The

steps are (1) a warm and sincere greeting, using the guest's name whenever possible; (2) the anticipation and compliance with guest needs, and lastly, (3) a fond farewell, giving them a warm good-bye and using their names whenever possible. These steps of service are combined with the Ritz-Carlton Basics. These are the 20 basic standards of conduct expected of any employee regardless of his or her position in the hotel. They include such things as: "All employees will know the needs of their internal and external customers (guests and employees) so that we may deliver the products and services they expect;" and, "Be an ambassador of your hotel in and outside the workplace. Always talk positively. No negative comments."

For the Ritz-Carlton Hotels quality management philosophy and systems to work, they must be lived from the top of the company throughout the whole organization. Horst Schulze teaches the "Gold Standards" himself, to every department, at every new hotel opening. At older properties, senior leadership teaches the Gold Standards to the new employees. For the new employees, it's the first thing they're learning. It is continually reinforced. There are daily meetings at every hotel for all employees and the basics are reinforced.

Once the standards are instilled at the hotel, it is the responsibility of local management to keep it going. There are feedback loops in the system that apprise management that they're on track. These are a series of surveys conducted by J.D. Power Associates that monitor the alignment between the plan and the delivery of the plan. The first feedback loop is the ongoing surveys of guests in relation to the Gold Standards. Management needs to know if the guest is experiencing what the system is trying to make happen through the standards. Second is the reality check through the employee surveys to make sure the plan is being followed. To provide management with incentive, there is a quarterly bonus based upon the results of the surveys.

One of the key features of the Ritz-Carlton system is its focus on continuous improvement. The standards must be constantly reassessed and reinterpreted in light of new information: Guest needs change, employees leave, and the competition improves. To be successful, a quality management system must be dynamic. According to Brian Bennett, Director of Quality at the Ritz-Carlton Naples, in traditional hotel management, the focus is on fixing the symptoms and finding someone to blame. It's almost "remedy first and diagnosis second." This doesn't work because planning (diagnosing and developing a solution) is separated from execution (implementing the solution). The individuals who develop the solution often have a single perspective and often don't understand issues of execution. There is no pride and joy in executing another's understanding of the problem and their solution to it.

The Ritz-Carlton Hotel Company's approach to quality improvement is based on the assumption that it happens on a project-by-project basis. Problems in a hotel are the end results of a complicated process across multiple departments. To solve them requires a team approach of individuals whose work lives are affected by the problem. The goal of the team is to isolate the problem, to understand why it is happening and to devise a solution that will solve it. It is not a simple activity and requires a lot of work on the part of employees. Quite often there is a lot of data that must be collected and analyzed. By joining the planning and the execution in the team approach, the pride and joy is returned and the probability for success of any solution is improved.

Quality at the Ritz-Carlton Naples: The management at the Ritz-Carlton Naples strives for a perfect alignment of the Ritz-Carlton quality system with the business plan for the hotel. From the general manager to individual employees, everybody is constantly trying to improve service quality. Using the results of guest and employee surveys, management identifies projects that will make a difference, those that are vital to customer satisfaction and where the hotel has a problem.

Presently, the hotel has projects in the following areas: anticipating guest needs; guest problem resolution in a personal and timely manner; meeting event difficulties; housekeeping difficulties (cleanliness); guestroom condition; and reducing difficulties of guestroom assignment. Note that all of the projects are complex and most have to do with service delivery issues, the most difficult challenges facing hotel managers. Note also that, if solved, these service delivery issues could have a tremendous impact on guest satisfaction. The Ritz-Carlton Naples has a plan to deliver in each of these areas. An executive committee member of the hotel leads each project. There is a director of quality at the hotel who works with each team providing expertise in quality management and keeping the team on track.

The Director of Quality is an important member of the management team at the Ritz-Carlton Naples. Mr. Bennett is part of the executive committee and is the quality advisor to the general manager. He has three crucial roles in the operation of the hotel. First, he facilitates the quality improvement teams. He teaches the team members how to apply the principles of quality management to their project and to operate on facts and not feelings. Second is a data feedback role. He interprets the data that has been collected and recommends other studies that may assist management and the project teams in making better decisions. Finally, he has a training role. He teaches the policies and procedures of quality to new employees.

For the system to work, the hotel needs employees who can take responsibility for their own behavior and who want to serve. As with the rest of the Ritz-Carlton quality system, employee selection is highly scientific. Each position in the hotel has a profile of excellence that has been developed for that position by an outside firm, Talent +. The initial candidate interview is to develop a profile of the applicant across a number of dimensions. This profile is then matched against the Gold Standards requirements to assess whether the applicant has the Ritz-Carlton attitude. If the answer is affirmative, the applicant's strengths are then matched against the profile of excellence for that position. Finally, there is an in-depth interview with the department where the position is located. The result of this careful selection process is that there has been a dramatic reduction in employee turnover. The company-wide rate is currently at 30 percent while employee associate satisfaction, according to the surveys, is above 90 percent. What the Ritz-Carlton Naples has learned from employees is that money is not the most important driver of their satisfaction; it is having the ability and freedom to serve guests.

Return on Quality for the Guest: Overall customer satisfaction and intent to return are excellent, according to internal data. The overall quality index for Ritz-Carlton company-wide, comprising employee turnover scores, guest satisfaction scores and employee satisfaction scores, has improved over a half of a percent per year for the last four years. According to Mr. Bennett, each one percent improvement translates into a 2.5 percent increase in RevPAR. Quality clearly translates into customer satisfaction and profit.

Return on Quality for the Owners: Owners understand the quality system and support it. How could an owner not like it: It's not short-term, it protects the asset and it directly affects revenue and profit. Here's an example. At the hotel, they were experiencing too many rooms out of service. This happens for a variety of reasons, usually because something is not working and engineering needs time to fix it. The revenue impact and the guest satisfaction impact can be detrimental, especially in high demand periods.

Ritz-Carlton developed a solution called CARE (clean and repair everything) in which a team inspects each guestroom in the hotel and cleans and repairs everything not working. The Ritz-Carlton Naples put two teams together to implement the program and work on the project of reducing the number of rooms out of service. Each team was made up of employees from the front office and engineering and each team does three guestrooms per day. No room in the hotel "ages" longer than three months before it is inspected cleaned and repaired.

The result is that due to CARE and high quality suppliers, the furniture, fixtures, and equipment last longer than normal.

Insights

According to Mr. Bennett, the benefits of quality management are available to anyone who wants to practice the principles. There are, however, some key success factors that must be observed. It must be run from the top, for you need alignment at all levels of the organization to succeed. It is a long-term process with financial implications. The relationship between quality and financial control must be understood. The director of quality and the financial controller must be partners. Finally, quality management is a new discipline. It requires effort and study to understand how to use it effectively. It is truly "a different way to manage."

Contact

Brian Bennett, Director of Quality
The Ritz-Carlton Naples
280 Vanderbilt Beach Road, Naples, FL 34108-2300
Ph: 941 598-3300   Fax: 941-598-6667

SLEEP INN

Overall Best-Practice Corporate Champion in Customer Service
"Customer Service is the Wild Card"

The Driving Source of Excellence

The hotel customer in the United States has many choices. According to Norm Cavin, vice president and brand manager of the Sleep Inn brand, a room is a room, and it is by shaping the way customers are made to feel from the time they check in to the time they check out that is the key to differentiating hotels. And Sleep Inn, a budget hotel chain, is proud to emphasize customer service as the core of its branding strategy. It may seem somewhat surprising since, by standard definition, a budget hotel is one that is "clean, well maintained, with a minimum of service and amenities to cater to price-sensitive customers." However, the customer-service strategy appears to have worked for Sleep Inn, leading to its unique position in the industry segment.

The Delivery of Excellence

The Sleep Inn Concept: Sleep Inn has no food and beverage outlets, offering guests only a continental breakfast. There is no bathtub in the guestroom, just an oversized shower, which is one of the brand's signature items. Public spaces are simple and limited in size. However, the rooms are ergonomically designed, and there are dataports for computer access. Since all the properties are new builds, properties are built to tight design specifications. At a price point of approximately $50, Sleep Inn rooms represent good value to the customer. However, in a competitive environment Sleep Inn management realizes that an excellent product alone is not enough.

The emphasis at Sleep Inn is not to sell a room to a customer but to "make the guest feel warm, like they're at home." Sleep Inn focuses on customer service to achieve this. New Sleep Inn franchisees are trained to appreciate the importance of customer service. A one-on-one orientation with the new owner explains the culture within the brand and the emphasis that is placed on customer service. The customer orientation is primarily reinforced through training, but the brand performs a number of additional activities that constantly reinforce the focus on service.

Customer Service Strategy: The core component of the Sleep Inn service strategy is the 100 percent satisfaction guarantee, which brings problems to the attention of management and protects the quality of the guest experience. The number of times the guarantee is invoked is low, approximately six per 1000 rooms occupied. Furthermore, the number of invocations decreased from 1997 to 1998, a period during which rooms added to the system increased by 35 percent.

In addition to the guarantee, a new initiative has just been launched that centers on customer service, but also includes financial management and housekeeping components. Mr. Cavin argues that in the hotel industry we emphasize training employees on the technical aspects of the job. A front desk employee is better at running a computer than dealing with a guest. Customer service is the "wild card," the one that, if played correctly, can win the game. He is convinced that training employees to deliver customer service can and will allow the Sleep Inn brand to win the game in their segment of the hotel industry.

The third component of the service strategy is the quality assurance reviews, which are on-property inspections done approximately every five months. These reviews focus primarily on the product and on the functional aspects of service related to the property's cleanliness and maintenance. Although the quality assurance reviews are expensive to conduct, Sleep Inn management believes that a quality product is part of excellent customer service.

Finally, the Sleep Inn service strategy is reinforced by the parent company, Choice Hotels International, which also has a customer relations department that emphasizes customer satisfaction. Choice offers a number of communication vehicles to the properties in each brand which are used to reinforce and grow the culture of customer satisfaction. In addition, Choice does follow-ups with each property and works to make certain that any customer issues are resolved, and, more importantly, that the problems do not reoccur. As part of its emphasis on customer service, Choice is presently building an internal research department to better understand and be able to respond to customer issues. Sleep Inn management is enthusiastic about such synergy.

Impact of the Service Strategy: The brand's major market segment, representing 60 percent, is the leisure traveler, typically an older couple. Business travelers account for the other 40 percent. Guests respond to the service strategy positively. Both customer segments find Sleep Inn hotels convenient, safe, and comfortable. Employees are the key to customer service.

Employees also benefit from the service culture. Focusing on customer service helps retain employees because they know their customer-oriented behavior is supported by management. There is not a formal employee empowerment program but the customer service culture acts as an informal one by creating a sense of community and common purpose, even a "feeling of fun."

Franchisees have also responded to the emphasis on customer service with enthusiasm. Not only are they for it, they sparked the issue within the company. They want the bar raised. As operators, they understand the financial impact of excellence in customer service. With a gross operating profit of 50 percent and a return on investment of 25 percent, the Sleep Inn brand is seen as an excellent investment. This ability to produce returns for the franchisees is one reason 45 new hotels opened in 1998, and why the pace of development is increasing.

Guest Perspective

Value Drivers in the Purchase Decision: The interviews we conducted with Sleep Inn customers confirm that the brand has carved a unique position in its segment by its joint emphasis on customer service and added value. This point is illustrated by the fact that, unlike our findings for other brands across all industry segments, convenient location did not play as significant a role as in determining the purchase decision for Sleep Inn customers. Instead, location represented a comparatively low proportion of the cited value drivers, particularly for the business customer, even among those market segments in which it was ranked first. Further, service (friendliness and overall) was the second value driver. Finding customer service to be the second hotel attribute driving customer purchase has been extremely rare in our survey, exceptions being primarily for brands in the much higher end of the lodging industry. Thus, the Sleep Inn brand customer service strategy appears to have permeated customer perceptions in an effective way. In third position as purchase motives, we

found attributes related to guestroom design and amenities (including specific recognition of the bathroom furnishings) and low prices. Cleanliness was the next hotel attribute driving purchase decision. Other value drivers mentioned with a certain frequency pertained to the constant availability of rooms, the brand name/reputation, and the quality of the physical property in general. The two customer segments basically valued the same attributes, except for some minor nuance in their order of influence. Sleep Inn hotels delivered on those attributes, driving their customers' purchase decision for 95 percent of our respondents.

Value Drivers in the Hotel Experience: The physical aspects of the property appear to create unique customer value during the hotel experience. One third of hotel attributes mentioned as value drivers were related to physical aspects of the property (primarily the guestroom and the bathroom, but also the physical property in general). Cleanliness came next, followed by staff friendliness. No important differences were observed across customer segments.

Customer Benefits and Outlook on Management Practices: Customer benefits that Sleep Inn hotels are able to create for their customers are simple but central for the service emphasis: a comfortable, restful stay that meets customer expectations. In terms of management practices, respondents saw the Sleep Inn brand's ability to create customer value as stemming from the interior designer guestrooms and properties in general, the staff knowledge and willingness to go beyond the call of duty, and the good property maintenance. Hence, a good congruency exists between customers' desires and managers' actions.

Intermediary Perspective

Value Drivers for Intermediaries: Travel agents recommend Sleep Inn hotels to their customers for two primary reasons: convenient location and low prices. Two other factors were noted, but had less effect on the travel agents' recommendations — the physical property and comments made by their satisfied customers after a stay. These satisfied customer comments included various aspects of customer service, guestroom design, and cleanliness. In their own dealings with Sleep Inn hotels, travel agents valued in particular the speed and friendliness of the service, the low prices and the constant availability of rooms. In terms of management practices, they highlighted

Sleep Inn promptness in paying commissions, and owners' investment in building and maintaining their properties.

Insights

Mr. Cavin is proud of the emphasis on customer service and the accomplishments of the Sleep Inn brand, but does not believe it is enough. The guest is still under-valued, he believes, throughout the hotel industry. He recognizes that many deficiencies in the guest's lodging experience can be overcome if the customer service is correct. Thus, he believes the brand needs even more tools to continue to do it right. Mr. Cavin recognizes that customer service is the wild card and he intends for the Sleep Inn brand to win the game.

Contact

Norm Cavin, Vice President and Brand Manager
Sleep Inn
10750 Columbia Pike, Silver Spring, MD 20901
Phone: 301-592-6052   Fax: 301-592-6176

SUPER 8 MOTELS, INC.

Overall Best-Practice Corporate Champion in Budget Segment
"A Focus on Hospitality"

The Driving Source of Excellence

Bob Weller, president of Super 8, says "We're pineapple kind of people," in reference to the universal symbol of hospitality. That is, Super 8 and its people represent a budget motel company providing a simple, hospitable place to stay. Because of the focus on hospitality, Super 8 has developed an enviable consistency in the definition of the product and service, which has resulted in three critical outcomes: continuity of ownership, a clear and specific market positioning, and positive relations with franchisees. This consistent focus also largely explains Super 8's success with its 1,760 properties and 106,000 rooms.

The Delivery of Excellence

Continuity of Ownership: In 25 years, only two companies have owned Super 8 Motels. Such continuity of ownership has led to stable senior management. The result is that the management team has had time to refine its philosophy and to support it.

Clear Positioning and Consistency: Throughout its history, Super 8 has been consistent in its definition of the product and service. It is in the middle of the economy segment and has occupied that niche since the beginning of the company. It has not wavered. Everyone in the company understands what the brand is and what it is not. Super 8 is also clearly positioned in the customer's mind. The brand offers a clean, comfortable room, friendly service, and the little extras that show hospitality and make the guest happy. All this is wrapped in extensive training, support, and inspections to ensure consistency for the guest.

Fifty-two percent of its customers are leisure and 48 percent business. Internal research at Super 8 shows all customers like the simplicity of the properties and the "down-home, friendly kind of environment." Customers have been very responsive and loyal to Super 8 over the years. To boost customer loyalty, Super 8 has established a V.I.P. club, open to any customer for a small fee. Benefits include a 10 percent discount on the room, being able to guarantee a reservation without a credit card, and to cash a personal check. The V.I.P. club has 5.7 million members and a growth rate of 13 percent in 1998; 53 percent of the reservations are made with the V.I.P. card. In addition, these loyal customers seem willing to pay a premium: the yield at Super 8 surpassed that of the competitive set.

Relations with Franchisees: For Super 8, the franchisees are customers, and everybody at Super 8 works hard to sell and retain them by maintaining positive relationships. Since good relations start with the right expectations, Super 8 communicates quite frequently with the franchisees to discuss and resolve common issues. Super 8 meets with its franchisee advisory board and its general manager advisory board quarterly. It also requires new owners to participate in a one-day orientation session to discuss the Super 8 philosophy of management and the operating principles of the company.

Super 8 recognizes that every franchisee is dependent upon the operating ability and the consistent execution of product and service delivery of every other franchisee. The company is determined to assist each property to be a strong link in the Super 8 chain. The company also conducts a series of courses, dubbed the "University of Pineapple" that relate to successful and profitable property management. General managers are required to attend one management class annually. The company has six franchise service managers whose mission is to respond to questions and solve problems for the franchisees, while other managers provide support in quality assurance and property openings. Super 8 also runs a series of regional meetings for general managers, owners, and employees to teach the nuts and bolts of operations. Most recently, the company has developed a series of training tapes on such techniques as housekeeping and front desk for use by franchisees.

Super 8 conducts unannounced property inspections on a quarterly basis. The management of Super 8 believes the inspections are important to maintain quality, and they assist owners by giving feedback on performance. In effect, the inspections are performed to protect the owner's investment; thus a positive approach is taken. If a property fails to meet standards, Super 8 offers to help by developing a work-out plan to assist the owner to come back into compliance, and it will work right along with the franchisee until it happens. However, Super 8 is firm about quality. If the property fails a second time, the property is in default and is in danger of being terminated. Super 8 celebrates the best properties in the system, annually awarding 600 awards, or 30 percent of the system, related to quality. These properties are publicly recognized and listed in the directory of properties so customers can also see who represents "the pride of Super 8." Firm but fair is the watchword of the relationship with franchisees.

Franchisees also recognize the value of the Super 8 brand, as reflected by the longevity and growth of the brand. In the last five years, the company's compounded annual growth rate has been over 15 percent. The franchisees know the management of Super 8 will not only treat them with respect and fairness, but listen and work with them. In addition, franchisees know that because of the construction standards and assistance, the operating system, the training, and the support of the parent company, Cendant Corporation, chances are extremely good that they'll make money. As one franchisee stated, "When I want to impress my neighbors, I build a Hampton Inn. When I want to make money, I build a Super 8."

The Strength of the Parent Company: Cendant has had a strong, positive influence on the brand. When Cendant purchased the brand, it took the time to analyze it and recognize what should and shouldn't be changed. Like all its hotel brands, Cendant allows Super 8 to operate independently of its other brands. The power of the Cendant relationship shows in the purchasing program, which has negotiated special arrangements with preferred vendors; this leads to significant savings for Super 8 as well as the other brands. Cendant also aggregates media purchases for all the brands resulting in savings for Super 8. Finally, the corporate parent has a low-interest loan program for franchisees to maintain their properties. It is a true partner to Super 8.

Guest Perspective

Value Drivers in the Purchase Decision: The customers we interviewed appear to be responding positively to Super 8's clear and simple promises. After convenient location, the top three motel attributes that drove purchase decision were low prices, cleanliness (both property and rooms), familiarity with the brand, and the loyalty program. This latter attribute is especially meaningful as loyalty programs have been rarely

found to be powerful drivers at purchase; this finding indicates that Super 8 must be providing unusual value for its members. Customers from the leisure and transient business segments showed a remarkable similarity in the motel attributes driving their purchase. Overall, 95 percent of the respondents affirmed that Super 8 delivered on these attributes driving their purchase decisions.

Value Drivers in the Motel Experience: The top sources of unique customer value during the motel stay proper were much in line with Super 8's brand position: cleanliness (property and room), friendliness of the staff, comfort of the room, bathroom furniture, and amenities. Again, the two customer segments were consistent.

Customer Benefits and Outlook on Management Practices: In our market research for this study, the benefits guests believed they derived from Super 8 were: convenience, comfort, a restful place, and a sense of security. Customers also identified those practices they believe Super 8 uses to create customer value: the free breakfast, the availability of non-smoking floors, the well-trained and knowledgeable staff, the consistency of operations, and the good property maintenance.

Intermediary Perspective

Value Drivers for Travel Agents: Travel agents we surveyed recommend Super 8 to their customers: first, for its low prices, and then, for the convenient locations. Other motives for recommending Super 8 ranged from the cleanliness of its property to its frequent stay program. Certain travel agents mentioned that the customers themselves often asked for Super 8. In their own experiences with Super 8, travel agents liked the friendliness of the motel staff and sales representatives, and the information they receive from the brand. They were also pleased with the attractiveness of the travel agent incentives.

Insights

Mr. Weller has these thoughts regarding motel management: Recognize that the "customer comes last." Get your employees to care about one another. Take the time to get them to buy into the philosophy and programs that are important for success. "Lead by following." If you take care of them and they care for one another, they will go out and take care of the customer. For those who wish to emulate the success of Super 8, start with a system and a plan. Be faithful to it. Get your people behind it. Most of all, remember it takes a long time to succeed and that "life belongs to the pluggers." That is a pineapple kind of person.

Contact

Robert N. Weller, President
Super 8 Motels, Inc.
339 Jefferson Rd., Parsippany, NJ 07054
Phone: 973-496-8415   Fax: 973-496-2305

TOWNEPLACE SUITES BY MARRIOTT BROOKFIELD, WISCONSIN

Overall Best-Practice Property Champion in Extended-Stay-Lower Tier Segment
"Remodeling the Property Hierarchical Structure"

The Driving Source of Excellence

Towneplace Suites by Marriott is a relatively new brand of Marriott Lodging. According to Tobin Williams, the general manager, the Brookfield property is positioned among the low- to mid-tier extended stay hotels, competing against such well-known brands as Homestead Village, Candlewood Suites, and StudioPlus. Their market is the business traveler staying longer than five nights. The value equation at Towneplace Suites is built upon a limited mix of products and services and a low price. What it offers is "friendly, clean, modern." This includes, in addition to a clean, comfortable guestroom, 24-hour staff availability, an exercise room, outdoor pool, gas barbecue grills and the Marriott Honored Guest Rewards program. What Towneplace Suites asks the extended-stay guest to give up is daily housekeeping (for semiweekly housekeeping), foodservice, hospitality hour, and grocery shopping services. The average property size is 95 units and with only 10-12 FTE, a staff-to-guest ratio that is not unusual in this industry segment. Towneplace Suites Brookfield has 112 units and 12 full-time employees. However, what differentiates Towneplace Suites from other brands is that it asks the guest to "give up services, not service." This case describes the model developed to deliver world-class customer service in an industry segment in which such standards may seem unusual.

The Delivery of Excellence

Empowerment Put to Action: At Towneplace Suites by Marriott in Brookfield, Wisconsin, the employees are empowered to create experiences that "wow" the guest. However, such "simplicity" is tied to many managerial decisions and actions aimed at having the employees look at their jobs in a different way. First, the hierarchical pyramid structure has been eliminated, replaced by a horizontal structure in which the hotel staff has a different relationship with management. Essentially, there are no employees; everyone is a "guest service team member." "Everybody walks the talk" on this team, Mr. Williams says.

Obviously, not everyone is good enough to make this team or even wants to join it. The human resources management model is special. The selection process targets individuals who can work without supervision. The hotel wants responsible, reliable individuals — those who want to be "delightfully subservient to guests." Compensation is competitive, the hotel does not pay a premium. The hotel also does not advertise for new employees. The staff knows the type of individuals who can be successful, and finds them from among their friends and neighbors.

The training creates the world-class service that Towneplace Suites provides, according to Mr. Williams. At this price point, though, there is not a lot of money available for training, so the culture is about training. Everyone is cross-trained in the technical aspects of all jobs. But the training emphasis is on customer service, how to interact and "wow" the guest. The four service principles behind the Towneplace Suites world-class service are:

Anticipate—plan ahead to meet guest needs
Satisfy—do what we promise
Solve—do whatever it takes to solve the problem
Surprise—wow them with random acts of kindness

On-the-Job Role Playing: The unique training method used at Towneplace Suites by Marriott property in Brookfield is on-the-job role-playing. The rules of the game are simple: Everybody on property wears a nametag. When a service team member (any staff member can role play at anytime) slips a colored piece of plastic over his nametag that is the cue that he is role-playing, and the color identifies the service principle that is being taught. He interacts with an employee for a short period of time and then they discuss what happened. In the de-briefing, the service team member explains what was done right and what the employee could improve. Employees do not have to go off-line in training sessions and the training is fun. The goal is to "keep it from being just a job." As any manager knows, though, this is difficult to do every day for "life intrudes on the staffing model."

The incidents of "wow" service take place at the hotel and the stories are repeated by the guests. As they are shared between guests, staff and management, over time, they grow into myths that become the backbone of the culture of world-class service. There is the story of the individual who walked in the hotel one Sunday morning, all upset because she had a flat tire on her car and did not know what to do. The front desk clerk calmed her down and fixed the tire himself. He never did find out if she was a guest. There is the story of the long-stay guest who had the flu and was stuck in bed. One of the front-desk clerks made chicken soup at home and brought it to her. On another occasion during a driving rainstorm, a service team member grabbed a large umbrella and went outside to help guests check in because she did not want them to get wet. That is service and when it is done routinely it becomes world-class service.

The Management Role: Mr. Williams sees his role as that of team leader, not manager. His behavior conveys his beliefs in providing customer service. Since this is a team, there is open communication on all issues. Mr. Williams holds a daily meeting with all employees that averages 15 minutes. Team members share guest comments, the previous day's financial results, operational issues, and anything the team needs to know to function effectively. Management understands that people only give authentic world-class service when they are led, not managed.

The Performance: The value equation proposed by Towneplace Suites by Marriott in Brookfield to their extended-stay customers appears to be profitable. It receives a rate premium for its competitive set and tries to remain $20-30 under the Residence Inn rate. Towneplace Suites guest satisfaction scores are very good but they are still working out the methodology to capture sufficient responses on a consistent basis. On the employee side, turnover is approximately 50 percent, which is much better than the industry average, and the gross operating profit for the hotel is between 64 to 70 percent, which is comfortable according to industry standards.

Guest Perspective

Value Drivers in the Purchase Decision: The efforts made by Towneplace Suites by Marriott in Brookfield to provide world-class service are noted by the guests we independently interviewed. In terms of purchase motives, service came in second position, not surprisingly, behind convenience of location and low prices, which were equally powerful attributes in influencing customers' decisions. Physical attributes recognized as purchase motives by customers were: the size of the guestroom, the kitchenette, the exercise room, and the guestroom entertainment system. Membership in the frequency program was also mentioned as source of value influencing purchase decision.

Value Drivers in the Hotel Experience: Interpersonal service attributes were ranked first in terms of creating unique value during the hotel experience. The service attributes specifically identified included: friendliness, genuineness, attentiveness, and the staff's ability to recognize guests and make them feel at home. Such an emphasis from the customers' perspective on what are, indeed, world-class service qualities, is remarkable for this industry segment. Two physical attributes, mentioned as unique sources of value during the hotel experience, were the exercise room and the guestroom entertainment system.

Insights

Mr. Williams believes that others can institute the Towneplace Suites model, but only if they throw out the old organizational structure. The pyramid doesn't work. The "workers circle," the team approach is the only way to achieve world-class service.

Contact

Tobin Williams, General Manager
Towneplace Suites by Marriott
600 North Calhoun Road, Brookfield, WI 53005
Phone: 414-748-8450   Fax: 414-784-8503

THE CUSTOMERS' PERSPECTIVES ON THE LODGING INDUSTRY'S BEST PRACTICES

Factors Driving Customer Value

Introduction

The presence of the customer at the core of service operations requires that a best-practice study include this critical perspective. In the Methodology chapter, we have described in detail how interviews were conducted to assess customers' perspectives on both the overall and functional best practices. To assess customers' perspectives on the overall best-practice champions, customers were asked to discuss their experience with one of the champions. In each of the overall best-practice champion case studies, we reported those hotel attributes that created value for the customers at the point of purchase and during their hotel experiences, identifying the set of benefits the champions were able to create for the customers. These detailed results have been presented in the individual case studies. In the first part of this chapter, we propose a comprehensive representation of customers' perspectives on the overall best practices in the lodging industry based on the study of the various sources of customers' value created by the champions within the various segments of this industry.

In contrast to the direct assessment performed on customers' perspective on overall practices, the assessment of customers' perspectives on the best functional practices in the lodging industry was not made in reference to the functional champions that were selected by the managers. Instead, customers' perspectives were presented from the point of view of what they consider the top performance in the lodging industry in a set of functional areas (e.g., personnel, check-in/out and in-stay services, marketing) that paralleled reasonably well the set of functional practices that emerged in Phase II. We explained the details of this methodological constraint earlier in the Methodology chapter. In the second section of this chapter, we identify the series of hotel attributes that drive the value customers derive from a top performance in a given functional area. In addition, we report on the specific hotel attributes, observed in these top performers, that were successful in creating a set of customer benefits often used in brand or hotel positioning (e.g., the personnel or some aspects of the guestroom that make business customers feel at home).

In the last section of this chapter, we compare managers' perspectives on best practices in the lodging industry, as pictured by the case studies developed in Phase II, to customers' perspectives, as assessed in Phase III. Discrepancies observed between the managers' and the customers' perspectives on best practices should provide useful managerial insights into strategic problems and market opportunities that may not be readily apparent from examining best practices in the lodging industry strictly from the management perspective.

A Comprehensive View of Customer Value

In the lodging industry, a satisfactory hotel experience, one that delivers customer value, is one in which the multitude of details unfold over the stay in a smooth, pleasant, efficient, and seamless fashion while creating the overall, unique character that differentiates the hotel concept from its competitors. These "details" permeate from functional and overall practices. Obviously, from the customer perspective, some of these "details" are deemed to be particularly powerful sources of value. Other "details" are likely to be particularly critical to the delivery of unique benefits promised by the brand (e.g., the promise of being pampered or having a worry-free stay). It is the effective translation of overall and functional best practices into customer value, benefits, purchase, and loyalty that ultimately determines hotel profitability.

In this research, we adopted the comprehensive view of customer value illustrated in Figure 1. According to this model, overall and functional practices, to create value for the customer, must translate into customer perceptions of the various hotel attributes that result from such practices. Hotel attributes are what constitutes, in a customer's mind, a given hotel experience, as shaped by the set of promises made by a brand or hotel name and by the actual delivery upon those promises during the stay proper. As argued above, all hotel attributes are not equal in the customer value they create. These factors that drive customer value are called "value drivers" (e.g., location, room size and comfort, friendly staff). These value drivers in turn create benefits of various kinds (e.g., feeling worry-free, pampered, saving time) and ultimately shape customers' purchase and loyalty decisions. This comprehensive view of value is used in this chapter to study customer perspective.

Figure 1: A Comprehensive View of Customer Value

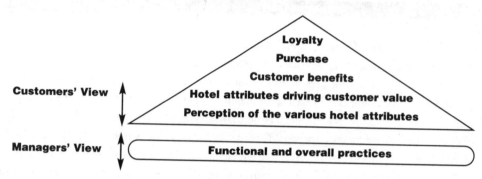

Results presented in this chapter were based uniquely on data from customer respondents who had been selected from a national list of end-users and intermediaries (see Methodology chapter). Interviews with 469 end-users (187 leisure, 168 business, 114 meeting/convention segments), 194 travel agents, and 123 meeting planners were conducted. Analyses were performed separately for end-users and intermediary customers.

Customer Value Created by Overall Best-Practice Champions

The content of customers' interviews was divided into distinct pieces of information. Each piece of information was assigned to a category of hotel attributes or customer benefits, according to the coding scheme presented in the Methodology chapter. We studied two distinct points of value creation in the service transaction: (1) when customers decide to book a room, and (2) as they stay at the hotel or, for the intermediary customers, as they do business with the hotel. We report first the results for end-user customers followed by those for intermediaries.

Value Created for End-User Customers

The results of this study indicate that the hotel attributes that drive customer purchase decisions are not the same attributes as those customers derive value from in the hotel experience proper. Moreover, our analyses reveal that unique customer value created during the experience significantly contributes to brand loyalty. After having elaborated on their purchase decisions regarding their last experience with one of the champions, responding customers were asked if something they had liked in particular stood out during their hotel experience and, if yes, to elaborate on which aspects of their stay had created value. Out of the 469 end-user customers we interviewed, 232 identified and elaborated on specific elements of the hotel stay that had created value for them; for the remaining respondents, no particular attribute significantly defined the hotel experience.

As a loyalty (intent) measure, all respondents were asked whether they were planning to stay at this hotel again on the next similar purchase occasion. The response options were "definitely yes," "definitely no," and "not sure." We compared the intentions of those who had derived some specific value from the hotel experience proper and those who did not. We found that creating value during a hotel experience significantly influenced customer loyalty. When unique customer value was created during the experience, 61 percent of the respondents stated that they would definitely stay at the same hotel on the next purchase occasion. When no particular value was created during the hotel experience (i.e., when customers were not able to remember anything they liked in particular during their stay at the hotel), the proportion expressing intent to return dropped to 41 percent. Translated in terms of revenues and profitability, a difference of such magnitude may be considerable.

In the next section of the report we present the value drivers in the purchase decision, followed by those tied to the hotel experience. We conclude with the various benefits (e.g., functional, psychological, social) derived from the hotel attributes creating value at the point of the purchase decision and the hotel experience.

Hotel Attributes Driving Purchase Decision

A total of 1,275 responses resulted in an average of 2.68 attributes being mentioned by each customer as factors driving the purchase decision. To keep the richness of customers' responses, hotel attribute categories were defined at a relatively specific level. To identify value drivers affecting the purchase decision, hotel attributes were grouped in the following set of general categories: location, value for money, brand name and reputation, physical property (exterior and public space), meeting rooms, guestroom, bathroom, service function, interpersonal service, food and beverage services, quality standards at in-stay services, and marketing. The other category grouped all infrequently mentioned hotel attributes. A description of these groupings is presented in Table 1.

Table 1: Specific Hotel Attributes within Value Driver Category

VALUE DRIVER CATEGORY	HOTEL ATTRIBUTES
Location	• Convenient location
Value for money	• Low/good prices • Value for money
Brand name and reputation	• Brand familiarity • Brand image/general • Recommendation/personal • Recommendation/travel agent • Brand image/segment • Brand image
Physical property (exterior and public space)	• Property/cleanliness • Property/overall • Property/aesthetics • Location/landscape • Property/size • Property/architecture • Property/public space
Guestroom design and amenities	• Room/overall • Room/size • Room/cleanliness • Room/comfort • Room/kitchenette • Room/aesthetics • Room/work equipment • Room/entertainment • Room/HVCA
Meeting room design and amenities	• Meeting room/overall • Meeting room/size • Meeting room/work equipment • Meeting room/furniture • Meeting room/clean linens

VALUE DRIVER CATEGORY	HOTEL ATTRIBUTES
Bathroom furniture and amenities	• Bathroom/amenities • Bathroom/size • Bathroom/furniture • Bathroom/overall • Bathroom/clean linens
Service, functional	• Service/overall • Service/speed • Service/efficiency • Check-in/check-out efficiency
Service, interpersonal	• Service/friendliness • Service/attentiveness • Service/professionalism • Service/customization • Personal recognition
F&B related services	• F&B/overall • F&B/quality • F&B/atmosphere • F&B/room service • F&B/variety • F&B/low or good prices
Quality standards at in-stay services	• Health club • Security • Variety of services • Housekeeping • Indoor pool • Executive floor • Business center
Marketing	• Room availability • Frequent-guest program • Discounts • Marketing
Other	• Event happening there • Client's choice

Figure 2 illustrates the top 10 hotel attributes driving customers' purchase decisions. As can be seen, results confirm the common belief that the key source of competitive advantage in the lodging industry is convenient location. Indeed, customers noted location as a primary determinant of their purchase decision in approximately one out of five responses.

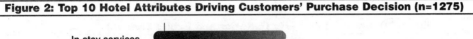

Figure 2: Top 10 Hotel Attributes Driving Customers' Purchase Decision (n=1275)

Brand name and reputation were mentioned with the second greatest frequency as source of customer value driving purchase. As can be seen in Figure 3A, the value associated with brand name and reputation was primarily derived from (1) customer familiarity with the brand, (2) customer perception of a positive and distinctive brand image, and (3) positive word-of-mouth from friends, family, and travel agents.

Figure 3A: Brand Name and Reputation (n=186)

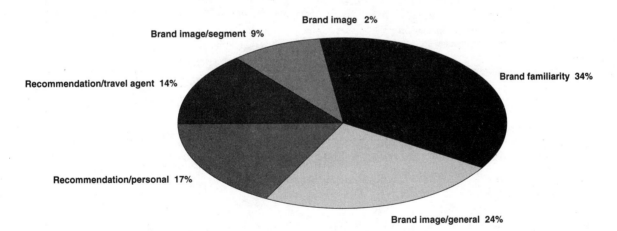

The physical appearance of the hotel exterior and public spaces as well as that of the guestroom were the next two most predominant hotel attributes driving customer purchase decisions. As Figure 3B reveals, close to 40 percent of customer responses in the hotel exterior/ public space category pertain to the cleanliness of the property. The overall quality of the physical properties and specific aesthetic aspects of the public spaces also were frequently identified as sources of customer value underlying purchase decisions.

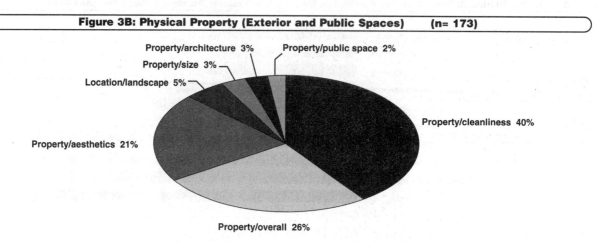

Figure 3B: Physical Property (Exterior and Public Spaces)   (n= 173)

Property/architecture 3%
Property/public space 2%
Property/size 3%
Location/landscape 5%
Property/cleanliness 40%
Property/aesthetics 21%
Property/overall 26%

Turning to the guestroom (see Figure 3C), customers noted with relatively equal frequency the overall quality of guestroom design and amenities, its size, cleanliness, and comfort. Guests also mentioned most room features, such as a kitchenette, work equipment, and entertainment.

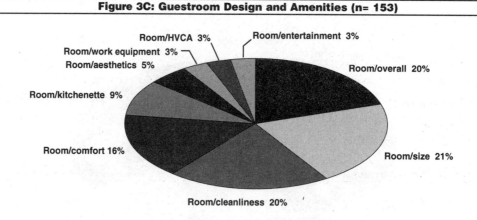

Figure 3C: Guestroom Design and Amenities (n= 153)

Room/HVCA 3%
Room/entertainment 3%
Room/work equipment 3%
Room/aesthetics 5%
Room/overall 20%
Room/kitchenette 9%
Room/size 21%
Room/comfort 16%
Room/cleanliness 20%

The fifth attribute driving a customer decision to stay at one of the overall practice champions comes from value for money, which in most instances focused on the price side of the value equation. It is interesting to note that functional and interpersonal aspects of services came in at sixth and seventh position as value drivers in the purchase decision. At the functional level, efficiency at check-in/out emerged as the hotel process most critical in driving customer purchase decision. Friendliness appeared to be the interpersonal dimension of service identified most frequently as a value driver at purchase, with less frequent mention of attentiveness and professionalism.

Of the marketing activities driving the customer purchase decision, an effective distribution system that makes rooms easily available was the most frequently mentioned marketing factor driving purchase, followed by frequent-stay programs. Discounts and advertising were less frequently mentioned.

In ninth position in the list of hotel attributes driving the purchase decision came quality standards of the various in-stay services, and their variety, and in tenth, food and beverage services. The presence of a health club, various security features, and the diversity of services offered are attributes that have bearing on the customer decision to stay in a hotel. Customers also listed various facets of food and beverage services as value drivers at purchase, with most references being made to the quality of food in general, and to a lesser extent, to room service.

To ascertain whether these value drivers at purchase generalized to all market segments, we compiled separately the relative predominance of these same set of core value driver categories in customers' purchase decisions from the leisure, business transient, and business meeting/convention market segments. As can be seen in Figure 4A, the hotel attributes driving leisure customers' purchase decision did not differ in significant ways from what was observed across the aggregated market segments.

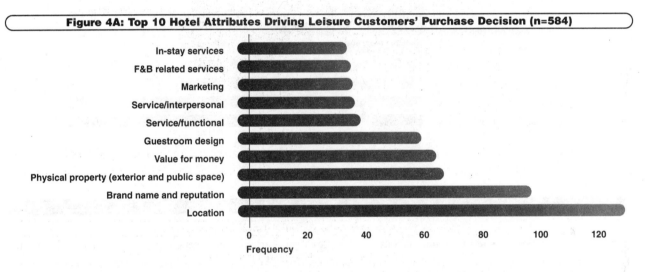

Figure 4A: Top 10 Hotel Attributes Driving Leisure Customers' Purchase Decision (n=584)

However, variations are observed for the two business segments. For transient-business customers, the supremacy of location as a value driver over any other hotel attribute is magnified, as revealed in Figure 4B. While brand name/reputation and physical aspects of the properties have about the same predominance as in the aggregate analysis, value for money and marketing efforts (in particular frequent-stay program) gained in the power of their effect on the purchase decision, to the detriment of services. Meeting rooms design, amenities, and service also emerged as sources of value driving the purchase decision.

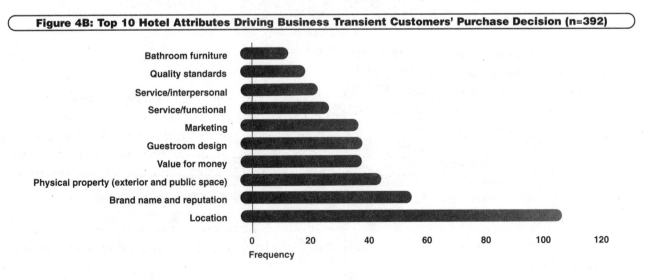

Figure 4B: Top 10 Hotel Attributes Driving Business Transient Customers' Purchase Decision (n=392)

The pattern of hotel attributes driving the purchase decision was even more differentiated for the business meeting and convention guests (see Figure 4C). The list of value drivers is now headed by the physical property, both in its public and private spaces. Location, brand name/reputation, value for money, and functional aspects of the service are much less predominant as value drivers for customers in the meeting and convention market than they were for the other two segments. Marketing had remarkably little influence on this segment.

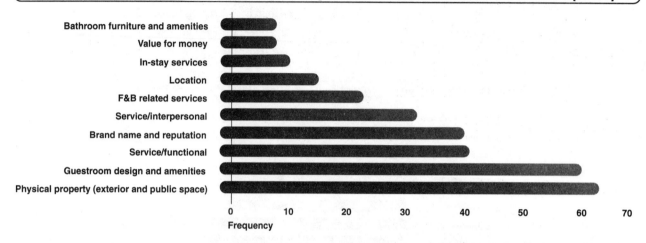

Figure 4C: Top 10 Hotel Attributes Driving Meeting/Convention Customers' Purchase Decision (n=299)

Value Drivers in the Hotel Experience

In this section, we report the results of our analysis of the value drivers derived from hotel experiences based on 232 customer respondents. The analyses mapped closely those reported for value drivers at purchase. Figure 5 presents the top 10 hotel attributes driving the creating of unique customer value during the hotel experience.

As can be seen in Figure 5, the top two most frequently mentioned sources of value during the hotel experience pertained to the physical quality of the property with guestroom design and amenities heading the list, followed very closely by exterior and public spaces.

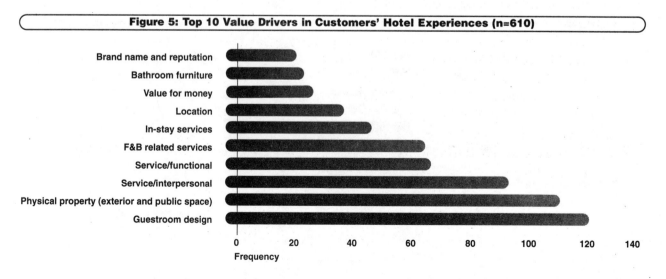

Figure 5: Top 10 Value Drivers in Customers' Hotel Experiences (n=610)

Figures 6A and 6B reveal that the specific guestroom and public space attributes creating customer value are the same regardless of where the customer is in the service transaction at the point of purchase decision or during the hotel stay.

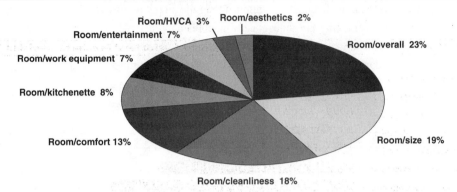

Figure 6A: Guestroom Design and Amenities (n=120)

Room/HVCA 3%
Room/aesthetics 2%
Room/entertainment 7%
Room/overall 23%
Room/work equipment 7%
Room/kitchenette 8%
Room/comfort 13%
Room/size 19%
Room/cleanliness 18%

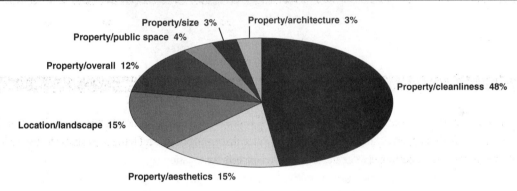

Figure 6B: Physical Property (Exterior and Public Space) (n=110)

Property/size 3%
Property/architecture 3%
Property/public space 4%
Property/overall 12%
Property/cleanliness 48%
Location/landscape 15%
Property/aesthetics 15%

Both interpersonal and functional aspects of service also were important sources of unique customer value during the hotel experience. While functional aspects of services surpassed the interpersonal components as sources of value in the purchase decision, the interpersonal aspects of services were mentioned more often as sources of value during the hotel stay than the functional aspects. The sources of customer value in terms of interpersonal services were more differentiated during the hotel experience than they were in the purchase decision. Service attentiveness, also present for the purchase decision, gained a larger share of value during the hotel experience. Customized service and personal recognition, which were absent in the purchase decision, were important as sources of value during the hotel experience.

The findings indicated that the functional service attributes creating value during the hotel experience remained more or less the same as for the purchase decision. That is, efficiency in check-in and check-out remained the only phase in the hotel process to be explicitly mentioned. Otherwise, 72% of the respondents referred to the overall service quality.

Food and beverage services, the next most frequently mentioned hotel attributes creating unique value during the stay, emerged as a more predominant source of value during the hotel experience than at the purchase decision. In fact, 10% of all mentions of components of hotel experiences that respondents particularly liked referred to food and beverage services. This proportion is twice as high as it was in the purchase-decision context. The relative contribution of specific attributes to value creation remains relatively unchanged except for room service being more frequently mentioned than the dining room/restaurant atmosphere as a source of value during the hotel stay, whereas both of them were about equally mentioned in the purchase-decision process.

Quality standards in various services during the stay also were valued by a reasonable number of customers. As Figure 6C revealed, the relative predominance of various services remained similar to that observed at purchase decision, with health clubs (39%) and the mere variety of services being offered (32%) heading the list of value drivers in this category.

Figure 6C: Quality Standards at In-Stay Services (n=44)

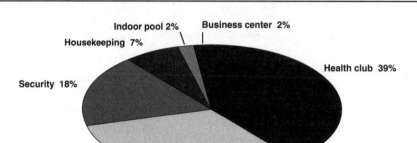

Indoor pool 2%   Business center 2%
Housekeeping 7%
Security 18%
Health club 39%
Variety of service 32%

The remaining hotel attributes that created unique customer value during the hotel experience, mentioned with less frequency, but nonetheless creating value for certain customers, were convenience of the location (for the guest who has to move around during the stay), bathroom fixtures and amenities, various marketing efforts, and meeting room design and amenities.

When hotel attributes creating unique value during the hotel experience were analyzed separately for the three market segments (see figures 7A, 7B, and 7C), physical aspects of the hotel were the primary value drivers in all market segments. However, leisure customers most valued exteriors and public spaces while both business segments valued various aspects of guestroom design and amenities more. Interpersonal aspects of services became the second value driver in all three segments. Food and beverage services retained its moderate status (i.e., fourth listed) as a value driver during the hotel experience for all three market segments.

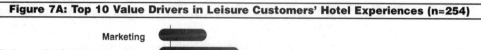

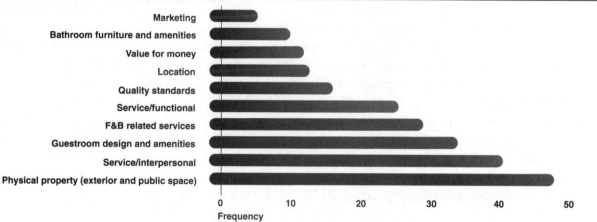

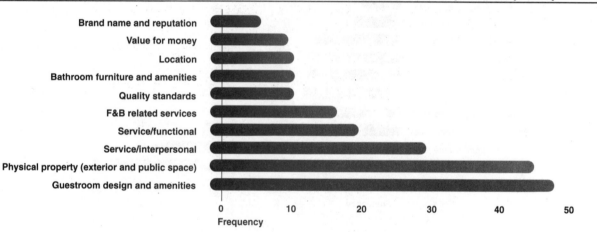

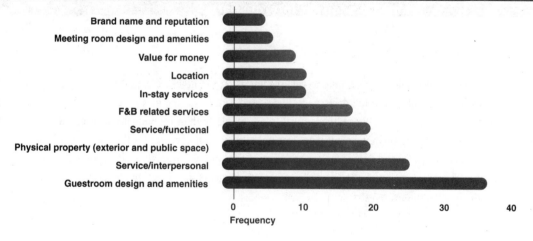

Customer Benefits

To better understand customer value, we inventoried the benefits that respondents associated with those hotel attributes they identified as value drivers at purchase or during the hotel stay. As argued earlier, these benefits often correspond to the way the hotel has positioned itself in the customer's mind through formal advertising campaigns. The top 10 most frequently mentioned benefits are presented in Figure 8. As can be seen, a large proportion of the customers could not specifically articulate the benefits they derived from various attributes of their hotel experience beyond saying that they were generally satisfied (that is, the hotel met their expectations). The next two benefits most often mentioned by customers are experiential in nature, specifically, a comfortable stay and an enjoyable experience. Two more functional benefits followed (i.e., having a convenient place to stay and a hassle-free stay). The next three, all with about equal salience, pertained to psychological benefits that hotels were able to induce, primarily by making customers feel secure, relaxed, and at home. In ninth and tenth positions were the two functional benefits of saving time and the ability to accumulate frequent-stay program points.

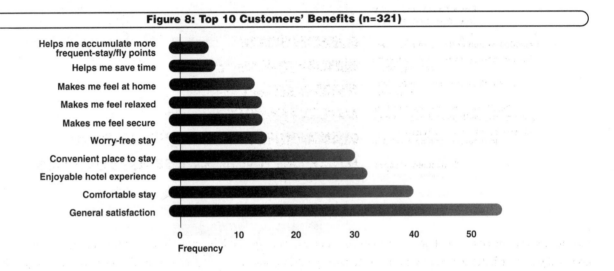

Figure 8: Top 10 Customers' Benefits (n=321)

Value Created for Intermediaries

Hotel Attributes

Hotel attributes driving purchase decision and creating unique value when using the hotel were analyzed for intermediaries. A grouping of specific attributes into a set of core value drivers was developed, similar to the grouping made for the end-users. However, because intermediaries do business with these hotels much more regularly than individual end-users, the distinction between value drivers at purchase and during the hotel experience was not as insightful as it was for the end-users. Therefore, we chose to combine the value drivers at purchase and during the experiencing of the hotel. On average, each respondent provided 1.44 hotel attributes. Figures 9A and 9B present the hotel attributes that drove travel agents' and meeting planners' perceptions of the value created by the overall practice champions.

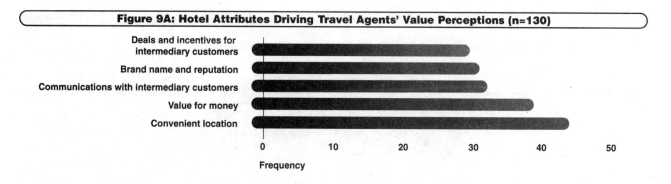

Figure 9A: Hotel Attributes Driving Travel Agents' Value Perceptions (n=130)

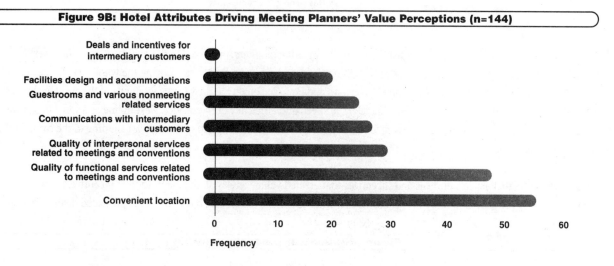

Figure 9B: Hotel Attributes Driving Meeting Planners' Value Perceptions (n=144)

As can be seen, convenient location is the dominant source of value for both intermediaries as it was for the end-users. For travel agents, three other hotel attributes were about equally significant sources of value: (1) the quality of communications with intermediaries, (2) the hotel brand name and reputation, and (3) the quality of the deals and incentives for intermediaries. For meeting planners, the functional quality of meeting/convention services emerged as the second most important source of value, followed at a reasonable distance by the interpersonal quality of meeting/convention services, the quality of communications with intermediaries, the quality of guestrooms and other nonmeeting related services, and the meeting room design and accommodations.

In analyzing in more detail the hotel attributes creating value, we have combined meeting planners and travel agents' responses whenever they mentioned attributes pertaining to the same value driver category. After convenient location, the second most important set of value drivers is the quality of communication with intermediaries. As can be seen in Figure 10A, three specific attributes contribute to such quality: namely, the efficiency of the computer systems for reservations, the quality of the sales representatives, and the quality of information follow-up on intermediary requests.

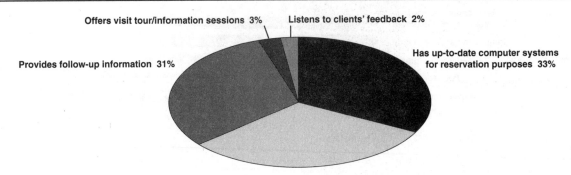

Figure 10A: Communication with Intermediary Customers (n=58)

Offers visit tour/information sessions 3%

Listens to clients' feedback 2%

Has up-to-date computer systems for reservation purposes 33%

Provides follow-up information 31%

Has good sales representatives 31%

The third source of value, mentioned almost exclusively by meeting planners, pertained to the quality of functional services related to meetings and conventions. Most respondents mentioned the service provided overall, during the whole event. The second hotel attribute to create value along this dimension was the food and beverage quality at the various functions of the event. A third attribute was efficient check-in/out. Mention also was made of the speed and efficiency of the service. Next in line as a value driver was value for money, with most intermediaries referring to low or good prices, with a small proportion (13%) alluding to the complete "value-for-money" equation.

Figure 10B shows that aspects of deals and incentives that created value were, first, the magnitude of incentives or commissions to the intermediary (50%), followed by the promptness of their payments (33%) and the value of the packaged deals (17%).

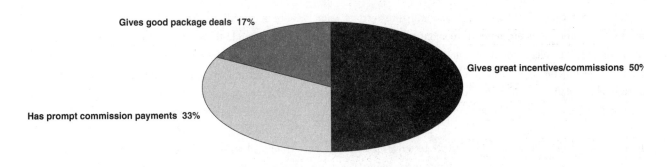

Figure 10B: Deals and Incentives (n=30)

Gives good package deals 17%

Gives great incentives/commissions 50%

Has prompt commission payments 33%

Turning to the interpersonal quality of services related to meetings and conventions, Figure 10C shows that the following qualities were mentioned in decreasing order of frequency: professionalism, friendliness, attentiveness, customization, and personal recognition.

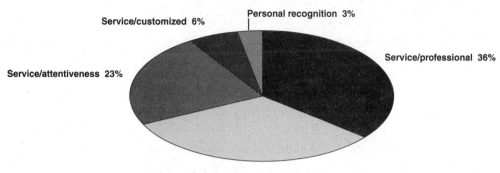

Figure 10C: Quality of Interpersonal Services Related to Meetings and Conventions (n=29)

Service/customized 6%
Personal recognition 3%
Service/professional 36%
Service/attentiveness 23%
Service/friendliness 32%

The eighth hotel attribute to create value for the intermediaries was guestroom and nonmeeting related services. The specific attributes included the overall quality of the guestrooms and specific aspects of the guestrooms, such as size, cleanliness, furniture comfort, work-related equipment, and kitchenette. Health clubs also were mentioned as a component of this value driver. Finally, various aspects of the physical facilities design and accommodations also were significant sources of value for intermediary customers. These were, in decreasing order of frequency, the hotel property overall, its aesthetics, its size, the size of meeting rooms, as well as the cleanliness of the property in general and of the public spaces.

Intermediaries' Outlook on Hotel Practices Underlying Value Drivers

Travel agents and meeting planners valued specific practices they perceive overall champions used. The top 10 most frequently mentioned practices are illustrated in Figure 11.

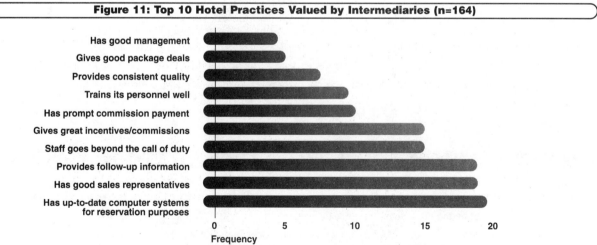

Figure 11: Top 10 Hotel Practices Valued by Intermediaries (n=164)

Has good management
Gives good package deals
Provides consistent quality
Trains its personnel well
Has prompt commission payment
Gives great incentives/commissions
Staff goes beyond the call of duty
Provides follow-up information
Has good sales representatives
Has up-to-date computer systems for reservation purposes

Frequency

The availability of technologically advanced and user-friendly computer systems for reservations is the most critical competency to creating value from the intermediaries' perspective. The hiring of good sales representatives and the availability of people and systems that allow a hotel to provide good follow-up information to intermediaries share the second position as needed hotel competencies.

Two other practices share the third position. Intermediaries recognized both the staff going beyond the line of duty, and the development of enticing incentive and commission schemes, as sources of value. The practices mentioned next, in decreasing order of frequency, were the promptness with which hotel companies were paying commissions and incentives, the way the hotel personnel were trained, various processes that enable the delivery of consistent quality, the compositions of package deals offered, and the overall quality of hotel management.

Intermediaries' Benefits

Figure 12 presents the benefits that travel agents and meeting planners associated with the hotel attributes they valued in our overall champions. As can be seen, one benefit clearly stood out. That is a worry-free, no-hassle transaction for the intermediary and the intermediary's customer (i.e., the end-user).

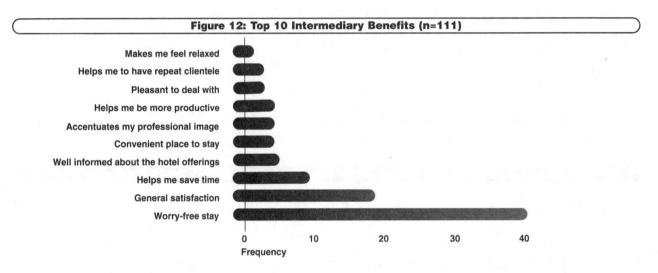

Figure 12: Top 10 Intermediary Benefits (n=111)

Around 20% of the intermediaries mentioned general satisfaction as a benefit. The next most frequently mentioned benefit pertained to saving time. A rich diversity of benefits were mentioned less frequently, and included being well-informed, convenience, accentuation of the intermediary's professional image, productivity, pleasure in dealing with them, help in building repeat clientele, and relaxation.

Customer Value Created by Top Performance in Functional Areas

In this section, we provide an in-depth analysis of the value customers derive from top performance in key functional areas of a hotel, with the objective of helping managers pinpoint those areas that have the strongest potential for improvement in terms of customer value and loyalty. We first evaluate the impact of a top performance in various functional areas on customer loyalty. Creating customer value per se is a laudable undertaking, but creating customer value that actually translates into customer loyalty is what maintains market share and profitability in the hypercompetitive condition of the current hotel market. Second, we identify those hotel attributes that created the most customer value in top performers in each functional area. Finally, we identify the hotel attributes that were able to create a set of customer benefits often used for positioning a brand or a hotel in the customers' minds.

End-users' Perspective

Loyalty Impact of Top Performance in Functional Areas

After having described the specific hotel attributes and the benefits created by their top performer on a given value driver, respondents were asked to indicate whether what they had just described would make them "give priority to this provider over other hotels on the next occasion." Respondents chose between "definitely yes," "definitely no," and "don't know." In Figure 13, we compare functional areas in terms of the proportion of end-user customers who declared that this would "definitely" make them remain loyal on the next occasion.

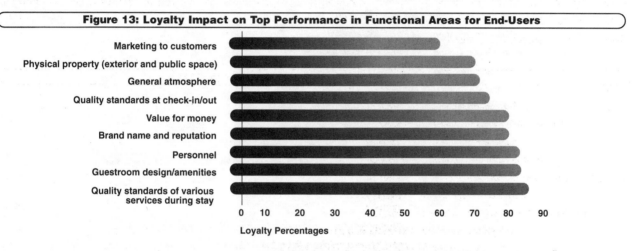

Figure 13: Loyalty Impact on Top Performance in Functional Areas for End-Users

In the preceding figure, the percentages represent portion of respondents for whom top performance in the functional area leads to loyalty

Different aspects of Figure 13 are worth highlighting. First, a top performance on any of the functional areas does create a tendency toward loyalty. The loyalty impact score, across functional area categories, ranges between 61% and 85%. The five functional areas that clearly have the largest loyalty impact are the quality standards of various services received during the hotel stay (loyalty impact score = 85%), the quality of the personnel (loyalty impact score = 83%), guestroom design/amenities (loyalty impact score = 83%), building brand name/reputation (loyalty impact score = 80%), and providing value for money (loyalty impact score = 80%).

Other powerful sources of customer loyalty were quality at check-in/out (loyalty impact score = 75%), as well as the general atmosphere (loyalty impact score = 71%) and the exterior/public spaces components of physical property (loyalty impact score = 70%). At the extreme end on the loyalty impact continuum, we can see that the type of functional practice that had the lowest loyalty impact was the marketing to the customers (loyalty impact score = 61%).

Hotel Attributes Driving Customer Value

In this section, we examine what specific hotel attributes, tied to each broad functional area of hotel management, create customer value. For each functional area, we illustrate the 10 most frequently mentioned attributes across all market segments. We present these functional areas in order of the loyalty impact of their top performance, with the most loyalty-inducing functional area being presented first; we also highlight similarities and differences across market segments.

Quality Standards in In-stay Services:

Figure 14A presents the most frequently mentioned hotel attributes creating customer value in the context of a top performance on the various services offered to the guest during the hotel stay. As can be seen, the largest number of respondents chose not to single out any specific quality of service or any part of the hotel experience, and instead identified the overall service quality of the hotel experience as that which created value.

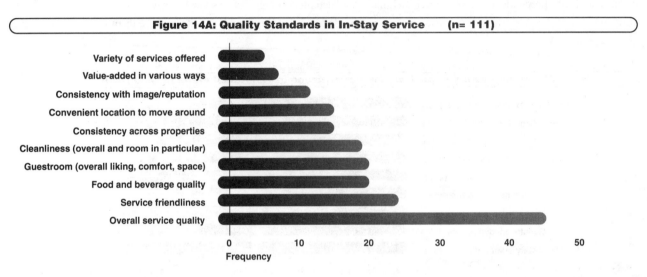

Figure 14A: Quality Standards in In-Stay Service (n= 111)

For those respondents who stated a specific quality of service as most critical, friendliness emerged as the most powerful source of customer value. Food and beverage quality, the guestroom experience (size and comfort), and the hotel cleanliness followed as other important sources of customer value during the hotel stay. Consistency in the delivery of these services across properties and with the brand image/reputation also created significant customer value. Finally, convenience of the hotel location in moving around during the stay and the variety of in-house services being offered also were attributes on which top performance created value. The predominance of overall service quality as being the most salient source of customer value during the hotel stay is constant across market segments. Market segments differed, though, in terms of their secondary value drivers: cleanliness for leisure guests, guestroom size and comfort for transient business guests, and low/good prices for various services during the stay for conventions/ meetings end-users.

Quality of the Personnel:

Figure 14B presents qualities of the service personnel most valued by customers. Many respondents did not refer to a specific dimension of service but instead alluded to the staff's ability to provide overall service quality. The most frequently mentioned characteristics regarding the quality of the service personnel were friendliness, attentiveness, consistency, efficiency, professionalism, clean appearance, and a distinctive personality. Friendliness and attentiveness are valued across all market segments, while professionalism emerged as a particularly important quality for the two business segments.

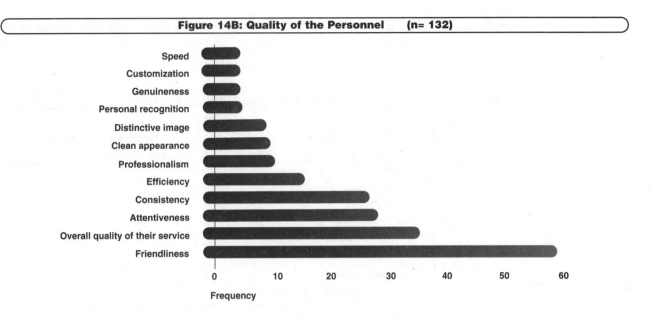

Figure 14B: Quality of the Personnel   (n= 132)

Guestroom Design and Amenities:

Figure 14C reveals the key features of the guestroom that are the most significant source of customer value, in decreasing order: the size of the room, its aesthetic quality, its cleanliness, the comfort of its furniture, the availability and quality of work-equipment, the presence of a kitchenette, the variety and quality of the bathroom amenities, and finally, its functional quality. The consistency of guestroom design across hotels for a given brand also was mentioned as an important source of customer value, figuring in the fourth position in Figure 14C.

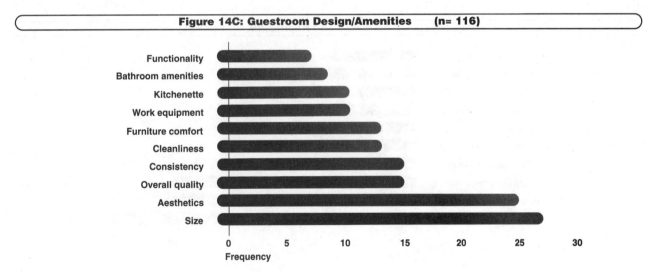

Figure 14C: Guestroom Design/Amenities   (n= 116)

The following table reveals numerous market segment differences in aspects of guestroom design/amenities that were sources of customer value. Leisure customers valued most functional aspects of the room whereas for both business travel segments, the room size and aesthetics were the two primary sources of value.

Table 2: Guestroom Design and Amenities, by Customer Segments		
Leisure end-users	**Business transient end-users**	**Meetings/conventions end-users**
Functionality	Size	Aesthetics
Cleanliness	Aesthetics	Size
Presence of kitchenette	Work equipment	Furniture comfort
Aesthetics	Overall quality of the room	Overall quality of the room
Size	Cleanliness	Consistency
Comfort	Consistency	Cleanliness
Bathroom amenities	Rooms on executive floors	

Brand Name and Reputation:

When asked to elaborate about top performance in terms of brand name and reputation, customers made two types of associations. Some pertained to the hotel attributes that contributed to establish the name or reputation. Others related to the qualities of a hotel that were derived from the hotel having a good brand name or reputation. For instance, in Figure 14D, service quality headed the list of attributes that creates a top brand name/reputation, particularly with the transient business customer segment. In addition, service friendliness figures the seventh in Figure 14D.

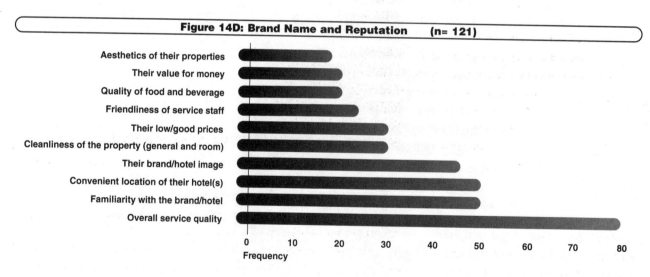

Figure 14D: Brand Name and Reputation   (n= 121)

The two following attributes sharing the second rank are derived from the hotel brand name and reputation: the sense of "knowing what to expect" that comes with familiarity, and the convenience of the hotel location. Familiarity was the most powerful value driver for the meeting/convention business segment whereas convenient location had the same moderate importance across all three segments. The next source of value comes from the actual image or reputation of the hotel/brand. Obviously, references were made to prestige and luxury image of certain hotels or a certain brand. However, references to high-quality levels or uniqueness of a hotel experience were made across all industry segments.

The next two hotel attributes to contribute the most to brand name and reputation were both of a functional nature: the cleanliness of the place, and low/good prices. For leisure customers, cleanliness was the hotel attribute associated most frequently with a top performance in brand name/reputation. As to the price aspect, the contribution of low/good prices to brand names may come from the relentless quest of various hotels to provide the same or more value to the customers at a lower price. Food and beverage, value for money, and aesthetics of the property completed the list of hotel attributes that contributed the most to the choice of a specific hotel as the top performer in terms of brand name/reputation.

Value for Money:

When including the provision of value for money as a distinct functional practice in this study, we were interested in learning whether "value of services" or the "price paid for services" would dominate in the equation used by customers to assess the best sources of value for a given purchase occasion. The most frequent associations customers made in accounting for their choice of their top performer on this value driver are presented in Figure 14E.

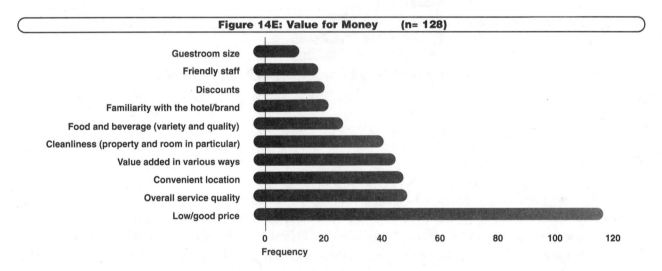

Figure 14E: Value for Money   (n= 128)

As can be seen in Figure 14E, customers did refer to both sides of the equation: The most frequently mentioned attribute was price, whether mentioned as a low price or a good price. This finding was consistent across all customer segments. The presence of discounts also emerged among the top 10 attributes most frequently mentioned. However, Figure 14E reveals a rich diversity of value-creating or value-adding hotel attributes, namely, overall service quality, convenient location, value added in various services during the stay, cleanliness, etc. In fact, fewer than one-third of customer responses represented in Figure 19 pertained to price and discount. There are interesting differences across segments in the various attributes that customers factor into their "value-for-money" equation. Service quality was the second source of customer value for leisure customers whereas this rank was occupied by convenient location for the two business segments. Leisure customers valued more cleanliness than various value-adding services during the stay — the converse was found for the two business segments.

Quality Standards at Check-in and Checkout:

The service qualities that customers associated with a top performance when they arrive at and leave the hotel (see Figure 14F) do not seem to be the same as those they revealed during their stay proper (see Figure 14A). At check-in and checkout time, what matters most is efficiency, which for some customers is translated to speed. These two service qualities combined represent close to 50% of all mentions of hotel attributes as a source of customer values represented in Figure 14F. Service friendliness, though, cannot be dismissed. It remains the third quality of service most frequently mentioned at the entry and exit points of the hotel experience. Overall service quality and consistency across hotels also were significant sources of customer value. Finally, the other attributes most frequently mentioned at check-in and checkout pertained to the aesthetics quality of the lobby and check-in counter, personal recognition, acknowledgement of frequent-stay program membership, and services customization, such as the choice of room at check-in or flexibility in checkout time. Except for acknowledgement of the frequent-stay program and lobby/check-in counter layout being respectively mentioned uniquely by transient and meeting/convention business segments, sources of customer value with top performance on this functional practice did not vary across market segments.

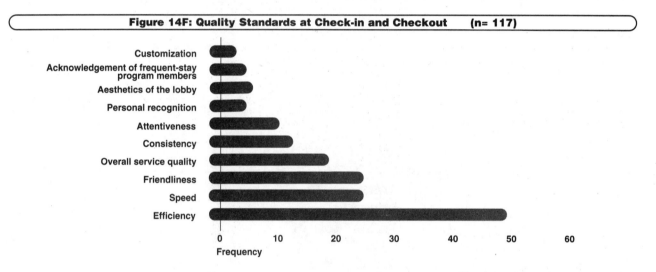

Figure 14F: Quality Standards at Check-in and Checkout   (n= 117)

General Atmosphere:

The functional practices related to the setting of the general atmosphere of the place are numerous and interrelated. Identifying which specific hotel attributes contribute the most to customer value for top performance on this practice is likely to be a challenge for customers and managers alike. Is it the place? Is it the people? It's hard to say. In Figure 14G, we illustrate those aspects of the hotel experience that were salient when customers were describing their experience at those hotels they had just chosen as the top performers in terms of general atmosphere.

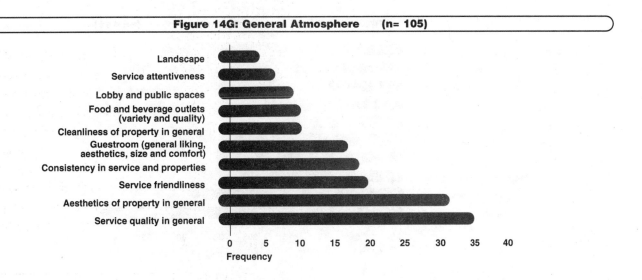

Figure 14G: General Atmosphere (n= 105)

Not surprisingly, the quality of service and the aesthetics of the property are almost face to face at the top of hotel attributes that contribute the most to the creation of customer value from top performance in terms of general atmosphere. Service seems to dominate physical property, though, as a source of customer value: Not only is overall service quality mentioned slightly more often than the aesthetic quality of the property but also the friendliness quality of service is the third attribute in Figure 14G. Moreover, service attentiveness is another quality of service to figure among the most frequently mentioned sources of customer value for hotel atmosphere.

Various aspects of guestrooms and, for hotel brands, consistency across properties were two other frequently mentioned sources of customer values. Next on the list come the pervasive cleanliness attribute, the variety and quality of food and beverage services available in-house, the various aspects of lobby and public spaces, and, finally, the landscape. Little difference was observed across market segments, with variations corresponding to a slightly different mixture of the basic ingredients mentioned above.

Physical Property (Exterior and Public Spaces):

Figure 14H presents the qualities of a hotel's physical property (other than those specifically tied to the guestroom) whose top performance contribute the most to customer value. As can be seen, the aesthetic quality of the property (be it in general, for the lobby and public spaces, or the landscape) surpassed functional aspects. Functional qualities mentioned as a source of value were primarily location, but also cleanliness and comfort. Among the public spaces, those that were mentioned most often as specific sources of customer values were the food and beverage outlets and the health club, the two being valued most by leisure customers. For both business segments, the two most powerful value drivers were aesthetics and a convenient location.

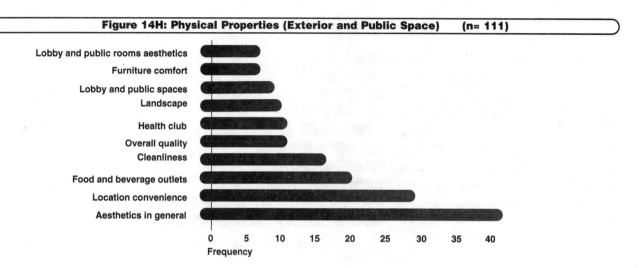

Figure 14H: Physical Properties (Exterior and Public Space)   (n= 111)

Marketing to the Customers:

As can be seen in Figure 14I, when respondents were asked to talk about customer value created by various marketing efforts (such as advertising, promotion, frequent-guest programs, etc.), they referred primarily to various aspects of their top performers' advertising and promotions. A good number of associations pertained to the appealing style and theme of these persuasive and informative communications; others related to the actual benefits being promoted or to the image that was conveyed. Interestingly, customers recognized the key "communication and promotional agent" role played by the contact staff with whom they interact on a day-to-day basis while they stay at the hotel. Staff communication appears second among the most frequently mentioned attributes presented in Figure 14I.

Customers also derived significant value from the sense of familiarity, "of knowing what will happen," that comes with a strong and positive brand image. Next in line as the source of customer value created along the standard marketing dimension came pricing and discount. Contrary to common belief, albeit figuring in the list of most frequently mentioned attributes, frequent-stay programs did not represent a very high proportion of customers' mentions as attributes creating value. In fact, it represents only 5 percent of all attribute mentions represented in Figure 14I. Other sources of customer value in this category were the depth of knowledge that the hotel had of its target customers as well as the word of mouth it was able to generate by travel agents and personal sources.

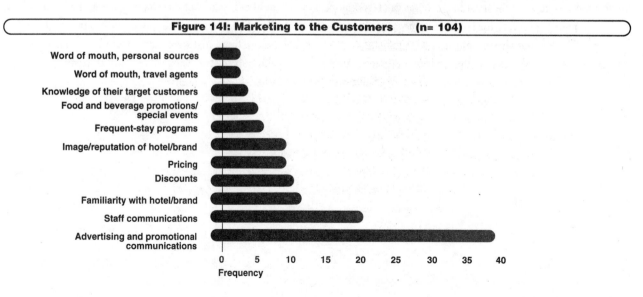

Figure 14I: Marketing to the Customers   (n= 104)

Table 3: Marketing to the Customers, by Customer Segments

Leisure end-users	Business transient end-users	Meetings/conventions end-users
Advertising and promotional communications	Advertising and promotional communications	Advertising and promotional communications
Staff communication	Staff communication	Image/reputation of the hotel/brand
Familiarity with the hotel/brand	Pricing	Discounts
Discounts	Frequent-stay programs	Pricing
	Image/reputation of the hotel/brand	Familiarity with the hotel/brand
	Discounts	

Customer Benefits

In this set of analyses, we identified those customer benefits most frequently created by top performances in the portfolio of functional areas covered in the survey. For those benefits that were most often mentioned, we proceeded to the detailed analysis of the various ways in which hotels were able to create such benefits. As depicted in Figure 15, respondents were able to describe precisely the functional, psychological, or social benefits they could derive from their favorite performers in the various functional areas.

Figure 15 reveals that of all the specific benefits end-users derive from a hotel stay, "no-worry, hassle-free stay" emerged clearly as the primary benefit sought by the customers of the American lodging industry, across market segments. This finding is highly consistent with earlier research focusing on the business luxury market in which Dubé et al. (1997) found that "having a worry-free stay" was the benefit most desired by American customers while being much less dominant in customers from other cultural backgrounds such as Asia.

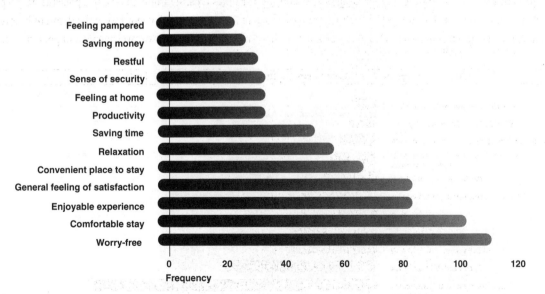

Figure 15: Customer Benefits Derived from Top Performance in Functional Areas   (n= 737)

Comfort emerged as the second benefit that customers derived from the value created by their favorite lodging providers. Two benefits shared the third position: (1) an enjoyable experience, i.e., various aspects of the hotel experience that have created enjoyment for the customer, and (2) a general sense of satisfaction, a feeling that customers got what they expected or what they needed. The next two benefits to appear in Figure 15 are of a functional nature: convenience and saving time. The split between experiential and functional benefits persists among the remaining benefits in Figure 15, some being experiential in nature (namely relaxation, rest, and feeling at home), some functional (productivity, security, and saving money). In addition, respondents also mentioned a restful stay, saving money, and feeling pampered as benefits occasionally created by a hotel experience.

Worry-Free Stay:

As can be seen in Figure 16A, there are various actions that hotel providers can do to make customers feel they are having a worry-free stay. The most frequently mentioned functional areas from which customers derived this benefit were, in decreasing order of frequency, the personnel's attitudes and actions, quality standards at check-in/out, the brand name/reputation of the hotel, and the guestroom design and amenities.

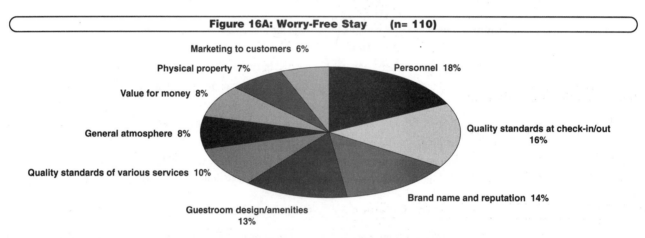

Figure 16A: Worry-Free Stay   (n= 110)

Marketing to customers 6%
Physical property 7%
Value for money 8%
General atmosphere 8%
Quality standards of various services 10%
Guestroom design/amenities 13%
Personnel 18%
Quality standards at check-in/out 16%
Brand name and reputation 14%

Comfortable Stay:

Figure 16B reveals that guestroom design and amenities most frequently provide guests with a sense of comfort, much more so than the public spaces. The other three functional areas that contributed the most to create comfort were the service provided by the personnel, value being added at various points of the hotel experience, and the quality standards upheld during the stay.

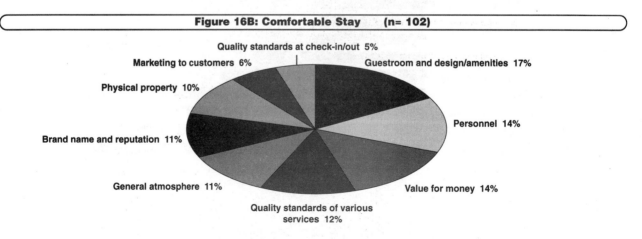

Figure 16B: Comfortable Stay   (n= 102)

Quality standards at check-in/out 5%
Marketing to customers 6%
Physical property 10%
Brand name and reputation 11%
General atmosphere 11%
Quality standards of various services 12%
Guestroom and design/amenities 17%
Personnel 14%
Value for money 14%

Enjoyable Experience:

The guestroom and its amenities are the hotel attributes most likely to create an enjoyable experience for the customer (see Figure 16C). The brand/hotel image and reputation as well as interaction with hotel personnel, perceived value for money, and various aspects of the physical properties also may shape an enjoyable experience.

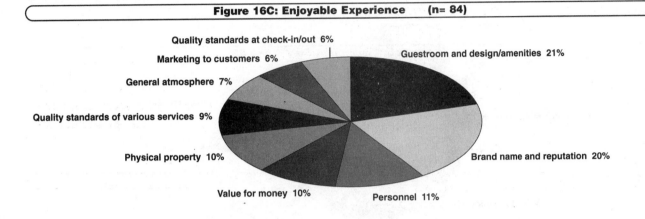

Figure 16C: Enjoyable Experience   (n= 84)

Quality standards at check-in/out 6%
Marketing to customers 6%
General atmosphere 7%
Quality standards of various services 9%
Physical property 10%
Value for money 10%
Personnel 11%
Guestroom and design/amenities 21%
Brand name and reputation 20%

General Feeling of Satisfaction:

In Figure 16D, we can observe the four functional areas that were most frequently recognized as creating general satisfaction for the guests. These areas consisted of the brand name or reputation, the personnel, the quality standards of various services during the stay, and the guestroom design/amenities.

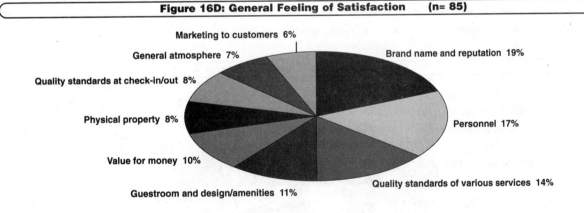

Figure 16D: General Feeling of Satisfaction   (n= 85)

Marketing to customers 6%
General atmosphere 7%
Quality standards at check-in/out 8%
Physical property 8%
Value for money 10%
Guestroom and design/amenities 11%
Brand name and reputation 19%
Personnel 17%
Quality standards of various services 14%

Convenient Stay:

From the pool of functional areas on which we surveyed the customers, the general atmosphere of the place and its quality standards on various services during the stay were the most powerful contributor to a convenient stay (see Figure 16E). Respondents also frequently mentioned certain marketing efforts to the customers (namely frequent-guest programs) and the brand image/reputation.

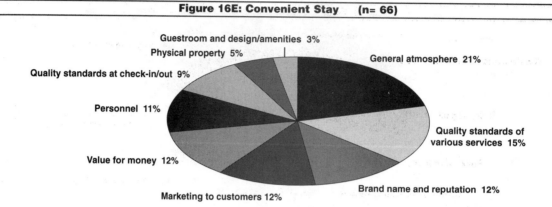

Figure 16E: Convenient Stay   (n= 66)

- Guestroom and design/amenities 3%
- Physical property 5%
- Quality standards at check-in/out 9%
- Personnel 11%
- Value for money 12%
- Marketing to customers 12%
- General atmosphere 21%
- Quality standards of various services 15%
- Brand name and reputation 12%

Saving Time:

The hotel functional area that customers saw as critically helping them save time was the quality standards at check-in/out. More than 50% of all respondents mentioned this practice, as presented in Figure 16F.

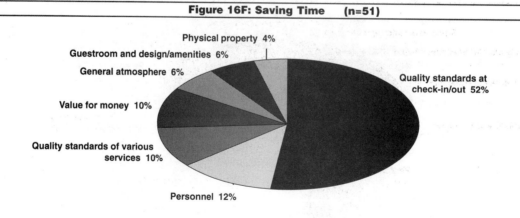

Figure 16F: Saving Time   (n=51)

- Physical property 4%
- Guestroom and design/amenities 6%
- General atmosphere 6%
- Value for money 10%
- Quality standards of various services 10%
- Personnel 12%
- Quality standards at check-in/out 52%

Relaxation:

According to the results presented in Figure 16G, guestroom design and amenities and the general atmosphere of the hotel create relaxation as a significant benefit to customers. Slightly less frequently mentioned, but equally important to a hotel's ability to induce customer relaxation as a benefit, were the brand name and reputation, the property's exterior (specifically landscape and view), and various actions or attitudes of the personnel.

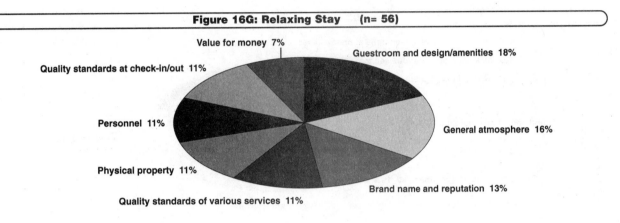

Figure 16G: Relaxing Stay   (n= 56)

Value for money 7%
Guestroom and design/amenities 18%
Quality standards at check-in/out 11%
Personnel 11%
General atmosphere 16%
Physical property 11%
Brand name and reputation 13%
Quality standards of various services 11%

Feeling at Home:

As can be seen in Figure 16H, it is the value-added features and the quality standards of the various services received during the stay that contribute the most to a feeling of being at home. Not surprisingly, the quality of the personnel and the general atmosphere of the place follow not far behind as important sources of this benefit as well.

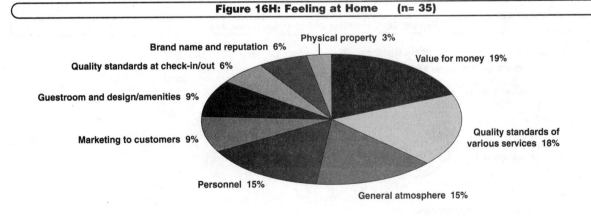

Figure 16H: Feeling at Home   (n= 35)

Brand name and reputation 6%
Physical property 3%
Quality standards at check-in/out 6%
Value for money 19%
Guestroom and design/amenities 9%
Quality standards of various services 18%
Marketing to customers 9%
Personnel 15%
General atmosphere 15%

Sense of Security:

Personnel plays a key role as the hotel attribute from which customers derive most of their sense of security during a hotel stay. One out of four respondents mentioned personnel as the value driver that antecedes this benefit (see Figure 16I). In terms of physical property, the exterior and public spaces were the second most frequently mentioned attribute inducing a sense of security, more so than the guestroom.

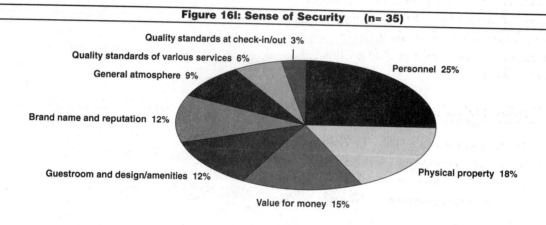

Figure 16I: Sense of Security   (n= 35)

Quality standards at check-in/out 3%
Quality standards of various services 6%
General atmosphere 9%
Brand name and reputation 12%
Guestroom and design/amenities 12%
Value for money 15%
Personnel 25%
Physical property 18%

Feeling Pampered:

As revealed in Figure 16J, customers equally mentioned the personnel and the general atmosphere as being key value drivers in a hotel's ability to make them feel pampered and special. Albeit less frequently, customers also mentioned various features of the guestroom design and specific steps in the check-in/out process as giving them this sense of being pampered and individually taken care of.

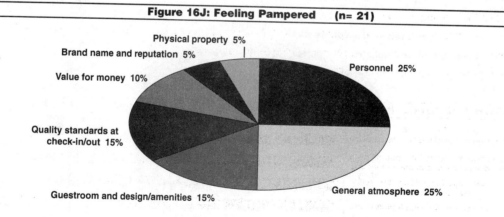

Figure 16J: Feeling Pampered   (n= 21)

Physical property 5%
Brand name and reputation 5%
Value for money 10%
Quality standards at check-in/out 15%
Guestroom and design/amenities 15%
Personnel 25%
General atmosphere 25%

Intermediaries' Perspective

Loyalty Impact of Top Performance on Functional Practices

The loyalty impact of functional areas was analyzed for intermediaries following the same approach as for the end-users. Analysis was performed separately for travel agents and meeting planners. Figure 17A presents, for the travel agents, the loyalty impacts of top performance in terms of brand name and reputation, value for money for the end-user, and promotion/incentives and communications with intermediaries. It is noteworthy that the loyalty impact score of functional areas was much weaker than it was for the end-users, with brand name and reputation and value for money both scoring 62% compared to a loyalty score of 80% for end-users. Even lower loyalty scores were observed for promotion-incentives to intermediaries (57%) and communication with intermediaries (48%).

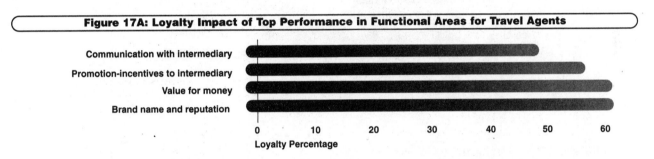

Figure 17A: Loyalty Impact of Top Performance in Functional Areas for Travel Agents

Figure 17B tells a very different story for meeting planners. For this type of intermediary customer, the functional areas that they deemed important — namely, quality of service related to meeting/conventions, meeting/conventions facility design and accommodations, promotion/incentives, communications with intermediaries, guestrooms, and various nonmeeting-related services and accommodations — were much more strongly tied to loyalty than they were for travel agents, with loyalty impact scores ranging between 69% and 83%. Moreover, two functional practices clearly distanced others in terms of loyalty impact. These were quality of services related to meeting and conventions, and the quality of communications with intermediaries, respectively scoring 83% and 82%. It seems that for meeting planners, service quality matters more than bricks, mortar, and technology. The loyalty impact of meeting/conventions facilities design and accommodations lags behind with a score of 70%. Finally, loyalty impact scores for guestrooms and various nonmeeting-related services and accommodations, and quality of promotions and incentives given to intermediaries, were respectively at 69% and 64%.

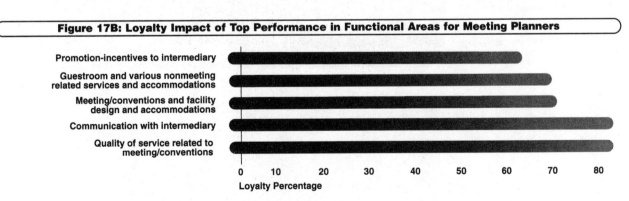

Figure 17B: Loyalty Impact of Top Performance in Functional Areas for Meeting Planners

Communication with Intermediaries:

As can be seen in Figure 18A, in addition to the overall quality of services provided by hotel sales representatives or the reservation staff, there are various qualities of service that can create value for the intermediaries. These are, in decreasing order of frequency, consistency, attentiveness, efficiency, speed, friendliness, and customization.

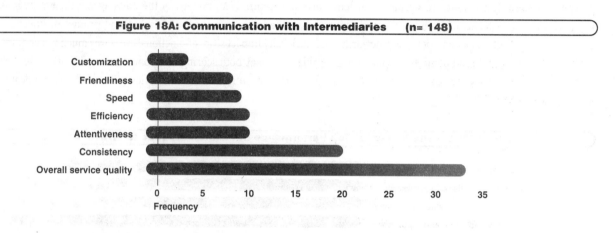

Figure 18A: Communication with Intermediaries (n= 148)

Promotions and Incentives for Intermediaries:

Interestingly, Figure 18B suggests that the most effective way to create value in terms of promotions or incentives is by providing intermediaries with either hotel rooms at a "good" regular price, hotel rooms at a discount, and/or presenting good value for money. These were the three most frequent responses when intermediaries were asked what is it that hotels do to be top performers in this functional area. Other attributes mentioned were attractive basic commission rates and incentive programs as well as the speed with which commissions and incentives were paid.

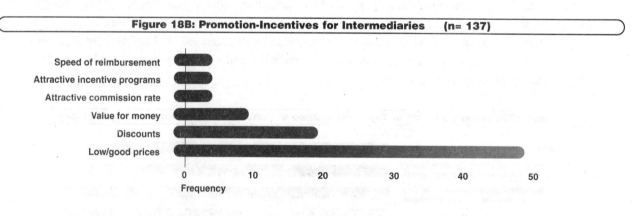

Figure 18B: Promotion-Incentives for Intermediaries (n= 137)

Quality of Services Related to Meetings and Conventions:

As can be seen in Figure 18C, in addition to the overall quality of the services provided by the sales representatives and the hotel staff involved in the event, respondents mentioned the specific qualities of these services as significant sources of value. These qualities included friendliness, attentiveness, consistency, professionalism, and efficiency. Value for meeting planners also was tied to the knowledge that the hotel representative and staff had of the precise needs of their target customers, and to the quality of food and beverage served in various social functions

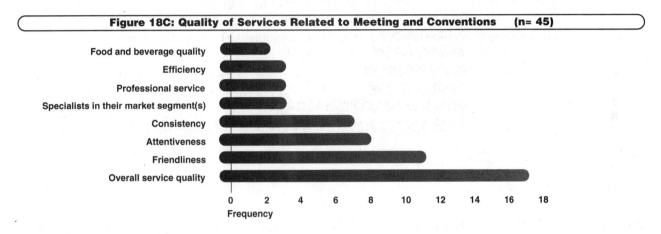

Figure 18C: Quality of Services Related to Meeting and Conventions   (n= 45)

Meeting and Convention Facility Design and Accommodations:

Figure 18D shows that of all hotel attributes, the fact that meeting planners know the type of meeting and convention facilities they will get from those hotels or brand of hotels with which they are familiar adds significant value. Not surprisingly, the convenience of the location of these facilities came in second as a source of value. The next four attributes, contributing equally to customer value, are the size of the property and three aspects of the meeting rooms, namely, overall room quality, room size, and room technological equipment. The speed of service on this equipment also was featured among the sources of value. The aesthetic quality of the property in general, that of the landscape, and of the meeting rooms all contributed to create value for the meeting planner.

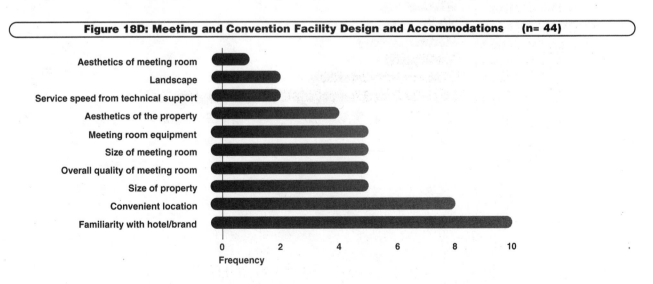

Figure 18D: Meeting and Convention Facility Design and Accommodations   (n= 44)

367

Quality of Guestroom and Various Nonmeeting Related Services and Accommodations:

In recommending or in choosing to hold a meeting or a convention at a given hotel, other aspects of the guest experience during the stay are factored in the meeting planner's decision. The overall quality of these services emerged as the most significant source of value. The general quality of the guestrooms and room aesthetics followed. Meeting planners also listed the rich diversity of services, guestrooms, and general physical property attributes as equally adding to their perception of value. For services, the important qualities were friendliness and attentiveness. For the guestroom, important attributes were related to its comfort and cleanliness. Finally, for the physical property in general, important attributes pertained to its overall quality, its aesthetics, and its cleanliness.

Travel Agents' Perspective on Hotel Practices in Terms of Brand Name/Reputation and Value for Money:

For travel agents, a hotel's top performance on brand name and reputation was primarily associated with overall service quality, ability to develop a brand image attuned to its specific market, low/good prices, convenient location, and the sense of familiarity that comes with a well-established name/reputation. In terms of attributes underlying top performance in value for money, travel agents also ranked the price side of the equation first, followed by service quality, convenient location, cleanliness of the property, and a variety of in-stay services, including food and beverage.

Intermediary Benefits

In elaborating upon the benefits created for travel agents and meeting planners by their favored top performers in the various functional areas, the types of benefits mentioned were not as diversified as those identified by end-users. The most frequently mentioned benefits are presented in Figure 19. As can be seen, beyond general satisfaction, the ability of a hotel to make hotel services completely hassle-free, with no worry, is a highly important benefit for the intermediary customers, as it was for end-users. With this one exception, benefits mentioned most often by an intermediary are of a strict functional nature: helping them to be more productive, to develop their repeat business, to help them know the products they are selling to their end-users, and saving time. Intermediary customers also mentioned "pleasant to do business with" as a significant benefit.

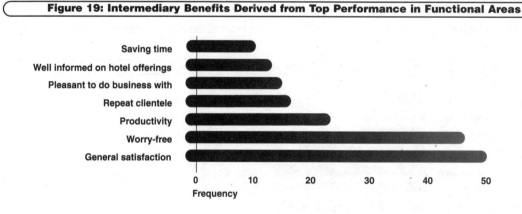

Figure 19: Intermediary Benefits Derived from Top Performance in Functional Areas (n= 165)

Comparing Customers' and Managers' Perspectives on the Lodging Industry Best Practices

Phase II of this research project reported on managers' perspectives on the best practices in the U.S. lodging industry. Phase III did the same, but from the perspective of the customers of businesses operating in the U.S. lodging industry. How do the two perspectives compare? The overall best practices presented can be seen as the reflection of the business strategies put in place by the champions in various industry segments to make their hotels compelling for the guests, the employees, and the investors. The portfolio of functional practices that emerged from Phase II represents these areas of practice that managers consider critical to achieving success in the lodging industry since these are the areas in which time, money, and efforts are invested in improvement and innovation. However, the overall and functional practices emphasized by industry managers may not be those deemed of importance by customers interviewed in Phase III; that is, a discrepancy between the perspectives may exist. Such a discrepancy, if it exists, may signal strategic opportunities or bring into question whether managers invest in developing those best practices with the highest return. In this section, we compare customers' and managers' perspectives on overall and functional best practices.

Comparison of Overall Best Practices

A short list of leading hotel attributes drove customers to purchase rooms at the overall best-practice champions. The five most powerful were location, brand name and reputation, public spaces (e.g., exteriors, lobby, and landscape), guestroom design and amenities, value for money and functional aspects of the service. Unique value during the hotel experience was primarily created by the public spaces, the guestroom, the interpersonal and the functional aspects of service as well as the hotel food and beverage services value built up loyalty. For a hotel company to be able to deliver on these prerequisites of customer purchase and loyalty, the set of managerial decisions must encompass real estate investment, property design and management, organizational culture of developing people, and processes to organize, manage, and improve upon. How consistent were the overall champions' business strategies with the decisions and actions necessary to deliver those hotel attributes driving their customers' purchase decisions and creating unique value during the hotel experience?

In reviewing the overall-best-practices case studies, there are striking similarities across most of the hotel brands designated as champions in the various segments of the lodging industry. Briefly stated, most of the overall champions had a strong and clear statement delineating the hotel concept or brand, and the champions had aligned properties, people, processes, marketing, and finances accordingly. Not surprisingly, when we turn to the customers' perspectives, we observe that the various factors driving value, as perceived by the customers, largely correspond with the practices the champions have instituted and the positioning of their hotels.

In fact, the close alignment between managers' views of practices that they believe add value and customers' perceptions of sources of value may be, indeed, a large part of what has driven these hotel brands and properties to the summit of their industry segment. While correspondence between the two views are close in terms of the hotel attributes driving customer value, there is still significant room for improvement in building up customer loyalty by providing unique customer value on every stay. We found that more than 50 percentage of the customers of overall champions were unable to think of anything in particular that had created unique value during their stay. Yet, creating unique value during the hotel stay was associated with a 20 percentage point increase in loyalty intent. Results of our analyses of the various hotel attributes that can induce specific customer benefits may be insightful for managers who want to improve upon the unique customer value they can create during the guest's stay at their hotel.

Comparison of Functional Best Practices

Consistent with the generally accepted belief that in services industries such as lodging, if management takes care of the employees, they will in turn take care of the customers, the largest portion of functional best practices to emerge was in the areas of process and human resources management. These noted practices were ultimately designed to improve service levels. Congruently, the results of our customers' survey indicate that service is, in the various ways in which it translates, a critical source of customer value. Functional and interpersonal aspects of services were respectively positioned at sixth and seventh as hotel attributes driving customers' purchase decision, and respectively positioned at third and fourth as a value driver during the hotel stay. In addition, personnel and the quality of various services during the stay were the two functional areas with the largest loyalty impact. Service was an even more powerful source of value for intermediary customers, in particular the meeting planners. Thus, in terms of service, we found a reasonably good alignment between customers' and managers' perspectives on functional best practices that create value for customers.

The second functional area in which many of the best practices emerged from the managers' side is that of traditional marketing activities, e.g., distribution system, pricing and revenue management, promotions, advertising, and loyalty or frequency programs. Here also, the customer's perspective is reasonably in line with the manager's. Many of these marketing practices aimed at developing brand name and reputation, ensuring the constant availability of rooms and providing value for money. These were all value drivers for the customers, be they end-users or intermediaries, in particular in their purchase decision. Frequency or loyalty programs were particularly valued by the business transient customer segments. It is important to note, though, in assessing the impact of these marketing practices on the customers, that these were associated with the lowest loyalty impact score.

Another area of functional practices in which customers' and managers' perspectives are reasonably in line is that related to the value-for-money aspect. A hotel's ability to deliver value for money, the fifth source of value driving the purchase decision, is tied to the cost-efficiency of its processes and its revenue management systems. A good number of best functional practices that emerged from managers were aimed precisely at this double objective.

A last area of functional practices in which customers' and managers' perspectives seem relatively aligned is that of food and beverage. From both perspectives, food and beverage services seem to be of moderate importance. One out of 10 hotel attributes mentioned as driving customer value during the hotel experience related to food and beverage services. A slightly lower proportion of managers' functional best practices focused on food and beverages. The banquet function area of food and beverage, however, may warrant further best-practice development. This domain of practice is noticeably absent from the managers' nominations for best practices, yet it is a significant source of value driving meeting planners' decisions.

A highly important area of divergence between customers' and managers' perspectives on functional practices falls into the realm of the physical aspects of lodging services. Only 4 percent functional best practices depicting managers' viewpoints on best practices related specifically to various aspects of the physical property. Yet, customers perceive that these hotel attributes are more powerful value drivers than service levels proper. Indeed, physical property elements represent three out of the top five value drivers at purchase. During the hotel experience, guestroom design/amenities and the exterior/public spaces are respectively positioned at first and second among the most frequently mentioned sources of value.

The discrepancy between customers and managers regarding the level of importance that physical property elements appear to play may be explained by two factors. First, delivering customer value on hotel attributes tied to physical quality are less dependent upon the day-to-day operations and therefore less urgent for managers who must regularly monitor the multiple ways in which people and processes can vary from one transaction to the next. Consequently, time-starved hotel managers are less likely to pay heed to physical property attributes. Second, another reason for managers' low priority on developing best practices to improve upon the physical side of products is related to the structural relationship between owners and managers in the lodging industry. Owners manage real estate, build, and renovate properties. Managers manage operations and maintain properties. As a result, architecture and design professionals typically decide issues that define the attractiveness of public spaces and guestrooms, with little input from managers and customers alike.

Nevertheless, the few best functional practices relating to physical aspects of hotels convincingly demonstrate that an industry refocus is possible. Consider the functional case reporting on the development of "Kidsuites" at Holiday Inn Hotel and Suites, Main Gate East. The operating partner and general manager teamed in the development of guestrooms that could best meet the demands of vacationing families in an innovative and profitable way. Similar integration of customers' views with managers' best practices in designing physical facilities is also evident in the other cases of functional best practices in this category; the design of Courtyard by Marriott is a convincing case in point.

In fact, the results of the customer survey and the insights provided by the few pioneers in the industry who have started to pave the way suggest that, at the level of the lodging industry as a whole, developing practices related to the physical components of a hotel stay may be a highly profitable agenda. In fact, in considering the overall practice champions that currently dominate in the various industry segments, one can observe a close integration of physical and service aspects of the lodging services at the core of their business strategies. For managers who wish to further the development of physical property best practices to create more value for their customers, the detailed analysis of the various features customers valued in public spaces and guestrooms may be insightful. These features were identified earlier in this chapter.

A tighter integration between customers' and managers' perspectives concerning the area of brand image and reputation also would benefit the lodging industry. Brand name and reputation came just after convenient location as a primary driver of customer value at purchase, and conformity to the brand image was important to the customer during the actual hotel experience. Yet, in spite of the fact that all managers interviewed on best functional practices were invited to elaborate on the ways in which the practice contributed to the hotel's ability to deliver the promises made to the customers, very few managers had a clear vision in this regard. Although the exception, a few functional best-practice cases, such as the Disney's Polynesian Resort, provided insightful examples of a well-integrated translation of a brand's promises to the customer. Our results on the diversity of functional practices that customers see as possible antecedents of benefits potentially used in brand positioning (e.g., feeling at home, saving time, etc.) may inspire managers who want to further the development of best practices in this direction. Interestingly, a tight integration between brand promises and aspects of operations and management was one of the most evident characteristics to transpire in the business strategies of the overall champions.

CONCLUSIONS

The purpose of this study has been to stimulate creativity and the development of ideas in the U.S. lodging industry by featuring best practices across functional areas, hotel segments, and operating structures. We hope that members of the lodging industry will learn from, adapt, and improve on the best practices we surfaced in this study, so that the industry as a whole may take great strides forward.

In reviewing the findings of our 115 functional best-practice case studies and our 29 overall best-practice case studies, we are able to draw some overall, although preliminary, conclusions regarding the emphasis and direction of current lodging industry practices. We begin with an examination of the functional cases followed by the overall cases, and end by drawing inferences based on the customers' perspectives.

The Functional Champions

In each of the following figures the percentages sum to 100%, and represent a variety of subclassifications of the original 115 functional cases. Many of the cases have applicability in more than one functional category. The figures to follow reflect an approach to data collection in which each best practice is counted in all of the appropriate functional categories. This approach to summarizing the functional case practices allows for a comprehensive and multi-functional counting for each case featured. Therefore, each of the functional cases may appear in numerous functional categories in the figures, so while sample sizes vary and are not included, the data rely on a case sample of 115 best-practice champions.

Figure 1: Functional Practice Tools

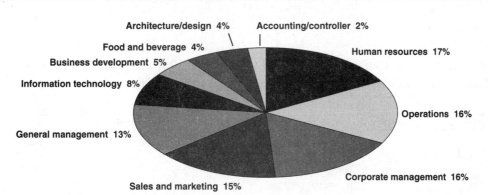

Architecture/design 4%
Accounting/controller 2%
Food and beverage 4%
Human resources 17%
Business development 5%
Information technology 8%
Operations 16%
General management 13%
Corporate management 16%
Sales and marketing 15%

The overwhelming emphasis in the lodging industry of best-practice champions in employee, operational, and customer practice areas is not surprising given how central these functions are to the success of services in general and hotel operations in particular. It is also the case that almost all of the best practices regardless of functional area were undertaken in order to improve customer service and satisfaction, enhance employee satisfaction, or increase sales and occupancy. Indeed, many champions voiced their belief in a direct connection among employee satisfaction, customer satisfaction, and hotel profitability. That is, they believed that by improving employee satisfaction, employee retention would increase. In turn, employee retention would enhance guest services resulting in increased customer satisfaction. Finally, customer satisfaction would lead to increased customer loyalty, occupancy, revenue per available customer, and ultimately, profitability.

Conclusions regarding the functional best practices can be further understood by looking at the champions in specific product segments, operating structures, and corporate versus property levels. The champions are examined in greater detail to provide further insight into the unique characteristics of best practices in various domains of the industry.

Functional Champions by Product Segment

The champions behind the functional best-practice cases can be classified according to the product segments in which they compete. The seven segments include (1) deluxe, (2) upscale, (3) midscale, (4) economy, (5) budget, (6) extended-stay upper tier, and (7) extended-stay lower tier. In some instances a champion is involved in several segments and is included in each segment in which it competes. A review of the various functional practices in the deluxe segment revealed that the largest percentage of best-practice champions were in operations and human resources as shown in Figure 2.

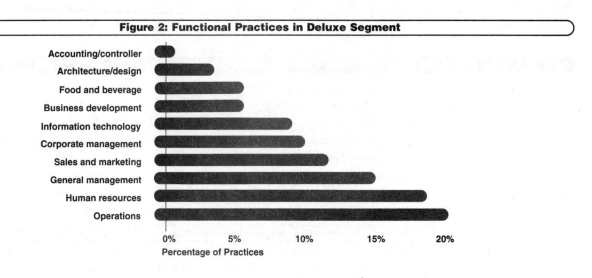

Figure 2: Functional Practices in Deluxe Segment

In Figure 3, the upscale segment best practices with the most champions were in the areas of corporate management and sales and marketing. In both deluxe and upscale segments, champions in accounting and food and beverage were infrequent.

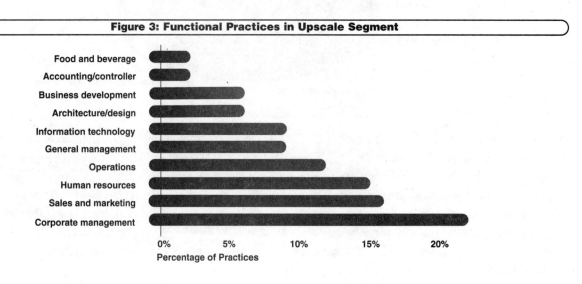

Figure 3: Functional Practices in Upscale Segment

In the midscale market, by far the most frequently surfaced best-practice champions were in the area of corporate management. Human resource practices were the second most frequently found category of excellence in this market segment. Figure 4 provides the percentage of practices in each of the ten functional areas for the midscale market with and without food and beverage.

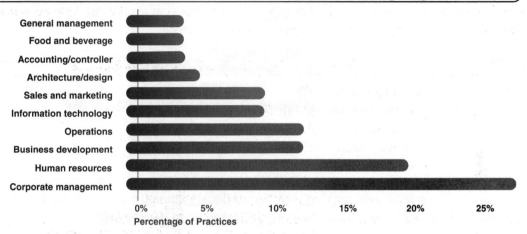

Figure 4: Functional Practices in Midscale with or without Food and Beverage Segment

Corporate management produced the largest percentage of best-practice champions for both the economy and the budget segments of the industry as Figure 5 and Figure 6 below show. Further, business development, human resources, and sales and marketing were strong areas for best-practice champions in both the economy and the budget segments.

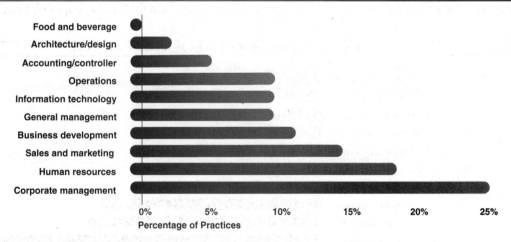

Figure 5: Functional Practices in Economy Segment

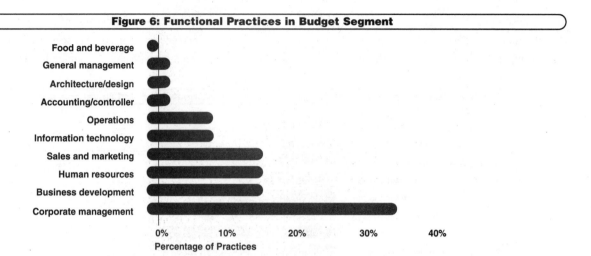

Figure 6: Functional Practices in Budget Segment

Extended stay was divided into upper-tier and lower-tier groupings of practices as shown in figures 7 and 8. While both tiers in this segment had the largest percentage of champions in corporate management, the lower-tier hotels were recognized for human resource champions, and the upper-tier hotels were extremely strong in business development practices.

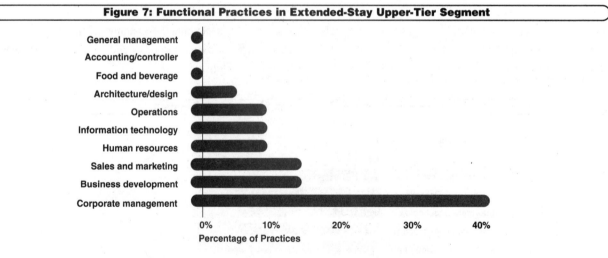

Figure 7: Functional Practices in Extended-Stay Upper-Tier Segment

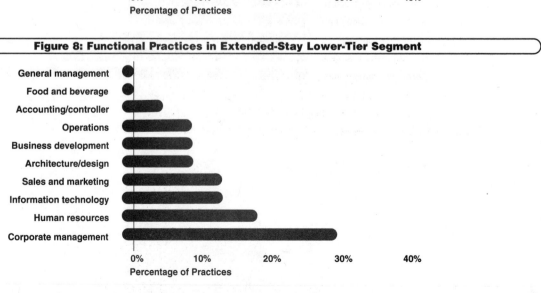

Figure 8: Functional Practices in Extended-Stay Lower-Tier Segment

As Figure 9 reveals, the number of best-practice champions surfaced in this study was not evenly distributed by product segment. The deluxe and midscale segments had the largest number of champions while the extended-stay upper and lower tiers had the fewest best-practice champions.

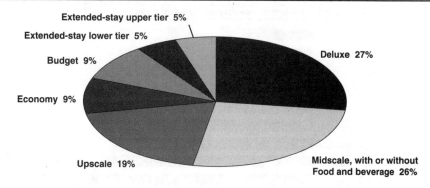

Figure 9: Functional Practices by Segment

In the previous figures the data show that a variety of different functional champions are found in the various segments of the industry. Corporate management practices were the most frequently identified practices in all segments with the exception of the luxury segment. Food and beverage, general management, and accounting were often the areas with the least number of practices depending on the segment, as the figures above reveal. In this section we have shown how the functional practices were distributed by product segment; in the next section the focus will be on the classification of practices by the operating structure of the champion.

Functional Champions by Operating Structure

The functional best-practice champions can be categorized according to their affiliation. The six most common approaches to structuring hotel operations used in this study include (1) chains, (2) management companies, (3) franchisees, (4) franchisors, (5) owners/operators, and (6) REITs. A summary of the best-practice champions by the category of operating structure and functions, shown in Figure 10, reveals that the largest percentage of practices are from owner/operators (28%) and chains (26%). Twenty-three percent of the champions were affiliated with management companies. Finally, franchisees (6%) and REITs (2%) produced the smallest number of best-practice champions.

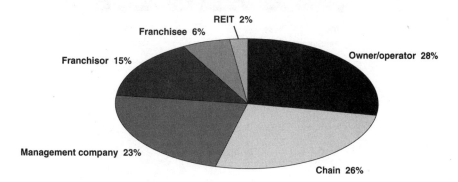

Figure 10: Functional Practices by Operating Structure

The next several figures show the percentage of practices in each functional area for each of the six operating structures. Figure 11 shows that the champions that were classified in chains were most often developing best practices in corporate management, human resources, and sales and marketing. Accounting and architecture best practices were the least frequently surfaced from the chain-affiliated champions.

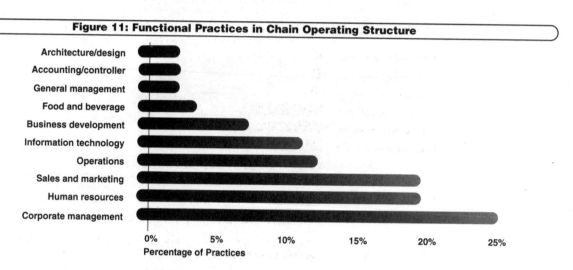

Figure 11: Functional Practices in Chain Operating Structure

The most frequently identified best practices for management companies were in the area of operations. Both human resources and corporate management practices also were frequently surfaced for management company champions as noted in Figure 12. Much like chain operators, the fewest champions were in accounting and architecture practices.

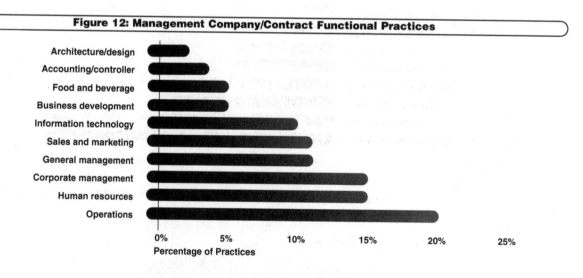

Figure 12: Management Company/Contract Functional Practices

Figures 13 and 14 show the functional champions for franchisees and franchisers. For franchisees, general management, human resources, and sales and marketing were the strongest areas of best practice. Franchisors excelled in corporate management in addition to human resources and sales and marketing. No food and beverage practice champions existed for companies with franchisee or franchiser status.

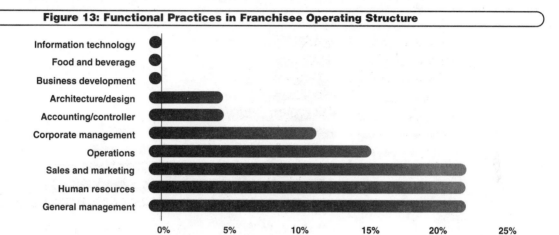

Figure 13: Functional Practices in Franchisee Operating Structure

Figure 14: Functional Practices in Franchisor Operating Structure

Owner/operators provided high numbers of best practices in general management, human resources, operations, and sales and marketing as is evident in Figure 15. Few best practices were found in accounting, business development, and food and beverage for owner/operators.

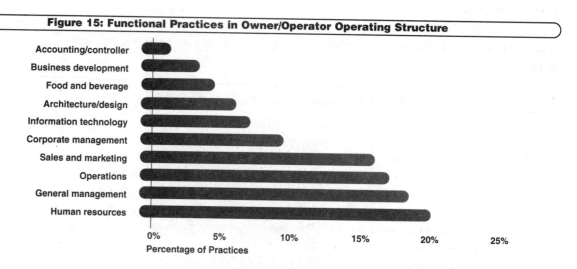

Figure 15: Functional Practices in Owner/Operator Operating Structure

Finally, the last operating structure explored in this study was REITs. This operating structure produced the smallest number of best practice champions. Accounting, architecture, and food and beverage were functions in which no best-practice champions existed in REITs, as Figure 16 shows.

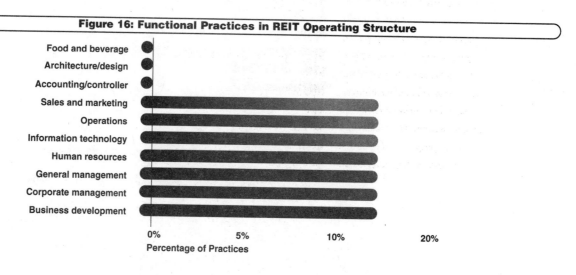

Figure 16: Functional Practices in REIT Operating Structure

By looking across the six operating structures comparisons also can be made. Chains produced the largest number of best practice champions in the areas of business development, corporate management, information technology, and sales and marketing. Management companies produced the largest number of best practice champions in accounting, food and beverage, and operations. Architecture, general management, and human resources were the functional areas in which owner/operators produced the largest number of champions.

Functional Champions by Corporate/Property Levels

A total of 63 functional best-practice champions were from the corporate level and 52 were from the property level. Large numbers of human resources, sales and marketing, and operations champions were found at both corporate and property levels as figure 17 shows. Accounting practices, business development, architecture, and information technology tended to be more often best practices associated with corporate champions. Property-level champions were most often found in the areas of general management and operations.

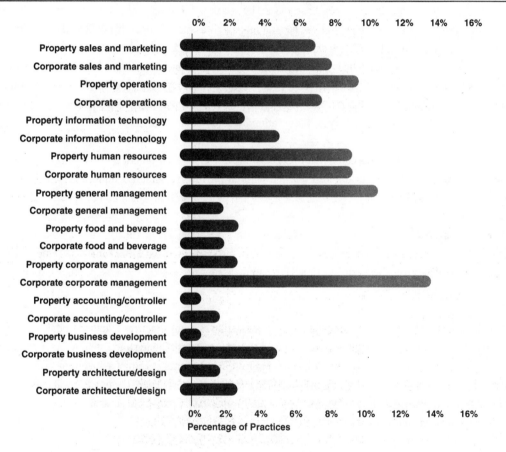

Figure 17: Corporate and Property Functional Practices

Percentage of Practices

Insights from the Functional Champions

Examination of the advice and insights offered by the contacts and champions in the case studies produced several consistent keys to successful implementation. Interestingly, a single individual who initially acted alone to build support for the idea within the organization nearly always championed best-practice ideas. Occasionally a team of two developed the best practice, but rarely did we find that the innovative ideas stemmed from groups larger than two. At the corporate level, approximately 63% of our functional best practices were derived from individuals at the vice-president level or above. The prominence of senior-level management as champions in the organizations we studied may suggest that they are most able to implement and gain support for their ideas.

Although some practices initially were developed and championed by people in the lower ranks of the corporation, innovators at the lower levels were rare. Similarly, at the property level, the general manager was most frequently noted as the individual behind the best practice, accounting for approximately 29 percentage of our best practices. Again, the general manager's position of power at the property level may facilitate the successful implementation of a new idea. While certainly not in the majority, we did find cases where the champions included a director of housekeeping, director of food and beverage, chief concierge, kitchen manager, chief engineer, night manager, and front-desk manager. Thus, we are encouraged by the possibility that the lodging industry can continue to improve as an industry by fostering creativity and innovation in employees at all levels.

A large number of functional champions observed that to successfully introduce their practice, the commitment and sponsorship of senior management was needed. Many champions felt that without the involvement and support of senior management the practice would not have been successful.

When asked about the outcomes of their efforts to implement their best practice, our functional champions most often cited increased profitability, improved customer satisfaction, lower employee turnover, improved quality, increased employee performance, increased occupancy, and enhanced employee satisfaction. The champions reported that for the most part the best practices appeared to have achieved their intended objectives.

Communication was viewed as the major glue that held the implementation of many practices together. Updated information along the way was key to success as was the sharing of information with the user and staff. Talking and listening to staff as well as keeping them challenged were essential components to careful execution, according to several champions. Involvement of the staff also was mentioned often as a key to success. As described by one champion, "Employees must believe the practice will make their job better." Champions felt that it was important to listen to managers and staff, empower employees to control critical implementation decisions, and experiment with a test hotel or a trial department.

It was interesting that several champions wished they had started the practice sooner, taken the process of introducing the practice slower, and involved more people in the early stages of implementation. Advice for others often revealed the importance of creating monitoring procedures for the practice and being tenacious.

Insights from the Overall Champions

Examination of the 29 overall champions revealed that they share a common quality: a relatively close correspondence between their management practices and business strategies, and the sources of value for customers and owners. The overall champions have a strong and clear statement delineating the hotel concept or brand, and align their properties, people, processes, marketing, and financial structures accordingly. In other words, the overall champions do not do one thing better than everyone else, rather they do many things extremely well. Consequently, in many cases, profits flow from getting a yield premium over the competitive set.

The champions seem ahead of others in understanding and executing on the basics. Execution is the key to success of the overall champions in the study. Over and over the champions noted that it is easy to formulate the ideas, but it is the execution "every day, every stay" that matters. Consistently executing on the details is viewed as essential to customer loyalty and, ultimately, profitability, according to the champions.

Regardless of the product segment, employees were viewed as central to achieving excellence. The overall champions recognize that to deliver on customer service, employees cannot be ordered or even managed to serve. They must want to do the job. The challenge is to help the employee want to serve the guest every day, even when "life intrudes upon the HR model." Throughout this study a variety of creative and innovative ideas were revealed for motivating, recruiting, selecting, training, compensating, and developing employees.

One factor common to the overall champions was the involvement and central role played by the general manager. For the champions, the general manager is a leader and a coach, not a boss. He or she sets the culture, the attitude, and the approach. General managers who are hands on, are involved, know names, and can explain in detail what is going on in an area are the key to property-level success. For many champions, the belief exists that without an involved GM nothing happens at the property level.

Another key to success is to understand customer needs and how to deliver value. All the overall champions had a depth of customer understanding and a model of how that knowledge leads to profit. All champions functioned with the belief that the business is about profit but long-term profit only comes from understanding and delivering value to the guests. Owner relations also are important. For the champions, owners are partners and must support and believe in the business model. Owners of the best-practice champions accept the business model, they invest, they stick with the organization or brand, they suggest improvements, and they maintain communication. In summary, the overall champions combine and fit customers', owners', and employees' needs into a business model focused on profitability. Good strategic business thinking, the development of a model of important relationships, and then consistent attention to execution are what keep these champions innovating.

Insights from the Customer Perspective

Regarding the customers' perspectives of value creation in the lodging industry, we provide a synthesized "voice of the customer" that conveys a few key messages and provides food for thought to the lodging industry.

"You don't have to be everything to have us stay at your hotel." Except for location, the set of hotel attributes that drove customers' purchase and loyalty decisions with the various overall champions varied importantly across hotels. We found that the key components of the branding and business strategies of the overall champion hotels were very much in line with the primary sources of value for their target customers.

"If you want us to be loyal, create unique value, every day, every stay." When the customers were able to remember something they liked in particular in their last stay at the champion hotel, they were 1.5 times more likely to remain loyal to that hotel. However, only one customer out of two has perceived such unique value. Thus, if the "every day, every stay" motto is present in some champion hotels, there seems to still be room for improvement on an industrywide basis. No chance to rest quietly on one's laurels!

"Top performance in key functions of your hotel pay, but all areas are not key." When customers recognized a hotel as the industrywide top performer on any of the functional areas, loyalty was created. The two functional areas in which top performance was most critical to customer loyalty were the quality standards of various services received during the hotel stay and the quality of the personnel. Not surprisingly, these are also areas in which management had developed numerous functional best practices. The functional area that had the lowest impact on loyalty was the formal marketing activities to the customers: A dose of realism is prescribed in estimating the customer impact of the large number of best functional practices that have emerged in this area as well.

"Service is important to us; when you work at it, we appreciate it." Functional and interpersonal aspects of customer service were critical sources of customer value. Service is also a key attribute in shaping the brand image and reputation, and an even more powerful source of value for intermediaries. Many of the hotel practices directly observed by the customers related to the personnel, often going beyond the call of duty. Therefore, management time and effort spent in developing best practices in human resource management do appear to create tangible value to the customers.

"But don't forget! We stay at your hotel and remain loyal also because of the physical product!" One of the functional areas in which only a few best practices emerged on the management side were those related to the physical product of the hotel (i.e., the room, the lobby, etc.). Yet, compared to service, physical product attributes have a more powerful influence on purchase decision and are more often sources of unique value during a hotel stay. Most of the overall practices presented a good balance between the physical and service hotel components. Some pioneer functional champions in this area show that best practices in this area can be developed as well. There may be an agenda here for the next millennium!

In Conclusion

It is important to appreciate that any effort to borrow and use the best practices of managers and organizations in the lodging industry must take into consideration the unique situations, resources, cultures, histories, and market factors that enabled the success of the practices featured here. A book such as this one in which a large number of practices are described is offered to inspire, excite, and stimulate the creation of future practices. It is through the modification of current practice, the creation of new innovations, the adjustment and adaptation of these ideas to your unique situation, and the courage to experiment and risk failure that you will begin your journey toward creating the next wave of excellence in the industry. We wish you luck!

REFERENCES

Ader, Jason N. and Robert A. Lafleur. 1997. "U.S. Lodging Almanac." New York: Bear, Stearns & Co.

Anderson, E. W., C. Fornell, and R. T. Rust. 1997. "Customer Satisfaction, Productivity, and Profitability: Differences between Goods and Services." *Marketing Science* 16 (2): 129-145.

Brown, Ed. 1997. "The Best Business Hotels." *Fortune* (March 17): 204-206.

Cline, Roger S., and Lalia Rach. 1996. *Hospitality 2000: A View to the Next Millennium.* Arthur Andersen.

Camp, Robert C. 1989. *Benchmarking: The Search for Industry Best Practices that Lead to Superior Performance.* Milwaukee, Wis.: Quality Press, American Society for Quality Control.

Dubé, Laurette, Amitava Chattopadhyay, Bernd H. Schmidt, and Ehsam El Huque. 1997. "Customer Expectations for Luxury Hotels: A Cross-cultural Comparison." Research report, Center for Hospitality Research, The School of Hotel Administration, Cornell University.

Dubé, Laurette, Michael D. Johnson, and Leo M. Renaghan. 1999. "Adapting the QFD Approach to Product Design in Extended Service Transactions: An Empirical Illustration with Luxury Business Hotels." Production and Operation Management: in press.

Enz, Cathy, and David Corsun. 1996. Cornell University Hotel Best Practices Survey: Practices for Improving Operations. Unpublished proprietary report.

Fornell, Claes, Michael D. Johnson, Eugene W. Anderson, Jaesung Cha, and Barbara Everitt Bryant. 1996. "The American Customer Satisfaction Index: Nature, Purpose, and Findings." *Journal of Marketing* 60 (October): 7-18.

Hequet, Marc. 1993. "The Limits of Benchmarking." *Training* 30 (February): 36-41.

Hiebeler, Robert, Thomas B. Kelly, and Charles Ketteman 1998. *Best Practices: Building Your Business with Customer-Focused Solutions.* New York: Simon & Schuster.

Holt, Blake. 1994. "Benchmarking Comes to HR." *Personnel Management* 26 (June): 32-35.

Keehley, Patricia, Stephen Medlin, Sue MacBride, and Laura Longmire. 1997. *Benchmarking for Best Practices in the Public Sector: Achieving Performance Breakthroughs in Federal, State and Local Agencies.* San Francisco: Jossey-Bass.

O'Dell, Carla and C. Jackson Grayson with Nilly Essaides 1998. *If Only We Knew What We Know: The Transfer of Internal Knowledge and Best Practices.* New York: The Free Press.

Parson, William T. 1995. "Best Practices in Retailing: Give the Lady What She Wants." *Chain Store Age* 71 (November): 86-88.

Renaghan, Leo M., and Cindy Green. 1993. Resort Hotel Benchmarking Study. Unpublished proprietary report conducted by Cornell School of Hotel Administration and Driving Revenue Consulting Company.

Rogers, Phillip B. 1997. "Raising the Bar." *Journal of Property Management* 62 (Nov/Dec): 48-51.

Roth, Aleda V., Richard B. Chase, and Chris Voss. 1997. "Service in the US: Progress Towards Global Service Leadership." Sponsored by Severn Trent Plc, UK Government's Department of Trade and Industry, Department of National Heritage.

Rucci, Anthony J., Steven P. Kirn, and Richard T. Quinn. 1998 "The Employee-Customer-Profit Chain at Sears." *Harvard Business Review* (Jan/Feb): 83-97.

Spendolini, Michael J. 1992. *The Benchmarking Book.* New York: AMACOM.

Stank, Theodore P., Dale S. Rogers, and Patricia J. Daugherty. 1994. "Benchmarking: Applications by Third Party Warehousing Firms." *Logistics and Transportation Review* 30 (March): 55-72.

Sullivan, David. 1995. "Benchmarking: Case Studies in Success." *National Petroleum News* 87 (February): 46-47.

Wright, P. 1980. "Message-Evoked Thoughts: Persuasion Research Using Thought Verbalizations." *Journal of Consumer Research* 7 (9): 151-175.

Young, Richard R. 1996. "Those Elusive Best Practices." *Distribution* 96 (September): 52.

Case Listings by Segment

Overall best-practice champions are noted with an asterisk (*) and are located alphabetically on pages 255 to 333. All others are functional best-practice champions and located on pages 33 to 248. Some individual placements may reflect typical practice based on a typical property and may not be actual practice for the listed individual property.

Deluxe

Accor North America..Formalizing The Relationship Selling Process And Sales Team Activities

Accor North America..Internal Customer Satisfaction

Ashley House Hotels-Keswick Hotel ....Quality Service Management Program For Employees

The Balsams Grand Resort Hotel.....................A Guest History System

The Boulders ....Self-Directed Housekeeping Teams

The Boulders ....Food Forager To Improve Quality In Food And Beverage

The Boulders ....Cornerstone Program: Developing A Service Culture

The Breakers Hotel..Annual F & B Staff Reorganization And Single-Theme Restaurant Concepts

Coastal Hotel Group ....Employees On Loan for Training With The Buddy System

Fairmont Copley Plaza Hotel............................Using A Property Management System To Improve Concierge Desk Excellence

The Farmington Inn..Writing Historical Fiction Books To Enhance Marketing

* Four Seasons and Regent Hotel & Resorts ....Consistency Over Time

Four Seasons and Regent Hotels & Resorts .....Designated Trainer Program For Front-Line Employees

Four Seasons and Regent Hotels & Resorts .....Developing A High Ratio Of Employees to Guests

Four Seasons and Regent Hotels & Resorts .....Ensuring A Luxury Hotel Experience

Four Seasons and Regent Hotels & Resorts .....Informal Dining Venues And Alternative Cuisine

* Four Seasons Hotel New York ....The Most Beautiful Stage Ever Performed Upon

* Four Seasons Hotel Washington D.C. ....A Passion To Serve

The Greenbrier ....Programs Establishing The Resort As A Center For Culinary Excellence

Hotel Bel Air ....Comprehensive Environmental Management

Hotel Bel Air ....Proactive Property-Maintenance Program

Hotel Nikko at Beverly Hills ....Portable Telephone System Throughout Hotel

* The Houstonian Hotel, Club & Spa................A Humanistic Approach To Profitability

Hyatt Arlington Hotel ....Redesigning And Revitalizing A Food And Beverage Outlet

Hyatt Hotels Corporation ....Survey-Based Guest-Satisfaction Program

Hyatt Regency Chicago.....................................Comprehensive Waste Reduction And Recycling Program

Hyatt Regency Scottsdale ....Developing An Environmental Recycling Program

Hyatt Regency Scottsdale ....Hospitality Training Program For High School Students

Inn at the Market..Outsourced Human Resources To Professional HR Consultant

Inter-Continental Hotels & Resorts.................Building A Global Marketing Database

* The Mansion on Turtle Creek ....Staffing Up To Customer Needs

* Marriott International, J.W. Marriott ....Success Is Never Final

Marriott International ....Revenue Management Systems For Revenue Enhancement

* Marriott International ....It's A Marathon Not A Sprint!

Marriott International ....Sales Innovations Strategies

Marriott International ....Aligning Information Technology With Corporate Strategy

Marriott International ....Leveraging Leadership Capacity And Building Future Leaders

Marriott International ....Developing Products To Meet The Needs Of Targeted Market Segments

Marriott International ....Successful Creation Of New Brands

Minneapolis-St. Paul Hilton ....Line Employee Empowerment

* Mirage Resorts ....Creating Artistically Pleasing Hotels For Guests And Employees

New York Marriott Financial Center.................Regular Status Meetings Between Executive And Department Staff

Newark Gateway Hilton ....Guest Check-In On Shuttle Bus

Omni Hotels...Integrated Property Management And Revenue Management System

* Ali Kasikci, The Peninsula Beverly Hills Hotel ..Every Day You Have To Re-Invent Yourself

The Peninsula Beverly Hills Hotel ....24-Hour Check-In/Checkout

The Pierre ....Implementing And Monitoring Cost-Plus Purchasing Agreements

The Pierre ....Maximizing Profitability By Managing The Sales Mix

Preferred Hotels & Resorts Worldwide, Inc.........Development Of Preferred Standards Of Excellence

Royal Palms Hotel & Casitas ....Restoration And Redesign Of Older Property For Residential Feel

The Ritz-Carlton Chicago ...."Compcierge" Position To Handle Guests' Computer Problems

The Ritz-Carlton Dearborn ....Special Check-In Service For Frequent Guests

* The Ritz-Carlton Hotel Co. ....Lead People, Manage Process

The Ritz-Carlton Hotel Co. ....Maximizing Guest Service

* The Ritz-Carlton Naples ....Quality…A Different Way To Manage

The Ritz-Carlton Tysons Corner ....Self-Directed Work Teams, Job Redesign, And Employee Empowerment

Sheraton - Denver West ....Job Sharing Between Sales Managers

Sheraton Elk Grove..Annual Implementation Of A Broad-Based Best Practice

Simpson House Inn ....Hospitality Training Curriculum With An Emphasis On Diversity

Sunstone Hotels ....Focused Growth Of Hotel Company Utilizing A REIT

Tishman Hotel Corporation ....Hotel Renovation: The Doral Park Avenue Hotel

The Waldorf-Astoria ....Gathering Customer Feedback And Coding Performance

The Waldorf-Astoria ....Revenue Maximization For The Food And Beverage Department

Windsor Court Hotel ....Sophisticated Guest-Recognition Program

Upscale

Abbey Group Resorts...................................Increasing Leisure Stays From Convention And Meetings Guests

Accor North America..................................Formalizing The Relationship Selling Process And Sales Team Activities

Accor North America..................................Internal Customer Satisfaction

The Barbizon Hotel and
   Empire Hotel New York ....Standardized Record Keeping For Operations And Guest Calls

* Bristol Hotels & Resorts ....Create A Culture Of Results, Not Of Trappings

Bristol Hotels & Resorts ....Streamlining The Operations Of Resource-Challenged Properties

* Caesars Palace Hotel & Casino ....Building A Hotel That Has...Mystique

Carlson Hospitality Worldwide....................World-Wide Reservation System

Cincinnati Marriott Northeast ....Treating Guests As Part Of The Family

Cincinnati Marriott Northeast ....We Are...Northeast

Clarion Hotel-Comfort Inn & Suites.............Generating Sales Leads From Employees: A Contest Approach Program

Coastal Hotel Group ....Employees On Loan For Training With The Buddy System

The Colony Hotel ....Guest-Friendly Environmental And Recycling Practices

Dahlmann Properties...................................Improving The Work Environment And Decrease Turnover

Disney's Polynesian Resort..........................A Value-Based Process Of Training And Selection

* Disney's Polynesian Resort.......................Creating And Delivering A Magical Experience

Embassy Suites - Greater Minneapolis.........Consolidation And Centralization Of Reservations Sales Office

Holiday Inn SunSpree Resort Lake
   Buena Vista and Holiday Inn Hotel &
   Suites Main Gate East...............................Specialized Suites To Meet The Demands Of The Vacationing Family

The Inn at Essex ....Advertising On City Buses To Create Awareness

The Inn at Essex ....Providing Absolute Guest Satisfaction

Kessler Enterprises, Inc. ....Development And Concept Of The Grand Theme Hotels

Kimpton Group Hotels and Restaurants
   and Outrigger Hotels and Resorts............Private Label Reservation System That Encourages Reservation Agent Upselling

* Marriott Hotels & Resorts ....It's A Marathon, Not A Sprint!

Marriott International..................................Revenue Management Systems For Revenue Enhancement

* Marriott International, Inc.,
   J.W. Marriott, Jr. ....Success Is Never Final

Marriott International ....Sales Innovations Strategies

Marriott International ....Aligning Information Technology Planning With Corporate Strategy

Marriott International ....Leveraging Leadership Capacity And Building Future Leaders

Marriott International ....Developing Products To Meet The Needs Of Targeted Market Segments

Marriott International ....Successful Creation Of New Brands

Marriott U.S. Postal Service
   Conference Center ....Express Check-In Service For Guests On Hotel Airport Shuttle Buses

* Mohonk Mountain House...........................Creating Profits By Not Focusing On The GOP

Palisades Executive Conference Center ....Experience Engineering And Integrative Design

Promus Hotel Corporation ....On-Line Integrated Payroll/Benefit Accounting System

Promus Hotel Corporation ....Guaranteed Customer Satisfaction

Radisson Worldwide......................................Reward Program For Travel Agents

SAI Luxury Hotels, Inc. ....Business Development/Renovation/Turnaround/Repositioning

Sonesta Hotels ....Creating A Profit Center Training Operation

Sunstone Hotels..Focused Growth Of Hotel Company Utilizing A REIT

Swissôtel..Creation Of A Revenue Manager Position To Increase Room Sales Revenues

Swissôtel..Implementing A Global Sales Effort

Tamar Inns..Implementation Of Self-Funded Health Insurance

Tishman Hotel Corporation ....Hotel Renovation: The Doral Park Avenue Hotel

Walt Disney World Resorts and
    Theme Parks...Providing A "Touchable" Dining Experience

Winegardner and Hammons
    Incorporated...Pre-Opening Handbook For New Hotel Properties

Wyndham Hotels & Resorts ....An Integrated Approach To Food And Beverage

Midscale, with and without Food and Beverage

* Bristol Hotels & Resorts ....Create A Culture Of Results, Not Of Trappings

Bristol Hotels & Resorts ....Streamlining The Operations Of Resource-Challenged Properties

Carlson Hospitality Worldwide....................World-Wide Reservation System

Cendant Corporation....................................Developing Preferred Alliances With National Vendors

Cendant Corporation....................................Integration Of All Hotel MIS Functions

Cendant Corporation....................................Comprehensive Diversity Initiative

Choice Hotels International...........................In-House Executive Training And Development

Club Hotel by Doubletree ....Employee Care Committees

Country Inns & Suites ....Successful Cobranding With Established Restaurant Concepts

* Courtyard by Marriott ....An Unfailing Desire To Listen To Our Guests

Courtyard by Marriott..................................Intranet Information Sharing

Day Hospitality Group ....Sabbatical Leave Program For General Managers

Grand Theme Hotels ....The Creation Of A Process To Track And Control Labor Costs

* Hampton Inn ....The Unconditional Guarantee As A Cultural Belief

* Holiday Inn Cincinnati Airport ....The Smartest Investment You Can Ever Make—The People

IMPAC Hotel Group ....A Lobby Kiosk Touch-Screen Guest Tracking System

Latham Hotel, Georgetown...........................Midscale Guestrooms Designed To Give An Upscale, Residential Feel

* Marriott International ....It's A Marathon Not A Sprint!

Marriott International ....Revenue Management Systems For Revenue Enhancement

* Marriott International, Inc.,

   J.W. Marriott, Jr. ....Success Is Never Final

Marriott International ....Sales Innovations Strategies

Marriott International ....Aligning Information Technology Planning With Corporate Strategy

Marriott International ....Leveraging Leadership Capacity And Building Future Leaders

Marriott International ....Developing Products To Meet The Needs Of Targeted Market Segments

Marriott International ....Successful Creation Of New Brands

Motel Properties Inc. ....Employee Recognition Program

Promus Hotel Corporation ....On-Line Integrated Payroll/Benefit Accounting System

Promus Hotel Corporation ....Guaranteed Customer Satisfaction

Ramada Franchise Systems, Inc. ....Employee Selection, Motivation, Training, And Satisfaction

SAI Luxury Hotels, Inc. ....Business Development/Renovation/Turnaround/Repositioning

Sunstone Hotels ....Focused Growth Of Hotel Company Utilizing A REIT

Tamar Inns ....Implementation Of Self-Funded Health Insurance

Tishman Hotel Corporation ....Hotel Renovation: The Doral Park Avenue Hotel

US Franchise Systems, Inc. ....Franchising Agreements At USFS

White Lodging Services ....Preshift Meetings For All Departments

Winegardner and Hammons

   Incorporated ....Pre-Opening Handbook For New Hotel Properties

Economy

AmericInn ....Solid Masonry Construction And Innovative Design

* Bristol Hotels & Resorts ....Create A Culture Of Results, Not Of Trappings

Bristol Hotels & Resorts ....Streamlining The Operations Of Resource-Challenged Properties

Cendant Corporation....................................Preferred Alliances/Cross Marketing

Cendant Corporation....................................Integration Of All Hotel MIS Functions

Cendant Corporation....................................Comprehensive Diversity Initiative

Choice Hotels International...........................In-House Executive Training And Development

Days Inn Altoona ....Integrated, Community-Based Marketing Plan

* Days Inn Altoona ....Professional Pride And Personal Values Forge Operating Philosophy

Holiday Inn Express, Cripple Creek, CO ....Making Every Employee's Job A Sales Job

Holiday Inn Express, Helena, MT ....Achieving Quality Customer Service At An Economy Property

* Marriott International, Inc.,

   J.W. Marriott, Jr. ....Success Is Never Final

Marriott International ....Revenue Management Systems For Revenue Enhancement

* Fairfield Inn by Marriott ....Impress More Guests, Sell More Rooms, Have More Fun

Marriott International ....Sales Innovations Strategies

Marriott International ....Aligning Information Technology With Corporate Strategy

Marriott International ....Leveraging Leadership Capacity And Building Future Leaders

Marriott International ....Developing Products To Meet The Needs Of Targeted Market Segments

Marriott International ....Successful Creation Of New Brands

Promus Hotel Corporation ....On-Line Integrated Payroll/Benefit Accounting System

Promus Hotel Corporation ....Guaranteed Customer Satisfaction

Rodeway Inn International Orlando ....Rewarding Employee Performance In An Economy Hotel

Tamar Inns ....Implementation Of Self-Funded Health Insurance Program

Budget

AIMS Inc. ....Making Unprofitable Hotels Profitable

Cendant Corporation...................................Developing Preferred Alliances With National Vendors

Cendant Corporation...................................Integration Of All Hotel MIS Functions

Cendant Corporation...................................Comprehensive Diversity Initiative

Choice Hotels International..........................In-House Executive Training And Development

Essex Partners ....Achieving Greater Profitability Through Budgeting, Cost Controls, And Team Building

Good Nite Inn ....Establishing Time Frames For Preventive Maintenance Tasks

Good Nite Inn ....Development Of Mobile Shop For Improved Guestroom Maintenance

Knights Inn Summerton (Preea, Inc.)..........Creating Your Own Mailing Lists To Increase Business

* Marriott Hotels & Resorts ....It's A Marathon Not A Sprint!

Marriott International ....Revenue Management Systems For Revenue Enhancement

* Marriott International, Inc.,

   J.W. Marriott, Jr. ....Success Is Never Final

Marriott International ....Sales Innovations

Marriott International ....Aligning Information Technology With Corporate Strategy

Marriott International ....Leveraging Leadership Capacity And Building Future Leaders

Marriott International ....Developing Products To Meet The Needs Of Targeted Market Segments

Marriott International ....Successful Creation Of New Brands

Motel 6...Developing A Memorable And Effective Advertising Message

Motel 6...Training Employees For General Management

* Sleep Inn ....Customer Service Is The Wild Card

* Super 8 Motel, Inc.....................................A Focus On Hospitality

Tamar Inns ....Implementation Of Self-Funded Health Insurance

Travelodge..Guest Loyalty At The Economy Level

Extended-Stay Upper Tier

* Embassy Suites ....When The Operating Strategy Is The Brand Strategy

* Homewood Suites, Alexandria ....On Being A Yes Hotel...

* Residence Inn by Marriott.......................A Relentless Focus On Extended-Stay

Residence Inn by Marriott..........................A Collaborative Approach To Quality Assurance In Extended-Stay Hotels

Residence Inn by Marriott...........................Sales Strategies For The Extended-Stay Market

White Lodging Services ....Preshift Meetings For All Departments

Extended-Stay Lower Tier

Candlewood Hotel Company ....Designing An Extended-Stay Hotel For A Single-Niche Market

Candlewood Hotel Company ....Electronic Record Management

Day Hospitality Group ....Sabbatical Leave Program For General Managers

* Extended StayAmerica ....To Be Leader In A New Industry Segment,
Build Market Share Faster And Deliver More Quality

Towneplace Suites by Marriott.....................Cross-Trained Staffing Model As Driver Of Revenue

* Towneplace Suites by Marriott-
Brookfield, Wisconsin...............................Remodeling The Property Hierarchical Structure

US Franchise Systems, Inc...........................Franchising Agreements At USFS

White Lodging Services ....Preshift Meetings For All Departments

Case Listings by Operating Structure

Overall best-practice champions are noted with an asterisk (*) and are located alphabetically on pages 255 to 333. All others are functional best-practice champions and located on pages 33 to 248. Some individual placements may reflect typical practice based on a typical property and may not be actual practice for the listed individual property.

Chain

Accor North America....................................Formalizing The Relationship Selling Process And Sales Team Activities

Accor North America....................................Internal Customer Satisfaction

Candlewood Hotel Company.........................Designing An Extended-Stay Hotel For A Single-Niche Market

Candlewood Hotel Company.........................Electronic Record Management

Carlson Hospitality Worldwide.....................World-Wide Reservation System

Carlson Hospitality Worldwide.....................Total Customer Satisfaction Via An On-Line Database And Employee Empowerment

Cendant Corporation....................................Developing Preferred Alliances With National Vendors

Cendant Corporation....................................Integration Of All Hotel MIS Functions

Cendant Corporation....................................Comprehensive Diversity Initiative

Choice Hotels International...........................In-House Executive Training And Development

Club Hotel by Doubletree ....Employee Care Committees

Country Inn & Suites....................................Successful Cobranding With Established Restaurant Concepts

Courtyard By Marriott..................................Intranet Information Sharing

*Four Seasons and Regent Hotels & Resorts..Consistency Over Time

Four Seasons and Regent Hotels & Resorts....Designated Trainer Program For Front-Line Employees

Four Seasons and Regent Hotels & Resorts....Developing A High Ratio Of Employees To Guests

Four Seasons and Regent Hotels & Resorts....Ensuring A Luxury Hotel Experience

Four Seasons and Regent Hotels & Resorts....Informal Dining Venue And Alternative Cuisine

Good Nite Inn..Establishing Time Frames For Preventive Maintenance Tasks

Good Nite Inn..Development Of Mobile Shop For Improved Guestroom Maintenance

Grand Theme Hotels ....The Creation Of A Process To Track And Control Labor Costs

Hyatt Hotels Corporation ....Survey-Based Guest-Satisfaction Program

Inter-Continental Hotels & Resorts................Building A Global Marketing Database

* Marriott International, Inc.,
   J.W. Marriott, Jr. ....Success Is Never Final

Marriott International ....Revenue Management Systems For Revenue Enhancement

* Marriott Hotels & Resorts ....It's A Marathon Not A Sprint!

Marriott International ....Sales Innovations Strategies

Marriott International ....Aligning Information Technology With Corporate Strategy

Marriott International ....Leveraging Leadership Capacity And Building Future Leaders

Marriott International ....Developing Products To Meet The Needs Of Targeted Market Segments

Marriott International ....Successful Creation Of New Brands

Motel 6 ....Developing A Memorable And Effective Advertising Message

Motel 6 ....Training Employees For General Management

Omni Hotels ....Integrated Property Management And Revenue Management System

Preferred Hotels & Resorts
   Worldwide, Inc. ....Development Of Preferred Standards Of Excellence

Promus Hotel Corporation ....On-Line Integrated Payroll/Benefit Accounting System

Promus Hotel Corporation ....Guaranteed Customer Satisfaction

Radisson Worldwide ....Reward Program For Travel Agents

Ramada Franchise Systems, Inc. ....Employee Selection, Motivation, Training, And Satisfaction

* Residence Inn by Marriott ....A Relentless Focus On Extended-Stay

Residence Inn by Marriott ....A Collaborative Approach To Quality Assurance In Extended-Stay Hotels

Residence Inn by Marriott ....Sales Strategies For The Extended-Stay Market

* The Ritz-Carlton Hotel Co. ....Lead People, Manage Process

The Ritz-Carlton Hotel Co. ....Maximizing Guest Service

Sonesta Hotels ....Creating A Profit Center Training Operation

Swissôtel ....Implementation Of A Global Sales Network

Swissôtel ....Creation Of A Revenue Manager Position To Increase Room Sales Revenues

Towneplace Suites by Marriott ....Cross-Trained Staffing Model As Driver of Revenue

Travelodge ....Guest Loyalty At The Economy Level

Wyndham Hotels & Resorts ....An Integrated Approach To Food And Beverage

Franchisee

Cincinnati Marriott Northeast ....Treating The Guest As Part Of The Family

* Cincinnati Marriott Northeast ....We Are...Northeast

Clarion Hotel-Comfort Inn & Suites ....Generating Sales Leads From Employees: A Contest Approach Program

* Days Inn Altoona ....Professional Pride And Personal Values Forge Operating Policy

Days Inn Altoona ....Integrated Community-Based Marketing Plan

Embassy Suites - Greater Minneapolis ....Consolidation And Centralization Of Reservations Sales Office

* Holiday Inn Cincinnati Airport ....The Smartest Investment You Can Ever Make—The People

Holiday Inn Express, Cripple Creek, CO ....Making Every Employee's Job A Sales Job

Holiday Inn Express, Helena, MT ....Achieving Quality Customer Service At An Economy Property

Holiday Inn SunSpree Resort Lake
   Buena Vista and Holiday Inn Hotel
   & Suites Main Gate East ....Specialized Suites To Meet The Demands Of The Vacationing Family

Knights Inn Summerton (Preea, Inc.)..........Creating Your Own Mailing Lists To Increase Business

Minneapolis-St. Paul Hilton ....Line Employee Empowerment

New York Marriott Financial Center............Regular Status Meetings Between Executive And Department Staffs

Rodeway Inn International Orlando ....Rewarding Employee Performance In An Economy Hotel

*Towneplace Suites by Marriott

    Brookfield, Wisconsin- ....Remodeling The Property Hierarchical Structure

Franchisor

AmericInn ....Solid Masonry Construction And Innovative Design

Carlson Hospitality Worldwide.....................World-Wide Reservation System

Carlson Hospitality Worldwide.....................Total Customer Satisfaction Via An On-Line Database And Employee Empowerment

Cendant Corporation....................................Developing Preferred Alliances With National Vendors

Cendant Corporation....................................Integration Of All Hotel MIS Functions Into One System

Cendant Corporation....................................Comprehensive Diversity Initiative

Choice Hotels International...........................In-House Executive Training And Development

* Courtyard by Marriott...............................An Unfailing Desire To Listen To Our Guests

Courtyard By Marriott.................................Intranet Information Sharing

* Embassy Suites..When The Operating Strategy Is The Brand Strategy

* Extended StayAmerica ....To Be Leader In A New Industry Segment,

    Build Market Share Faster And Deliver Quality

* Fairfield Inn by Marriott ....Impress More Guests, Sell More Rooms, Have More Fun

* Hampton Inn ....The Unconditional Guarantee As A Cultural Belief

* Homewood Suites, Alexandria ....On Being A Yes Hotel…

* Marriott International, Inc.,

    J.W. Marriott, Jr. ....Success Is Never Final

Marriott International ....Revenue Management Systems For Revenue Enhancement

* Marriott Hotels & Resorts ....It's A Marathon, Not A Sprint!

Marriott International ....Sales Innovations Strategies

Marriott International ....Aligning Information Technology With Corporate Strategy

Marriott International ....Leveraging Leadership Capacity And Building Future Leaders

Marriott International ....Developing Products To Meet The Needs Of Targeted Market Segments

Marriott International ....Successful Creation Of New Brands

Motel 6 ....Developing A Memorable And Effective Advertising Message

Motel 6 ....Training Employees For General Management

Motel Properties Inc. ....Employee Recognition Program

Omni Hotels..Integrated Property Management And Revenue Management System

Promus Hotel Corporation ....On-Line Integrated Payroll/Benefit Accounting System

Promus Hotel Corporation ....Guaranteed Customer Satisfaction

Radisson Worldwide......................................Reward Program For Travel Agents

Ramada Franchise Systems, Inc. ....Employee Selection, Motivation, Training, And Satisfaction

* Residence Inn by Marriott..........................A Relentless Focus On Extended-Stay

Residence Inn by Marriott.............................A Collaborative Approach To Quality Assurance In Extended-Stay Hotels

Residence Inn by Marriott.............................Sales Strategies For The Extended-Stay Market

* Sleep Inn...Customer Service Is The Wild Card

* Super 8 Motel, Inc.....................................A Focus On Hospitality

Towneplace Suites by Marriott.....................Cross-Trained Staffing Model As Driver Of Revenue

US Franchise Systems, Inc............................Franchising Agreements At USFS

Management Company/Management Contract

The Boulders ....Self-Directed Housekeeping Teams

The Boulders ....Food Forager To Improve Quality In Food And Beverage

The Boulders ....Cornerstone Program: Developing A Service Culture

* Bristol Hotels & Resorts ....Create A Culture Of Results, Not Of Trappings

Bristol Hotels & Resorts ....Streamlining The Operations Of Resource-Challenged Properties

Coastal Hotel Group ....Managers On Loan For Training With The Buddy System

Essex Partners ....Achieving Greater Profitability Through Budgeting, Cost Controls, And Team Building

Holiday Inn Express, Cripple Creek, CO ....Making Every Employee's Job A Sales Job

Hotel Nikko at Beverly Hills ....Portable Telephone System Throughout Hotel

Hyatt Arlington Hotel ....Redesigning And Revitalizing A Food And Beverage Outlet

Hyatt Hotels Corporation ....Survey-Based Guest-Satisfaction Program

Hyatt Regency Chicago.................................Comprehensive Waste Reduction And Recycling Program

Hyatt Regency Scottsdale ....Environmental Leadership

Hyatt Regency Scottsdale ....Hospitality Training Program For High School Students

IMPAC Hotel Group ....A Lobby Kiosk Touch-Screen Guest Tracking System

Inter-Continental Hotels & Resorts ....Building A Global Marketing Database

* Kimpton Group..Differentiation To The Extreme

Kimpton Group Hotels and Restaurants
    and Outrigger Hotels and Resorts ....Private Label Reservation System To Encourage Upselling

* Marriott International, Inc.,
    J.W. Marriott, Jr. ....Success Is Never Final

Marriott International ....Revenue Management Systems For Revenue Enhancement

Marriott International ....Sales Innovations Strategies

Marriott International ....Aligning Information Technology Planning With Corporate Strategic Planning

Marriott International ....Leveraging Leadership Capacity And Building Future Leaders

Marriott International ....Developing Products To Meet The Needs Of Targeted Market Segments

* Marriott Hotels & Resorts ....It's A Marathon Not A Sprint!

Marriott International ....Successful Creation Of New Brands

Marriott U.S. Postal Service
   Conference Center ....Express Check-In Service For Guests On Hotel Airport Shuttle Buses

Motel 6 ....Developing A Memorable And Effective Advertising Message

Motel 6 ....Training Employees For General Management

Newark Gateway Hilton ....Guest Check-In On The Shuttle Bus

The Pierre ....Implementing And Monitoring Cost-Plus Purchasing Agreements

The Pierre ....Maximizing Profitability By Managing The Sales Mix

Promus Hotel Corporation ....On-Line Integrated Payroll/Benefit Accounting System

Promus Hotel Corporation ....Guaranteed Customer Satisfaction

The Ritz-Carlton Chicago ...."Compcierge" Position To Handle Guests' Computer Problems

The Ritz-Carlton Dearborn ....Special Check-In Service For Frequent Guests

* The Ritz-Carlton Hotel Co. ....Lead People, Manage Process

The Ritz-Carlton Hotel Co. ....Maximizing Guest Service

* The Ritz-Carlton Naples ....Quality...A Different Way To Manage

The Ritz-Carlton Tysons Corner ....Self-Directed Work Teams, Job Redesign, And Employee Empowerment

Tamar Inns ....Implementation Of Self-Funded Health Insurance

Tishman Hotel Corporation ....Hotel Renovation: The Doral Park Avenue Hotel

White Lodging Services ....Preshift Meetings For All Departments

Winegardner and Hammons Incorporated .....Pre-Opening Handbook For New Hotel Properties

Wyndham Hotels & Resorts ....An Integrated Approach To Food And Beverage

Owner/Operator

Abbey Group Resorts...................................Increasing Leisure Stays From Convention And Meeting Guests

AIMS Inc. ....Making Unprofitable Hotels Profitable

Ashley House Hotels-Keswick Hotel.............Quality Service Management Program For Employees

The Balsams Grand Resort Hotel ....A Guest History System

The Barbizon Hotel and
   Empire Hotel New York ....Standardized Recordkeeping For Operations And Guest Calls

The Breakers Hotel......................................Annual F&B Staff Reorganization And Single-Theme Restaurant Concepts

The Colony Hotel ....Guest-Friendly Environmental And Recycling Practices

Dahlmann Properties ....Improving The Work Environment And Decreasing Turnover

Day Hospitality Group ....Sabbatical Leave Program For General Managers

Days Inn Altoona ....Integrated, Community-Based Marketing Plan

*Days Inn Altoona ....Professional Pride And Personal Values

Disney's Polynesian Resort...........................A Value-Based Process Of Training And Selection

* Disney's Polynesian Resort......................Creating And Delivering A Magical Experience

Embassy Suites - Greater Minneapolis.........Consolidation And Centralization Of Reservations Sales Office

Fairmont Copley Plaza Hotel.......................Using A Property Management System To Improve Concierge Desk Excellence

The Farmington Inn....................................Writing Historical Fiction Books To Enhance Marketing

Four Seasons and Regent Hotels & Resorts....Designated Trainer Program For Front-Line Employees

* Four Seasons and Regent Hotels & Resorts...Developing A High Ratio Of Employees To Guests

Four Seasons and Regent Hotels & Resorts....Ensuring A Luxury Hotel Experience

Four Seasons and Regent Hotels & Resorts....Informal Dining Venue And Alternative Cuisine

* Four Seasons New York.............................The Most Beautiful Stage Ever Performed Upon

* Four Seasons Washington, DC...................A Passion To Serve

Good Nite Inn..Establishing Time Frames For Preventive Maintenance Tasks

Good Nite Inn..Development Of Mobile Shop For Improved Guestroom Maintenance

Grand Theme Hotels ....The Creation Of A Process To Track And Control Labor Costs

The Greenbrier ....Programs Establishing The Resort As A Center For Culinary Excellence

Hotel Bel Air ....Comprehensive Environmental Management

Hotel Bel Air ....Proactive Property-Maintenance Program

* The Houstonian Hotel, Club & Spa............A Humanistic Approach To Profitability

The Inn at Essex ....Advertising On City Buses To Create Awareness

The Inn at Essex ....Providing Absolute Guest Satisfaction

Inn at the Market...Outsourced Human Resources To Professional HR Consultant

Inter-Continental Hotels & Resorts..............Building A Global Marketing Database

Kessler Enterprises, Inc. ....Development And Concept Of The Grand Theme Hotels

* Kimpton Group...Differentiation To The Extreme

Kimpton Group Hotels and Restaurants
    and Outrigger Hotels and Resorts...........Private Label Reservation System To Encourage Upselling

Latham Hotel, Georgetown..........................Midscale Guestrooms Designed To Give An Upscale, Residential Feel

Minneapolis-St. Paul Hilton ....Line Employee Empowerment

* The Mansion on Turtle Creek ....Staffing Up To Customer Needs

* Mirage Resorts ....Creating Artistically Pleasing Hotels For Guests And Employees

* Mohonk Mountain House.........................Creating Profits By Not Focusing On The GOP

Motel 6..Developing A Memorable And Effective Advertising Message

Motel 6..Training Employees For General Management

New York Marriott Financial Center............Regular Status Meetings Between Executive And Department Staffs

Omni Hotels...Integrated Property Management And Revenue Management System

Palisades Executive Conference Center ....Experience Engineering And Integrative Design

* The Peninsula Beverly Hills Hotel,
   Ali Kasikci ....Every Day You Have To Re-Invent Yourself

The Peninsula Beverly Hills Hotel ....24-Hour Check-In/Checkout

Royal Palms Hotel & Casitas ....Restoration And Redesign Of Older Property For Residential Feel

SAI Luxury Hotels, Inc. ....Business Development/Renovation/Turnaround/Repositioning

Sheraton - Denver West ....Job Sharing Between Sales Managers

Sheraton Elk Grove ....Annual Implementation Of A Broad-Based Best Practice

Simpson House Inn ....Hospitality Training Curriculum With An Emphasis On Diversity

Swissôtel ....Implementing A Global Sales Effort

Swissôtel ....Creation Of A Revenue Manager Position To Increase Room Sales Revenues

Tamar Inns ....Implementation Of Self-Funded Health Insurance

The Waldorf-Astoria....................................Gathering Customer Feedback And Coding Performances

The Waldorf-Astoria ....Revenue Maximization For The Food And Beverage Department

Tishman Hotel Corporation ....Hotel Renovation: The Doral Park Avenue Hotel

Walt Disney World Resorts and
   Theme Parks...Providing A "Touchable" Dining Experience

White Lodging Services ....Preshift Meetings For All Departments

Windsor Court Hotel ....Sophisticated Guest-Recognition Program

REIT

* Caesars Palace Hotel & Casino ....Building A Hotel That Has…Mystique

Sheraton - Denver West ....Job Sharing Between Sales Managers

Sheraton Elk Grove ....Annual Implementation Of A Broad-Based Best Practice

Sunstone Hotels ....Focused Growth Of Hotel Company Utilizing A REIT

BIOGRAPHIES OF PRINCIPAL INVESTIGATORS

Laurette Dubé: Laurette Dubé is an associate professor of marketing at the Faculty of Management, McGill University, Montreal, Canada. Dr. Dubé received her Ph.D. from Cornell University at the School of Hotel Administration in 1990. Her work focuses on diverse aspects of consumer behavior (specifically, expectations, consumption experience, satisfaction, and loyalty) and their link with strategic and operation management practice in service industries. Dr. Dubé has published more than 20 research articles in top academic journals including *Journal of Consumer Research*, *Journal of Marketing Research*, *Journal of Personality and Social Psychology*, *Marketing Letters*, and *Psychology & Marketing*. Her research has been supported by grants from national agencies in Canada, by the Marketing Science Institute, and the Center for Hospitality Research of the Cornell School of Hotel Administration (Palace Hotel competition). Dr. Dubé teaches services marketing and management from a multidisciplinary perspective at the undergraduate, MBA, and Ph.D. levels. She also teaches consumer behavior and marketing research. Dr. Dubé has an ongoing interest in food. She worked 10 years as a foodservice manager before joining academia. She also has made significant contributions in the domain of food marketing, producing scientific and applied articles, writing a book on food cost and quality control, and chairing in 1994 the first international symposium on the topic.

Cathy A. Enz: Cathy A. Enz is the Lewis G. Schaenman Jr. Professor of Innovation and Dynamic Management at the School of Hotel Administration at Cornell University. Dr. Enz received her Ph.D. in organizational behavior from the Ohio State University Graduate School of Business in 1985, and previously was on the faculty of the Graduate School of Business at Indiana University. She has published more than 40 journal articles in the areas of strategic management and human resources. Her expertise focuses on issues of change management, organizational design, employee empowerment, service quality, and corporate culture. She is a research fellow for the Center for Hospitality Research and on the editorial review board of five journals including the *Journal of Hospitality and Tourism Research*. She has been a co-investigator on more than ten funded research grants, and recently completed a best-practices study with an international hotel chain. Professor Enz recently designed and taught a course titled "Best Practices and the Management of Change for High Performance," and is currently teaching a course titled "Innovation & Dynamic Management." She is the developer of the Hospitality Change Simulation, a learning tool for the introduction of effective change. In addition to teaching graduates and undergraduates she coordinates the senior level Advanced Management Executive Program at SHA and consults extensively in Europe, Asia, and Central America. Professor Enz recently completed a study of best practices for improved operations that examined the impact of 57 best practices on property-level performance, customer satisfaction, and employee satisfaction.

Leo M. Renaghan: Leo M. Renaghan is the former director of the Center For Hospitality Research at the Cornell School of Hotel Administration and an associate professor of services marketing at the Hotel School. He received his Ph.D. in marketing from Pennsylvania State University. His area of expertise is services marketing, and his intellectual and research efforts focus primarily on the translation of services marketing theory to management practice, especially in the hospitality industry. He teaches services marketing, and most recently, a new required graduate course in the Hotel School on managing for service excellence. This course integrates concepts and principles in marketing, organizational behavior, and operations management to capture the complexity of the hospitality industry to better understand and profitably manage hospitality operations. He has consulted with major hotel companies for the past 15 years on various marketing and sales issues and has implemented marketing planning systems in six international hotel companies. In 1993 he conducted a sales and marketing best-practices study for a group of independent resorts in the United States. He is a director of the board for Radisson-SAS Hotels in Brussels, Belgium, a position he has held for the past seven years.

Judy A. Siguaw: Judy A. Siguaw is an associate professor of marketing in the School of Hotel Administration at Cornell University. Professor Siguaw completed her D.B.A. degree in marketing in 1991. Prior to entering academia, Professor Siguaw spent more than 10 years in the corporate sector in the employ of Conoco Inc. and General Foods Corporation, where she established a new sales record. Professor Siguaw is an accomplished researcher and has published more than 35 articles, including those in the *Journal of Marketing Research, Journal of Marketing, Journal of Strategic Marketing, Industrial Management,* and *Journal of Business Ethics.* She is a contributor to two textbooks. She is also the recipient of a prestigious Marketing Science Institute research award, a Jane Fenyo Award from the Academy of Marketing Science, a research fellowship, a CIBER travel award from Duke University, and the recipient of six university research grants. She is an expert in sales management and currently teaches hospitality sales and hospitality marketing management. In addition, she has served as a sales/sales management consultant for international organizations, one of which has one of the largest sales forces in the world, and has conducted sales seminars for several national industry associations. Her current research interests include antecedents to customer satisfaction and customer loyalty, and the relationship of the latter variables to sales performance measures.